CRIMINAL PROCEDURE: ADJU

ASPEN CASEBOOK SERIES

CRIMINAL PROCEDURE: ADJUDICATION
Second Edition

Erwin Chemerinsky

Dean and Distinguished Professor of Law
University of California at Irvine School of Law

Laurie L. Levenson

Professor of Law, William M. Rains Fellow
and David W. Burcham Chair in Ethical Advocacy
Loyola Law School

Wolters Kluwer
Law & Business

Library of Congress Cataloging-in-Publication Data

Chemerinsky, Erwin.
    Criminal procedure : adjudication / Erwin Chemerinsky, Dean and Distinguished Professor of Law, University of California at Irvine School of Law; Laurie L. Levenson, Professor of Law, William M. Rains, Fellow and David W. Burcham Chair in Ethical Advocacy, Loyola Law School. — Second Edition.
        pages cm
    Includes index.
    ISBN 978-1-4548-0712-4
    1. Criminal procedure — United States. 2. Criminal procedure — United States — Cases. I. Levenson, Laurie L., 1956- II. Title.
        KF9619.C482 2013
        345.73'05 — dc23

                                                                                    2013023534

For our families and for our students

SUMMARY OF CONTENTS

About Wolters Kluwer Law & Business

Wolters Kluwer Law & Business is a leading global provider of intelligent information and digital solutions for legal and business professionals in key specialty areas, and respected educational resources for professors and law students. Wolters Kluwer Law & Business connects legal and business professionals as well as those in the education market with timely, specialized authoritative content and information-enabled solutions to support success through productivity, accuracy and mobility.

Serving customers worldwide, Wolters Kluwer Law & Business products include those under the Aspen Publishers, CCH, Kluwer Law International, Loislaw, ftwilliam.com and MediRegs family of products.

CCH products have been a trusted resource since 1913, and are highly regarded resources for legal, securities, antitrust and trade regulation, government contracting, banking, pension, payroll, employment and labor, and healthcare reimbursement and compliance professionals.

Aspen Publishers products provide essential information to attorneys, business professionals and law students. Written by preeminent authorities, the product line offers analytical and practical information in a range of specialty practice areas from securities law and intellectual property to mergers and acquisitions and pension/benefits. Aspen's trusted legal education resources provide professors and students with high-quality, up-to-date and effective resources for successful instruction and study in all areas of the law.

Kluwer Law International products provide the global business community with reliable international legal information in English. Legal practitioners, corporate counsel and business executives around the world rely on Kluwer Law journals, looseleafs, books, and electronic products for comprehensive information in many areas of international legal practice.

Loislaw is a comprehensive online legal research product providing legal content to law firm practitioners of various specializations. Loislaw provides attorneys with the ability to quickly and efficiently find the necessary legal information they need, when and where they need it, by facilitating access to primary law as well as state-specific law, records, forms and treatises.

ftwilliam.com offers employee benefits professionals the highest quality plan documents (retirement, welfare and non-qualified) and government forms (5500/PBGC, 1099 and IRS) software at highly competitive prices.

MediRegs products provide integrated health care compliance content and software solutions for professionals in healthcare, higher education and life sciences, including professionals in accounting, law and consulting.

Wolters Kluwer Law & Business, a division of Wolters Kluwer, is headquartered in New York. Wolters Kluwer is a market-leading global information services company focused on professionals.

CONTENTS

CHAPTER 1

INTRODUCTION TO CRIMINAL PROCEDURE   1

CHAPTER 4

DISCOVERY   **101**

CHAPTER 5

PLEA BARGAINING AND GUILTY PLEAS   **137**

CHAPTER 6

SPEEDY TRIAL RIGHTS   **179**

CHAPTER 7

RIGHT TO COUNSEL   **209**

CHAPTER 8

TRIAL   251

CHAPTER 9

SENTENCING 367

CHAPTER 10

DOUBLE JEOPARDY   471

CHAPTER 11

PREFACE

Our goal is to write the most student-friendly book we can to help teach students about the fascinating area of criminal procedure. Between us, we have over 50 years of experience in teaching in law schools. We have used many different casebooks in teaching criminal procedure and other subjects. We have consistently seen that students strongly prefer a casebook that presents the material in a clear and well-organized fashion and that does not hide the law. That is our goal for this book.

In aspiring to provide such a book, we have made several choices. First, the book focuses on the key cases regarding each issue of criminal procedure. To help students in understanding these cases and provide a context for understanding them, we include brief comments before and after the cases. We recognize that professors have different ways in which they like to discuss these cases. Therefore, rather than providing lengthy notes and questions after each case, we provide suggested discussion questions in our teacher's manual. This method has the benefit of not limiting professors in how they approach the discussion. Also, our experience is that students often find notes filled with rhetorical questions frustrating, and only occasionally do they reflect the questions that the instructor wants to raise.

Second, there are no long passages excerpting the scholarly literature. There is a rich scholarly literature concerning almost every aspect of criminal procedure. At many places, we provide brief essays that describe and cite to this literature. But we have eschewed providing long block quotes of this material and make no pretense of being comprehensive in summarizing the literature. Our goal is to provide a casebook, not a reference tool.

Third, we decided to include "practical" materials in a supplement rather than in the casebook. For example, we think it is useful for students in studying the Fourth Amendment to see a search warrant or in learning about the Fifth Amendment to see an indictment. We considered including these in the casebook but decided for reasons of length to place them in a separate supplement. We recognize that instructors vary as to how they wish to use this material, and having the materials in a supplement was the best solution. We also provide material using other media, such as PowerPoint slides, for professors who wish to use them.

Fourth, the major cases are presented in slightly longer form, with a bit less editing than in many other books. Criminal procedure, of course, is an area of constitutional law, and the law is very much the product of the Supreme Court's decisions. Lawyers practicing criminal law base their arguments on these decisions, and thus we believe that it is desirable to expose students to the cases in their fuller form. Space constraints required more editing than we would have liked, but we have done our best to present the cases in as accurate and full a form as possible.

We do not indicate deletions of material in the cases by ellipses. Our experience is that the necessary frequent use of ellipses is distracting and does not provide useful information to the students. On the other hand, any addition, however small, is indicated by brackets.

Finally, our goal is to be comprehensive on adjudication in criminal procedure. We have organized the book roughly along the chronology of a criminal case. Chapter 1 is an introduction and includes an overview of the stages of the criminal justice system. Subsequent chapters examine each step of criminal proceedings, beginning in Chapter 2 with initiating prosecution and concluding in Chapter 11 with habeas corpus. We were careful in writing the book to be sure that each chapter is independent so that professors can cover the material in any order and use those chapters that fit their curriculum.

Criminal procedure, of course, is an area in which there are constantly new developments. We are grateful to all who sent us comments on the first edition. We plan to provide an annual supplement and write new editions of this book about every four years. We, of course, continue to welcome comments and suggestions from faculty and students who use it. Our goal is to provide the best possible teaching tool for criminal procedure, and we very much would appreciate any ideas for how to better accomplish this objective.

Erwin Chemerinsky
Laurie L. Levenson

June 2013

ACKNOWLEDGMENTS

This book is the product of our having taught this material for many years. We are very grateful to our students, who have constantly challenged us to think about this material in new ways. It is to them that we dedicate this book. We also dedicate this book to our families, whose patience, support, and love made this book — and everything else we do — possible.

We are also very grateful to Marcy Strauss for her detailed comments on the first edition and to many users who sent us valuable suggestions. In addition, we thank the following sources for permission to reprint portions of their work:

Inmate Convicted of Indecent Exposure. Used with permission of The Associated Press. © 2007.

Judge Dismisses Molestation Case — Again. Copyright © 2008 The New Mexican, Inc. Reprinted with permission. All rights reserved.

Lawyer Disbarred over Lacrosse Rape Case. Used with permission of The Associated Press. © 2007.

Mandatory 55-Year Sentence "Extreme"? Reprinted with permission of the Salt Lake Tribune.

Right to a Speedy Trial? Justice Delayed. The Atlanta Journal-Constitution, Copyright © 2007.

State Loses Appeal in Child-Rape Case. Copyright © The Albuquerque Journal, Mountain View Telegraph. Reprinted with permission. Permission does not imply endorsement.

THE CONSTITUTION OF THE UNITED STATES

We the People of the United States, in Order to form a more perfect Union, establish Justice, insure domestic Tranquility, provide for the common defense, promote the general Welfare, and secure the Blessings of Liberty to ourselves and our Posterity, do ordain and establish this Constitution for the United States of America.

ARTICLE I

Section 1. All legislative Powers herein granted shall be vested in a Congress of the United States, which shall consist of a Senate and House of Representatives.

Section 2. [1] The House of Representatives shall be composed of Members chosen every second Year by the People of the several States, and the Electors in each State shall have the Qualifications requisite for Electors of the most numerous Branch of the State Legislature.

[2] No Person shall be a Representative who shall not have attained to the Age of twenty five Years, and been seven Years a Citizen of the United States, and who shall not, when elected, be an Inhabitant of that State in which he shall be chosen.

[3] Representatives and direct Taxes shall be apportioned among the several States which may be included within this Union, according to their respective Numbers, which shall be determined by adding to the whole Number of free Persons, including those bound to Service for a Term of Years, and excluding Indians not taxed, three fifths of all other Persons. The actual Enumeration shall be made within three Years after the first Meeting of the Congress of the United States, and within every subsequent Term of ten Years, in such Manner as they shall by Law direct. The Number of Representatives shall not exceed one for every thirty Thousand, but each State shall have at Least one Representative; and until such enumeration shall be made, the State of New Hampshire shall be entitled to chuse three, Massachusetts eight, Rhode Island and Providence Plantations one, Connecticut five, New York six, New Jersey four, Pennsylvania eight, Delaware one, Maryland six, Virginia ten, North Carolina five, South Carolina five, and Georgia three.

[4] When vacancies happen in the Representation from any State, the Executive Authority thereof shall issue Writs of Election to fill such Vacancies.

[5] The House of Representatives shall chuse their Speaker and other Officers; and shall have the sole Power of Impeachment.

Section 3. [1] The Senate of the United States shall be composed of two Senators from each State, chosen by the Legislature thereof, for six Years; and each Senator shall have one Vote.

[2] Immediately after they shall be assembled in Consequence of the first Election, they shall be divided as equally as may be into three Classes. The Seats of the Senators of the first Class shall be vacated at the Expiration of the second Year, of the second Class at the Expiration of the fourth Year, and of the third Class at the Expiration of the sixth Year, so that one third may be chosen every second Year; and if Vacancies happen by Resignation, or otherwise, during the Recess of the Legislature of any State, the Executive thereof may make temporary Appointments until the next Meeting of the Legislature, which shall then fill such Vacancies.

[3] No Person shall be a Senator who shall not have attained to the Age of thirty Years, and been nine Years a Citizen of the United States, and who shall not, when elected, be an Inhabitant of that State for which he shall be chosen.

[4] The Vice President of the United States shall be President of the Senate, but shall have no Vote, unless they be equally divided.

[5] The Senate shall chuse their other Officers, and also a President pro tempore, in the absence of the Vice President, or when he shall exercise the Office of President of the United States.

[6] The Senate shall have the sole Power to try all Impeachments. When sitting for that Purpose, they shall be on Oath or Affirmation. When the President of the United States is tried, the Chief Justice shall preside: And no Person shall be convicted without the Concurrence of two thirds of the Members present.

[7] Judgment in Cases of Impeachment shall not extend further than to removal from Office, and disqualification to hold and enjoy any Office of honor, Trust or Profit under the United States: but the Party convicted shall nevertheless be liable and subject to Indictment, Trial, Judgment and Punishment, according to Law.

Section 4. [1] The Times, Places and Manner of holding Elections for Senators and Representatives, shall be prescribed in each State by the Legislature thereof; but the Congress may at any time by Law make or alter such Regulations, except as to the Places of chusing Senators.

[2] The Congress shall assemble at least once in every Year, and such Meeting shall be on the first Monday in December, unless they shall by Law appoint a different Day.

Section 5. [1] Each House shall be the Judge of the Elections, Returns and Qualifications of its own Members, and a Majority of each shall constitute a Quorum to do Business; but a smaller Number may adjourn from day to day, and may be authorized to compel the Attendance of absent Members, in such Manner, and under such Penalties as each House may provide.

[2] Each House may determine the Rules of its Proceedings, punish its Members for disorderly Behaviour, and, with the Concurrence of two thirds, expel a Member.

[3] Each House shall keep a Journal of its Proceedings, and from time to time publish the same, excepting such Parts as may in their Judgment require Secrecy; and the Yeas and Nays of the Members of either House on any question shall, at the Desire of one fifth of those Present, be entered on the Journal.

[4] Neither House, during the Session of Congress, shall, without the Consent of the other, adjourn for more than three days, nor to any other Place than that in which the two Houses shall be sitting.

Section 6. [1] The Senators and Representatives shall receive a Compensation for their Services, to be ascertained by Law, and paid out of the Treasury of the United States. They shall in all Cases, except Treason, Felony and Breach of the Peace, be privileged from Arrest during their Attendance at the Session of their respective Houses, and in going to and returning from the same; and for any Speech or Debate in either House, they shall not be questioned in any other Place.

[2] No Senator or Representative shall, during the Time for which he was elected, be appointed to any civil Office under the Authority of the United States, which shall have been created, or the Emoluments whereof shall have been increased during such time; and no Person holding any Office under the United States, shall be a Member of either House during his Continuance in Office.

Section 7. [1] All Bills for raising Revenue shall originate in the House of Representatives; but the Senate may propose or concur with Amendments as on other Bills.

[2] Every Bill which shall have passed the House of Representatives and the Senate, shall, before it become a Law, be presented to the President of the United States; If he approve he shall sign it, but if not he shall return it, with his Objections to that House in which it shall have originated, who shall enter the Objections at large on their Journal, and proceed to reconsider it. If after such Reconsideration two thirds of that House shall agree to pass the Bill, it shall be sent, together with the Objections, to the other House, by which it shall likewise be reconsidered, and if approved by two thirds of that House, it shall become a Law. But in all such Cases the Votes of both Houses shall be determined by Yeas and Nays, and the Names of the Persons voting for and against the Bill shall be entered on the Journal of each House respectively. If any Bill shall not be returned by the President within ten Days (Sundays excepted) after it shall have been presented to him, the Same shall be a Law, in like Manner as if he had signed it, unless the Congress by their Adjournment prevent its Return, in which Case it shall not be a Law.

[3] Every Order, Resolution, or Vote to which the Concurrence of the Senate and House of Representatives may be necessary (except on a question of Adjournment) shall be presented to the President of the United States; and before the Same shall take Effect, shall be approved by him, or being

disapproved by him, shall be repassed by two thirds of the Senate and House of Representatives, according to the Rules and Limitations prescribed in the Case of a Bill.

Section 8. [1] The Congress shall have Power To lay and collect Taxes, Duties, Imposts and Excises, to pay the Debts and provide for the common Defence and general Welfare of the United States; but all Duties, Imposts and Excises shall be uniform throughout the United States;

[2] To borrow money on the credit of the United States;

[3] To regulate Commerce with foreign Nations, and among the several States, and with the Indian Tribes;

[4] To establish an uniform Rule of Naturalization, and uniform Laws on the subject of Bankruptcies throughout the United States;

[5] To coin Money, regulate the Value thereof, and of foreign Coin, and fix the Standard of Weights and Measures;

[6] To provide for the Punishment of counterfeiting the Securities and current Coin of the United States;

[7] To establish Post Offices and post Roads;

[8] To promote the Progress of Science and useful Arts, by securing for limited Times to Authors and Inventors the exclusive Right to their respective Writings and Discoveries;

[9] To constitute Tribunals inferior to the supreme Court;

[10] To define and punish Piracies and Felonies committed on the high Seas, and Offences against the Law of Nations;

[11] To declare War, grant Letters of Marque and Reprisal, and make Rules concerning Captures on Land and Water;

[12] To raise and support Armies, but no Appropriation of Money to that Use shall be for a longer Term than two Years;

[13] To provide and maintain a Navy;

[14] To make Rules for the Government and Regulation of the land and naval Forces;

[15] To provide for calling forth the Militia to execute the Laws of the Union, suppress Insurrections and repel Invasions;

[16] To provide for organizing, arming, and disciplining, the Militia, and for governing such Part of them as may be employed in the Service of the United States, reserving to the States respectively, the Appointment of the Officers, and the Authority of training the Militia according to the discipline prescribed by Congress;

[17] To exercise exclusive Legislation in all Cases whatsoever, over such District (not exceeding ten Miles square) as may, by Cession of particular States, and the Acceptance of Congress, become the Seat of the Government of the United States, and to exercise like Authority over all Places purchased by the Consent of the Legislature of the State in which the Same shall be, for the Erection of Forts, Magazines, Arsenals, dock-Yards, and other needful Buildings;—And

[18] To make all Laws which shall be necessary and proper for carrying into Execution the foregoing Powers, and all other Powers vested by this

Constitution in the Government of the United States, or in any Department or Officer thereof.

Section 9. [1] The Migration or Importation of such Persons as any of the States now existing shall think proper to admit, shall not be prohibited by the Congress prior to the Year one thousand eight hundred and eight, but a Tax or duty may be imposed on such Importation, not exceeding ten dollars for each Person.

[2] The Privilege of the Writ of Habeas Corpus shall not be suspended, unless when in Cases of Rebellion or Invasion the public Safety may require it.

[3] No Bill of Attainder or ex post facto Law shall be passed.

[4] No Capitation, or other direct, Tax shall be laid, unless in Proportion to the Census or Enumeration herein before directed to be taken.

[5] No Tax or Duty shall be laid on Articles exported from any State.

[6] No Preference shall be given by any Regulation of Commerce or Revenue to the Ports of one State over those of another: nor shall Vessels bound to, or from, one State, be obliged to enter, clear, or pay Duties in another.

[7] No Money shall be drawn from the Treasury, but in Consequence of Appropriations made by Law; and a regular Statement and Account of the Receipts and Expenditures of all public Money shall be published from time to time.

[8] No Title of Nobility shall be granted by the United States: And no Person holding any Office of Profit or Trust under them, shall, without the Consent of the Congress, accept of any present, Emolument, Office, or Title, of any kind whatever, from any King, Prince, or foreign State.

Section 10. [1] No State shall enter into any Treaty, Alliance, or Confederation; grant Letters of Marque and Reprisal; coin Money; emit Bills of Credit; make any Thing but gold and silver Coin a Tender in Payment of Debts; pass any Bill of Attainder, ex post facto Law, or Law impairing the Obligation of Contracts, or grant any Title of Nobility.

[2] No State shall, without the Consent of the Congress, lay any Imposts or Duties on Imports or Exports, except what may be absolutely necessary for executing its inspection Laws: and the net Produce of all Duties and Imposts, laid by any State on Imports or Exports, shall be for the Use of the Treasury of the United States; and all such Laws shall be subject to the Revision and Controul of the Congress.

[3] No State shall, without the Consent of Congress, lay any Duty of Tonnage, keep Troops, or Ships of War in time of Peace, enter into any Agreement or Compact with another State, or with a foreign Power, or engage in War, unless actually invaded, or in such imminent Danger as will not admit of delay.

ARTICLE II

Section 1. [1] The executive Power shall be vested in a President of the United States of America. He shall hold his Office during the Term of four

Years, and, together with the Vice President, chosen for the same Term, be elected, as follows:

[2] Each State shall appoint, in such Manner as the Legislature thereof may direct, a Number of Electors, equal to the whole Number of Senators and Representatives to which the State may be entitled in the Congress: but no Senator or Representative, or Person holding an Office of Trust or Profit under the United States, shall be appointed an Elector.

[3] The Electors shall meet in their respective States, and vote by Ballot for two Persons, of whom one at least shall not be an Inhabitant of the same State with themselves. And they shall make a List of all the Persons voted for, and of the Number of Votes for each; which List they shall sign and certify, and transmit sealed to the Seat of the Government of the United States, directed to the President of the Senate. The President of the Senate shall, in the Presence of the Senate and House of Representatives, open all the Certificates, and the Votes shall then be counted. The Person having the greatest Number of Votes shall be the President, if such Number be a Majority of the whole Number of Electors appointed; and if there be more than one who have such Majority, and have an equal Number of Votes, then the House of Representatives shall immediately chuse by Ballot one of them for President; and if no Person have a Majority, then from the five highest on the List the said House shall in like Manner chuse the President. But in chusing the President, the Votes shall be taken by States, the Representation from each State having one Vote; a quorum for this Purpose shall consist of a Member or Members from two thirds of the States, and a Majority of all the States shall be necessary to a Choice. In every Case, after the Choice of the President, the Person having the greatest Number of Votes of the Electors shall be the Vice President. But if there should remain two or more who have equal Votes, the Senate shall chuse from them by Ballot the Vice President.

[4] The Congress may determine the Time of chusing the Electors, and the Day on which they shall give their Votes; which Day shall be the same throughout the United States.

[5] No Person except a natural born Citizen, or a Citizen of the United States, at the time of the Adoption of this Constitution, shall be eligible to the Office of President; neither shall any Person be eligible to that Office who shall not have attained to the Age of thirty five Years, and been fourteen Years a Resident within the United States.

[6] In Case of the Removal of the President from Office, or of his Death, Resignation, or Inability to discharge the Powers and Duties of the said Office, the Same shall devolve on the Vice President, and the Congress may by Law provide for the Case of Removal, Death, Resignation or Inability, both of the President and Vice President, declaring what Officer shall then act as President, and such Officer shall act accordingly, until the Disability be removed, or a President shall be elected.

[7] The President shall, at stated Times, receive for his Services, a Compensation, which shall neither be increased nor diminished during the

Period for which he shall have been elected, and he shall not receive within that Period any other Emolument from the United States, or any of them.

[8] Before he enter on the Execution of his Office, he shall take the following Oath or Affirmation: "I do solemnly swear (or affirm) that I will faithfully execute the Office of President of the United States, and will to the best of my Ability, preserve, protect and defend the Constitution of the United States."

Section 2. [1] The President shall be Commander in Chief of the Army and Navy of the United States, and of the Militia of the several States, when called into the actual Service of the United States; he may require the Opinion, in writing, of the principal Officer in each of the executive Departments, upon any subject relating to the Duties of their respective Offices, and he shall have Power to grant Reprieves and Pardons for Offences against the United States, except in Cases of Impeachment.

[2] He shall have Power, by and with the Advice and Consent of the Senate, to make Treaties, provided two thirds of the Senators present concur; and he shall nominate, and by and with the Advice and Consent of the Senate, shall appoint Ambassadors, other public Ministers and Consuls, Judges of the supreme Court, and all other Officers of the United States, whose Appointments are not herein otherwise provided for, and which shall be established by Law: but the Congress may by Law vest the Appointment of such inferior Officers, as they think proper, in the President alone, in the Courts of Law, or in the Heads of Departments.

[3] The President shall have Power to fill up all Vacancies that may happen during the Recess of the Senate, by granting Commissions which shall expire at the End of their next Session.

Section 3. He shall from time to time give to the Congress Information of the State of the Union, and recommend to their Consideration such Measures as he shall judge necessary and expedient; he may, on extraordinary Occasions, convene both Houses, or either of them, and in Case of Disagreement between them, with Respect to the Time of Adjournment, he may adjourn them to such Time as he shall think proper; he shall receive Ambassadors and other public Ministers; he shall take Care that the Laws be faithfully executed, and shall Commission all the Officers of the United States.

Section 4. The President, Vice President and all civil Officers of the United States, shall be removed from Office on Impeachment for, and Conviction of, Treason, Bribery, or other high Crimes and Misdemeanors.

ARTICLE III

Section 1. The judicial Power of the United States shall be vested in one supreme Court, and in such inferior Courts as the Congress may from time to time ordain and establish. The Judges, both of the supreme and inferior Courts, shall hold their Offices during good Behaviour, and shall, at stated

Times, receive for their Services a Compensation, which shall not be diminished during their Continuance in Office.

Section 2. [1] The Judicial Power shall extend to all Cases, in Law and Equity, arising under this Constitution, the Laws of the United States, and Treaties made, or which shall be made, under their Authority; — to all Cases affecting Ambassadors, other public Ministers and Consuls; — to all Cases of admiralty and maritime Jurisdiction; — to Controversies to which the United States shall be a Party; — to Controversies between two or more States; — between a State and Citizens of another State; — between Citizens of different States; — between Citizens of the same State claiming Lands under Grants of different States, and between a State, or the Citizens thereof, and foreign States, Citizens or Subjects.

[2] In all Cases affecting Ambassadors, other public Ministers and Consuls, and those in which a State shall be Party, the supreme Court shall have original Jurisdiction. In all the other Cases before mentioned, the supreme Court shall have appellate Jurisdiction, both as to Law and Fact, with such Exceptions, and under such Regulations as the Congress shall make.

[3] The Trial of all Crimes, except in Cases of Impeachment, shall be by Jury; and such Trial shall be held in the State where the said Crimes shall have been committed; but when not committed within any State, the Trial shall be at such Place or Places as the Congress may by Law have directed.

Section 3. [1] Treason against the United States, shall consist only in levying War against them, or in adhering to their Enemies, giving them Aid and Comfort. No Person shall be convicted of Treason unless on the Testimony of two Witnesses to the same overt Act, or on Confession in open Court.

[2] The Congress shall have Power to declare the Punishment of Treason, but no Attainder of Treason shall work Corruption of Blood, or Forfeiture except during the Life of the Person attainted.

ARTICLE IV

Section 1. Full Faith and Credit shall be given in each State to the public Acts, Records, and judicial Proceedings of every other State. And the Congress may by general Laws prescribe the Manner in which such Acts, Records and Proceedings shall be proved, and the Effect thereof.

Section 2. [1] The Citizens of each State shall be entitled to all Privileges and Immunities of Citizens in the several States.

[2] A Person charged in any State with Treason, Felony, or other Crime, who shall flee from Justice, and be found in another State, shall on demand of the executive Authority of the State from which he fled, be delivered up, to be removed to the State having Jurisdiction of the Crime.

[3] No Person held to Service or Labour in one State, under the Laws thereof, escaping into another, shall, in Consequence of any Law or Regulation therein, be discharged from such Service or Labour, but shall be delivered up on Claim of the Party to whom such Service or Labour may be due.

Section 3. [1] New States may be admitted by the Congress into this Union; but no new State shall be formed or erected within the Jurisdiction of any other State; nor any State be formed by the Junction of two or more States, or Parts of States, without the Consent of the Legislatures of the States concerned as well as of the Congress.

[2] The Congress shall have Power to dispose of and make all needful Rules and Regulations respecting the Territory or other Property belonging to the United States; and nothing in this Constitution shall be so construed as to Prejudice any Claims of the United States, or of any particular State.

Section 4. The United States shall guarantee to every State in this Union a Republican Form of Government, and shall protect each of them against Invasion; and on Application of the Legislature, or of the Executive (when the Legislature cannot be convened) against domestic Violence.

ARTICLE V

The Congress, whenever two thirds of both Houses shall deem it necessary, shall propose Amendments to this Constitution, or, on the Application of the Legislatures of two thirds of the several States, shall call a Convention for proposing Amendments, which, in either Case, shall be valid to all Intents and Purposes, as Part of this Constitution, when ratified by the Legislatures of three fourths of the several States, or by Conventions in three fourths thereof, as the one or the other Mode of Ratification may be proposed by the Congress; Provided that no Amendment which may be made prior to the Year One thousand eight hundred and eight shall in any Manner affect the first and fourth Clauses in the Ninth Section of the first Article; and that no State, without its Consent, shall be deprived of its equal Suffrage in the Senate.

ARTICLE VI

[1] All Debts contracted and Engagements entered into, before the Adoption of this Constitution, shall be as valid against the United States under this Constitution, as under the Confederation.

[2] This Constitution, and the Laws of the United States which shall be made in Pursuance thereof; and all Treaties made, or which shall be made, under the Authority of the United States, shall be the supreme Law of the Land; and the Judges in every State shall be bound thereby, any Thing in the Constitution or Laws of any State to the Contrary notwithstanding.

[3] The Senators and Representatives before mentioned, and the Members of the several State Legislatures, and all executive and judicial Officers, both of the United States and of the several States, shall be bound by Oath or

Affirmation, to support this Constitution; but no religious Test shall ever be required as a Qualification to any Office or public Trust under the United States.

ARTICLE VII

The Ratification of the Conventions of nine States, shall be sufficient for the Establishment of this Constitution between the States so ratifying the Same.

Done in Convention by the Unanimous Consent of the States present the Seventeenth Day of September in the Year of our Lord one thousand seven hundred and Eighty seven and of the Independence of the United States of America the Twelfth.

ARTICLES IN ADDITION TO, AND AMENDMENT OF THE CONSTI-TUTION OF THE UNITED STATES OF AMERICA, PROPOSED BY CON-GRESS, AND RATIFIED BY THE LEGISLATURES OF THE SEVERAL STATES, PURSUANT TO THE FIFTH ARTICLE OF THE ORIGINAL CONSTITUTION.

AMENDMENT I [1791]

Congress shall make no law respecting an establishment of religion, or prohibiting the free exercise thereof; or abridging the freedom of speech, or of the press; or the right of the people peaceably to assemble, and to petition the Government for a redress of grievances.

AMENDMENT II [1791]

A well regulated Militia, being necessary to the security of a free State, the right of the people to keep and bear Arms, shall not be infringed.

AMENDMENT III [1791]

No Soldier shall, in time of peace be quartered in any house, without the consent of the Owner, nor in time of war, but in a manner to be prescribed by law.

AMENDMENT IV [1791]

The right of the people to be secure in their persons, houses, papers, and effects, against unreasonable searches and seizures, shall not be violated, and no Warrants shall issue, but upon probable cause, supported by Oath or affirmation, and particularly describing the place to be searched, and the persons or things to be seized.

AMENDMENT V [1791]

No person shall be held to answer for a capital, or otherwise infamous crime, unless on a presentment or indictment of a Grand Jury, except in cases arising in the land or naval forces, or in the Militia, when in actual service in time of War or public danger; nor shall any person be subject for the same offence to be twice put in jeopardy of life or limb; nor shall be compelled in any criminal case to be a witness against himself, nor be deprived of life, liberty, or property, without due process of law; nor shall private property be taken for public use, without just compensation.

AMENDMENT VI [1791]

In all criminal prosecutions, the accused shall enjoy the right to a speedy and public trial, by an impartial jury of the State and district wherein the crime shall have been committed, which district shall have been previously ascertained by law, and to be informed of the nature and cause of the accusation; to be confronted with the witnesses against him; to have compulsory process for obtaining witnesses in his favor, and to have the Assistance of Counsel for his defence.

AMENDMENT VII [1791]

In Suits at common law, where the value in controversy shall exceed twenty dollars, the right of trial by jury shall be preserved, and no fact tried by a jury, shall be otherwise reexamined in any Court of the United States, than according to the rules of the common law.

AMENDMENT VIII [1791]

Excessive bail shall not be required, nor excessive fines imposed, nor cruel and unusual punishments inflicted.

AMENDMENT IX [1791]

The enumeration in the Constitution, of certain rights, shall not be construed to deny or disparage others retained by the people.

AMENDMENT X [1791]

The powers not delegated to the United States by the Constitution, nor prohibited by it to the States, are reserved to the States respectively, or to the people.

AMENDMENT XI [1798]

The Judicial power of the United States shall not be construed to extend to any suit in law or equity, commenced or prosecuted against one of the United States by Citizens of another State, or by Citizens or Subjects of any Foreign State.

AMENDMENT XII [1804]

The Electors shall meet in their respective states and vote by ballot for President and Vice-President, one of whom, at least, shall not be an inhabitant of the same state with themselves; they shall name in their ballots the person voted for as President, and in distinct ballots the person voted for as Vice-President, and they shall make distinct lists of all persons voted for as President, and of all persons voted for as Vice-President, and of the number of votes for each, which lists they shall sign and certify, and transmit sealed to the seat of the government of the United States, directed to the President of the Senate;—The President of the Senate shall, in the presence of the Senate and House of Representatives, open all the certificates and the votes shall then be counted;—The person having the greatest number of votes for President, shall be the President, if such number be a majority of the whole number of Electors appointed; and if no person have such majority, then from the persons having the highest numbers not exceeding three on the list of those voted for as President, the House of Representatives shall choose immediately, by ballot, the President. But in choosing the President, the votes shall be taken by states, the representation from each state having one vote; a quorum for this purpose shall consist of a member or members from two-thirds of the states, and a majority of all the states shall be necessary to a choice. And if the House of Representatives shall not choose a President whenever the right of choice shall devolve upon them, before the fourth day of March next following, then the Vice-President shall act as President, as in case of the death or other constitutional disability of the President.—The person having the greatest number of votes as Vice-President, shall be the Vice-President, if such number be a majority of the whole number of Electors appointed, and if no person have a majority, then from the two highest numbers on the list, the Senate shall choose the Vice-President; a quorum for the purpose shall consist of two-thirds of the whole number of Senators, and a majority of the whole number shall be necessary to a choice. But no person constitutionally ineligible to the office of President shall be eligible to that of Vice-President of the United States.

AMENDMENT XIII [1865]

Section 1. Neither slavery nor involuntary servitude, except as a punishment for crime whereof the party shall have been duly convicted, shall exist within the United States, or any place subject to their jurisdiction.

Section 2. Congress shall have power to enforce this article by appropriate legislation.

AMENDMENT XIV [1868]

Section 1. All persons born or naturalized in the United States, and subject to the jurisdiction thereof, are citizens of the United States and of the State wherein they reside. No State shall make or enforce any law which shall abridge the privileges or immunities of citizens of the United States; nor shall any State deprive any person of life, liberty, or property, without due process of law; nor deny to any person within its jurisdiction the equal protection of the laws.

Section 2. Representatives shall be apportioned among the several States according to their respective numbers, counting the whole number of persons in each State, excluding Indians not taxed. But when the right to vote at any election for the choice of electors for President and Vice-President of the United States, Representatives in Congress, the Executive and Judicial officers of a State, or the members of the Legislature thereof, is denied to any of the male inhabitants of such State, being twenty-one years of age, and citizens of the United States, or in any way abridged, except for participation in rebellion, or other crime, the basis of representation therein shall be reduced in the proportion which the number of such male citizens shall bear to the whole number of male citizens twenty-one years of age in such State.

Section 3. No person shall be a Senator or Representative in Congress, or elector of President and Vice-President, or hold any office, civil or military, under the United States, or under any State, who, having previously taken an oath, as a member of Congress, or as an officer of the United States, or as a member of any State legislature, or as an executive or judicial officer of any State, to support the Constitution of the United States, shall have engaged in insurrection or rebellion against the same, or given aid or comfort to the enemies thereof. But Congress may by a vote of two-thirds of each House, remove such disability.

Section 4. The validity of the public debt of the United States, authorized by law, including debts incurred for payment of pensions and bounties for services in suppressing insurrection or rebellion, shall not be questioned.

But neither the United States nor any State shall assume or pay any debt or obligation incurred in aid of insurrection or rebellion against the United States, or any claim for the loss or emancipation of any slave; but all such debts, obligations and claims shall be held illegal and void.

Section 5. The Congress shall have the power to enforce, by appropriate legislation, the provisions of this article.

AMENDMENT XV [1870]

Section 1. The right of citizens of the United States to vote shall not be denied or abridged by the United States or by any State on account of race, color, or previous condition of servitude.

Section 2. The Congress shall have the power to enforce this article by appropriate legislation.

AMENDMENT XVI [1913]

The Congress shall have power to lay and collect taxes on incomes, from whatever source derived, without apportionment among the several States, and without regard to any census or enumeration.

AMENDMENT XVII [1913]

[1] The Senate of the United States shall be composed of two Senators from each State, elected by the people thereof, for six years; and each Senator shall have one vote. The electors in each State shall have the qualifications requisite for electors of the most numerous branch of the State legislatures.

[2] When vacancies happen in the representation of any State in the Senate, the executive authority of such State shall issue writs of election to fill such vacancies: *Provided,* That the legislature of any State may empower the executive thereof to make temporary appointments until the people fill the vacancies by election as the legislature may direct.

[3] This amendment shall not be so construed as to affect the election or term of any Senator chosen before it becomes valid as part of the Constitution.

AMENDMENT XVIII [1919]

Section 1. After one year from the ratification of this article the manufacture, sale, or transportation of intoxicating liquors within, the importation thereof into, or the exportation thereof from the United States and all territory subject to the jurisdiction thereof for beverage purposes is hereby prohibited.

Section 2. The Congress and the several States shall have concurrent power to enforce this article by appropriate legislation.

Section 3. This article shall be inoperative unless it shall have been ratified as an amendment to the Constitution by the legislatures of the several States, as provided in the Constitution, within seven years from the date of the submission hereof to the States by the Congress.

AMENDMENT XIX [1920]

[1] The right of citizens of the United States to vote shall not be denied or abridged by the United States or by any State on account of sex.

[2] Congress shall have power to enforce this article by appropriate legislation.

AMENDMENT XX [1933]

Section 1. The terms of the President and the Vice President shall end at noon on the 20th day of January, and the terms of Senators and Representatives at noon on the 3d day of January, of the years in which such terms would have ended if this article had not been ratified; and the terms of their successors shall then begin.

Section 2. The Congress shall assemble at least once in every year, and such meeting shall begin at noon on the 3d day of January, unless they shall by law appoint a different day.

Section 3. If, at the time fixed for the beginning of the term of the President, the President elect shall have died, the Vice President elect shall become President. If a President shall not have been chosen before the time fixed for the beginning of his term, or if the President elect shall have failed to qualify, then the Vice President elect shall act as President until a President shall have qualified; and the Congress may by law provide for the case wherein neither a President elect nor a Vice President shall have qualified, declaring who shall then act as President, or the manner in which one who is to act shall be selected, and such person shall act accordingly until a President or Vice President shall have qualified.

Section 4. The Congress may by law provide for the case of the death of any of the persons from whom the House of Representatives may chuse a President whenever the right of choice shall have devolved upon them, and for the case of the death of any of the persons from whom the Senate may choose a Vice President whenever the right of choice shall have devolved upon them.

Section 5. Sections 1 and 2 shall take effect on the 15th day of October following the ratification of this article.

Section 6. This article shall be inoperative unless it shall have been ratified as an amendment to the Constitution by the legislatures of three-fourths of the several States within seven years from the date of its submission.

AMENDMENT XXI [1933]

Section 1. The eighteenth article of amendment to the Constitution of the United States is hereby repealed.

Section 2. The transportation or importation into any State, Territory, or Possession of the United States for delivery or use therein of intoxicating liquors, in violation of the laws thereof, is hereby prohibited.

Section 3. This article shall be inoperative unless it shall have been ratified as an amendment to the Constitution by conventions in the several States, as provided in the Constitution, within seven years from the date of the submission hereof to the States by the Congress.

AMENDMENT XXII [1951]

Section 1. No person shall be elected to the office of the President more than twice, and no person who has held the office of President, or acted as President, for more than two years of a term to which some other person was elected President shall be elected to the office of President more than once. But this Article shall not apply to any person holding the office of President when this Article was proposed by Congress, and shall not prevent any person who may be holding the office of President, or acting as President, during the term within which this Article becomes operative from holding the office of President or acting as President during the remainder of such term.

Section 2. This article shall be inoperative unless it shall have been ratified as an amendment to the Constitution by the legislatures of three-fourths of the several States within seven years from the date of its submission to the States by the Congress.

AMENDMENT XXIII [1961]

Section 1. The District constituting the seat of Government of the United States shall appoint in such manner as Congress may direct: A number of electors of President and Vice President equal to the whole number of Senators and Representatives in Congress to which the District would be entitled if it were a State, but in no event more than the least populous State; they shall be in addition to those appointed by the States, but they shall be considered, for the purposes of the election of President and Vice President, to be electors appointed by a State; and they shall meet in the District and perform such duties as provided by the twelfth article of amendment.

Section 2. The Congress shall have power to enforce this article by appropriate legislation.

AMENDMENT XXIV [1964]

Section 1. The right of citizens of the United States to vote in any primary or other election for President or Vice President, for electors for President or Vice President, or for Senator or Representative in Congress, shall not be denied or abridged by the United States or any State by reason of failure to pay poll tax or other tax.

Section 2. The Congress shall have power to enforce this article by appropriate legislation.

AMENDMENT XXV [1967]

Section 1. In case of the removal of the President from office or of his death or resignation, the Vice President shall become President.

Section 2. Whenever there is a vacancy in the office of the Vice President, the President shall nominate a Vice President who shall take office upon confirmation by a majority vote of both Houses of Congress.

Section 3. Whenever the President transmits to the President pro tempore of the Senate and the Speaker of the House of Representatives his written declaration that he is unable to discharge the powers and duties of his office, and until he transmits to them a written declaration to the contrary, such powers and duties shall be discharged by the Vice President as Acting President.

Section 4. Whenever the Vice President and a majority of either the principal officers of the executive departments or of such other body as Congress may by law provide, transmit to the President pro tempore of the Senate and the Speaker of the House of Representatives their written declaration that the President is unable to discharge the powers and duties of his office, the Vice President shall immediately assume the powers and duties of the office as Acting President.

Thereafter, when the President transmits to the President pro tempore of the Senate and the Speaker of the House of Representatives his written declaration that no inability exists, he shall resume the powers and duties of his office unless the Vice President and a majority of either the principal officers of the executive department or of such other body as Congress may by law provide, transmit within four days to the President pro tempore of the Senate and the Speaker of the House of Representatives their written declaration that the President is unable to discharge the powers and duties of his office. Thereupon Congress shall decide the issue, assembling within forty-eight hours for that purpose if not in session. If the Congress, within twenty-one days after receipt of the latter written declaration, or, if Congress is not in session, within twenty-one days after Congress is required to assemble, determines by two-thirds vote of both Houses that the President is unable to discharge the powers and duties of his office, the Vice President shall continue to discharge the same as Acting President; otherwise, the President shall resume the powers and duties of his office.

AMENDMENT XXVI [1971]

Section 1. The right of citizens of the United States, who are eighteen years of age or older, to vote shall not be denied or abridged by the United States or by any State on account of age.

Section 2. The Congress shall have power to enforce this article by appropriate legislation.

AMENDMENT XXVII [1992]

No law, varying the compensation for the services of the Senators and Representatives, shall take effect, until an election of representatives shall have intervened.

CRIMINAL PROCEDURE: ADJUDICATION

CHAPTER
1

INTRODUCTION TO CRIMINAL PROCEDURE

Criminal procedure covers the rules and practices that govern the investigation and prosecution of criminal cases. "Investigatory criminal procedure" generally refers to the rules governing police conduct in investigating a case. These rules derive from the Fourth, Fifth, and Sixth Amendments to the United States Constitution. "Accusatory criminal procedure" generally refers to the rights of a defendant as a case proceeds through the criminal justice system. The rules governing this stage of the criminal process generally derive from the Fifth and Fourteenth Amendment rights to due process, the Sixth Amendment right to counsel and a speedy and public trial, the Eighth Amendment prohibition of excessive bail and double jeopardy, and the rules of procedure enacted by Congress or the states. Although federal constitutional rules govern these areas of criminal procedure, there are other laws that may control, including federal statutory laws, state constitutions, state laws, court rules of procedure, and ethical codes.

Section A of this introduction reviews the roles of the various participants in the criminal justice process. Section B provides an overview of how a case progresses through the criminal justice system. Section C then discusses why procedural rules are important, and section D sets forth the governing constitutional principles. Finally, section E discusses the applicability of constitutional rights to the states through the Incorporation Doctrine, with section F addressing the test for determining when new procedural rules are to be applied retroactively.

A. THE PARTICIPANTS IN THE CRIMINAL JUSTICE SYSTEM

Many types of individuals play a role in the criminal justice system. The rules of procedure constantly attempt to address the needs of each of these participants while also respecting the rights and interests of the others.

1. Defendants

All defendants have an interest in ensuring that their constitutional rights are respected, and that they have an opportunity to zealously contest the charges brought against them. To ensure that they receive fair trials, defendants will ordinarily be represented by defense counsel — either retained or appointed by the court (see Chapter 7). Moreover, although some refer to the adversarial system as a "search for the truth," criminal defendants' main interest and goal is to avoid conviction.

2. Defense Counsel

Defense counsel represents defendants in criminal actions. Unlike prosecutors, who must serve the "interests of justice" regardless of whether doing so entails convicting or acquitting a defendant, "[t]he basic duty defense counsel owe[] to the administration of justice and as . . . officer[s] of the court is to serve as [defendants'] counselor[s] and advocate[s] with courage and devotion and to render effective, quality representation." ABA Standards Relating to the Administration of Criminal Justice, Defense Standard 4-1.2(b).

Many defendants cannot afford a lawyer, yet a lawyer is critical to having a fair adversarial process. Accordingly, the Supreme Court has recognized a right to the assistance of counsel in all cases in which the defendant faces incarceration. The right to counsel and the standards for effective assistance of counsel are discussed in Chapter 7.

3. Prosecutors

Currently, prosecutors file over 10 million criminal cases annually in the United States.[1] Prosecutors represent the community in criminal actions. Federal prosecutors represent the United States and are assigned by either the local U.S. Attorney's Office or the Department of Justice. City attorneys, district attorneys, and county prosecutors represent local jurisdictions; the state attorney general represents the state at large. Unlike U.S. Attorneys, most states' prosecutors are elected officials.

The prosecutor has a unique role in the criminal justice system. "The prosecutor is an administrator of justice, an advocate, and an officer of the court. . . . The duty of the prosecutor is to seek justice, not merely to convict." ABA Standards Relating to the Administration of Criminal Justice, Prosecution Standard 3-1.2(b)–(c).

---

1. For more information regarding criminal caseloads in state courts, *see* National Center for State Courts, *Examining the Work of State Courts, 2005: A National Perspective from the Court Statistics Project*, http://cdm16501.contentdm.oclc.org/cdm/singleitem/collection/ctadmin/id/412/rec/19.

Prosecutors enjoy great discretion in the exercise of their duties. As discussed in Chapter 2, prosecutors can decide which cases and defendants to charge, what charges to bring, and how serious a sentence to seek.

If a case goes to trial, the prosecutor has a duty to represent the government in those prosecutions. Moreover, during the investigative phase of trial, a prosecutor may also be responsible for supervising the work of police and investigators. This duty may require the prosecutor to prepare search warrants, issue subpoenas, and supervise grand jury proceedings.

4. Victims

Victims' interests are represented in criminal cases by the prosecutor. Prosecutors, not victims, decide which cases to charge, whether to plea bargain, trial strategies, and even sentencing recommendations. Criminal victims' roles are circumscribed. Some states have passed laws, or even constitutional amendments, that provide victims a limited right to observe criminal proceedings, *see, e.g.*, Ariz. Const. art. II, §2.1(3), and to speak at sentencing, *see, e.g.*, N.Y. Crim. Proc. Law §380.50(2) (McKinney 2007). However, because a crime is considered to be an offense against the entire community and not just individual victims, victims do not control the handling of criminal cases.

5. Police and Other Law Enforcement Officers

Police officers are on the front line of the criminal justice system. They serve several purposes, from ensuring the public's safety to investigating allegations of crimes to apprehending individuals responsible for those crimes. Police officers, like prosecutors, wield an enormous amount of discretion. They make the initial decision of whether to investigate a case, and whether to arrest and charge an individual with an offense. Police officers make these decisions even though they are not ordinarily lawyers.

The focus of police officers is on the safety of the community. Although they may be aware of defendants' constitutional rights, the pressure on police officers to ensure community safety and their eagerness to secure convictions may lead to violation of these rights.

Investigative criminal procedure focuses on what procedures police may use when apprehending and investigating defendants. Specifically, it addresses the rules for searches, seizures, and interrogations of defendants.

There are many different types of law enforcement officers in the United States. Each jurisdiction is likely to have its own police force. Currently, there are over 18,000 law enforcement agencies in the United States, with over 15,000 of them consisting of municipal police departments. The primary federal law enforcement agencies include the Federal Bureau of Investigation (FBI), the Secret Service, the Drug Enforcement Administration (DEA), the Bureau of Alcohol, Tobacco and Firearms (ATF), the Bureau of Customs and Borders Prosecution (CBP), Immigration and Customs Enforcement (ICE), and the Securities and Exchange Commission (SEC).

6. Magistrates and Judges

Magistrates and judges are the neutral decision makers in the criminal justice system. One crucial aspect of their role is to ensure that defendants' constitutional rights are respected. Thus, in federal courts, magistrates determine whether search or arrest warrants should issue, whether there is sufficient evidence to hold an arrested defendant, and even whether bail should be granted. Both magistrates and judges may review police conduct to determine if evidence should be suppressed because of constitutional violations. Judges have the additional responsibility of supervising criminal trials. Magistrates and judges must perform their responsibilities both efficiently and fairly, and are often faced with huge dockets of cases to process through their courts.

The method of selecting judges and holding them accountable varies. In federal court, federal district court and federal court of appeals judges are appointed by the president and must be confirmed by the Senate; once confirmed, they serve for life unless they resign or are impeached and removed from office. Federal magistrate judges are appointed by the district courts and sit for eight-year terms. Many states elect their state court judges through many different types of election systems, and other states have appointed judges.

7. Jurors

There are two types of jurors in the criminal justice system: grand jurors and trial jurors. Grand jurors (discussed in Chapter 2) oversee investigations of cases and decide whether to return indictments against individuals for specific crimes. Trial jurors (discussed in Chapter 8), by contrast, are the fact-finders in most criminal trials. After listening to all of the evidence, they decide whether there is sufficient evidence to convict a defendant. To make this decision, trial jurors ordinarily have to make key credibility decisions in the case by deciding which side's witnesses to believe.

8. Corrections Officials

Once defendants are convicted, corrections officials have the responsibility of supervising defendants' incarceration or release on parole or probation. Like police officers and prosecutors, corrections officials often have huge caseloads. In 2010, there were close to 5 million individuals on probation or parole in the United States.[2]

9. Public

The general public also has an interest in the criminal justice system. Indeed, one of the primary concerns for members of the public is their safety.[3] The public also has a financial interest in ensuring that cases are efficiently processed, and that government officials respect the constitutional rights of citizens. In a criminal prosecution, the prosecutor has the responsibility of representing the interests of the public. However, the legislature also represents the public by enacting the laws that, to a large extent, govern the prosecutor's and judge's authority.

10. Media

Finally, the media has an interest in covering criminal cases and serving as a check on government powers. However, the First Amendment rights and interests of the media easily come into conflict with a defendant's Sixth Amendment right to a fair trial. As discussed in Chapter 7, judges must ensure, to the greatest extent possible, that both the media's and defendants' constitutional rights are respected.

B. STAGES OF THE CRIMINAL JUSTICE PROCESS

Before embarking on a detailed discussion of the rules governing criminal procedure, it is helpful to understand how a case proceeds through the criminal justice system. Although there may be slight variations in the process depending on the nature of a particular case and the jurisdiction in which it is adjudicated,[4] the typical route for criminal cases is as follows:

1. Step 1: Pre-Arrest Investigation

If a crime occurs, the police may have little time to investigate the case. When time is of the essence, police officers may have to make their own

---

2. Department of Justice, Bureau of Justice Statistics, *Sourcebook of Criminal Justice Statistics Online*, Table 6.1.2010, http://www.albany.edu/sourcebook/pdf/t612010.pdf.

3. *See, e.g.*, Lydia Saad, *Worry About Crime Remains at Last Year's Elevated Levels*, Gallup, Oct. 19, 2006, http://www.gallup.com/poll/25078/Worry-About-Crime-Remains-Last-Years-Elevated-Levels.aspx.

4. There are 52 different jurisdictions (each state, the District of Columbia, and federal prosecutions), each having its own rules of procedure.

observations, or use the accounts of others at the scene, to gather the minimal amount of information necessary to execute an arrest. For these on-the-scene arrests, the majority of the investigation will occur after the suspect is already in custody. Such investigations may include witness and victim interviews, interrogations of the suspect, identification procedures, undercover follow-up investigations, searches, and issuance of evidence sub-poenas. Close to 50 percent of all criminal cases are handled in this manner. Thus, police officers will often have only a few minutes to decide whether to arrest a suspect, and their ability to conduct a pre-arrest investigation will be greatly limited.

In the remainder of cases, however, a lengthy investigation will typically occur before a suspect is arrested. Police will use their investigative tools, such as search warrants, interviews, informants, and evidence collection, to seek formal charges against the suspect before they execute an arrest. A magistrate may then issue an arrest warrant, together with a formal complaint filed by the prosecution, or the prosecution will obtain an arrest warrant in conjunction with a grand jury indictment. When there has been a grand jury indictment, months or years of pre-arrest investigation may have occurred, including witnesses testifying before the grand jury.

2. Step 2: Arrest

Police have enormous discretion to decide whether to arrest a suspect. When an arrest occurs, it may be with or without a warrant. Once a suspect is taken into custody, he begins his journey through the criminal justice process. If the police did not use an arrest warrant, they must file an affidavit with the court setting forth the probable cause for the arrest and getting a complaint to hold the defendant for further proceedings. Even if the police did use an arrest warrant, the defendant has the right to appear before a judge, be informed of his constitutional rights, be advised of the charges against him, and be assigned counsel.

For some minor offenses, a suspect may merely receive a citation and will not be formally arrested. A citation or summons requires that the suspect appear at a later date to answer the charges against him. Likewise, if a suspect is not a flight risk, an indictment may be issued along with a summons for the suspect to appear instead of an authorization for an arrest warrant.

If a suspect is arrested, he is taken to the police station for booking. Once his picture and background information is taken, the suspect is placed into a holding facility. Depending on the offense, the suspect may be able to post bail based on an approved bail schedule. If the suspect posts bail, he will be ordered to appear in court on a specific date for further proceedings. If the suspect does not post bail, he will be held in jail until he is released by the court.

3. Step 3: Filing the Complaint[5]

For police to be able to hold a suspect after arrest, the prosecution must file charges. Once the prosecution does so, it takes over the decision-making process from the police, and has discretion as to which charges to file. If the suspect has not been indicted, the prosecutor will use a complaint to file initial charges against the suspect. The complaint must be supported by a showing of probable cause based on a sworn affidavit by law enforcement officers.

4. Step 4: Gerstein Review

The magistrate judge must review the prosecution's complaint and support-ing affidavit to determine whether there is probable cause supporting the initial charges against the defendant. This review is called a "*Gerstein* review" because it was first prescribed by the Supreme Court in Gerstein v. Pugh, 420 U.S. 103 (1975). The magistrate's review for probable cause is done ex parte and is based on the filings alone — no evidentiary hearing is required. Often, the court will conduct a *Gerstein* review at the time of the defendant's first appearance, as long as that first appearance occurs within 48 hours of the defendant's arrest, as required by the Supreme Court in County of Riverside v. McLaughlin, 500 U.S. 44 (1991).

5. Step 5: First Appearance/Arraignment on Complaint

Once the prosecution files a complaint, the defendant is also entitled to appear before the court to be advised of the charges against him, have an opportunity to seek bail, and be advised of his right to retain counsel or to have counsel assigned. For example, Rule 5 of the Federal Rules of Criminal Procedure requires that arresting officers bring the accused before a mag-istrate judge "without unnecessary delay." Ordinarily, the first appearance, sometimes called an "initial arraignment" or "preliminary arraignment," depending on the jurisdiction, will occur within 48 hours of the defendant's arrest. This proceeding is usually a brief one and is merely a minimal check to ensure that a basis for the defendant's arrest exists.

---

5. See Chapter 2.

6. *Step 6: Grand Jury or Preliminary Hearing*[6]

Before a defendant is required to stand trial, there must be another screening of the cases that establishes the charges the defendant will face at trial. The Fifth Amendment promises that for all federal felonies, a defendant is entitled to grand jury indictment. With ancient roots in British common law, the grand jury serves as a screening process to formalize charges for trial. It serves as a minimum check on the prosecutor's decision to bring charges.

A grand jury consists of 23 members of the community who listen to evidence presented by the prosecution and decide whether there is probable cause to prosecute the defendant. There is no judge in the grand jury, nor is the defendant or defense counsel entitled to be present.

The prosecutor generally directs the grand jury operations. If there is probable cause, the grand jury issues an indictment, or "true bill." The indictment sets forth the charges the defendant will face at trial. If the grand jury does not want to indict, it issues a "no bill." Grand juries also have the power to investigate cases by calling witnesses or issuing subpoenas.

Although some states choose to use grand juries in felony prosecutions, they are not bound to do so by the Fifth Amendment. In addition, they need not use the same procedures as federal grand juries. Thus, unlike federal grand juries, some states may limit the type of evidence that grand juries may hear or give the defense a greater opportunity to present evidence to the grand jury. A detailed analysis of grand jury procedures is set forth in Chapter 2.

Another mechanism to screen cases before trial is the preliminary hearing. The Constitution does not require preliminary hearings, but a majority of jurisdictions use them to decide whether there is enough evidence to hold a defendant for trial and to settle on which charges the prosecution will bring. A preliminary hearing is very different from a grand jury proceeding. No jury is present during a preliminary hearing. The judge presiding over the hearing decides whether there is probable cause to "bind the case over" for trial. Although procedures can differ by jurisdiction, both sides are generally given an opportunity to present evidence during the preliminary hearing. In some jurisdictions, hearsay evidence can be used to establish probable cause. As an adversarial process, both sides have an opportunity to cross-examine witnesses. The preliminary hearing gives the defendant a preview of the prosecution's case. If the prosecution does not establish probable cause for a particular charge, the court can reject that charge. If all charges are rejected, the court may order the case dismissed. If the defendant is bound over for trial, however, the court will replace the complaint with a formal information charging the defendant with the offenses he will face at trial. Preliminary hearings are also discussed in Chapter 2.

6. See Chapter 2.

7. Step 7: Arraignment on Indictment or Information

Once an indictment or information is filed, the defendant will appear for arraignment on those charges. At the arraignment, the defendant will typically be asked to enter a plea of guilty or not guilty, be advised of the charges against him, and be assigned counsel if counsel has not yet been assigned. The court will then assign a trial date. The trial date must comply with constitutional standards for a speedy trial (see Chapter 6) and any applicable Speedy Trial Acts.

8. Step 8: Discovery[7]

To prepare for trial, the parties will engage in discovery. Discovery is the process by which the parties seek to examine the evidence that the other party is likely to use at trial. Statutes and procedural rules often govern discovery. However, defendants also have a due process right to exculpatory evidence and evidence that may impeach the prosecution's witnesses (see Chapter 4).

In the federal system, discovery of witness statements is covered by separate statutes. In state courts, comprehensive discovery statutes often cover both inculpatory and exculpatory evidence, including witness statements.

9. Step 9: Pretrial Motions

Frequently, the parties will file pretrial motions regarding a variety of issues. The defense will seek to suppress evidence illegally obtained by the prosecution, move to change venue, and seek dismissal for speedy trial violations or problems with the charges. The prosecution will also have an opportunity to file pretrial motions. For example, the prosecution may file pretrial motions *in limine* to get pretrial rulings on key evidentiary issues in the case. Pretrial motions help the parties define the scope of their own cases, and to assess the relative strength of the other side's case.

10. Step 10: Plea Bargaining and Guilty Pleas[8]

More than 90 percent of all criminal cases never go to trial. Rather, the vast majority of cases—97 percent in federal court and 94 percent in state courts—end with a guilty or *nolo contendere* (no contest) plea. During the plea bargaining process, prosecutors may choose to reduce the charges or sentence exposure for a defendant in exchange for the defendant's guilty

---

7. See Chapter 4.
8. See Chapter 5.

plea, and oftentimes, the defendant's cooperation. Anticipating that plea bargaining will occur, it is not unusual for prosecutors to load up charges against the defendant so that there is room to compromise during plea bargaining.

If a defendant decides to plead guilty, a formal hearing is held for the defendant to enter his plea. A guilty plea is both an admission that the defendant committed the crime, and a waiver of all of the rights the defendant would have had if he proceeded to trial. Thus, at a guilty plea hearing, the defendant will be advised of his right to counsel, right to confront witnesses, right to present evidence, right to a jury, and privilege against self-incrimination. If the defendant waives these rights, the court will ask for a factual basis for the plea. Either the prosecutor or the defense may provide the recitation necessary to establish that there is a basis for the plea. The court will also determine whether the plea is voluntary, and the nature of any inducements for the plea. Finally, the court will advise the defendant of the consequences of pleading guilty. If the defendant's guilty plea is knowing and voluntary, the court will accept the plea. The guilty plea obviates the need for a trial.

A defendant may also enter a *nolo contendere* plea. A *nolo contendere* plea has the same effect in the criminal case as a guilty plea. The defendant can receive the same criminal punishment as a defendant who enters a guilty plea. However, unlike a guilty plea, which serves as an admission for a civil case that the defendant is responsible, a *nolo contendere* plea has no impact on any companion civil case. Both guilty pleas and *nolo contendere* pleas are examined in Chapter 5.

11.   Step 11: Trial[9]

If a defendant does not plead guilty, the case proceeds to trial. A trial may be a court ("bench") trial or jury trial. If the case is going to be decided by a judge alone, both sides must agree to waive the right to jury trial. The judge will then hear the evidence adduced at trial, and decide whether there is proof beyond reasonable doubt for each of the charges.

The right to jury trial is guaranteed by the Sixth Amendment for all serious offenses, which the Supreme Court has defined as offenses that carry a possible sentence of more than six months in custody. Although there is a popular notion that 12 persons must sit on a jury, the Supreme Court has held to the contrary. States may choose to have juries as small as six persons for noncapital felony cases. Moreover, there is no constitutional requirement that the jurors' verdict be unanimous. Depending on the size of the jury, a nonunanimous jury may be sufficient.

---

9. See Chapter 7.

The jury selection process begins with a panel of jurors (called the "venire") being summoned for jury selection. Potential jurors are questioned in a process called "voir dire" to reveal their backgrounds, attitudes, and any possible biases they may hold. The parties can excuse jurors from the jury by using challenges for cause, or by exercising peremptory challenges. Challenges for cause are allegations that specific jurors cannot be fair. Each side has an unlimited number of challenges for cause. By contrast, each party will have a limited number of peremptory challenges. Peremptory challenges need not be supported by a showing of actual bias by the juror. Each side has wide discretion in exercising peremptory challenges, although it is improper to use them in a discriminatory manner. Once jurors are finally chosen to sit on a case, they are referred to as the "petit" jury.

It is the jury's job to listen to all of the evidence, consider the court's jury instructions, and decide whether the defendant is guilty beyond a reasonable doubt. If the jury is not able to reach a decision, it constitutes a hung jury, and the court will declare a mistrial. In general, the prosecution can retry a defendant following a hung jury.

12. Step 12: Sentencing[10]

If the defendant is convicted, he will be sentenced by the court, ordinarily at a separate sentencing hearing. Before deciding on a sentence, the court will receive reports by the probation officer and input from the parties. At the sentencing hearing, the defendant has an opportunity to address the court. Sentencing systems vary greatly in the United States. In some jurisdictions, judges have broad discretion in imposing a sentence. In other jurisdictions, sentencing guidelines and mandatory sentences control a judge's sentence. If the judge's sentence must be based on specific factual findings other than a defendant's prior criminal record, the trier of fact must find the existence of those facts beyond a reasonable doubt if they will increase the defendant's sentence beyond the presumptive sentence for that crime.

13. Step 13: Appeals and Habeas Corpus[11]

Finally, a defendant is entitled to challenge his conviction on direct appeal or through collateral proceedings known as habeas corpus proceedings. On direct appeal, the defendant may challenge errors by the court or prosecution at trial. A defendant has the right to an initial appeal to an intermediate court. Unless otherwise provided by statute, a defendant does not have the right to review by the state's high court. On appeal, the burden shifts to the

---

10. See Chapter 8.
11. See Chapter 11.

defendant to demonstrate why he did not receive a fair trial, or that there was insufficient evidence to support the jury's verdict.

After all direct appeals are completed, a defendant also may challenge constitutional violations in his case through a habeas corpus petition. These are sometimes called forms of "collateral review." Habeas corpus petitions are suits that allege that the defendant is being held unconstitutionally. Both state and federal courts have procedures for collateral review; in federal court it is via a petition for a writ of habeas corpus. One of the primary grounds for habeas corpus petitions is ineffective assistance of counsel. Fourth Amendment search and seizure issues are not sufficient bases for habeas corpus challenges. In a habeas corpus petition, the court may hold an evidentiary hearing to determine whether there has been a constitutional violation. However, most habeas petitions are decided without a hearing. Because habeas corpus petitions are considered civil proceedings, defendants are not constitutionally entitled to the assistance of counsel. Habeas corpus is discussed in Chapter 11.

If a defendant succeeds on appeal or with a habeas corpus petition, the ordinary remedy is a retrial. However, if the appellate court finds that there was insufficient evidence to support the verdict, the defendant may not be retried because of double jeopardy principles.

C. THE PURPOSE OF PROCEDURAL RULES

To understand why procedural rules are important, it is helpful to consider situations in which fair procedures are not afforded to defendants. In the infamous "Scottsboro trial," nine young black men were accused of raping two white women on a train from Chattanooga to Memphis, Tennessee. The train was intercepted as it traveled through Alabama, and the boys were captured and nearly lynched. There, they faced trial. Newspapers decried them as guilty, and all of the ugly traits of racism in the South in 1931 took hold. The defendants were brought to trial six days after they were indicted. The newspapers proclaimed them guilty of their "atrocious crime" even before the trial began. The judge perfunctorily appointed the entire local bar to represent the boys, although none of them investigated the case or assumed the role of zealous representatives of the defendants. The defendants were convicted and sentenced to death after a one-day trial before an all-white jury. During the trial, the credibility of the alleged victims was seriously impeached. Even though the victims, Victoria Price and Ruby Bates, were known prostitutes and transients, and Bates later recanted her testimony, it took years before the defendants' sentences were finally vacated.

As you read the Supreme Court's decision in their appeal, consider the importance of the rights to a fair trial, effective counsel, discovery, and due process. Consider also the role that race and economic status play in the criminal justice system.

POWELL v. ALABAMA
287 U.S. 45 (1932)

Justice SUTHERLAND delivered the opinion of the Court.

The petitioners, hereinafter referred to as defendants, are negroes charged with the crime of rape, committed upon the persons of two white girls. The crime is said to have been committed on March 25, 1931. The indictment was returned in a state court of first instance on March 31, and the record recites that on the same day the defendants were arraigned and entered pleas of not guilty. There is a further recital to the effect that upon the arraignment they were represented by counsel. But no counsel had been employed, and aside from a statement made by the trial judge several days later during a colloquy immediately preceding the trial, the record does not disclose when, or under what circumstances, an appointment of counsel was made, or who was appointed.

Each of the three trials was completed within a single day. Under the Alabama statute the punishment for rape is to be fixed by the jury, and in its discretion may be from ten years imprisonment to death. The juries found defendants guilty and imposed the death penalty upon all.

In this court the judgments are assailed upon the grounds that the defendants, and each of them, were denied due process of law and the equal protection of the laws, in contravention of the Fourteenth Amendment, specifically as follows: (1) they were not given a fair, impartial and deliberate trial; (2) they were denied the right of counsel, with the accustomed incidents of consultation and opportunity of preparation for trial; and (3) they were tried before juries from which qualified members of their own race were systematically excluded.

The only one of the assignments which we shall consider is the second, in respect of the denial of counsel; and it becomes unnecessary to discuss the facts of the case or the circumstances surrounding the prosecution except in so far as they reflect light upon that question.

The record shows that on the day when the offense is said to have been committed, these defendants, together with a number of other negroes, were upon a freight train on its way through Alabama. On the same train were seven white boys and the two white girls. A fight took place between the negroes and the white boys, in the course of which the white boys, with the exception of one named Gilley, were thrown off the train. A message was sent ahead, reporting the fight and asking that every negro be gotten off the train. The participants in the fight, and the two girls, were in an open gondola car. The two girls testified that each of them was assaulted by six different negroes in turn, and they identified the seven defendants as having been among the number. None of the white boys was called to testify, with the exception of Gilley, who was called in rebuttal.

Before the train reached Scottsboro, Alabama, a sheriff's posse seized the defendants and two other negroes. Both girls and the negroes then were taken to Scottsboro, the county seat. Word of their coming and of the alleged assault had preceded them, and they were met at Scottsboro by a large crowd. The sheriff thought it necessary to call for the militia to assist in safeguarding the prisoners. It is perfectly apparent that the proceedings, from beginning to end, took place in an atmosphere of tense, hostile and excited public sentiment. [T]he record clearly indicates that most, if not all, of them were youthful, and they are constantly referred to as "the boys." They were ignorant and illiterate. All of them were residents of other states, where alone members of their families or friends resided.

However guilty defendants, upon due inquiry, might prove to have been, they were, until convicted, presumed to be innocent. It was the duty of the court having their cases in charge to see that they were denied no necessary incident of a fair trial. With any error of the state court involving alleged contravention of the state statutes or constitution we, of course, have nothing to do. The sole inquiry which we are permitted to make is whether the federal Constitution was contravened and as to that, we confine ourselves, as already suggested, to the inquiry whether the defendants were in substance denied the right of counsel, and if so, whether such denial infringes the due process clause of the Fourteenth Amendment.

First. The record shows that immediately upon the return of the indictment defendants were arraigned and pleaded not guilty. Apparently they were not asked whether they had, or were able to employ, counsel, or wished to have counsel appointed; or whether they had friends or relatives who might assist in that regard if communicated with. "They were nonresidents," he said, "and had little time or opportunity to get in touch with their families and friends who were scattered throughout two other states, and time has demonstrated that they could or would have been represented by able counsel had a better opportunity been given by a reasonable delay in the trial of the cases. . . ."

April 6, six days after indictment, the trials began. When the first case was called, the court inquired whether the parties were ready for trial. The state's attorney replied that he was ready to proceed. No one answered for the defendants or appeared to represent or defend them. Mr. Roddy, a Tennessee lawyer not a member of the local bar, addressed the court, saying that he had not been employed, but that people who were interested had spoken to him about the case. He was asked by the court whether he intended to appear for the defendants, and answered that he would like to appear along with counsel that the court might appoint. The record then proceeds:

Mr. Roddy: Your Honor has appointed counsel, is that correct?
The Court: I appointed all the members of the bar for the purpose of arraigning the defendants and then of course I anticipated them to continue to help them if no counsel appears.
Mr. Roddy: Then I don't appear then as counsel but I do want to stay in and not be ruled out in this case.

I merely came down here as a friend of the people who are interested and not as paid counsel I am merely here at the solicitation of people who have become interested in this case without any payment of fee and without any preparation for trial and I think the boys would be better off if I step entirely out of the case according to my way of looking at it and according to my lack of preparation of it and not being familiar with the procedure in Alabama, . . .

The Court: All right.

It thus will be seen that until the very morning of the trial no lawyer had been named or definitely designated to represent the defendants. Prior to that time, the trial judge had "appointed all the members of the bar" for the limited "purpose of arraigning the defendants."

That this action of the trial judge in respect of appointment of counsel was little more than an expansive gesture, imposing no substantial or definite obligation upon any one, is borne out by the fact that prior to the calling of the case for trial on April 6, a leading member of the local bar accepted employment on the side of the prosecution and actively participated in the trial. [T]he circumstance lends emphasis to the conclusion that during perhaps the most critical period of the proceedings against these defendants, that is to say, from the time of their arraignment until the beginning of their trial, when consultation, thoroughgoing investigation and preparation were vitally important, the defendants did not have the aid of counsel in any real sense. . . .

Under the circumstances disclosed, we hold that defendants were not accorded the right of counsel in any substantial sense. To decide otherwise, would simply be to ignore actualities.

In the light of the facts outlined in the forepart of this opinion — the ignorance and illiteracy of the defendants, their youth, the circumstances of public hostility, the imprisonment and the close surveillance of the defendants by the military forces, the fact that their friends and families were all in other states and communication with them necessarily difficult, and above all that they stood in deadly peril of their lives — we think the failure of the trial court to give them reasonable time and opportunity to secure counsel was a clear denial of due process.

Judgments reversed.

———————————

Why are procedures so important? As *Powell* demonstrates, without fair procedures and respect for constitutional rights, there is a strong likelihood that the defendants will not be treated fairly, and that persons will be held accountable for crimes they did not commit. Procedural rules thus play a crucial role in ensuring the fair and efficient processing of cases, as well as the perception of the public and defendants that the criminal justice system has acted in a reliable and fair manner.

Even today, there are numerous obstacles to the fair handling of criminal investigations and prosecutions. Many defendants are poor and do not receive effective representation in asserting their rights. A large percentage of defendants are uneducated, unemployed, and have a substance abuse problem. Law enforcement officials are often overworked and undertrained. Racial stereotypes permeate society, including the criminal justice system. There can also be political pressure on prosecutors to secure convictions. All of these factors may impact how effectively our laws are implemented.

Moreover, it is not just the courts who must abide by fair procedures. Much of criminal procedure is devoted to ensuring that law enforcement officers respect the rights of defendants during the investigative phase of cases. Consider how police conduct affects the likelihood of reaching a correct and fair result in a case.

PATTERSON v. FORMER CHICAGO POLICE LT. JON BURGE

328 F. Supp. 2d 878 (N.D. Ill. 2004)

Opinion by Joan B. GOTTSCHALL:

After being convicted for the 1986 murders of Rafaela and Vincent Sanchez and spending 13 years on death row, plaintiff Aaron Patterson was pardoned by Illinois Governor George Ryan on January 10, 2003. Patterson filed this civil action in June of 2003, asserting that defendants, individually and in conspiracy, violated his rights under the United States Constitution when they knowingly filed false charges and framed him for the Sanchez murders, tortured and beat him at Chicago Police Department's Area 2 headquarters, fabricated his "confession" and falsified inculpatory evidence, coerced witnesses to testify against him, gave perjured testimony, published defamatory statements regarding his guilt, and obstructed justice and suppressed exculpatory evidence throughout his suppression hearing, trial, and post-conviction proceedings.

I. BACKGROUND

On April 19, 1986, Chicago Police Department officers discovered the dead bodies of Rafaela and Vincent Sanchez in their apartment at 8849 South Burley. Officers and defendants Lt. Jon Burge, Sgt. John Byrne, Detectives James Pienta, William Marley, Daniel McWeeny, Joseph Danzl (collectively, "Area 2 defendants"), and other Area 2 detectives were assigned to investigate the Sanchez murders. On April 21, Danzl allegedly coerced and intimidated 16 year-old Marva Hall, whose uncle was a suspect in the murders, into falsely implicating Patterson. On April 22, Burge and another Area 2 detective took a different suspect, Michael Arbuckle, into custody at Area 2 headquarters. Burge allegedly told Arbuckle that they "really wanted to get Aaron Patterson" and wanted Arbuckle to say that Patterson was involved in the murders. When Arbuckle refused to implicate Patterson and asked for his lawyer, Burge threatened him with electrocution and lethal injection and told him that they would get Arbuckle to "cooperate one way or another." Still, Arbuckle denied his and Patterson's involvement.

On or about April 23, McWeeny, Byrne, and other Area 2 detectives on the case were informed by several persons that Willie Washington and his brother killed Rafaela and Vincent Sanchez. Nevertheless, for the next week, Byrne, McWeeny, and other Area 2 detectives searched unsuccessfully for Patterson. On April 30, Patterson was arrested on an outstanding warrant by Chicago Police Department officers from the Fourth District. Defendants Pienta, Marley, and Pedersen were called to transport Patterson from the Fourth District police station to Area 2. During the ride, Pienta allegedly told Patterson that if he had arrested him, he would have killed him.

At Area 2 Patterson was placed in an interview room, handcuffed to the wall, and questioned by Area 2 detectives about the Sanchez murders for about an hour. Patterson denied any involvement. He was then taken to 11th and State before being returned to the interview room at Area 2. After brief questioning, Pienta told Patterson that he was "tired of this bullshit," left the room, and came back with a grey typewriter cover. When Patterson refused to implicate himself in the murders, the Area 2 defendants, including Pienta, Marley, and Pedersen, handcuffed him behind his back, turned out the lights, and repeatedly beat him in the chest and suffocated him by holding the typewriter cover over his face and ears for at least a minute. Pienta continued to urge Patterson to "cooperate," and when he refused, the Area 2 defendants again turned out the lights and suffocated Patterson with the plastic cover. The second time, the "bagging" and beating lasted for over two minutes. Patterson found the abuse unbearable and told the detectives he would "say anything you say" if they would stop the suffocation and beating.

After Patterson agreed to cooperate, the Area 2 defendants left the room to get a state's attorney from the felony review division to take his statement. While alone in the room, Patterson used a paper clip to scratch into the interview room bench that he was "suffocated with plastic" and that his statement to the police was false. Defendant Burge returned with an Assistant State's Attorney ("ASA") who said that Burge told him Patterson wanted to make a statement. After Burge left the room at Patterson's request, Patterson told the ASA that he had nothing to say. The ASA left and told Burge that Patterson refused to confess. Burge then returned to the room, told Patterson "you're fucking up," placed his handgun on the table in front of Patterson, and said "we told you if you don't do what we tell you to, you're going to get something worse than before—it will have been a snap compared to what you will get." He also told Patterson that if he revealed the torture, "it's your word against ours and who are they going to believe, you or us." Burge then told Patterson that they could do anything they wanted to him.

Next, defendant Peter Troy, an ASA with the State's Attorney's Office ("SAO"), entered the interview room with Area 2 defendant Madigan. Initially, Patterson agreed to make a statement in exchange for phone privileges, but he refused to sign the statement Troy had written out after the Area 2 defendants terminated his calls. In an attempt to make Patterson sign the statement, Troy and Madigan physically attacked Patterson. McWeeny entered the room at this time, professing not to be involved in the prior beatings and suffocation, and urged Patterson to cooperate because the other defendants "could do something serious to him if he didn't." As a result of this coercion and under threat of continued torture, Patterson said he would agree with whatever the Area 2 defendants and Troy said had happened.

Around the same time, defendant Pienta arrested Eric Caine, Patterson's co-defendant in the Sanchez murder prosecution. Caine was interrogated and beaten and told that if he did not make a statement he would get the same treatment as Patterson. Caine initially gave a statement, but when he tried to repudiate it Madigan hit Caine with his open hand over his ear and cheekbone, causing a loud pop and rupturing his ear drum. Caine screamed in pain; he later gave and signed a court-reported statement prepared by the Area 2 defendants which falsely implicated Patterson in the murders.

The Area 2 defendants, together with SAO defendants Troy and William Lacy, allegedly fabricated oral admissions and reduced these "admissions" to false reports implicating Patterson and Caine in the Sanchez murders. Defendants communicated these false reports to the prosecuting attorneys, who used them at Patterson's suppression hearing and at trial. Defendants also testified falsely about the fabricated admissions and the torture and abuse which produced them throughout Patterson's prosecution. No physical evidence linking Patterson to the murders was ever discovered, though a bloody fingerprint that was not Patterson's was found at the scene and not introduced at trial. Patterson was convicted for the Sanchez murders on the basis of his false confession and the testimony of Marva Hall and defendants. Patterson was sentenced to death, and after his conviction was affirmed on appeal, spent over 13 years incarcerated on death row until his pardon in January of 2003.

In a televised interview in December of 1999 defendant Byrne made defamatory statements concerning Patterson's protestations of his innocence and claims of torture at Area 2, including that Patterson was "without a doubt" "guilty of the [Sanchez] murders" and that "the detectives who worked with him would not" and did not torture suspects. On January 10, 2003, then Governor of Illinois George Ryan granted Patterson and three other death row victims allegedly tortured by Burge and other Area 2 detectives pardons on the basis of innocence. In granting the pardons Governor Ryan announced that "the category of horrors was hard to believe," and the evidence showed that the four men — Patterson, Madison Hobley, Leroy Orange, and Stanley Howard — had been "beaten and tortured and convicted on the basis of confessions they allegedly provided." In response, State's Attorney Devine publicly condemned the pardons of the four men, whom he referred to as "evil" and "convicted murderers," as "outrageous" and "unconscionable."

As *Patterson* illustrates, constitutional rights are not just formalities. They are critical to ensuring that police respect people's rights and that the right people are held responsible for criminal actions.

D. KEY PROVISIONS OF THE BILL OF RIGHTS

The Bill of Rights protects individuals against the power of the State. Fundamental rights ensured by a number of the first ten amendments have been made applicable to the states under the Fourteenth Amendment's Due Process Clause. The following key constitutional provisions are covered in this book.

AMENDMENT IV
The right of the people to be secure in their persons, houses, papers, and effects, against unreasonable searches and seizures, shall not be violated, and no Warrants shall issue but upon probable cause, supported by Oath or affirmation, and particularly describing the place to be searched, and the persons or things to be seized.

The Fourth Amendment is the key constitutional provision governing police conduct during searches and arrest. The amendment has been interpreted as generally requiring a warrant based on probable cause for a search or arrest. However, there are numerous exceptions that allow for warrantless searches and stops as long as they are "reasonable."

AMENDMENT V
No person shall be held to answer for a capital, or otherwise infamous crime, unless on a presentment or indictment of a Grand Jury . . . ; nor shall any person be subject for the same offense to be twice put in jeopardy of life or limb; nor shall be compelled in any criminal case to be a witness against himself, nor be deprived of life, liberty, or property, without due process of law.

There are several aspects to the Fifth Amendment. It sets forth the right in federal cases to indictment by a grand jury (see Chapter 2). It also provides for the right against double jeopardy (Chapter 10), the privilege against self-incrimination, and the general right of due process in criminal cases.

AMENDMENT VI
In all criminal prosecutions, the accused shall enjoy the right to a speedy and public trial, by an impartial jury of the State and district wherein the crime shall have been committed, which district shall have been previously ascertained by law; and to be informed of the nature and cause of the accusation; to be confronted with the witnesses against him; to have compulsory process for obtaining witnesses in his favor, and to have the Assistance of Counsel for his defense.

The Sixth Amendment guarantees a defendant the right to a speedy and public jury trial. (See Chapter 8.) It also requires that the defendant be given an opportunity to confront the witnesses against him and to call his own witnesses. However, the most important right that the defendant enjoys under the Sixth Amendment is the right to assistance of counsel. (See Chapter 7.) Through counsel's diligent efforts, a defendant can preserve his other rights.

AMENDMENT VIII
Excessive bail shall not be required, nor excessive fines imposed, nor cruel and unusual punishment inflicted.

The Eighth Amendment prohibits cruel and unusual punishment. (See Chapter 9.) The standard for "cruel and unusual punishment" evolves. Generally, the term "cruel and unusual punishment" relates to the proportionality of the sentence, not just the manner in which the sentence is imposed.

E. THE APPLICATION OF THE BILL OF RIGHTS TO THE STATES

1. *The Provisions of the Bill of Rights and the Idea of "Incorporation"*

There are a few criminal procedure protections in the first seven articles of the Constitution, such as the prohibition on Congress suspending the writ of habeas corpus found in Article I, section 9, and the assurance of trial by jury in Article III. But the key protections of criminal procedure examined through this book are found in the Fourth, Fifth, Sixth, and Eighth Amendments.

In understanding the material in this book, it is important to know that these provisions of the Bill of Rights did not apply to state governments until the twentieth century and generally not until the second half of the twentieth century. Initially, it was thought that the Bill of Rights was meant just to limit the federal government; state constitutions were deemed adequate to protect people from abuses by state and local governments.

In Barron v. Mayor & City of Baltimore, 32 U.S. (7 Pet.) 243 (1833), the Supreme Court held that the Bill of Rights did not apply to the states. The specific issue was whether the states had to comply with the Fifth Amendment's prohibition of the taking of private property without just compensation. The Court, in an opinion by Chief Justice John Marshall, declared, "The question thus presented is, we think, of great importance, but not of much difficulty. The constitution was ordained and established by the people of the United States for themselves, for their own government, and not for the government of the individual states." The Court held that the Bill of Rights simply did not apply to the States: "If these propositions be correct, the fifth amendment must be understood as restraining the power of the general government, not as applicable to the states. In their several constitutions, they have imposed such restrictions on their respective governments, as their own wisdom suggested; such as they deemed most proper for themselves."

In the late nineteenth century, the Supreme Court suggested an alternate approach: finding that at least some of the Bill of the Rights provisions are part of the liberty protected from state interference by the Due Process Clause of the Fourteenth Amendment. In other words, the Court indicated that the Due Process Clause of the Fourteenth Amendment, which applies to state and local governments, incorporates and protects at least some of the Bill of Rights.

In 1897, in Chicago, Burlington & Quincy Railroad Co. v. City of Chicago, 166 U.S. 226 (1897), the Supreme Court ruled that the Due Process Clause of the Fourteenth Amendment prevents states from taking property without just compensation. Although the Court did not speak explicitly of the Fourteenth Amendment incorporating the Takings Clause, that was the practical effect of the decision.

In Twining v. New Jersey, 211 U.S. 78 (1908), the Supreme Court first expressly discussed applying the Bill of Rights to the states through the process of incorporation. The specific issue was whether a jury in state court could draw an adverse inference against a criminal defendant for failing to testify. Although the Court held that this does not apply to the states (a conclusion that the Court later would reverse in Griffin v. California, 380 U.S. 609 (1965)), it stated, "[I]t is possible that some of the personal rights safeguarded by the first eight Amendments against national action may also be safeguarded against state action, because a denial of them would be a denial of due process of law. If this is so, it is not because those rights are enumerated in the first eight Amendments, but because they are of such a nature that they are included in the conception of due process of law."

Twining expressly opened the door to the Supreme Court applying provisions of the Bill of Rights to the states by finding them to be included — incorporated — into the Due Process Clause of the Fourteenth Amendment. Soon the Court began to use this door. In Gitlow v. New York, 268 U.S. 652 (1925), the Court for the first time said that the First Amendment's protection of freedom of speech applies to the states through its incorporation into the Due Process Clause of the Fourteenth Amendment. The Court declared, "For present purposes we may and do assume that freedom of speech and of the press — which are protected by the First Amendment from abridgment by Congress — are among the fundamental personal rights and liberties protected by the due process clause of the Fourteenth Amendment from impairment by the States." In *Gitlow*, the Court actually rejected the constitutional challenge to a state law that made it a crime to advocate the violent overthrow of government by force or violence. Two years later, in Fiske v. Kansas, 274 U.S. 380 (1927), the Court for the first time found that a state law regulating speech violated the Due Process Clause of the Fourteenth Amendment.

In 1933, in Powell v. Alabama, 287 U.S. 45 (1932), which is presented above, the Court found that a state's denial of counsel in a capital case denied due process, thereby in essence applying the Sixth Amendment to the states in capital cases. The infamous Scottsboro trial involved two African American men who were convicted of rape without the assistance of an attorney at trial and with a jury from which all blacks had been excluded. The Supreme Court concluded that the Due Process Clause of the Fourteenth Amendment protects fundamental rights from state interference and that this can include Bill of Rights provisions. But the Court said that "[i]f this is so, it is not because those rights are enumerated in the first eight Amendments, but because they are of such a nature that they are included in the 'conception of due process of law.'" The Court held that in a capital case, "it [is] clear that the right to the aid of counsel is of this fundamental character."

2. The Debate over Incorporation

Once the Court found that the Due Process Clause of the Fourteenth Amendment protected fundamental rights from state infringement, there was a major debate over which liberties are safeguarded. For many years, this debate raged among Justices and commentators. On the one side, there were the total incorporationists who believed that all of the Bill of Rights should be deemed to be included in the Due Process Clause of the Fourteenth Amendment. Justices Black and Douglas were the foremost advocates of this position.[12]

On the other side, there were the selective incorporationists who believed that only some of the Bill of Rights were sufficiently fundamental to apply to state and local governments. Justice Cardozo, for example, wrote that "[t]he process of absorption . . . [applied to rights where] neither liberty nor justice would exist if they were sacrificed."[13] Justice Cardozo said that the Due Process Clause included "principles of justice so rooted in the tradition and conscience of our people as to be ranked as fundamental" and that were therefore "implicit in the concept of ordered liberty."[14] Justice Frankfurter said that due process precludes those practices that "offend those canons of decency and fairness which express the notions of justice of English-speaking peoples."[15]

The debate between total and selective incorporation was extremely important because it determined the reach of the Bill of Rights and the extent to which individuals could turn to the federal courts for protection from state and local governments.

For example, in Palko v. Connecticut, 302 U.S. 319 (1937), the Court held the prohibition of double jeopardy, which keeps states from appealing

---

12. *See, e.g.*, Adamson v. California, 332 U.S. 46, 71-72 (1947) (Black, J., dissenting).
13. 302 U.S. 319, 326 (1937).
14. *Id.* at 325.
15. Adamson v. California, 332 U.S. 46, 67 (1947) (Frankfurter, J., concurring).

acquittals in criminal cases, does not apply to the states. Justice Cardozo, writing for the Court, stated, "Is [allowing the State to appeal the] kind of double jeopardy to which the statute has subjected him a hardship so acute and shocking that our policy will not endure it? Does it violate those 'fundamental principles of liberty and justice which lie at the base of all our civil and political institutions'? The answer surely must be 'no.' There is here no seismic innovation. The edifice of justice stands."

Similarly, in Adamson v. California, 332 U.S. 46 (1947), the Court held that states were not obligated to follow the Fifth Amendment's prohibition on a prosecutor's commenting on a criminal defendant's failure to take the witness stand. Justice Black wrote a famous dissent. He declared:

> The first 10 amendments were proposed and adopted largely because of fear that Government might unduly interfere with prized individual liberties. . . . My study of the historical events that culminated in the Fourteenth Amendment, and the expressions of those who sponsored and favored, as well as those who opposed its submission and passage, persuades me that one of the chief objects that the provisions of the Amendment's first section, separately, and as a whole, were intended to accomplish was to make the Bill of Rights applicable to the states. With full knowledge of the import of the *Barron* decision, the framers and backers of the Fourteenth Amendment proclaimed its purpose to be to overturn the constitutional rule that case had announced. This historical purpose has never received full consideration or exposition in any opinion of this Court interpreting the Amendment.[16]

The debate over incorporation primarily was centered on three issues.[17] First, the debate was over history and whether the framers of the Fourteenth Amendment intended for it to apply the Bill of Rights to the states. Both sides of the debate claimed that history supported their view.

Second, the incorporation debate was over federalism. Applying the Bill of Rights to the states imposes a substantial set of restrictions on state and local governments. Not surprisingly, opponents of total incorporation argued based on federalism: the desirability of preserving state and local governing autonomy by freeing them from the application of the Bill of Rights. Defenders of total incorporation responded that federalism is not a sufficient reason for tolerating violations of fundamental liberties.

Third, the debate was over the appropriate judicial role. Advocates of total incorporation, such as Justice Black, claimed that allowing the Court to pick and choose which rights to incorporate left too much to the subjective preference of the justices. In contrast, advocates of selective incorporation denied this and maintained that total incorporation would mean more

---

16. In Griffin v. California, 380 U.S. 609 (1965), the Supreme Court overruled *Adamson* and held that the Due Process Clause of the Fourteenth Amendment was violated by a prosecutor's comments on a defendant's silence.

17. For a detailed description of the debate and the issues, *see* Jerold Israel, *Selective Incorporation Revisited*, 71 Geo. L.J. 253, 336-338 (1982).

judicial oversight of state and local actions and thus less room for democracy to operate.

3. *The Current Law as to What's Incorporated*

The selective incorporationists prevailed in this debate in that the Supreme Court never has accepted the total incorporationist approach. However, from a practical perspective, the total incorporationists largely succeeded in their objective because, one by one, the Supreme Court found almost all of the provisions to be incorporated. This is reflected in the following case, Duncan v. Louisiana, which summarizes the many decisions, particularly of the Warren Court during the 1950s and 1960s, finding almost all of the Bill of Rights to be incorporated.

DUNCAN v. LOUISIANA

391 U.S. 145 (1968)

Justice WHITE delivered the opinion of the Court.

Appellant, Gary Duncan, was convicted of simple battery in the Twenty-fifth Judicial District Court of Louisiana. Under Louisiana law simple battery is a misdemeanor, punishable by a maximum of two years' imprisonment and a $300 fine. Appellant sought trial by jury, but because the Louisiana Constitution grants jury trials only in cases in which capital punishment or imprisonment at hard labor may be imposed, the trial judge denied the request. Appellant was convicted and sentenced to serve 60 days in the parish prison and pay a fine of $150.

The Fourteenth Amendment denies the States the power to "deprive any person of life, liberty, or property, without due process of law." In resolving conflicting claims concerning the meaning of this spacious language, the Court has looked increasingly to the Bill of Rights for guidance; many of the rights guaranteed by the first eight Amendments to the Constitution have been held to be protected against state action by the Due Process Clause of the Fourteenth Amendment. That clause now protects the right to compensation for property taken by the State, Chicago, B. & Q.R. Co. v. City of Chicago (1897); the rights of speech, press, and religion covered by the First Amendment, see, e.g., Fiske v. State of Kansas (1927); the Fourth Amendment rights to be free from unreasonable searches and seizures and to have excluded from criminal trials any evidence illegally seized, Mapp v. State of Ohio (1961); the right guaranteed by the Fifth Amendment to be free of compelled self-incrimination, Malloy v. Hogan (1964); and the Sixth Amendment rights to counsel, Gideon v. Wainwright (1963); to a speedy, Klopfer v. State of North Carolina (1967) and public trial, In re Oliver (1948); to confrontation of opposing witnesses, Pointer v. State of

Texas (1965); and to compulsory process for obtaining witnesses, Washington v. State of Texas (1967).

The test for determining whether a right extended by the Fifth and Sixth Amendments with respect to federal criminal proceedings is also protected against state action by the Fourteenth Amendment has been phrased in a variety of ways in the opinions of this Court. The question has been asked whether a right is among those "fundamental principles of liberty and justice which lie at the base of all our civil and political institutions," Powell v. State of Alabama, (1932); whether it is "basic in our system of jurisprudence," In re Oliver (1948); and whether it is "a fundamental right, essential to a fair trial," Gideon v. Wainwright (1963).

The claim before us is that the right to trial by jury guaranteed by the Sixth Amendment meets these tests. The position of Louisiana, on the other hand, is that the Constitution imposes upon the States no duty to give a jury trial in any criminal case, regardless of the seriousness of the crime or the size of the punishment which may be imposed. Because we believe that trial by jury in criminal cases is fundamental to the American scheme of justice, we hold that the Fourteenth Amendment guarantees a right of jury trial in all criminal cases which—were they to be tried in a federal court—would come within the Sixth Amendment's guarantee.

The guarantees of jury trial in the Federal and State Constitutions reflect a profound judgment about the way in which law should be enforced and justice administered. A right to jury trial is granted to criminal defendants in order to prevent oppression by the Government. Those who wrote our constitutions knew from history and experience that it was necessary to protect against unfounded criminal charges brought to eliminate enemies and against judges too responsive to the voice of higher authority. The framers of the constitutions strove to create an independent judiciary but insisted upon further protection against arbitrary action. Providing an accused with the right to be tried by a jury of his peers gave him an inestimable safeguard against the corrupt or overzealous prosecutor and against the compliant, biased, or eccentric judge. If the defendant preferred the common-sense judgment of a jury to the more tutored but perhaps less sympathetic reaction of the single judge, he was to have it. Beyond this, the jury trial provisions in the Federal and State Constitutions reflect a fundamental decision about the exercise of official power—a reluctance to entrust plenary powers over the life and liberty of the citizen to one judge or to a group of judges. Fear of unchecked power, so typical of our State and Federal Governments in other respects, found expression in the criminal law in this insistence upon community participation in the determination of guilt or innocence. The deep commitment of the Nation to the right of jury trial in serious criminal cases as a defense against arbitrary law enforcement qualifies for protection under the Due Process Clause of the Fourteenth Amendment, and must therefore be respected by the States.

Justice BLACK, with whom Justice DOUGLAS joins, concurring.

The Court today holds that the right to trial by jury guaranteed defendants in criminal cases in federal courts by Art. III of the United States Constitution and by the Sixth Amendment is also guaranteed by the Fourteenth Amendment to defendants tried in state courts. With this holding I agree for reasons given by the Court.

I am very happy to support this selective process through which our Court has since the *Adamson* case held most of the specific Bill of Rights' protections applicable to the States to the same extent they are applicable to the Federal Government. All of these holdings making Bill of Rights' provisions applicable as such to the States mark, of course, a departure from the *Twining* doctrine holding that none of those provisions were enforceable as such against the States.

My view has been and is that the Fourteenth Amendment, as a whole, makes the Bill of Rights applicable to the States. This would certainly include the language of the Privileges and Immunities Clause, as well as the Due Process Clause. I can say only that the words "No State shall make or enforce any law which shall abridge the privileges or immunities of citizens of the United States" seem to me an eminently reasonable way of expressing the idea that henceforth the Bill of Rights shall apply to the States. What more precious "privilege" of American citizenship could there be than that privilege to claim the protections of our great Bill of Rights? I suggest that any reading of "privileges or immunities of citizens of the United States" which excludes the Bill of Rights' safeguards renders the words of this section of the Fourteenth Amendment meaningless. Senator Howard, who introduced the Fourteenth Amendment for passage in the Senate, certainly read the words this way.

Finally I want to add that I am not bothered by the argument that applying the Bill of Rights to the States "according to the same standards that protect those personal rights against federal encroachment," interferes with our concept of federalism in that it may prevent States from trying novel social and economic experiments. I have never believed that under the guise of federalism the States should be able to experiment with the protections afforded our citizens through the Bill of Rights.

In closing I want to emphasize that I believe as strongly as ever that the Fourteenth Amendment was intended to make the Bill of Rights applicable to the States. I have been willing to support the selective incorporation doctrine, however, as an alternative, although perhaps less historically supportable than complete incorporation. The selective incorporation process, if used properly, does limit the Supreme Court in the Fourteenth Amendment field to specific Bill of Rights' protections only and keeps judges from roaming at will in their own notions of what policies outside the Bill of Rights are desirable and what are not. And, most importantly for me, the selective incorporation process has the virtue of having already worked to make most of the Bill of Rights' protections applicable to the States.

There are still four provisions of the Bill of Rights that never have been incorporated and do not apply to state and local governments. First, the Third Amendment right to not have soldiers quartered in a person's home never has been deemed incorporated. The reason almost certainly is that a Third Amendment case presenting the incorporation question never has reached the Supreme Court. If ever such a case would arise, the Supreme Court surely would find this provision applies to the states.[18]

Second, the Court has held that the Fifth Amendment's right to a grand jury indictment in criminal cases is not incorporated.[19] Thus, states need not use grand juries and can choose alternatives such as preliminary hearings and prosecutorial information.

Third, the Court has ruled that the Seventh Amendment right to jury trial in civil cases is not incorporated.[20] States therefore can eliminate juries in some or even all civil suits without violating the United States Constitution.

Finally, the Court never has ruled as to whether the prohibition of excessive fines in the Eighth Amendment is incorporated.[21]

All of the rest of the Bill of Rights, as detailed above, have been deemed incorporated. Technically, the Bill of Rights still applies directly only to the federal government; Barron v. Mayor & City Council of Baltimore never has been expressly overruled. Therefore, whenever a case involves a state or local violation of a Bill of Rights provision, to be precise, it involves that provision as applied to the states through the Due Process Clause of the Fourteenth Amendment.

4. The Content of Incorporated Rights

If a provision of the Bill of Rights applies to the states, is its content identical as to when it is applied to the federal government? Or as it is sometimes phrased, does the Bill of Rights provision apply "jot for jot"?[22]

The Supreme Court has not consistently answered these questions. In some cases, the Court has expressly stated that the Bill of Rights provision applied in exactly the same manner whether it is a federal or a state government action. For example, the Supreme Court has declared that it is "firmly embedded in our constitutional jurisprudence ... that the several States have no greater power to restrain the individual freedoms protected by the First Amendment than does the Congress of the United States."[23]

---

18. *See* Engblom v. Carey, 677 F.2d 957 (2d Cir. 1982) (finding that the Third Amendment is incorporated).

19. Hutardo v. California, 110 U.S. 516 (1884).

20. Minneapolis & St. Louis Railroad Co. v. Bombolis, 241 U.S. 211 (1916).

21. Browning-Ferris Industries of Vt., Inc. v. Kelco Disposal, Inc., 492 U.S. 257, 262, 276 n.2 (1989).

22. *See* Duncan v. Louisiana, 391 U.S. at 181 (Harlan, J., dissenting) (using the "jot-for-jot" language).

23. Wallace v. Jaffree, 472 U.S. 38, 48-49 (1985).

Similarly, the Court has said that "the guarantees of the First Amendment, the prohibition of unreasonable searches and seizures of the Fourth Amendment, and the right to counsel guaranteed by the Sixth Amendment, are all to be enforced against the States under the Fourteenth Amendment according to the same standards that protect those personal rights against federal encroachment."[24] The Court said that it "rejected the notion that the Fourteenth Amendment applies to the states only a watered-down, subjective version of the individual guarantees of the Bill of Rights."[25]

However, in other instances, the Court has ruled that some Bill of Rights provisions apply differently to the states than to the federal government. In Williams v. Florida, 399 U.S. 78 (1970), the Supreme Court held that states need not use 12-person juries in criminal cases, even though that is required by the Sixth Amendment for federal trials. The Court upheld the constitutionality of six-person juries in state criminal trials and explained that the jury of 12 was "a historical accident, unnecessary to effect the purposes of the jury system."

In Apodaca v. Oregon, 406 U.S. 404 (1972), and Johnson v. Louisiana, 406 U.S. 356 (1972), the Supreme Court held that states may allow nonunanimous jury verdicts in criminal cases. Although the Sixth Amendment has been interpreted to require unanimous juries in federal criminal trials, the Supreme Court ruled that states may allow convictions based on 11-1 or 10-2 jury votes. However, the Court has ruled that conviction by a nonunanimous six-person jury violates due process.[26]

From a practical perspective, except for the requirements of a 12-person jury and a unanimous verdict, the Bill of Rights provisions that have been incorporated apply to the states exactly as they apply to the federal government. This might be criticized on federalism grounds as unduly limiting the states. But rights such as freedom of speech are fundamental liberties and there is no reason why their content should vary depending on the level of government.

Of course, apart from the Bill of Rights, there are many differences between criminal procedure in federal and state courts. The Federal Rules of Criminal Procedure, mentioned at many points throughout this book, are sometimes different than the rules followed in many states. Also, the Supreme Court often articulates requirements as part of its supervisory role over federal courts in areas where states are free to follow their own procedures. For example, the contempt powers of a federal court, as defined by the Supreme Court, may be different than those in a state court.

Although the debate over incorporation raged among justices and scholars during the 1940s, 1950s, and 1960s, now the issue seems settled. Except for the few provisions mentioned above, the Bill of Rights do apply to state

24. Malloy v. Hogan, 378 U.S. at 10.
25. *Id.* at 10-11 (citations omitted).
26. Burch v. Louisiana, 441 U.S. 130 (1979).

and local governments and, in almost all instances, with the same content regardless of whether it is a challenge to federal, state, or local actions.

F.   RETROACTIVITY

In reading the cases throughout this book, it is important to keep in mind that generally criminal procedure decisions apply only in that case and in future ones; they do not apply retroactively to already decided cases. Actually, to be more precise, a Supreme Court decision recognizing a right of criminal procedure generally applies to that case, to any cases pending at the time (in a trial court or on appeal, but not to those pending on habeas corpus), and to future cases. Generally, Supreme Court criminal procedure rulings do not apply retroactively to cases where the appeals have already been completed.

It is easy to understand the reason for this. If Supreme Court decisions recognizing new criminal procedure rights applied retroactively, hundreds or thousands of convicted criminals would seek to reopen their cases to take advantage of the new right. The burden on the courts, depending on the new right, would be enormous. In many instances, the government simply could not retry the person because witnesses would no longer be available. But there is a serious cost to not applying Supreme Court decisions retroactively: People remain in prison, or even are executed, in violation of the Constitution. An accident of timing is determinative; those whose appeals are pending get the benefit of the new right, which could lead to the reversal of their conviction, but those whose appeal is over are out of luck in taking advantage of the new right.

Occasionally, though rarely, the Supreme Court will apply a criminal procedure protection retroactively. The Court has identified two situations in which this will occur. One situation is where a Supreme Court decision places a matter beyond the reach of the criminal law; that is, the Court holds that certain behavior cannot be criminally punished. For instance, in Lawrence v. Texas, 539 U.S. 558 (2003), the Court held that states may not punish private consensual homosexual activity between adults. This obviously puts such conduct beyond the reach of the criminal law and thus the decision would apply retroactively.

Second, the Supreme Court has said that a "watershed" rule of criminal procedure would apply retroactively. Rarely, though, has the Supreme Court found any decision to constitute a watershed rule of criminal procedure.

In Whorton v. Bocking, 549 U.S. 406 (2007), the Supreme Court elaborated that it must be a "'watershed rul[e] of criminal procedure' implicating the fundamental fairness and accuracy of the criminal proceeding."[27] The

_____

27. Whorton v. Bocking involved whether a major Supreme Court decision concerning the Confrontation Clause of the Sixth Amendment applies retroactively. Crawford v. Washington, 541 U.S. 36 (2004), held that a prosecutor could not use "testimonial" statements against a

Court said that "[t]his exception is 'extremely narrow.'" Justice Alito, writing for a unanimous Court, stated, "In order to qualify as watershed, a new rule must meet two requirements. First, the rule must be necessary to prevent an 'impermissibly large risk' of an inaccurate conviction. Second, the rule must 'alter our understanding of the bedrock procedural elements essential to the fairness of a proceeding.'"

In theory, it is possible that a criminal procedure decision would apply retroactively. Gideon v. Wainwright, 372 U.S. 335 (1963), which held that criminal defendants have a right to counsel at trial in any case where the sentence potentially includes imprisonment, is often mentioned as the classic example of a decision that would apply retroactively. Without counsel there is an impermissibly large risk of a wrongful conviction and *Gideon* altered the basic understanding "of the bedrock procedural elements essential to the fairness of a proceeding." But this is the exception; in reality, almost always, criminal procedure rulings, such as those in this book, apply only prospectively.

---

criminal defendant that had been made by a witness who was unavailable at trial on the grounds that they were reliable. In *Whorton*, the Court unanimously held that *Crawford* does not apply retroactively to those whose convictions were final before it was decided.

CHAPTER

2

INITIATING PROSECUTION

This chapter focuses on mechanisms used to charge defendants with offenses. Initially, police officers will use their discretion to decide when to arrest a suspect. In most jurisdictions, initial charges are filed in a complaint or information. The complaint must be supported by an affidavit that sets forth the evidence supporting the charges. Based on this ex parte showing, the suspect may be held until more formal charges are filed through indictment (for a felony) or information.

Once initial charges are filed, a defendant has the right to have a judge assess whether there is probable cause for the charges. If the defendant has not been arrested with a warrant, this probable cause review must ordinarily be done within 48 hours of a defendant's arrest. *See* Gerstein v. Pugh, 420 U.S. 103 (1975) (defendant arrested without a warrant is entitled to "prompt" post-arrest assessment of probable cause by a magistrate); County of Riverside v. McLaughlin, 500 U.S. 44 (1991) (probable cause review should be conducted within 48 hours of arrest).

Assuming that there is probable cause, prosecutors have enormous discretion in deciding what charges to bring and against whom.[1] As long as there is probable cause to support the charges, prosecutors can decide how many counts to bring, the severity of the crime to charge, and which suspects to use as witnesses and which to charge as defendants. United States v. Batchelder, 442 U.S. 114 (1979) (prosecutors are not required to use the most lenient statute in charging a defendant).

Because of separation of powers, if judges disagree with a prosecutor's charging decision, they can decide to dismiss charges, but they cannot order prosecutors to bring other charges. As Judge Posner has stated, "A judge in our system does not have the authority to tell prosecutors which crimes to prosecute or when to prosecute them. Prosecutorial discretion resides in the executive, not in the judicial branch."[2] Although prosecutors have broad discretion in deciding what to charge, their decisions are not

---

1. *See generally* Wayne R. LaFave, *The Prosecutor's Discretion in the United States*, 18 Am. J. Comp. L. 532, 533-539 (1970).
2. United States v. Giannattasio, 979 F.2d 98 (7th Cir. 1992).

necessarily easy ones. Section A of this chapter discusses the complexities of the prosecutor's decision to file charges.

Section B then details the constitutional, statutory, and ethical limits on prosecutorial discretion. In particular, it focuses on the doctrines of selective and vindictive prosecution. Although prosecutors have broad discretion in charging cases, they cannot bring charges based on impermissible criteria, such as race or religion. They also cannot retaliate against the defendant for the exercise of a constitutional right. Prosecutors must abide by statutory, ethical, and administrative standards in making their charging decisions.

Once a decision has been made to charge a defendant, there are two primary procedures to screen which cases should be formally charged — the grand jury and the preliminary hearing. These procedures are discussed in section C. The Fifth Amendment provides a right to grand jury indictment for federal felonies. However, because this portion of the Fifth Amendment has not been incorporated under the Fourteenth Amendment, states are not required to use grand juries. Instead, many states use another mechanism — the preliminary hearing — to screen cases. Defendants have the right to waive preliminary hearing and frequently do so when they reach an early plea bargain in the case or are not yet prepared to contest the prosecution's case or do not want to disclose their likely defenses.

In addition, there are fairness considerations that may impact how a defendant is charged. Section D discusses the issues of severance and joinder. Courtroom efficiencies may favor the joinder of defendants or offenses for trial, but these benefits must be weighed against the concern of unduly prejudicing a defendant's right to a fair trial.

Finally, this chapter ends with a brief word on how charges can be corrected if mistakes are found before trial. Amendments and variances are addressed in section E of the chapter.

A. THE CHARGING DECISION

By some estimates, less than 2 percent of all crimes are actually prosecuted in the United States.[3] That means that throughout the criminal justice process, both the police and prosecutors are using their discretion to decide which cases warrant prosecution. Prosecutors have this broad discretion even though they have relatively little accountability to the public. They are often guided by abstract standards like "seeking justice" or being "fair" or "neutral." In reality, these terms are just "proxies for a constellation of other, sometimes equally vague, normative expectations about how prosecutors should make decisions." Bruce A. Green & Fred C. Zacharias, *Prosecutorial Neutrality*, 2004 Wis. L. Rev. 837, 902-903.

---

3. *See* Sara Sun Beale, *Essay: The Many Faces of Overcriminalization*, 54 Am. U. L. Rev. 747, 757 (2005).

Several factors influence the decision of whether to prosecute a case. First, there are the economic realities. There are not enough prosecutors, police, or courts to prosecute all of the crimes that are committed. For most prosecution offices, there is only one prosecutor for every 4,000 people in their district. Many prosecution offices have small operating budgets.[4] There are only 800,000 full-time sworn law enforcement officers in the United States for a population of over 300 million people. Thus, prosecutors and police must select very carefully the cases they want to prosecute.

Second, prosecutors must assess which prosecutions are likely to bring the greatest benefit to the community. Depending on community interests, prosecutors will set the priorities for their jurisdictions. In the 1980s, prosecutors launched the "war on drugs." Today, prosecutorial priorities are also focusing on terrorism crimes and Internet violations. According to government statistics, approximately one-quarter of all felony defendants are charged with violent offenses. Those charged with murder (0.8 percent) and rape (1.3 percent) account for a small percentage of defendants overall.[5] That means that three-quarters of defendants were charged with a nonviolent felony, with a majority of these being narcotics-related offenses. Nonviolent crimes can range from multimillion dollar fraud schemes to shoplifting offenses. Prosecution priorities may be influenced by political decisions of both the legislature and individual government officials. These individuals generally don't want to be viewed as "soft on crime," especially since most District Attorneys are elected officials.

Third, prosecutors must evaluate the merits and strengths of each individual case. Prosecutors only need probable cause to charge a defendant. However, they need proof beyond a reasonable doubt to succeed at trial. Typically, prosecutorial offices enjoy a conviction rate of over 90 percent because they can pick and choose the cases they prosecute. In doing so, they must consider the impact of a trial on prosecution witnesses, the strength of their evidence, the deterrence value of the case, and the harm caused by the crime.

It is not unusual for prosecutors to tack on additional charges so as to create an incentive for the defendant to cooperate and/or to plead guilty. "If the prosecutor charges five offenses instead of two, he may get the defendant to agree to plead guilty to three charges in exchange for his agreement to dismiss two, even if he would have a difficult time proving the two charges before a judge or jury."[6]

Prosecutors will also evaluate the background of individual defendants before deciding whether to prosecute a case. More than one-third of the defendants prosecuted already have an active criminal justice status at the

---

4. Bureau of Justice Statistics, *Prosecutors in State Courts, 2007 — Statistical Tables*, December 2011, http://bjs.gov/content/pub/pdf/psc07st.pdf (reporting that more than half of prosecution offices had a total budget of $526,000 or less).

5. *See* Department of Justice, Bureau of Justice Statistics, *Sourcebook of Criminal Justice Statistics Online*, Table 5.44.2006, http://www.albany.edu/sourcebook/pdf/t5442006.pdf.

6. Angela J. Davis, Arbitrary Justice: The Power of the American Prosecution (Oxford University Press 2007).

time of the new charged offense.[7] Of course, with the power to individually evaluate each case comes the danger that prosecutors will use improper factors in making their decisions. Currently, one out of every three young African American males is a defendant in the criminal justice system.[8] Based on current rates of incarceration, an estimated 32 percent of black males will enter state or federal prison during their lifetime, compared to 17 percent of Hispanic males and 5.9 percent of white males.[9] These statistics prompt important questions about conscious and unconscious racial bias in policing and charging decisions.[10] The Supreme Court has repeatedly stated that "prosecutorial discretion cannot be exercised on the basis of race," McClesky v. Kemp, 481 U.S. 279 (1987), yet statistical studies have shown that race has an impact on how a defendant is treated by the criminal justice system. For example, according to the Baldus study cited in McClesky v. Kemp, "prosecutors seek the death penalty for 70% of black defendants with white victims, but for only 15% of black defendants with black victims, and only 19% of white defendants with black victims." As the dissent in that case noted, "racial and other forms of discrimination still remain a fact of life, in the administration of justice as in our society as a whole." *Id.* at 332 (Brennan, J., dissenting).

Finally, prosecutors should factor in the overall impact of their decision to prosecute or drop a case. This includes the impact on the victims, their families, law enforcement, and all members of the broader community. There are more than enough criminal codes to prosecute defendants, but prosecutors must consider whether it is in the public interest to bring a charge. Consider the following prosecution and whether it was a prudent exercise of prosecutorial discretion.

INMATE CONVICTED OF INDECENT EXPOSURE

Associated Press, July 25, 2007

Terry Lee Alexander thought he was having a private moment in his jail cell. But a deputy jailer thought otherwise. Alexander, 20, was sitting on his bunk alone in his cell masturbating when a female deputy, monitoring his cell by video camera from a nearby control room, took offense. Today he's scheduled to go to trial to fight a misdemeanor indecent exposure charge.

Taxpayers have been footing the bill — $91.29 a day — to keep Alexander in the main jail. The grand total for Alexander's incarceration in that

---

7. *Id.*

8. *See* Marc Mauer & Tracy Huling, Young Black Americans and the Criminal Justice System (Oct. 1995).

9. Twenty-eight percent of all arrests and 31.1 percent of juvenile arrests in 2010 were of black suspects. *See* Department of Justice, Bureau of Justice Statistics, *Sourcebook of Criminal Justice Statistics Online*, Table 4.10.2010, http://www.albany.edu/sourcebook/pdf/t4102010.pdf.

10. *See* Angela J. Davis, *Prosecution and Race: The Power and Privilege of Discretion*, 67 Fordham L. Rev. 13 (1998).

case is nearly $21,000. On top of that, the public will pay $1,150 for his attorney.

Critics are appalled at what they call a deputy's "moral crusade" and question the value of prosecuting such cases. "I would think [taxpayers] would be upset that this is how their money is being spent," said Betsy Benson, a Broward assistant public defender.[11]

Prosecutorial charging discretion can also give prosecutors considerable power to influence sentencing. Consider the next example and how the prosecutor's power to charge controlled the judge's sentencing decision.

MANDATORY 55-YEAR SENTENCE "EXTREME"?

Salt Lake Tribune, Dec. 4, 2007

Lawyers for a Utah record producer serving 55 years in prison for carrying a firearm while dealing pot filed a request Monday for a resentencing, saying the punishment is "extreme" and unconstitutional.

"As a result of three sales of small amounts of marijuana to a paid informant and the suspect charging decisions by federal prosecutors, Angelos received a 55-year sentence that highlights the most unjust and arbitrary aspects of the federal criminal justice system and mandatory minimum sentencing provisions," the motion for resentencing says.

The motion was filed in U.S. District Court in Salt Lake City, where Judge Paul Cassell reluctantly imposed the mandatory term almost four years ago. Cassell described the sentence as "unjust, cruel and irrational," but said he had no choice under the law but to impose it.

Angelos was accused of selling eight ounces of marijuana for $350 in each sale. At one sale, he had a gun strapped to his ankle and there were firearms in the vicinity during the other drug buys, according to court records.

Monday's motion — filed by a team of lawyers that recently stepped into the case — says recent statistics show that the vast majority of all felony marijuana trafficking convictions result in a prison term of less than one year.

Angelos' sentencing sparked a national debate on mandatory sentences and prompted dozens of former judges and prosecutors to join in friend-of-the-court briefs to the 10th Circuit and the U.S. Supreme Court seeking reversal of the punishment.

------

11. In deciding whether the prosecutor used good judgment in bringing the charges, consider that all of the prospective jurors had to be asked about their attitudes toward masturbation and whether they engaged in it. *See* Robert Santiago, *Jury Panel Queried in Masturbation Trial,* Miami Herald, July 24, 2007.

The charging decision is one of the most important determinations a prosecutor makes. Whereas police officers must decide on the spot whether to arrest someone, the prosecutor has the time and ability to do a closer evaluation of a case to determine whether charges are warranted. A decision to charge an individual means, at minimum, that individual will confront the expense and stress of facing trial. Because of the high rate of guilty pleas, the charging decision frequently predetermines the outcome of a criminal case. It vests enormous power in the hands of the prosecutor.

In addition to deciding when and whom to charge, prosecutors have the power to decide *not* to charge a case. Generally, judges do not have the power to second-guess decisions by the prosecution not to charge a case.

INMATES OF ATTICA CORRECTIONAL FACILITY v. ROCKEFELLER
477 F.2d 375 (2d Cir. 1973)

Circuit Judge MANSFIELD delivered the opinion of the court.

This appeal raises the question of whether the federal judiciary should, at the instance of victims, compel federal and state officials to investigate and prosecute persons who allegedly have violated certain federal and state criminal statutes. Plaintiffs are certain present and former inmates of New York State's Attica Correctional Facility [and] the mother of an inmate who was killed when Attica was retaken after the inmate uprising in September 1971. They appeal from an order of the district court dismissing their complaint. We affirm.

[F]ederal courts have traditionally and, to our knowledge, uniformly refrained from overturning, at the instance of a private person, discretionary decisions of federal prosecuting authorities not to prosecute persons regarding whom a complaint of criminal conduct is made.

The primary ground upon which this traditional judicial aversion to compelling prosecutions has been based is the separation of powers doctrine.

> Although as a member of the bar, the attorney for the United States is an officer of the court, he is nevertheless an executive official of the Government, and it is as an officer of the executive department that he exercises discretion as to whether or not there shall be a prosecution in a particular case. It follows, as an incident of the constitutional separation of powers, that the courts are not to interfere with the free exercise of the discretionary powers of the attorneys of the United States in their control over criminal prosecutions.

Nor is it clear what the judiciary's role of supervision should be were it to undertake such a review. At what point would the prosecutor be entitled to call a halt to further investigation as unlikely to be productive? What evidentiary standard would be used to decide whether prosecution should be compelled? How much judgment would the United States Attorney be allowed? What collateral factors would be permissible bases for a decision not to prosecute, e.g., the pendency of another criminal proceeding elsewhere against the same parties? With limited personnel and facilities at his disposal, what priority would the prosecutor be required to give to cases in which investigation or prosecution was directed by the court?

These difficult questions engender serious doubts as to the judiciary's capacity to review and as to the problem of arbitrariness inherent in any judicial decision to order prosecution. On balance, we believe that substitution of a court's decision to compel prosecution for the U.S. Attorney's decision not to prosecute, even upon an abuse of discretion standard of review and even if limited to directing that a prosecution be undertaken in good faith would be unwise.

Generally, prosecutors have both the responsibility and discretion to file criminal charges. In some jurisdictions, private citizens can file misdemeanor complaints (with judicial approval), but the most significant charging decisions rest in the hands of prosecutors.

B. LIMITS ON PROSECUTORIAL DISCRETION

Although prosecutors enjoy broad discretion in charging cases, there are statutory, administrative, ethical, and constitutional limits on prosecutorial discretion.

1. Statutory and Administrative Limits

Prosecutors can only charge conduct that the legislature has designated as a crime. Each jurisdiction has governing statutes for its criminal offenses. Federal prosecutions are brought by the United States Attorney's Office or the Department of Justice. Criminal offenses are listed in the United States Code. Generally, prosecutors will have numerous charges to choose from in deciding which charges to bring. As long as the charges are supported by probable cause, it is within the prosecutor's discretion to decide whether to bring a charge with a greater or lesser potential punishment.

Local offenses are charged by state district attorneys, city attorneys, and state attorneys general. The offenses they can charge are listed in the penal codes for those jurisdictions. In some cases, a crime may be charged by state prosecutors, federal prosecutors, or both. As discussed in Chapter 9, federal double jeopardy law does not bar separate sovereigns from charging the same offense. Thus, unless a state provides greater double jeopardy protection, both state and federal officials may charge a violation of law if there are applicable statutes.

Even prosecution of criminal contempt cases arising out of private disputes should be handled by public prosecutors. In Young v. United States ex rel. Vuitton et Fils S.A., 481 U.S. 787 (1987), the Court held that Federal Rule of Criminal Procedure 42(b) allows for the prosecution of criminal contempt, but it does not allow the victim to be the prosecutor.

> The prosecutor is appointed solely to pursue the public interest in vindication of the court's authority. A private attorney appointed to prosecute a criminal contempt therefore certainly should be as disinterested as a public prosecutor who undertakes such a prosecution. . . . A prosecutor exercises considerable discretion in [determining] which persons should be targets of investigation, what methods of investigation should be used, what information will be sought as evidence, which persons should be charged with what offenses, which persons should be utilized as witnesses, whether to enter into plea bargains and the terms on which they will be established, and whether any individuals should be granted immunity. These decisions, critical to the conduct of a prosecution, [require a disinterested prosecutor].

Id. at 804-805.

Prosecutors may adopt guidelines for their decisions to prosecute. For example, federal prosecutors have the U.S. Attorney's Manual, which guides their prosecutorial decisions. These guidelines typically leave a great deal of discretion for the prosecutor's decision, although they may require approval by superiors before certain types of cases are brought. However, violation of these internal guidelines does not afford the defendant grounds to contest the charges. As internal guidelines, they do not create independent rights for the defendant.

2. Ethical Limits

Prosecutors are also governed by ethical rules. The Supreme Court has repeatedly recognized that prosecutors have special ethical responsibilities because of the power they wield:

> The United States Attorney is the representative not of an ordinary party to a controversy, but of a sovereignty whose obligation to govern impartially is as compelling as its obligation to govern at all; and whose interest, therefore, in a criminal prosecution is not that it shall win a case, but that justice shall be done. As such, he is in a peculiar and very definite sense the servant of the law, the twofold aim of which is that guilt shall not escape nor innocence suffer.

Berger v. United States, 295 U.S. 78, 88 (1935).

The unique responsibilities of prosecutors are expressed in Ethical Consideration (EC) 7-13 of Canon 7 of the American Bar Association (ABA) Model Code of Professional Responsibility (1982): "The responsibility of a public prosecutor differs from that of the usual advocate; his duty is to seek justice, not merely to convict."

For charging decisions, ABA Standards for Criminal Justice: The Prosecution Function, Standard 3-3.9 (Discretion in the Charging Decision) provides:

> (a) A prosecutor should not institute, or cause to be instituted, or permit the continued pendency of criminal charges when the prosecutor knows that the charges are not supported by probable cause. A prosecutor should not institute, cause to be instituted, or permit the continued pendency of criminal charges in the absence of sufficient admissible evidence to support conviction.
>
> (b) The prosecutor is not obliged to present all charges which the evidence might support. The prosecutor may in some circumstances and for good cause consistent with the public interest decline to prosecute, notwithstanding that sufficient evidence may exist which would support a conviction. Illustrative of the factors which the prosecutor may properly consider in exercising his or her discretion are:
>
> (i) the prosecutor's reasonable doubt that the accused is in fact guilty;
>
> (ii) the extent of the harm caused by the offense;
>
> (iii) the disproportion of the authorized punishment in relation to the particular offense or the offender;
>
> (iv) possible improper motives of a complainant;
>
> (v) reluctance of the victim to testify;
>
> (vi) cooperation of the accused in the apprehension or conviction of others;
>
> (vii) availability and likelihood of prosecution by another jurisdiction.
>
> (c) A prosecutor should not be compelled by his or her supervisor to prosecute a case in which he or she has a reasonable doubt about the guilt of the accused.
>
> (d) In making the decision to prosecute, the prosecutor should give no weight to the personal or political advantages which might be involved or to a desire to enhance his or her record of conviction.
>
> (e) In cases which involve a serious threat to the community, the prosecutor should not be deterred from prosecution by the fact that in the jurisdiction juries have tended to acquit persons accused of the particular criminal act in question.
>
> (f) The prosecutor should not bring or seek charges greater in number or degree than can be supported with evidence at trial or than are necessary to fairly reflect the gravity of the offense.

Prosecutors who do not honor these ethical obligations risk causing a grave injustice to others and professional consequences to themselves. One particularly notorious case involved rape charges filed against three Duke University lacrosse players by a politically ambitious prosecutor. The prosecutor, Michael Nifong, aggressively pursued charges against the players as he ran for office. Nifong was aware of serious problems with the case. Nonetheless, he portrayed himself as the crusader for minorities and continued with the prosecution. After the defendants' reputations were tarnished, and millions of dollars were spent on their defense, North Carolina's attorney general found that there was no evidence to support the charges and dismissed them. Michael Nifong ended up being disbarred. Nifong's case, although relatively rare, offers important lessons about the role of ethics in prosecutors' charging decisions.

LAWYER DISBARRED OVER LACROSSE RAPE CASE

Associated Press, June 18, 2007

Raleigh, North Carolina: A disgraced North Carolina lawyer has been disbarred for his "selfish" rape prosecution of three lacrosse players at a top U.S. university, bringing to an end an American saga about race and class that sparked a bitter national debate.

Hours after he was found guilty of ethics violations in his prosecution of three white Duke University lacrosse players falsely accused of raping a black stripper at an off-campus house party in March last year, Durham County District Attorney Michael Nifong at the weekend surrendered his law license to the state bar and said he would waive his right to appeal.

A three-person North Carolina State Bar disciplinary panel, on the fifth day of an ethics hearing, said the evidence showed that Mr. Nifong had withheld crucial information from the students' defence lawyers and engaged in "dishonesty, fraud, deceit or misrepresentation" during his prosecution of the case.

It is the first time a sitting district attorney has been disbarred in North Carolina.

"This matter has been a fiasco. There's no doubt about it," said F. Lane Williamson, chair of the disciplinary committee. The committee said Mr. Nifong manipulated the investigation to boost his chances of winning his first election for Durham County district attorney.

Mr. Williamson specifically cited Mr. Nifong's comments in the early days of the case, which included a confident proclamation that he would not allow Durham to become known for "a bunch of lacrosse players from Duke raping a black girl." He also called the Duke lacrosse team "a bunch of hooligans."

Appointed district attorney in 2005, Mr. Nifong was in a tight race for the office when a stripper told police she had been raped at the party. "At the time he was facing a primary, and yes, he was politically naive," Mr. Williamson said.

"But we can draw no other conclusion than [that] those initial statements he made were to further his political ambitions."

The case stirred furious debate over race, class and the privileged status of college athletes, and heightened longstanding tensions in Durham between its large working-class black population and the mostly white, mostly affluent students at the private, elite university.

During the ethics trial, Mr. Nifong acknowledged he knew there was no DNA evidence connecting Duke students Reade Seligmann and Collin Finnerty to the 28-year-old accuser when he indicted them on charges of rape, sexual offence and kidnapping. Mr. Nifong later charged Dave Evans with the same crimes.

But months later, state prosecutors concluded the players were innocent and in a blistering assessment of the case Attorney-General Roy Cooper dropped all charges in April.

"This case shows the enormous consequences of overreaching by a prosecutor," he said. "In the rush to condemn, a community and a state lost the ability to see clearly."

———————

By most accounts, what happened to the prosecutor in the Nifong case was highly unusual. Prosecutors are rarely disciplined for improper charging of cases. The ABA ethical rules are only aspirational, and prosecutors are rarely called on to justify their charging decisions.

3.   Constitutional Limits[12]

Although prosecutorial discretion is broad, it is not unlimited. Prosecutors cannot use unconstitutional motives to charge a defendant. A defendant who is prosecuted because of his race, religion, or other classification, in violation of the Fourteenth Amendment's Equal Protection Clause, can move to dismiss for selective or discriminatory enforcement. A defendant who is prosecuted in retaliation for the defendant's exercise of a constitutional right, such as the First Amendment right to free speech, can move to dismiss for vindictive prosecution.

a.   Selective or Discriminatory Enforcement

There is a general presumption that prosecutors will exercise their discretion in good faith. However, if a defendant can show that the prosecution used an impermissible motive to prosecute, such as prosecuting a defendant because of his race or exercise of his First Amendment rights, then the prosecution can be dismissed. As the next two cases — Wayte v. United States and United States v. Armstrong — illustrate, not only has the Supreme Court set a high standard for defendants claiming selective prosecution, but it has

---

12. This chapter focuses on due process and equal protection limits on prosecutorial discretion. In addition, Article I, section 9, clause 3 of the Constitution prohibits bills of attainder and ex post facto laws. "A *bill of attainder* is a legislative act which inflicts punishment without judicial trial and includes any legislative act which takes away the life, liberty or property of a particular named or easily ascertainable person or group of persons because the legislature thinks them guilty of conduct which deserves punishment." Cummings v. Missouri, 71 U.S. 277 (1867) (emphasis added). An *ex post facto law* is a law that punishes acts that were legal at the time they were committed. *See generally* Calder v. Bull, 3 Dall. 386 (1798). The prohibition on ex post facto laws also bars laws that increase the punishment of an act after it was committed or retroactively extend the statute of limitations so that a defendant can be charged with a crime. *See* Stogner v. California, 539 U.S. 607 (2003) (state law that sought to resurrect prosecution of child molestation cases that were otherwise time-barred violated the Ex Post Facto Clause). However, the rule does not bar the retroactive application of registration laws, such as laws requiring sex offenders to register their whereabouts. *See* Smith v. Doe, 538 U.S. 84 (2003). The prohibition on bills of attainder and ex post facto laws applies to the states pursuant to Article I, section 10, clause 1 of the federal Constitution.

imposed a significant burden on defendants seeking discovery to support a claim of discriminatory prosecution.

WAYTE v. UNITED STATES
470 U.S. 598 (1985)

Justice POWELL delivered the opinion of the Court.

[David Wayte was a war protestor. When he refused to register for the Selective Service System, he was warned that he could be prosecuted for violating the Military Selective Service Act. Nonetheless, Wayte continued to protest the war and refused to register. In a letter to the Selective Service System and president, Wayte stated, "I decided to obey my conscience rather than your law. I did not register for your draft. I will never register for your draft. Nor will I ever cooperate with yours or any other military system, despite the laws I might break or the consequences which may befall me." Ultimately, he was indicted. He then moved for dismissal, contending that he was "selectively prosecuted" for resisting the system. The district court granted the motion. The respondent government appealed, asserting that the petitioner did not prove a prima facie case of discrimination.]

The question presented is whether a passive enforcement policy under which the Government prosecutes only those who report themselves as having violated the law, or who are reported by others, violates the First and Fifth Amendments.

Petitioner moved to dismiss the indictment on the ground of selective prosecution. He contended that he and the other [13] indicted nonregistrants were "vocal" opponents of the registration program who had been impermissibly targeted (out of an estimated 674,000 nonregistrants) for prosecution on the basis of their exercise of First Amendment rights.

In our criminal justice system, the Government retains "broad discretion" as to whom to prosecute. "[So] long as the prosecutor has probable cause to believe that the accused committed an offense defined by statute, the decision whether or not to prosecute, and what charge to file or bring before a grand jury, generally rests entirely in his discretion." This broad discretion rests largely on the recognition that the decision to prosecute is particularly ill-suited to judicial review. Such factors as the strength of the case, the prosecution's general deterrence value, the Government's enforcement priorities, and the case's relationship to the Government's overall enforcement plan are not readily susceptible to the kind of analysis the courts are competent to undertake. Judicial supervision in this area, moreover, entails systemic costs of particular concern. Examining the basis of a prosecution delays the criminal proceeding, threatens to chill law enforcement by subjecting the prosecutor's motives and decisionmaking to outside inquiry, and may undermine prosecutorial effectiveness by revealing the Government's enforcement policy. All these are substantial concerns that make the courts properly hesitant to examine the decision whether to prosecute.

As we have noted in a slightly different context, however, although prosecutorial discretion is broad, it is not "'unfettered.' Selectivity in the enforcement of criminal laws is ... subject to constitutional constraints." In particular, the decision to prosecute may not be "'deliberately based upon an unjustifiable standard such as race, religion, or other arbitrary classification,'" including the exercise of protected statutory and constitutional rights.

It is appropriate to judge selective prosecution claims according to ordinary equal protection standards. Under our prior cases, these standards require petitioner to show both that the passive enforcement system had a discriminatory effect and that it was motivated by a discriminatory purpose.[13] All petitioner has shown here is that those eventually prosecuted, along with many not prosecuted, reported themselves as having violated the law. He has not shown that the enforcement policy selected nonregistrants for prosecution on the basis of their speech. Indeed, he could not have done so given the way the "beg" policy[14] was carried out. The Government did not prosecute those who reported themselves but later registered. Nor did it prosecute those who protested registration but did not report themselves or were not reported by others. In fact, the Government did not even investigate those who wrote letters to Selective Service criticizing registration unless their letters stated affirmatively that they had refused to comply with the law. The Government, on the other hand, did prosecute people who reported themselves or were reported by others but who did not publicly protest. These facts demonstrate that the Government treated all reported nonregistrants similarly. It did not subject vocal nonregistrants to any special burden. Indeed, those prosecuted in effect selected themselves for prosecution by refusing to register after being reported and warned by the Government.

Even if the passive policy had a discriminatory effect, petitioner has not shown that the Government intended such a result. The evidence he presented demonstrated only that the Government was aware that the passive enforcement policy would result in prosecution of vocal objectors and that they would probably make selective prosecution claims. As we have noted, however: "'Discriminatory purpose' ... implies more than ... intent as awareness of consequences. It implies that the decisionmaker ... selected or reaffirmed a particular course of action at least in part 'because of,' not merely 'in spite of,' its adverse effects upon an identifiable group." In the present case, petitioner has not shown that the Government prosecuted him

---

13. A showing of discriminatory intent is not necessary when the equal protection claim is based on an overtly discriminatory classification. *See* Strauder v. West Virginia, (1880). [No such claim was presented by Wayte.] [Footnote by the Court.]

14. Pursuant to the Department of Justice "beg" policy, those referred were not immediately prosecuted. Instead, the appropriate United States Attorney was required to notify identified nonregistrants by registered mail that, unless they registered within a specified time, prosecution would be considered. In addition, an FBI agent was usually sent to interview the nonregistrant before prosecution was instituted. This effort to persuade nonregistrants to change their minds became known as the "beg" policy. [Footnote by casebook authors.]

because of his protest activities. Absent such a showing, his claim of selective prosecution fails.[15]

Justice MARSHALL, with whom Justice BRENNAN joins, dissenting.

The Court decides today that petitioner "has not shown that the Government prosecuted him because of his protest activities," and it remands to permit his prosecution to go forward. However interesting the question decided by the Court may be, it is not necessary to the disposition of this case. Instead, the issue this Court must grapple with is far less momentous but no less deserving of thoughtful treatment. What it must decide is whether Wayte has earned the right to discover Government documents relevant to his claim of selective prosecution.

The District Court ordered such discovery, the Government refused to comply, and the District Court dismissed the indictment. The Court of Appeals reversed on the grounds that Wayte had failed to prevail on the merits of his selective prosecution claim, and that the discovery order was improper. If Wayte is entitled to obtain evidence currently in the Government's possession, the Court cannot dismiss his claim on the basis of only the evidence now in the record. To prevail here, then, all that Wayte needs to show is that the District Court applied the correct legal standard and did not abuse its discretion in determining that he had made a nonfrivolous showing of selective prosecution entitling him to discovery.

There can be no doubt that Wayte has sustained his burden. Therefore, his claim cannot properly be dismissed at this stage in the litigation. I respectfully dissent from this Court's decision to do so.

The discovery issue that Justice Marshall raised in his dissent came before the Court in United States v. Armstrong. There the Court dealt with an issue much more common in selective prosecution cases: When do racial disparities in prosecutions constitute selective/discriminatory prosecution?

UNITED STATES v. ARMSTRONG

517 U.S. 456 (1996)

Chief Justice REHNQUIST delivered the opinion of the Court.

In this case, we consider the showing necessary for a defendant to be entitled to discovery on a claim that the prosecuting attorney singled him out for prosecution on the basis of his race. We conclude that respondents

---

15. Wayte also challenged his prosecution directly on First Amendment grounds. However, this claim also failed because the incidental restriction on his speech was essential to further the government's legitimate interest in having people comply with the registration laws. [Footnote by casebook authors.]

failed to satisfy the threshold showing: They failed to show that the Government declined to prosecute similarly situated suspects of other races.

In April 1992, respondents were indicted on charges of conspiring to possess with intent to distribute more than 50 grams of cocaine base (crack) and conspiring to distribute the same and federal firearms offenses. In response to the indictment, respondents filed a motion for discovery or for dismissal of the indictment, alleging that they were selected for federal prosecution because they are black. In support of their motion, they offered only an affidavit by a "Paralegal Specialist," employed by the Office of the Federal Public Defender representing one of the respondents. The only allegation in the affidavit was that, in every one of the 24 [narcotics] cases closed by the office during 1991, the defendant was black. Accompanying the affidavit was a "study" listing the 24 defendants, their race, whether they were prosecuted for dealing cocaine as well as crack, and the status of each case.

The Government opposed the discovery motion, arguing, among other things, that there was no evidence or allegation "that the Government has acted unfairly or has prosecuted non-black defendants or failed to prosecute them."

A selective-prosecution claim is not a defense on the merits to the criminal charge itself, but an independent assertion that the prosecutor has brought the charge for reasons forbidden by the Constitution. Our cases delineating the necessary elements to prove a claim of selective prosecution have taken great pains to explain that the standard is a demanding one.

A selective-prosecution claim asks a court to exercise judicial power over a "special province" of the Executive. The Attorney General and United States Attorneys retain "broad discretion" to enforce the Nation's criminal laws. Wayte v. United States (1985). They have this latitude because they are designated by statute as the President's delegates to help him discharge his constitutional responsibility to "take Care that the Laws be faithfully executed." U.S. Const., Art. II, §3. As a result, "the presumption of regularity supports" their prosecutorial decisions and, "in the absence of clear evidence to the contrary, courts presume that they have properly discharged their official duties." "[S]o long as the prosecutor has probable cause to believe that the accused committed an offense defined by statute, the decision whether or not to prosecute, and what charge to file or bring before a grand jury, generally rests entirely in his discretion." Bordenkircher v. Hayes (1978).

Of course, a prosecutor's discretion is "subject to constitutional constraints." One of these constraints, imposed by the equal protection component of the Due Process Clause of the Fifth Amendment is that the decision whether to prosecute may not be based on "an unjustifiable standard such as race, religion, or other arbitrary classification." A defendant may demonstrate that the administration of a criminal law is "directed so exclusively against a particular class of persons . . . with a mind so unequal and oppressive" that the system of prosecution amounts to "a practical denial" of equal protection of the law. Yick Wo v. Hopkins (1886).

In order to dispel the presumption that a prosecutor has not violated equal protection, a criminal defendant must present "clear evidence to the contrary." The requirements for a selective-prosecution claim draw on "ordinary equal protection standards." The claimant must demonstrate that the federal prosecutorial policy "had a discriminatory effect and that it was motivated by a discriminatory purpose." To establish a discriminatory effect in a race case, the claimant must show that similarly situated individuals of a different race were not prosecuted.

The similarly situated requirement does not make a selective-prosecution claim impossible to prove. In *Hunter*, we invalidated a state law disenfranchising persons convicted of crimes involving moral turpitude. Our holding was consistent with ordinary equal protection principles, including the similarly situated requirement. There was convincing direct evidence that the State had enacted the provision for the purpose of disenfranchising blacks and indisputable evidence that the state law had a discriminatory effect on blacks as compared to similarly situated whites: Blacks were "by even the most modest estimates at least 1.7 times as likely as whites to suffer disfranchisement under" the law in question.

Having reviewed the requirements to prove a selective-prosecution claim, we turn to the showing necessary to obtain discovery in support of such a claim. If discovery is ordered, the Government must assemble from its own files documents which might corroborate or refute the defendant's claim. Discovery thus imposes many of the costs present when the Government must respond to a prima facie case of selective prosecution. It will divert prosecutors' resources and may disclose the Government's prosecutorial strategy. The justifications for a rigorous standard for the elements of a selective-prosecution claim thus require a correspondingly rigorous standard for discovery in aid of such a claim.

The parties, and the Courts of Appeals which have considered the requisite showing to establish entitlement to discovery, describe this showing with a variety of phrases, like "colorable basis," "substantial threshold showing," "substantial and concrete basis," or "reasonable likelihood." However, the many labels for this showing conceal the degree of consensus about the evidence necessary to meet it. The Courts of Appeals "require some evidence tending to show the existence of the essential elements of the defense," discriminatory effect and discriminatory intent.

In this case we consider what evidence constitutes "some evidence tending to show the existence" of the discriminatory effect element. The Court of Appeals held that a defendant may establish a colorable basis for discriminatory effect without evidence that the Government has failed to prosecute others who are similarly situated to the defendant. We think it was mistaken in this view. The Court of Appeals reached its decision in part because it started "with the presumption that people of all races commit all types of crimes—not with the premise that any type of crime is the exclusive province of any particular racial or ethnic group." It cited no authority for this proposition, which seems contradicted by the most recent statistics of the

United States Sentencing Commission. Those statistics show: More than 90% of the persons sentenced in 1994 for crack cocaine trafficking were black, 93.4% of convicted LSD dealers were white, and 91% of those convicted for pornography or prostitution were white. Presumptions at war with presumably reliable statistics have no proper place in the analysis of this issue.

The Court of Appeals also expressed concern about the "evidentiary obstacles defendants face." But all of its sister Circuits that have confronted the issue have required that defendants produce some evidence of differential treatment of similarly situated members of other races or protected classes. In the present case, if the claim of selective prosecution were well founded, it should not have been an insuperable task to prove that persons of other races were being treated differently than respondents. For instance, respondents could have investigated whether similarly situated persons of other races were prosecuted by the State of California and were known to federal law enforcement officers, but were not prosecuted in federal court. We think the required threshold — a credible showing of different treatment of similarly situated persons — adequately balances the Government's interest in vigorous prosecution and the defendant's interest in avoiding selective prosecution.

In the case before us, respondents' "study" did not constitute "some evidence tending to show the existence of the essential elements of" a selective-prosecution claim. The study failed to identify individuals who were not black and could have been prosecuted for the offenses for which respondents were charged, but were not so prosecuted. The newspaper article, which discussed the discriminatory effect of federal drug sentencing laws, was not relevant to an allegation of discrimination in decisions to prosecute. Respondents' affidavits, which recounted one attorney's conversation with a drug treatment center employee and the experience of another attorney defending drug prosecutions in state court, recounted hearsay and reported personal conclusions based on anecdotal evidence. The judgment of the Court of Appeals is therefore reversed, and the case is remanded for proceedings consistent with this opinion.

Justice STEVENS, dissenting.

Federal prosecutors are respected members of a respected profession. Despite an occasional misstep, the excellence of their work abundantly justifies the presumption that "they have properly discharged their official duties." Nevertheless, the possibility that political or racial animosity may infect a decision to institute criminal proceedings cannot be ignored. For that reason, it has long been settled that the prosecutor's broad discretion to determine when criminal charges should be filed is not completely unbridled.

The United States Attorney is a member and an officer of the bar of that District Court. As such, she has a duty to the judges of that Court to maintain the standards of the profession in the performance of her official functions. If a District Judge has reason to suspect that she, or a member of her staff, has singled out particular defendants for prosecution on the basis of their race, it is surely appropriate for the judge to determine whether there is a factual basis for such a concern. I agree with the Court that Rule 16 of the Federal Rules of Criminal Procedure is not the source of the District Court's power to make the necessary inquiry. I disagree, however, with its implicit assumption that a different, relatively rigid rule needs to be crafted to regulate the use of this seldom-exercised inherent judicial power.

The District Judge's order should be evaluated in light of three circumstances that underscore the need for judicial vigilance over certain types of drug prosecutions. First, the Anti-Drug Abuse Act of 1986 and subsequent legislation established a regime of extremely high penalties for the possession and distribution of so-called "crack" cocaine. Those provisions treat one gram of crack as the equivalent of 100 grams of powder cocaine.

Second, the disparity between the treatment of crack cocaine and powder cocaine is matched by the disparity between the severity of the punishment imposed by federal law and that imposed by state law for the same conduct. For a variety of reasons, often including the absence of mandatory minimums, the existence of parole, and lower baseline penalties, terms of imprisonment for drug offenses tend to be substantially lower in state systems than in the federal system. The difference is especially marked in the case of crack offenses. The majority of States draw no distinction between types of cocaine in their penalty schemes; of those that do, none has established as stark a differential as the Federal Government.

Finally, it is undisputed that the brunt of the elevated federal penalties falls heavily on blacks. While 65% of the persons who have used crack are white, in 1993 they represented only 4% of the federal offenders convicted of trafficking in crack. Eighty-eight percent of such defendants were black. Those figures represent a major threat to the integrity of federal sentencing reform, whose main purpose was the elimination of disparity (especially racial) in sentencing.[16]

The extraordinary severity of the imposed penalties and the troubling racial patterns of enforcement give rise to a special concern about the fairness of charging practices for crack offenses. In my view, the District Judge, who has sat on both the federal and the state benches in Los Angeles, acted well within her discretion to call for the development of facts that would demonstrate what standards, if any, governed the choice of forum where similarly situated offenders are prosecuted.

---

16. It took many years to reform the laws applicable to crack and powder cocaine offenses. In 2007, the Congress and the U.S. Sentencing Commission finally amended the crack cocaine guidelines. The Fair Sentencing Act of 2010 reduced from 100:1 to 18:1 the ratio used to punish crack cocaine offenders more harshly than those violating laws with commensurate amounts of powder cocaine. *See* http://www.justice.gov/oip/docs/fair-sentencing-act-memo.pdf. [Footnote by casebook authors.]

The problem of racial disparity in prosecutions continues to be significant. While the legal standard requires that defendants show intentional discrimination, critics charge that unintentional discrimination poses significant challenges. Every day, prosecutors may make decisions that unintentionally discriminate. "This discriminatory impact may occur because of unconscious racism — a phenomenon that plays a powerful role in so many discretionary decisions in the criminal process — and because the lack of power and disadvantaged circumstances of so many African-American defendants and victims make it more likely that prosecutors will treat them less well than whites."[17] Nonetheless, under the Court's equal protection standards, only the most egregious situations of discrimination are likely to meet legal standards for selective prosecution motions.

b. Vindictive Prosecution

A prosecutor's decision to increase the number or severity of charges against a defendant may also be challenged as violating due process if it penalizes a defendant's exercise of constitutional or statutory rights. The mere increase in charges does not satisfy the standard. Rather, a defendant must show actual vindictiveness.

Pretrial decisions by prosecutors are generally not considered to be vindictive. For example, there is no presumption of vindictiveness when a prosecutor threatens to increase charges if a defendant does not accept a plea offer. *See* Bordenkircher v. Hayes, 434 U.S. 357 (1978). Such threats are accepted as part of the plea bargaining process. Likewise, there is no presumption of vindictiveness when additional charges are added after a defendant requests a jury trial. *See* United States v. Goodwin, 457 U.S. 368 (1982).

However, there are certain situations, especially when a defendant is reindicted, in which the court is willing to presume vindictiveness. The Court discussed the issue of vindictive prosecution in Blackledge v. Perry.

BLACKLEDGE v. PERRY

417 U.S. 21 (1974)

Justice STEWART delivered the opinion of the Court.

[Perry was an inmate in a North Carolina prison where he got into a fight with another inmate. Perry was charged with misdemeanor assault with a deadly weapon. After he was convicted by a lower trial court, he exercised his statutory right to appeal his conviction and seek a trial de novo before a

---

17. *See* Angela J. Davis, *Prosecution and Race: The Power and Privilege of Discretion*, 67 Fordham L. Rev. 13 (1998).

higher court. While that appeal was pending, the prosecutor obtained an indictment charging Perry with felony assault with intent to kill. Perry claimed vindictive prosecution.]

[Perry] urges that the indictment on the felony charge constituted a penalty for his exercising his statutory right to appeal, and thus contravened the Due Process Clause of the Fourteenth Amendment. Perry's due process arguments are derived substantially from North Carolina v. Pearce and its progeny. In *Pearce*, the Court considered the constitutional problems presented when, following a successful appeal and reconviction, a criminal defendant was subjected to a greater punishment than that imposed at the first trial. While we concluded that such a harsher sentence was not absolutely precluded by either the Double Jeopardy or Due Process Clause, we emphasized that "imposition of a penalty upon the defendant for having successfully pursued a statutory right of appeal or collateral remedy would be . . . a violation of due process of law." Because "vindictiveness against a defendant for having successfully attacked his first conviction must play no part in the sentence he receives after a new trial," we held that an increased sentence could not be imposed upon retrial unless the sentencing judge placed certain specified findings on the record.

[T]he Due Process Clause is not offended by all possibilities of increased punishment upon retrial after appeal, but only by those that pose a realistic likelihood of "vindictiveness." The question is whether the opportunities for vindictiveness in this situation are such as to impel the conclusion that due process of law requires a rule analogous to that of the *Pearce* case. We conclude that the answer must be in the affirmative.

A prosecutor clearly has a considerable stake in discouraging convicted misdemeanants from appealing and thus obtaining a trial de novo in the Superior Court, since such an appeal will clearly require increased expenditures of prosecutorial resources before the defendant's conviction becomes final, and may even result in a formerly convicted defendant's going free. And, if the prosecutor has the means readily at hand to discourage such appeals—by "upping the ante" through a felony indictment whenever a convicted misdemeanant pursues his statutory appellate remedy—the State can insure that only the most hardy defendants will brave the hazards of a de novo trial.

There is, of course, no evidence that the prosecutor in this case acted in bad faith or maliciously in seeking a felony indictment against Perry. The rationale of our judgment in the *Pearce* case, however, was not grounded upon the proposition that actual retaliatory motivation must inevitably exist. Rather, we emphasized that "since the fear of such vindictiveness may unconstitutionally deter a defendant's exercise of the right to appeal or collaterally attack his first conviction, due process also requires that a defendant be freed of apprehension of such a retaliatory motivation on the part of the sentencing judge." We think it clear that the same considerations apply here. A person convicted of an offense is entitled to pursue his statutory right to a trial de novo, without apprehension that the

State will retaliate by substituting a more serious charge for the original one, thus subjecting him to a significantly increased potential period of incarceration.

Due process of law requires that such a potential for vindictiveness must not enter into North Carolina's two-tiered appellate process. We hold, therefore, that it was not constitutionally permissible for the State to respond to Perry's invocation of his statutory right to appeal by bringing a more serious charge against him prior to the trial de novo.[18]

It is rare for a vindictive trial motion to be granted. Most cases are not like *Blackledge*, and judges do not assume that the prosecutor had an impermissible motive for enhancing charges. Rather, judges generally give wide latitude to prosecutors to reevaluate their charging decisions. Thus, in United States v. Goodwin, 457 U.S. 368 (1982), the Court held that there is no presumption of vindictiveness if the prosecution increases charges pretrial because they have the right to reevaluate their case as they prepare for trial. Accordingly, there is also no violation of a defendant's rights when a prosecutor threatens to add more charges during plea bargain negotiations. Moreover, even in the post-trial context, a claim of vindictiveness is easily rebutted if prosecutors can show that new evidence or a reevaluation of the case justified the imposition of the new charges. Lower courts continue to limit the impact of *Blackledge* by finding that it does not apply when a prosecutor escalates charges following a mistrial or files additional charges after an acquittal.[19]

C. FORMAL CHARGING MECHANISMS

American courts rely on two different mechanisms to screen cases before they are set for trial and to formalize the charges the defendant will face. Both the grand jury and preliminary hearing are designed to protect citizens from unjust prosecutions, but they use very different procedures to accomplish this goal.

---

18. In its decision, the Court noted that a claim of prosecutorial vindictiveness would be overcome if the state could show "that it was impossible to proceed on the more serious charge at the outset" because, for example, the victim did not die until after the initial charges were brought. *See* Diaz v. United States, 223 U.S. 442 (1912). However, the prosecution in *Blackledge* had made no attempt to rebut the claim of vindictiveness. [Footnote by casebook authors.]

19. For a discussion of cases limiting the doctrine of vindictive prosecution, *see* C. Peter Erlinder & David C. Thomas, *Prohibiting Prosecutorial Vindictiveness While Protecting Prosecutorial Discretion: Toward a Principled Resolution of a Due Process Dilemma*, 76 J. Crim. L. & C. 341 (1985); Barbara A. Schwartz, *The Limits of Prosecutorial Vindictiveness*, 69 Iowa L. Rev. 127 (1983).

1. *The Grand Jury*

The modern grand jury descends from the English grand jury used more than 800 years ago.[20] The grand jury consisted of a group of citizens who would act as a buffer between the Crown and the accused. Acting in secrecy, the grand jury would decide when individuals should be charged with crimes. American colonists adopted the grand jury as part of the common law system. In the famous Zenger case, a grand jury refused to indict newspaper publisher John Peter Zenger for libel after he criticized the governor of New York, although the grand jurors themselves were threatened with incarceration.

The right to a grand jury was incorporated into the Fifth Amendment. It provides that, except in military cases, "no person shall be held to answer for a capital, or otherwise infamous crime, unless on a presentment or indictment of a grand jury." Presentments, which were charges initiated by the grand jury, are no longer used. However, grand jury indictments are still the primary mechanism for bringing federal charges.

The right to an indictment only applies to "infamous crimes." A crime is "infamous" if it can result in imprisonment in a penitentiary or hard labor. Ex parte Wilson, 114 U.S. 417 (1885). Thus, federal felony charges are brought by way of indictment. Misdemeanor charges can be filed directly by the prosecutor by information.

The right to a grand jury indictment only applies to federal prosecutions. In Hurtado v. California, 110 U.S. 516 (1884), the Supreme Court held that the right to a grand jury is not incorporated under the Fourteenth Amendment. Thus, states are free to bring charges for serious crimes without using a grand jury or by using a grand jury that has different procedures from a federal grand jury. Only about one-third of the states have grand juries, and some states use their grand juries primarily to conduct civil investigations of government agencies.

While the primary function of a grand jury is to screen cases and decide which should be indicted, the grand jury also performs an important investigative role. The grand jury has the power to subpoena witnesses and documents. It is an effective tool for prosecutors because they can conduct their investigations in secret without the defense being present.

Pursuant to Federal Rule of Criminal Procedure 6(a), 23 citizens sit on a grand jury. They are selected from a cross-section of the community. Grand jurors typically serve for 6 months, but their service can extend for as long as 18 months. If a grand jury refuses to issue an indictment, prosecutors can represent the same case to another grand jury.

Although the grand jury is considered to be an independent screening body, the reality is that the grand jury is directed in its operations by the prosecutor. Prosecutors suggest what cases the grand jury should investigate,

---

20. For a summary of the history and purpose of the grand jury, *see* United States v. Navarro-Vargas, 408 F.3d 1184 (9th Cir. 2005).

prepare the subpoenas for their signature, draft the indictments, and advise the grand jurors of the law. It is therefore extremely rare for a grand jury to refuse to issue an indictment requested by a prosecutor. If the grand jury refuses to indict, it issues a "no bill." However, many people perceive the modern grand jury as nothing more than a "rubber stamp" for prosecutors.

Grand jurors do not have the power to bring charges without the agreement of the prosecutor. If the grand jury returns an indictment, and the prosecution disagrees with its decision, it may refuse to sign the indictment or issue a *nolle prosequi*, which dismisses the charges. There have been situations of "runaway" grand juries, but courts have held that grand jurors do not have independent power to bring a prosecution.[21]

A defendant can waive grand jury indictment and opt to have the prosecution file formal charges by information. Fed. R. Crim. P. 7(b). Waiver of indictment often signals that a defendant is cooperating in the government's investigation.

a. Operation of the Grand Jury

Grand jury operations are an ex parte process. Only the prosecutor is represented in grand jury proceedings. During the typical grand jury proceeding, the prosecutor calls and examines witnesses before the grand jury. Then, if the prosecutor wants to secure an indictment, the prosecutor presents a typed indictment to the grand jury, instructs them on the applicable law, and steps out when the grand jurors are asked to deliberate to determine whether there is probable cause to support the charges.

Neither the defendant nor his counsel has the right to be present in the grand jury. There is also no judge present for grand jury proceedings. The grand jury is considered to be an independent body that investigates and screens cases.

Individuals who are the focus of a grand jury investigation are typically referred to as "targets" of the grand jury. It is rare, although not prohibited, for the target of a grand jury to be called as a witness in the grand jury because an individual has the Fifth Amendment right to refuse to testify before the grand jury.

Some prosecutors also refer to "subjects" of a grand jury investigation. A subject is also a person who may be charged with a crime, but is not as likely to be indicted as the identified "target" of the investigation. Prosecutors are not required to tell individuals that they are the target or suspect of a grand

---

21. The most infamous case of a runaway grand jury involved an investigation of Rockwell International for operating its Rocky Flats nuclear-weapons plant in a manner that included dumping nuclear waste into the environment. The prosecutor declined to sign a grand jury indictment against Rockwell, instead reaching a financial settlement with the company. Incensed by the prosecutor's refusal, the grand jurors tried to bring charges on their own, but the court refused to intervene in the prosecutor's decision. *See* Jim Hughes, *Grand Jurors Hope to Go Public and Ask Congress to Decide in Rocky Flats Case*, Denver Post, March 14, 2004, B-04.

jury investigation. Moreover, because of secrecy rules, Department of Justice guidelines advise prosecutors not to confirm an ongoing grand jury investigation.

Grand jury transcripts remain secret until ordered released by the court. In federal court, the testimony of a grand jury witness is not discoverable unless that witness testifies at trial or the requesting party shows a particularized need for release of the transcript. Fed. R. Crim. P. 6(e). Some states routinely release grand jury transcripts to the public once a case has been indicted.

Violations of grand jury procedures generally become moot once the defendant is convicted. For example, in United States v. Mechanik, 475 U.S. 66 (1986), the prosecution arguably violated Federal Rule of Criminal Procedure 6(d) by having two witnesses testify at once before the grand jury. The Supreme Court held that while such a procedural error could influence a grand jury to indict the defendant, once the petit jury returned a guilty verdict, there was proof beyond a reasonable doubt that such charges were warranted. Thus, any error in the grand jury proceeding was harmless.

Moreover, even if a defendant raises a claim of grand jury error before a case is tried, grand jury violations are not grounds for dismissing an indictment absent a showing of prejudice. Thus, in Bank of Nova Scotia v. United States, 487 U.S. 250 (1988), the district court found a variety of alleged violations of grand jury procedures, including unauthorized disclosures of grand jury materials to civil government employees and improper disclosure of the targets of the grand jury. Nonetheless, the Supreme Court held that dismissal is still not a proper remedy unless the defendant can demonstrate prejudice from the violations. Writing for the majority, Justice Kennedy stated, "We conclude that the District Court had no authority to dismiss the indictment on the basis of prosecutorial misconduct absent a finding that petitioners were prejudiced by such misconduct. The prejudicial inquiry must focus on whether any violations had an effect on the grand jury's decision to indict."

b. Screening Function of the Grand Jury

The role of the grand jury is to screen cases before defendants are required to stand trial. Yet it is not bound by the same rules of evidence and procedure that will govern the trial jury's decision. In light of the next two cases, how effectively do you believe the grand jury screens cases before trial?

COSTELLO v. UNITED STATES
350 U.S. 359 (1956)

Justice BLACK delivered the opinion of the Court.

We granted certiorari in this case to consider a single question: "May a defendant be required to stand trial and a conviction be sustained where only hearsay evidence was presented to the grand jury which indicted him?"

Petitioner, Frank Costello, was indicted for willfully attempting to evade payment of income taxes. Petitioner promptly filed a motion for inspection of the minutes of the grand jury and for a dismissal of the indictment. His motion was based on an affidavit stating that he was firmly convinced there could have been no legal or competent evidence before the grand jury which indicted him since he had reported all his income and paid all taxes due. The motion was denied. At the trial which followed the Government offered evidence designed to show increases in Costello's net worth in an attempt to prove that he had received more income during the years in question than he had reported. To establish its case the Government called and examined 144 witnesses and introduced 368 exhibits. All of the testimony and documents related to business transactions and expenditures by petitioner and his wife. The prosecution concluded its case by calling three government agents. Their investigations had produced the evidence used against petitioner at the trial. They were allowed to summarize the vast amount of evidence already heard and to introduce computations showing, if correct, that petitioner and his wife had received far greater income than they had reported. We have held such summarizations admissible in a "net worth" case like this.

Counsel for petitioner asked each government witness at the trial whether he had appeared before the grand jury which returned the indictment. This cross-examination developed the fact that the three investigating officers had been the only witnesses before the grand jury. After the Government concluded its case, petitioner again moved to dismiss the indictment on the ground that the only evidence before the grand jury was "hearsay," since the three officers had no firsthand knowledge of the transactions upon which their computations were based. Nevertheless the trial court again refused to dismiss the indictment, and petitioner was convicted. The Court of Appeals affirmed, holding that the indictment was valid even though the sole evidence before the grand jury was hearsay. Petitioner here urges: (1) that an indictment based solely on hearsay evidence violates that part of the Fifth Amendment providing that "No person shall be held to answer for a capital, or otherwise infamous crime, unless on a presentment or indictment of a Grand Jury . . ." and (2) that if the Fifth Amendment does not invalidate an indictment based solely on hearsay we should now lay down such a rule for the guidance of federal courts.

The Fifth Amendment provides that federal prosecutions for capital or otherwise infamous crimes must be instituted by presentments or indictments of grand juries. But neither the Fifth Amendment nor any other constitutional provision prescribes the kind of evidence upon which grand juries must act. The grand jury is an English institution, brought to this country by the early colonists and incorporated in the Constitution by the Founders. There is every reason to believe that our constitutional grand jury was intended to operate substantially like its English progenitor. The basic purpose of the English grand jury was to provide a fair method for instituting criminal proceedings against persons believed to have committed crimes. Grand jurors were selected from the body of the people and their work was not hampered by rigid procedural or evidential rules. In fact, grand jurors could act on their own knowledge and were free to make their presentments or indictments on such information as they deemed satisfactory. Despite its broad power to institute criminal proceedings the grand jury grew in popular favor with the years. It acquired an independence in England free from control by the Crown or judges. Its adoption in our Constitution as the sole method for preferring charges in serious criminal cases shows the high place it held as an instrument of justice. And in this country as in England of old the grand jury has convened as a body of laymen, free from technical rules, acting in secret, pledged to indict no one because of prejudice and to free no one because of special favor.

In Holt v. United States, this Court had to decide whether an indictment should be quashed because supported in part by incompetent evidence. The Court refused to hold that such an indictment should be quashed. If indictments were to be held open to challenge on the ground that there was inadequate or incompetent evidence before the grand jury, the resulting delay would be great indeed. The result of such a rule would be that before trial on the merits a defendant could always insist on a kind of preliminary trial to determine the competency and adequacy of the evidence before the grand jury. This is not required by the Fifth Amendment. An indictment returned by a legally constituted and unbiased grand jury, like an information drawn by the prosecutor, if valid on its face, is enough to call for trial of the charge on the merits. The Fifth Amendment requires nothing more.

Petitioner urges that this Court should exercise its power to supervise the administration of justice in federal courts and establish a rule permitting defendants to challenge indictments on the ground that they are not supported by adequate or competent evidence. No persuasive reasons are advanced for establishing such a rule. It would run counter to the whole history of the grand jury institution, in which laymen conduct their inquiries unfettered by technical rules. Neither justice nor the concept of a fair trial requires such a change. In a trial on the merits, defendants are entitled to a strict observance of all the rules designed to bring about a fair verdict. Defendants are not entitled, however, to a rule which would result in interminable delay but add nothing to the assurance of a fair trial.

In order for grand juries to be more exacting in their screening of cases, states can mandate that only admissible evidence may be presented to the grand jury to establish grounds for an indictment. *See, e.g.*, Cal. Penal Code §939.6(b). Yet, as *Costello* discussed, there is no constitutional bar to having a grand jury consider hearsay evidence in deciding whether to indict. Moreover, grand jurors can also hear evidence that would be excludable by a motion to suppress. In United States v. Calandra, 414 U.S. 338 (1974), the

Supreme Court held that illegally seized evidence can also be used in a grand jury proceeding.

Not only is the grand jury not required to consider only admissible evidence; it is not, as the next case demonstrates, required to consider defense evidence that could be presented at trial. The grand jury is not an adversarial proceeding. It is a modest screening mechanism to ensure that cases that do proceed to trial are supported by probable cause.

UNITED STATES v. WILLIAMS
504 U.S. 36 (1992)

Justice SCALIA delivered the opinion of the Court.

The question presented in this case is whether a district court may dismiss an otherwise valid indictment because the Government failed to disclose to the grand jury "substantial exculpatory evidence" in its possession.

Respondent does not contend that the Fifth Amendment itself obliges the prosecutor to disclose substantial exculpatory evidence in his possession to the grand jury. Instead, building on our statement that the federal courts "may, within limits, formulate procedural rules not specifically required by the Constitution or the Congress," he argues that imposition of [a] disclosure rule is supported by the courts' "supervisory power." We think not. Bank of Nova Scotia v. United States (1988) makes clear that the supervisory power can be used to dismiss an indictment because of misconduct before the grand jury, at least where that misconduct amounts to a violation of one of those "few, clear rules which were carefully drafted and approved by this Court and by Congress to ensure the integrity of the grand jury's functions."[22] We did not hold in *Bank of Nova Scotia*, however, that the courts' supervisory power could be used, not merely as a means of enforcing or vindicating legally compelled standards of prosecutorial conduct before the grand jury, but as a means of prescribing those standards of prosecutorial conduct in the first instance — just as it may be used as a means of establishing standards of prosecutorial conduct before the courts themselves.

"Rooted in long centuries of Anglo-American history," the grand jury is mentioned in the Bill of Rights, but not in the body of the Constitution. It has not been textually assigned, therefore, to any of the branches described in the first three Articles. It "is a constitutional fixture in its own right." In fact the whole theory of its function is that it belongs to no branch of the institutional Government, serving as a kind of buffer or referee between the Government and the people. Although the grand jury normally operates, of course, in the courthouse and under judicial auspices, its institutional relationship with the Judicial Branch has traditionally been, so to speak, at arm's

---

22. These rules are set forth in Federal Rule of Criminal Procedure 6 in the Statutory Supplement, including rules on grand jury secrecy and the persons who may be present during grand jury deliberations. [Footnote by casebook authors.]

length. Judges' direct involvement in the functioning of the grand jury has generally been confined to the constitutive one of calling the grand jurors together and administering their oaths of office.

The grand jury's functional independence from the Judicial Branch is evident both in the scope of its power to investigate criminal wrongdoing and in the manner in which that power is exercised. "Unlike [a] court, whose jurisdiction is predicated upon a specific case or controversy, the grand jury 'can investigate merely on suspicion that the law is being violated, or even because it wants assurance that it is not.'" It need not identify the offender it suspects, or even "the precise nature of the offense" it is investigating. The grand jury requires no authorization from its constituting court to initiate an investigation, nor does the prosecutor require leave of court to seek a grand jury indictment. And in its day-to-day functioning, the grand jury generally operates without the interference of a presiding judge.

We have insisted that the grand jury remain "free to pursue its investigations unhindered by external influence or supervision so long as it does not trench upon the legitimate rights of any witness called before it." Recognizing this tradition of independence, we have said that the Fifth Amendment's "constitutional guarantee presupposes an investigative body 'acting independently of either prosecuting attorney or judge.' . . ."

We have twice suggested, though not held, that the Sixth Amendment right to counsel does not attach when an individual is summoned to appear before a grand jury, even if he is the subject of the investigation. And although "the grand jury may not force a witness to answer questions in violation of [the Fifth Amendment's] constitutional guarantee" against self-incrimination, our cases suggest that an indictment obtained through the use of evidence previously obtained in violation of the privilege against self-incrimination "is nevertheless valid."

Given the grand jury's operational separateness from its constituting court, it should come as no surprise that we have been reluctant to invoke the judicial supervisory power as a basis for prescribing modes of grand jury procedure.

Respondent makes a generalized appeal to functional notions: Judicial supervision of the quantity and quality of the evidence relied upon by the grand jury plainly facilitates, he says, the grand jury's performance of its twin historical responsibilities, i.e., bringing to trial those who may be justly accused and shielding the innocent from unfounded accusation and prosecution. We do not agree. The rule would neither preserve nor enhance the traditional functioning of the institution that the Fifth Amendment demands. To the contrary, requiring the prosecutor to present exculpatory as well as inculpatory evidence would alter the grand jury's historical role, transforming it from an accusatory to an adjudicatory body.

It is axiomatic that the grand jury sits not to determine guilt or innocence, but to assess whether there is adequate basis for bringing a criminal charge. As a consequence, neither in this country nor in England has the suspect under investigation by the grand jury ever been thought to have a right to testify or to have exculpatory evidence presented.

Imposing upon the prosecutor a legal obligation to present exculpatory evidence in his possession would be incompatible with this system. If a "balanced" assessment of the entire matter is the objective, surely the first thing to be done—rather than requiring the prosecutor to say what he knows in defense of the target of the investigation—is to entitle the target to tender his own defense. To require the former while denying (as we do) the latter would be quite absurd. It would also be quite pointless, since it would merely invite the target to circumnavigate the system by delivering his exculpatory evidence to the prosecutor, whereupon it would have to be passed on to the grand jury—unless the prosecutor is willing to take the chance that a court will not deem the evidence important enough to qualify for mandatory disclosure.

Respondent acknowledges (as he must) that the "common law" of the grand jury is not violated if the grand jury itself chooses to hear no more evidence than that which suffices to convince it an indictment is proper. Respondent insists, however, that courts must require the modern prosecutor to alert the grand jury to the nature and extent of the available exculpatory evidence, because otherwise the grand jury "merely functions as an arm of the prosecution." We reject the attempt to convert a non-existent duty of the grand jury itself into an obligation of the prosecutor.

[I]n Costello v. United States, we held that "it would run counter to the whole history of the grand jury institution" to permit an indictment to be challenged "on the ground that there was inadequate or incompetent evidence before the grand jury." It would make little sense, we think, to abstain from reviewing the evidentiary support for the grand jury's judgment while scrutinizing the sufficiency of the prosecutor's presentation. A complaint about the quality or adequacy of the evidence can always be recast as a complaint that the prosecutor's presentation was "incomplete" or "misleading." Our words in *Costello* bear repeating: Review of facially valid indictments on such grounds "would run counter to the whole history of the grand jury institution[,] [and] neither justice nor the concept of a fair trial requires [it]."

[R]espondent argues that a rule requiring the prosecutor to disclose exculpatory evidence to the grand jury would, by removing from the docket unjustified prosecutions, save valuable judicial time. That depends, we suppose, upon what the ratio would turn out to be between unjustified prosecutions eliminated and grand jury indictments challenged—for the latter as well as the former consume "valuable judicial time." We need not pursue the matter; if there is an advantage to the proposal, Congress is free to prescribe it. For the reasons set forth above, however, we conclude that courts have no authority to prescribe such a duty pursuant to their inherent supervisory authority over their own proceedings.

Justice STEVENS, with whom Justice BLACKMUN and Justice O'CONNOR join, and with whom Justice THOMAS joins in part, dissenting.

Like the Hydra slain by Hercules, prosecutorial misconduct has many heads. [T]he prosecutor has [a] duty to refrain from improper methods calculated to produce a wrongful indictment. Indeed, the prosecutor's duty to protect the fundamental fairness of judicial proceedings assumes special importance when he is presenting evidence to a grand jury. "The costs of continued unchecked prosecutorial misconduct" before the grand jury are particularly substantial because there:

> the prosecutor operates without the check of a judge or a trained legal adversary, and virtually immune from public scrutiny. The prosecutor's abuse of his special relationship to the grand jury poses an enormous risk to defendants as well. For while in theory a trial provides the defendant with a full opportunity to contest and disprove the charges against him, in practice, the handing up of an indictment will often have a devastating personal and professional impact that a later dismissal or acquittal can never undo. Where the potential for abuse is so great, and the consequences of a mistaken indictment so serious, the ethical responsibilities of the prosecutor, and the obligation of the judiciary to protect against even the appearance of unfairness, are correspondingly heightened.
>
> The ex parte character of grand jury proceedings makes it peculiarly important for a federal prosecutor to remember that, in the familiar phrase, the interest of the United States "in a criminal prosecution is not that it shall win a case, but that justice shall be done."

We do not protect the integrity and independence of the grand jury by closing our eyes to the countless forms of prosecutorial misconduct that may occur inside the secrecy of the grand jury room. After all, the grand jury is not merely an investigatory body; it also serves as a "protector of citizens against arbitrary and oppressive governmental action."

It blinks reality to say that the grand jury can adequately perform this important historic role if it is intentionally misled by the prosecutor — on whose knowledge of the law and facts of the underlying criminal investigation the jurors will, of necessity, rely.

Unlike the Court, I am unwilling to hold that countless forms of prosecutorial misconduct must be tolerated — no matter how prejudicial they may be, or how seriously they may distort the legitimate function of the grand jury — simply because they are not proscribed by Rule 6 of the Federal Rules of Criminal Procedure or a statute that is applicable in grand jury proceedings. Such a sharp break with the traditional role of the federal judiciary is unprecedented, unwarranted, and unwise. Unrestrained prosecutorial misconduct in grand jury proceedings is inconsistent with the administration of justice in the federal courts and should be redressed in appropriate cases by the dismissal of indictments obtained by improper methods.

c. Grand Jury Reform

There continue to be calls for grand jury reform, but these generally go unheeded by Congress and the Supreme Court. The ABA Criminal Justice Section Committee on the Grand Jury has proposed the following reforms:

1. Witnesses before the grand jury be afforded the right to be accompanied by counsel in the grand jury room;

2. Prosecutors be required to advise the grand jury of any known exculpatory information;

3. Prosecutors not be permitted to present to the grand jury evidence that would be inadmissible at trial;

4. Targets of a grand jury investigation be given the right to testify;

5. Grand jury witnesses be provided with transcripts of their own testimony; and

6. Grand juries not name persons in an indictment as an unindicted co-conspirator.

Thus far, these reforms have not been adopted in federal court; the Supreme Court's holding in United States v. Mandujano, 425 U.S. 564 (1976) — that a grand jury witness has no constitutional right to have counsel present during grand jury proceedings — remains in effect.

2. Preliminary Hearing

Another mechanism available to screen cases is the preliminary hearing. In federal court, preliminary hearings are governed by Federal Rule of Criminal Procedure 5.1 and are only used to hold a defendant until an indictment can be obtained.

However, states routinely rely on preliminary hearings in lieu of or in addition to grand jury proceedings. Approximately two-thirds of the states permit felony prosecutions to be initiated by information or indictment. Once the magistrate or judge finds probable cause, the defendant is "bound over" for trial on charges filed by the prosecutor in an information.

A preliminary hearing is fundamentally different from a grand jury proceeding. Preliminary hearings are more akin to "mini-trials." A judge presides over the preliminary hearing; it is an adversarial process. The defendant has the right to be present and to be represented by counsel. Coleman v. Alabama, 399 U.S. 1 (1970). Preliminary hearings are generally open to the public. The prosecution bears the burden at a preliminary hearing to present probable cause supporting the charges.

Different states use different evidentiary standards for preliminary hearings, depending on how exacting they want the case screening procedure to be. If a state wants a screening process that will authorize charges only when there is a strong chance of conviction at trial, it requires that the evidence at the preliminary hearing meet the same evidentiary standards it will have to meet for trial. Hearsay evidence is not allowed. However, many states view the preliminary hearing as a more modest check on prosecutorial discretion. In those venues, hearsay evidence may be presented at the preliminary hearing and the defense has a more limited opportunity to cross-examine the prosecution's witnesses. See also Fed. R. Evid. 1101(d)(3) (rules of evidence do not apply to federal preliminary hearings).

Following a preliminary hearing, the court's decision to bind a defendant over for trial generally triggers a more intense effort at plea negotiations.

Having seen a preview of the prosecution's case, defense counsel is in a better position to assess a defendant's case than counsel might be if the defendant were indicted in secret by the grand jury.

If a magistrate refuses to bind over a defendant for trial, prosecutors may present their case to the grand jury or move to dismiss it and refile before a different judge. Any errors at the preliminary hearing are generally considered harmless once the defendant is tried and convicted.

In addition to screening cases for trial, a preliminary hearing is also crucial to preserving evidence for trial. In Crawford v. Washington, 541 U.S. 36 (2004), the Supreme Court held that testimonial hearsay statements cannot be presented at trial unless the declarant is unavailable and the defendant has had the opportunity to cross-examine the declarant before the statement is introduced. Thus, if a witness provides a formal statement before trial but then does not appear to testify, that statement cannot be used as evidence unless the defendant had an opportunity to cross-examine the victim regarding the statement. A preliminary hearing can provide the means to preserve that witness's testimony for trial by giving the defendant a pretrial opportunity to cross-examine the witness. Although the Supreme Court has held that the Sixth Amendment Confrontation Clause is a trial right and does not apply to the preliminary hearing (*see* Goldsby v. United States, 160 U.S. 70 (1895)), states now provide defendants the right to cross-examine pursuant to local or state rule.

D. SEVERANCE AND JOINDER

One of the decisions a prosecutor must make in deciding how to charge a case is whether to join charges and defendants for trial. Prosecutors generally favor trying defendants together. As Justice Scalia wrote in Richardson v. Marsh, 481 U.S. 200 (1987), there are advantages in joining defendants:

> Joint trials play a vital role in the criminal justice system. It would impair both the efficiency and the fairness of the criminal justice system to require . . . that prosecutors bring separate proceedings, presenting the same evidence again and again, requiring victims and witnesses to repeat the inconvenience (and sometimes trauma) of testifying, and randomly favoring the last-tried defendants who have the advantage of knowing the prosecution's case beforehand. Joint trials generally serve the interests of justice by avoiding inconsistent verdicts and enabling more accurate assessment of relative culpability — advantages which sometimes operate to the defendant's benefit. Even apart from these tactical considerations, joint trials generally serve the interests of justice by avoiding the scandal and inequity of inconsistent verdicts.

Yet there are also downsides to trying defendants together. Defendants may be tainted by the evidence against their codefendants. The mere fact that the defendants are charged together, or are facing multiple counts, can suggest to the jury that each defendant was part of a larger criminal scheme.

1. *Federal Rules of Criminal Procedure 8 and 14*

Federal Rules of Criminal Procedure 8 and 14 govern the issues of joinder and severance of criminal cases in federal court. Rule 8(a) permits the joinder of offenses that "are of the same or similar character, or are based on the same act or transaction, or are connected with or constitute parts of a common scheme or plan." Rule 8(b) permits two or more defendants to be charged together if they have participated in the same act or transaction, or in the same series of acts or transactions. The defendants may be charged in one or more counts together. All defendants need not be charged in each count.

Rule 14 provides relief from prejudicial joinder. "If the joinder of offenses or defendants in an indictment, or information, or a consolidation for trial, appears to prejudice a defendant or the government, the court may order separate trials of counts, sever the defendants' trials, or provide any other relief that justice requires."

2. *Irreconcilable Conflicts and* **Bruton** *Problems*

Two common grounds are offered in support of a defendant's motion to sever defendants who have been joined for trial: (1) finger-pointing at trial by one defendant against another and (2) introduction of confessions that implicate codefendants in a manner that violates the codefendant's right of confrontation. Generally, courts will not sever a case unless the conflict between defendants is irreconcilable.

a. **Conflicting Defenses**

ZAFIRO v. UNITED STATES

506 U.S. 534 (1993)

Justice O'CONNOR delivered the opinion of the Court.

Rule 8(b) of the Federal Rules of Criminal Procedure provides that defendants may be charged together "if they are alleged to have participated in the same act or transaction or in the same series of acts or transactions constituting an offense or offenses." Rule 14 of the Rules, in turn, permits a district court to grant a severance of defendants if "it appears that a defendant or the government is prejudiced by a joinder." In this case, we consider whether Rule 14 requires severance as a matter of law when codefendants present "mutually antagonistic defenses."

Gloria Zafiro, Jose Martinez, Salvador Garcia, and Alfonso Soto were accused of distributing illegal drugs in the Chicago area, operating primarily out of Soto's bungalow in Chicago and Zafiro's apartment in Cicero, a nearby suburb. One day, Government agents observed Garcia and Soto place a large box in Soto's car and drive from Soto's bungalow to Zafiro's apartment. The agents followed the two as they carried the box up the stairs. When the agents identified themselves, Garcia and Soto dropped the box and ran into the apartment. The agents entered the apartment in pursuit and found the four petitioners in the living room. The dropped box contained 55 pounds of cocaine.

The four petitioners were indicted and brought to trial together. At various points during the proceeding, Garcia and Soto moved for severance, arguing that their defenses were mutually antagonistic. Soto testified that he knew nothing about the drug conspiracy. He claimed that Garcia had asked him for a box, which he gave Garcia, and that he (Soto) did not know its contents until they were arrested. Garcia did not testify, but his lawyer argued that Garcia was innocent: The box belonged to Soto and Garcia was ignorant of its contents.

Zafiro and Martinez also repeatedly moved for severance on the ground that their defenses were mutually antagonistic. Zafiro testified that she was merely Martinez's girlfriend and knew nothing of the conspiracy. She claimed that Martinez stayed in her apartment occasionally, kept some clothes there, and gave her small amounts of money. Although she allowed Martinez to store a suitcase in her closet, she testified, she had no idea that the suitcase contained illegal drugs. Like Garcia, Martinez did not testify. But his lawyer argued that Martinez was only visiting his girlfriend and had no idea that she was involved in distributing drugs.

The District Court denied the motions for severance. The jury convicted all four petitioners of conspiring to possess cocaine, heroin, and marijuana with the intent to distribute. Petitioners appealed their convictions.

Rule 8(b) states that "two or more defendants may be charged in the same indictment or information if they are alleged to have participated in the same act or transaction or in the same series of acts or transactions constituting an offense or offenses." There is a preference in the federal system for joint trials of defendants who are indicted together. Joint trials "play a vital role in the criminal justice system." Richardson v. Marsh (1987). They promote efficiency and "serve the interests of justice by avoiding the scandal and inequity of inconsistent verdicts." For these reasons, we repeatedly have approved of joint trials. But Rule 14 recognizes that joinder, even when proper under Rule 8(b), may prejudice either a defendant or the Government. Thus, the Rule provides: "If it appears that a defendant or the government is prejudiced by a joinder of . . . defendants . . . for trial together, the court may order an election or separate trials of counts, grant a severance of defendants or provide whatever other relief justice requires."

In interpreting Rule 14, the Courts of Appeals frequently have expressed the view that "mutually antagonistic" or "irreconcilable" defenses may be so prejudicial in some circumstances as to mandate severance. Notwithstanding such assertions, the courts have reversed relatively few convictions for failure to grant a severance on grounds of mutually antagonistic or irreconcilable defenses. The low rate of reversal may reflect the inability of defendants to prove a risk of prejudice in most cases involving conflicting defenses.

Nevertheless, petitioners urge us to adopt a bright-line rule, mandating severance whenever codefendants have conflicting defenses. We decline to do so. Mutually antagonistic defenses are not prejudicial per se. Moreover, Rule 14 does not require severance even if prejudice is shown; rather, it leaves the tailoring of the relief to be granted, if any, to the district court's sound discretion.

We believe that, when defendants properly have been joined under Rule 8(b), a district court should grant a severance under Rule 14 only if there is a serious risk that a joint trial would compromise a specific trial right of one of the defendants, or prevent the jury from making a reliable judgment about guilt or innocence. [For example,] evidence that is probative of a defendant's guilt but technically admissible only against a codefendant also might present a risk of prejudice. *See* Bruton v. United States (1968). The risk of prejudice will vary with the facts in each case, and district courts may find prejudice in situations not discussed here. When the risk of prejudice is high, a district court is more likely to determine that separate trials are necessary, but, less drastic measures, such as limiting instructions, often will suffice to cure any risk of prejudice.

Turning to the facts of this case, we note that petitioners do not articulate any specific instances of prejudice. Instead they contend that the very nature of their defenses, without more, prejudiced them. Their theory is that when two defendants both claim they are innocent and each accuses the other of the crime, a jury will conclude (1) that both defendants are lying and convict them both on that basis, or (2) that at least one of the two must be guilty without regard to whether the Government has proved its case beyond a reasonable doubt.

As to the first contention, it is well settled that defendants are not entitled to severance merely because they may have a better chance of acquittal in separate trials. As to the second contention, the short answer is that petitioners' scenario simply did not occur here. The Government argued that all four petitioners were guilty and offered sufficient evidence as to all four petitioners; the jury in turn found all four petitioners guilty of various offenses. Moreover, even if there were some risk of prejudice, here it is of the type that can be cured with proper instructions, and "juries are presumed to follow their instructions."

Rule 14 leaves the determination of risk of prejudice and any remedy that may be necessary to the sound discretion of the district courts. Because petitioners have not shown that their joint trial subjected them to any legally cognizable prejudice, we conclude that the District Court did not abuse its discretion in denying petitioners' motions to sever.

Justice STEVENS, concurring in the judgment.

When two people are apprehended in possession of a container filled with narcotics, it is probable that they both know what is inside. The inference of knowledge is heightened when, as in this case, both people flee when confronted by police officers, or both people occupy the premises in which the container is found. At the same time, however, it remains entirely possible that one person did not have such knowledge. That, of course, is the argument made by each of the defendants in this case: that he or she did not know what was in the crucial box or suitcase.

Most important here, it is also possible that both persons lacked knowledge of the contents of the relevant container. Moreover, that hypothesis is compatible with individual defenses of lack of knowledge. There is no logical inconsistency between a version of events in which one person is ignorant, and a version in which the other is ignorant; unlikely as it may seem, it is at least theoretically possible that both versions are true, in that both persons are ignorant. In other words, dual ignorance defenses do not necessarily translate into "mutually antagonistic" defenses, as that term is used in reviewing severance motions, because acceptance of one defense does not necessarily preclude acceptance of the other and acquittal of the codefendant.

I agree with the Court that a "bright-line rule, mandating severance whenever codefendants have conflicting defenses" is unwarranted. [But] I think district courts must retain their traditional discretion to consider severance whenever mutually antagonistic defenses are presented. Accordingly, I would refrain from announcing a preference for joint trials, or any general rule that might be construed as a limit on that discretion.

b. *Bruton* Problems

As noted in *Zafiro*, there are situations in which the introduction of a confession by one defendant may implicate a codefendant and poses a Confrontation Clause problem because the codefendant has not had an opportunity to cross-examine the defendant on his confession. This is known as a *Bruton* problem. While the confessing defendant's statement may be admissible against the defendant who confessed, introducing the statement would violate the codefendant's right of confrontation because he has never had an opportunity to cross-examine the defendant who implicated him. In such situations, either the prosecution must redact the statement so that it does not implicate any codefendants or bring two separate trials.

BRUTON v. UNITED STATES

391 U.S. 123 (1968)

Justice BRENNAN delivered the opinion of the Court.

This case presents the question whether the conviction of a defendant at a joint trial should be set aside although the jury was instructed that a codefendant's confession inculpating the defendant had to be disregarded in determining his guilt or innocence.

A joint trial of petitioner and one Evans resulted in the conviction of both by a jury on a federal charge of armed postal robbery. A postal inspector testified that Evans orally confessed to him that Evans and petitioner committed the armed robbery. We hold that, because of the substantial risk that the jury, despite instructions to the contrary, looked to the incriminating extrajudicial statements in determining petitioner's guilt, admission of Evans' confession in this joint trial violated petitioner's right of cross-examination secured by the Confrontation Clause of the Sixth Amendment. We therefore overrule [our prior decision in] *Delli Paoli* and reverse.

The basic premise of *Delli Paoli* was that it is "reasonably possible for the jury to follow" sufficiently clear instructions to disregard the confessor's extrajudicial statement that his codefendant participated with him in committing the crime. If it were true that the jury disregarded the reference to the codefendant, no question would arise under the Confrontation Clause. But since *Delli Paoli* was decided this Court has effectively repudiated its basic premise. "It is impossible realistically to suppose that when the twelve good men and women [have a defendant's confession in the privacy of the jury room, they will not use it to implicate the codefendant]."

Those who have defended reliance on the limiting instruction in this area have cited several reasons in support. Judge Learned Hand, a particularly severe critic of the proposition that juries could be counted on to disregard inadmissible hearsay, . . . [called the] limiting instruction, . . . a "recommendation to the jury of a mental gymnastic which is beyond, not only their powers, but anybody's else." Judge Hand referred to the instruction as a "placebo," medically defined as "a medicinal lie." Judge Jerome Frank suggested that its legal equivalent "is a kind of 'judicial lie.'"

Another reason cited in defense of *Delli Paoli* is the justification for joint trials in general, the argument being that the benefits of joint proceedings should not have to be sacrificed by requiring separate trials in order to use the confession against the declarant. Joint trials do conserve state funds, diminish inconvenience to witnesses and public authorities, and avoid delays in bringing those accused of crime to trial. But the answer to this argument was cogently stated by Judge Lehman in People v. Fisher:

> We still adhere to the rule that an accused is entitled to confrontation of the witnesses against him and the right to cross-examine them. . . . We destroy the age-old rule which in the past has been regarded as a fundamental principle of our jurisprudence by a legalistic formula, required of the judge, that the jury may not consider any admissions against any party who did not join in them. We secure greater speed, economy and convenience in the administration of the law at the price of fundamental principles of constitutional liberty. That price is too high.

Despite the concededly clear instructions to the jury to disregard Evans' inadmissible hearsay evidence inculpating petitioner, in the context of a joint trial we cannot accept limiting instructions as an adequate substitute for petitioner's constitutional right of cross-examination.

Justice WHITE, dissenting.

I dissent from this excessively rigid rule. There is nothing in this record to suggest that the jury did not follow the trial judge's instructions. There has been no new learning since *Delli Paoli* indicating that juries are less reliable than they were considered in that case to be. There is nothing in the prior decisions of this Court which supports this new constitutional rule.

The Court concedes that there are many instances in which reliance on limiting instructions is justified, The Court asserts, however, that the hazards to the defendant of permitting the jury to hear a codefendant's confession implicating him are so severe that we must assume the jury's inability to heed a limiting instruction. There are good reasons, however, for distinguishing the codefendant's confession from that of the defendant himself and for trusting in the jury's ability to disregard the former when instructed to do so.

First, the defendant's own confession is probably the most probative and damaging evidence that can be admitted against him. Though itself an out-of-court statement, it is admitted as reliable evidence because it is an admission of guilt by the defendant and constitutes direct evidence of the facts to which it relates. Even the testimony of an eyewitness may be less reliable than the defendant's own confession.

The rule which the Court announces today will severely limit the circumstances in which defendants may be tried together for a crime which they are both charged with committing. Unquestionably, joint trials are more economical and minimize the burden on witnesses, prosecutors, and courts. They also avoid delays in bringing those accused of crime to trial. This much the Court concedes. It is also worth saying that separate trials are apt to have varying consequences for legally indistinguishable defendants. The unfairness of this is confirmed by the common prosecutorial experience of seeing codefendants who are tried separately strenuously jockeying for position with regard to who should be the first to be tried.

In view of the practical difficulties of separate trials and their potential unfairness, I am disappointed that the Court has not spelled out how the federal courts might conduct their business consistent with today's opinion. I would suppose that it will be necessary to exclude all extrajudicial confessions unless all portions of them which implicate defendants other than the declarant are effectively deleted. Effective deletion will probably require not only omission of all direct and indirect inculpations of codefendants but also of any statement that could be employed against those defendants once their identity is otherwise established. Of course, the deletion must not be such that it will distort the statements to the substantial prejudice of either the declarant or the Government. If deletion is not feasible, then the Government will have to choose either not to use the confession at all or to try the defendants separately. To save time, money, and effort, the Government might best seek a ruling at the earliest possible stage of the trial proceedings as to whether the confession is admissible once offending portions are deleted. Oral statements, such as that involved in the present case, will present special problems, for there is a risk that the witness in testifying will inadvertently exceed permissible limits. Except for recommending that caution be used with regard to such oral statements, it is difficult to anticipate the issues which will arise in concrete factual situations.

As Justice White predicted, courts have had to fashion other alternatives to the *Bruton* problem. Prosecutors have a few options:

1. They can agree to separate trials for the defendants.
2. They can try the defendants jointly but forgo use of the confession.
3. They can redact the confession to remove all references to the existence of a non-confessing defendant.

In redacting the confession, prosecutors must be careful to ensure that a non-testifying codefendant's confession still cannot be construed as implicating the defendant. In the next two cases, Richardson v. Marsh, 481 U.S. 200 (1987) and Gray v. Maryland, 523 U.S. 185 (1998), the Court provided guidance as to what kinds of redacted confessions interfere with a codefendant's Sixth Amendment confrontation rights.

RICHARDSON v. MARSH
481 U.S. 200 (1987)

Justice SCALIA delivered the opinion of the Court.

In Bruton v. United States (1968), we held that a defendant is deprived of his rights under the Confrontation Clause when his nontestifying codefendant's confession naming him as a participant in the crime is introduced at their joint trial, even if the jury is instructed to consider that confession only against the codefendant. Today we consider whether *Bruton* requires the same result when the codefendant's confession is redacted to omit any reference to the defendant, but the defendant is nonetheless linked to the confession by evidence properly admitted against him at trial.

I

Respondent Clarissa Marsh, Benjamin Williams, and Kareem Martin were charged with assaulting Cynthia Knighton and murdering her 4-year-old son, Koran, and her aunt, Ollie Scott. Respondent and Williams were tried jointly, over her objection. (Martin was a fugitive at the time of trial.) At the trial, Knighton testified as follows: On the evening of October 29, 1978, she and her son were at Scott's home when respondent and her boyfriend Martin visited. After a brief conversation in the living room, respondent announced that she had come to "pick up something" from Scott and rose from the couch. Martin then pulled out a gun, pointed it at Scott and the Knightons, and said that "someone had gotten killed and [Scott] knew something about it." Respondent immediately walked to the front door and peered out the peephole. The doorbell rang, respondent opened the door, and Williams walked in, carrying a gun. As Williams passed respondent, he asked, "Where's the money?" Martin forced Scott upstairs, and Williams went into the kitchen, leaving respondent alone with the Knightons. Knighton and her son attempted to flee, but respondent grabbed Knighton and held her until Williams returned. Williams ordered the Knightons to lie on the floor and then went upstairs to assist Martin. Respondent, again left alone with the Knightons, stood by the front door and occasionally peered out the peephole. A few minutes later, Martin, Williams, and Scott came down the stairs, and Martin handed a paper grocery bag to respondent. Martin and Williams then forced Scott and the Knightons into the basement, where Martin shot them. Only Cynthia Knighton survived.

In addition to Knighton's testimony, the State introduced (over respondent's objection) a confession given by Williams to the police shortly after his arrest. The confession was redacted to omit all reference to respondent—indeed, to omit all indication that anyone other than Martin and Williams participated in the crime. At the time the confession was admitted, the jury was admonished not to use it in any way against respondent. Williams did not testify.

During his closing argument, the prosecutor admonished the jury not to use Williams' confession against respondent. After closing arguments, the judge again instructed the jury that Williams' confession was not to be considered against respondent. The jury convicted respondent of two counts of felony murder in the perpetration of an armed robbery and one count of assault with intent to commit murder.

Respondent then filed a petition for a writ of habeas corpus. She alleged that introduction of Williams' confession at the joint trial had violated her rights under the Confrontation Clause.

II

The Confrontation Clause of the Sixth Amendment, extended against the States by the Fourteenth Amendment, guarantees the right of a criminal defendant "to be confronted with the witnesses against him." The right of confrontation includes the right to cross-examine witnesses. Therefore, where two defendants are tried jointly, the pretrial confession of one cannot be admitted against the other unless the confessing defendant takes the stand.

Ordinarily, a witness whose testimony is introduced at a joint trial is not considered to be a witness "against" a defendant if the jury is instructed to consider that testimony only against a codefendant. This accords with the almost invariable assumption of the law that jurors follow their instructions which we have applied in many varying contexts. In *Bruton*, however, we recognized a narrow exception to this principle: We held that a defendant is deprived of his Sixth Amendment right of confrontation when the facially incriminating confession of a nontestifying codefendant is introduced at their joint trial, even if the jury is instructed to consider the confession only against the codefendant.

There is an important distinction between this case and *Bruton*, which causes it to fall outside the narrow exception we have created. In *Bruton*, the codefendant's confession "expressly implicat[ed]" the defendant as his accomplice. Thus, at the time that confession was introduced there was not the slightest doubt that it would prove "powerfully incriminating." By contrast, in this case the confession was not incriminating on its face, and became so only when linked with evidence introduced later at trial (the defendant's own testimony).

The rule that juries are presumed to follow their instructions is a pragmatic one, rooted less in the absolute certitude that the presumption is true than in the belief that it represents a reasonable practical accommodation of the interests of the state and the defendant in the criminal justice process. On the precise facts of *Bruton*, involving a facially incriminating confession, we found that accommodation inadequate. As our discussion above shows, the calculus changes when confessions that do not name the defendant are at issue. While we continue to apply *Bruton* where we have found that its rationale validly applies, we decline to extend it further. We hold that the Confrontation Clause is not violated by the admission of a nontestifying codefendant's confession with a proper limiting instruction when, as here, the confession is redacted to eliminate not only the defendant's name, but any reference to his or her existence.

Compare the type of redacted confession approved by the Supreme Court in Richardson v. Marsh with the redacted confession rejected by the Court in the next case of Gray v. Maryland.

GRAY v. MARYLAND

523 U.S. 185 (1998)

Justice BREYER delivered the opinion of the Court.

The issue in this case concerns the application of Bruton v. United States (1968). The case before us differs from *Bruton* in that the prosecution here redacted the codefendant's confession by substituting for the defendant's name in the confession a blank space or the word "deleted." We must decide whether these substitutions make a significant legal difference. We hold that they do not and that *Bruton*'s protective rule applies.

I

In 1993, Stacy Williams died after a severe beating. Anthony Bell gave a confession, to the Baltimore City police, in which he said that he (Bell), Kevin Gray, and Jacquin "Tank" Vanlandingham had participated in the beating that resulted in Williams' death. Vanlandingham later died. A Maryland grand jury indicted Bell and Gray for murder. The State of Maryland tried them jointly.

The trial judge, after denying Gray's motion for a separate trial, permitted the State to introduce Bell's confession into evidence at trial. But the judge ordered the confession redacted. Consequently, the police detective who read the confession into evidence said the word "deleted" or "deletion" whenever Gray's name or Vanlandingham's name appeared. Immediately after the police detective read the redacted confession to the jury, the prosecutor asked, "after he gave you that information, you subsequently were able to arrest Mr. Kevin Gray; is that correct?" The officer responded, "That's correct."

When instructing the jury, the trial judge specified that the confession was evidence only against Bell; the instructions said that the jury should not use the confession as evidence against Gray. The jury convicted both Bell and Gray. Gray appealed.

We granted certiorari in order to consider *Bruton*'s application to a redaction that replaces a name with an obvious blank space or symbol or word such as "deleted."

II

In deciding whether *Bruton*'s protective rule applies to the redacted confession before us, we must consider both *Bruton*, and a later case, Richardson v. Marsh (1987), which limited *Bruton*'s scope.

Bruton, as we have said, involved two defendants — Evans and Bruton — tried jointly for robbery. Evans did not testify, but the Government introduced into evidence Evans' confession, which stated that both he (Evans) and Bruton together had committed the robbery. The trial judge told the jury it could consider the confession as evidence only against Evans, not against Bruton.

This Court held that, despite the limiting instruction, the introduction of Evans' out-of-court confession at Bruton's trial had violated Bruton's right, protected by the Sixth Amendment, to cross-examine witnesses. [The Court said that]

> there are some contexts in which the risk that the jury will not, or cannot, follow instructions is so great, and the consequences of failure so vital to the defendant, that the practical and human limitations of the jury system cannot be ignored. Such a context is presented here, where the powerfully incriminating extrajudicial statements of a codefendant, who stands accused side-by-side with the defendant, are deliberately spread before the jury in a joint trial.

In *Richardson v. Marsh*, the Court considered a redacted confession. The case involved a joint murder trial of Marsh and Williams. The State had redacted the confession of one defendant, Williams, so as to "omit all reference" to his codefendant, Marsh — "indeed, to omit all indication that anyone other than . . . Williams" and a third person had "participated in the crime." The trial court also instructed the jury not to consider the confession against Marsh. As redacted, the confession indicated that Williams and the third person had discussed the murder in the front seat of a car while they traveled to the victim's house. The redacted confession contained no indication that Marsh — or any other person — was in the car.

The Court held that this redacted confession fell outside *Bruton*'s scope and was admissible (with appropriate limiting instructions) at the joint trial. The Court added: "We express no opinion on the admissibility of a confession in which the defendant's name has been replaced with a symbol or neutral pronoun."

III

[U]nlike *Richardson*'s redacted confession, this confession refers directly to the "existence" of the nonconfessing defendant. The State has simply replaced the nonconfessing defendant's name with a kind of symbol, namely the word "deleted" or a blank space set off by commas. We therefore must decide a question that *Richardson* left open, namely whether redaction that replaces a defendant's name with an obvious indication of deletion, such as a blank space, the word "deleted," or a similar symbol, still falls within *Bruton*'s protective rule. We hold that it does.

Redactions that simply replace a name with an obvious blank space or a word such as "deleted" or a symbol or other similarly obvious indications of alteration, however, leave statements that, considered as a class, so closely resemble *Bruton*'s unredacted statements that, in our view, the law must require the same result.

For one thing, a jury will often react similarly to an unredacted confession and a confession redacted in this way, for the jury will often realize that the confession refers specifically to the defendant. This is true even when the State does not blatantly link the defendant to the deleted name, as it did in this case by asking whether Gray was arrested on the basis of information in Bell's confession as soon as the officer had finished reading the redacted statement. Consider a simplified but typical example, a confession that reads "I, Bob Smith, along with Sam Jones, robbed the bank." To replace the words "Sam Jones" with an obvious blank will not likely fool anyone. A juror somewhat familiar with criminal law would know immediately that the blank, in the phrase "I, Bob Smith, along with _____, robbed the bank," refers to defendant Jones. A juror who does not know the law and who therefore wonders to whom the blank might refer need only lift his eyes to Jones, sitting at counsel table, to find what will seem the obvious answer, at least if the juror hears the judge's instruction not to consider the confession as evidence against Jones, for that instruction will provide an obvious reason for the blank. A more sophisticated juror, wondering if the blank refers to someone else, might also wonder how, if it did, the prosecutor could argue the confession is reliable, for the prosecutor, after all, has been arguing that Jones, not someone else, helped Smith commit the crime.

IV

For these reasons, we hold that the confession here at issue, which substituted blanks and the word "delete" for the respondent's proper name, falls within the class of statements to which *Bruton*'s protections apply.

   Justice SCALIA, with whom Chief Justice REHNQUIST, Justice KENNEDY and Justice THOMAS join, dissenting.
   We declined in *Richardson* . . . to extend *Bruton* to confessions that incriminate only by inference from other evidence. When incrimination is inferential, "it is a less valid generalization that the jury will not likely obey the instruction to disregard the evidence." Today the Court struggles to decide whether a confession redacted to omit the defendant's name is incriminating on its face or by inference. The Court should have stopped with its concession: the statement "Me, deleted, deleted, and a few other guys" does not facially incriminate anyone but the speaker.
   The Court's extension of *Bruton* to name-redacted confessions "as a class" will seriously compromise "society's compelling interest in finding, convicting, and punishing those who violate the law."
   The United States Constitution guarantees, not a perfect system of criminal justice (as to which there can be considerable disagreement), but a minimum standard of fairness.

E. AMENDMENTS AND VARIANCES

Not all mistakes in the charges against a defendant will result in dismissal of a case. Federal Rule of Criminal Procedure 7(c) does not require that formal, legal language be used in an indictment. Rather, an indictment is sufficient if it is "a plain, concise, and definite written statement of the essential facts constituting the offense charged." The indictment or information need only inform a defendant of the charge the defendant must defend and provide sufficient detail that the defendant can raise a double jeopardy objection to a future prosecution for the same offense. *See* Hamling v. United States, 418 U.S. 87 (1974).
   A defendant may request a *bill of particulars* to ascertain more details regarding the charged offense. The court has discretion pursuant to Federal Rule of Criminal Procedure 7(e) to grant a bill of particulars. Alternatively, the prosecution may provide such information through discovery. See Chapter 4.

Defendants may challenge indictments on *duplicity* grounds if they charge two or more distinct offenses in a single count of the indictment. Generally, duplicity is not fatal to an indictment. The government can correct the problem by selecting a single basis on which it will try the case.

Defendants may also challenge an indictment because a single offense is charged in multiple counts of an indictment. The simple solution to the problem of *multiplicity* is for the court to order the government to elect which count it will use and dismiss the remaining counts.

If there is a defect in an indictment, the prosecutor may seek to re-present the case to the grand jury for a *superseding indictment*. There is no limit on the number of times a prosecutor can return to the grand jury for a superseding indictment. If the original grand jury is no longer available, the prosecutor can re-present the case in summary fashion to a new grand jury. Superseding indictments are typically used to add new defendants or charges to an indictment or to correct errors before trial.

Indictments can also be *amended* to correct obvious clerical errors or delete surplusage from the indictment. However, it is improper to substantively amend an indictment because a defendant in federal court has a Fifth Amendment right to be tried only for those offenses charged by the grand jury. *See* Stirone v. United States, 361 U.S. 212 (1960).

A *variance* occurs when the evidence at trial proves facts other than those alleged in the indictment. For example, there may be a variance in the time of the crime charged or the number of conspiracies. If a defendant can demonstrate prejudice from a variance, the conviction cannot stand.

CHAPTER
3

BAIL AND PRETRIAL RELEASE

A. INTRODUCTION

After a suspect is arrested and booked on charges, he or she will typically seek release by posting bail. Defendants want bail for many reasons. First and foremost, no one wants to be incarcerated. The conditions in many jails are deplorable and the very loss of liberty is demoralizing, especially for a defendant who has not yet been convicted of a crime. Second, it is much more difficult to prepare for trial when a defendant is incarcerated. Behind bars the defendant is limited in how much he can assist his lawyer and it is much more cumbersome for defense counsel to meet with the client when the client is incarcerated. Third, defendants who remain in pretrial custody face the loss of income, social consequences, and even the loss of support by their families. Finally, there are the intangible effects of a defendant remaining in pretrial custody. A defendant can become demoralized and fear that he will be incarcerated for a long period of time.

On the other side of the ledger, there may be legitimate reasons that the prosecution wants the defendant to remain in pretrial custody. The defendant may pose a threat to society or prosecutors may worry that the defendant is a flight risk if not kept incarcerated before trial.

Very little guidance is given in the Constitution regarding bail. The Eighth Amendment simply states that "[e]xcessive bail shall not be required." This does not provide answers as to the types of cases where bail is allowed or what is considered to be excessive. In Stack v. Boyle, 342 U.S. 1 (1951), the Supreme Court held that the Eighth Amendment did not guarantee the right to bail in all cases. Rather, it said that the Eighth Amendment provides that where bail is permitted, it cannot be excessive. It also noted that bail need not be allowed in capital offense cases.

In addition, the Supreme Court has never held that the "no excessive bail" clause of the Eighth Amendment applies to state prosecutions. Rather, it has been left to statutes and lower court decisions to sort out when bail is permitted and what factors may be considered in deciding to grant, or not grant, bail. The current standard directs the court to evaluate whether the defendant is a flight risk or a danger to the community.

Bail in the federal system is governed by the Bail Reform Act of 1984, 18 U.S.C. §§3142 and 3144. States have their own statutes governing the granting of bail. In most jurisdictions, the police have a *bail schedule* that they can use to release a suspect on bail even before the defendant has made a court appearance. However, in more serious cases, the court will determine whether there will be bail and, if so, what will be the amount.

There are many types of bail.[1] *Own recognizance (OR)* or *personal recognizance (PR)* release permits a defendant to be released upon a mere promise to appear in court. Under *conditions of pretrial release* a defendant may be subject to supervision, or perhaps a rehabilitation program, before trial. Failure to comply with the terms of supervision, including failure to report to probation officers or to have drug testing, can result in the defendant's reincarceration.

A financial bond requires a defendant to post money with the court. The posting of a bond may be handled by a bail bondsman, a third party, or the defendant. There are two basic types of bonds: a *secured bond*, usually secured by a deed to property, and an *unsecured bond*, which is based on a cash deposit and a promise to pay the remainder if the defendant fails to appear. If a bail bondsman posts bond for a defendant, the bondsman will typically take 10 percent of the amount of the bond to be posted with the court as his fee. If a defendant or family member posts bond for the defendant, and the defendant satisfies all of the conditions for pretrial release (including appearing for trial), the cash deposit is refunded by the court.[2]

Judges can take steps to prevent defendants from posting money or property derived from illegal proceeds. The court has the right to reject illegally derived funds as bail. To determine whether the proceeds being posted as bond are from an illegal source, the court may hold a special hearing referred to as a *Nebbia hearing*. In United States v. Nebbia, 357 F.2d 303 (2d Cir. 1966), the court held that a court does not need to accept a cash bond if it was illegally obtained because that is not the type of bail that is likely to secure a defendant's presence.

A court can impose many different types of conditions on a defendant posting bond. They may include drug testing, restrictions on travel, surrender of passport, counseling, lack of contact with witnesses and victims, home confinement, and other similar measures. Sometimes, individuals are placed under house arrest and a monitoring device is placed on their body to monitor their presence. Effective defense lawyers try to fashion a bail package that imposes those conditions that will assure the court that it is in the court's and defendant's best interest to grant bail.

If a defendant fails to comply with the terms of bail, such as not appearing at trial, bail may be forfeited. Forfeiture is governed by Federal Rule of Criminal Procedure 46(f).[3]

---

1. *See generally* Mary A. Tuborg, *Pretrial Release: A National Evaluation of Practices and Outcomes* (National Institute of Justice, 1981), 7, 9.

2. Sample bail schedules and 10 percent bail plans are set forth in the Statutory Supplement.

3. Federal Rule of Criminal Procedure 46 is set forth in the Statutory Supplement.

B. PREVENTIVE DETENTION

1. Pretrial Detention

The issue of bail pending trial raises the basic question of whether it is fair to hold a defendant in custody before he has been adjudged guilty of a crime. Prior to the Bail Reform Act of 1984,[4] the sole factor that courts were to consider was whether the defendant was a flight risk. However, in the 1984 Act, Congress added a second factor — danger to the community.

Prior to the Bail Reform Act, prosecutors would include concerns over dangerousness by claiming that a person who is dangerous to the community is a person who is unlikely to follow the laws and therefore unlikely to appear for trial. Following the 1984 Bail Reform Act, danger to the community became an express factor for denying bail. Given that the defendant has not been convicted, does it violate the presumption of innocence and due process to use danger to the community as a factor to deny or raise the amount of bail? The Supreme Court answered that question in United States v. Salerno.

UNITED STATES v. SALERNO

481 U.S. 739 (1987)

Chief Justice REHNQUIST delivered the opinion of the Court.

The Bail Reform Act of 1984 (Act) allows a federal court to detain an arrestee pending trial if the Government demonstrates by clear and convincing evidence after an adversary hearing that no release conditions "will reasonably assure . . . the safety of any other person and the community." The United States Court of Appeals for the Second Circuit struck down this provision of the Act as facially unconstitutional, because, in that court's words, this type of pretrial detention violates "substantive due process." We granted certiorari because of a conflict among the Courts. We hold that, as against the facial attack mounted by these respondents, the Act fully comports with constitutional requirements. We therefore reverse.

Responding to "the alarming problem of crimes committed by persons on release," Congress formulated the Bail Reform Act of 1984, 18 U.S.C. §3141 et seq., as the solution to a bail crisis in the federal courts. The Act represents the National Legislature's considered response to numerous perceived deficiencies in the federal bail process. By providing for sweeping changes in both the way federal courts consider bail applications and the circumstances under which bail is granted, Congress hoped to "give the courts adequate authority to make release decisions that give appropriate recognition to the danger a person may pose to others if released."

---

4. The Bail Reform Act of 1984, 18 U.S.C. §3141, is set forth in the Statutory Supplement.

To this end, §3141(a) of the Act requires a judicial officer to determine whether an arrestee shall be detained. Section 3142(e) provides that "if, after a hearing pursuant to the provisions of subsection (f), the judicial officer finds that no condition or combination of conditions will reasonably assure the appearance of the person as required and the safety of any other person and the community, he shall order the detention of the person prior to trial." Section 3142(f) provides the arrestee with a number of procedural safeguards. He may request the presence of counsel at the detention hearing, he may testify and present witnesses in his behalf, as well as proffer evidence, and he may cross-examine other witnesses appearing at the hearing. If the judicial officer finds that no conditions of pretrial release can reasonably assure the safety of other persons and the community, he must state his findings of fact in writing, §3142(i), and support his conclusion with "clear and convincing evidence," §3142(f).

The judicial officer is not given unbridled discretion in making the detention determination. Congress has specified the considerations relevant to that decision. These factors include the nature and seriousness of the charges, the substantiality of the Government's evidence against the arrestee, the arrestee's background and characteristics, and the nature and seriousness of the danger posed by the suspect's release. §3142(g). Should a judicial officer order detention, the detainee is entitled to expedited appellate review of the detention order. §§3145(b), (c).

Respondents Anthony Salerno and Vincent Cafaro were arrested on March 21, 1986, after being charged in a 29-count indictment alleging various Racketeer Influenced and Corrupt Organizations Act (RICO) violations, mail and wire fraud offenses, extortion, and various criminal gambling violations. The RICO counts alleged 35 acts of racketeering activity, including fraud, extortion, gambling, and conspiracy to commit murder. At respondents' arraignment, the Government moved to have Salerno and Cafaro detained pursuant to §3142(e), on the ground that no condition of release would assure the safety of the community or any person. The District Court held a hearing at which the Government made a detailed proffer of evidence. The Government's case showed that Salerno was the "boss" of the Genovese crime family of La Cosa Nostra and that Cafaro was a "captain" in the Genovese family. According to the Government's proffer, based in large part on conversations intercepted by a court-ordered wiretap, the two respondents had participated in wide-ranging conspiracies to aid their illegitimate enterprises through violent means. The Government also offered the testimony of two of its trial witnesses, who would assert that Salerno personally participated in two murder conspiracies. Salerno opposed the motion for detention, challenging the credibility of the Government's witnesses. He offered the testimony of several character witnesses as well as a letter from his doctor stating that he was suffering from a serious medical condition. Cafaro presented no evidence at the hearing, but instead characterized the wiretap conversations as merely "tough talk."

The District Court granted the Government's detention motion, concluding that the Government had established by clear and convincing evidence that no condition or combination of conditions of release would ensure the safety of the community or any person: "The activities of a criminal organization such as the Genovese Family do not cease with the arrest of its principals and their release on even the most stringent of bail conditions. The illegal businesses, in place for many years, require constant attention and protection, or they will fail. Under these circumstances, this court recognizes a strong incentive on the part of its leadership to continue business as usual. When business as usual involves threats, beatings, and murder, the present danger such people pose in the community is self-evident."

Respondents appealed, contending that to the extent that the Bail Reform Act permits pretrial detention on the ground that the arrestee is likely to commit future crimes, it is unconstitutional on its face. Over a dissent, the United States Court of Appeals for the Second Circuit agreed.

The court concluded that the Government could not, consistent with due process, detain persons who had not been accused of any crime merely because they were thought to present a danger to the community. It reasoned that our criminal law system holds persons accountable for past actions, not anticipated future actions. Although a court could detain an arrestee who threatened to flee before trial, such detention would be permissible because it would serve the basic objective of a criminal system — bringing the accused to trial.

Respondents present two grounds for invalidating the Bail Reform Act's provisions permitting pretrial detention on the basis of future dangerousness. First, they rely upon . . . the Due Process Clause of the Fifth Amendment. Second, they contend that the Act contravenes the Eighth Amendment's proscription against excessive bail. We treat these contentions in turn.

A

The Due Process Clause of the Fifth Amendment provides that "No person shall . . . be deprived of life, liberty, or property, without due process of law. . . ." This Court has held that the Due Process Clause protects individuals against two types of government action. So-called "substantive due process" prevents the government from engaging in conduct that "shocks the conscience." When government action depriving a person of life, liberty, or property survives substantive due process scrutiny, it must still be implemented in a fair manner. This requirement has traditionally been referred to as "procedural" due process.

Respondents first argue that the Act violates substantive due process because the pretrial detention it authorizes constitutes impermissible punishment before trial. The Government, however, has never argued that pretrial detention could be upheld if it were "punishment." The Court of Appeals assumed that pretrial detention under the Bail Reform Act is regulatory, not penal, and we agree that it is.

As an initial matter, the mere fact that a person is detained does not inexorably lead to the conclusion that the government has imposed punishment. To determine whether a restriction on liberty constitutes impermissible punishment or permissible regulation, we first look to legislative intent. Unless Congress expressly intended to impose punitive restrictions, the punitive/regulatory distinction turns on "whether an alternative purpose to which [the restriction] may rationally be connected is assignable for it, and whether it appears excessive in relation to the alternative purpose assigned [to it]."

We conclude that the detention imposed by the Act falls on the regulatory side of the dichotomy. The legislative history of the Bail Reform Act clearly indicates that Congress did not formulate the pretrial detention provisions as punishment for dangerous individuals. Congress instead perceived pretrial detention as a potential solution to a pressing societal problem. There is no doubt that preventing danger to the community is a legitimate regulatory goal.

Moreover, the conditions of confinement envisioned by the Act "appear to reflect the regulatory purposes relied upon by the" Government. The statute at issue here requires that detainees be housed in a "facility separate, to the extent practicable, from persons awaiting or serving sentences or being held in custody pending appeal." 18 U.S.C. §3142(i)(2). We conclude, therefore, that the pretrial detention contemplated by the Bail Reform Act is regulatory in nature, and does not constitute punishment before trial in violation of the Due Process Clause.

We have repeatedly held that the Government's regulatory interest in community safety can, in appropriate circumstances, outweigh an individual's liberty interest. For example, in times of war or insurrection, when society's interest is at its peak, the Government may detain individuals whom the Government believes to be dangerous. Even outside the exigencies of war, we have found that sufficiently compelling governmental interests can justify detention of dangerous persons. Thus, we have found no absolute constitutional barrier to detention of potentially dangerous resident aliens pending deportation proceedings. We have also held that the government may detain mentally unstable individuals who present a danger to the public. We have approved of post-arrest regulatory detention of juveniles when they present a continuing danger to the community. Even competent adults may face substantial liberty restrictions as a result of the operation of our criminal justice system. If the police suspect an individual of a crime, they may arrest and hold him until a neutral magistrate determines whether probable cause exists.

The government's interest in preventing crime by arrestees is both legitimate and compelling. The Government must first of all demonstrate probable cause to believe that the charged crime has been committed by the arrestee, but that is not enough. In a full-blown adversary hearing, the Government must convince a neutral decisionmaker by clear and convincing evidence that no conditions of release can reasonably assure the safety of the community or any person.

On the other side of the scale, of course, is the individual's strong interest in liberty. We do not minimize the importance and fundamental nature of this right. But, as our cases hold, this right may, in circumstances where the government's interest is sufficiently weighty, be subordinated to the greater needs of society. When the Government proves by clear and convincing evidence that an arrestee presents an identified and articulable threat to an individual or the community, we believe that, consistent with the Due Process Clause, a court may disable the arrestee from executing that threat.

Under the Bail Reform Act, the procedures by which a judicial officer evaluates the likelihood of future dangerousness are specifically designed to further the accuracy of that determination. Detainees have a right to counsel at the detention hearing. They may testify in their own behalf, present information by proffer or otherwise, and cross-examine witnesses who appear at the hearing. The Government must prove its case by clear and convincing evidence. Finally, the judicial officer must include written findings of fact and a written statement of reasons for a decision to detain. The Act's review provisions provide for immediate appellate review of the detention decision.

We think these extensive safeguards suffice to repel a facial challenge. Given the legitimate and compelling regulatory purpose of the Act and the procedural protections it offers, we conclude that the Act is not facially invalid under the Due Process Clause of the Fifth Amendment.

B

Respondents also contend that the Bail Reform Act violates the Excessive Bail Clause of the Eighth Amendment. We think that the Act survives a challenge founded upon the Eighth Amendment.

The Eighth Amendment addresses pretrial release by providing merely that "excessive bail shall not be required." This Clause, of course, says nothing about whether bail shall be available at all. Respondents nevertheless contend that this Clause grants them a right to bail calculated solely upon considerations of flight. They rely on Stack v. Boyle (1951), in which the Court stated that "bail set at a figure higher than an amount reasonably calculated [to ensure the defendant's presence at trial] is 'excessive' under the Eighth Amendment." Respondents concede that the right to bail they have discovered in the Eighth Amendment is not absolute. A court may, for example, refuse bail in capital cases.

While we agree that a primary function of bail is to safeguard the courts' role in adjudicating the guilt or innocence of defendants, we reject the proposition that the Eighth Amendment categorically prohibits the government from pursuing other admittedly compelling interests through regulation of pretrial release. The above-quoted dictum in Stack v. Boyle is far too slender a reed on which to rest this argument. The Court in *Stack* had no occasion to consider whether the Excessive Bail Clause requires courts to admit all defendants to bail, because the statute before the Court in that case in fact allowed the defendants to be bailed.

III

In our society liberty is the norm, and detention prior to trial or without trial is the carefully limited exception. We hold that the provisions for pretrial detention in the Bail Reform Act of 1984 fall within that carefully limited exception. The Act authorizes the detention prior to trial of arrestees charged with serious felonies who are found after an adversary hearing to pose a threat to the safety of individuals or to the community which no condition of release can dispel. The numerous procedural safeguards detailed above must attend this adversary hearing. We are unwilling to say that this congressional determination, based as it is upon that primary concern of every government—a concern for the safety and indeed the lives of its citizens—on its face violates either the Due Process Clause of the Fifth Amendment or the Excessive Bail Clause of the Eighth Amendment.

Justice MARSHALL, dissenting.

This case brings before the Court for the first time a statute in which Congress declares that a person innocent of any crime may be jailed indefinitely, pending the trial of allegations which are legally presumed to be untrue, if the Government shows to the satisfaction of a judge that the accused is likely to commit crimes, unrelated to the pending charges, at any time in the future. Such statutes, consistent with the usages of tyranny and the excesses of what bitter experience teaches us to call the police state, have long been thought incompatible with the fundamental human rights protected by our Constitution. Today a majority of this Court holds otherwise. Its decision disregards basic principles of justice established centuries ago and enshrined beyond the reach of governmental interference in the Bill of Rights.

The essence of this case may be found, ironically enough, in a provision of the Act to which the majority does not refer. Title 18 U.S.C. §3142(j) provides that "nothing in this section shall be construed as modifying or limiting the presumption of innocence." But the very pith and purpose of this statute is an abhorrent limitation of the presumption of innocence. The majority's untenable conclusion that the present Act is constitutional arises from a specious denial of the role of the Bail Clause and the Due Process Clause in protecting the invaluable guarantee afforded by the presumption of innocence.

"The principle that there is a presumption of innocence in favor of the accused is the undoubted law, axiomatic and elementary, and its enforcement lies at the foundation of the administration of our criminal law." The statute now before us declares that persons who have been indicted may be detained if a judicial officer finds clear and convincing evidence that they pose a danger to individuals or to the community.

As Chief Justice Vinson wrote for the Court in Stack v. Boyle: "Unless th[e] right to bail before trial is preserved, the presumption of innocence, secured only after centuries of struggle, would lose its meaning."

Throughout the world today there are men, women, and children interned indefinitely, awaiting trials which may never come or which may be a mockery of the word, because their governments believe them to be "dangerous." Our Constitution, whose construction began two centuries ago, can shelter us forever from the evils of such unchecked power. Over 200 years it has slowly, through our efforts, grown more durable, more expansive, and more just. But it cannot protect us if we lack the courage, and the self-restraint, to protect ourselves. Today a majority of the Court applies itself to an ominous exercise in demolition. Theirs is truly a decision which will go forth without authority, and come back without respect.

Salerno cleared the way for courts to consider both a defendant's *flight risk* and *future danger to the community* in deciding bail. Some crimes, such as violent offenses and drug trafficking, may even carry a rebuttable presumption that detention is warranted.

In general, courts will consider several factors in determining whether the defendant should be granted bail and the amount of that bail:

1. The seriousness of the offense
2. The punishment the defendant faces
3. Defendant's prior criminal record
4. Defendant's ties to the community
5. Defendant's character
6. Defendant's financial status
7. Any other information relevant to its determination of whether defendant is a flight risk or poses a future risk to the community

Bail pending appeal does not pose the same issues as bail before trial because the defendant no longer enjoys a presumption of innocence. Thus, under the Bail Reform Act of 1984, the burden shifts to the defendant to show why he should be released pending appeal. Under the Bail Reform Act, a defendant may only be released pending appeal if the court finds "by clear and convincing evidence that the person is not likely to flee or pose a danger to the safety of another person or the community" and "the appeal is not for purposes of delay and raises a substantial question of law or fact likely to result in reversal or an order for a new trial."

With such a high standard, it is extremely difficult for defendants to secure pending appeal. A good example is the recent case of presidential advisor I. Lewis Libby, who was convicted of lying to a grand jury regarding its probe into persons leaking information regarding CIA operative Valerie Plame. *See* United States v. Libby, 2007 U.S. Dist. LEXIS 4463 (D.D.C. 2007). In denying Libby's motion for bail pending appeal, the court held that even though Libby was not a flight risk, the burden had shifted to the defendant to show why he should be released pending appeal. The court rejected Libby's challenge to the appointment of Special Prosecutor Patrick Fitzgerald, finding that the appellate issue raised by Libby did not present a "substantial question of law or fact likely to result in . . . reversal."

2.   *Other Types of Preventive Detention*

Salerno had a dramatic impact on courts' attitudes toward preventive detention. Not only may defendants now be detained because they pose a risk of future danger to the community, but persons who are not being held on criminal charges may also be detained. This may include preventative detention of material witnesses, sexual predators, psychiatric patients, persons subject to deportation and removal proceedings, and individuals designated as enemy combatants. Each of these situations requires a balancing of the detainee's liberty interests with the government's reasons for seeking detention.

a.   Detention of Material Witnesses

Pursuant to 18 U.S.C. §3144, persons designated as "material witnesses" may be detained pretrial. A material witness is an individual who has information regarding a criminal proceeding whose appearance "may become impracticable to secure . . . by subpoena." These individuals are not themselves accused of any crime; however, they are kept in custody because they may have information regarding a crime that was committed and their appearance at trial cannot otherwise be secured. After the terrorist attacks of September 11, 2001, the government increased its use of the material witness statute and sought to use it for both trial and grand jury witnesses. This led to additional challenges to the use of preventive detention. Not surprisingly, the balance in these cases fell in favor of the government, especially when the court was convinced that the statute provided sufficient procedural protections for the detainee before the detention was ordered. In the next case, the court discussed why it would permit preventive detention of material witnesses in grand jury proceedings.

UNITED STATES v. OSAMA AWADALLAH

349 F.3d 42 (2d Cir. 2003)

JACOBS, Circuit Judge:

This appeal, which arises from the government's investigation of the September 11, 2001 terrorist attacks, presents questions about the scope of the federal material witness statute and the government's powers of arrest and detention thereunder. *See* 18 U.S.C. §3144. The district court ruled that the statute cannot be applied constitutionally to a grand jury witness such as the defendant-appellee, Osama Awadallah, and dismissed the perjury indictment against him as fruit of an illegal detention.

We conclude that these rulings must be reversed and the indictment reinstated.

BACKGROUND

In the days immediately following September 11, 2001, the United States Attorney for the Southern District of New York initiated a grand jury investigation into the terrorist attacks. Investigators quickly identified Nawaf Al-Hazmi and Khalid Al-Mihdhar as two of the hijackers on American Airlines Flight 77, which crashed into the Pentagon. The Justice Department released the identities of all nineteen hijackers on Friday, September 14, 2001, and news media around the country publicized their names and photographs the following day.

A search of the car Al-Hazmi abandoned at Dulles Airport in Virginia produced a piece of paper with the notation, "Osama 589-5316." Federal agents tracked this number to a San Diego address at which the defendant, Osama Awadallah, had lived approximately eighteen months earlier. Al-Hazmi and Al-Mihdhar also had lived in the San Diego vicinity around that time.

On the morning of September 20, 2001, federal agents went to Awadallah's current residence in San Diego. When the agents arrived at the apartment, Awadallah was attending a course in English as a second language at nearby Grossmont College, where he was enrolled. The agents interviewed Awadallah's roommate in their apartment for several hours.

When Awadallah came home at around 2:00 P.M. that afternoon, several agents approached him as he entered the parking lot and got out of his car (a gray Honda). They questioned him in the parking lot for a few minutes and then told him that he had to accompany them to the FBI office for questioning. Awadallah insisted on returning to his apartment first to observe the afternoon Muslim prayer, which he did as the agents watched. When Awadallah went into the bathroom, the agents insisted that the bathroom door be left open.

Before leaving for the FBI office, an agent asked Awadallah to sign a consent form allowing them to search his apartment and car. Otherwise, the agent told him, they would get a warrant and "tear up" his home. Believing he had no choice, Awadallah signed the form without reading it. The agents then put him in their car and drove him to the FBI office. Awadallah told them that he had to return in time for a 6:00 P.M. computer class; they told him that would be no problem.

At the FBI office, agents offered Awadallah a drink, but he declined because he was fasting. They asked him to sign another consent form for the search of his second car, an inoperative white Honda in the parking lot of his apartment building. This time, Awadallah read the form and learned that he had a right to refuse consent; and though he signed the consent form for his second car, he explicitly revoked his consent for the search of the first car. An agent tried to reach the agents at the apartment building by cell phone, but did not reach them until fifteen minutes later, after the search of the first car had been completed. The agents at the scene then searched the apartment and the second car. The search of Awadallah's home produced several computer-generated photographs of Osama bin Laden; the searches of his cars produced two videotapes on Bosnia and one on Islam and a retractable razor which could be described as a box-cutter or a carpet knife.

Awadallah was alone in a locked interview room for a while, until agents arrived to question him. They did not advise him of his rights or tell him that he could leave. They asked him about the September 11 hijackers and about his life and acquaintances. He told the agents that he knew Al-Hazmi, and that he had frequently seen another man with him, whose name he did not know.

The district court found that Awadallah was "cooperative" throughout this questioning. When 6:00 P.M. approached, the agents told Awadallah that they had called his school and that it was alright for him to miss class. They told him he would "have to stay" with them until they were finished. The entire interview lasted approximately six hours, ending at nearly 11:00 P.M. Before allowing Awadallah to leave, the agents scheduled a polygraph examination for the next morning.

At 6:30 A.M. the following day, September 21, 2001, Awadallah called the FBI and refused to come in for the polygraph test until he had a lawyer. The agent told him they would get an arrest warrant. Believing he had no choice, Awadallah went with two agents who picked him up at his apartment at 7:00 A.M.

At the FBI office, agents advised Awadallah of his rights and he signed an advice-of-rights acknowledgment form. The polygraph exam lasted one-and-a-half to two hours. Afterward, the agents told Awadallah that the polygraph registered lies in response to two questions: whether he had advance knowledge of the September 11 attacks and whether he had participated in them in any way. It is unclear whether these were in fact the results. The conversation became heated as the agents accused Awadallah of being a terrorist. They refused Awadallah's requests to call a lawyer and his brother, and did not release him in time for Friday prayer.

Throughout the questioning that day, the FBI agents in San Diego had been in contact with an Assistant United States Attorney ("AUSA") in New York. At approximately 2:00 P.M. Eastern time, the AUSA instructed the agents to arrest Awadallah as a material witness. The agents handcuffed Awadallah and took him to the San Diego correctional center for booking.

During the period of his detention, Awadallah spent time in four prisons as he was transferred to the New York correctional center by way of Oklahoma City. He alleges that he received harsh and improper treatment during this period. Awadallah spent most of his time in solitary confinement; at times lacked access to his family, his lawyer, or a phone; and was repeatedly strip-searched. The government did not dispute that, by October 4, 2001, "Awadallah had bruises on his upper arms," and an agent's report indicated several other injuries on his shoulder, ankles, hand, and face. Awadallah sometimes refrained from eating because the meals provided did not comply with his religious dietary restrictions.

On October 10, 2001, twenty days after his arrest as a material witness, Awadallah testified before the grand jury in the Southern District of New York. The prosecutor questioned him for most of the day. In the course of his testimony, Awadallah denied knowing anyone named Khalid Al-Mihdhar or Khalid. The government then showed him an examination booklet he had written in September, which the government obtained from his English teacher in San Diego. The booklet contained the following handwritten sentence: "One of the quietest people I have met is Nawaf. Another one his name Khalid. They have stayed in S.D. [San Diego] for 6 months." Awadallah acknowledged that it was his examination booklet, and that most of the writing in it was his own, but he denied that the name Khalid and a few other words on the page were written in his handwriting. On October 15, 2001, when Awadallah again appeared before the grand jury, he stated that his recollection of Khalid's name had been refreshed by his October 10 testimony and that the disputed writing in the exam booklet was in fact his own. However, he did not admit to making false statements in his first grand jury appearance.

The United States Attorney for the Southern District of New York filed charges against Awadallah on two counts of making false statements to the grand jury in violation of 18 U.S.C. §1623: falsely denying that he knew Khalid Al-Mihdhar; and falsely denying that the handwriting in the exam booklet was his own.

On November 27, 2001, the district court (Scheindlin, J.) granted Awadallah's bail application. He satisfied the bail conditions and was released approximately two weeks later.

In December 2001, Awadallah moved to dismiss the indictment. The court ruled that the federal material witness statute, 18 U.S.C. §3144, did not apply to grand jury witnesses. Judge Scheindlin ruled that Awadallah's perjured grand jury testimony had to be suppressed as fruit of this illegal arrest and detention. The government filed a timely notice of appeal.

DISCUSSION

APPLICABILITY OF 18 U.S.C. §3144

The first issue presented is whether the federal material witness statute, 18 U.S.C. §3144, allows the arrest and detention of grand jury witnesses. As discussed at oral argument, we might evade this issue by holding that Awadallah's allegedly false testimony should not have been suppressed as fruit of the poisonous tree even if his detention under §3144 was improper, and that the indictment therefore should not have been dismissed. We reach the issue, however, because the present split within our Circuit on the scope

of §3144 affects the liberty interests of persons identified as material witnesses, the security and law enforcement interests of the government, and
the ability of courts to make prompt and fair rulings on present and future
detentions.

Section 3144, titled "release or detention of a material witness," provides
in its entirety:

> If it appears from an affidavit filed by a party that the testimony of a person is
> material in a criminal proceeding, and if it is shown that it may become imprac-
> ticable to secure the presence of the person by subpoena, a judicial officer may
> order the arrest of the person and treat the person in accordance with the provi-
> sions of section 3142 of this title. No material witness may be detained because of
> inability to comply with any condition of release if the testimony of such witness can
> adequately be secured by deposition, and if further detention is not necessary to
> prevent a failure of justice. Release of a material witness may be delayed for a
> reasonable period of time until the deposition of the witness can be taken pursuant
> to the Federal Rules of Criminal Procedure.

The statute is cast in terms of a material witness in "a criminal proceeding." The decisive question here is whether that term encompasses proceedings before a grand jury.

Given the broad language of the statute, its legislative history . . . , the
substantial body of case law indicating that there is no constitutional impediment to detention of grand jury witnesses, and the unquestioned application of the statute to grand jury witnesses over a period of decades before
Awadallah, to perceive a Congressional intention that grand jury witnesses
be excluded from the reach of section 3144 is to perceive something that is
not there. [W]e conclude that the district court's ruling in this case must be
reversed.

[Section] 3144 applies to witnesses whose testimony is material in "a
criminal proceeding." "Criminal proceeding" is a broad and capacious
term, and there is good reason to conclude that it includes a grand jury
proceeding. [T]he term "criminal proceeding" has been construed in
other statutes to encompass grand jury proceedings. Notwithstanding this
support for the general view that "criminal proceedings" encompass grand
jury proceedings, however, we cannot say that the statutory wording alone
compels that conclusion. Black's Law Dictionary defines a "criminal proceeding" as "[a] proceeding instituted to determine a person's guilt or
innocence or to set a convicted person's punishment; a criminal hearing
or trial." Defined this way, a grand jury proceeding is not a "proceeding
instituted to determine a person's guilt or innocence or to set a convicted
person's punishment," but rather a proceeding to "decide whether to issue
indictments." For these reasons, we must look beyond the text of §3144 to
discern the meaning of "criminal proceeding."

In surveying legislative history we have repeatedly stated that the authoritative source for finding the Legislature's intent lies in the Committee

Reports on the bill. . . . Here, the Senate committee report states in so many words the intent to include grand jury proceedings within the ambit of the statute — an intent that is consistent with the statute's language, even if not compelled by it.

The Fourth Amendment prohibits "unreasonable searches and seizures." Determining the reasonableness of a seizure involves a balancing of competing interests: "The essential purpose of the proscriptions in the Fourth Amendment is to impose a standard of 'reasonableness' upon the exercise of discretion by government officials, including law enforcement agents, in order 'to safeguard the privacy and security of individuals against arbitrary invasions. . . .' Thus, the permissibility of a particular law enforcement practice is judged by balancing its intrusion on the individual's Fourth Amendment interests against its promotion of legitimate governmental interests."

In its balancing analysis, the district court found that "the only legitimate reason to detain a grand jury witness is to aid in 'an ex parte investigation to determine whether a crime has been committed and whether criminal proceedings should be instituted against any person.'" This is no small interest. The grand jury is an integral part of our constitutional heritage which was brought to this country with the common law. Indispensable to the exercise of its power is the authority to compel the attendance and the testimony of witnesses.

The district court noted (and we agree) that it would be improper for the government to use §3144 for other ends, such as the detention of persons suspected of criminal activity for which probable cause has not yet been established. However, the district court made no finding (and we see no evidence to suggest) that the government arrested Awadallah for any purpose other than to secure information material to a grand jury investigation. Moreover, that grand jury was investigating the September 11 terrorist attacks. The particular governmental interests at stake therefore were the indictment and successful prosecution of terrorists whose attack, if committed by a sovereign, would have been tantamount to war, and the discovery of the conspirators' means, contacts, and operations in order to forestall future attacks.

On the other side of the balance, the district court found in essence that §3144 was not calibrated to minimize the intrusion on the liberty of a grand jury witness. We agree with the district court, of course, that arrest and detention are significant infringements on liberty, but we conclude that §3144 sufficiently limits that infringement and reasonably balances it against the government's countervailing interests. [Given the procedural safeguards of §3144 that provide that] "no material witness may be detained because of inability to comply with any condition of release if the testimony of such witness can adequately be secured by deposition," and that detention must be necessary to prevent a failure of justice, [we disagree with the district court's balancing of interests].

b. Preventive Detention of Sexual Predators

The concept of preventive detention is also used to incarcerate other types of individuals who do not face criminal charges but continue to pose a danger to society. In response to the growing number of sexual offenders, states have passed "sexual predator" laws that allow the ongoing detention of defendants after they have completed their sentences for sexual offenses. The Supreme Court upheld the constitutionality of this type of preventive detention in Kansas v. Hendricks by once again, in its substantive due process analysis, balancing the need for detention against the defendant's liberty interests.

KANSAS v. HENDRICKS
521 U.S. 346 (1996)

Justice THOMAS delivered the opinion of the Court.

In 1994, Kansas enacted the Sexually Violent Predator Act, which establishes procedures for the civil commitment of persons who, due to a "mental abnormality" or a "personality disorder," are likely to engage in "predatory acts of sexual violence." The State invoked the Act for the first time to commit Leroy Hendricks, an inmate who had a long history of sexually molesting children, and who was scheduled for release from prison shortly after the Act became law. Hendricks challenged his commitment on, inter alia, "substantive" due process, double jeopardy, and ex post facto grounds. The Kansas Supreme Court invalidated the Act, holding that its pre-commitment condition of a "mental abnormality" did not satisfy what the court perceived to be the "substantive" due process requirement that involuntary civil commitment must be predicated on a finding of "mental illness." The State of Kansas petitioned for certiorari. We now reverse the judgment below.

I

The Kansas Legislature enacted the Sexually Violent Predator Act (Act) in 1994 to grapple with the problem of managing repeat sexual offenders. Although Kansas already had a statute addressing the involuntary commitment of those defined as "mentally ill," the legislature determined that existing civil commitment procedures were inadequate to confront the risks presented by "sexually violent predators." In the Act's preamble, the legislature explained: "[A] small but extremely dangerous group of sexually violent predators exist who do not have a mental disease or defect that renders them appropriate for involuntary treatment pursuant to the [general involuntary civil commitment statute]. . . . In contrast to persons appropriate for civil commitment under the [general involuntary civil commitment statute], sexually violent predators generally have anti-social personality features which are unamenable to existing mental illness treatment modalities and those features render them likely to engage in sexually violent behavior."

As a result, the Legislature found it necessary to establish "a civil commitment procedure for the long-term care and treatment of the sexually violent predator." The Act's civil commitment procedures pertained to: (1) a presently confined person who, like Hendricks, "has been convicted of a sexually violent offense" and is scheduled for release; (2) a person who has been "charged with a sexually violent offense" but has been found incompetent to stand trial; (3) a person who has been found "not guilty by reason of insanity of a sexually violent offense"; and (4) a person found "not guilty" of a sexually violent offense because of a mental disease or defect. [The Act] was designed to initiate a specific series of procedures. The custodial agency was required to notify the local prosecutor 60 days before the anticipated release of a person who might have met the Act's criteria. The prosecutor was then obligated, within 45 days, to decide whether to file a petition in state court seeking the person's involuntary commitment. If such a petition were filed, the court was to determine whether "probable cause" existed to support a finding that the person was a "sexually violent predator" and thus eligible for civil commitment. Upon such a determination, transfer of the individual to a secure facility for professional evaluation would occur. After that evaluation, a trial would be held to determine beyond a reasonable doubt whether the individual was a sexually violent predator. If that determination were made, the person would then be transferred to the custody of the Secretary of Social and Rehabilitation Services (Secretary) for "control, care and treatment until such time as the person's mental abnormality or personality disorder has so changed that the person is safe to be at large."

Once an individual was confined, confined persons were afforded three different avenues of review, [including an annual review] to determine whether continued detention was warranted.

B

In 1984, Hendricks was convicted of taking "indecent liberties" with two 13-year-old boys. After serving nearly 10 years of his sentence, he was slated for release to a halfway house. Shortly before his scheduled release, however, the State filed a petition in state court seeking Hendricks' civil confinement as a sexually violent predator.

Hendricks subsequently requested a jury trial to determine whether he qualified as a sexually violent predator. During that trial, Hendricks' own testimony revealed a chilling history of repeated child sexual molestation and abuse, beginning in 1955 when he exposed his genitals to two young girls. At that time, he pleaded guilty to indecent exposure. Then, in 1957, he was convicted of lewdness involving a young girl and received a brief jail sentence. In 1960, he molested two young boys while he worked for a carnival. After serving two years in prison for that offense, he was paroled, only to be rearrested for molesting a 7-year-old girl. Attempts were made to treat him for his sexual deviance, and in 1965 he was considered "safe to be at large," and was discharged from a state psychiatric hospital.

Shortly thereafter, however, Hendricks sexually assaulted another young boy and girl — he performed oral sex on the 8-year-old girl and fondled the 11-year-old boy. He was again imprisoned in 1967, but refused to participate in a sex offender treatment program, and thus remained incarcerated until his parole in 1972. Diagnosed as a pedophile, Hendricks entered into, but then abandoned, a treatment program. He testified that despite having received professional help for his pedophilia, he continued to harbor sexual desires for children. Indeed, soon after his 1972 parole, Hendricks began to abuse his own stepdaughter and stepson. He forced the children to engage in sexual activity with him over a period of approximately four years. Then, as noted above, Hendricks was convicted of "taking indecent liberties" with two adolescent boys after he attempted to fondle them. As a result of that conviction, he was once again imprisoned, and was serving that sentence when he reached his conditional release date in September 1994.

The jury unanimously found beyond a reasonable doubt that Hendricks was a sexually violent predator. The trial court subsequently determined, as a matter of state law, that pedophilia qualifies as a "mental abnormality" as defined by the Act, and thus ordered Hendricks committed to the Secretary's custody.

Hendricks appealed, claiming, among other things, that application of the Act to him violated the Federal Constitution's Due Process clause. The Kansas Supreme Court accepted Hendricks' due process claim.

II

A

Kansas argues that the Act's definition of "mental abnormality" satisfies "substantive" due process requirements. We agree. Although freedom from physical restraint "has always been at the core of the liberty protected by the Due Process Clause from arbitrary governmental action," that liberty interest is not absolute. The Court has recognized that an individual's constitutionally protected interest in avoiding physical restraint may be overridden even in the civil context:

> The liberty secured by the Constitution of the United States to every person within its jurisdiction does not import an absolute right in each person to be, at all times and in all circumstances, wholly free from restraint. There are manifold restraints to which every person is necessarily subject for the common good. On any other basis organized society could not exist with safety to its members.

Accordingly, States have in certain narrow circumstances provided for the forcible civil detainment of people who are unable to control their behavior and who thereby pose a danger to the public health and safety. We have consistently upheld such involuntary commitment statutes provided the confinement takes place pursuant to proper procedures and evidentiary standards. It thus cannot be said that the involuntary civil confinement of a limited subclass of dangerous persons is contrary to our understanding of ordered liberty.

The challenged Act unambiguously requires a finding of dangerousness either to one's self or to others as a prerequisite to involuntary confinement. Commitment proceedings can be initiated only when a person "has been convicted of or charged with a sexually violent offense," and "suffers from a mental abnormality or personality disorder which makes the person likely to engage in the predatory acts of sexual violence." The statute thus requires proof of more than a mere predisposition to violence; rather, it requires evidence of past sexually violent behavior and a present mental condition that creates a likelihood of such conduct in the future if the person is not incapacitated. These added statutory requirements serve to limit involuntary civil confinement to those who suffer from a volitional impairment rendering them dangerous beyond their control. The Kansas Act is plainly of a kind with these other civil commitment statutes: It requires a finding of future dangerousness, and then links that finding to the existence of a "mental abnormality" or "personality disorder" that makes it difficult, if not impossible, for the person to control his dangerous behavior. The pre-commitment requirement of a "mental abnormality" or "personality disorder" is consistent with the requirements of these other statutes that we have upheld in that it narrows the class of persons eligible for confinement to those who are unable to control their dangerousness.

B

We granted Hendricks' cross-petition to determine whether the Act violates the Constitution's double jeopardy prohibition or its ban on ex post facto lawmaking. The thrust of Hendricks' argument is that the Act establishes criminal proceedings; hence confinement under it necessarily constitutes punishment. He contends that where, as here, newly enacted "punishment" is predicated upon past conduct for which he has already been convicted and forced to serve a prison sentence, the Constitution's Double Jeopardy and Ex Post Facto Clauses are violated. We are unpersuaded by Hendricks' argument that Kansas has established criminal proceedings.

The categorization of a particular proceeding as civil or criminal "is first of all a question of statutory construction." Here, Kansas' objective to create a civil proceeding is evidenced by its placement of the Sexually Violent Predator Act within the Kansas probate code, instead of the criminal code, as well as its description of the Act as creating a "civil commitment procedure." Nothing on the face of the statute suggests that the legislature sought to create anything other than a civil commitment scheme designed to protect the public from harm.

Although we recognize that a "civil label is not always dispositive," we will reject the legislature's manifest intent only where a party challenging the statute provides "the clearest proof" that "the statutory scheme [is] so punitive either in purpose or effect as to negate [the State's] intention" to deem it "civil." In those limited circumstances, we will consider the statute to have established criminal proceedings for constitutional purposes. Hendricks, however, has failed to satisfy this heavy burden.

As a threshold matter, commitment under the Act does not implicate either of the two primary objectives of criminal punishment: retribution or deterrence. The Act's purpose is not retributive because it does not affix culpability for prior criminal conduct. In addition, the Kansas Act does not make a criminal conviction a prerequisite for commitment—persons absolved of criminal responsibility may nonetheless be subject to confinement under the Act. An absence of the necessary criminal responsibility suggests that the State is not seeking retribution for a past misdeed. Thus, the fact that the Act may be "tied to criminal activity" is "insufficient to render the statute punitive."

Although the civil commitment scheme at issue here does involve an affirmative restraint, "the mere fact that a person is detained does not inexorably lead to the conclusion that the government has imposed punishment." United States v. Salerno (1987). The State may take measures to restrict the freedom of the dangerously mentally ill. This is a legitimate non-punitive governmental objective and has been historically so regarded. If detention for the purpose of protecting the community from harm necessarily constituted punishment, then all involuntary civil commitments would have to be considered punishment. But we have never so held.

[A claim] that treatment is not possible for this category of individuals does not obligate us to adopt its legal conclusions. We have already observed that, under the appropriate circumstances and when accompanied by proper procedures, incapacitation may be a legitimate end of the civil law. Accordingly, the Kansas court's determination that the Act's "overriding concern" was the continued "segregation of sexually violent offenders" is consistent with our conclusion that the Act establishes civil proceedings. Accord Compagnie Francaise de Navigation a Vapeur v. Louisiana Bd. of Health (1902) (permitting involuntary quarantine of persons suffering from communicable diseases). What is significant, however, is that Hendricks was placed under the supervision of the Kansas Department of Health and Social and Rehabilitative Services, housed in a unit segregated from the general prison population and operated not by employees of the Department of Corrections, but by other trained individuals.

Where the State has "disavowed any punitive intent"; limited confinement to a small segment of particularly dangerous individuals; provided strict procedural safeguards; directed that confined persons be segregated from the general prison population and afforded the same status as others who have been civilly committed; recommended treatment if such is possible; and permitted immediate release upon a showing that the individual is no longer dangerous or mentally impaired, we cannot say that it acted with punitive intent. We therefore hold that the Act does not establish criminal proceedings and that involuntary confinement pursuant to the Act is not punitive. Our conclusion that the Act is nonpunitive thus removes an essential prerequisite for both Hendricks' double jeopardy and ex post facto claims.

The Double Jeopardy Clause provides: "Nor shall any person be subject for the same offence to be twice put in jeopardy of life or limb." Because we have determined that the Kansas Act is civil in nature, initiation of its commitment proceedings does not constitute a second prosecution.

Hendricks' ex post facto claim is similarly flawed. The Ex Post Facto Clause, which "forbids the application of any new punitive measure to a crime already consummated," has been interpreted to pertain exclusively to penal statutes. As we have previously determined, the Act does not impose punishment; thus, its application does not raise ex post facto concerns.

We hold that the Kansas Sexually Violent Predator Act comports with due process requirements and neither runs afoul of double jeopardy principles nor constitutes an exercise in impermissible ex post facto lawmaking. Accordingly, the judgment of the Kansas Supreme Court is reversed.

Justice KENNEDY, concurring.

I join the opinion of the Court in full and add these additional comments. My brief, further comment is to caution against dangers inherent when a civil confinement law is used in conjunction with the criminal process, whether or not the law is given retroactive application.

Notwithstanding its civil attributes, the practical effect of the Kansas law may be to impose confinement for life. A common response to this may be, "A life term is exactly what the sentence should have been anyway," or, in the words of a Kansas task force member, "So be it." The point, however, is not how long Hendricks and others like him should serve a criminal sentence. With his criminal record, after all, a life term may well have been the only sentence appropriate to protect society and vindicate the wrong. The concern instead is whether it is the criminal system or the civil system which should make the decision in the first place. If the civil system is used simply to impose punishment after the State makes an improvident plea bargain on the criminal side, then it is not performing its proper function. These concerns persist whether the civil confinement statute is put on the books before or after the offense. We should bear in mind that while incapacitation is a goal common to both the criminal and civil systems of confinement, retribution and general deterrence are reserved for the criminal system alone.

c. Preventive Detention for Immigration Detainees

Immigrants illegally in the United States may also be detained by the government even if they have not been convicted of or charged with a specific crime. For example, in Zadvydas v. Davis, 533 U.S. 678 (2001), the Supreme Court addressed a statute that provides for the detention of aliens who have been ordered removed but cannot be deported because there is no receiving country. The statute permitted the aliens to be detained whenever they are "determined by the Attorney General to be a risk to the community or unlikely to comply with the order of removal." Aliens complained that, under the statute, they could be held indefinitely. Using a due process analysis, the Supreme Court held that civil confinement may be justified by the government's regulatory needs, but that indefinite detention without court review would violate due process. Thus, it held that an alien not removed within the 90-day period of the statute could file a habeas corpus action to determine if his continued detention was unreasonable.

Zadvydas was decided before September 11, 2001. In 2003, the Supreme Court decided Denmore v. Kim, 538 U.S. 510 (2003). Kim, a citizen of South Korea, challenged an immigration law that provides that an alien subject to removal must be detained pending removal proceedings. Kim had been convicted of burglary and petty theft and was therefore subject to removal. He complained that the immigration law violated due process because there had never been a determination that he posed a danger to society or flight risk. The Supreme Court rejected his challenge. Noting the ongoing need by the government to detain deportable aliens for a limited period because more than 20 percent of them fail to appear for their removal hearings, the Court held that detention was permissible. "[D]etention necessarily serves the purpose of preventing deportable criminal aliens from fleeing prior to or during their removal proceedings, thus increasing the chance that, if ordered removed, the aliens will be successfully removed."

d. Enemy Combatants

The doctrine of preventative detention most dramatically affects individuals who are not charged in the criminal justice system or protected by immigration procedures. It allows for the ongoing detention of individuals, including American citizens, suspected of terrorism whom the president designates to be enemy combatants.

In Rasul v. Bush, 542 U.S. 466 (2004), the Supreme Court held that foreign nationals detained at the military base in Guantanamo Bay, Cuba, have the right to challenge the legality of their long-term detention. The Court did not, however, establish what constitutional limits there would be on their continued detention.

In Hamdi v. Rumsfeld, 542 U.S. 507 (2004), the Court held that it had jurisdiction to review the legality of a citizen's designation and detention as an enemy combatant. It held that "due process demands that a citizen held in the United States as an enemy combatant be given a meaningful opportunity to contest the factual basis for that detention before a neutral decision maker." Once again, the Court left open what kind of process was required for enemy combatants.

The Court again examined the rights of detainees in Hamdan v. Rumsfeld, 126 S. Ct. 2749 (2006). It held that the military commissions convened to try enemy combatants violated the Uniform Code of Military Justice and the Geneva Convention. However, it did not identify exactly what procedures would satisfy due process concerns in the indefinite detention of enemy combatants and left that decision to future cases. Meanwhile, Congress passed the Military Commission Act of 2006, setting forth new procedural protections for enemy combatants but depriving the courts of jurisdiction to hear challenges by the detainees. In Boumediene v. Bush, 553 U.S. 723 (2008), the Court ruled that the Military Commission Act of 2006 violated the detainee's rights by unconstitutionally suspending the right of habeas corpus. A full discussion of that case is in Chapter 11 ("Habeas Corpus"). Thus, although detainees now have some access to the courts, judges are still extremely deferential to the executive branch's decision to detain enemy combatants.

CHAPTER

4

DISCOVERY

A. INTRODUCTION

Imagine trying to play a baseball game blindfolded. Faced with such a scenario, the crowd would quickly cry, "Not fair!" There is much more at stake in a criminal trial than in a sporting event, and a fundamental principle of fairness is that there should not be trial by ambush.

Discovery in criminal cases serves many important purposes. First, it gives the prosecution and defense an idea of the evidence that the other side will present at trial. This allows the parties to prepare ahead of time and to be more efficient in their presentation of trials. Second, discovery leads to pretrial settlement of cases. More than 90 percent of criminal cases are settled before trial. Discovery provides valuable information to the parties for assessing the strength of their cases, thereby facilitating the plea bargaining process. Third, discovery allows each party to contest evidence before it is presented to the court. Using pretrial *motions in limine*, the parties can bring to the court's attention evidence they want to introduce or preclude at trial. Finally, discovery creates more of a level playing field for trial.

Prosecutors have many tools they can use to obtain evidence prior to and after the filing of charges. Before trial, they can use grand jury subpoenas, search warrants, surveillance, and government investigators to investigate cases. While defense counsel can use private or court-appointed investigators, their investigative resources are more limited. Discovery gives the defense an opportunity to see the evidence that the prosecution has uncovered.

Despite these benefits, criminal cases do not have unlimited discovery. Only a few jurisdictions currently have "open-file" discovery,[1] a procedure that allows the defense access to everything in the prosecutor's files. However, most jurisdictions limit the discovery available to the defense, in part because of concerns about witness intimidation and the fabrication of

---

1. For example, in 2004 North Carolina enacted a law for open-file discovery in order to reduce the number of wrongful convictions. The law was modified in 2007 to require the sharing of witness statements, although it still has an exception for information regarding confidential informants. *See* N.C. Gen. Stat. §15A-501(6).

evidence. Conversely, concerns about interference with the defendant's Fifth Amendment privilege against self-incrimination limit the prosecutor's right to reciprocal discovery from the defense.

In learning the rules of discovery, it is helpful to think of its two primary aspects. First, some discovery rules are statutory. These rules generally cover the inculpatory evidence the prosecutor must disclose to the defense. Inculpatory evidence is evidence the prosecution will use to prove its case-in-chief at trial. Statutory discovery also covers the defense's reciprocal discovery obligations, such as the obligation to make available expert reports or physical evidence the defense will introduce in its case-in-chief at trial. In addition, there are statutory rules that govern the disclosure of witness statements that each side plans to use.

The second type of discovery is mandated by the defendant's constitutional right to a fair trial. Pursuant to the Fifth and Fourteenth Amendments, the defendant has a due process right to the discovery of exculpatory information. Exculpatory evidence is evidence that undermines the prosecution's case either by supporting the defendant's claim of innocence or by impeaching the prosecution's witnesses. Constitutional discovery applies only to the defendant because the government has no due process rights under the Constitution. Rather, the government must rely on statutes and rules to provide it a right of discovery.

Section B of this chapter begins with a review of the statutory rights to discovery of both the government and the defense. Pursuant to rules of procedure, each side may be entitled to examine certain types of evidence that the other side plans to introduce at trial.

Section C then focuses on the defendant's constitutional right to discovery. As set forth in the seminal cases of Brady v. Maryland, 373 U.S. 83 (1963), United States v. Bagley, 473 U.S. 667 (1985), and Giglio v. United States, 405 U.S. 150 (1972), the government has an obligation to disclose evidence favorable to the defense.

Section D briefly discusses what discovery rights defendants have before entering guilty pleas. Although defendants going to trial have the full panoply of constitutional discovery rights, a defendant pleading guilty has more limited rights to discovery.

Finally, section E of this chapter examines the defendant's limited right to have evidence preserved for trial. Although the Supreme Court held in California v. Trombetta, 467 U.S. 479 (1984), that the Constitution requires the government to preserve evidence "that might be expected to play a significant role in the suspect's defense," its later decision in Arizona v. Youngblood, 488 U.S. 51 (1988), clarified that a failure to preserve potentially useful evidence does not constitute a denial of due process absent a showing of bad faith by the police.

Discovery is a critical part of the criminal justice process. Unfortunately, it is also a part of the criminal justice system that is particularly prone to violations. In 2007, the failure of North Carolina District Attorney Michael Nifong to abide by his discovery obligations led to three white Duke lacrosse players being falsely charged with rape by a black exotic dancer who accused them of abusing her at an off-campus party. Nifong failed to disclose to the defendants that laboratory tests indicated that the DNA found on the alleged victim did not come from the defendants. Outrage over the incident led to Nifong's disbarment and increased public attention to the need to adhere to discovery rules.[2]

According to one study, at least 381 defendants nationally have had a homicide conviction thrown out because prosecutors concealed evidence of a defendant's innocence or knowingly presented perjured testimony.[3] The Innocence Project reports that 38 percent of all prosecutorial misconduct cases involve suppression of exculpatory evidence.[4] If prosecutors do not abide by their discovery obligations, the chances of wrongful conviction increase dramatically.

The prosecutor's violations were discovered in the Duke lacrosse case because the defendants came from affluent families who could afford expensive investigations and representation by defense counsel. However, as commentators have recognized, race and financial means can have a dramatic impact on whether defendants' rights are respected by the criminal justice system.[5]

It is also critical that defense lawyers abide by their discovery obligations. While the federal constitutional right to discovery applies only to prosecutors, general policy interests in fair and expeditious proceedings also support the prosecution's right to statutory and rule discovery. Specifically, defense discovery to the prosecution can (1) prevent surprise at trial, (2) deter perjured testimony, and (3) reduce trial delay.[6]

B. STATUTORY AND RULE DISCOVERY: A TWO-WAY STREET

Unlike Constitution-based discovery, statutory rules of discovery are ordinarily two-way streets. These rules require prosecutors and defense attorneys to disclose to each other certain types of evidence that they plan to use in their respective cases-in-chief.

---

2. For an excellent discussion of this incident, *see* Robert P. Mosteller, *Exculpatory Evidence, Ethics, and the Road to the Disbarment of Mike Nifong: The Critical Importance of Full Open-File Discovery,* 76 Fordham L. Rev. 1337 (2007).

3. *See* Ken Armstrong & Steve Mills, *Death Row Justice Derailed,* Chicago Tribune, Nov. 14, 1999, 1C.

4. *See* Emily M. West, *Court Findings of Prosecutorial Misconduct Claims in Post-Conviction Appeals and Civil Suits Among the First 255 DNA Exoneration Cases,* Aug. 2010, http://www.innocenceproject.org/docs/Innocence_Project_Pros_Misconduct.pdf.

5. *See generally* Angela J. Davis, *Arbitrary Justice: The Power of the American Prosecutor* (Oxford Univ. Press 2007).

6. *See* Robert P. Mosteller, *Discovery Against the Defense: Tilting the Adversarial Balance,* 74 Cal. L. Rev. 1567, 1674 (1986) (describing "revolutionary expansion" in defense discovery obligations during the early 1970s).

Every jurisdiction has rules governing discovery. For example, in federal court, Federal Rule of Criminal Procedure 16(a)[7] requires that the prosecution disclose to the defense all statements of the defendant, the defendant's prior criminal record, documents and physical objects the prosecutor will seek to introduce during trial, experts' reports, and the bases of experts' opinions. Rule 26.2, also known as the *Jencks Act*, requires that the prosecutor disclose a witness's pretrial statements after the witness testifies on direct examination so that these statements are available for impeachment. However, because defense counsel needs time to review these statements, and judges do not want mid-trial delays, it is the practice of many to make earlier disclosure of witness statements. Unlike in civil cases, depositions are rarely used by prosecutors or defense counsel in criminal prosecutions.[8]

Under the Federal Rules of Criminal Procedure, the defense also has statutory duties to disclose certain types of evidence that it plans to use at trial. Under Rule 16(b), if the defense requests discovery from the prosecution, the defense has a reciprocal duty to provide documents and tangible objects it intends to introduce in its case-in-chief, as well as access to experts' reports and the bases for their testimony. In addition, Rule 26.2 requires that the defense provide a copy of its witnesses' pretrial statements after defense witnesses testify on direct examination.

The Federal Rules of Criminal Procedure also contain notice requirements that both sides must follow. Rule 12.1 requires the defense, upon the government's request, to provide written notice of an intention to offer an alibi defense. Once the defense provides such notice, the prosecution has a duty to provide to the defense information regarding rebuttal witnesses it will use to establish the defendant's presence at the scene of the crime or to rebut the testimony of the defendant's alibi witnesses. Similarly, Rule 12.2 requires that the defendant give notice of an intention to rely on a mental defense at trial. Once the defense provides such notice, the government has an opportunity to have its expert examine the defendant so that it can prepare for the defense's case.

If there is a violation of the statutory rules of discovery, the court has broad discretion in ordering a remedy. The court may exclude the evidence, grant an appropriate continuance, or sanction counsel. Courts generally will impose the least severe sanction that will accomplish the goal of compliance with the discovery rules. However, in Taylor v. Illinois, 484 U.S. 400 (1988), the Supreme Court held that a defendant's Sixth Amendment right to compel witnesses is not violated if a court bars a defense witness from testifying because the defense has not complied with a valid court discovery order. In deciding what, if any, sanction to impose on parties that violate discovery

---

7. Federal Rules of Criminal Procedure 12.1, 12.2, 16, and 26.2 are set forth in the Statutory Supplement.

8. The limited circumstances for depositions in criminal cases are set forth in Federal Rule of Criminal Procedure 15. The use of depositions is limited by the rule and the defendant's Sixth Amendment right of confrontation.

rules, courts consider whether the violating party acted in bad faith and whether the opposing party suffered any prejudice as a result of the violation.

Defendants have been unsuccessful in attacking discovery rules that require early notification of the evidence that the defense plans to use in its case-in-chief. *See* Michigan v. Lucas, 500 U.S. 145 (1991) (upholding statute that requires disclosure of evidence defense plans to offer regarding rape victim's sexual history). Although the Fifth Amendment confers on defendants a right not to incriminate themselves, this right does not permit defendants to refuse to comply with discovery rules. Discovery rules are designed to prevent either side from being ambushed at trial.

WILLIAMS v. FLORIDA
399 U.S. 78 (1970)

Justice WHITE delivered the opinion of the Court.

[Before trial, Williams sought an order excusing him from complying with a Florida discovery rule that requires a defendant, upon written demand of the prosecuting attorney, to give pretrial notice if the defendant intends to claim an alibi, and to furnish the prosecuting attorney with information regarding the defendant's location and with the names and addresses of the alibi witnesses he intends to use. In his motion Williams openly declared his intent to claim an alibi, but objected to the further disclosure requirements on the ground that the rule "compels the Defendant in a criminal case to be a witness against himself" in violation of his Fifth and Fourteenth Amendment rights.]

We need not linger over the suggestion that the discovery permitted the State against petitioner in this case deprived him of "due process" or a "fair trial." Florida law provides for liberal discovery by the defendant against the State and the notice-of-alibi rule is itself carefully hedged with reciprocal duties requiring state disclosure to the defendant. Given the ease with which an alibi can be fabricated, the State's interest in protecting itself against an eleventh-hour defense is both obvious and legitimate. The adversary system of trial is hardly an end in itself; it is not yet a poker game in which players enjoy an absolute right always to conceal their cards until played. We find ample room in that system, at least as far as "due process" is concerned, for the instant Florida rule, which is designed to enhance the search for truth in the criminal trial by insuring both the defendant and the State ample opportunity to investigate certain facts crucial to the determination of guilt or innocence.

Petitioner's major contention is that he was "compelled . . . to be a witness against himself" contrary to the commands of the Fifth and Fourteenth Amendments because the notice-of-alibi rule required him to give the State the name and address of [his alibi witness] in advance of trial and thus to furnish the State with information useful in convicting him.

We conclude, however, as has apparently every other court that has considered the issue that the privilege against self-incrimination is not violated by a requirement that the defendant give notice of an alibi defense and disclose his alibi witnesses.

The defendant in a criminal trial is frequently forced to testify himself and to call other witnesses in an effort to reduce the risk of conviction. That the defendant faces such a dilemma demanding a choice between complete silence and presenting a defense has never been thought an invasion of the privilege against compelled self-incrimination. The pressures generated by the State's evidence may be severe but they do not vitiate the defendant's choice to present an alibi defense and witnesses to prove it, even though the attempted defense ends in catastrophe for the defendant.

In the case before us, the notice-of-alibi rule by itself in no way affected petitioner's crucial decision to call alibi witnesses or added to the legitimate pressures leading to that course of action. At most, the rule only compelled petitioner to accelerate the timing of his disclosure, forcing him to divulge at an earlier date information that the petitioner from the beginning planned to divulge at trial. Nothing in the Fifth Amendment privilege entitles a defendant as a matter of constitutional right to await the end of the State's case before announcing the nature of his defense, any more than it entitles him to await the jury's verdict on the State's case-in-chief before deciding whether or not to take the stand himself.

Chief Justice BURGER, concurring.

I join fully in [the] opinion for the Court. I see an added benefit to the notice-of-alibi rule in that it will serve important functions by way of disposing of cases without trial in appropriate circumstances — a matter of considerable importance when courts, prosecution offices, and legal aid and defender agencies are vastly overworked. The prosecutor upon receiving notice will, of course, investigate prospective alibi witnesses. If he finds them reliable and unimpeachable he will doubtless re-examine his entire case and this process would very likely lead to dismissal of the charges. In turn he might be obliged to determine why false charges were instituted and where the breakdown occurred in the examination of evidence that led to a charge.

On the other hand, inquiry into a claimed alibi defense may reveal it to be contrived and fabricated and the witnesses accordingly subject to impeachment or other attack. In this situation defense counsel would be obliged to re-examine his case and, if he found his client has proposed the use of false testimony, either seek to withdraw from the case or try to persuade his client to enter a plea of guilty, possibly by plea discussions which could lead to disposition on a lesser charge.

In either case the ends of justice will have been served and the processes expedited. These are the likely consequences of an enlarged and truly reciprocal pretrial disclosure of evidence and the move away from the "sporting contest" idea of criminal justice.

Justice BLACK, with whom Justice DOUGLAS, joins, concurring in part and dissenting in part.

The Court . . . holds that a State can require a defendant in a criminal case to disclose in advance of trial the nature of his alibi defense and give the names and addresses of witnesses he will call to support that defense. This decision, in my view, is a radical and dangerous departure from the historical and constitutionally guaranteed right of a defendant in a criminal case to remain completely silent, requiring the State to prove its case without any assistance of any kind from the defendant himself.

The core of the majority's decision is an assumption that compelling a defendant to give notice of an alibi defense before a trial is no different from requiring a defendant, after the State has produced the evidence against him at trial, to plead alibi before the jury retires to consider the case.

When a defendant is required to indicate whether he might plead alibi in advance of trial, he faces a vastly different decision from that faced by one who can wait until the State has presented the case against him before making up his mind. Before trial the defendant knows only what the State's case might be. Therefore any appraisal of the desirability of pleading alibi will be beset with guesswork and gambling. . . . Any lawyer who has actually tried a case knows that, regardless of the amount of pretrial preparation, a case looks far different when it is actually being tried than when it is only being thought about.

[T]he Fifth Amendment itself clearly provides that "no person . . . shall be compelled in any criminal case to be a witness against himself." If words are to be given their plain and obvious meaning, that provision, in my opinion, states that a criminal defendant cannot be required to give evidence, testimony, or any other assistance to the State to aid it in convicting him of crime. The Florida notice-of-alibi rule in my opinion is a patent violation of that constitutional provision because it requires a defendant to disclose information to the State so that the State can use that information to destroy him.

A criminal trial is in part a search for truth. But it is also a system designed to protect "freedom" by insuring that no one is criminally punished unless the State has first succeeded in the admittedly difficult task of convincing a jury that the defendant is guilty. The Framers decided that the benefits to be derived from the kind of trial required by the Bill of Rights were well worth any loss in "efficiency" that resulted. Their decision constitutes the final word on the subject, absent some constitutional amendment. That decision should not be set aside as the Court does today.

C. CONSTITUTIONAL DISCOVERY: A ONE-WAY STREET

In addition to statutory rights to discovery, defendants also have a constitutional right to certain types of evidence. The Bill of Rights does not refer explicitly to "the right to discovery." Rather, the Court has fashioned the right to discovery from the defendant's right of due process. Because only defendants have constitutional due process rights, constitutional discovery rights are a one-way street—the prosecutor must give evidence to the defense that may help the defendant avoid conviction, but there is no corresponding obligation for the defense to give evidence to the prosecution that may help secure a conviction.

Why does the prosecution have an obligation to help the defense by providing exculpatory evidence if we have an adversarial system? Shouldn't each side have the responsibility of finding the evidence it needs to win the case? The Supreme Court answered this question in its historic case of Brady v. Maryland.

BRADY v. MARYLAND
373 U.S. 83 (1963)

Justice DOUGLAS' opinion was announced by Justice BRENNAN.

Petitioner and a companion, Boblit, were found guilty of murder in the first degree and were sentenced to death. Their trials were separate, [Brady] being tried first. At his trial Brady took the stand and admitted his participation in the crime, but he claimed that Boblit did the actual killing. And, in his summation to the jury, Brady's counsel conceded that Brady was guilty of murder in the first degree, asking only that the jury return that verdict "without capital punishment." Prior to the trial petitioner's counsel had requested the prosecution to allow him to examine Boblit's extrajudicial statements. Several of those statements were shown to him; but one . . . in which Boblit admitted the actual homicide, was withheld by the prosecution and did not come to petitioner's notice until after he had been tried, convicted, and sentenced.

We agree with the Court of Appeals that suppression of the confession was a violation of the Due Process Clause of the Fourteenth Amendment. This ruling is an extension of Mooney v. Holohan (1935) where the court ruled [that a prosecutor could not knowingly present perjured testimony] and Napue v. Illinois (1959) [where the Court barred the State from allowing unsolicited false evidence to go uncorrected].

We now hold that the suppression by the prosecution of evidence favorable to an accused upon request violates due process where the evidence is material either to guilt or to punishment, irrespective of the good faith or bad faith of the prosecution.

The principle . . . is not punishment of society for misdeeds of a prosecutor but avoidance of an unfair trial to the accused. Society wins not only when the guilty are convicted but when criminal trials are fair; our system of the administration of justice suffers when any accused is treated unfairly. An inscription on the walls of the Department of Justice states the proposition candidly for the federal domain: "The United States wins its point whenever justice is done its citizens in the courts." A prosecution that withholds evidence on demand of an accused which, if made available, would tend to exculpate him or educe the penalty . . . casts the prosecutor in the role of an architect of a proceeding that does not comport with standards of justice.

───────────

Brady implicitly recognizes that practical obstacles, including lack of resources and law enforcement's zeal to win, often make it difficult for defendants to discover evidence to support their cases. Yet the decision does not depend on the good or bad faith of the prosecutor in withholding discovery. What is important is what possible effect the exculpatory evidence may have had on the defendant's guilt or punishment.

Under *Brady*, the prosecutor has the responsibility of anticipating what defenses might be presented in a case. Regardless of whether the defense requests discovery, the prosecutor has the constitutional duty to provide exculpatory evidence.

Brady did not set forth a requirement that exculpatory evidence be provided at a particular time, as long as it is provided in sufficient time for the defense to use it at trial. It also did not establish how "material" the withheld evidence needs to be. That is an issue the Court would address in future cases, beginning with United States v. Bagley, *infra.*

Thus, while *Brady* was an important step toward ensuring the defendant a fair trial, its effectiveness continues to depend on the judgment and ethics of the prosecutor. Nothing in *Brady* itself prohibited prosecutors from taking their chances by withholding exculpatory evidence and later arguing that the withheld evidence would not have affected the verdict. Subsequent ethical rules have filled in that gap by directing a prosecutor to "make timely disclosure to the defense all evidence or information known to the prosecutor that tends to negate the guilt of the accused or mitigates the offense [or could impact on sentencing]." ABA Model Rule of Professional Conduct 3.8(d).

Shortly after *Brady*, the Supreme Court extended the constitutional right to discovery to not only evidence that tends to exculpate the defendant but also evidence that undermines the prosecution's case by impeaching its witnesses.

GIGLIO v. UNITED STATES

405 U.S. 150 (1972)

Chief Justice BURGER delivered the opinion of the Court.

Petitioner was convicted of passing forged money orders and sentenced to five years' imprisonment. While appeal was pending in the Court of Appeals, defense counsel discovered new evidence indicating that the Government had failed to disclose an alleged promise made to its key witness that he would not be prosecuted if he testified for the Government. We granted certiorari to determine whether the evidence not disclosed was such as to require a new trial under the due process criteria of . . . Brady v. Maryland (1963).

The controversy in this case centers around the testimony of Robert Taliento, [Giglio's alleged coconspirator and the prosecution's key witness in the case against Giglio. Taliento testified that Giglio participated in a scheme to pass forged money orders. When he was cross-examined by defense counsel, Taliento denied that he had been promised leniency in a scheme to pass forged money orders. After trial, however, the defense discovered that a prosecutor had promised Taliento that if he testified before the grand jury and at trial, he would not be prosecuted. That prosecutor ended up not trying the case and the trial prosecutor, whether purposely or inadvertently, did not reveal to the defense that Taliento had been promised immunity.]

As long ago as Mooney v. Holohan (1935), this Court made clear that deliberate deception of a court and jurors by the presentation of known false evidence is incompatible with "rudimentary demands of justice." In Napue v. Illinois (1959), we said, "the same result obtains when the State, although not soliciting false evidence, allows it to go uncorrected when it appears." Thereafter Brady v. Maryland held that suppression of material evidence justifies a new trial "irrespective of the good faith or bad faith of the prosecution." When the "reliability of a given witness may well be determinative of guilt or innocence," nondisclosure of evidence affecting credibility falls within this general rule. We do not, however, automatically require a new trial whenever "a combing of the prosecutors' files after the trial has disclosed evidence possibly useful to the defense but not likely to have changed the verdict. . . ." A finding of materiality of the evidence is required under *Brady*.

The prosecutor's office is an entity and as such it is the spokesman for the Government. A promise made by one attorney must be attributed, for these purposes, to the Government. To the extent this places a burden on the large prosecution offices, procedures and regulations can be established to carry that burden and to insure communication of all relevant information on each case to every lawyer who deals with it.

Here the Government's case depended almost entirely on Taliento's testimony; without it there could have been no indictment and no evidence to carry the case to the jury. Taliento's credibility as a witness was therefore an important issue in the case, and evidence of any understanding or agreement as to a future prosecution would be relevant to his credibility and the jury was entitled to know of it.

For these reasons, the due process requirements enunciated in *Napue* and the other cases cited earlier require a new trial.

Although the Court in *Brady* and *Giglio* established the due process right of discovery of exculpatory and impeachment evidence, it limited its holdings to "material" evidence. It took 20 years for the Court to agree on a standard for materiality. What circumstances and what types of withheld evidence trigger a defendant's right to a new trial under the Due Process Clause? The justices debated this issue and ultimately resolved it in United States v. Bagley.

UNITED STATES v. BAGLEY
473 U.S. 667 (1985)

Justice BLACKMUN delivered the opinion of the Court, except as to Part III.

In Brady v. Maryland (1963), this Court held that "the suppression by the prosecution of evidence favorable to an accused upon request violates due process where the evidence is material either to guilt or punishment." The issue in the present case concerns the standard of materiality to be applied in determining whether a conviction should be reversed because the prosecutor failed to disclose requested evidence that could have been used to impeach Government witnesses.

I

Bagley was indicted on 15 charges of violating federal narcotics and firearms statutes. [Twenty-four] days before trial, he filed a discovery motion. [He requested, among other things]: "The names and addresses of witnesses that the government intends to call at trial. Also the prior criminal records of witnesses, and any deals, promises or inducements made to witnesses in exchange for their testimony."

The Government's two principal witnesses at the trial were James F. O'Connor and Donald E. Mitchell. The Government's response to the discovery motion did not disclose that any "deals, promises or inducements" had been made to O'Connor or Mitchell. In apparent reply to a [defendant's discovery] request, the Government produced a series of affidavits that O'Connor and Mitchell had signed that concluded with the statement, "I made this statement freely and voluntarily without any threats or rewards, or promises of reward having been made to me in return for it."

Respondent waived his right to a jury trial and was tried before the court in December 1977. At the trial, O'Connor and Mitchell testified about both the firearms and the narcotics charges. [T]he court found respondent guilty on the narcotics charges, but not guilty on the firearms charges.

In mid-1980, respondent filed requests for information pursuant to the Freedom of Information Act. He received in response copies of ATF form contracts that O'Connor and Mitchell had signed on May 3, 1977. Each form was entitled "Contract for Purchase of Information and Payment of Lump

Sum Therefor." The printed portion of the form stated that the vendor "will provide" information to ATF and that "upon receipt of such information . . . the United States will pay to said vendor a sum commensurate with services and information rendered." The figure "$300.00" was handwritten in each form on a line entitled "Sum to Be Paid to Vendor."

Because these contracts had not been disclosed to respondent in response to his pretrial discovery motion, [Bagley] alleged that the Government's failure to disclose the contracts, which he could have used to impeach O'Connor and Mitchell, violated his right to due process under Brady v. Maryland. [The Court of Appeals held that the failure to provide this information required automatic reversal of Bagley's conviction.]

II

The holding in Brady v. Maryland requires disclosure only of evidence that is both favorable to the accused and "material either to guilt or to punishment." The Court explained in United States v. Agurs (1976): "A fair analysis of the holding in *Brady* indicates that implicit in the requirement of materiality is a concern that the suppressed evidence might have affected the outcome of the trial."

The *Brady* rule is based on the requirement of due process. Its purpose is not to displace the adversary system as the primary means by which truth is uncovered, but to ensure that a miscarriage of justice does not occur. Thus, the prosecutor is not required to deliver his entire file to defense counsel, but only to disclose evidence favorable to the accused that, if suppressed, would deprive the defendant of a fair trial.[9]

In *Brady* and *Agurs*, the prosecutor failed to disclose exculpatory evidence. In the present case, the prosecutor failed to disclose evidence that the defense might have used to impeach the Government's witnesses by showing bias or interest. Impeachment evidence, however, as well as exculpatory evidence, falls within the *Brady* rule. See *Giglio* (1972). Such evidence is "evidence favorable to an accused," so that, if disclosed and used effectively, it may make the difference between conviction and acquittal.

The Court of Appeals treated impeachment evidence as constitutionally different from exculpatory evidence. According to that court, failure to disclose impeachment evidence is "even more egregious" than failure to disclose exculpatory evidence "because it threatens the defendant's right to confront adverse witnesses." Relying on Davis v. Alaska, 415 U.S. 308 (1974), the Court of Appeals held that the Government's failure to disclose requested impeachment evidence that the defense could use to conduct an

---

9. By requiring the prosecutor to assist the defense in making its case, the *Brady* rule represents a limited departure from a pure adversary model. The Court has recognized, however, that the prosecutor's role transcends that of an adversary: He "is the representative not of an ordinary party to a controversy, but of a sovereignty . . . whose interest . . . in a criminal prosecution is not that it shall win a case, but that justice shall be done." Berger v. United States (1935). [Footnote by the Court.]

effective cross-examination of important prosecution witnesses constitutes "'constitutional error of the first magnitude'" requiring automatic reversal.

This Court has rejected any such distinction between impeachment evidence and exculpatory evidence. Thus, the Court of Appeals' holding is inconsistent with our precedents.

Moreover, the court's reliance on Davis v. Alaska for its "automatic reversal" rule is misplaced. In *Davis*, the defense sought to cross-examine a crucial prosecution witness concerning his probationary status as a juvenile delinquent. Pursuant to a state rule of procedure . . . , the trial judge prohibited the defense from conducting the cross-examination. This Court reversed the defendant's conviction, ruling that the direct restriction on the scope of cross-examination denied the defendant "the right of effective cross-examination which would be constitutional error of the first magnitude and no amount of showing of want of prejudice would cure it."

The present case, in contrast, does not involve any direct restriction on the scope of cross-examination. The defense was free to cross-examine the witnesses on any relevant subject, including possible bias or interest resulting from inducements made by the Government. The constitutional error, if any, in this case was the Government's failure to assist the defense by disclosing information that might have been helpful in conducting the cross-examination. As discussed above, such suppression of evidence amounts to a constitutional violation only if it deprives the defendant of a fair trial. [A] constitutional error occurs, and the conviction must be reversed, only if the evidence is material in the sense that its suppression undermines confidence in the outcome of the trial.

III

It remains to determine the standard of materiality applicable to the nondisclosed evidence at issue in this case. Our starting point is the framework for evaluating the materiality of *Brady* evidence established in United States v. Agurs. The Court in *Agurs* distinguished three situations involving the discovery, after trial, of information favorable to the accused that had been known to the prosecution but unknown to the defense. The first situation was the prosecutor's knowing use of perjured testimony or, equivalently, the prosecutor's knowing failure to disclose that testimony used to convict the defendant was false. The Court noted the well-established rule that "a conviction obtained by the knowing use of perjured testimony is fundamentally unfair, and must be set aside if there is any reasonable likelihood that the false testimony could have affected the judgment of the jury."

At the other extreme is the situation in *Agurs* itself, where the defendant does not make a *Brady* request and the prosecutor fails to disclose certain evidence favorable to the accused. The Court rejected a harmless-error rule in that situation. The Court reasoned: "If the standard applied to the usual motion for a new trial based on newly discovered evidence were the same when the evidence was in the State's possession as when it was found in a neutral source, there would be no special significance to the prosecutor's obligation to serve the cause of justice." The standard of materiality applicable in the absence of a specific *Brady* request is therefore stricter than the harmless-error standard but more lenient to the defense than the newly-discovered-evidence standard.

The third situation identified by the Court in *Agurs* is where the defense makes a specific request and the prosecutor fails to disclose responsive evidence. The Court . . . suggested that the standard might be more lenient to the defense than in the situation in which the defense makes no request or only a general request.

The Court has relied on and reformulated the *Agurs* standard for the materiality of undisclosed evidence in two subsequent cases arising outside the *Brady* context. In [one of them], Strickland v. Washington (1984), the Court held that a new trial must be granted when evidence is not introduced because of the incompetence of counsel only if "there is a reasonable probability that, but for counsel's unprofessional errors, the result of the proceeding would have been different." The *Strickland* Court defined a "reasonable probability" as "a probability sufficient to undermine confidence in the outcome."

We find the *Strickland* formulation of the *Agurs* test for materiality sufficiently flexible to cover the "no request," "general request," and "specific request" cases of prosecutorial failure to disclose evidence favorable to the accused: The evidence is material only if there is a reasonable probability that, had the evidence been disclosed to the defense, the result of the proceeding would have been different. A "reasonable probability" is a probability sufficient to undermine confidence in the outcome.

The Government suggests that a materiality standard more favorable to the defendant reasonably might be adopted in specific request cases. The Government notes that an incomplete response to a specific request not only deprives the defense of certain evidence, but also has the effect of representing to the defense that the evidence does not exist. In reliance on this misleading representation, the defense might abandon lines of independent investigation, defenses, or trial strategies that it otherwise would have pursued.

We agree that the prosecutor's failure to respond fully to a *Brady* request may impair the adversary process in this manner. And the more specifically the defense requests certain evidence, thus putting the prosecutor on notice of its value, the more reasonable it is for the defense to assume from the nondisclosure that the evidence does not exist, and to make pretrial and trial decisions on the basis of this assumption. This possibility of impairment does not necessitate a different standard of materiality, however, for under the *Strickland* formulation the reviewing court may consider directly any adverse effect that the prosecutor's failure to respond might have had on the preparation or presentation of the defendant's case. The reviewing court should assess the possibility that such effect might have occurred in light of the totality of the circumstances and with an awareness of the difficulty of reconstructing in a post-trial proceeding the course that the defense and the trial would have taken had the defense not been misled by the prosecutor's incomplete response.

In the present case, we think that there is a significant likelihood that the prosecutor's response to respondent's discovery motion misleadingly induced defense counsel to believe that O'Connor and Mitchell could not be impeached on the basis of bias or interest arising from inducements offered by the Government.

The District Court, nonetheless, found beyond a reasonable doubt that, had the information that the Government held out the possibility of reward to its witnesses been disclosed, the result of the criminal prosecution would not have been different [because O'Connor's and Mitchell's testimony was directed at the weapons charges on which Bagley was acquitted].

[The Supreme Court reversed the Circuit Court's holding that Bagley's case should be automatically reversed for a *Brady* violation and remanded the case to the lower court to decide whether the withheld evidence was "material" under the standard it established in this opinion.]

Justice White, with whom Chief Justice Burger and Justice Rehnquist join, concurring in part and concurring in the judgment.

I agree with the Court that respondent is not entitled to have his conviction overturned unless he can show that the evidence withheld by the Government was "material," and I therefore join Parts I and II of the Court's opinion. I also agree . . . that for purposes of this inquiry, "evidence is material only if there is a reasonable probability that, had the evidence been disclosed to the defense, the result of the proceeding would have been different." As the Justice correctly observes, this standard is "sufficiently flexible" to cover all instances of prosecutorial failure to disclose evidence favorable to the accused. Given the flexibility of the standard and the inherently fact-bound nature of the cases to which it will be applied, however, I see no reason to attempt to elaborate on the relevance to the inquiry of the specificity of the defense's request for disclosure, either generally or with respect to this case. I would hold simply that the proper standard is one of reasonable probability and that the Court of Appeals' failure to apply this standard necessitates reversal. I therefore concur in the judgment.

Justice Marshall, with whom Justice Brennan joins, dissenting.

When the Government withholds from a defendant evidence that might impeach the prosecution's only witnesses, that failure to disclose cannot be deemed harmless error. Because that is precisely the nature of the undisclosed evidence in this case, I would affirm the judgment of the Court of Appeals and would not remand for further proceedings.

The record plainly demonstrates that on the two counts for which Bagley received sentences of imprisonment, the Government's entire case hinged on the testimony of O'Connor and Mitchell.

Whenever the Government fails, in response to a request, to disclose impeachment evidence relating to the credibility of its key witnesses, the truth-finding process of trial is necessarily thrown askew. The failure to disclose evidence affecting the overall credibility of witnesses corrupts the process to some degree in all instances.

Instead of affirming, the Court today chooses to reverse and remand the case for application of its newly stated standard to the facts of this case. While I believe that the evidence at issue here, which remained undisclosed despite a particular request, undoubtedly was material under the Court's standard, I also have serious doubts whether the Court's definition of the constitutional right at issue adequately takes account of the interests this Court sought to protect in its decision in Brady v. Maryland (1963).

I begin from the fundamental premise, which hardly bears repeating, that "[the] purpose of a trial is as much the acquittal of an innocent person as it is the conviction of a guilty one." When evidence favorable to the defendant is known to exist, disclosure only enhances the quest for truth; it takes no direct toll on that inquiry. Moreover, the existence of any small piece of evidence favorable to the defense may, in a particular case, create just the doubt that prevents the jury from returning a verdict of guilty. The private whys and wherefores of jury deliberations pose an impenetrable barrier to our ability to know just which piece of information might make, or might have made, a difference.

When the state does not disclose information in its possession that might reasonably be considered favorable to the defense, it precludes the trier of fact from gaining access to such information and thereby undermines the reliability of the verdict. . . . With a minimum of effort, the state could improve the real and apparent fairness of the trial enormously, by assuring that the defendant may place before the trier of fact favorable evidence known to the government. This proposition is not new. We have long recognized that, within the limit of the state's ability to identify so-called exculpatory information, the state's concern for a fair verdict precludes it from withholding from the defense evidence favorable to the defendant's case in the prosecutor's files.

This recognition no doubt stems in part from the frequently considerable imbalance in resources between most criminal defendants and most prosecutors' offices. Many, perhaps most, criminal defendants in the United States are represented by appointed counsel, who often are paid minimal wages and operate on shoestring budgets. In addition, unlike police, defense counsel generally is not present at the scene of the crime, or at the time of arrest, but instead comes into the case late. Moreover, unlike the government, defense counsel is not in the position to make deals with witnesses to gain evidence. Thus, an inexperienced, unskilled, or unaggressive attorney often is unable to amass the factual support necessary to a reasonable defense. When favorable evidence is in the hands of the prosecutor but not disclosed, the result may well be that the defendant is deprived of a fair chance before the trier of fact, and the trier of fact is deprived of the ingredients necessary to a fair decision. This grim reality, of course, poses a direct challenge to the traditional model of the adversary criminal process, and perhaps because this reality so directly questions the fairness of our longstanding processes, change has been cautious and halting. Thus, the Court has not gone the full road and expressly required that the state provide to the defendant access to the prosecutor's complete files, or investigators who will assure that the defendant has an opportunity to discover every existing piece of helpful evidence. Instead, in acknowledgment of the fact that important interests are served when potentially favorable evidence is disclosed, the Court has fashioned a compromise, requiring that the prosecution identify and disclose to the defendant favorable material that it possesses. This requirement is but a small, albeit important, step toward equality of justice.

At the trial level, the duty of the state to effectuate *Brady* devolves into the duty of the prosecutor; the dual role that the prosecutor must play poses a serious obstacle to implementing *Brady*. The prosecutor is by trade, if not necessity, a zealous advocate. He is a trained attorney who must aggressively seek convictions in court on behalf of a victimized public. At the same time, as a representative of the state, he must place foremost in his hierarchy of interests the determination of truth. Thus, for purposes of *Brady*, the prosecutor must abandon his role as an advocate and pore through his files, as objectively as possible, to identify the material that could undermine his case. Given this obviously unharmonious role, it is not surprising that these advocates oftentimes overlook or downplay potentially favorable evidence, often in cases in which there is no doubt that the failure to disclose was a result of absolute good faith.

The prosecutor surely greets the moment at which he must turn over *Brady* material with little enthusiasm. In perusing his files, he must make the often difficult decision as to whether evidence is favorable, and must decide on which side to err when faced with doubt. In his role as advocate, the answers are clear. In his role as representative of the state, the answers should be equally clear, and often to the contrary. Evidence that is of doubtful worth in the eyes of the prosecutor could be of inestimable value to the defense, and might make the difference to the trier of fact.

Once the prosecutor suspects that certain information might have favorable implications for the defense, either because it is potentially exculpatory or relevant to credibility, I see no reason why he should not be required to disclose it. After all, favorable evidence indisputably enhances the truthseeking process at trial. And it is the job of the defense, not the prosecution, to decide whether and in what way to use arguably favorable evidence. In addition, to require disclosure of all evidence that might reasonably be considered favorable to the defendant would have the precautionary effect of assuring that no information of potential consequence is mistakenly overlooked. By requiring full disclosure of favorable evidence in this way, courts could begin to assure that a possibly dispositive piece of information is not withheld from the trier of fact by a prosecutor who is torn between the two roles he must play. A clear rule of this kind, coupled with a presumption in favor of disclosure, also would facilitate the prosecutor's admittedly difficult task by removing a substantial amount of unguided discretion.

Under the foregoing analysis, the prosecutor's duty is quite straightforward: he must divulge all evidence that reasonably appears favorable to the defendant, erring on the side of disclosure.

The Court, however, offers a complex alternative. [T]he Court holds that due process does not require the prosecutor to turn over evidence unless the evidence is "material," and the Court states that evidence is "material" "only if there is a reasonable probability that, had the evidence been disclosed to the defense, the result of the proceeding would have been different."

The standard for disclosure that the Court articulates today enables prosecutors to avoid disclosing obviously exculpatory evidence while acting well within the bounds of their constitutional obligation.

The Court's definition poses other, serious problems. Besides legitimizing the nondisclosure of clearly favorable evidence, the standard set out by the Court also asks the prosecutor to predict what effect various pieces of evidence will have on the trial. He must evaluate his case and the case of the defendant — of which he presumably knows very little — and perform the impossible task of deciding whether a certain piece of information will have a significant impact on the trial, bearing in mind that a defendant will later shoulder the heavy burden of proving how it would have affected the outcome. At best, this standard places on the prosecutor a responsibility to speculate, at times without foundation, since the prosecutor will not normally know what strategy the defense will pursue or what evidence the defense will find useful. At worst, the standard invites a prosecutor, whose interests are conflicting, to gamble, to play the odds, and to take a chance that evidence will later turn out not to have been potentially dispositive. One Court of Appeals has recently vented its frustration at these unfortunate consequences:

> The Court's standard also encourages the prosecutor to assume the role of the jury, and to decide whether certain evidence will make a difference. In our system of justice, that decision properly and wholly belongs to the jury. The prosecutor, convinced of the guilt of the defendant and of the truthfulness of his witnesses, may all too easily view as irrelevant or unpersuasive evidence that draws his own judgments into question. Accordingly he will decide the evidence need not be disclosed. But the ideally neutral trier of fact, who approaches the case from a wholly different perspective, is by the prosecutor's decision denied the opportunity to consider the evidence.

I simply cannot agree with the Court that the due process right to favorable evidence recognized in *Brady* was intended to become entangled in prosecutorial determinations of the likelihood that particular information would affect the outcome of trial. Almost a decade of lower court practice with *Agurs* convinces me that courts and prosecutors have come to pay "too much deference to the federal common law policy of discouraging discovery in criminal cases, and too little regard to due process of law for defendants." Eager to apply the "materiality" standard at the pretrial stage, as the Court permits them to do, prosecutors lose sight of the basic principles underlying the doctrine. I would return to the original theory and promise of *Brady* and reassert the duty of the prosecutor to disclose all evidence in his files that might reasonably be considered favorable to the defendant's case. No prosecutor can know prior to trial whether such evidence will be of consequence at trial; the mere fact that it might be, however, suffices to mandate disclosure.

In so saying, I recognize that a failure to divulge favorable information should not result in reversal in all cases. It may be that a conviction should be affirmed on appeal despite the prosecutor's failure to disclose evidence that reasonably might have been deemed potentially favorable prior to trial. However, in making the determination of harmlessness, I would apply our normal constitutional error test and reverse unless it is clear beyond a reasonable doubt that the withheld evidence would not have affected the outcome of the trial.

In practical effect, it might be argued, there is little difference between the rule I propose — that a prosecutor must disclose all favorable evidence in his files, subject to harmless-error review — and the rule the Court adopts — that the prosecutor must disclose only the favorable information that might affect the outcome of the trial. According to this argument, if a constitutional right to all favorable evidence leads to reversal only when the withheld evidence might have affected the outcome of the trial, the result will be the same as with a constitutional right only to evidence that will affect the trial outcome. For several reasons, however, I disagree. First, I have faith that a prosecutor would treat a rule requiring disclosure of all information of a certain kind differently from a rule requiring disclosure only of some of that information. Second, persistent or egregious failure to comply with the constitutional duty could lead to disciplinary actions by the courts. Third, the standard of harmlessness I adopt is more protective of the defendant than that chosen by the Court, placing the burden on the prosecutor, rather than the defendant, to prove the harmlessness of his actions. It would be a foolish prosecutor who gambled too glibly with that standard of review.

[O]nly a strict appellate standard, which places on the prosecutor a burden to defend his decisions, will remove the incentive to gamble on a finding of harmlessness. Any lesser standard, and especially one in which the defendant bears the burden of proof, provides the prosecutor with ample room to withhold favorable evidence, and provides a reviewing court with a simple means to affirm whenever in its view the correct result was reached. This is especially true given the speculative nature of retrospective review.

The Court's *Brady/Bagley* standard requires judges to evaluate on a case-by-case basis whether withheld information would have had a reasonable probability of affecting the defendant's case. Ten years after *Bagley*, the Court reaffirmed this approach in Kyles v. Whitley, taking the opportunity to clarify some of the details of the materiality standard and how the *Brady/Bagley* rule should be applied. Rather than requiring that any individual piece of withheld evidence be enough to change the outcome of the defendant's case, the Court emphasized "that the favorable evidence [withheld should] be taken to put the whole case in such a different light as to undermine confidence in the verdict." Kyles v. Whitley, 514 U.S. 419, 435 (1995).

KYLES v. WHITLEY
514 U.S. 419 (1995)

Justice SOUTER delivered the opinion of the Court.

After his first trial in 1984 ended in a hung jury, petitioner Curtis Lee Kyles was tried again, convicted of first-degree murder, and sentenced to death. Because the net effect of the evidence withheld by the State in this case raises a reasonable probability that its disclosure would have produced a different result, Kyles is entitled to a new trial.

[I]

A

The record indicates that, at about 2:20 P.M. on Thursday, September 20, 1984, 60-year-old Dolores Dye left the Schwegmann Brothers' store (Schwegmann's) on Old Gentilly Road in New Orleans after doing some food shopping. As she put her grocery bags into the trunk of her red Ford LTD, a man accosted her and after a short struggle drew a revolver, fired into her left temple, and killed her. The gunman took Dye's keys and drove away in the LTD.

New Orleans police took statements from six eyewitnesses, who offered various descriptions of the gunman. They agreed that he was a black man, and four of them said that he had braided hair. The witnesses differed significantly, however, in their descriptions of height, age, weight, build, and hair length. Two reported seeing a man of 17 or 18, while another described the gunman as looking as old as 28. One witness described him as 5'4" or 5'5", medium build, 140-150 pounds; another described the man as slim and close to six feet. One witness said he had a mustache; none of the others spoke of any facial hair at all. One witness said the murderer had shoulder-length hair; another described the hair as "short."

Since the police believed the killer might have driven his own car to Schwegmann's and left it there when he drove off in Dye's LTD, they recorded the license numbers of the cars remaining in the parking lots around the store at 9:15 P.M. on the evening of the murder. Matching these numbers with registration records produced the names and addresses of the owners of the cars, with a notation of any owner's police record. Despite this list and the eyewitness descriptions, the police had no lead to the gunman until the Saturday evening after the shooting.

At 5:30 P.M., on September 22, a man identifying himself as James Joseph called the police and reported that on the day of the murder he had bought a red Thunderbird from a friend named Curtis, whom he later identified as petitioner, Curtis Kyles. He said that he had subsequently read about Dye's murder in the newspapers and feared that the car he purchased was the victim's. He agreed to meet with the police.

A few hours later, the informant met New Orleans Detective John Miller, who was wired with a hidden body microphone, through which the ensuing conversation was recorded. The informant now said his name was Joseph Banks and that he was called Beanie. His actual name was Joseph Wallace.

His story, as well as his name, had changed since his earlier call. In place of his original account of buying a Thunderbird from Kyles on Thursday, Beanie told Miller that he had not seen Kyles at all on Thursday and had bought a red LTD the previous day, Friday. Beanie led Miller to the parking lot of a nearby bar, where he had left the red LTD, later identified as Dye's.

Beanie told Miller that he lived with Kyles's brother-in-law (later identified as Johnny Burns), whom Beanie repeatedly called his "partner." Beanie described Kyles as slim, about 6-feet tall, 24 or 25 years old, with a "bush" hairstyle. When asked if Kyles ever wore his hair in plaits, Beanie said that he did but that he "had a bush" when Beanie bought the car.

During the conversation, Beanie repeatedly expressed concern that he might himself be a suspect in the murder. He explained that he had been seen driving Dye's car on Friday evening in the French Quarter, admitted that he had changed its license plates, and worried that he "could have been charged" with the murder on the basis of his possession of the LTD. He asked if he would be put in jail. Miller acknowledged that Beanie's possession of the car would have looked suspicious, but reassured him that he "didn't do anything wrong," *id.*

Beanie seemed eager to cast suspicion on Kyles, who allegedly made his living by "robbing people," and had tried to kill Beanie at some prior time. Beanie said that Kyles regularly carried two pistols, a .38 and a .32, and that if the police could "set him up good," they could "get that same gun" used to kill Dye. Beanie rode with Miller and Miller's supervisor, Sgt. James Eaton, in an unmarked squad car to Desire Street, where he pointed out the building containing Kyles's apartment.

Beanie told the officers that after he bought the car, he and his "partner" (Burns) drove Kyles to Schwegmann's about 9 P.M. on Friday evening to pick up Kyles's car, described as an orange four-door Ford.[10] When asked where Kyles's car had been parked, Beanie replied that it had been "on the same side [of the lot] where the woman was killed at." The officers later drove

10. According to photographs later introduced at trial, Kyles's car was actually a Mercury and, according to trial testimony, a two-door model. [Footnote by the Court.]

Beanie to Schwegmann's, where he indicated the space where he claimed Kyles's car had been parked. Beanie went on to say that when he and Burns had brought Kyles to pick up the car, Kyles had gone to some nearby bushes to retrieve a brown purse, which Kyles subsequently hid in a wardrobe at his apartment. Beanie said that Kyles had "a lot of groceries" in Schwegmann's bags and a new baby's potty "in the car." Beanie told Eaton that Kyles's garbage would go out the next day and that if Kyles was "smart" he would "put [the purse] in [the] garbage." Beanie made it clear that he expected some reward for his help, saying at one point that he was not "doing all of this for nothing." The police repeatedly assured Beanie that he would not lose the $400 he paid for the car.

After the visit to Schwegmann's, Eaton and Miller took Beanie to a police station where Miller interviewed him again on the record, which was transcribed and signed by Beanie, using his alias "Joseph Banks." This statement, Beanie's third (the telephone call being the first, then the recorded conversation), repeats some of the essentials of the second one. Portions of the third statement, however, embellished or contradicted Beanie's preceding story and were even internally inconsistent.

Although the police did not thereafter put Kyles under surveillance, they learned about events at his apartment from Beanie, who went there twice on Sunday. According to a fourth statement by Beanie, this one given to the chief prosecutor in November (between the first and second trials), he first went to the apartment about 2 P.M., after a telephone conversation with a police officer who asked whether Kyles had the gun that was used to kill Dye. Beanie stayed in Kyles's apartment. [Thereafter,] Sgt. Eaton wrote in an interoffice memorandum, he had "reason to believe the victims [sic] personal papers and the Schwegmann's bags will be in the trash."

At 10:40 A.M., Kyles was arrested as he left the apartment, which was then searched under a warrant. Behind the kitchen stove, the police found a .32-caliber revolver containing five live rounds and one spent cartridge. Ballistics tests later showed that this pistol was used to murder Dye. In a wardrobe in a hallway leading to the kitchen, the officers found a homemade shoulder holster that fit the murder weapon. In a bedroom dresser drawer, they discovered two boxes of ammunition, one containing several .32-caliber rounds of the same brand as those found in the pistol. Back in the kitchen, various cans of cat and dog food, some of them of the brands Dye typically purchased, were found in Schwegmann's sacks. No other groceries were identified as possibly being Dye's, and no potty was found. Later that afternoon at the police station, police opened the rubbish bags and found the victim's purse, identification, and other personal belongings wrapped in a Schwegmann's sack.

The gun, the LTD, the purse, and the cans of pet food were dusted for fingerprints. The gun had been wiped clean. Several prints were found on the purse and on the LTD, but none was identified as Kyles's. Dye's prints were not found on any of the cans of pet food. Kyles's prints were found, however, on a small piece of paper taken from the front passenger-side floorboard of the LTD. A second Schwegmann's receipt was found in the trunk of the LTD, but Kyles's prints were not found on it. Beanie's fingerprints were not compared to any of the fingerprints found.

The lead detective on the case, John Dillman, put together a photo lineup that included a photograph of Kyles (but not of Beanie) and showed the array to five of the six eyewitnesses who had given statements. Three of them picked the photograph of Kyles; the other two could not confidently identify Kyles as Dye's assailant.

B

Kyles was indicted for first-degree murder. Before trial, his counsel filed a lengthy motion for disclosure by the State of any exculpatory or impeachment evidence. The prosecution responded that there was "no exculpatory evidence of any nature," despite the government's knowledge of the following evidentiary items: (1) the six contemporaneous eyewitness statements taken by police following the murder; (2) records of Beanie's initial call to the police; (3) the tape recording of the Saturday conversation between Beanie and officers Eaton and Miller; (4) the typed and signed statement given by Beanie on Sunday morning; (5) the computer printout of license numbers of cars parked at Schwegmann's on the night of the murder, which did not list the number of Kyles's car; (6) the internal police memorandum calling for the seizure of the rubbish after Beanie had suggested that the purse might be found there; and (7) evidence linking Beanie to other crimes at Schwegmann's and to the unrelated murder of one Patricia Leidenheimer, committed in January before the Dye murder.

At the first trial, in November, the heart of the State's case was eyewitness testimony from four people who were at the scene of the crime. Kyles maintained his innocence, offered supporting witnesses, and supplied an alibi that he had been picking up his children from school at the time of the murder. The theory of the defense was that Kyles had been framed by Beanie, who had planted evidence in Kyles's apartment and his rubbish for the purposes of shifting suspicion away from himself, removing an impediment to romance with Pinky Burns, and obtaining reward money. Beanie did not testify as a witness for either the defense or the prosecution.

Because the State withheld evidence, its case was much stronger, and the defense case much weaker, than the full facts would have suggested. Even so, after four hours of deliberation, the jury became deadlocked on the issue of guilt, and a mistrial was declared.

After the mistrial, the chief trial prosecutor, Cliff Strider, interviewed Beanie. Strider's notes show that Beanie again changed important elements of his story. Notwithstanding the many inconsistencies and variations among Beanie's statements, neither Strider's notes nor any of the other notes and transcripts were given to the defense.

In December 1984, Kyles was tried a second time. Again, the heart of the State's case was the testimony of four eyewitnesses who positively identified Kyles in front of the jury. Once again, Beanie did not testify.

As in the first trial, the defense contended that the eyewitnesses were mistaken. Kyles's counsel called several individuals, including Kevin Black, who testified to seeing Beanie, with his hair in plaits, driving a red car similar to the victim's about an hour after the killing. Another witness testified that Beanie, with his hair in braids, had tried to sell him the car on Thursday evening, shortly after the murder. Another witness testified that Beanie, with his hair in a "Jheri curl," had attempted to sell him the car on Friday. One witness, Beanie's "partner," Burns, testified that he had seen Beanie on Sunday at Kyles's apartment, stooping down near the stove where the gun was eventually found, and the defense presented testimony that Beanie was romantically interested in Pinky Burns. To explain the pet food found in Kyles's apartment, there was testimony that Kyles's family kept a dog and cat and often fed stray animals in the neighborhood.

Finally, Kyles again took the stand. Denying any involvement in the shooting, he explained his fingerprints on the cash register receipt found in Dye's car by saying that Beanie had picked him up in a red car on Friday, September 21, and had taken him to Schwegmann's, where he purchased transmission fluid and a pack of cigarettes. He suggested that the receipt may have fallen from the bag when he removed the cigarettes.

On rebuttal, the prosecutor had Beanie brought into the courtroom. All of the testifying eyewitnesses, after viewing Beanie standing next to Kyles, reaffirmed their previous identifications of Kyles as the murderer. Kyles was convicted of first-degree murder and sentenced to death.

Following direct appeal, it was revealed in the course of state collateral review that the State had failed to disclose evidence favorable to the defense. After exhausting state remedies, Kyles sought relief on federal habeas. Although the United States District Court denied relief and the Fifth Circuit affirmed, Judge King dissented, writing that "for the first time in my fourteen years on this court . . . I have serious reservations about whether the State has sentenced to death the right man."

[II]

The prosecution's affirmative duty to disclose evidence favorable to a defendant can trace its origins to early 20th-century strictures against misrepresentation and is of course most prominently associated with this Court's decision in Brady v. Maryland (1963). *Brady* held "that the suppression by the prosecution of evidence favorable to an accused upon request violates due process where the evidence is material either to guilt or to punishment, irrespective of the good faith or bad faith of the prosecution."

[In] United States v. Bagley (1985), the Court disavowed any difference between exculpatory and impeachment evidence for *Brady* purposes, and it abandoned the distinction between the . . . "specific-request" and "general- or no-request" situations. *Bagley* held that regardless of request, favorable evidence is material, and constitutional error results from its suppression by the government, "if there is a reasonable probability that, had the evidence been disclosed to the defense, the result of the proceeding would have been different."

Four aspects of materiality under *Bagley* bear emphasis. Although the constitutional duty is triggered by the potential impact of favorable but undisclosed evidence, a showing of materiality does not require demonstration by a preponderance that disclosure of the suppressed evidence would have resulted ultimately in the defendant's acquittal. *Bagley*'s touchstone of materiality is a "reasonable probability" of a different result, and the adjective is important. The question is not whether the defendant would more likely than not have received a different verdict with the evidence, but whether in its absence he received a fair trial, understood as a trial resulting in a verdict worthy of confidence. A "reasonable probability" of a different result is accordingly shown when the government's evidentiary suppression "undermines confidence in the outcome of the trial."

The second aspect of *Bagley* materiality bearing emphasis here is that it is not a sufficiency of evidence test. A defendant need not demonstrate that after discounting the inculpatory evidence in light of the undisclosed evidence, there would not have been enough left to convict. The possibility of an acquittal on a criminal charge does not imply an insufficient evidentiary basis to convict. One does not show a *Brady* violation by demonstrating that some of the inculpatory evidence should have been excluded, but by showing that the favorable evidence could reasonably be taken to put the whole case in such a different light as to undermine confidence in the verdict.

Third, we note that, contrary to the assumption made by the Court of Appeals once a reviewing court applying *Bagley* has found constitutional error there is no need for further harmless-error review.

The fourth and final aspect of *Bagley* materiality to be stressed here is its definition in terms of suppressed evidence considered collectively, not item by item.

[III]

In this case, disclosure of the suppressed evidence to competent counsel would have made a different result reasonably probable.

As the District Court put it, "the essence of the State's case" was the testimony of eyewitnesses, who identified Kyles as Dye's killer. Disclosure of their statements would have resulted in a markedly weaker case for the prosecution and a markedly stronger one for the defense. To begin with, the value of two of those witnesses would have been substantially reduced or destroyed.

The State rated Henry Williams as its best witness, who testified that he had seen the struggle and the actual shooting by Kyles. The jury would have found it helpful to probe this conclusion in the light of Williams's contemporaneous statement, in which he told the police that the assailant was "a black male, about 19 or 20 years old, about 5′4″ or 5′5″, 140 to 150 pounds, medium build" and that "his hair looked like it was platted." If cross-examined on this description, Williams would have had trouble explaining how he could have described Kyles, 6-feet tall and thin, as a man more than half a foot shorter with a medium build.[11] Indeed, since Beanie was 22 years old, 5'5" tall, and 159 pounds, the defense would have had a compelling argument that Williams's description pointed to Beanie but not to Kyles.[12]

The trial testimony of a second eyewitness, Isaac Smallwood, was equally damning to Kyles. Smallwood's statement taken at the parking lot, however, was vastly different. . . . A jury would reasonably have been troubled by the adjustments to Smallwood's original story by the time of the second trial.[13]

Damage to the prosecution's case would not have been confined to evidence of the eyewitnesses, for Beanie's various statements would have raised opportunities to attack not only the probative value of crucial physical evidence and the circumstances in which it was found, but the thoroughness and even the good faith of the investigation, as well.

If the defense had called Beanie as an adverse witness, he could not have said anything of any significance without being trapped by his inconsistencies.

Even if Kyles's lawyer had followed the more conservative course of leaving Beanie off the stand, though, the defense could have examined the police to good effect on their knowledge of Beanie's statements and so have attacked the reliability of the investigation in failing even to consider Beanie's possible guilt and in tolerating (if not countenancing) serious possibilities that incriminating evidence had been planted.

By demonstrating the detectives' knowledge of Beanie's affirmatively self-incriminating statements, the defense could have laid the foundation for a vigorous argument that the police had been guilty of negligence.

Exposure to Beanie's own words, even through cross-examination of the police officers, would have made the defense's case more plausible and reduced its vulnerability to credibility attack.

In assessing the significance of the evidence withheld, one must of course bear in mind that not every item of the State's case would have been directly undercut if the *Brady* evidence had been disclosed. It is significant, however, that the physical evidence remaining unscathed would, by the State's own admission, hardly have amounted to overwhelming proof that Kyles was the murderer. Ammunition and a holster were found in Kyles's apartment, but if the jury had suspected the gun had been planted the significance of these

---

11. The record makes numerous references to Kyles being approximately six feet tall and slender; photographs in the record tend to confirm these descriptions. The description of Beanie in the text comes from his police file. Record photographs of Beanie also depict a man possessing a medium build. [Footnote by the Court.]

12. The defense could have further underscored the possibility that Beanie was Dye's killer through cross-examination of the police on their failure to direct any investigation against Beanie. [Footnote by the Court.]

13. The implication of coaching would have been complemented by the fact that Smallwood's testimony at the second trial was much more precise and incriminating than his testimony at the first, which produced a hung jury. [Footnote by the Court.]

items might have been left in doubt. The fact that pet food was found in Kyles's apartment was consistent with the testimony of several defense witnesses that Kyles owned a dog and that his children fed stray cats.

Similarly undispositive is the small Schwegmann's receipt on the front passenger floorboard of the LTD, the only physical evidence that bore a fingerprint identified as Kyles's. Kyles explained that Beanie had driven him to Schwegmann's on Friday to buy cigarettes and transmission fluid, and he theorized that the slip must have fallen out of the bag when he removed the cigarettes. This explanation is consistent with the location of the slip when found and with its small size.

The inconclusiveness of the physical evidence does not, to be sure, prove Kyles's innocence. . . . But the question is not whether the State would have had a case to go to the jury if it had disclosed the favorable evidence, but whether we can be confident that the jury's verdict would have been the same. [Finding in favor of Kyles, the Court reversed the lower court's decision and remanded the case for a new trial in compliance with *Brady* and *Bagley*.]

Justice SCALIA, with whom Chief Justice REHNQUIST, Justice KENNEDY, and Justice THOMAS join, dissenting.

In any analysis of this case, the desperate implausibility of the theory that petitioner put before the jury must be kept firmly in mind. The first half of that theory — designed to neutralize the physical evidence . . . was that petitioner was the victim of a "frame-up" by the police informer and evil genius, Beanie. Now it is not unusual for a guilty person who knows that he is suspected of a crime to try to shift blame to someone else; and it is less common, but not unheard of, for a guilty person who is neither suspected nor subject to suspicion (because he has established a perfect alibi), to call attention to himself by coming forward to point the finger at an innocent person. But petitioner's theory is that the guilty Beanie, who could plausibly be accused of the crime . . . , but who was not a suspect any more than Kyles was (the police as yet had no leads), injected both Kyles and himself into the investigation in order to get the innocent Kyles convicted. If this were not stupid enough, the wicked Beanie is supposed to have suggested that the police search his victim's premises a full day before he got around to planting the incriminating evidence on the premises.

The second half of petitioner's theory was that he was the victim of a quadruple coincidence, in which four eyewitnesses to the crime mistakenly identified him as the murderer — three picking him out of a photo array without hesitation, and all four affirming their identification in open court after comparing him with Beanie. The extraordinary mistake petitioner had to persuade the jury these four witnesses made was not simply to mistake the real killer, Beanie, for the very same innocent third party (hard enough to believe), but in addition to mistake him for the very man Beanie had chosen to frame — the last and most incredible level of coincidence. However small the chance that the jury would believe any one of those improbable scenarios, the likelihood that it would believe them all together is far smaller. The Court concludes that it is "reasonably probable" the undisclosed witness interviews would have persuaded the jury of petitioner's implausible theory of mistaken eyewitness testimony, and then argues that it is "reasonably probable" the undisclosed information regarding Beanie would have persuaded the jury of petitioner's implausible theory regarding the incriminating physical evidence. I think neither of those conclusions is remotely true, but even if they were the Court would still be guilty of a fallacy in declaring victory on each implausibility in turn, and thus victory on the whole, without considering the infinitesimal probability of the jury's swallowing the entire concoction of implausibility squared.

The State presented to the jury a massive core of evidence (including four eyewitnesses) showing that petitioner was guilty of murder, and that he lied about his guilt. The effect that the *Brady* materials would have had in chipping away at the edges of the State's case can only be called immaterial. For the same reasons I reject petitioner's claim that the *Brady* materials would have created a "residual doubt" sufficient to cause the sentencing jury to withhold capital punishment.

———

As *Kyles* demonstrates, *Brady* inquiries are extremely fact-intensive. In deciding whether there has been a *Brady* violation, the focus should be on the collective impact of the withheld evidence and whether it undermines confidence in the verdict. The prosecutors' duty to provide exculpatory and impeachment materials includes evidence not directly in the prosecution's possession, such as evidence that the prosecutor can obtain from his or her investigating officers.

Courts tend to scrutinize cases most closely when the death sentence is imposed. For example, in Banks v. Dretke, 540 U.S. 668 (2004), the Supreme Court reversed Bank's death sentence because the prosecutor failed to disclose that its key witness, Bank's associate, was paid $200 for his testimony. Yet even in death penalty cases, the concept of "materiality" requires a judgment call that can be influenced by the gruesome nature of the case and the strength of the other evidence presented by the prosecution and defense.

BANKS v. DRETKE

540 U.S. 668 (2004)

Justice GINSBURG delivered the opinion of the Court.

Here, the State elected to call Farr as a witness. Indeed, he was a key witness at both guilt and punishment phases of Banks's capital trial. Farr's status as a paid informant was unquestionably "relevant"; similarly beyond doubt, disclosure of Farr's status would have been "helpful to [Banks's] defense." Nothing in [any] decision of this Court suggests that the State can examine an informant at trial, withholding acknowledgment of his informant status in the hope that defendant will not catch on, so will make no disclosure motion.

Banks's prosecutors represented at trial and in state postconviction proceedings that the State had held nothing back. . . . Because Banks had no criminal record, Farr's testimony about Banks's propensity to commit violent acts was crucial to the prosecution. Without that testimony, the State could not have underscored, as it did three times in the penalty phase, that Banks would use the gun fetched in Dallas to "take care" of trouble arising during the robberies. The stress placed by the prosecution on this part of Farr's testimony, uncorroborated by any other witness, belies the State's suggestion that "Farr's testimony was adequately corroborated." The prosecution's penalty-phase summation, moreover, left no doubt about the importance the State attached to Farr's testimony. What Farr told the jury, the prosecution urged, was "of the utmost significance" to show "[Banks] is a danger to friends and strangers, alike."

The jury, moreover, did not benefit from customary, truth-promoting precautions that generally accompany the testimony of informants. This Court has long recognized the "serious questions of credibility" informers pose.

At least as to the penalty phase, in sum, one can hardly be confident that Banks received a fair trial, given the jury's ignorance of Farr's true role in the investigation and trial of the case.

Justice THOMAS, with whom Justice SCALIA joins, concurring in part and dissenting in part.

Although I find it to be a very close question, I cannot conclude that the nondisclosure of Farr's informant status was prejudicial under Kyles v. Whitley (1995), and *Brady*.

To demonstrate prejudice, Banks must show that "the favorable evidence could reasonably be taken to put the whole case in such a different light as to undermine confidence in the verdict."

I do not believe that there is a reasonable probability that the jury would have altered its finding. The jury was presented with the facts of a horrible crime. Banks, after meeting the victim, Richard Whitehead, a 16-year-old boy who had the misfortune of owning a car that Banks wanted, decided "to kill the person for the hell of it" and take his car. Banks proceeded to shoot Whitehead three times, twice in the head and once in the upper back. Banks fired one of the shots only 18 to 24 inches away from Whitehead. The jury was thus presented with evidence showing that Banks, apparently on a whim, executed Whitehead simply to get his car.

The jury was also presented with evidence, in the form of Banks' own testimony, that he was willing to abet another individual in obtaining a gun, with the full knowledge that this gun would aid future armed robberies.

Accordingly, the jury was also presented with Banks' willingness to assist others in committing deadly crimes. . . . The jury also heard testimony that

Banks had violently pistol-whipped and threatened to kill his brother-in-law one week before the murder.

In sum, the jury knew that Banks had murdered a 16-year-old on a whim, had violently attacked and threatened a relative shortly before the murder, and was willing to assist another individual in committing armed robberies by providing the "means and possible death weapon" for these robberies. Even if the jury were to discredit entirely Farr's testimony that Banks was planning more robberies, in all likelihood the jury still would have found "beyond a reasonable doubt" that there "[was] a probability that [Banks] would commit criminal acts of violence that would constitute a continuing threat to society." The randomness and wantonness of the murder would perhaps, standing alone, mandate such a finding. Accordingly, I cannot find that the nondisclosure of the evidence was prejudicial.

It took more than 40 years, but the Supreme Court has finally established through this series of cases the contours of the defendant's due process right to discovery. Under *Brady*, due process requires the prosecutor to disclose evidence favorable to an accused when such evidence is material to guilt or innocence. As established in *Bagley*, evidence is "material" if there is a reasonable probability that disclosure of the evidence would have changed the outcome of the proceeding. A "reasonable probability" is defined as a probability sufficient to undermine confidence in the outcome. Per *Kyle*, the focus should be on the collective impact of the withheld evidence. A defendant's due process right to discovery does not depend on whether the prosecutor acts in good faith or bad faith, or whether there is a defense request for the evidence. Both of these may be used to argue whether the evidence was material, but they are not by themselves separate threshold requirements for constitutional discovery.

Because the focus of the constitutional standard is on the "materiality" of the evidence not disclosed, there is no *Brady* violation if the prosecution fails to disclose speculative or irrelevant information, or information the defense already possesses or could obtain from other sources. But, as established in *Kyles*, a prosecutor's duty extends beyond disclosure of evidence already in the prosecutor's possession and includes the duty to learn of and disclose any favorable evidence possessed by government agents or police working on the case. It is also imperative for the government to disclose problems with eyewitness testimony. In Smith v. Cain, 132 S. Ct. 627 (2012), the Court reversed a murder conviction because the prosecutors failed to disclose notes undermining defendant's identification by the government's only eyewitness. The Court held that it was material that the witness had said the night of the crime that he "could not ID anyone because [he] couldn't see faces" and "would not know them if [he] saw them."

Late disclosure of *Brady* material, while not in the spirit of the Court's holding, will not necessarily result in a reversal unless the defendant can show that the delay denied him or her a fair trial. A defendant must show specifically how he or she was prejudiced by the late disclosure of the discovery.

Finally, the remedy for a *Brady* violation is the grant of a new trial at which the defendant will be able to use the previously undisclosed exculpatory evidence. Thus, even when a defendant has been improperly convicted because of a clear *Brady* violation, a defendant may still not be able to sue the individual prosecutor for violation of the defendant's due process rights. *See* Connick v. Thompson, 131 S. Ct. 1350 (2011).

D.   DISCOVERY FOR GUILTY PLEAS

The focus of the *Brady* line of cases was on whether a defendant received enough information to have a fair trial or sentencing proceeding. However, these cases never addressed whether due process requires disclosure of exculpatory and impeachment materials if a defendant is willing to plead guilty and admit his guilt. That question was decided by the Court in United States v. Ruiz, 536 U.S. 622 (2002).

In *Ruiz*, immigration agents caught Angela Ruiz with 30 kilograms of marijuana. As part of the prosecution's "fast track" plea bargain program, she was offered a deal in which prosecutors would recommend a lesser sentence if she agreed to plead guilty. Under the details of the agreement, the government would provide Ruiz with information of factual innocence, but she had to waive the right to receive impeachment information. Ruiz refused to do so. The government withdrew its offer, but she pled guilty anyway. When the court refused to give her the same sentencing reduction she would have received under the plea bargain, Ruiz appealed.

Justice Breyer, writing for a unanimous Supreme Court, held that due process does not require that the government disclose impeachment evidence before a defendant's guilty plea. Disclosure of impeachment evidence is required to ensure a fair trial, but a guilty plea may be voluntary without it. "It is particularly difficult to characterize impeachment information as critical information of which the defendant must always be aware prior to pleading guilty given the random way in which such information may, or may not, help a particular defendant."

Moreover, requiring the prosecution to disclose impeachment evidence may render the prosecution less likely to engage in plea bargains, because disclosure would impose additional preparation burdens on the prosecution and put its witnesses and ongoing investigations at risk. "[A] constitutional obligation to provide impeachment information during plea bargaining, prior to entry of a guilty plea, could seriously interfere with the Government's interest in securing those guilty pleas that are factually justified, desired by defendants, and help to secure the efficient administration of justice. . . . These considerations, taken together, lead us to conclude that the Constitution does not require the Government to disclose material impeachment evidence prior to entering a plea agreement with a criminal defendant."

Although the Supreme Court held that due process does not require disclosure of material exculpatory evidence before a guilty plea, the prosecution's failure to disclose such evidence may affect whether the court finds that there was a "knowing and voluntary" guilty plea.[14] If a defendant is unaware of evidence that could support a defense, it is easier for the defendant to claim that he or she did not enter a valid guilty plea.

E.   DUTY TO PRESERVE EVIDENCE

Brady and its progeny hold that the government has a duty to disclose exculpatory evidence. However, is a prosecutor obliged to preserve evidence that *may be* exculpatory? The Supreme Court addressed the extent of the prosecution's responsibility to preserve potentially exculpatory evidence in another line of cases.

First, in California v. Trombetta, 467 U.S. 479 (1984), the Supreme Court, in a unanimous decision written by Justice Marshall, held that due process did not require the police to preserve breath samples collected from drunk drivers because the preserved samples were unlikely to help the suspect's defense. In addition, the state had developed procedures to ensure that the alcohol tests that were used on the defendant were accurate.

Then, in Arizona v. Youngblood, the Court expanded on its ruling in *Trombetta*, setting forth the standard to be used when a defendant claims that the government's failure to preserve evidence has denied him the right to a fair trial.

ARIZONA v. YOUNGBLOOD

488 U.S. 51 (1988)

Chief Justice REHNQUIST delivered the opinion of the Court.

Respondent Larry Youngblood was convicted by a Pima County, Arizona, jury of child molestation, sexual assault, and kidnaping. The Arizona Court of Appeals reversed his conviction on the ground that the State had failed to preserve semen samples from the victim's body and clothing. We granted certiorari to consider the extent to which the Due Process Clause of the Fourteenth Amendment requires the State to preserve evidentiary material that might be useful to a criminal defendant.

On October 29, 1983, David L., a 10-year-old boy, attended a church service with his mother. After he left the service at about 9:30 P.M., the boy went to a carnival behind the church, where he was abducted by a middle-aged

---

14. Guilty pleas are discussed in more detail in Chapter 5.

man of medium height and weight. The assailant drove the boy to a secluded area near a ravine and molested him. He then took the boy to an unidentified, sparsely furnished house where he sodomized the boy [five times]. He threatened to kill the boy if he told anyone about the attack. The entire ordeal lasted about 1½ hours.

After the boy made his way home, his mother took him to Kino Hospital. At the hospital, a physician treated the boy for rectal injuries. The physician also used a "sexual assault kit" to collect evidence of the attack. Here, the physician used the swab to collect samples from the boy's rectum and mouth. The police placed the kit in a secure refrigerator at the police station. At the hospital, the police also collected the boy's underwear and T-shirt. This clothing was not refrigerated or frozen.

Nine days after the attack, on November 7, 1983, the police asked the boy to pick out his assailant from a photographic lineup. The boy identified respondent as the assailant. Respondent was not located by the police until four weeks later; he was arrested on December 9, 1983.

On November 8, 1983, Edward Heller, a police criminologist, examined the sexual assault kit. After he determined that such contact had occurred, the criminologist did not perform any other tests, although he placed the assault kit back in the refrigerator. He testified that tests to identify blood group substances were not routinely conducted during the initial examination of an assault kit and in only about half of all cases in any event. He did not test the clothing at this time.

Respondent was indicted on charges of child molestation, sexual assault, and kidnaping. The State moved to compel respondent to provide blood and saliva samples for comparison with the material gathered through the use of the sexual assault kit, but the trial court denied the motion on the ground that the State had not obtained a sufficiently large semen sample to make a valid comparison.

In January 1985, the police criminologist examined the boy's clothing for the first time. He found one semen stain on the boy's underwear and another on the rear of his T-shirt. The criminologist tried to obtain blood group substances from both stains using the ABO technique, but was unsuccessful. He also performed a P-30 protein molecule test on the stains, which indicated that only a small quantity of semen was present on the clothing; it was inconclusive as to the assailant's identity. The Tucson Police Department had just begun using this test, which was then used in slightly more than half of the crime laboratories in the country.

Respondent's principal defense at trial was that the boy had erred in identifying him as the perpetrator of the crime. In this connection, both a criminologist for the State and an expert witness for respondent testified as to what might have been shown by tests performed on the samples shortly after they were gathered, or by later tests performed on the samples from the boy's clothing had the clothing been properly refrigerated. The court instructed the jury that if they found the State had destroyed or lost evidence, they might "infer that the true fact is against the State's interest."

The jury found respondent guilty as charged, but the Arizona Court of Appeals reversed the judgment of conviction. It stated that "when identity is an issue at trial and the police permit the destruction of evidence that could eliminate the defendant as the perpetrator, such loss is material to the defense and is a denial of due process." The Court of Appeals reached this conclusion even though it did "not imply any bad faith on the part of the State." We now reverse.

Decision of this case requires us to again consider "what might loosely be called the area of constitutionally guaranteed access to evidence." In Brady v. Maryland (1963), we held that "the suppression by the prosecution of evidence favorable to the accused upon request violates due process where the evidence is material either to guilt or to punishment, irrespective of the good faith or bad faith of the prosecution."

There is no question but that the State complied with *Brady* here. The State disclosed relevant police reports to respondent, which contained information about the existence of the swab and the clothing, and the boy's examination at the hospital. The State provided respondent's expert with the laboratory reports and notes prepared by the police criminologist, and respondent's expert had access to the swab and to the clothing.

If respondent is to prevail on federal constitutional grounds, then, it must be because of some constitutional duty over and above that imposed by cases such as *Brady*. Our most recent decision in this area of the law, California v. Trombetta (1984), arose out of a drunken driving prosecution in which the State had introduced test results indicating the concentration of alcohol in the blood of two motorists. The defendants sought to suppress the test results on the ground that the State had failed to preserve the breath samples used in the test. We rejected this argument for several reasons: first, "the officers here were acting in 'good faith and in accord with their normal practice'"; second, in the light of the procedures actually used the chances that preserved samples would have exculpated the defendants were slim; and, third; even if the samples might have shown inaccuracy in the tests, the defendants had "alternative means of demonstrating their innocence."

Our decisions in related areas have stressed the importance for constitutional purposes of good or bad faith on the part of the Government when the claim is based on loss of evidence attributable to the Government.

The Due Process Clause of the Fourteenth Amendment, as interpreted in *Brady*, makes the good or bad faith of the State irrelevant when the State fails to disclose to the defendant material exculpatory evidence. But we think the Due Process Clause requires a different result when we deal with the failure of the State to preserve evidentiary material of which no more can be said than that it could have been subjected to tests, the results of which might have exonerated the defendant. Part of the reason for the difference in treatment is found in the observation made by the Court in *Trombetta*, that "[w]henever potentially exculpatory evidence is permanently lost, courts face the treacherous task of divining the import of materials whose contents are unknown and, very often, disputed." Part of it stems from our unwillingness to read the "fundamental fairness" requirement of the Due Process Clause, as imposing on the police an undifferentiated and absolute duty to retain and to preserve all material that might be of conceivable evidentiary significance in a particular prosecution. We think that requiring a defendant to show bad faith on the part of the police both limits the extent of the police's obligation to preserve evidence to reasonable bounds and confines it to that class of cases where the interests of justice most clearly require it, i.e., those cases in which the police themselves by their conduct indicate that the evidence could form a basis for exonerating the defendant. We therefore hold that unless a criminal defendant can show bad faith on the part of the police, failure to preserve potentially useful evidence does not constitute a denial of due process of law.

In this case, the police collected the rectal swab and clothing on the night of the crime; respondent was not taken into custody until six weeks later. The failure of the police to refrigerate the clothing and to perform tests on the semen samples can at worst be described as negligent. None of this information was concealed from respondent at trial, and the evidence — such as it was — was made available to respondent's expert who declined to perform any tests on the samples. [T]here was no suggestion of bad faith on the part of the police. It follows, therefore, from what we have said, that there was no violation of the Due Process Clause.

Justice BLACKMUN, with whom Justice BRENNAN and Justice MARSHALL join, dissenting.

The Constitution requires that criminal defendants be provided with a fair trial, not merely a "good faith" try at a fair trial. Respondent here, by what may have been nothing more than police ineptitude, was denied the opportunity to present a full defense. That ineptitude, however, deprived respondent of his guaranteed right to due process of law.

I recognize the difficulties presented by such a situation. The societal interest in seeing criminals punished rightly requires that indictments be dismissed only when the unavailability of the evidence prevents the defendant from receiving a fair trial. [I]n a situation like the present one [which is unlike *Trombetta* where there was alternative evidence available to the defense], due process requires something more. Rather than allow a State's ineptitude to saddle a defendant with an impossible burden, a court should focus on the type of evidence, the possibility it might prove exculpatory, and the existence of other evidence going to the same point of contention in determining whether the failure to preserve the evidence in question violated due process. To put it succinctly, where no comparable evidence is likely to be available to the defendant, police must preserve physical evidence of a type that they reasonably should know has the potential, if tested, to reveal immutable characteristics of the criminal, and hence to exculpate a defendant charged with the crime.

Youngblood was decided before post-conviction DNA testing became prevalent. The first DNA exoneration took place in 1989, the year after *Youngblood* was decided. Since then, DNA has exonerated defendants in 31 states, including 15 people serving time on death row. Since 2000, there have been at least 147 exonerations from DNA testing. Given this experience with DNA testing, one might question whether the Court was correct to assume in *Youngblood* that just because evidence is only "potentially" exculpatory, failure to preserve it will not deprive the defendant of a fair trial unless officers or prosecutors act out of bad faith. DNA testing has shown that evidence that is only potentially exculpatory today could be the key to overturning a wrongful conviction in the future. As a result, many states have now passed laws requiring law enforcement to preserve biological materials for future testing. *See* Cynthia E. Jones, *Evidence Destroyed, Innocence Lost: The Preservation of Biological Evidence Under Innocence Protection Statutes,* 42 Am. Crim. L. Rev. 129 (2005).[15] While most states have enacted laws authorizing post-conviction DNA testing, the Supreme Court declined to hold that due process requires such testing. *See* District Attorney's Office for the Third Judicial Dist. v. Osborne, 557 U.S. 52 (2009).

F.   FINAL NOTE

Both statutes and the Supreme Court's decisions have created duties for the prosecution to provide discovery to the defense, and the defense has a responsibility to provide limited discovery to the prosecution. Nevertheless, very few jurisdictions have adopted an "open-file" approach. The prevailing approach is still rooted in the adversarial system but with a recognition that a defendant has a due process right to a fair trial. The Court has not required the prosecution to disclose evidence that it will use to impeach defense witnesses (unless required under alibi discovery rules). Further, neither side is required to disclose matters covered by other privileges, such as the attorney-client privilege and the defendant's Fifth Amendment privilege against self-incrimination. Finally, neither side has the right to know the other's trial strategy.

---

15. *See also* D. Michael Risinger, *Innocents Convicted: An Empirically Justified Factual Wrongful Conviction Rate,* 97 J. Crim. L. & Criminology 61 (2007).

CHAPTER
5

PLEA BARGAINING AND GUILTY PLEAS

A.   INTRODUCTION

In a criminal case, there are three types of pleas: not guilty, guilty, or *nolo contendere*. A plea of not guilty does not mean "I didn't do it." Rather, it means "Prosecutor, prove your case." A guilty plea, on the other hand, is an admission by the defendant that he committed the crime and waives his right to trial. A *nolo contendere* is a no-contest plea by the defendant: The defendant does not admit guilt to the charged offense but may be sentenced the same as if he pled guilty. Because a *nolo contendere* plea is not an admission, it does not result in an automatic judgment against the defendant in any companion civil case.

By most accounts, more than 90 percent of all criminal cases never go to trial. In federal court, 97 percent of all of the defendants who are convicted are convicted by their own no-contest or guilty pleas.[1] Nevertheless, plea bargaining remains a controversial practice. Opponents of the practice argue that plea bargaining compromises the criminal justice system by allowing defendants to escape full punishment for their crimes. Other opponents worry that plea bargaining will do exactly the opposite — pressure innocent defendants to plead guilty. Supporters of plea bargaining argue that the practice enables the criminal justice system to process a high volume of cases, while allowing disposition of cases to be tailored to the specific situations of individual defendants.

Section B of this chapter examines the role of plea bargaining in the American criminal justice system and the arguments for and against its use. It also reviews the Supreme Court's decisions upholding the constitutionality of plea bargaining. Section C analyzes the constitutional standards for a valid guilty plea. Section D provides an overview of the practical steps of entering a guilty plea, as set forth in Federal Rule of Criminal Procedure 11.

---

1. *See* Missouri v. Frye, 132 S. Ct. 1407, citing Department of Justice, Bureau of Justice Statistics, *Sourcebook of Criminal Justice Statistics Online*, Table 5.22.2009, http://www.albany.edu/sourcebook/pdf/t5222009.pdf.

Section E sets forth the consequences of breaching a plea agreement. Finally, section F discusses when and how a defendant can seek to withdraw a guilty plea.

B. PLEA BARGAINING

Plea bargaining is the process through which the defendant agrees to admit guilt in exchange for some concession from the government. There are two main types of plea bargaining: (1) bargaining that reduces the number or severity of the charges the defendant faces and (2) bargaining that reduces the defendant's sentence or the government's recommendation for a sentence.

1. History of Plea Bargaining

The practice of plea bargaining stems back to the earliest days of the common law. Generally, courts did not support the practice. Rather, judges would counsel defendants to plead not guilty and proceed to trial. At the time, there were fewer institutional pressures for a defendant to plead guilty because trials were relatively short and did not consume much of the court's time.[2] When defendants began to plead guilty, judges openly feared that innocent defendants would be forced into pleas, including guilty pleas for capital offenses.

The legal landscape for plea bargaining changed significantly in the second half of the nineteenth century. Magistrates, prosecutors, and even police officers became "fixers." For a price, they would arrange for defendants to plead guilty and receive lesser punishments. Pressure was placed on innocent defendants to plead guilty. As a result, states began to impose specific requirements for guilty pleas in order to safeguard "the protection of prisoners and of the public" in response "to serious abuses caused by [prosecutors] procuring prisoners to plead guilty when a fair trial might show they were not guilty."[3]

By the 1920s, plea bargaining had become an integral part of the judicial system. The number of prosecutions grew and the guilty plea rate in some jurisdictions jumped from 25 percent in 1839 to 90 percent of the convictions in 1920. A commission study at the time noted that the major inducement for a defendant to plead guilty was not necessarily his actual guilt but the kind of bargain the defendant could make with the state.

---

2. For an excellent discussion of the history of plea bargaining, *see* Albert W. Alschuler, *Plea Bargaining and Its History*, 13 Law & Soc'y Rev. 211 (1979).

3. *See* Douglas D. Guidorizzi, *Should We Really "Ban" Plea Bargaining?: The Core Concerns of Plea Bargaining Critics*, 47 Emory L.J. 753, 759 (1998).

For the last 100 years, plea bargaining has continued to be one of the essential, yet most controversial, aspects of the American criminal justice system. Even though some jurisdictions have tried to ban or limit the practice,[4] the reality of growing caseloads has pretty much guaranteed that the practice will not disappear in the near future.

2.   The Pros and Cons of Plea Bargaining

a.   Support for Plea Bargaining

Plea bargaining supporters argue that plea bargaining offers crucial advantages to both the prosecution and the defense. For the prosecution, plea bargaining ensures a conviction, reduces the stress on government resources, and relieves victims of the burden of testifying in court. It allows prosecutors to concentrate their resources and efforts on more serious and high profile cases. It also provides benefits to the police, especially if there were problems in the investigation. By allowing the defendant to plead guilty pursuant to a plea bargain, law enforcement can avoid airing their mistakes in public.

Supporters argue that plea bargaining also benefits the defense. By plea bargaining, defendants and their lawyers expend fewer resources, reduce the defendant's punishment exposure, and provide greater certainty to the outcome of their cases. Defendants need not go through the anxious process of a trial. By pleading guilty, a defendant can assert more control over his or her fate. A plea bargain can help individualize the criminal justice system's response to the defendant's case.

Judges also tend to support plea bargaining. Quick disposition of cases eases court congestion and reduces the cost of providing jury trials. It also shifts the public's attention from the judge to the decisions and practices of prosecutors.

Finally, plea bargaining can benefit the victims in a case. If there is no trial, victims are spared the agony, inconvenience, and embarrassment of trial proceedings. Plea bargaining provides victims with some assurance that the defendant will be held responsible for his crime.

b.   Criticisms of Plea Bargaining

Despite these advantages, there are a number of strong arguments against plea bargaining. First, plea bargaining can pressure innocent persons to

---

4. *See, e.g.,* Cal. Penal Code §1192.7 (creating plea bargain limitations for serious felonies); DOJ Policy Concerning Charging Criminal Offenses, Disposition of Charges, and Sentencing (Attorney General John Ashcroft, Sept. 22, 2003) (general order to charge and pursue most serious offenses, unless limited exceptions exist).

plead guilty to avoid the consequences of conviction on more serious charges. This has been the concern with plea bargaining since its earliest use. Guilty pleas are one of the principal causes for wrongful convictions. One critic has written:

> Plea bargains have corrupted the justice system by creating fictional crimes in place of real ones. The practice of having people admit to what did not happen in order to avoid charges for what did happen creates a legal culture that elevates fiction over truth. By making the facts of the case malleable, plea bargains enable prosecutors to supplement weak evidence with psychological pressure. Legal scholar John Langbein compares "the modern American plea bargaining system" with "the ancient system of judicial torture." Many innocent people cop a plea just to end their ordeal. Confession and self-incrimination have replaced the jury trial. Just as Bentham wanted, torture has been resurrected as a principal method of conviction. As this legal culture now operates, it permits prosecutors to bring charges in the absence of crimes.
>
> Plea bargaining is a major cause of wrongful conviction. First, plea bargains undermine police investigative work. Because few cases go to trial, police have learned that their evidence is seldom tested in the courtroom. Carelessness creeps in. Sloppy investigations are less likely to lead to apprehension of the guilty party. Second, plea bargaining greatly increases the number of cases that can be prosecuted. Prosecutors have found that they can coerce a plea and elevate their conviction rate by raising the number and seriousness of the charges that they throw at a defendant. Counsel advises defendants that conviction at trial on even one charge can carry more severe punishment than a plea to a lesser charge. The sentencing differential alone is enough to make plea bargaining coercive.[5]

Although courts discuss plea bargains as a "contract" or "agreement" between the prosecutor and the defendant, the reality is that "the prosecutor substantially dictates the terms of plea agreements in most cases." There is often relatively little "give-and-take," as there is in settlement discussions for civil cases, because of the disparity in bargaining power between the prosecutor and defendant.[6] Prosecutors have an overwhelming bargaining advantage and can bring enormous institutional pressures on the defendant to agree to the plea bargain. Defense lawyers regularly acquiesce to the prosecutor's wishes. For example, as Professor Alschuler discussed in his classic work, *The Defense Attorney's Role in Plea Bargaining*, 84 Yale L.J. 1179 (1975), defense lawyers will plead for months with their clients to plead guilty, and if that doesn't work, they will call in family members to talk about how hard it would be to collect the defendant's body after he had been electrocuted. *See* United States ex rel. Brown v. LaValle, 424 F.2d 457 (2d Cir.), *cert. denied*, 401 U.S. 942 (1972).

Second, plea bargaining is also criticized because it frequently takes place outside the public view. Not only does it allow police to cover up mistakes and abuses, but it shields from public scrutiny the process that prosecutors

---

5. Paul Craig Roberts, *The Causes of Wrongful Conviction*, 4 The Indep. Rev. No. 4 (Spring 2003).

6. *See generally* Donald G. Gifford, *Meaningful Reform of Plea Bargaining: The Control of Prosecutorial Discretion*, 1983 U. Ill. L. Rev. 37 (1983).

use to evaluate their cases. "The sub rosa nature of plea bargaining and the lack of citizen participation reduce public confidence that justice has been done." *Gifford, supra* at 71.

Third, some of the strongest arguments made against plea bargaining stem from the belief that the practice subverts the values of the criminal justice system; in essence, plea bargaining allows a defendant to escape full accountability for his actions by receiving a "discount on justice." As one critic of plea bargaining observed, "the plea bargain convinces criminals that the majesty of the law is a fraud, that the law is like a Turkish bazaar."[7] Because a defendant is not held fully responsible for his or her acts, plea bargaining reduces the deterrent effect of punishment. The not-so-subtle message of the plea deal is that the defendant can "get away" with something because it is too much trouble for the government to pursue him.

Fourth, plea bargaining can be particularly frustrating for victims. They are ordinarily not direct participants in the process and must stand by as defendants plead guilty to crimes that do not reflect the seriousness of the offense or receive sentences less severe than what the victims believe they deserved. While there are growing efforts to notify victims before plea deals are reached,[8] the ultimate power to decide whether to accept a plea agreement rests with the prosecutor, not the victim.

Finally, plea bargaining is criticized because of the discriminatory impact it can have on defendants. Defendants who have greater resources to challenge the prosecution secure more favorable resolutions than those who cannot mount such a challenge. "[D]efendants perceive plea bargaining as a 'game' where the most important factors are money and luck." *Gifford, supra* at 73. Because judges typically are not involved in the plea negotiations, they have little way of preventing prosecutorial prejudices from influencing the plea bargaining process.[9]

c. Evaluating a Plea Bargain

Plea bargaining must be evaluated through the eyes of those it affects. Given the arguments for and against it, it is often helpful to ask how various constituents of the criminal justice system would react to a proposed plea bargain in any given case. What would the victim's reaction be? Why would the police and prosecutor support it? What concerns would the defense lawyer have? What would be the public's reaction? Should the court accept the plea bargain?

Jurisdictions differ on how much involvement the judge may have in the plea bargaining process. Federal Rule of Criminal Procedure 11(c)(1) bars the court from participating in plea discussions. Some states, however,

---

7. John Kaplan, *American Merchandising and the Guilty Plea: Replacing the Bazaar with the Department Store*, 5 Am. J. Crim. L. 215, 218 (1977).

8. *See* U.S. Dept. of Justice, Victim Input into Plea Agreements (2002).

9. *See* Angela J. Davis, Arbitrary Justice: The Power of the American Prosecutor 43-59, 140-141 (Oxford Univ. Press 2007).

authorize the judge to take part in the negotiations. *See* N.C. Gen. Stat. 15-1021(a). Most states neither bar nor encourage court involvement in plea negotiations.

3. Bans on Plea Bargaining

Over time, there have been efforts to limit or eliminate plea bargaining. "District attorneys and attorneys general have instituted plea cut-off dates, bans on plea bargaining after a felony indictment, total bans on plea bargaining, as well as replacing plea bargaining with the jury waiver or the 'slow plea.'" Guidorizzi, *supra* at 772-773. In 1975, Alaska experimented with an attempt to abolish plea bargaining. The changed policy prohibited both charge- and sentence-related bargaining. Contrary to predictions, the ban did not cause significant backlogs in criminal cases or an increased dismissal rate of cases. Nonetheless, Alaska relaxed its prohibition in the 1980s when it adopted presumptive sentencing guidelines that gave prosecutors increased flexibility in deciding which charges to pursue.

Despite efforts to restrict plea bargaining in both state and federal prosecutions, the practice persists today.[10] Rather than eliminate plea bargaining, jurisdictions tend to try to regulate its use. Ultimately, it is a habit that is hard to break, especially when the parties perceive benefits in engaging in the practice.

4. The Legality of Plea Bargaining

The constitutionality of plea bargaining was not addressed by the Supreme Court until the practice was in full swing. In United States v. Jackson, 390 U.S. 570 (1968), the Court invalidated a statute that put undue pressure on a defendant to plead guilty because it made defendants eligible for the death penalty only if they were convicted in a jury trial. The Court struck down the statute because it chilled a defendant's assertion of his right to pursue a jury trial.

Yet soon thereafter, the Court refused to go the next step and invalidate all plea bargaining simply because it put pressure on a defendant to forgo his right to a jury trial.

BRADY v. UNITED STATES
397 U.S. 742 (1970)

Justice WHITE delivered the opinion of the Court.

In 1959, petitioner was charged with kidnaping in violation of 18 U.S.C. §1201(a). Since the indictment charged that the victim of the kidnaping was

---

10. *See generally* George Fisher, *Plea Bargaining's Triumph*, 109 Yale L.J. 857 (2000).

not liberated unharmed, petitioner faced a maximum penalty of death if the verdict of the jury should so recommend. Petitioner, represented by competent counsel throughout, first elected to plead not guilty. Apparently because the trial judge was unwilling to try the case without a jury, petitioner made no serious attempt to reduce the possibility of a death penalty by waiving a jury trial. Upon learning that his codefendant, who had confessed to the authorities, would plead guilty and be available to testify against him, petitioner changed his plea to guilty. His plea was accepted after the trial judge twice questioned him as to the voluntariness of his plea. Petitioner was sentenced to 50 years' imprisonment, later reduced to 30.

In 1967, petitioner sought relief under 28 U.S.C. §2255, claiming that his plea of guilty was not voluntarily given because §1201(a) operated to coerce his plea, because his counsel exerted impermissible pressure upon him, and because his plea was induced by representations with respect to reduction of sentence and clemency. It was also alleged that the trial judge had not fully complied with Rule 11 of the Federal Rules of Criminal Procedure.[11]

After a hearing, the District Court for the District of New Mexico denied relief. According to the District Court's findings, petitioner's counsel did not put impermissible pressure on petitioner to plead guilty. The court concluded that "the plea was voluntarily and knowingly made."

The Court of Appeals for the Tenth Circuit affirmed, [and the Supreme Court granted review].

[In United States v. Jackson (1968), defendants were indicted under §1201(a), the same statute charged against Brady.] The District Court dismissed the §1201(a) count of the indictment, holding the statute unconstitutional because it permitted imposition of the death sentence only upon a jury's recommendation and thereby made the risk of death the price of a jury trial. This Court held the statute valid, except for the death penalty provision. [The statute makes the death penalty] applicable only to those defendants who assert the right to contest their guilt before a jury. The inevitable effect of the provision was said to be to discourage assertion of the Fifth Amendment right not to plead guilty and to deter exercise of the Sixth Amendment right to demand a jury trial. Because the legitimate goal of limiting the death penalty to cases in which a jury recommends it could be achieved without penalizing those defendants who plead not guilty and elect a jury trial, the death penalty provision "needlessly penalize[d] the assertion of a constitutional right," and was therefore unconstitutional.

Since the "inevitable effect" of the death penalty provision of §1201(a) was said by the Court to be the needless encouragement of pleas of guilty and waivers of jury trial, Brady contends that *Jackson* requires the invalidation of

---

11. When petitioner pleaded guilty, Rule 11 read as follows: "A defendant may plead not guilty, guilty or, with the consent of the court, nolo contendere. The court may refuse to accept a plea of guilty, and shall not accept the plea without first determining that the plea is made voluntarily with understanding of the nature of the charge. If a defendant refuses to plead or if the court refuses to accept a plea of guilty or if a defendant corporation fails to appear, the court shall enter a plea of not guilty." [Footnote by the Court.]

every plea of guilty entered under that section, at least when the fear of death is shown to have been a factor in the plea. Petitioner, however, has read far too much into the *Jackson* opinion.

Jackson ruled neither that all pleas of guilty encouraged by the fear of a possible death sentence are involuntary pleas nor that such encouraged pleas are invalid whether involuntary or not. *Jackson* prohibits the imposition of the death penalty under §1201(a), but that decision neither fashioned a new standard for judging the validity of guilty pleas nor mandated a new application of the test theretofore fashioned by courts and since reiterated that guilty pleas are valid if both "voluntary" and "intelligent." Boykin v. Alabama (1969).

That a guilty plea is a grave and solemn act to be accepted only with care and discernment has long been recognized. Central to the plea and the foundation for entering judgment against the defendant is the defendant's admission in open court that he committed the acts charged in the indictment. He thus stands as a witness against himself and he is shielded by the Fifth Amendment from being compelled to do so — hence the minimum requirement that his plea be the voluntary expression of his own choice. But the plea is more than an admission of past conduct; it is the defendant's consent that judgment of conviction may be entered without a trial — a waiver of his right to trial before a jury or a judge. Waivers of constitutional rights not only must be voluntary but must be knowing, intelligent acts done with sufficient awareness of the relevant circumstances and likely consequences. On neither score was Brady's plea of guilty invalid.

The voluntariness of Brady's plea can be determined only by considering all of the relevant circumstances surrounding it. One of these circumstances was the possibility of a heavier sentence following a guilty verdict after a trial. It may be that Brady, faced with a strong case against him and recognizing that his chances for acquittal were slight, preferred to plead guilty and thus limit the penalty to life imprisonment rather than to elect a jury trial which could result in a death penalty. But even if we assume that Brady would not have pleaded guilty except for the death penalty provision of §1201(a), [this] does not necessarily prove that the plea was coerced and invalid as an involuntary act.

The State to some degree encourages pleas of guilty at every important step in the criminal process. For some people, their breach of a State's law is alone sufficient reason for surrendering themselves and accepting punishment. For others, apprehension and charge, both threatening acts by the Government, jar them into admitting their guilt. In still other cases, the post-indictment accumulation of evidence may convince the defendant and his counsel that a trial is not worth the agony and expense to the defendant and his family. All these pleas of guilty are valid in spite of the State's responsibility for some of the factors motivating the pleas; the pleas are no more improperly compelled than is the decision by a defendant at the close of the State's evidence at trial that he must take the stand or face certain conviction.

Of course, the agents of the State may not produce a plea by actual or threatened physical harm or by mental coercion overbearing the will of the defendant. But nothing of the sort is claimed in this case; nor is there evidence that Brady was so gripped by fear of the death penalty or hope of leniency that he did not or could not, with the help of counsel, rationally weigh the advantages of going to trial against the advantages of pleading guilty. Brady's claim is of a different sort: that it violates the Fifth Amendment to influence or encourage a guilty plea by opportunity or promise of leniency and that a guilty plea is coerced and invalid if influenced by the fear of a possibly higher penalty for the crime charged if a conviction is obtained after the State is put to its proof.

Insofar as the voluntariness of his plea is concerned, there is little to differentiate Brady from (1) the defendant, in a jurisdiction where the judge and jury have the same range of sentencing power, who pleads guilty because his lawyer advises him that the judge will very probably be more lenient than the jury; (2) the defendant, in a jurisdiction where the judge alone has sentencing power, who is advised by counsel that the judge is normally more lenient with defendants who plead guilty than with those who go to trial; (3) the defendant who is permitted by prosecutor and judge to plead guilty to a lesser offense included in the offense charged; and (4) the defendant who pleads guilty to certain counts with the understanding that other charges will be dropped. In each of these situations, as in Brady's case, the defendant might never plead guilty absent the possibility or certainty that the plea will result in a lesser penalty than the sentence that could be imposed after a trial and a verdict of guilty. We decline to hold, however, that a guilty plea is compelled and invalid under the Fifth Amendment whenever motivated by the defendant's desire to accept the certainty or probability of a lesser penalty rather than face a wider range of possibilities extending from acquittal to conviction and a higher penalty authorized by law for the crime charged.

The issue we deal with is inherent in the criminal law and its administration because guilty pleas are not constitutionally forbidden, because the criminal law characteristically extends to judge or jury a range of choice in setting the sentence in individual cases, and because both the State and the defendant often find it advantageous to preclude the possibility of the maximum penalty authorized by law. For a defendant who sees slight possibility of acquittal, the advantages of pleading guilty and limiting the probable penalty are obvious — his exposure is reduced, the correctional processes can begin immediately, and the practical burdens of a trial are eliminated. For the State there are also advantages — the more promptly imposed punishment after an admission of guilt may more effectively attain the objectives of punishment; and with the avoidance of trial, scarce judicial and prosecutorial resources are conserved for those cases in which there is a substantial issue of the defendant's guilt or in which there is substantial doubt that the State can sustain its burden of proof. It is this mutuality of advantage that perhaps explains the fact that at present well over three-fourths of the criminal convictions in this country rest on pleas of guilty, a great many of them no doubt motivated at least in part by the hope or assurance of a lesser penalty than might be imposed if there were a guilty verdict after a trial to judge or jury.[12]

Of course, that the prevalence of guilty pleas is explainable does not necessarily validate those pleas or the system which produces them. But we cannot hold that it is unconstitutional for the State to extend a benefit to a defendant who in turn extends a substantial benefit to the State and who demonstrates by his plea that he is ready and willing to admit his crime and to enter the correctional system in a frame of mind that affords hope for success in rehabilitation over a shorter period of time than might otherwise be necessary.

A contrary holding would require the States and Federal Government to forbid guilty pleas altogether, to provide a single invariable penalty for each crime defined by the statutes, or to place the sentencing function in a separate authority having no knowledge of the manner in which the conviction in each case was obtained. In any event, it would be necessary to forbid prosecutors and judges to accept guilty pleas to selected counts, to lesser included offenses, or to reduced charges. The Fifth Amendment does not reach so far.

Brady first pleaded not guilty; prior to changing his plea to guilty he was subjected to no threats or promises in face-to-face encounters with the authorities. He had competent counsel and full opportunity to assess the advantages and disadvantages of a trial as compared with those attending a plea of guilty; there was no hazard of an impulsive and improvident response to a seeming but unreal advantage. His plea of guilty was entered in open court and before a judge obviously sensitive to the requirements of the law with respect to guilty pleas. Brady's plea . . . was voluntary.

The standard as to the voluntariness of guilty pleas must be essentially that defined by Judge Tuttle of the Court of Appeals for the Fifth Circuit:

> [A] plea of guilty entered by one fully aware of the direct consequences, including the actual value of any commitments made to him by the court, prosecutor, or his own counsel, must stand unless induced by threats (or promises to discontinue improper harassment), misrepresentation (including unfulfilled or unfulfillable promises), or perhaps by promises that are by their nature improper as having no proper relationship to the prosecutor's business (e.g. bribes).

Under this standard, a plea of guilty is not invalid merely because entered to avoid the possibility of a death penalty.

---

12. It has been estimated that about 90 percent, and perhaps 95 percent, of all criminal convictions are by pleas of guilty; between 70 percent and 85 percent of all felony convictions are estimated to be by guilty plea. D. Newman, Conviction, The Determination of Guilt or Innocence Without Trial 3 and n. 1 (1966). [Footnote by the Court.]

The record before us also supports the conclusion that Brady's plea was intelligently made. He was advised by competent counsel, he was made aware of the nature of the charge against him, and there was nothing to indicate that he was incompetent or otherwise not in control of his mental faculties; once his confederate had pleaded guilty and became available to testify, he chose to plead guilty, perhaps to ensure that he would face no more than life imprisonment or a term of years. Brady was aware of precisely what he was doing when he admitted that he had kidnaped the victim and had not released her unharmed.

It is true that Brady's counsel advised him that §1201(a) empowered the jury to impose the death penalty and that nine years later in United States v. Jackson, the Court held that the jury had no such power as long as the judge could impose only a lesser penalty if trial was to the court or there was a plea of guilty. But these facts do not require us to set aside Brady's conviction.

Often the decision to plead guilty is heavily influenced by the defendant's appraisal of the prosecution's case against him and by the apparent likelihood of securing leniency should a guilty plea be offered and accepted. [J]udgments may be made that in the light of later events seem improvident, although they were perfectly sensible at the time. The rule that a plea must be intelligently made to be valid does not require that a plea be vulnerable to later attack if the defendant did not correctly assess every relevant factor entering into his decision. A defendant is not entitled to withdraw his plea merely because he discovers long after the plea has been accepted that his calculus misapprehended the quality of the State's case or the likely penalties attached to alternative courses of action. More particularly, absent misrepresentation or other impermissible conduct by state agents, a voluntary plea of guilty intelligently made in the light of the then applicable law does not become vulnerable because later judicial decisions indicate that the plea rested on a faulty premise.

The fact that Brady did not anticipate United States v. Jackson, does not impugn the truth or reliability of his plea. We find no requirement in the Constitution that a defendant must be permitted to disown his solemn admissions in open court that he committed the act with which he is charged simply because it later develops that the State would have had a weaker case than the defendant had thought or that the maximum penalty then assumed applicable has been held inapplicable in subsequent judicial decisions.

This is not to say that guilty plea convictions hold no hazards for the innocent or that the methods of taking guilty pleas presently employed in this country are necessarily valid in all respects. This mode of conviction is no more foolproof than full trials to the court or to the jury. Accordingly, we take great precautions against unsound results, and we should continue to do so, whether conviction is by plea or by trial. In the case before us, nothing in the record impeaches Brady's plea or suggests that his admissions in open court were anything but the truth.

Although Brady's plea of guilty may well have been motivated in part by a desire to avoid a possible death penalty, we are convinced that his plea was voluntarily and intelligently made and we have no reason to doubt that his solemn admission of guilt was truthful.

Affirmed.

After *Jackson* and *Brady*, what kind of pressure can be asserted on defendants to encourage them to accept a plea deal? The Supreme Court addressed this issue in Bordenkircher v. Hayes, 434 U.S. 357 (1978).

In *Bordenkircher*, a grand jury indicted Paul Lewis Hayes on a charge of uttering a forged instrument in the amount of $88.30, an offense then punishable by a term of two to ten years in prison. After arraignment, Hayes, his retained counsel, and the Commonwealth's Attorney met to discuss a possible plea agreement. During these conferences the prosecutor offered to recommend a sentence of five years in prison if Hayes would plead guilty to the indictment. He also said that if Hayes did not plead guilty and "save the court the inconvenience and necessity of a trial," he would return to the grand jury to seek an indictment under the Kentucky Habitual Criminal Act, which would subject Hayes to a mandatory sentence of life imprisonment by reason of his two prior felony convictions. Hayes chose not to plead guilty, and the prosecutor did obtain an indictment charging him under the Habitual Criminal Act. Hayes complained that the prosecution's plea negotiations violated his right to due process.

The Supreme Court, in a 5-4 decision, held that prosecutors have the option of either charging the defendant at the outset with the most serious crimes and then reducing those charges as part of a plea bargain or charging the defendant with lesser charges and then threatening more serious charges if the defendant refuses its plea offer. In upholding the defendant's guilty plea, Justice Stewart, writing for the majority, stated:

> To punish a person because he has done what the law plainly allows him to do is a due process violation of the most basic sort, *see* North Carolina v. Pearce (1969), and for an agent of the State to pursue a course of action whose objective is to penalize a person's reliance on his legal rights is "patently unconstitutional." But in the "give-and-take" of plea bargaining, there is no such element of punishment or retaliation so long as the accused is free to accept or reject the prosecution's offer.
>
> Plea bargaining flows from "the mutuality of advantage" to defendants and prosecutors, each with his own reasons for wanting to avoid trial. Indeed, acceptance of the basic legitimacy of plea bargaining necessarily implies rejection of any notion that a guilty plea is involuntary in a constitutional sense simply because it is the end result of the bargaining process. By hypothesis, the plea may have been induced by promises of a recommendation of a lenient sentence or a reduction of charges, and thus by fear of the possibility of a greater penalty upon conviction after a trial.
>
> While confronting a defendant with the risk of more severe punishment clearly may have a "discouraging effect on the defendant's assertion of his trial rights, the

imposition of these difficult choices [is] an inevitable" — and permissible — "attribute of any legitimate system which tolerates and encourages the negotiation of pleas." It follows that, by tolerating and encouraging the negotiation of pleas, this Court has necessarily accepted as constitutionally legitimate the simple reality that the prosecutor's interest at the bargaining table is to persuade the defendant to forgo his right to plead not guilty.

It is not disputed here that Hayes was properly chargeable under the recidivist statute, since he had in fact been convicted of two previous felonies. In our system, so long as the prosecutor has probable cause to believe that the accused committed an offense defined by statute, the decision whether or not to prosecute, and what charge to file or bring before a grand jury, generally rests entirely in his discretion. "[T]he conscious exercise of some selectivity in enforcement is not in itself a federal constitutional violation" so long as "the selection was [not] deliberately based upon an unjustifiable standard such as race, religion, or other arbitrary classification." A rigid constitutional rule that would prohibit a prosecutor from acting forthrightly in his dealings with the defense could only invite unhealthy subterfuge that would drive the practice of plea bargaining back into the shadows from which it has so recently emerged.

But Justice Blackmun, joined by Justices Brennan and Marshall, dissented. They argued:

> Even if overcharging is to be sanctioned, there are strong reasons of fairness why the charge should be presented at the beginning of the charging process, rather than as a filliped thread at the end. First, it means that a prosecutor is required to reach a charging decision without any knowledge of the particular defendant's willingness to plead guilty; hence the defendant who truly believes himself to be innocent, and wishes for that reason to go to trial, is not likely to be subject to quite such a devastating gamble since the prosecutor has fixed the incentives for the average case.
>
> Second, it is healthful to keep charging practices visible to the general public, so that political bodies can judge whether the policy being followed is a fair one. Visibility is enhanced if the prosecutor is required to lay his cards on the table with an indictment of public record at the beginning of the bargaining process, rather than making use of unrecorded verbal warnings of more serious indictments yet to come.
>
> Finally, I would question whether it is fair to pressure defendants to plead guilty by threat of reindictment on an enhanced charge for the same conduct when the defendant has no way of knowing whether the prosecutor would indeed be entitled to bring him to trial on the enhanced charge.

In a separate dissent, Justice Powell acknowledged the constitutionality of plea bargaining in general, but argued that the situation in this case violated the defendant's due process rights:

> No explanation appears in the record for the prosecutor's decision to escalate the charge against respondent other than respondent's refusal to plead guilty. It seems to me that the question to be asked under the circumstances is whether the prosecutor reasonably might have charged respondent under the Habitual Criminal Act in the first place. The deference that courts properly accord the exercise of a prosecutor's discretion perhaps would foreclose judicial criticism if the prosecutor

originally had sought an indictment under that Act, as unreasonable as it would have seemed. But here the prosecutor evidently made a reasonable, responsible judgment not to subject an individual to a mandatory life sentence when his only new offense had societal implications as limited as those accompanying the uttering of a single $88 forged check. I think it may be inferred that the prosecutor himself deemed it unreasonable and not in the public interest to put this defendant in jeopardy of a sentence of life imprisonment.

There may be situations in which a prosecutor would be fully justified in seeking a fresh indictment for a more serious offense. Here, any inquiry into the prosecutor's purpose is made unnecessary by his candid acknowledgment that he threatened to procure and in fact procured the habitual criminal indictment because of respondent's insistence on exercising his constitutional rights.

The plea-bargaining process, as recognized by this Court, is essential to the functioning of the criminal-justice system. It normally affords genuine benefits to defendants as well as to society. And if the system is to work effectively, prosecutors must be accorded the widest discretion, within constitutional limits, in conducting bargaining. Only in the most exceptional case should a court conclude that the scales of the bargaining are so unevenly balanced as to arouse suspicion. In this case, the prosecutor's actions denied respondent due process because their admitted purpose was to discourage and then to penalize with unique severity his exercise of constitutional rights. Implementation of a strategy calculated solely to deter the exercise of constitutional rights is not a constitutionally permissible exercise of discretion.

Given the Court's decisions, prosecutors today have considerable leverage in the plea bargaining process. They may use the threat of mandatory minimum sentences, including mandatory life sentences under "three strikes" laws, to encourage defendants to plead guilty. *See* Chris Kemmitt, *Function over Form: Reviving the Criminal Jury's Historical Role as a Sentencing Body*, 40 U. Mich. J.L. Reform 93, 138 (Fall 2006) ("Prosecutors can now afford to threaten defendants with more oppressive punishments than under earlier sentencing regimes because the jury is ignorant of the sentencing consequences faced by defendants and the judge lacks the power to rein them in. By threatening more oppressive punishment if defendants risk trial, prosecutors can coerce defendants into accepting less favorable sentencing terms through plea bargaining").

Jurisdictions vary as to what role, if any, the judge may play in the plea bargaining process. In federal courts, judges may not participate in the plea bargaining process because of a concern that the court may have undue influence on the defendant's decision to accept a plea offer. *See* Fed. R. Crim. P. 11(c). However, many states allow court participation.

Under the Federal Rules of Criminal Procedure, the court has the power to accept, reject, or defer its decision as to whether to be bound by the parties' proposed plea agreement. Fed. R. Crim. P. 11(c)(3). Ordinarily, plea agreements do not bind a court in its sentencing decision. Rather, they merely commit the prosecution to make certain sentencing recommendations. However, pursuant to Rule 11(c)(1)(C), a defendant can plead guilty contingent to the court's acceptance of a binding sentence plea agreement.

5.   *Effective Assistance of Counsel for Plea Bargaining*

Although the Supreme Court has never held that there is a constitutional right to a plea bargain, it has recognized a right to effective assistance of counsel during the plea bargaining process. In the recent companion cases of Missouri v. Frye, 132 S. Ct. 1399 (2012), and Lafler v. Cooper, 132 S. Ct. 1376 (2012), the Court held that a claim of ineffective assistance of counsel can be made when defense counsel gives bad advice during the plea bargaining process.

MISSOURI v. FRYE
─────────────────
132 S. Ct. 1399 (2012)

Justice KENNEDY delivered the opinion of the Court.

The *Sixth Amendment,* applicable to the States by the terms of the *Fourteenth Amendment,* provides that the accused shall have the assistance of counsel in all criminal prosecutions. The right to counsel is the right to effective assistance of counsel. See *Strickland v. Washington (1984).* This case arises in the context of claimed ineffective assistance that led to the lapse of a prosecution offer of a plea bargain, a proposal that offered terms more lenient than the terms of the guilty plea entered later. The initial question is whether the constitutional right to counsel extends to the negotiation and consideration of plea offers that lapse or are rejected. If there is a right to effective assistance with respect to those offers, a further question is what a defendant must demonstrate in order to show that prejudice resulted from counsel's deficient performance. Other questions relating to ineffective assistance with respect to plea offers, including the question of proper remedies, are considered in a second case decided today. See *Lafler v. Cooper.*

I

In August 2007, respondent Galin Frye was charged with driving with a revoked license. Frye had been convicted for that offense on three other occasions, so the State of Missouri charged him with a class D felony, which carries a maximum term of imprisonment of four years.

On November 15, the prosecutor sent a letter to Frye's counsel offering a choice of two plea bargains. The prosecutor first offered to recommend a 3-year sentence if there was a guilty plea to the felony charge, without a recommendation regarding probation but with a recommendation that Frye serve 10 days in jail as so-called "shock" time. The second offer was to reduce the charge to a misdemeanor and, if Frye pleaded guilty to it, to recommend a 90-day sentence. The misdemeanor charge of driving with a revoked license carries a maximum term of imprisonment of one year. The letter stated both offers would expire on December 28. Frye's attorney did not advise Frye that the offers had been made. The offers expired.

Frye's preliminary hearing was scheduled for January 4, 2008. On December 30, 2007, less than a week before the hearing, Frye was again arrested for driving with a revoked license. At the January 4 hearing, Frye waived his right to a preliminary hearing on the charge arising from the August 2007 arrest. He pleaded not guilty at a subsequent arraignment but then changed his plea to guilty. There was no underlying plea agreement. The state trial court accepted Frye's guilty plea. The prosecutor recommended a 3-year sentence, made no recommendation regarding probation, and requested 10 days shock time in jail. The trial judge sentenced Frye to three years in prison.

Frye filed for postconviction relief in state court. He alleged his counsel's failure to inform him of the prosecution's plea offer denied him the effective assistance of counsel. At an evidentiary hearing, Frye testified he would have entered a guilty plea to the misdemeanor had he known about the offer.

II

A

It is well settled that the right to the effective assistance of counsel applies to . . . all "'critical" stages of the criminal proceedings. Critical stages include arraignments, postindictment interrogations, postindictment lineups, and the entry of a guilty plea.

With respect to the right to effective counsel in plea negotiations, a proper beginning point is to discuss two cases from this Court considering the role of counsel in advising a client about a plea offer and an ensuing guilty plea: *Hill v. Lockhart* (1985); and *Padilla v. Kentucky* (2010).

Hill established that claims of ineffective assistance of counsel in the plea bargain context are governed by the two-part test set forth in *Strickland*. In *Hill*, the decision turned on the second part of the *Strickland* test. There, a defendant who had entered a guilty plea claimed his counsel had misinformed him of the amount of time he would have to serve before he became eligible for parole. But the defendant had not alleged that, even if adequate advice and assistance had been given, he would have elected to plead not guilty and proceed to trial. Thus, the Court found that no prejudice from the inadequate advice had been shown or alleged.

In *Padilla*, the Court again discussed the duties of counsel in advising a client with respect to a plea offer that leads to a guilty plea. *Padilla* held that a guilty plea, based on a plea offer, should be set aside because counsel misinformed the defendant of the immigration consequences of the conviction.

In the case now before the Court the State, as petitioner, points out that the legal question presented is different from that in *Hill* and *Padilla*. In those cases the claim was that the prisoner's plea of guilty was invalid because counsel had provided incorrect advice pertinent to the plea. In the instant case, by contrast, the guilty plea that was accepted, and the plea proceedings concerning it in court, were all based on accurate advice and information from counsel. The challenge is not to the advice pertaining to the plea that was accepted but rather to the course of legal representation that preceded it with respect to other potential pleas and plea offers.

[T]he State urges that there is no right to a plea offer or a plea bargain in any event. See *Weatherford v.* Bursey (1977). It claims Frye therefore was not deprived of any legal benefit to which he was entitled. Under this view, any wrongful or mistaken action of counsel with respect to earlier plea offers is beside the point.

The State is correct to point out that . . . [b]efore a guilty plea is entered the defendant's understanding of the plea and its consequences can be established on the record. This affords the State substantial protection against later claims that the plea was the result of inadequate advice.

When a plea offer has lapsed or been rejected, however, no formal court proceedings are involved. Indeed, discussions between client and defense counsel are privileged. So the prosecution has little or no notice if something may be amiss and perhaps no capacity to intervene in any event. And, as noted, the State insists there is no right to receive a plea offer. For all these reasons, the State contends, it is unfair to subject it to the consequences of defense counsel's inadequacies, especially when the opportunities for a full and fair trial, or, as here, for a later guilty plea albeit on less favorable terms, are preserved.

The State's contentions are neither illogical nor without some persuasive force, yet they do not suffice to overcome a simple reality. Ninety-seven percent of federal convictions and ninety-four percent of state convictions are the result of guilty pleas. The reality is that plea bargains have become so central to the administration of the criminal justice system that defense counsel have responsibilities in the plea bargain process, responsibilities that must be met to render the adequate assistance of counsel that the *Sixth Amendment* requires in the criminal process at critical stages. Because ours "is for the most part a system of pleas, not a system of trials," it is insufficient simply to point to the guarantee of a fair trial as a backstop that inoculates any errors in the pretrial process. "To a large extent . . . horse trading [between prosecutor and defense counsel] determines who goes to jail and for how long. That is what plea bargaining is. It is not some adjunct to the criminal justice system; it *is* the criminal justice system." In today's criminal justice system, therefore, the negotiation of a plea bargain, rather than the unfolding of a trial, is almost always the critical point for a defendant.

To note the prevalence of plea bargaining is not to criticize it. The potential to conserve valuable prosecutorial resources and for defendants to admit their crimes and receive more favorable terms at sentencing means that a plea agreement can benefit both parties. In order that these benefits can be realized, however, criminal defendants require effective counsel during plea negotiations. "Anything less . . . might deny a defendant 'effective representation by counsel at the only stage when legal aid and advice would help him.'"

B

The inquiry then becomes how to define the duty and responsibilities of defense counsel in the plea bargain process. This is a difficult question. Bargaining is, by its nature, defined to a substantial degree by personal style. The alternative courses and tactics in negotiation are so individual that it may be neither prudent nor practicable to try to elaborate or define detailed standards for the proper discharge of defense counsel's participation in the process.

This case presents neither the necessity nor the occasion to define the duties of defense counsel in those respects, however. Here the question is whether defense counsel has the duty to communicate the terms of a formal offer to accept a plea on terms and conditions that may result in a lesser sentence, a conviction on lesser charges, or both.

This Court now holds that, as a general rule, defense counsel has the duty to communicate formal offers from the prosecution to accept a plea on terms and conditions that may be favorable to the accused. Any exceptions to that rule need not be explored here, for the offer was a formal one with a fixed expiration date. When defense counsel allowed the offer to expire without advising the defendant or allowing him to consider it, defense counsel did not render the effective assistance the Constitution requires.

Here defense counsel did not communicate the formal offers to the defendant. As a result of that deficient performance, the offers lapsed. Under *Strickland*, the question then becomes what, if any, prejudice resulted from the breach of duty.

C

To show prejudice from ineffective assistance of counsel where a plea offer has lapsed or been rejected because of counsel's deficient performance, defendants must demonstrate a reasonable probability they would have accepted the earlier plea offer had they been afforded effective assistance of counsel. Defendants must also demonstrate a reasonable probability the plea would have been entered without the prosecution canceling it or the trial court refusing to accept it, if they had the authority to exercise that discretion under state law.

III

These standards must be applied to the instant case.

There appears to be a reasonable probability Frye would have accepted the prosecutor's original offer of a plea bargain if the offer had been communicated to him, because he pleaded guilty to a more serious charge, with no promise of a sentencing recommendation from the prosecutor.

The Court of Appeals failed, however, to require Frye to show that the first plea offer, if accepted by Frye, would have been adhered to by the prosecution and accepted by the trial court. Whether the prosecution and trial court are required to do so is a matter of state law, and it is not the place of this Court to settle those matters.

We remand for the Missouri Court of Appeals to consider these state-law questions, because they bear on the federal question of *Strickland* prejudice. If, as the Missouri court stated here, the prosecutor could have canceled the plea agreement, and if Frye fails to show a reasonable probability the prosecutor would have adhered to the agreement, there is no *Strickland* prejudice.

Justice SCALIA, with whom THE CHIEF JUSTICE, Justice THOMAS, and Justice ALITO join, dissenting.

The Court acknowledges, moreover, that Frye's conviction was untainted by attorney error: "[T]he guilty plea that was accepted, and the plea proceedings concerning it in court, were all based on accurate advice and information from counsel." Given the "ultimate focus" of our ineffective-assistance cases on "the fundamental fairness of the proceeding whose result is being challenged," that should be the end of the matter.

The plea-bargaining process is a subject worthy of regulation, since it is the means by which most criminal convictions are obtained. It happens not to be, however, a subject covered by the *Sixth Amendment*, which is concerned not with the fairness of bargaining but with the fairness of conviction.

LAFLER v. COOPER

132 S. Ct. 1376 (2012)

Justice KENNEDY delivered the opinion of the Court.

In this case, as in *Missouri* v. *Frye,* also decided today, a criminal defendant seeks a remedy when inadequate assistance of counsel caused nonacceptance of a plea offer and further proceedings led to a less favorable outcome. In *Frye,* defense counsel did not inform the defendant of the plea offer; and after the offer lapsed the defendant still pleaded guilty, but on more severe terms. Here, the favorable plea offer was reported to the client but, on advice of counsel, was rejected. In *Frye* there was a later guilty plea. Here, after the plea offer had been rejected, there was a full and fair trial before a jury. After a guilty verdict, the defendant received a sentence harsher than that offered in the rejected plea bargain. The instant case comes to the Court with the concession that counsel's advice with respect to the plea offer fell below the standard of adequate assistance of counsel guaranteed by the *Sixth Amendment,* applicable to the States through the *Fourteenth Amendment.*

I

On the evening of March 25, 2003, respondent pointed a gun toward Kali Mundy's head and fired. [T]he shot missed and Mundy fled. Respondent followed in pursuit, firing repeatedly. Mundy was shot in her buttock, hip, and abdomen but survived the assault.

Respondent was charged under Michigan law with assault with intent to murder, possession of a firearm by a felon, possession of a firearm in the commission of a felony, misdemeanor possession of marijuana, and for being a habitual offender. On two occasions, the prosecution offered to dismiss two of the charges and to recommend a sentence of 51 to 85 months for the other two, in exchange for a guilty plea. In a communication with the court respondent admitted guilt and expressed a willingness to accept the offer. Respondent, however, later rejected the offer on both occasions, allegedly after his attorney convinced him that the prosecution would be unable to establish his intent to murder Mundy because she had been shot below the waist. After trial, respondent was convicted on all counts and received a mandatory minimum sentence of 185 to 360 months' imprisonment.

II

A

Defendants have a *Sixth Amendment* right to counsel, a right that extends to the plea-bargaining process. In this case all parties agree the performance of respondent's counsel was deficient when he advised respondent to reject the plea offer on the grounds he could not be convicted at trial. In light of this concession, it is unnecessary for this Court to explore the issue.

The question for this Court is how to apply *Strickland*'s prejudice test where ineffective assistance results in a rejection of the plea offer and the defendant is convicted at the ensuing trial.

B

To establish *Strickland* prejudice a defendant must "show that there is a reasonable probability that, but for counsel's unprofessional errors, the result of the proceeding would have been different."

In contrast to *Hill*, here the ineffective advice led not to an offer's acceptance but to its rejection. Having to stand trial, not choosing to waive it, is the prejudice alleged.

Petitioner and the Solicitor General propose a different, far more narrow, view of the *Sixth Amendment*. They contend there can be no finding of *Strickland* prejudice arising from plea bargaining if the defendant is later convicted at a fair trial. The three reasons petitioner and the Solicitor General offer for their approach are unpersuasive.

First, petitioner and the Solicitor General claim that the sole purpose of the *Sixth Amendment* is to protect the right to a fair trial. Errors before trial, they argue, are not cognizable under the *Sixth Amendment* unless they affect the fairness of the trial itself. The *Sixth Amendment*, however, is not so narrow in its reach. The *Sixth Amendment* requires effective assistance of counsel at critical stages of a criminal proceeding. The constitutional guarantee applies to pretrial critical stages that are part of the whole course of a criminal proceeding, a proceeding in which defendants cannot be presumed to make critical decisions without counsel's advice.

In the instant case respondent went to trial rather than accept a plea deal, and it is conceded this was the result of ineffective assistance during the plea negotiation process. Respondent received a more severe sentence at trial, one 3½ times more severe than he likely would have received by pleading guilty. Far from curing the error, the trial caused the injury from the error. Even if the trial itself is free from constitutional flaw, the defendant who goes to trial instead of taking a more favorable plea may be prejudiced from either a conviction on more serious counts or the imposition of a more severe sentence.

[Second], [i]t is, of course, true that defendants have "no right to be offered a plea . . . nor a federal right that the judge accept it." In the circumstances here, that is beside the point. If no plea offer is made, or a plea deal is accepted by the defendant but rejected by the judge, the issue raised here simply does not arise. [But] "[w]hen a State opts to act in a field where its action has significant discretionary elements, it must nonetheless act in accord with the dictates of the Constitution."

Third, petitioner seeks to preserve the conviction obtained by the State by arguing that the purpose of the *Sixth Amendment* is to ensure "the reliability of [a] conviction following trial." This argument, too, fails to comprehend the full scope of the *Sixth Amendment's* protections; and it is refuted by precedent.

In the end, petitioner's three arguments amount to one general contention: A fair trial wipes clean any deficient performance by defense counsel during plea bargaining. That position ignores the reality that criminal justice today is for the most part a system of pleas, not a system of trials. Ninety-seven percent of federal convictions and ninety-four percent of state convictions are the result of guilty pleas. As explained in *Frye*, the right to adequate assistance of counsel cannot be defined or enforced without taking account of the central role plea bargaining plays in securing convictions and determining sentences.

C

Even if a defendant shows ineffective assistance of counsel has caused the rejection of a plea leading to a trial and a more severe sentence, there is the question of what constitutes an appropriate remedy. That question must now be addressed.

The specific injury suffered by defendants who decline a plea offer as a result of ineffective assistance of counsel and then receive a greater sentence as a result of trial can come in at least one of two forms. In some cases, the sole advantage a defendant would have received under the plea is a lesser sentence. In this situation the court may conduct an evidentiary hearing to determine whether the defendant has shown a reasonable probability that but for counsel's errors he would have accepted the plea. If the showing is made, the court may exercise discretion in determining whether the defendant should receive the term of imprisonment the government offered in the plea, the sentence he received at trial, or something in between.

[In other situations,] the proper exercise of discretion to remedy the constitutional injury may be to require the prosecution to reoffer the plea proposal.

Justice SCALIA, with whom Justice THOMAS joins, and with whom THE CHIEF JUSTICE joins as to all but Part IV, dissenting.

Anthony Cooper received a full and fair trial, was found guilty of all charges by a unanimous jury, and was given the sentence that the law prescribed.

It is impossible to conclude discussion of today's extraordinary opinion without commenting upon the remedy it provides for the unconstitutional conviction. It is a remedy unheard-of in American jurisprudence—and, I would be willing to bet, in the jurisprudence of any other country.

The Court requires Michigan to "reoffer the plea agreement" that was rejected because of bad advice from counsel. [T]he acceptance or rejection of a plea agreement that has no status whatever under the United States Constitution.

I suspect that the Court's squeamishness in fashioning a remedy, and the incoherence of what it comes up with, is attributable to its realization, deep down, that there is no real constitutional violation here anyway. The defendant has been fairly tried, lawfully convicted, and properly sentenced, and *any* "remedy" provided for this will do nothing but undo the just results of a fair adversarial process.

In the United States, we have plea bargaining aplenty, but until today it has been regarded as a necessary evil. It presents grave risks of prosecutorial overcharging that effectively compels an innocent defendant to avoid massive risk by pleading guilty to a lesser offense; and for guilty defendants it often-perhaps usually-results in a sentence well below what the law prescribes for the actual crime. But even so, we accept plea bargaining because many believe that without it our long and expensive process of criminal trial could not sustain the burden imposed on it, and our system of criminal justice would grind to a halt.

Today, however, the Supreme Court of the United States elevates plea bargaining from a necessary evil to a constitutional entitlement. It is no longer a somewhat embarrassing adjunct to our criminal justice system; rather, as the Court announces in the companion case to this one, "'it *is* the criminal justice system.'" Thus, even though there is no doubt that the respondent here is guilty of the offense with which he was charged; even though he has received the exorbitant gold standard of American justice—a full-dress criminal trial with its innumerable constitutional and statutory limitations upon the evidence that the prosecution can bring forward, and (in Michigan as in most States) the requirement of a unanimous guilty verdict by impartial jurors—the Court says that his conviction is invalid because he was deprived of his *constitutional entitlement* to plea-bargain.

I am less saddened by the outcome of this case than I am by what it says about this Court's attitude toward criminal justice. The Court today embraces the sporting chance theory of criminal law, in which the State functions like a conscientious casino-operator, giving each player a fair chance to beat the house, that is, to serve less time than the law says he deserves. And when a player is excluded from the tables, his *constitutional rights* have been violated. I do not subscribe to that theory. No one should, least of all the Justices of the Supreme Court.

C. GUILTY PLEAS

What is a guilty plea? It is more than just a confession or a waiver of the right to a jury trial. Rather, it is a combination of both. A guilty plea is a waiver of the right to trial (and all of the rights that go with it), as well as an admission that the defendant committed the crime to which he is pleading guilty. The requirements for a constitutionally valid guilty plea were set forth by the Court in Boykin v. Alabama.

BOYKIN v. ALABAMA
395 U.S. 238 (1969)

Justice DOUGLAS delivered the opinion of the Court.

In the spring of 1966, within the period of a fortnight, a series of armed robberies occurred in Mobile, Alabama. [A] local grand jury returned five indictments against petitioner, a 27-year-old Negro, for common-law robbery—an offense punishable in Alabama by death.

Before the matter came to trial, the court determined that petitioner was indigent and appointed counsel to represent him. Three days later, at his arraignment, petitioner pleaded guilty to all five indictments. So far as the record shows, the judge asked no questions of petitioner concerning his plea, and petitioner did not address the court.

A plea of guilty is more than a confession which admits that the accused did various acts; it is itself a conviction; nothing remains but to give judgment and determine punishment. Admissibility of a confession must be based on a "reliable determination on the voluntariness issue which satisfies the constitutional rights of the defendant." The requirement that the prosecution spread on the record the prerequisites of a valid waiver is no constitutional innovation. "Presuming waiver from a silent record is impermissible. The record must show, or there must be an allegation and evidence which show, that an accused was offered counsel but intelligently and understandingly rejected the offer. Anything less is not waiver."

We think that the same standard must be applied to determining whether a guilty plea is voluntarily made. For, as we have said, a plea of guilty is more than an admission of conduct; it is a conviction. Ignorance, incomprehension, coercion, terror, inducements, subtle or blatant threats might be a perfect cover-up of unconstitutionality. The question of an effective waiver of a federal constitutional right in a proceeding is of course governed by federal standards.

Several federal constitutional rights are involved in a waiver that takes place when a plea of guilty is entered in a state criminal trial. First, is the privilege against compulsory self-incrimination guaranteed by the Fifth Amendment and applicable to the States by reason of the Fourteenth. Second, is the right to trial by jury. Third, is the right to confront one's accusers. We cannot presume a waiver of these three important federal rights from a silent record.

What is at stake for an accused facing death or imprisonment demands the utmost solicitude of which courts are capable in canvassing the matter with the accused to make sure he has a full understanding of what the plea connotes and of its consequence. When the judge discharges that function, he leaves a record adequate for any review that may be later sought and forestalls the spin-off of collateral proceedings that seek to probe murky memories.[13]

[Because the trial court failed to obtain from the defendant a full waiver of his rights, the conviction was overturned.]

Justice HARLAN, whom Justice BLACK joins, dissenting.

The Court today holds that petitioner Boykin was denied due process of law, and that his robbery convictions must be reversed outright, solely because "the record [is] inadequate to show that petitioner . . . intelligently and knowingly pleaded guilty." The Court thus in effect fastens upon the States, as a matter of federal constitutional law, the rigid prophylactic requirements of Rule 11 of the Federal Rules of Criminal Procedure. Moreover, the Court does all this at the behest of a petitioner who has never at any time alleged that his guilty plea was involuntary or made without knowledge of the consequences. I cannot possibly subscribe to so bizarre a result.

So far as one can make out from the Court's opinion, what is now in effect being held is that the prophylactic procedures of Criminal Rule 11 are substantially applicable to the States as a matter of federal constitutional due process.

I would hold that petitioner Boykin is not entitled to outright reversal of his conviction simply because of the "inadequacy" of the record pertaining to his guilty plea.

---

13. A majority of criminal convictions are obtained after a plea of guilty. If these convictions are to be insulated from attack, the trial court is best advised to conduct an on the record examination of the defendant which should include, inter alia, an attempt to satisfy itself that the defendant understands the nature of the charges, his right to a jury trial, the acts sufficient to constitute the offenses for which he is charged and the permissible range of sentences. [Footnote by the Court.]

How informed must a defendant be to enter a "knowing and voluntary" guilty plea? In Henderson v. Morgan, 426 U.S. 637 (1976), the Court held that a defendant must understand the nature of the offense to which he pleads.

HENDERSON v. MORGAN

426 U.S. 637 (1976)

Justice STEVENS delivered the opinion of the Court.

The question presented is whether a defendant may enter a voluntary plea of guilty to a charge of second-degree murder without being informed that intent to cause the death of his victim was an element of the offense.

I

On April 6, 1965, respondent killed Mrs. Ada Francisco in her home.

When he was in seventh grade, respondent was committed to the Rome State School for Mental Defectives where he was classified as "retarded." He was released to become a farm laborer and ultimately went to work on Mrs. Francisco's farm. Following an argument, she threatened to return him to state custody. He then decided to abscond. During the night he entered Mrs. Francisco's bedroom with a knife, intending to collect his earned wages before leaving; she awoke, began to scream, and he stabbed her. He took a small amount of money, fled in her car, and became involved in an accident about 80 miles away. The knife was found in the glove compartment of her car. He was promptly arrested and made a statement to the police. He was then 19 years old and substantially below average intelligence.

Respondent was indicted for first-degree murder. Defense counsel held a series of conferences with the prosecutors, with the respondent, and with members of his family. The lawyers "thought manslaughter first would satisfy the needs of justice." They therefore endeavored to have the charge reduced to manslaughter, but the prosecution would agree to nothing less than second-degree murder and a minimum sentence of 25 years. The lawyers gave respondent advice about the different sentences which could be imposed for the different offenses, but, as the District Court found, did not explain the required element of intent.

On June 8, 1965, respondent appeared in court with his attorneys and entered a plea of guilty to murder in the second degree in full satisfaction of the first-degree murder charge made in the indictment. In direct colloquy with the trial judge respondent stated that his plea was based on the advice of his attorneys, that he understood he was accused of killing Mrs. Francisco in Fulton County, that he was waiving his right to a jury trial, and that he would be sent to prison. There was no discussion of the elements of the offense of second-degree murder, no indication that the nature of the offense had ever been discussed with respondent, and no reference of any kind to the requirement of intent to cause the death of the victim.

At the sentencing hearing a week later his lawyers made a statement explaining his version of the offense, particularly noting that respondent "meant no harm to that lady" when he entered her room with the knife.[14] After studying the probation officer's report, the trial judge pronounced sentence.

At the evidentiary hearing [where respondent challenged his plea, he] testified that he would not have pleaded guilty if he had known that an intent to cause the death of his victim was an element of the offense of second-degree murder. The District Judge did not indicate whether or not he credited this testimony.

II

We assume, as petitioner argues, that the prosecutor had overwhelming evidence of guilt available. Nevertheless, such a plea cannot support a judgment of guilt unless it was voluntary in a constitutional sense. And clearly the plea could not be voluntary in the sense that it constituted an intelligent admission that he committed the offense unless the defendant received "real notice of the true nature of the charge against him, the first and most universally recognized requirement of due process."[15]

The charge of second-degree murder was never formally made. Had it been made, it necessarily would have included a charge that respondent's assault was "committed with a design to effect the death of the person killed." [A]n admission by respondent that he killed Mrs. Francisco does not necessarily also admit that he was guilty of second-degree murder.

---

14. The attorney described the incident, in part, in these words:

He awakened Mrs. Francisco for the purpose of obtaining the money which was rightfully his, and which he had a right to. Of course it was an unusual hour to do it, but he had returned home late, and he had been threatened with that other thing on the part of Mrs. Francisco of returning him to the Rome School. So I assume, putting all of those factors together, the one idea in his mind was to take his money and get away as far as he could to avoid being transferred back.

Now, Mrs. Francisco was awakened. Apparently he had stayed there in the house, and she had no fear of him because her bedroom was open. There was no door on it. No locks at all. So when he awakened her, instead of responding to him, she merely started to scream. Now, I assume if she had talked to him that night in a normal tone, this thing would never have happened. But the minute she screamed, of course with his uncontrollable and ungovernable temper, and the idea in mind of perhaps she may awaken the people who were living in the other apartment of the house — there was a man and his wife who were working there for Mrs. Francisco and living in the house — in order to stop the screaming and in the excitement and tension of it all, the assault occurred and as a result Mrs. Francisco met her death. [Footnote by the Court.]

15. A plea may be involuntary either because the accused does not understand the nature of the constitutional protections that he is waiving, or because he has such an incomplete understanding of the charge that his plea cannot stand as an intelligent admission of guilt. Without adequate notice of the nature of the charge against him, or proof that he in fact understood the charge, the plea cannot be voluntary in this latter sense. [Footnote by the Court.]

There is nothing in this record that can serve as a substitute for either a finding after trial, or a voluntary admission, that respondent had the requisite intent. Defense counsel did not purport to stipulate to that fact; they did not explain to him that his plea would be an admission of that fact; and he made no factual statement or admission necessarily implying that he had such intent. In these circumstances it is impossible to conclude that his plea to the unexplained charge of second-degree murder was voluntary.[16]

Normally the record contains either an explanation of the charge by the trial judge, or at least a representation by defense counsel that the nature of the offense has been explained to the accused. Moreover, even without such an express representation, it may be appropriate to presume that in most cases defense counsel routinely explain the nature of the offense in sufficient detail to give the accused notice of what he is being asked to admit. This case is unique because the trial judge found as a fact that the element of intent was not explained to respondent. Moreover, respondent's unusually low mental capacity provides a reasonable explanation for counsel's oversight; it also forecloses the conclusion that the error was harmless beyond a reasonable doubt, for it lends at least a modicum of credibility to defense counsel's appraisal of the homicide as a manslaughter rather than a murder.

Since respondent did not receive adequate notice of the offense to which he pleaded guilty, his plea was involuntary and the judgment of conviction was entered without due process of law.

Justice REHNQUIST, with whom Chief Justice BURGER joins, dissenting.

There was no contention in the federal habeas court that respondent's guilty plea was not "voluntary" in the normal sense of that word. There was no hint of physical or psychological coercion, and respondent was represented by not one but two admittedly capable defense attorneys.

But the Court refers to "voluntary in a constitutional sense" stating that the term includes the requirement of "'real notice of the true nature of the . . .' charge." [T]he test to be applied is not whether respondent's attorneys mechanically recited to him the elements of the crime with which he was charged as those elements would have been set forth in black letter law in a criminal law hornbook, but rather it is a test based on the practices of reasonably competent attorneys experienced in the day-to-day business of representing criminal defendants in a trial court.

His attorneys were motivated by the eminently reasonable tactical judgment on their part that he should plead guilty to second-degree murder in order to avoid the possibility of conviction for first-degree murder with its more serious attendant penalties. Since the Court concedes both the

---

16. There is no need in this case to decide whether notice of the true nature, or substance, of a charge always requires a description of every element of the offense; we assume it does not. Nevertheless, intent is such a critical element of the offense of second-degree murder that notice of that element is required. [Footnote by the Court.]

competence of respondent's counsel and the wisdom of their advice, that should be the end of the inquiry.

———————

Although the Court in *Henderson* struck down the defendant's plea, it is not always easy to get a guilty plea overturned. Even outside the plea bargaining context, a defendant must also show that he would not have pled guilty absent counsel's improper advice. Only significant errors, such as when defense counsel fails to advise the defendant of the deportation consequences of his plea, are likely to lead to reversal.

HILL v. LOCKHART
474 U.S. 52 (1985)

Justice REHNQUIST delivered the opinion of the Court.

Petitioner William Lloyd Hill pleaded guilty in the Arkansas trial court to charges of first-degree murder and theft of property. More than two years later he sought federal habeas relief on the ground that his court-appointed attorney had failed to advise him that, as a second offender, he was required to serve one-half of his sentence before becoming eligible for parole. [W]e conclude that petitioner failed to allege the kind of prejudice from the allegedly incompetent advice of counsel that would have entitled him to a hearing.

Under Arkansas law, the murder charge to which petitioner pleaded guilty carried a potential sentence of 5 to 50 years or life in prison, along with a fine of up to $15,000. Petitioner's court-appointed attorney negotiated a plea agreement pursuant to which the State, in return for petitioner's plea of guilty to both the murder and theft charges, agreed to recommend that the trial judge impose concurrent prison sentences of 35 years for the murder and 10 years for the theft. Petitioner signed a written "plea statement" indicating that he understood the charges against him and the consequences of pleading guilty, that his plea had not been induced "by any force, threat, or promise" apart from the plea agreement itself, that he realized that the trial judge was not bound by the plea agreement and retained the sole "power of sentence," and that he had discussed the plea agreement with his attorney and was satisfied with his attorney's advice. The last two lines of the "plea statement," just above petitioner's signature, read: "I am aware of everything in this document. I fully understand what my rights are, and I voluntarily plead guilty because I am guilty as charged."

Petitioner appeared before the trial judge at the plea hearing, recounted the events that gave rise to the charges against him, affirmed that he had signed and understood the written "plea statement," reiterated that no "threats or promises" had been made to him other than the plea agreement itself, and entered a plea of guilty to both charges. The trial judge accepted the guilty plea and sentenced petitioner in accordance with the State's recommendations. The trial judge also granted petitioner credit for the time he had already served in prison, and told petitioner that "[you] will be required to serve at least one-third of your time before you are eligible for parole."

More than two years later petitioner filed a federal habeas corpus petition alleging, inter alia, that his guilty plea was involuntary by reason of ineffective assistance of counsel because his attorney had misinformed him as to his parole eligibility date. According to petitioner, his attorney had told him that if he pleaded guilty he would become eligible for parole after serving one-third of his prison sentence. In fact, because petitioner previously had been convicted of a felony in Florida, he was classified under Arkansas law as a "second offender" and was required to serve one-half of his sentence before becoming eligible for parole. Petitioner asked the United States District Court to reduce his sentence to a term of years that would result in his becoming eligible for parole in conformance with his original expectations.

The District Court denied habeas relief without a hearing. The court noted that neither Arkansas nor federal law required that petitioner be informed of his parole eligibility date prior to pleading guilty, and concluded that, even if petitioner was misled by his attorney's advice, parole eligibility "is not such a consequence of [petitioner's] guilty plea that such misinformation renders his plea involuntary." The court also held that "even if an attorney's advice concerning such eligibility is not wholly accurate, such advice does not render that attorney's performance constitutionally inadequate."

The longstanding test for determining the validity of a guilty plea is "whether the plea represents a voluntary and intelligent choice among the alternative courses of action open to the defendant." Here petitioner does not contend that his plea was "involuntary" or "unintelligent" simply because the State through its officials failed to supply him with information about his parole eligibility date. We have never held that the United States Constitution requires the State to furnish a defendant with information about parole eligibility in order for the defendant's plea of guilty to be voluntary, and indeed such a constitutional requirement would be inconsistent with the current rules of procedure governing the entry of guilty pleas in the federal courts. Instead, petitioner relies entirely on the claim that his plea was "involuntary" as a result of ineffective assistance of counsel because his attorney supplied him with information about parole eligibility that was erroneous. Where, as here, a defendant is represented by counsel during the plea process and enters his plea upon the advice of counsel, the voluntariness of the plea depends on whether counsel's advice "was within the range of competence demanded of attorneys in criminal cases."

Attorney errors come in an infinite variety and are as likely to be utterly harmless in a particular case as they are to be prejudicial. Representation is an art, and an act or omission that is unprofessional in one case may be sound or even brilliant in another. "Even if a defendant shows that particular errors of counsel were unreasonable, therefore, the defendant must show that they actually had an adverse effect on the defense."

[As stated] in United States v. Timmreck, 441 U.S. 780 (1979):

> Every inroad on the concept of finality undermines confidence in the integrity of our procedures; and, by increasing the volume of judicial work, inevitably delays and impairs the orderly administration of justice. The impact is greatest when new grounds for setting aside guilty pleas are approved because the vast majority of criminal convictions result from such pleas.

We hold, therefore, that . . . in order to satisfy the "prejudice" requirement, the defendant must show that there is a reasonable probability that, but for counsel's errors, he would not have pleaded guilty and would have insisted on going to trial.

Petitioner did not allege in his habeas petition that, had counsel correctly informed him about his parole eligibility date, he would have pleaded not guilty and insisted on going to trial. He alleged no special circumstances that might support the conclusion that he placed particular emphasis on his parole eligibility in deciding whether or not to plead guilty. Indeed, petitioner's mistaken belief that he would become eligible for parole after serving one-third of his sentence would seem to have affected not only his calculation of the time he likely would serve if sentenced pursuant to the proposed plea agreement, but also his calculation of the time he likely would serve if he went to trial and were convicted.

Because petitioner in this case failed to allege the kind of "prejudice" necessary to satisfy [his burden, his petition was properly denied].

PADILLA v. KENTUCKY

130 S. Ct. 1473 (2010)

Justice STEVENS delivered the opinion of the Court.

Petitioner Jose Padilla, a native of Honduras, has been a lawful permanent resident of the United States for more than 40 years. Padilla served this Nation with honor as a member of the U. S. Armed Forces during the Vietnam War. He now faces deportation after pleading guilty to the transportation of a large amount of marijuana in his tractor-trailer in the Commonwealth of Kentucky.

In this postconviction proceeding, Padilla claims that his counsel not only failed to advise him of this consequence prior to his entering the plea, but also told him that he "did not have to worry about immigration status since he had been in the country so long." Padilla relied on his counsel's erroneous advice when he pleaded guilty to the drug charges that made his deportation virtually mandatory. He alleges that he would have insisted on going to trial if he had not received incorrect advice from his attorney.

Assuming the truth of his allegations, the Supreme Court of Kentucky denied Padilla postconviction relief without the benefit of an evidentiary hearing. The court held that the *Sixth Amendment's* guarantee of effective assistance of counsel does not protect a criminal defendant from erroneous advice about deportation because it is merely a "collateral" consequence of his conviction. In its view, neither counsel's failure to advise petitioner about the possibility of removal, nor counsel's incorrect advice, could provide a basis for relief.

We granted certiorari, to decide whether, as a matter of federal law, Padilla's counsel had an obligation to advise him that the offense to which he was pleading guilty would result in his removal from this country. We agree with Padilla that constitutionally competent counsel would have advised him that his conviction for drug distribution made him subject to automatic deportation. Whether he is entitled to relief depends on whether he has been prejudiced, a matter that we do not address.

I

The landscape of federal immigration law has changed dramatically over the last 90 years. While once there was only a narrow class of deportable offenses and judges wielded broad discretionary authority to prevent deportation, immigration reforms over time have expanded the class of deportable offenses and limited the authority of judges to alleviate the harsh consequences of deportation. The "drastic measure" of deportation or removal is now virtually inevitable for a vast number of noncitizens convicted of crimes.

[C]hanges to our immigration law have dramatically raised the stakes of a noncitizen's criminal conviction. The importance of accurate legal advice for noncitizens accused of crimes has never been more important. These changes confirm our view that as a matter of federal law, deportation is an integral part—indeed, sometimes the most important part—of the penalty that may be imposed on noncitizen defendants who plead guilty to specified crimes.

II

Before deciding whether to plead guilty, a defendant is entitled to "the effective assistance of competent counsel." The Supreme Court of Kentucky rejected Padilla's ineffectiveness claim on the ground that the advice he sought about the risk of deportation concerned only collateral matters, *i.e.*, those matters not within the sentencing authority of the state trial court.

We, however, have never applied a distinction between direct and collateral consequences to define the scope of constitutionally "reasonable professional assistance" required under *Strickland.* Whether that distinction is appropriate is a question we need not consider in this case because of the unique nature of deportation.

We have long recognized that deportation is a particularly severe "penalty," but it is not, in a strict sense, a criminal sanction. Although removal proceedings are civil in nature, deportation is nevertheless intimately related to the criminal process. Our law has enmeshed criminal convictions and the penalty of deportation for nearly a century. And, importantly, recent changes in our immigration law have made removal nearly an automatic result for a broad class of noncitizen offenders. Thus, we find it "most difficult" to divorce the penalty from the conviction in the deportation context.

Deportation as a consequence of a criminal conviction is, because of its close connection to the criminal process, uniquely difficult to classify as either a direct or a collateral consequence. The collateral versus direct distinction is thus ill-suited to evaluating a *Strickland* claim concerning the specific risk of deportation. We conclude that advice regarding deportation is not categorically removed from the ambit of the *Sixth Amendment* right to counsel. *Strickland* applies to Padilla's claim.

III

Under *Strickland,* we first determine whether counsel's representation "fell below an objective standard of reasonableness." Then we ask whether "there is a reasonable probability that, but for counsel's unprofessional errors, the result of the proceeding would have been different."

The weight of prevailing professional norms supports the view that counsel must advise her client regarding the risk of deportation. "[A]uthorities of every stripe — including the American Bar Association, criminal defense and public defender organizations, authoritative treatises, and state and city bar publications — universally require defense attorneys to advise as to the risk of deportation consequences for non-citizen clients. . . ."

In the instant case, the terms of the relevant immigration statute are succinct, clear, and explicit in defining the removal consequence for Padilla's conviction. Padilla's counsel could have easily determined that his plea would make him eligible for deportation simply from reading the text of the statute, which addresses not some broad classification of crimes but specifically commands removal for all controlled substances convictions except for the most trivial of marijuana possession offenses. Instead, Padilla's counsel provided him false assurance that his conviction would not result in his removal from this country. This is not a hard case in which to find deficiency: The consequences of Padilla's plea could easily be determined from reading the removal statute, his deportation was presumptively mandatory, and his counsel's advice was incorrect.

V

[W]e have little difficulty concluding that Padilla has sufficiently alleged that his counsel was constitutionally deficient. Whether Padilla is entitled to relief will depend on whether he can demonstrate prejudice. The judgment of the Supreme Court of Kentucky is reversed, and the case is remanded for further proceedings not inconsistent with this opinion.

Although a defendant may claim ineffective assistance of counsel to challenge a guilty plea, the primary protection for a defendant lies not in a subsequent constitutional challenge but in reliance on statutory rules designed to protect a defendant's constitutional rights. In the federal system, Federal Rule of Criminal Procedure 11 governs the procedures required for a valid guilty plea.

D.   RULE 11 AND THE PROCEDURAL REQUIREMENTS FOR ENTERING GUILTY PLEAS

A guilty plea is valid only if it demonstrates on the record that the defendant has knowingly and voluntarily waived his constitutional rights. Federal Rule of Criminal Procedure 11 is designed to accomplish this goal. Rule 11(b)(1) requires that the judge address the defendant personally in open court to inform the defendant, and to determine that the defendant personally understands, that the defendant will be waiving the following rights by pleading guilty:[17]

1.   The right not to plead guilty
2.   The right to a jury trial
3.   The right to be represented by counsel
4.   The nature of the charge to which the defendant is pleading
5.   Any mandatory minimum penalty
6.   Any maximum possible penalty
7.   The defendant's waiver of certain appeal rights
8.   The government's right to use the defendant's statements in a perjury prosecution

The court must also advise the defendant of the likely consequences of pleading guilty and establish that there is a factual basis for the plea. In addition, the court must ensure that the plea is voluntary and did not result from force, threats of force, or promises other than those in a plea agreement. Finally, the plea must be entered on the record.

Ordinarily, the defendant will establish the factual basis for the guilty plea by briefly describing his criminal actions. In some courts, however, the prosecutor will set forth the factual basis for the plea. In North Carolina v. Alford,

---

17. A sample guilty plea transcript is set forth in the Statutory Supplement.

400 U.S. 25 (1970), the Court held that as long as the record reflects a factual basis for a guilty plea, the defendant need not personally admit his guilt for the guilty plea to be valid. Alford, who was indicted for first-degree murder, chose to plead guilty to avoid the death penalty. Although Alford was not willing to admit that he committed the murder, the court was presented with testimony that strongly indicated the defendant's guilt. Alford later claimed that his plea was not voluntary because he had not admitted to the murder. Justice White, expressing the view of six members of the court, held that there was no constitutional error in accepting a guilty plea that contained a protestation of innocence when, as in Alford's case, the defendant intelligently concluded that his interests required entry of a guilty plea and the record before the judge contained strong evidence of actual guilt.

A defendant must be mentally competent to plead guilty. In Godinez v. Moran, 509 U.S. 389 (1993), the Supreme Court held that the competency standard for pleading guilty is no higher than the competency standard for standing trial. That standard requires that the defendant understand the proceedings against him and be able to consult with his lawyer with a reasonable degree of rational understanding. *See generally* Dusky v. United States, 362 U.S. 402 (1960) (per curiam).

Finally, a defendant has only limited discovery rights before pleading guilty. As discussed in Chapter 4, in United States v. Ruiz, 536 U.S. 622 (2002), the Supreme Court held that the Constitution does not require prosecutors to disclose "impeachment information relating to any informants or other witnesses" before entering into a binding plea agreement with the defendant. The Supreme Court has not yet decided whether directly exculpatory evidence must be revealed, but lower courts have allowed defendants to withdraw their guilty pleas when the prosecutor failed to disclose exculpatory information prior to the defendant's guilty plea. *See, e.g.,* State v. Harris, 266 Wis. 2d 200, 667 N.W. 813 (Wis. App. 2003). Given that innocent people sometimes plead guilty,[18] it is important to consider carefully how much information a defendant should have before entering a knowing and voluntary plea.

E. REMEDIES FOR VIOLATIONS OF PLEA AGREEMENTS

Plea agreements are treated as contracts and are enforceable under contract principles. Thus, if a guilty plea is based on a plea agreement, both the prosecution and defense have the right to enforce that agreement.

---

18. *See generally* Andrew D. Leipold, *How the Pretrial Process Contributes to Wrongful Convictions*, 42 Am. Crim. L. Rev. 1123 (2005).

SANTOBELLO v. NEW YORK
404 U.S. 257 (1971)

Chief Justice BURGER delivered the opinion of the Court.

We granted certiorari in this case to determine whether the State's failure to keep a commitment concerning the sentence recommendation on a guilty plea required a new trial.

The facts are not in dispute. The State of New York indicted petitioner in 1969 on two felony counts, Promoting Gambling in the First Degree, and Possession of Gambling Records in the First Degree. Petitioner first entered a plea of not guilty to both counts. After negotiations, the Assistant District Attorney in charge of the case agreed to permit petitioner to plead guilty to a lesser-included offense, Possession of Gambling Records in the Second Degree, conviction of which would carry a maximum prison sentence of one year. The prosecutor agreed to make no recommendation as to the sentence.

On June 16, 1969, petitioner accordingly withdrew his plea of not guilty and entered a plea of guilty to the lesser charge. At [sentencing], another prosecutor had replaced the prosecutor who had negotiated the plea. The new prosecutor recommended the maximum one-year sentence. In making this recommendation, he cited petitioner's criminal record and alleged links with organized crime. Defense counsel immediately objected on the ground that the State had promised petitioner before the plea was entered that there would be no sentence recommendation by the prosecution. He sought to adjourn the sentence hearing in order to have time to prepare proof of the first prosecutor's promise. The second prosecutor, apparently ignorant of his colleague's commitment, argued that there was nothing in the record to support petitioner's claim of a promise, but the State, in subsequent proceedings, has not contested that such a promise was made.

The sentencing judge ended discussion, with the following statement, quoting extensively from the presentence report:

"[Defense Counsel], I am not at all influenced by what the District Attorney says, so that there is no need to adjourn the sentence, and there is no need to have any testimony. It doesn't make a particle of difference what the District Attorney says he will do, or what he doesn't do.

"I have here . . . a probation report. I have here a history of a long, long serious criminal record. I have here a picture of the life history of this man. . . .

"'He is unamenable to supervision in the community. He is a professional criminal.'" Under the plea, I can only send him to the New York City Correctional Institution for men for one year, which I am hereby doing."

The judge then imposed the maximum sentence of one year.

This record represents another example of an unfortunate lapse in orderly prosecutorial procedures, in part, no doubt, because of the enormous increase in the workload of the often understaffed prosecutor's offices.

The heavy workload may well explain these episodes, but it does not excuse them. The disposition of criminal charges by agreement between the prosecutor and the accused, sometimes loosely called "plea bargaining," is an essential component of the administration of justice. Properly administered, it is to be encouraged. If every criminal charge were subjected to a full-scale trial, the States and the Federal Government would need to multiply by many times the number of judges and court facilities.

Disposition of charges after plea discussions is not only an essential part of the process but a highly desirable part for many reasons. It leads to prompt and largely final disposition of most criminal cases; it avoids much of the corrosive impact of enforced idleness during pretrial confinement for those who are denied release pending trial; it protects the public from those accused persons who are prone to continue criminal conduct even while on pretrial release; and, by shortening the time between charge and disposition, it enhances whatever may be the rehabilitative prospects of the guilty when they are ultimately imprisoned. *See* Brady v. United States (1970). [W]hen a plea rests in any significant degree on a promise or agreement of the prosecutor, so that it can be said to be part of the inducement or consideration, such promise must be fulfilled.

On this record, petitioner "bargained" and negotiated for a particular plea in order to secure dismissal of more serious charges, but also on condition that no sentence recommendation would be made by the prosecutor. It is now conceded that the promise to abstain from a recommendation was made, and at this stage the prosecution is not in a good position to argue that its inadvertent breach of agreement is immaterial. The staff lawyers in a prosecutor's office have the burden of "letting the left hand know what the right hand is doing" or has done. That the breach of agreement was inadvertent does not lessen its impact.

We need not reach the question whether the sentencing judge would or would not have been influenced had he known all the details of the negotiations for the plea. He stated that the prosecutor's recommendation did not influence him and we have no reason to doubt that. Nevertheless, we conclude that the interests of justice and appropriate recognition of the duties of the prosecution in relation to promises made in the negotiation of pleas of guilty will be best served by remanding the case to the state courts for further consideration. The ultimate relief to which petitioner is entitled we leave to the discretion of the state court, which is in a better position to decide whether the circumstances of this case require only that there be specific performance of the agreement on the plea, in which case petitioner should be resentenced by a different judge, or whether, in the view of the state court, the circumstances require granting the relief sought by petitioner, i.e., the opportunity to withdraw his plea of guilty. We emphasize that this is in no sense to question the fairness of the sentencing judge; the fault here rests on the prosecutor, not on the sentencing judge.

The judgment is vacated and the case is remanded for reconsideration not inconsistent with this opinion.

Justice DOUGLAS, concurring.

I join the opinion of the Court and add only a word. [There] is no excuse for the default merely because a member of the prosecutor's staff who was not a party to the "plea bargain" was in charge of the case when it came before the New York court. The staff of the prosecution is a unit and each member must be presumed to know the commitments made by any other member.

[It] is . . . clear that a prosecutor's promise may deprive a guilty plea of the "character of a voluntary act." Where the "plea bargain" is not kept by the prosecutor, the sentence must be vacated and the state court will decide in light of the circumstances of each case whether due process requires (a) that there be specific performance of the plea bargain or (b) that the defendant be given the option to go to trial on the original charges. One alternative may do justice in one case, and the other in a different case. In choosing a remedy, however, a court ought to accord a defendant's preference considerable, if not controlling, weight inasmuch as the fundamental rights flouted by a prosecutor's breach of a plea bargain are those of the defendant, not of the State.

Just as the Court found in Santobello v. New York that a defendant is entitled to have a plea agreement enforced, the Court held in Ricketts v. Adamson that the defendant can be held to his side of the bargain.

RICKETTS v. ADAMSON
483 U.S. 1 (1987)

Justice WHITE delivered the opinion of the Court.

The question for decision is whether the Double Jeopardy Clause bars the prosecution of respondent for first-degree murder following his breach of a plea agreement. The Court of Appeals for the Ninth Circuit held that the prosecution of respondent violated double jeopardy principles and directed the issuance of a writ of habeas corpus. We reverse.

In 1976, Donald Bolles, a reporter for the Arizona Republic, was fatally injured when a dynamite bomb exploded underneath his car. Respondent was arrested and charged with first-degree murder in connection with Bolles' death. Shortly after his trial had commenced, while jury selection was underway, respondent and the state prosecutor reached an agreement whereby respondent agreed to plead guilty to a charge of second-degree murder and to testify against two other individuals — Max Dunlap and James Robison — who were allegedly involved in Bolles' murder. Specifically, respondent agreed to "testify fully and completely in any Court, State or Federal, when requested by proper authorities against any and all parties involved in the murder of Don Bolles. . . ." The agreement provided that "should the defendant refuse to testify or should he at any time testify untruthfully . . . then this entire agreement is null and void and the original charge will be automatically reinstated." The parties agreed that respondent would receive a prison sentence of 48-49 years, with a total incarceration time of 20 years and 2 months. In January 1977, the state trial court accepted the plea agreement and the proposed sentence, but withheld imposition of the sentence. Thereafter, respondent testified as obligated under the agreement, and both Dunlap and Robison were convicted of the first-degree murder of Bolles. While their convictions and sentences were on appeal, the trial court, upon motion of the State, sentenced respondent. In February 1980, the Arizona Supreme Court reversed the convictions of Dunlap and Robison and remanded their cases for retrial. This event sparked the dispute now before us.

The State sought respondent's cooperation and testimony in preparation for the retrial of Dunlap and Robison. On April 3, 1980, however, respondent's counsel informed the prosecutor that respondent believed his obligation to provide testimony under the agreement had terminated when he was sentenced. Respondent would again testify against Dunlap and Robison only if certain conditions were met, including, among others, that the State release him from custody following the retrial. The State then informed respondent's attorney on April 9, 1980, that it deemed respondent to be in breach of the plea agreement. On April 18, 1980, the State called respondent to testify in pretrial proceedings. In response to questions, and upon advice of counsel, respondent invoked his Fifth Amendment privilege against self-incrimination.

On May 8, 1980, the State filed a new information charging respondent with first-degree murder. Respondent's motion to quash the information on double jeopardy grounds was denied. The court rejected respondent's double jeopardy claim, holding that the plea agreement "by its very terms waives the defense of double jeopardy if the agreement is violated."

After these rulings, respondent offered to testify at the retrials, but the State declined his offer. Respondent was then convicted of first-degree murder and sentenced to death.

Under the terms of the plea agreement, both parties bargained for and received substantial benefits. The State obtained respondent's guilty plea and his promise to testify against "any and all parties involved in the murder of Don Bolles" and in certain specified other crimes. Respondent, a direct participant in a premeditated and brutal murder, received a specified prison sentence accompanied with a guarantee that he would serve actual incarceration time of 20 years and 2 months. He further obtained the State's promise that he would not be prosecuted for his involvement in certain other crimes.

The agreement specifies in two separate paragraphs the consequences that would flow from respondent's breach of his promises. Paragraph 5 provides that if respondent refused to testify, "this entire agreement is null and void and the original charge will be automatically reinstated."

Similarly, Paragraph 15 of the agreement states that "in the event this agreement becomes null and void, then the parties shall be returned to the positions they were in before this agreement." Respondent unquestionably understood the meaning of these provisions. At the plea hearing, the trial judge read the plea agreement to respondent, line by line, and pointedly asked respondent whether he understood the provisions in Paragraphs 5 and 15. Respondent replied "Yes, sir," to each question.

The State did not force the breach; respondent chose, perhaps for strategic reasons or as a gamble, to advance an interpretation of the agreement that proved erroneous. And, there is no indication that respondent did not fully understand the potential seriousness of the position he adopted. In the April 3 letter, respondent's counsel advised the prosecutor that respondent "is fully aware of the fact that your office may feel that he has not completed his obligations under the plea agreement . . . and, further, that your office may attempt to withdraw the plea agreement from him, [and] that he may be prosecuted for the killing of Donald Bolles on a first degree murder charge." This statement of respondent's awareness of the operative terms of the plea agreement only underscores that which respondent's plea hearing made evident: respondent clearly appreciated and understood the consequences were he found to be in breach of the agreement.

Finally, it is of no moment that following the Arizona Supreme Court's decision respondent offered to comply with the terms of the agreement. At this point, respondent's second-degree murder conviction had already been ordered vacated and the original charge reinstated. The parties did not agree that respondent would be relieved from the consequences of his refusal to testify if he were able to advance a colorable argument that a testimonial obligation was not owing. The parties could have struck a different bargain, but permitting the State to enforce the agreement the parties actually made does not violate the Double Jeopardy Clause.

Justice BRENNAN, with whom Justice MARSHALL, Justice BLACKMUN, and Justice STEVENS join, dissenting.

The critical question in this case is whether Adamson ever breached his plea agreement. Only by demonstrating that such a breach occurred can it plausibly be argued that Adamson waived his rights under the Double Jeopardy Clause. By simply assuming that such a breach occurred, the Court ignores the only important issue in this case.

[T]he agreement does not contain an explicit waiver of all double jeopardy protection. Adamson's interpretation of the agreement — that he was not required to testify at the retrials of Max Dunlap and James Robison — was reasonable. Nothing in the plea agreement explicitly stated that Adamson was required to provide testimony should retrials prove necessary. At the time the State demanded that Adamson testify in the retrials, Adamson had been transferred from the custody of the Pima County Sheriff. Adamson therefore could reasonably conclude that he had provided all the testimony required by the agreement, and that, as he communicated to the State by letter of

April 3, 1980, the testimony demanded by the State went beyond his duties under the agreement.[19] Adamson's interpretation of the agreement was "reasonabl[e]," and was supported by the plain language of the agreement, "logic, and common sense."

[T]he law of commercial contract may in some cases prove useful as an analogy or point of departure in construing a plea agreement, or in framing the terms of the debate. [But] the values that underlie commercial contract law, and that govern the relations between economic actors, are not coextensive with those that underlie the Due Process Clause. Unlike some commercial contracts, plea agreements must be construed in light of the rights and obligations created by the Constitution.

Even if one assumes, *arguendo*, that Adamson breached his plea agreement by offering an erroneous interpretation of that agreement, it still does not follow that the State was entitled to retry Adamson on charges of first-degree murder. [I]mmediately following the decision of the Arizona Supreme Court adopting the State's construction of the plea agreement, Adamson sent a letter to the State stating that he was ready and willing to testify. At this point, there was no obstacle to proceeding with the retrials of Dunlap and Robison; each case had been dismissed without prejudice to refiling, and only about one month's delay had resulted from the dispute over the scope of the plea agreement. Thus, what the State sought from Adamson — testimony in the Dunlap and Robison trials — was available to it.

The State decided instead to abandon the prosecution of Dunlap and Robison, and to capitalize on what it regarded as Adamson's breach by seeking the death penalty against him. No doubt it seemed easier to proceed against Adamson at that point, since the State had the benefit of his exhaustive testimony about his role in the murder of Don Bolles. But even in the world of commercial contracts it has long been settled that the party injured by a breach must nevertheless take all reasonable steps to minimize the consequent damage.

The Court's decision flouts the law of contract, due process, and double jeopardy. It reflects a world where individuals enter agreements with the State only at their peril, where the Constitution does not demand of the State the minimal good faith and responsibility that the common law imposes on commercial enterprises, and where, in blind deference to state courts and prosecutors, this Court abdicates its duty to uphold the Constitution. I dissent.

---

19. Prior to sentencing, Adamson had provided extensive testimony for the State. He testified that he had "made 14 court appearances . . . on five separate cases consisting of approximately 31 days of testimony. . . . Of the 81 or so jurors who have heard my testimony all have returned guilty verdicts in each case resulting in seven convictions. I have been cross-examined under oath for approximately 190 hours . . . by 22 different attorneys. . . . I have cooperated in approximately 205 interrogative sessions. . . . Fifty-five of these have been formal face-to-face in-depth question and answer sessions, approximately." [Footnote by the Court.]

F. WITHDRAWAL OF GUILTY PLEAS

Ordinarily, after a defendant pleads guilty, the final step in the criminal process is for the defendant to be sentenced. A guilty plea is a waiver of the defendant's right to challenge the prosecution's case, unless the defendant has entered a conditional plea reserving issues for appeal.

Occasionally, defendants want to withdraw their guilty pleas after they are entered. Federal Rule of Criminal Procedure 11 provides that, before a guilty plea is accepted, the defendant may withdraw a guilty plea for any reason. However, once a defendant has entered his plea and the court has accepted it, a guilty plea may be withdrawn only for a "fair and just" reason.

Judges have broad latitude in deciding whether to allow the withdrawal of a guilty plea after they have accepted it. In making this decision, a court must consider the need for finality in guilty pleas, the defendant's reasons for withdrawing the plea, and the prejudice to the prosecution by allowing withdrawal of the plea.

If a defendant is not allowed to withdraw a guilty plea, his only options are to appeal the court's decision or to raise a collateral challenge to the plea. Not all errors in guilty pleas will result in reversals of convictions, however. Errors that do not affect a defendant's "substantial rights" are regarded as harmless. While the reviewing court will ordinarily rely only on the transcript of a plea to determine whether the plea was properly entered, if a defendant does not object to his plea, the court can look outside the transcript.

For example, in United States v. Vonn, 535 U.S. 55 (2002), defendant Alphonso Vonn did not object when the judge took his guilty plea to a firearm charge, even though the judge failed to mention that Vonn had a right to counsel if he went to trial. Instead, Vonn raised the issue on appeal after the trial court denied Vonn's motion to withdraw his guilty plea. The Supreme Court held that because defendant did not make an objection to the trial court, it was his burden to satisfy the plain-error rule. The Supreme Court found that Vonn could not satisfy that burden because transcripts of other proceedings in his case demonstrated that Vonn had been advised on multiple occasions of his right to counsel. He was advised at his initial appearance before the magistrate judge and twice at his first arraignment. At least four times Vonn or his counsel either affirmed that Vonn had heard or read a statement of his rights and understood what they were. Because the overall record of the case demonstrated that Vonn knew he had the right to counsel, the trial court's failure to advise Vonn of this right at the guilty plea hearing did not undermine his guilty plea. As Justice Souter wrote for a unanimous Court, a defendant must be "on his toes" to ensure that the court correctly conducts the plea hearing. If a defendant is aware of a mistake in the plea procedures at the time they are conducted, he must object when the problem can still be fixed. Otherwise, the court will look to the rest of the defendant's case record to determine whether the defendant was aware of his rights at the time of the guilty plea.

CHAPTER
6

SPEEDY TRIAL RIGHTS

A. INTRODUCTION

The Sixth Amendment provides that "[i]n all criminal prosecutions, the accused shall enjoy the right to a speedy and public trial."[1] The Framers considered the right to a speedy trial to be so important that they included it as a basic guarantee in the Bill of Rights. Yet they did not spell out in the Sixth Amendment what standard should be used to determine whether a defendant's right has been violated. Rather, like other constitutional rights, it was left to the Supreme Court to determine the contours of the right to a speedy trial. In making this decision, the Court turned to the purposes served by a speedy trial right.

Section B of this chapter focuses on the policy concerns underlying the right to a speedy trial. Whose interests does it serve? Why is it so important that criminal cases be processed in an expeditious manner? These policy interests underlie the standards created by the Court for speedy trial rights.

Although we speak generally about the "right to a speedy trial," there are really two standards at issue: (1) rules governing delay during the period from the commitment of the crime until arrest or formal charging and (2) rules governing delays during the period from charging until trial. Section C examines each of these types of delay and the standards that apply.

Finally, section D discusses the remedy for a speedy trial violation and how that remedy affects the standards used to determine whether a defendant's speedy trial rights have been violated.

B. WHY SPEEDY TRIAL RIGHTS MATTER

To understand why speedy trial rights matter, it is useful to put oneself in the shoes of those most affected by the criminal justice process. If a crime occurs

---

1. The Sixth Amendment right to a speedy trial is a fundamental right that applies to states. *See* Klopfer v. North Carolina, 386 U.S. 213 (1967).

and it takes years for it to be charged or to go to trial, how are the interests of the defendant, victim, prosecutor, witnesses, and public affected? In making that determination, consider the speedy trial concerns raised by the following two cases.

RIGHT TO A SPEEDY TRIAL? JUSTICE DELAYED

The Atlanta Journal-Constitution, Oct. 14, 2007

With his monotone speech, robotic movements, and a plastic tube snaking from his nostrils to a battery-powered oxygen source, Edward Kramer is beginning to resemble the science-fiction characters he writes about.

He's well-known as a science-fiction author and founder of DragonCon, a sci-fi, fantasy and gaming convention that brings thousands of visitors and millions of dollars to Atlanta every year.

Yet Kramer is also known for something else: Investigators say he molested three teenage boys.

Kramer maintains his innocence.

Police first arrested Kramer on Aug. 25, 2000 — more than seven years ago — but the case has not yet gone to trial.

Legal experts say a seven-year delay is unusual and potentially damaging, as memories fade and evidence deteriorates. Former U.S. Rep. Bob Barr, a former federal prosecutor, filed court papers this year that decry "an overwhelming sense of injustice" toward Kramer.

Prosecutors say Kramer has mischaracterized his illness and orchestrated several delays to stave off a possible 60-year prison sentence.

Nevertheless, "the amount of time here raises eyebrows," said Ron Carlson, a criminal law professor at the University of Georgia.

As he waits for his day in court, Kramer lives in his two-story home in Duluth, where he's been under house arrest since early 2001.

He has shelled out more than $250,000 in legal fees, according to a Web site his supporters maintain, and he says he's running out of money.

He no longer has an active role with DragonCon — Kramer said he resigned as convention chairman in 2000 to avoid bringing the event negative publicity.

"I'm a whole lot weaker now than I was before," Kramer said in an interview this month as he sat tethered to an oxygen tank under the shade of a patio umbrella.

He said he suffers debilitating back pain, the result of spinal injuries he suffered in jail and in a subsequent car accident. The spinal injuries caused a partial paralysis of his diaphragm, which makes it difficult to breathe.

"It's like my life has essentially halted for seven years waiting for this to end," Kramer said.

The lives of two brothers also have changed. They were 13 and 15 when Kramer began dating their mother.

Kramer dazzled them with action figures, sci-fi memorabilia and celebrity connections, their mother said. The boys told police that Kramer took advantage of them during sleepovers.

Now the brothers are in their 20s and in the Army. One serves in South Korea. The other will be deployed to Iraq in February.

STATE LOSES APPEAL IN CHILD-RAPE CASE

Kate Wilson, Albuquerque Journal, Oct. 14, 2006

The New Mexico Court of Appeals has upheld a 2005 ruling by Santa Fe state District Judge Michael Vigil, who threw out a case of alleged sex abuse after he found the defendant's speedy trial rights had been violated.

Paul Stock sat in jail for nearly 3 1/2 years while a series of overburdened public defenders failed to move the case along.

Stock had been charged with raping a preteen.

"The delay is in part attributable to the neglect of his overworked public defenders," Appeals Court Judge Lynn Pickard states in the Sept. 29 ruling.

But prosecutors were also to blame, the appeals court judge wrote.

"It is ultimately the state's burden to make sure that defendants are brought to trial in a timely manner," Pickard wrote.

"Throughout this case, the state did little or nothing to ascertain what was happening in the case or to move the case forward. . . . We think the state's inaction in this case can be characterized as "bureaucratic indifference," which we have held to weigh against the state more heavily than mere negligence."

The delays in the case started in February 2001, when Stock's defense counsel requested an extension of time so Stock's competency could be evaluated.

At [a] hearing [regarding the delay] in August 2005, Stock's series of three attorneys testified. They carried heavy case loads, often up to 300 each. They said they didn't have the resources to both pursue the issue of competency and investigate the merits of the case.

After the hearing, Vigil dismissed the case again, saying, "It is humanly impossible for lawyers to practice law under the conditions that we're asking them to practice law."

Vigil said he would continue dismissing cases that were not properly prosecuted.

JUDGE DISMISSES MOLESTATION CASE — AGAIN

Jason Auslander, Santa Fe New Mexican, Aug. 24, 2005

The girl's father said after Tuesday's hearing that the dismissal felt "like an injustice" to his daughter, whom Stock was accused of abusing beginning when she was 7, as well as the rest of his family. He said his daughter has been in therapy for five years, and is undergoing treatment at a voluntary foster-care facility. He said he placed 70 percent of the blame for the dismissal on the defense and 30 percent on the prosecution.

In the end, Vigil dismissed the case against Stock "reluctantly," saying he felt badly that the alleged victim in the case wouldn't get her day in court. He also chastised prosecutors for letting Stock sit in jail for so long, saying they had an obligation to schedule a hearing to determine the status of the case.

"The Constitution requires minimum standards be followed and this case falls way below them," Vigil said.

———————

As these excerpts highlight, delay in the criminal justice process can detrimentally affect the defense, the prosecution, victims, witnesses, courts, and the public.

1. Impact on the Defendant

There are many ways that a defendant can be prejudiced by pretrial delay. First, and foremost, if a defendant is in custody, he loses his liberty even though a jury has not found him guilty of any crime. While in custody, a defendant may lose his livelihood and the support of his family and community. Pretrial delay also prolongs the anxiety a defendant faces before trial. Even defendants who are not in custody suffer from this anxiety and must bear the stigma of being charged with a crime. Long-term pretrial delay is demoralizing; a defendant must live under a cloud of suspicion until his name is cleared.

Second, pretrial delay can result in the loss of evidence. Witnesses' memories tend to fade with time. Physical evidence may disappear and a defendant's own memory of what occurred may become blurred. A defendant has a due process right to present a defense, but this cannot be done if pretrial delay has made it impossible to secure the evidence needed for a defense.

2. Impact on the Prosecution and Witnesses

Defendants, of course, are not the only ones who suffer from pretrial delay. In fact, sometimes defendants want a delay so that it will be harder for the prosecution to present its case and meet its burden of proof beyond a reasonable doubt.

By its terms, the Sixth Amendment, like other guarantees in the Bill of Rights, only affords defendants the right to a speedy trial. This does not mean, however, that the prosecution and the public don't also have strong policy interests in a speedy trial. In addition to wanting to preserve evidence and witness testimony, prosecutors must also be concerned about the emotional toll of long delays on victims and other witnesses. Victims cannot put their experiences behind them if the criminal matter is still not resolved by the court.

3.   Impact on the Public

Finally, delays in pursuing cases can impact on the public's confidence in the criminal justice system. Justice delayed is frequently viewed as justice denied. The longer it takes for a case to grind through the criminal justice system, the more resources are dedicated to that case and thus unavailable for other matters. Speedy trial delay causes congestion in the courts and undermines the efficiency of the criminal justice system.

C.   DUE PROCESS AND SPEEDY TRIAL RIGHTS

There are two periods of delay that may occur in a criminal proceeding. First, there is the period of time from commitment of the crime until charges are filed. This is referred to as "pre-charging delay." Although this delay may have an impact on a defendant's right to a fair trial, it is not covered by the defendant's Sixth Amendment right to a speedy trial. Rather, for reasons explained in the next section, the Supreme Court has held that speedy trial rights are not triggered until after a defendant has been formally charged. The period of pre-charge delay is covered by statutes of limitations and the constitutional right to due process.

The second period of delay runs from the filing of charges until the time that trial begins. This period of time is covered by the Sixth Amendment right to a speedy trial. It is often covered by Speedy Trial Acts that provide statutory limits on pretrial delay.

1.   Pre-Charging Delay, Due Process Rights, and Statutes of Limitations

The Sixth Amendment right to a speedy trial does not cover all delay from the time that a defendant commits a crime until the defendant is brought to trial. Rather, the time from when a defendant commits a crime until the defendant is charged is treated differently. In United States v. Marion, the Supreme Court explained when speedy trials actually begin and what, if any, constitutional protection there is for a defendant for pre-charge delay.

UNITED STATES v. MARION
404 U.S. 307 (1971)

Justice WHITE delivered the opinion of the Court.

[Appellees] claim that their rights to a speedy trial were violated by the period of approximately three years between the end of the criminal [fraud] scheme charged and the return of the indictment; it is argued that this delay is so substantial and inherently prejudicial that the Sixth Amendment required the dismissal of the indictment. In our view, however, the Sixth

Amendment speedy trial provision has no application until the putative defendant in some way becomes an "accused," an event that occurred in this case only when the appellees were indicted.

The Sixth Amendment provides that "in all criminal prosecutions, the accused shall enjoy the right to a speedy and public trial. . . ." On its face, the protection of the Amendment is activated only when a criminal prosecution has begun and extends only to those persons who have been "accused" in the course of that prosecution. These provisions would seem to afford no protection to those not yet accused, nor would they seem to require the Government to discover, investigate, and accuse any person within any particular period of time. The Amendment would appear to guarantee to a criminal defendant that the Government will move with the dispatch that is appropriate to assure him an early and proper disposition of the charges against him.

The framers could hardly have selected less appropriate language if they had intended the speedy trial provision to protect against pre-accusation delay. No opinions of this Court intimate support for appellees' thesis, and the courts of appeals that have considered the question in constitutional terms have never reversed a conviction or dismissed an indictment solely on the basis of the Sixth Amendment's speedy trial provision where only pre-indictment delay was involved.

III

Invocation of the speedy trial provision thus need not await indictment, information, or other formal charge. But we decline to extend the reach of the amendment to the period prior to arrest. Until this event occurs, a citizen suffers no restraints on his liberty and is not the subject of public accusation: his situation does not compare with that of a defendant who has been arrested and held to answer. Passage of time, whether before or after arrest, may impair memories, cause evidence to be lost, deprive the defendant of witnesses, and otherwise interfere with his ability to defend himself. But this possibility of prejudice at trial is not itself sufficient reason to wrench the Sixth Amendment from its proper context.

The law has provided other mechanisms to guard against possible as distinguished from actual prejudice resulting from the passage of time between crime and arrest or charge. As we said, "the applicable statute of limitations . . . is . . . the primary guarantee against bringing overly stale criminal charges." Such statutes represent legislative assessments of relative interests of the State and the defendant in administering and receiving justice; they "are made for the repose of society and the protection of those who may [during the limitation] . . . have lost their means of defence." These statutes provide predictability by specifying a limit beyond which there is an irrebuttable presumption that a defendant's right to a fair trial would be prejudiced. As this Court observed [previously]:

> The purpose of a statute of limitations is to limit exposure to criminal prosecution to a certain fixed period of time following the occurrence of those acts the legislature has decided to punish by criminal sanctions. Such a limitation is designed to protect individuals from having to defend themselves against charges when the basic facts may have become obscured by the passage of time and to minimize the danger of official punishment because of acts in the far-distant past. Such a time limit may also have the salutary effect of encouraging law enforcement officials promptly to investigate suspected criminal activity.

There is thus no need to press the Sixth Amendment into service to guard against the mere possibility that pre-accusation delays will prejudice the defense in a criminal case since statutes of limitation already perform that function.

[T]he Government [also] concedes that the Due Process Clause of the Fifth Amendment would require dismissal of the indictment if it were shown at trial that the pre-indictment delay in this case caused substantial prejudice to appellees' rights to a fair trial and that the delay was an intentional device to gain tactical advantage over the accused. However, we need not, and could not now, determine when and in what circumstances actual prejudice resulting from pre-accusation delays requires the dismissal of the prosecution. Actual prejudice to the defense of a criminal case may result from the shortest and most necessary delay; and no one suggests that every delay-caused detriment to a defendant's case should abort a criminal prosecution. To accommodate the sound administration of justice to the rights of the defendant to a fair trial will necessarily involve a delicate judgment based on the circumstances of each case. It would be unwise at this juncture to attempt to forecast our decision in such cases.

The 38-month delay between the end of the scheme charged in the indictment and the date the defendants were indicted did not extend beyond the period of the applicable statute of limitations here. Appellees have not, of course, been able to claim undue delay pending trial, since the indictment was brought on April 21, 1970, and dismissed on June 8, 1970. Nor have appellees adequately demonstrated that the pre-indictment delay by the Government violated the Due Process Clause. No actual prejudice to the conduct of the defense is alleged or proved, and there is no showing that the Government intentionally delayed to gain some tactical advantage over appellees or to harass them. Appellees rely solely on the real possibility of prejudice inherent in any extended delay: that memories will dim, witnesses become inaccessible, and evidence be lost. In light of the applicable statute of limitations, however, these possibilities are not in themselves enough to demonstrate that appellees cannot receive a fair trial and to therefore justify the dismissal of the indictment.

Justice DOUGLAS, with whom Justice BRENNAN and Justice MARSHALL join, concurring in the result.

Much is made of the history of the Sixth Amendment as indicating that the speedy trial guarantee had no application to pre-prosecution delays.

There are two answers to that proposition. First, British courts historically did consider delay as a condition to issuance of an information. . . . Second, and more basically, the 18th century criminal prosecution at the common law was in general commenced in a completely different way from that with which we are familiar today. By the common law of England which was brought to the American colonies, the ordinary criminal prosecution was conducted by a private prosecutor, in the name of the King. In case the victim of the crime or someone interested came forward to prosecute, he retained his own counsel and had charge of the case as in the usual civil proceeding. . . . Procedurally, the criminal prosecution was commenced by the filing of a lawsuit, and thereafter the filing of an application for criminal prosecution. . . . The English common law, with which the Framers were familiar, conceived of a criminal prosecution as being commenced prior to indictment. Thus in that setting the individual charged as the defendant in a criminal proceeding could and would be an "accused" prior to formal indictment.

"The Speedy Trial Clause protects societal interests, as well as those of the accused. The public is concerned with the effective prosecution of criminal cases, both to restrain those guilty of crime and to deter those contemplating it. Just as delay may impair the ability of the accused to defend himself, so it may reduce the capacity of the government to prove its case. Moreover, while awaiting trial, an accused who is at large may become a fugitive from justice or commit other criminal acts. And the greater the lapse of time between commission of an offense and the conviction of the offender, the less the deterrent value of his conviction."

At least some of these values served by the right to a speedy trial are not unique to any particular stage of the criminal proceeding. Undue delay may be as offensive to the right to a speedy trial before as after an indictment or information. The anxiety and concern attendant on public accusation may weigh more heavily upon an individual who has not yet been formally indicted or arrested for, to him, exoneration by a jury of his peers may be only a vague possibility lurking in the distant future. Indeed, the protection underlying the right to a speedy trial may be denied when a citizen is damned by clandestine innuendo and never given the chance promptly to defend himself in a court of law. Those who are accused of crime but never tried may lose their jobs or their positions of responsibility, or become outcasts in their communities.

The impairment of the ability to defend oneself may become acute because of delays in the pre-indictment stage. Those delays may result in the loss of alibi witnesses, the destruction of material evidence, and the blurring of memories. At least when a person has been accused of a specific crime, he can devote his powers of recall to the events surrounding the alleged occurrences. When there is no formal accusation, however, the State may proceed methodically to build its case while the prospective defendant proceeds to lose his.

In the present case, two to three years elapsed between the time the District Court found that the charges could and should have been brought and the actual return of the indictment. The justifications offered were that the United States Attorney's office was "not sufficiently staffed to proceed as expeditiously" as desirable and that priority had been given to other cases. . . . They argue that there is a great likelihood that the recollection of such events will be blurred or erased by the frailties of the human memory. If this were a simpler crime, I think the British precedent which I have cited would warrant dismissal of the indictment because of the speedy trial guarantee of the Sixth Amendment. But we know from experience that the nature of the crime charged here often has vast interstate aspects, the victims are often widely scattered and hard to locate, and the reconstruction of the total scheme of the fraudulent plan takes time. . . . I think a three-year delay even in that kind of case goes to the edge of a permissible delay. But on the bare bones of this record I hesitate to say that the guarantee of a speedy trial has been violated.

As established in *Marion*, the Sixth Amendment's speedy trial right does not apply to pre-charging delay. Rather, a defendant's rights during that time period are protected by statutes of limitations and the right to due process. A charge cannot be filed outside the statute of limitations. Different jurisdictions set different statutes of limitations for crimes. The length of time selected reflects the seriousness of the crime and how long it might take to investigate it. For example, consider the following sampling of federal statute of limitations laws and why Congress set the time periods they did in each statute.

FEDERAL STATUTES OF LIMITATION

18 U.S.C. §3281. Capital offenses

An indictment for any offense punishable by death may be found at any time without limitation.

18 U.S.C. §3282. Offenses not capital

(a) In general—Except as otherwise expressly provided by law, no person shall be prosecuted, tried or punished for any offense, not capital, unless the indictment is found or the information is instituted within five years next after such offense shall have been committed.

18 U.S.C. §3283. Offenses against children

No statute of limitations that would otherwise preclude prosecution for an offense involving the sexual or physical abuse, or kidnapping, of a child under the age of 18 years shall preclude such prosecution during the life of the child, or for ten years after the offense, whichever is longer.

18 U.S.C. §3286. Extension of statute of limitation for certain terrorism offenses

(a) Eight-year limitation—Notwithstanding section 3282, no person shall be prosecuted, tried, or punished for any noncapital offense involving [certain terrorism crimes], unless the indictment is found or the information is instituted within 8 years after the offense was committed.

(b) No limitation—Notwithstanding any other law, an indictment may be found or any information instituted at any time without limitation for any [terrorism offense], if the commission of such offense resulted in, or created a foreseeable risk of, death or serious bodily injury to another person.

18 U.S.C. §3290. Fugitive from justice

No statute of limitations shall extend to any person fleeing from justice.

18 U.S.C. §3293. Financial institution offenses

No person shall be prosecuted, tried, or punished for a violation of, or a conspiracy to violate—[certain offenses affecting financial institutions] unless the indictment is returned or the information is filed within 10 years after the commission of the offense.

18 U.S.C. §3294. Theft of major artwork

No person shall be prosecuted, tried, or punished for a violation of or conspiracy [to steal major art works] unless the indictment is returned or the information is filed within 20 years after the commission of the offense.

18 U.S.C. §3297. Cases involving DNA evidence

In a case in which DNA testing implicates an identified person in the commission of a felony, no statute of limitations that would otherwise preclude prosecution of the offense shall preclude such prosecution until a period of time following the implication of the person by DNA testing has elapsed that is equal to the otherwise applicable limitation period.

Although protection from pre-charging delay lies with the statute of limitations, a defendant also has a constitutional right to argue a due process violation if the delay is too long. As the court briefly explained in *Marion*, the due process standard is a high one. Mere possibility of prejudice is insufficient. The defendant must show intentional delay to give the government a tactical advantage and actual prejudice caused by the delay.

Six years after *Marion*, the Supreme Court took a closer look at due process challenges to pre-charging delay, elaborating on why it had set the standard so high for claims of pre-charging delay.

UNITED STATES v. LOVASCO

431 U.S. 783 (1977)

Justice MARSHALL delivered the opinion of the Court.

On March 6, 1975, respondent was indicted for possessing eight firearms stolen from the United States mails, and for dealing in firearms without a license. The offenses were alleged to have occurred between July 25 and August 31, 1973, more than 18 months before the indictment was filed. Respondent moved to dismiss the indictment due to the delay.

The District Court conducted a hearing on respondent's motion at which the respondent sought to prove that the delay was unnecessary and that it had prejudiced his defense. In an effort to establish the former proposition, respondent presented a Postal Inspector's report on his investigation that was prepared one month after the crimes were committed, and a stipulation concerning the post-report progress of the probe. The report stated, in brief, that within the first month of the investigation respondent had admitted to Government agents that he had possessed and then sold five of the stolen guns, and that the agents had developed strong evidence linking respondent to the remaining three weapons. The report also stated, however, that the agents had been unable to confirm or refute respondent's claim that he had found the guns in his car when he returned to it after visiting his son, a mail handler, at work. [L]ittle additional information concerning the crimes was uncovered in the 17 months following the preparation of the Inspector's report.

To establish prejudice to the defense, respondent testified that he had lost the testimony of two material witnesses due to the delay. The first witness, Tom Stewart, died more than a year after the alleged crimes occurred. At the hearing respondent claimed that Stewart had been his source for two or three of the guns. The second witness, respondent's brother, died in April 1974, eight months after the crimes were completed. Respondent testified that his brother was present when respondent called Stewart to secure the guns, and witnessed all of respondent's sales. Respondent did not state how the witnesses would have aided the defense had they been willing to testify.

Government made no systematic effort in the District Court to explain its long delay. The Assistant United States Attorney did expressly disagree, however, with defense counsel's suggestion that the investigation had ended after the Postal Inspector's report was prepared.

II

In United States v. Marion (1971), this Court considered the significance, for constitutional purposes, of a lengthy preindictment delay. We held that as far as the Speedy Trial Clause of the Sixth Amendment is concerned, such delay is wholly irrelevant, since our analysis of the language, history, and purposes of the Clause persuaded us that only "a formal indictment or information or else the actual restraints imposed by arrest and holding to answer a criminal charge . . . engage the particular protections" of that provision. We went on to note that statutes of limitations, which provide predictable, legislatively enacted limits on prosecutorial delay, provide "the primary guarantee against bringing overly stale criminal charges." But we did acknowledge that the "statute of limitations does not fully define [defendants'] rights with respect to the events occurring prior to indictment," and that the Due Process Clause has a limited role to play in protecting against oppressive delay.

Thus *Marion* makes clear that proof of prejudice is generally a necessary but not sufficient element of a due process claim, and that the due process inquiry must consider the reasons for the delay as well as the prejudice to the accused.

The Court of Appeals found that the sole reason for the delay here was "a hope on the part of the Government that others might be discovered who may have participated in the theft. . . ." It concluded that this hope did not justify the delay, and therefore affirmed the dismissal of the indictment. But the Due Process Clause does not permit courts to abort criminal prosecutions simply because they disagree with a prosecutor's judgment as to when to seek an indictment.

It might be argued that once the Government has assembled sufficient evidence to prove guilt beyond a reasonable doubt, it should be constitutionally required to file charges promptly, even if its investigation of the entire criminal transaction is not complete. Adopting such a rule, however, would have many of the same consequences as adopting a rule requiring immediate prosecution upon probable cause.

First, compelling a prosecutor to file public charges as soon as the requisite proof has been developed against one participant on one charge would cause numerous problems in those cases in which a criminal transaction involves more than one person or more than one illegal act. In some instances, an immediate arrest or indictment would impair the prosecutor's ability to continue his investigation, thereby preventing society from bringing lawbreakers to justice. In other cases, the prosecutor would be able to obtain additional indictments despite an early prosecution, but the necessary result would be multiple trials involving a single set of facts. Such trials place needless burdens on defendants, law enforcement officials, and courts.

Second, insisting on immediate prosecution once sufficient evidence is developed to obtain a conviction would pressure prosecutors into resolving doubtful cases in favor of early — and possibly unwarranted — prosecutions.

Finally requiring the Government to make charging decisions immediately upon assembling evidence sufficient to establish guilt would preclude the Government from giving full consideration to the desirability of not prosecuting in particular cases.

In our view, investigative delay is fundamentally unlike delay undertaken by the Government solely "to gain tactical advantage over the accused," precisely because investigative delay is not so one-sided. Rather than deviating from elementary standards of "fair play and decency," a prosecutor abides by them if he refuses to seek indictments until he is completely satisfied that he should prosecute and will be able promptly to establish guilt beyond a reasonable doubt. Penalizing prosecutors who defer action for these reasons would subordinate the goal of "orderly expedition" to that of "mere speed." This the Due Process Clause does not require. We therefore hold that to prosecute a defendant following investigative delay does not deprive him of due process, even if his defense might have been somewhat prejudiced by the lapse of time.

Justice STEVENS, dissenting.

If the record presented the question which the Court decides today, I would join its well-reasoned opinion. I am unable to do so because I believe [the record does not support the majority's findings].

After a thorough hearing on the respondent's motion to dismiss the indictment for prejudicial preindictment delay—a hearing at which both sides were given every opportunity to submit evidence concerning the question—the District Court found that "[t]he Government's delay ha[d] not been explained or justified and [was] unnecessary and unreasonable."

The findings of the District Court, as approved by the Court of Appeals, establish four relevant propositions: (1) this is a routine prosecution; (2) after the Government assembled all of the evidence on which it expects to establish respondent's guilt, it waited almost 18 months to seek an indictment; (3) the delay was prejudicial to respondent's defense; and (4) no reason whatsoever explains the delay. We may reasonably infer that the prosecutor was merely busy with other matters that he considered more important than this case.

The question presented by those facts is not an easy one. Nevertheless, unless we are to conclude that the Constitution imposes no constraints on the prosecutor's power to postpone the filing of formal charges to suit his own convenience, I believe we must affirm the judgment of the Court of Appeals.

The requirement of speedy justice has been part of the Anglo-American common law tradition since the Magna Carta. It came to this country and was embodied in the early state constitutions and later in the Sixth Amendment to the United States Constitution. As applied to this case, in which respondent made numerous anxious inquiries of the Postal Inspectors concerning whether he would be indicted, in which the delay caused substantial prejudice to the respondent, and in which the Government has offered no justification for the delay, the right to speedy justice should be honored.

There are benefits and burdens of extensive pre-indictment investigation. Sometimes, additional investigation can lead to the discovery of evidence that will show that the defendant was not responsible for the alleged crime. By awaiting this additional information, the prosecution prevents faulty prosecutions and the defendant avoids prosecution.

However, lengthy investigative delay also gives the prosecution additional time to find more evidence to prove its case. Moreover, if exculpatory evidence is not found during that time, it makes it difficult for the defense to argue that the prosecution conducted a rushed and inadequate investigation.

2.   Post-Charging Delay and Speedy Trial Rights

The Sixth Amendment right to a speedy trial applies to the period of time from arrest or formal charging until the beginning of trial. Where the pre-charging period is governed by statutory protections in the form of statutes of limitations and the constitutional protections of due process, the period from formal charges to trial is likewise controlled by statutes and constitutional protections.

a.   Statutory Protections

Each jurisdiction has a Speedy Trial Act that commonly prescribes the time period for bringing an accused to trial. For example, under the federal Speedy Trial Act, 18 U.S.C. §3161, trial must begin within 70 days of the filing of an information or indictment or the defendant's initial appearance, unless there is excludable delay.[2] The Act then defines what constitutes "excludable delay." This may include delay due to pretrial motions (18 U.S.C. §3161(h)(1)(F)) or the unavailability of the defendant or an essential witness (18 U.S.C. §3161(h)(3)(A)). There is also a catch-all provision that allows for excludable delay when the court determines it is necessary to serve "the ends of justice" (18 U.S.C. §3161(h)(8)).

If there is a violation of the Speedy Trial Act, the judge must decide whether to dismiss with or without prejudice. In making this decision, the court must consider, among other things, "the seriousness of the offense; the facts and circumstances of the case which led to the dismissal; and the impact of reprosecution on the administration of [the Speedy Trial Act] and on the administration of justice." 18 U.S.C. §3162(a)(2).

The purpose of the Speedy Trial Act is not just to protect a defendant's right to a speedy trial; it is also designed to protect the public's interest in a speedy trial. There are many defendants, especially those on pretrial release,

---

2. The federal Speedy Trial Act is set forth in the Statutory Supplement.

who may welcome lengthy pretrial delay. However, the public continues to have an interest in the expeditious processing of cases. Because of this public interest, the Supreme Court held in Zedner v. United States, 547 U.S. 489 (2006), that a defendant cannot prospectively waive application of the Speedy Trial Act. It also held in Bloate v. United States, 129 S. Ct. 1345 (2010), that the act's provisions for allowing excludable time should be read narrowly and do not automatically exclude time used to prepare defense pretrial motions.

b. Constitutional Protection

The Sixth Amendment provides for a speedy trial once a person has been formally accused. Thus, apart from the Speedy Trial Act, a defendant has a right to contest a lengthy post-charging delay as a violation of the defendant's right to a speedy trial. However, the language of the Sixth Amendment does not define how long a delay is too long. When does post-charge delay become a Sixth Amendment violation and what approach should be used to make this determination?

BARKER v. WINGO
407 U.S. 514 (1972)

Justice POWELL delivered the opinion of the Court.

Although a speedy trial is guaranteed the accused by the Sixth Amendment to the Constitution, this Court has dealt with that right on infrequent occasions. [I]n none of our cases have we attempted to set out the criteria by which the speedy trial right is to be judged. This case compels us to make such an attempt.

I

On July 20, 1958, in Christian County, Kentucky, an elderly couple was beaten to death by intruders wielding an iron tire tool. Two suspects, Silas Manning and Willie Barker, the petitioner, were arrested shortly thereafter. The grand jury indicted them on September 15. Counsel was appointed on September 17, and Barker's trial was set for October 21. The Commonwealth had a stronger case against Manning, and it believed that Barker could not be convicted unless Manning testified against him. Manning was naturally unwilling to incriminate himself. Accordingly, on October 23, the day Silas Manning was brought to trial, the Commonwealth sought and obtained the first of what was to be a series of 16 continuances of Barker's trial. Barker made no objection. By first convicting Manning, the Commonwealth would remove possible problems of self-incrimination and would be able to assure his testimony against Barker.

The Commonwealth encountered more than a few difficulties in its pros-ecution of Manning. The first trial ended in a hung jury. A second trial resulted in a conviction, but the Kentucky Court of Appeals reversed because of the admission of evidence obtained by an illegal search. At his third trial, Manning was again convicted, and the Court of Appeals again reversed because the trial court had not granted a change of venue. A fourth trial resulted in a hung jury. Finally, after five trials, Manning was convicted, in March 1962, of murdering one victim, and after a sixth trial, in December 1962, he was convicted of murdering the other.

The Christian County Circuit Court holds three terms each year — in February, June, and September. Barker's initial trial was to take place in the September term of 1958. The first continuance postponed it until the February 1959 term. The second continuance was granted for one month only. Every term thereafter for as long as the Manning prosecutions were in process, the Commonwealth routinely moved to continue Barker's case to the next term. When the case was continued from the June 1959 term until the following September, Barker, having spent 10 months in jail, obtained his release by posting a $5,000 bond. He thereafter remained free in the community until his trial. Barker made no objection, through his counsel, to the first 11 continuances.

When on February 12, 1962, the Commonwealth moved for the twelfth time to continue the case until the following term, Barker's counsel filed a motion to dismiss the indictment. The motion to dismiss was denied two weeks later, and the Commonwealth's motion for a continuance was granted. The Commonwealth was granted further continuances in June 1962 and September 1962, to which Barker did not object.

In February 1963, the first term of court following Manning's final con-viction, the Commonwealth moved to set Barker's trial for March 19. But on the day scheduled for trial, it again moved for a continuance until the June term. It gave as its reason the illness of the ex-sheriff who was the chief investigating officer in the case. To this continuance, Barker objected unsuccessfully.

The witness was still unable to testify in June, and the trial, which had been set for June 19, was continued again until the September term over Barker's objection. This time the court announced that the case would be dismissed for lack of prosecution if it were not tried during the next term. The final trial date was set for October 9, 1963. On that date, Barker again moved to dismiss the indictment, and this time specified that his right to a speedy trial had been violated. The motion was denied; the trial commenced with Manning as the chief prosecution witness; Barker was convicted and given a life sentence.

The right to a speedy trial is generically different from any of the other rights enshrined in the Constitution for the protection of the accused. In addition to the general concern that all accused persons be treated accord-ing to decent and fair procedures, there is a societal interest in providing a speedy trial which exists separate from, and at times in opposition to, the interests of the accused. The inability of courts to provide a prompt trial has contributed to a large backlog of cases in urban courts which, among other things, enables defendants to negotiate more effectively for pleas of guilty to lesser offenses and otherwise manipulate the system. In addition, persons released on bond for lengthy periods awaiting trial have an opportunity to commit other crimes. It must be of little comfort to the residents of Christian County, Kentucky, to know that Barker was at large on bail for over four years while accused of a vicious and brutal murder of which he was ultimately convicted. Moreover, the longer an accused is free awaiting trial, the more tempting becomes his opportunity to jump bail and escape. Finally, delay between arrest and punishment may have a detrimental effect on rehabilitation.

If an accused cannot make bail, he is generally confined, as was Barker for 10 months, in a local jail. This contributes to the overcrowding and generally deplorable state of those institutions. Lengthy exposure to these conditions "has a destructive effect on human character and makes the rehabilitation of the individual offender much more difficult." At times the result may even be violent rioting. Finally, lengthy pretrial detention is costly. . . . In addition, society loses wages which might have been earned, and it must often support families of incarcerated breadwinners.

A second difference between the right to speedy trial and the accused's other constitutional rights is that deprivation of the right may work to the accused's advantage. Delay is not an uncommon defense tactic. As the time between the commission of the crime and trial lengthens, witnesses may become unavailable or their memories may fade. If the witnesses support the prosecution, its case will be weakened, sometimes seriously so. And it is the prosecution which carries the burden of proof. Thus, unlike the right to counsel or the right to be free from compelled self-incrimination, deprivation of the right to speedy trial does not per se prejudice the accused's ability to defend himself.

Finally, and perhaps most importantly, the right to speedy trial is a more vague concept than other procedural rights. It is, for example, impossible to determine with precision when the right has been denied. We cannot definitely say how long is too long in a system where justice is supposed to be swift but deliberate. As a consequence, there is no fixed point in the criminal process when the State can put the defendant to the choice of either exercising or waiving the right to a speedy trial.

The amorphous quality of the right also leads to the unsatisfactorily severe remedy of dismissal of the indictment when the right has been deprived. This is indeed a serious consequence because it means that a defendant who may be guilty of a serious crime will go free, without having been tried. Such a remedy is more serious than an exclusionary rule or a reversal for a new trial, but it is the only possible remedy.

III

Perhaps because the speedy trial right is so slippery, two rigid approaches are urged upon us as ways of eliminating some of the uncertainty which courts experience in protecting the right. The first suggestion is that we hold that the Constitution requires a criminal defendant to be offered a trial within a specified time period. The result of such a ruling would have the virtue of clarifying when the right is infringed and of simplifying courts' application of it. Recognizing this, some legislatures have enacted laws, and some courts have adopted procedural rules which more narrowly define the right.

But such a result would require this Court to engage in legislative or rulemaking activity, rather than in the adjudicative process to which we should confine our efforts.

The second suggested alternative would restrict consideration of the right to those cases in which the accused has demanded a speedy trial. Most States have recognized what is loosely referred to as the "demand rule." It is not clear, however, precisely what is meant by that term.

Such an approach, by presuming waiver of a fundamental right from inaction, is inconsistent with this Court's pronouncements on waiver of constitutional rights. "Presuming waiver from a silent record is impermissible. The record must show, or there must be an allegation and evidence which show, that an accused was offered counsel but intelligently and understandably rejected the offer. Anything less is not waiver."

We, therefore, reject both of the inflexible approaches — the fixed-time period because it goes further than the Constitution requires; the demand-waiver rule because it is insensitive to a right which we have deemed fundamental. The approach we accept is a balancing test, in which the conduct of both the prosecution and the defendant are weighed.

IV

A balancing test necessarily compels courts to approach speedy trial cases on an ad hoc basis. We can do little more than identify some of the factors which courts should assess in determining whether a particular defendant has been deprived of his right. [W]e identify four such factors: Length of delay, the reason for the delay, the defendant's assertion of his right, and prejudice to the defendant.

The length of the delay is to some extent a triggering mechanism. Until there is some delay which is presumptively prejudicial, there is no necessity for inquiry into the other factors that go into the balance. Nevertheless, because of the imprecision of the right to speedy trial, the length of delay that will provoke such an inquiry is necessarily dependent upon the peculiar circumstances of the case.[3] To take but one example, the delay that can be tolerated for an ordinary street crime is considerably less than for a serious, complex conspiracy charge.

Closely related to length of delay is the reason the government assigns to justify the delay. Here, too, different weights should be assigned to different reasons. A deliberate attempt to delay the trial in order to hamper the

---

3. For example, the First Circuit thought a delay of nine months overly long, absent a good reason, in a case that depended on eyewitness testimony. [Footnote by the Court.]

defense should be weighted heavily against the government. A more neutral reason such as negligence or overcrowded courts should be weighted less heavily but nevertheless should be considered since the ultimate responsibility for such circumstances must rest with the government rather than with the defendant. Finally, a valid reason, such as a missing witness, should serve to justify appropriate delay.

We have already discussed the third factor, the defendant's responsibility to assert his right. Whether and how a defendant asserts his right is closely related to the other factors we have mentioned. The strength of his efforts will be affected by the length of the delay, to some extent by the reason for the delay, and most particularly by the personal prejudice, which is not always readily identifiable, that he experiences. The more serious the deprivation, the more likely a defendant is to complain. The defendant's assertion of his speedy trial right, then, is entitled to strong evidentiary weight in determining whether the defendant is being deprived of the right. We emphasize that failure to assert the right will make it difficult for a defendant to prove that he was denied a speedy trial.

A fourth factor is prejudice to the defendant. Prejudice, of course, should be assessed in the light of the interests of defendants which the speedy trial right was designed to protect. This Court has identified three such interests: (i) to prevent oppressive pretrial incarceration; (ii) to minimize anxiety and concern of the accused; and (iii) to limit the possibility that the defense will be impaired. Of these, the most serious is the last, because the inability of a defendant adequately to prepare his case skews the fairness of the entire system. If witnesses die or disappear during a delay, the prejudice is obvious. There is also prejudice if defense witnesses are unable to recall accurately events of the distant past. Loss of memory, however, is not always reflected in the record because what has been forgotten can rarely be shown.

We have discussed previously the societal disadvantages of lengthy pretrial incarceration, but obviously the disadvantages for the accused who cannot obtain his release are even more serious. The time spent in jail awaiting trial has a detrimental impact on the individual. It often means loss of a job; it disrupts family life; and it enforces idleness. Most jails offer little or no recreational or rehabilitative programs. The time spent in jail is simply dead time. Moreover, if a defendant is locked up, he is hindered in his ability to gather evidence, contact witnesses, or otherwise prepare his defense.[4] Imposing those consequences on anyone who has not yet been convicted is serious. It is especially unfortunate to impose them on those persons who are ultimately found to be innocent. Finally, even if an accused is not incarcerated prior to trial, he is still disadvantaged by restraints on his liberty and by living under a cloud of anxiety, suspicion, and often hostility.

---

4. There is statistical evidence that persons who are detained between arrest and trial are more likely to receive prison sentences than those who obtain pretrial release, although other factors bear upon this correlation. *See* Wald, *Pretrial Detention and Ultimate Freedom: A Statistical Study*, 39 N.Y.U. L. Rev. 631 (1964) [Footnote by the Court.]

We regard none of the four factors identified above as either a necessary or sufficient condition to the finding of a deprivation of the right of speedy trial. Rather, they are related factors and must be considered together with such other circumstances as may be relevant. In sum, these factors have no talismanic qualities; courts must still engage in a difficult and sensitive balancing process.

V

The difficulty of the task of balancing these factors is illustrated by this case, which we consider to be close. It is clear that the length of delay between arrest and trial—well over five years—was extraordinary. Only seven months of that period can be attributed to a strong excuse, the illness of the ex-sheriff who was in charge of the investigation.

Two counterbalancing factors, however, outweigh these deficiencies. The first is that prejudice was minimal. [T]here is no claim that any of Barker's witnesses died or otherwise became unavailable owing to the delay. The trial transcript indicates only two very minor lapses of memory—one on the part of a prosecution witness—which were in no way significant to the outcome.

More important than the absence of serious prejudice, is the fact that Barker did not want a speedy trial. [T]he record shows no action whatever taken between October 21, 1958, and February 12, 1962, that could be construed as the assertion of the speedy trial right.

The probable reason for Barker's attitude was that he was gambling on Manning's acquittal. The evidence was not very strong against Manning, as the reversals and hung juries suggest, and Barker undoubtedly thought that if Manning were acquitted, he would never be tried.

We do not hold that there may never be a situation in which an indictment may be dismissed on speedy trial grounds where the defendant has failed to object to continuances. There may be a situation in which the defendant was represented by incompetent counsel, was severely prejudiced, or even cases in which the continuances were granted ex parte. But barring extraordinary circumstances, we would be reluctant indeed to rule that a defendant was denied this constitutional right on a record that strongly indicates, as does this one, that the defendant did not want a speedy trial. We hold, therefore, that Barker was not deprived of his due process right to a speedy trial.

[The concurring opinion of Justice White and Justice Brennan is omitted.]

———————————

Barker provided a four-factor test for deciding whether there has been a constitutional speedy trial violation. To decide whether there has been a Sixth Amendment speedy trial violation, courts must consider:

1. The length of the delay
2. The reason for the delay

3. Whether, when, and how the defendant asserted his right to speedy trial
4. Whether the defendant was prejudiced by the delay

The first factor — the length of the delay — is a triggering mechanism. Unless there is some significant delay, the courts will not even examine the other factors.

Barker v. Wingo was decided three years before the enactment of the federal Speedy Trial Act in 1975. However, the Speedy Trial Act did not replace the constitutional right to a speedy trial. Rather, it provided statutory direction as to when a trial must occur. Regardless of whether statutory requirements were met, a defendant may still invoke his Sixth Amendment right to a speedy trial.

In Doggett v. United States, 505 U.S. 647 (1992), the Supreme Court revisited the speedy trial issue and gave more guidance as to what kind of delay triggers a Sixth Amendment violation and whether a showing of actual prejudice was required to prove a speedy trial violation.

DOGGETT v. UNITED STATES
505 U.S. 647 (1992)

Justice SOUTER delivered the opinion of the Court.

In this case we consider whether the delay of 8½ years between petitioner's indictment and arrest violated his Sixth Amendment right to a speedy trial. We hold that it did.

I

[Doggett was indicted with conspiring to distribute cocaine. He admitted that he knew nothing about the indictment during the lengthy delay before he was arrested. Shortly after he was indicted, Doggett left the country. When he returned two years later, he passed without trouble through Customs. He lived openly under his own name for the next six years in the United States. During that time, he got married, attended college, got a job, and had no trouble with the law. Finally, six years later, the Marshal's Service ran a credit check on several thousands of people. They found the outstanding warrant on Doggett and within minutes arrested him. On September 5, 1988, nearly six years after his return to the United States and eight and one-half years after his indictment, Doggett was arrested.]

II

The Sixth Amendment guarantees that, "in all criminal prosecutions, the accused shall enjoy the right to a speedy . . . trial. . . ." On its face, the Speedy Trial Clause is written with such breadth that, taken literally, it would forbid the government to delay the trial of an "accused" for any reason at all. Our cases, however, have qualified the literal sweep of the provision by specifically recognizing the relevance of four separate enquiries: whether delay before trial was uncommonly long, whether the government or the criminal defendant is more to blame for that delay, whether, in due course, the defendant asserted his right to a speedy trial, and whether he suffered prejudice as the delay's result.

The first of these is actually a double enquiry. Simply to trigger a speedy trial analysis, an accused must allege that the interval between accusation and trial has crossed the threshold dividing ordinary from "presumptively prejudicial" delay. If the accused makes this showing, the court must then consider, as one factor among several, the extent to which the delay stretches beyond the bare minimum needed to trigger judicial examination of the claim. In this case, the extraordinary $8^{1}/_{2}$-year lag between Doggett's indictment and arrest clearly suffices to trigger the speedy trial enquiry.[5]

As for *Barker*'s second criterion, the Government claims to have sought Doggett with diligence. For six years, the Government's investigators made no serious effort to test their progressively more questionable assumption that Doggett was living abroad, and, had they done so, they could have found him within minutes. While the Government's lethargy may have reflected no more than Doggett's relative unimportance in the world of drug trafficking, it was still findable negligence, and the finding stands.

The Government goes against the record again in suggesting that Doggett knew of his indictment years before he was arrested. Were this true, *Barker*'s third factor, concerning invocation of the right to a speedy trial, would be weighed heavily against him. But here again, the Government is trying to revisit the facts. [The record was unrebutted that Doggett did not know he was wanted on the indictment.]

III

The Government is left, then, with its principal contention: that Doggett fails to make out a successful speedy trial claim because he has not shown precisely how he was prejudiced by the delay between his indictment and trial.

We have observed in prior cases that unreasonable delay between formal accusation and trial threatens to produce more than one sort of harm, including "oppressive pretrial incarceration," "anxiety and concern of the accused," and "the possibility that the [accused's] defense will be impaired" by dimming memories and loss of exculpatory evidence. Of these forms of prejudice, "the most serious is the last, because the inability of a defendant adequately to prepare his case skews the fairness of the entire system." Doggett claims this kind of prejudice, and there is probably no other kind that he can claim, since he was subjected neither to pretrial

---

5. Depending on the nature of the charges, the lower courts have generally found postaccusation delay "presumptively prejudicial" at least as it approaches one year. [Footnote by the Court.]

detention nor, he has successfully contended, to awareness of unresolved charges against him.

[T]he Government claims Doggett has failed to make any affirmative showing that the delay weakened his ability to raise specific defenses, elicit specific testimony, or produce specific items of evidence. Though Doggett did indeed come up short in this respect, affirmative proof of particularized prejudice is not essential to every speedy trial claim. *Barker* explicitly recognized that impairment of one's defense is the most difficult form of speedy trial prejudice to prove because time's erosion of exculpatory evidence and testimony "can rarely be shown." Thus, we generally have to recognize that excessive delay presumptively compromises the reliability of a trial in ways that neither party can prove or, for that matter, identify.

This brings us to an enquiry into the role that presumptive prejudice should play in the disposition of Doggett's speedy trial claim. [I]n this case, if the Government had pursued Doggett with reasonable diligence from his indictment to his arrest, his speedy trial claim would fail. The Government concedes, on the other hand, that Doggett would prevail if he could show that the Government had intentionally held back in its prosecution of him to gain some impermissible advantage at trial.

Between diligent prosecution and bad-faith delay, official negligence in bringing an accused to trial occupies the middle ground. *Barker* made it clear that "different weights [are to be] assigned to different reasons" for delay. Although negligence is obviously to be weighed more lightly than a deliberate intent to harm the accused's defense, it still falls on the wrong side of the divide between acceptable and unacceptable reasons for delaying a criminal prosecution once it has begun. [O]ur toleration of such negligence varies inversely with its protractedness.

[T]he Government's egregious persistence in failing to prosecute Doggett is clearly sufficient. The lag between Doggett's indictment and arrest was 8½ years, and he would have faced trial 6 years earlier than he did but for the Government's inexcusable oversights. The portion of the delay attributable to the Government's negligence far exceeds the threshold needed to state a speedy trial claim; indeed, we have called shorter delays "extraordinary." [The Court held that Doggett was entitled to dismissal of the indictment.]

Justice THOMAS, with whom Chief Justice REHNQUIST and Justice SCALIA join, dissenting.

Just as "bad facts make bad law," so too odd facts make odd law. Doggett's 8½-year odyssey from youthful drug dealing in the tobacco country of North Carolina, through stints in a Panamanian jail and in Colombia, to life as a computer operations manager, homeowner, and registered voter in suburban Virginia is extraordinary. But even more extraordinary is the Court's conclusion that the Government denied Doggett his Sixth Amendment right to a speedy trial despite the fact that he has suffered none of the harms that the right was designed to prevent.

There is no basis for concluding that the disruption of an accused's life years after the commission of his alleged crime is an evil independently protected by the Speedy Trial Clause. Such disruption occurs regardless of whether the individual is under indictment during the period of delay. To recognize a constitutional right to repose is to recognize a right to be tried speedily after the offense. That would, of course, convert the Speedy Trial Clause into a constitutional statute of limitations—a result with no basis in the text or history of the Clause or in our precedents.

II

So engrossed is the Court in applying the multifactor balancing test set forth in *Barker* that it loses sight of the nature and purpose of the speedy trial guarantee set forth in the Sixth Amendment. *Barker* does not apply at all—when an accused is entirely unaware of a pending indictment against him.

Today's opinion, I fear, will transform the courts of the land into boards of law enforcement supervision. For the Court compels dismissal of the charges against Doggett not because he was harmed in any way by the delay between his indictment and arrest, but simply because the Government's efforts to catch him are found wanting. By divorcing the Speedy Trial Clause from all considerations of prejudice to an accused, the Court positively invites the Nation's judges to indulge in ad hoc and result-driven second-guessing of the government's investigatory efforts. Our Constitution neither contemplates nor tolerates such a role.

Many observers were surprised by the result in *Doggett,* especially given the emphasis the Supreme Court in *Barker* had placed on the requirement that there be prejudice for Barker to prove a constitutional violation. To what extent do you think that the Court was concerned about negligent police officers and their lack of professionalism during a "war on drugs"?

More recently, the Court faced another issue arising with more frequency in speedy trial challenges. Should delays by appointed defense counsel be weighed as a factor against a defendant's motion for dismissal? The Supreme Court decided the issue in Vermont v. Brillon.

VERMONT v. BRILLON
556 U.S. 81 (2009)

Justice GINSBURG delivered the opinion of the Court.

This case concerns the *Sixth Amendment* guarantee that "[i]n all criminal prosecutions, the accused shall enjoy the right to a speedy . . . trial." Michael

Brillon, defendant below, respondent here, was arrested in July 2001 on felony domestic assault and habitual offender charges. Nearly three years later, in June 2004, he was tried by jury, found guilty as charged, and sentenced to 12 to 20 years in prison. The Vermont Supreme Court vacated Brillon's conviction and held that the charges against him must be dismissed because he had been denied his right to a speedy trial.

During the time between Brillon's arrest and his trial, at least six different attorneys were appointed to represent him. Brillon "fired" the first, who served from July 2001 to February 2002. His third lawyer, who served from March 2002 until June 2002, was allowed to withdraw when he reported that Brillon had threatened his life. The Vermont Supreme Court charged against Brillon the delays associated with those periods, but charged against the State periods in which assigned counsel failed "to move the case forward."

We hold that the Vermont Supreme Court erred in ranking assigned counsel essentially as state actors in the criminal justice system. Assigned counsel, just as retained counsel, act on behalf of their clients, and delays sought by counsel are ordinarily attributable to the defendants they represent. For a total of some six months of the time that elapsed between Brillon's arrest and his trial, Brillon lacked an attorney. The State may be charged with those months if the gaps resulted from the trial court's failure to appoint replacement counsel with dispatch. Similarly, the State may bear responsibility if there is "a breakdown in the public defender system." But, as the Vermont Supreme Court acknowledged, the record does not establish any such institutional breakdown.

I

On July 27, 2001, Michael Brillon was arrested after striking his girlfriend. Three days later he was arraigned in state court in Bennington County, Vermont and charged with felony domestic assault. His alleged status as a habitual offender exposed him to a potential life sentence. The court ordered him held without bail.

Richard Ammons, from the county public defender's office, was assigned on the day of arraignment as Brillon's first counsel. In October, Ammons filed a motion to recuse the trial judge. It was denied the next month and trial was scheduled for February 2002. In mid-January, Ammons moved for a continuance, but the State objected, and the trial court denied the motion.

On February 22, four days before the jury draw, Ammons again moved for a continuance, citing his heavy workload and the need for further investigation. Ammons acknowledged that any delay would not count (presumably against the State) for speedy-trial purposes. The State opposed the motion, and at the conclusion of a hearing, the trial court denied it. Brillon, participating in the proceedings through interactive television, then announced: "You're fired, Rick." Three days later, the trial court — over the State's objection — granted Ammons' motion to withdraw as counsel, citing Brillon's termination of Ammons and Ammons' statement that he could no longer zealously represent Brillon. The trial court warned Brillon that further delay would occur while a new attorney became familiar with the case. The same day, the trial court appointed a second attorney, but he immediately withdrew based on a conflict.

On March 1, 2002, Gerard Altieri was assigned as Brillon's third counsel. On May 20, Brillon filed a motion to dismiss Altieri for, among other reasons, failure to file motions, "[v]irtually no communication whatsoever," and his lack of diligence "because of heavy case load." At a June 11 hearing, Altieri denied several of Brillon's allegations, noted his disagreement with Brillon's trial strategy, and insisted he had plenty of time to prepare. The State opposed Brillon's motion as well. Near the end of the hearing, however, Altieri moved to withdraw on the ground that Brillon had threatened his life during a break in the proceedings. The trial court granted Brillon's motion to dismiss Altieri, but warned Brillon that "this is somewhat of a dubious victory in your case because it simply prolongs the time that you will remain in jail until we can bring this matter to trial."

That same day, the trial court appointed Paul Donaldson as Brillon's fourth counsel. At an August 5 status conference, Donaldson requested additional time to conduct discovery in light of his caseload. A few weeks later, Brillon sent a letter to the court complaining about Donaldson's unresponsiveness and lack of competence. Two months later, Brillon filed a motion to dismiss Donaldson — similar to his motion to dismiss Altieri — for failure to file motions and "virtually no communication whatsoever." At a November 26 hearing, Donaldson reported that his contract with the Defender General's office had expired in June and that he had been in discussions to have Brillon's case reassigned. The trial court released Donaldson from the case "[w]ithout making any findings regarding the adequacy of [Donaldson]'s representation."

Brillon's fifth counsel, David Sleigh, was not assigned until January 15, 2003; Brillon was without counsel during the intervening two months. On February 25, Sleigh sought extensions of various discovery deadlines, noting that he had been in trial out of town. On April 10, however, Sleigh withdrew from the case, based on "modifications to [his] firm's contract with the Defender General."

Brillon was then without counsel for the next four months. On June 20, the Defender General's office notified the court that it had received "funding from the legislature" and would hire a new special felony unit defender for Brillon. On August 1, Kathleen Moore was appointed as Brillon's sixth counsel. The trial court set November 7 as the deadline for motions, but granted several extensions in accord with the parties' stipulation. On February 23, 2004, Moore filed a motion to dismiss for lack of a speedy trial. The trial court denied the motion on April 19.

The case finally went to trial on June 14, 2004. Brillon was found guilty and sentenced to 12 to 20 years in prison. The trial court denied a post-trial motion to dismiss for want of a speedy trial, concluding that the delay in Brillon's trial was "in large part the result of his own actions" and that Brillon had "failed to demonstrate prejudice as a result of [the] pre-trial delay."

II

The *Sixth Amendment* guarantees that "[i]n all criminal prosecutions, the accused shall enjoy the right to a speedy . . . trial." The speedy-trial right is "amorphous," "slippery," and "necessarily relative." In *Barker*, the Court refused to "quantif[y]" the right "into a specified number of days or months" or to hinge the right on a defendant's explicit request for a speedy trial. Rejecting such "inflexible approaches," *Barker* established a "balancing test, in which the conduct of both the prosecution and the defendant are weighed." "[S]ome of the factors" that courts should weigh include "[l]ength of delay, the reason for the delay, the defendant's assertion of his right, and prejudice to the defendant."

Primarily at issue here is the reason for the delay in Brillon's trial. Because "the attorney is the [defendant's] agent when acting, or failing to act, in furtherance of the litigation," delay caused by the defendant's counsel is also charged against the defendant. The same principle applies whether counsel is privately retained or publicly assigned, for "[o]nce a lawyer has undertaken the representation of an accused, the duties and obligations are the same whether the lawyer is privately retained, appointed, or serving in a legal aid or defender program."

III

An assigned counsel's failure "to move the case forward" does not warrant attribution of delay to the State. Contrary to the Vermont Supreme Court's analysis, assigned counsel generally are not state actors for purposes of a speedy-trial claim. While the Vermont Defender General's office is indeed "part of the criminal justice system," the individual counsel here acted only on behalf of Brillon, not the State. Most of the delay that the Vermont Supreme Court attributed to the State must therefore be attributed to Brillon as delays caused by his counsel.

A contrary conclusion could encourage appointed counsel to delay proceedings by seeking unreasonable continuances, hoping thereby to obtain a dismissal of the indictment on speedy-trial grounds. Trial courts might well respond by viewing continuance requests made by appointed counsel with skepticism, concerned that even an apparently genuine need for more time is in reality a delay tactic.

The general rule attributing to the defendant delay caused by assigned counsel is not absolute. Delay resulting from a systemic "breakdown in the public defender system," could be charged to the State. But the Vermont Supreme Court made no determination, and nothing in the record suggests, that institutional problems caused any part of the delay in Brillon's case.

In sum, delays caused by defense counsel are properly attributed to the defendant, even where counsel is assigned.

c.   Other Speedy Trial Rules and Laws

In addition to constitutional protections and rights under the Speedy Trial Act, other federal statutes contain provisions to prevent post-accusation delay. For example, Federal Rule of Criminal Procedure 48(b) grants trial courts the discretion to dismiss a case if there is "unnecessary delay" in bringing a defendant to trial. The court may dismiss the case with or without prejudice. Generally, this rule is only used if a delay is not covered by other statutory provisions.

Also, the Interstate Agreement on Detainer Act, 18 U.S.C. app. §2 (2000), provides time limits for a defendant's transfer from one jurisdiction to another to commence trial. The Juvenile Delinquency and Justice Act, 18 U.S.C. §§5031-5042 (2000), establishes time limits for various pretrial proceedings in juvenile cases that take into account the special nature of those cases.

D.   REMEDIES FOR SPEEDY TRIAL VIOLATIONS

As we have seen, the remedy for violations of Speedy Trial Acts and governing federal rules is dismissal with or without prejudice. A dismissal without prejudice allows the government to refile charges. However, the remedy for a constitutional speedy trial violation is more limited. In Strunk v. United States, 412 U.S. 434 (1973), the Supreme Court held that the only remedy that makes sense for violations of the Sixth Amendment right to speedy trial is dismissal with prejudice. By definition, once the court finds there has been a violation of the defendant's constitutional right to a speedy trial, it is too late to try the defendant.

Given the extreme remedy, it is not surprising that courts are reluctant to find that there has been a violation of the constitutional right to a speedy trial. Finding a constitutional speedy trial violation means that there will never be a trial to resolve a case. Victims may continue to be frustrated because they never have had their day in court. It also can mean that a defendant who is responsible for a serious crime will be rereleased into society because the criminal justice system failed to safeguard his constitutional rights.

The Supreme Court noted these concerns in *Strunk*, in which it rejected an argument that it should use a balancing approach to derive different remedies for a speedy trial violation. Chief Justice Burger quoted the lower court in his opinion when he recognized that "[t]he remedy for a violation of this constitutional right has traditionally been the dismissal of the indictment or the vacation of the sentence. Perhaps the severity of that remedy has caused courts to be extremely hesitant in finding a failure to afford a speedy trial." *Id.* at 438. Nonetheless, although dismissal of an indictment for denial of a speedy trial is an "unsatisfactorily severe remedy" and in practice, "it means that a defendant who may be guilty of a serious crime will go free, without having been tried[,]" such severe remedies are not unique in the application of constitutional standards. In light of the policies which underlie the right to a speedy trial, dismissal must remain, as *Barker* noted, "the only possible remedy."

CHAPTER
7

RIGHT TO COUNSEL

A. INTRODUCTION

Of all the defendant's constitutional rights, none is more important than the defendant's right to counsel. With the assistance of counsel, a defendant can protect all of his other rights. From beginning to end, the defense lawyer serves as an advocate for the accused, ensuring that both law enforcement and prosecutors comply with the defendants' constitutional rights. This chapter focuses on the right to counsel at trial and pretrial proceedings.

Before examining the scope of the right to counsel, it is worth considering the practical challenges in providing quality counsel to the accused. Nationally, there is a shortage of funds to pay the fees for indigent counsel. As a result, in some areas of the country, defense lawyers are paid as little as $50 to handle a criminal case.[1] Not surprisingly, the low pay and demanding nature of the job make it difficult to recruit experienced and qualified lawyers to handle indigent criminal cases. While there are many dedicated public defenders who work countless hours of unpaid overtime, there continues to be a shortage of capable defense counsel. As this chapter discusses, the right to counsel is a crucial right, but it involves more than just the right to appointment of a lawyer. The Sixth Amendment provides for the right to the "effective" assistance of counsel.

Section B begins with the landmark case of Gideon v. Wainwright, 372 U.S. 335 (1963). As discussed in the notes preceding *Gideon*, the right to counsel under the Sixth Amendment was not always applied to the states. Rather, representation by counsel was considered an aspect of the right to due process. It was not until *Gideon* that the Supreme Court recognized an independent right to counsel under the Sixth Amendment.

---

1. *See* Adam Gershowitz, *Raise the Proof: A Default Rule for Indigent Defense*, 40 Conn. L. Rev. 85 (2007). Defense lawyers are often outspent by a 3:1 margin. For a detailed study of public defender systems throughout the country, *see* Alissa Pollitz Worden, Andrew Lucas Blaize Davies & Elizabeth K. Brown, *A Patchwork of Policies: Justice, Due Process and Public Defense Across American States*, 74 Alb. L. Rev. 1423 (2010).

Section C then discusses when the right to counsel is triggered. The right to counsel is available for all "critical stages" of a prosecution. Critical stages begin before trial and last through the initial appeal. Not all proceedings related to criminal cases qualify as "prosecutions" for purposes of the Sixth Amendment. Specifically, the Supreme Court does not recognize a Sixth Amendment right to counsel in misdemeanor cases in which no imprisonment is imposed or in post-conviction proceedings, such as parole hearings or habeas corpus cases.

Section D discusses the standard to be used to measure whether the defendant has been afforded "effective" assistance of counsel. How good of a lawyer is a defendant entitled to under the Sixth Amendment? What resources should be available to a defense lawyer in representing his or her client? Does the right to counsel include the right to experts to assist counsel in his or her representation of the defendant?

Section E addresses the right of self-representation. Although a defendant has the Sixth Amendment right to counsel, a competent defendant can waive the right and represent himself. Finally, section F briefly discusses the situation of enemy combatants and the nature of the right to counsel.

B. APPOINTMENT OF COUNSEL

Prior to *Gideon*, many states were providing counsel to indigent defendants but only in the most serious cases, such as death penalty cases. In Powell v. Alabama, 287 U.S. 45, 64-65 (1932),[2] the Court recognized the importance of counsel. Powell and his codefendants were young, black men accused of raping two white girls in Alabama. In what was to become the infamous "Scottsboro Boys" trial, no lawyer was designated to represent the defendants until the morning of trial. With no time to prepare, and facing an ignorant and hostile community, it was no surprise that the defendants were convicted. On appeal, the Supreme Court found that the defendants' due process rights were violated. Justice Sutherland wrote, "[W]e are of the opinion that, under the circumstances [of this case], the necessity of counsel was so vital and imperative that the failure of the trial court to make an effective appointment of counsel was . . . a denial of due process within the meaning of the Fourteenth Amendment."

In Betts v. Brady, 316 U.S. 455 (1942), the Court expressly refused to find that the Fourteenth Amendment incorporated the Sixth Amendment right to counsel to the states. As a result, the Court needed to decide on a case-by-case basis whether the lack of counsel denied the defendant due process at trial. Not surprisingly, this led to a flood of cases in which each defendant claimed that denial of counsel in his or her case denied the defendant due

---

2. This case is also discussed in Chapter 1.

process. Courts were inconsistent in their rulings and the time became ripe for the Court to reexamine the issue. It did so in Gideon v. Wainwright.

GIDEON v. WAINWRIGHT
372 U.S. 335 (1963)

Justice BLACK delivered the opinion of the Court.

Petitioner was charged in a Florida state court with having broken and entered a poolroom with intent to commit a misdemeanor. This offense is a felony under Florida law. Appearing in court without funds and without a lawyer, petitioner asked the court to appoint counsel for him, whereupon the following colloquy took place:

The COURT: Mr. Gideon, I am sorry, but I cannot appoint Counsel to represent you in this case. Under the laws of the State of Florida, the only time the Court can appoint Counsel to represent a Defendant is when that person is charged with a capital offense. I am sorry, but I will have to deny your request to appoint Counsel to defend you in this case.

The DEFENDANT: The United States Supreme Court says I am entitled to be represented by Counsel.

Put to trial before a jury, Gideon conducted his defense about as well as could be expected from a layman. He made an opening statement to the jury, cross-examined the State's witnesses, presented witnesses in his own defense, declined to testify himself, and made a short argument "emphasizing his innocence to the charge contained in the Information filed in this case." The jury returned a verdict of guilty, and petitioner was sentenced to serve five years in the state prison. Later, petitioner filed in the Florida Supreme Court this habeas corpus petition attacking his conviction and sentence on the ground that the trial court's refusal to appoint counsel for him denied him rights "guaranteed by the Constitution and the Bill of Rights by the United States Government."[3] Treating the petition for habeas corpus as properly before it, the State Supreme Court, "upon consideration thereof" but without an opinion, denied all relief. Since 1942, when Betts v. Brady was decided by a divided Court, [the rule has been that there is no automatic right to counsel unless counsel is needed to ensure due process to the defendant in his particular case]. [W]e appointed counsel to represent [Gideon] and requested both sides to discuss in their briefs and oral arguments the following: "Should this Court's holding in Betts v. Brady be reconsidered?"

The Sixth Amendment provides, "In all criminal prosecutions, the accused shall enjoy the right . . . to have the Assistance of Counsel for his

---

3. The Supreme Court accepted a handwritten petition Gideon wrote for himself. He stated, "I, Clarence Earl Gideon, claim that I was denied the rights of the 4th, 5th and 14th amendments of the Bill of Rights." See original opinion, fn.2. [Footnote by casebook authors.]

defence." Betts argued that this right is extended to indigent defendants in state courts by the Fourteenth Amendment. On the basis of . . . historical data the Court concluded that "appointment of counsel is not a fundamental right, essential to a fair trial."

We accept Betts v. Brady's assumption, based as it was on our prior cases, that a provision of the Bill of Rights which is "fundamental and essential to a fair trial" is made obligatory upon the States by the Fourteenth Amendment. We think the Court in *Betts* was wrong, however, in concluding that the Sixth Amendment's guarantee of counsel is not one of these fundamental rights.

"[The assistance of counsel] is one of the safeguards of the Sixth Amendment deemed necessary to insure fundamental human rights of life and liberty. . . . The Sixth Amendment stands as a constant admonition that if the constitutional safeguards it provides be lost, justice will not 'still be done.'" Johnson v. Zerbst (1938).

The fact is that in deciding as it did — that "appointment of counsel is not a fundamental right, essential to a fair trial" — the Court in Betts v. Brady made an abrupt break with its own well-considered precedents. In returning to these old precedents, sounder we believe than the new, we but restore constitutional principles established to achieve a fair system of justice. Not only these precedents but also reason and reflection require us to recognize that in our adversary system of criminal justice, any person haled into court, who is too poor to hire a lawyer, cannot be assured a fair trial unless counsel is provided for him. This seems to us to be an obvious truth. Governments, both state and federal, quite properly spend vast sums of money to establish machinery to try defendants accused of crime. Lawyers to prosecute are everywhere deemed essential to protect the public's interest in an orderly society. Similarly, there are few defendants charged with crime, few indeed, who fail to hire the best lawyers they can get to prepare and present their defenses. That government hires lawyers to prosecute and defendants who have the money hire lawyers to defend are the strongest indications of the widespread belief that lawyers in criminal courts are necessities, not luxuries. The right of one charged with crime to counsel may not be deemed fundamental and essential to fair trials in some countries, but it is in ours. From the very beginning, our state and national constitutions and laws have laid great emphasis on procedural and substantive safeguards designed to assure fair trials before impartial tribunals in which every defendant stands equal before the law. This noble ideal cannot be realized if the poor man charged with crime has to face his accusers without a lawyer to assist him. A defendant's need for a lawyer is nowhere better stated than in the moving words of Mr. Justice Sutherland in Powell v. Alabama:

> The right to be heard would be, in many cases, of little avail if it did not comprehend the right to be heard by counsel. Even the intelligent and educated layman has small and sometimes no skill in the science of law. If charged with crime, he is incapable, generally, of determining for himself whether the indictment is good or bad. He is unfamiliar with the rules of evidence. Left without the aid of counsel he may be put on trial without a proper charge, and convicted upon incompetent

evidence, or evidence irrelevant to the issue or otherwise inadmissible. He lacks both the skill and knowledge adequately to prepare his defense, even though he have a perfect one. He requires the guiding hand of counsel at every step in the proceedings against him. Without it, though he be not guilty, he faces the danger of conviction because he does not know how to establish his innocence.

The Court in Betts v. Brady departed from the sound wisdom upon which the Court's holding in Powell v. Alabama rested. *Betts* was "an anachronism when handed down" and . . . it should now be overruled.

Gideon was afforded a new trial with counsel. Upon retrial, he was acquitted.

The right to counsel is so important that it is automatically triggered by the prosecution of the defendant and does not depend on the defendant's request for a lawyer. Brewer v. Williams, 430 U.S. 387, 404 (1977). As *Gideon* established, if a defendant cannot afford his own lawyer, the court must appoint counsel for him.

C. WHEN THE RIGHT TO COUNSEL APPLIES

The Sixth Amendment provides that "[i]n all criminal prosecutions, the accused shall enjoy the right . . . to have the Assistance of Counsel for his defense." The Court has interpreted this language to mean that the absolute right to counsel applies to all "critical stages" of a criminal prosecution after the filing of formal charges. Kirby v. Illinois, 406 U.S. 682 (1972) (plurality opinion). Critical stages may occur before trial. Defense counsel can play a critical role before trial in the investigation of a case and in plea bargaining discussions with the prosecutor.

The Court has expressly held that the right to counsel attaches at all post-indictment pretrial lineups (United States v. Wade, 388 U.S. 218 (1967)), preliminary hearings (Coleman v. Alabama, 399 U.S. 1 (1970)), post-indictment interrogations (Massiah v. United States, 377 U.S. 201 (1964)), and arraignments (Hamilton v. Alabama, 368 U.S. 52 (1961)). In Rothgery v. Gillespie County, 554 U.S. 191 (2008), the Court clarified that the Sixth Amendment right to counsel attaches at the defendant's first appearance before a judicial officer after a formal charge is made, regardless of whether a prosecutor is present.

The right to counsel applies to a defendant's first appeal of right. *See* Douglas v. California, 372 U.S. 353 (1963); Evitts v. Lucey, 469 U.S. 387 (1985). This includes the first-tier of discretionary appeals. Halbert v. Michigan, 545 U.S. 605 (2005). Even if a defendant's appeal does not have merit, the defendant is entitled to appointed counsel who will examine the record carefully to identify any nonfrivolous issues for the appellate court to review. Anders v. California, 386 U.S. 738 (1967).

By contrast, there is no right to counsel for second-tier discretionary state appeals or petitions for review to the United States Supreme Court. Ross v. Moffitt, 417 U.S. 600 (1974). The right to counsel also does not attach at parole hearings or probation revocation hearings (Gagnon v. Scarpelli, 411 U.S. 778 (1973)) or in civil matters such as habeas corpus proceedings (Pennsylvania v. Finley, 481 U.S. 551 (1987)). By the terms of the Sixth Amendment, the right to assistance of counsel does not apply in civil cases but only "[i]n all criminal prosecutions."

As for parole and probation revocation hearings, the Supreme Court refused to create a per se requirement for the appointment of counsel. Rather, using a due process case-by-case approach, the Court held that appointment of counsel was not automatically required by the Sixth Amendment. Justice Powell wrote:

> [T]he "purpose is to help individuals reintegrate into society as constructive individuals as soon as they are able. . . ." The introduction of counsel into a revocation proceeding will alter significantly the nature of the proceeding. If counsel is provided for the probationer or parolee, the State in turn will normally provide its own counsel; lawyers, by training and disposition, are advocates and bound by professional duty to present all available evidence and arguments in support of their clients' positions and to contest with vigor all adverse evidence and views. The role of the hearing body itself, aptly described as being "predictive and discretionary" as well as factfinding, may become more akin to that of a judge at a trial, and less attuned to the rehabilitative needs of the individual probationer or parolee. In the greater self-consciousness of its quasi-judicial role, the hearing body may be less tolerant of marginal deviant behavior and feel more pressure to reincarcerate than to continue nonpunitive rehabilitation. Certainly, the decisionmaking process will be prolonged, and the financial cost to the State — for appointed counsel, counsel for the State, a longer record, and the possibility of judicial review — will not be insubstantial.
>
> In some cases, these modifications in the nature of the revocation hearing must be endured and the costs borne because the probationer's or parolee's version of a disputed issue can fairly be represented only by a trained advocate. But due process is not so rigid as to require that the significant interests in informality, flexibility, and economy must always be sacrificed.
>
> In so concluding, we are of course aware that the case-by-case approach to the right to counsel in felony prosecutions adopted in Betts v. Brady (1942), was later rejected in favor of a per se rule in Gideon v. Wainwright (1963). *See also* Argersinger v. Hamlin (1972). We do not, however, draw from [these cases] the conclusion that a case-by-case approach to furnishing counsel is necessarily inadequate to protect constitutional rights: there are critical differences between criminal trials and probation or parole revocation hearings, and both society and the probationer or parolee have stakes in preserving these differences.

Gagnon v. Scarpelli, 411 U.S. at 783-791.

A defendant has a Sixth Amendment right to counsel in any felony case or in a misdemeanor case if a sentence of incarceration is actually imposed. Argersinger v. Hamlin, 407 U.S. 25, 40 (1972). This includes cases in which the defendant received a suspended sentence and was later incarcerated for a probation violation. Alabama v. Shelton, 535 U.S. 654, 674 (2002).

As detailed in Chapter 8, there is no right to a jury trial for petty offenses. *See* Blanton v. City of North Las Vegas, 489 U.S. 538, 541-542 (1989). By contrast, there is a right to counsel if the defendant is sentenced to jail. Why? Once again, the answer lies in the role defense counsel plays in a case.

ARGERSINGER v. HAMLIN
407 U.S. 25 (1972)

Justice DOUGLAS delivered the opinion of the Court.

Petitioner, an indigent, was charged in Florida with carrying a concealed weapon, an offense punishable by imprisonment up to six months, a $1,000 fine, or both. The trial was to a judge, and petitioner was unrepresented by counsel. He was sentenced to serve 90 days in jail, and brought this habeas corpus action alleging that being deprived of his right to counsel, he was unable as an indigent layman properly to raise and present to the trial court good and sufficient defenses to the charge for which he stands convicted.

While there is historical support for limiting the "deep commitment" to trial by jury to "serious criminal cases," there is no such support for a similar limitation on the right to assistance of counsel:

> Originally, in England, a person charged with treason or felony was denied the aid of counsel, except in respect of legal questions which the accused himself might suggest. At the same time parties in civil cases and persons accused of misdemeanors were entitled to the full assistance of counsel. . . .

The Sixth Amendment thus extended the right to counsel beyond its common-law dimensions. But there is nothing in the language of the Amendment, its history, or in the decisions of this Court, to indicate that it was intended to embody a retraction of the right in petty offenses wherein the common law previously did require that counsel be provided.

We reject, therefore, the premise that since prosecutions for crimes punishable by imprisonment for less than six months may be tried without a jury, they may also be tried without a lawyer.

> The assistance of counsel is often a requisite to the very existence of a fair trial.[4] In our adversary system of criminal justice, any person haled into court, who is too poor to hire a lawyer, cannot be assured a fair trial unless counsel is provided for

---

4. [The Sixth Amendment] embodies a realistic recognition of the obvious truth that the average defendant does not have the professional legal skill to protect himself when brought before a tribunal with power to take his life or liberty, wherein the prosecution is represented by experienced and learned counsel. That which is simple, orderly and necessary to the lawyer, to the untrained layman may appear intricate, complex and mysterious.

Johnson v. Zerbst, 304 U.S. 458, 462-463 (1938). [Footnote by the Court.]

him. This seems to us to be an obvious truth. Governments, both state and federal, quite properly spend vast sums of money to establish machinery to try defendants accused of crime. Lawyers to prosecute are everywhere deemed essential to protect the public's interest in an orderly society. Similarly, there are few defendants charged with crime, few indeed, who fail to hire the best lawyers they can get to prepare and present their defenses. That government hires lawyers to prosecute and defendants who have the money hire lawyers to defend are the strongest indications of the widespread belief that lawyers in criminal courts are necessities, not luxuries. The right of one charged with crime to counsel may not be deemed fundamental and essential to fair trials in some countries, but it is in ours.

The requirement of counsel may well be necessary for a fair trial even in a petty-offense prosecution. We are by no means convinced that legal and constitutional questions involved in a case that actually leads to imprisonment even for a brief period are any less complex than when a person can be sent off for six months or more. The trial of vagrancy cases is illustrative. While only brief sentences of imprisonment may be imposed, the cases often bristle with thorny constitutional questions.

Beyond the problem of trials and appeals is that of the guilty plea, a problem which looms large in misdemeanor as well as in felony cases. Counsel is needed so that the accused may know precisely what he is doing, so that he is fully aware of the prospect of going to jail or prison, and so that he is treated fairly by the prosecution.

In addition, the volume of misdemeanor cases, far greater in number than felony prosecutions, may create an obsession for speedy dispositions, regardless of the fairness of the result. An inevitable consequence of volume that large is the almost total preoccupation in such a court with the movement of cases. The calendar is long, speed often is substituted for care, and casually arranged out-of-court compromise too often is substituted for adjudication. Inadequate attention tends to be given to the individual defendant, whether in protecting his rights, sifting the facts at trial, deciding the social risk he presents, or determining how to deal with him after conviction. The frequent result is futility and failure. As Dean Edward Barrett recently observed:

> Wherever the visitor looks at the system, he finds great numbers of defendants being processed by harassed and overworked officials. Police have more cases than they can investigate. Prosecutors walk into courtrooms to try simple cases as they take their initial looks at the files. Defense lawyers appear having had no more than time for hasty conversations with their clients. Judges face long calendars with the certain knowledge that their calendars tomorrow and the next day will be, if anything, longer, and so there is no choice but to dispose of the cases.
>
> Suddenly it becomes clear that for most defendants in the criminal process, there is scant regard for them as individuals. They are numbers on dockets, faceless ones to be processed and sent on their way. The gap between the theory and the reality is enormous.

There is evidence of the prejudice which results to misdemeanor defendants from this "assembly-line justice." One study concluded that "misdemeanants represented by attorneys are five times as likely to emerge from police court with all charges dismissed as are defendants who face similar charges without counsel."

We must conclude, therefore, that the problems associated with misdemeanor and petty offenses often require the presence of counsel to insure the accused a fair trial.

We hold, therefore, that absent a knowing and intelligent waiver, no person may be imprisoned for any offense, whether classified as petty, misdemeanor, or felony, unless he was represented by counsel at his trial.

Despite the important role of counsel — even in misdemeanor prosecutions — the Supreme Court reaffirmed in Scott v. Illinois, 440 U.S. 567 (1979), that the right to counsel in misdemeanor cases applies only where a term of imprisonment is imposed. A court may impose a fine regardless of whether the defendant was represented by counsel. As Justice Rehnquist wrote, "[T]he central premise of *Argersinger* — that actual imprisonment is a penalty different in kind from fines or the mere threat of imprisonment — is eminently sound and warrants adoption of actual imprisonment as the line defining the constitutional right to appointment of counsel."

D. STANDARD FOR "EFFECTIVE ASSISTANCE" OF COUNSEL

Following *Gideon,* the courts struggled with the issue of how competent counsel must be to satisfy Sixth Amendment standards. Is the defendant entitled to a lawyer who makes no mistakes? What if the lawyer makes mistakes but those mistakes were unlikely to affect the outcome of the defendant's trial? What does the Sixth Amendment mean when it guarantees the right to "effective" assistance of counsel? The Court settled on its standard for effective assistance of counsel in Strickland v. Washington.

STRICKLAND v. WASHINGTON
466 U.S. 668 (1984)

Justice O'CONNOR delivered the opinion of the Court.

This case requires us to consider the proper standards for judging a criminal defendant's contention that the Constitution requires a conviction or death sentence to be set aside because counsel's assistance at the trial or sentencing was ineffective.

I

During a 10-day period in September 1976, respondent planned and committed three groups of crimes, which included three brutal stabbing murders, torture, kidnaping, severe assaults, attempted murders, attempted extortion, and theft. After his two accomplices were arrested, respondent surrendered to police and voluntarily gave a lengthy statement confessing to the third of the criminal episodes. The State of Florida indicted respondent for kidnaping and murder and appointed an experienced criminal lawyer to represent him.

Counsel actively pursued pretrial motions and discovery. He cut his efforts short, however, and he experienced a sense of hopelessness about the case, when he learned that, against his specific advice, respondent had also confessed to the first two murders. By the date set for trial, respondent was subject to indictment for three counts of first-degree murder and multiple counts of robbery, kidnaping for ransom, breaking and entering and assault, attempted murder, and conspiracy to commit robbery. Respondent waived his right to a jury trial, again acting against counsel's advice, and pleaded guilty to all charges, including the three capital murder charges.

In the plea colloquy, respondent told the trial judge that, although he had committed a string of burglaries, he had no significant prior criminal record and that at the time of his criminal spree he was under extreme stress caused by his inability to support his family. He also stated, however, that he accepted responsibility for the crimes. The trial judge told respondent that he had "a great deal of respect for people who are willing to step forward and admit their responsibility" but that he was making no statement at all about his likely sentencing decision.

Counsel advised respondent to invoke his right under Florida law to an advisory jury at his capital sentencing hearing. Respondent rejected the advice and waived the right. He chose instead to be sentenced by the trial judge without a jury recommendation.

In preparing for the sentencing hearing, counsel spoke with respondent about his background. He also spoke on the telephone with respondent's wife and mother, though he did not follow up on the one unsuccessful effort to meet with them. He did not otherwise seek out character witnesses for respondent. Nor did he request a psychiatric examination, since his conversations with his client gave no indication that respondent had psychological problems.

Counsel decided not to present and hence not to look further for evidence concerning respondent's character and emotional state. That decision reflected trial counsel's sense of hopelessness about overcoming the evidentiary effect of respondent's confessions to the gruesome crimes. It also reflected the judgment that it was advisable to rely on the plea colloquy for evidence about respondent's background and about his claim of emotional stress: the plea colloquy communicated sufficient information about these subjects, and by forgoing the opportunity to present new evidence on these subjects, counsel prevented the State from cross-examining respondent on his claim and from putting on psychiatric evidence of its own.

Counsel also excluded from the sentencing hearing other evidence he thought was potentially damaging. He successfully moved to exclude respondent's "rap sheet." Because he judged that a presentence report might prove more detrimental than helpful, as it would have included respondent's criminal history and thereby would have undermined the claim of no significant history of criminal activity, he did not request that one be prepared.

At the sentencing hearing, counsel's strategy was based primarily on the trial judge's remarks at the plea colloquy as well as on his reputation as a sentencing judge who thought it important for a convicted defendant to own up to his crime. Counsel argued that respondent's remorse and acceptance of responsibility justified sparing him from the death penalty. Counsel also argued that respondent had no history of criminal activity and that respondent committed the crimes under extreme mental or emotional disturbance, thus coming within the statutory list of mitigating circumstances. He further argued that respondent should be spared death because he had surrendered, confessed, and offered to testify against a codefendant and because respondent was fundamentally a good person who had briefly gone badly wrong in extremely stressful circumstances. The State put on evidence and witnesses largely for the purpose of describing the details of the crimes. Counsel did not cross-examine the medical experts who testified about the manner of death of respondent's victims.

The trial judge found several aggravating circumstances with respect to each of the three murders. He found that all three murders were especially heinous, atrocious, and cruel, all involving repeated stabbings. All three murders were committed in the course of at least one other dangerous and violent felony, and since all involved robbery, the murders were for pecuniary gain. All three murders were committed to avoid arrest for the accompanying crimes and to hinder law enforcement. In the course of one of the murders, respondent knowingly subjected numerous persons to a grave risk of death by deliberately stabbing and shooting the murder victim's sisters-in-law, who sustained severe — in one case, ultimately fatal — injuries.

With respect to mitigating circumstances, the trial judge made the same findings for all three capital murders. First, although there was no admitted evidence of prior convictions, respondent had stated that he had engaged in a course of stealing. In any case, even if respondent had no significant history of criminal activity, the aggravating circumstances "would still clearly far outweigh" that mitigating factor. Second, the judge found that, during all three crimes, respondent was not suffering from extreme mental or emotional disturbance and could appreciate the criminality of his acts. Third, none of the victims was a participant in, or consented to, respondent's conduct. Fourth, respondent's participation in the crimes was neither minor nor the result of duress or domination by an accomplice.

In short, the trial judge found numerous aggravating circumstances and no (or a single comparatively insignificant) mitigating circumstance. With respect to each of the three convictions for capital murder, the trial judge concluded: "A careful consideration of all matters presented to the court impels the conclusion that there are insufficient mitigating circumstances ... to outweigh the aggravating circumstances." He therefore sentenced respondent to death on each of the three counts of murder and to prison terms for the other crimes.

Respondent subsequently sought collateral relief in state court on numerous grounds, among them that counsel had rendered ineffective assistance at the sentencing proceeding. Respondent challenged counsel's assistance in six respects. He asserted that counsel was ineffective because he failed to move for a continuance to prepare for sentencing, to request a psychiatric report, to investigate and present character witnesses, to seek a presentence investigation report, to present meaningful arguments to the sentencing judge, and to investigate the medical examiner's reports or cross-examine the medical experts. In support of the claim, respondent submitted 14 affidavits from friends, neighbors, and relatives stating that they would have testified if asked to do so. He also submitted one psychiatric report and one psychological report stating that respondent, though not under the influence of extreme mental or emotional disturbance, was "chronically frustrated and depressed because of his economic dilemma" at the time of his crimes.

The trial court denied relief.

In assessing attorney performance, all the Federal Courts of Appeals and all but a few state courts have now adopted the "reasonably effective assistance" standard in one formulation or another. Yet this Court has not had occasion squarely to decide whether that is the proper standard. [W]e granted certiorari to consider the standards by which to judge a contention that the Constitution requires that a criminal judgment be overturned because of the actual ineffective assistance of counsel.

II

In a long line of cases that includes ... Gideon v. Wainwright (1963), this Court has recognized that the Sixth Amendment right to counsel exists, and is needed, in order to protect the fundamental right to a fair trial. The Constitution guarantees:

> In all criminal prosecutions, the accused shall enjoy the right to a speedy and public trial, by an impartial jury of the State and district wherein the crime shall have been committed, which district shall have been previously ascertained by law, and to be informed of the nature and cause of the accusation; to be confronted with the witnesses against him; to have compulsory process for obtaining witnesses in his favor, and to have the Assistance of Counsel for his defence.

Thus, a fair trial is one in which evidence subject to adversarial testing is presented to an impartial tribunal for resolution of issues defined in advance of the proceeding. The right to counsel plays a crucial role in the adversarial system embodied in the Sixth Amendment, since access to counsel's skill and knowledge is necessary to accord defendants the "ample opportunity to meet the case of the prosecution" to which they are entitled.

Because of the vital importance of counsel's assistance, this Court has held that, with certain exceptions, a person accused of a federal or state crime has the right to have counsel appointed if retained counsel cannot be obtained. *See* Argersinger v. Hamlin (1972). That a person who happens to be a lawyer is present at trial alongside the accused, however, is not enough to satisfy the constitutional command. The Sixth Amendment recognizes the right to the assistance of counsel because it envisions counsel's playing a role that is critical to the ability of the adversarial system to produce just results. An accused is entitled to be assisted by an attorney, whether retained or appointed, who plays the role necessary to ensure that the trial is fair.

For that reason, the Court has recognized that "the right to counsel is the right to the effective assistance of counsel." Government violates the right to effective assistance when it interferes in certain ways with the ability of counsel to make independent decisions about how to conduct the defense. *See, e.g.,* Geders v. United States (1976) (bar on attorney-client consultation during overnight recess). Counsel, however, can also deprive a defendant of the right to effective assistance, simply by failing to render "adequate legal assistance," Cuyler v. Sullivan (actual conflict of interest adversely affecting lawyer's performance renders assistance ineffective).

The Court has not elaborated on the meaning of the constitutional requirement of effective assistance in the latter class of cases — that is, those presenting claims of "actual ineffectiveness." In giving meaning to the requirement, however, we must take its purpose — to ensure a fair trial — as the guide. The benchmark for judging any claim of ineffectiveness must be whether counsel's conduct so undermined the proper functioning of the adversarial process that the trial cannot be relied on as having produced a just result.

The same principle applies to a capital sentencing proceeding such as that provided by Florida law. We need not consider the role of counsel in an ordinary sentencing, which may involve informal proceedings and standardless discretion in the sentencer, and hence may require a different approach to the definition of constitutionally effective assistance. A capital sentencing proceeding like the one involved in this case, however, is sufficiently like a trial in its adversarial format and in the existence of standards for decision, that counsel's role in the proceeding is comparable to counsel's role at trial — to ensure that the adversarial testing process works to produce a just result under the standards governing decision. For purposes of describing counsel's duties, therefore, Florida's capital sentencing proceeding need not be distinguished from an ordinary trial.

III

A convicted defendant's claim that counsel's assistance was so defective as to require reversal of a conviction or death sentence has two components. First, the defendant must show that counsel's performance was deficient. This requires showing that counsel made errors so serious that counsel was not functioning as the "counsel" guaranteed the defendant by the Sixth Amendment. Second, the defendant must show that the deficient performance prejudiced the defense. This requires showing that counsel's errors were so serious as to deprive the defendant of a fair trial, a trial whose result is reliable. Unless a defendant makes both showings, it cannot be said that the conviction or death sentence resulted from a breakdown in the adversary process that renders the result unreliable.

A

As all the Federal Courts of Appeals have now held, the proper standard for attorney performance is that of reasonably effective assistance. . . . When a convicted defendant complains of the ineffectiveness of counsel's assistance, the defendant must show that counsel's representation fell below an objective standard of reasonableness.

More specific guidelines are not appropriate. The Sixth Amendment refers simply to "counsel," not specifying particular requirements of effective assistance. It relies instead on the legal profession's maintenance of standards sufficient to justify the law's presumption that counsel will fulfill the role in the adversary process that the Amendment envisions. The proper measure of attorney performance remains simply reasonableness under prevailing professional norms.

Representation of a criminal defendant entails certain basic duties. Counsel's function is to assist the defendant, and hence counsel owes the client a duty of loyalty, a duty to avoid conflicts of interest. From counsel's function as assistant to the defendant derive the overarching duty to advocate the defendant's cause and the more particular duties to consult with the defendant on important decisions and to keep the defendant informed of important developments in the course of the prosecution. Counsel also has a duty to bring to bear such skill and knowledge as will render the trial a reliable adversarial testing process.

These basic duties neither exhaustively define the obligations of counsel nor form a checklist for judicial evaluation of attorney performance. In any case presenting an ineffectiveness claim, the performance inquiry must be whether counsel's assistance was reasonable considering all the circumstances. Prevailing norms of practice as reflected in American Bar Association standards and the like are guides to determining what is reasonable, but they are only guides. No particular set of detailed rules for counsel's conduct can satisfactorily take account of the variety of circumstances faced by defense counsel or the range of legitimate decisions regarding how best to represent a criminal defendant. Any such set of rules would interfere with the constitutionally protected independence of counsel and restrict the wide latitude counsel must have in making tactical decisions.

Judicial scrutiny of counsel's performance must be highly deferential. It is all too tempting for a defendant to second-guess counsel's assistance after conviction or adverse sentence, and it is all too easy for a court, examining counsel's defense after it has proved unsuccessful, to conclude that a particular act or omission of counsel was unreasonable. A fair assessment of attorney performance requires that every effort be made to eliminate the distorting effects of hindsight, to reconstruct the circumstances of counsel's challenged conduct, and to evaluate the conduct from counsel's perspective at the time. Because of the difficulties inherent in making the evaluation, a court must indulge a strong presumption that counsel's conduct falls within the wide range of reasonable professional assistance; that is, the defendant must overcome the presumption that, under the circumstances, the challenged action "might be considered sound trial strategy." There are countless ways to provide effective assistance in any given case. Even the best criminal defense attorneys would not defend a particular client in the same way.

The availability of intrusive post-trial inquiry into attorney performance or of detailed guidelines for its evaluation would encourage the proliferation of ineffectiveness challenges. Criminal trials resolved unfavorably to the defendant would increasingly come to be followed by a second trial, this one of counsel's unsuccessful defense. Counsel's performance and even willingness to serve could be adversely affected. Intensive scrutiny of counsel and rigid requirements for acceptable assistance could dampen the ardor and impair the independence of defense counsel, discourage the acceptance of assigned cases, and undermine the trust between attorney and client.

Thus, a court deciding an actual ineffectiveness claim must judge the reasonableness of counsel's challenged conduct on the facts of the particular case, viewed as of the time of counsel's conduct. A convicted defendant making a claim of ineffective assistance must identify the acts or omissions of counsel that are alleged not to have been the result of reasonable professional judgment. The court must then determine whether, in light of all the circumstances, the identified acts or omissions were outside the wide range of professionally competent assistance. In making that determination, the court should keep in mind that counsel's function, as elaborated in prevailing professional norms, is to make the adversarial testing process work in the particular case. At the same time, the court should recognize that counsel is strongly presumed to have rendered adequate assistance and made all significant decisions in the exercise of reasonable professional judgment.

These standards require no special amplification in order to define counsel's duty to investigate, the duty at issue in this case. [C]ounsel has a duty to make reasonable investigations or to make a reasonable decision that makes particular investigations unnecessary.

The reasonableness of counsel's actions may be determined or substantially influenced by the defendant's own statements or actions. Counsel's actions are usually based, quite properly, on informed strategic choices made by the defendant and on information supplied by the defendant. In particular, what investigation decisions are reasonable depends critically on such information. For example, when the facts that support a certain potential line of defense are generally known to counsel because of what the defendant has said, the need for further investigation may be considerably diminished or eliminated altogether. And when a defendant has given counsel reason to believe that pursuing certain investigations would be fruitless or even harmful, counsel's failure to pursue those investigations may not later be challenged as unreasonable. In short, inquiry into counsel's conversations with the defendant may be critical to a proper assessment of counsel's investigation decisions, just as it may be critical to a proper assessment of counsel's other litigation decisions.

B

An error by counsel, even if professionally unreasonable, does not warrant setting aside the judgment of a criminal proceeding if the error had no effect on the judgment. The purpose of the Sixth Amendment guarantee of counsel is to ensure that a defendant has the assistance necessary to justify reliance on the outcome of the proceeding. Accordingly, any deficiencies in counsel's performance must be prejudicial to the defense in order to constitute ineffective assistance under the Constitution.

In certain Sixth Amendment contexts, prejudice is presumed. Actual or constructive denial of the assistance of counsel altogether is legally presumed to result in prejudice. So are various kinds of state interference with counsel's assistance. Prejudice in these circumstances is so likely that case-by-case inquiry into prejudice is not worth the cost. Moreover, such circumstances involve impairments of the Sixth Amendment right that are easy to identify and, for that reason and because the prosecution is directly responsible, easy for the government to prevent.

One type of actual ineffectiveness claim warrants a similar, though more limited, presumption of prejudice. In Cuyler v. Sullivan, the Court held that prejudice is presumed when counsel is burdened by an actual conflict of interest. In those circumstances, counsel breaches the duty of loyalty, perhaps the most basic of counsel's duties. Moreover, it is difficult to measure the precise effect on the defense of representation corrupted by conflicting interests. Given the obligation of counsel to avoid conflicts of interest and the ability of trial courts to make early inquiry in certain situations likely to give rise to conflicts, *see, e.g.*, Fed. Rule Crim. Proc. 44(c), it is reasonable for the criminal justice system to maintain a fairly rigid rule of presumed prejudice for conflicts of interest.

Conflict of interest claims aside, actual ineffectiveness claims alleging a deficiency in attorney performance are subject to a general requirement that the defendant affirmatively prove prejudice. The government is not responsible for, and hence not able to prevent, attorney errors that will result in reversal of a conviction or sentence. Attorney errors come in an infinite variety and are as likely to be utterly harmless in a particular case as they are to be prejudicial. They cannot be classified according to likelihood of causing prejudice. Nor can they be defined with sufficient precision to inform defense attorneys correctly just what conduct to avoid. Representation is an art, and an act or omission that is unprofessional in one case may be sound or even brilliant in another. Even if a defendant shows that particular errors of counsel were unreasonable, therefore, the defendant must show that they actually had an adverse effect on the defense.

It is not enough for the defendant to show that the errors had some conceivable effect on the outcome of the proceeding. Virtually every act or omission of counsel would meet that test, and not every error that conceivably could have influenced the outcome undermines the reliability of the result of the proceeding. Respondent suggests requiring a showing that the errors "impaired the presentation of the defense." That standard, however, provides no workable principle. Since any error, if it is indeed an error, "impairs" the presentation of the defense, the proposed standard is inadequate because it provides no way of deciding what impairments are sufficiently serious to warrant setting aside the outcome of the proceeding.

On the other hand, we believe that a defendant need not show that counsel's deficient conduct more likely than not altered the outcome in the case. . . . The result of a proceeding can be rendered unreliable, and hence the proceeding itself unfair, even if the errors of counsel cannot be shown by a preponderance of the evidence to have determined the outcome.

Accordingly, the appropriate test for prejudice finds its roots in the test for materiality of exculpatory information not disclosed to the defense by the prosecution. The defendant must show that there is a reasonable probability that, but for counsel's unprofessional errors, the result of the proceeding would have been different. A reasonable probability is a probability sufficient to undermine confidence in the outcome.

When a defendant challenges a conviction, the question is whether there is a reasonable probability that, absent the errors, the factfinder would have had a reasonable doubt respecting guilt. When a defendant challenges a death sentence such as the one at issue in this case, the question is whether there is a reasonable probability that, absent the errors, the sentencer — including an appellate court, to the extent it independently reweighs the evidence — would have concluded that the balance of aggravating and mitigating circumstances did not warrant death.

In making this determination, a court hearing an ineffectiveness claim must consider the totality of the evidence before the judge or jury. Some of the factual findings will have been unaffected by the errors, and factual findings that were affected will have been affected in different ways. Some errors will have had a pervasive effect on the inferences to be drawn from the evidence, altering the entire evidentiary picture, and some will have had an isolated, trivial effect. Moreover, a verdict or conclusion only weakly supported by the record is more likely to have been affected by errors than one with overwhelming record support. Taking the unaffected findings as a given, and taking due account of the effect of the errors on the remaining findings, a court making the prejudice inquiry must ask if the defendant has met the burden of showing that the decision reached would reasonably likely have been different absent the errors.

IV

A number of practical considerations are important for the application of the standards we have outlined. Most important, in adjudicating a claim of actual ineffectiveness of counsel, a court should keep in mind that the principles we have stated do not establish mechanical rules. Although those principles should guide the process of decision, the ultimate focus of inquiry must be on the fundamental fairness of the proceeding whose result is being challenged. In every case the court should be concerned with whether, despite the strong presumption of reliability, the result of the particular proceeding is unreliable because of a breakdown in the adversarial process that our system counts on to produce just results.

Although we have discussed the performance component of an ineffectiveness claim prior to the prejudice component, there is no reason for a court deciding an ineffective assistance claim to approach the inquiry in the same order or even to address both components of the inquiry if the defendant makes an insufficient showing on one. In particular, a court need not determine whether counsel's performance was deficient before examining the prejudice suffered by the defendant as a result of the alleged deficiencies. The object of an ineffectiveness claim is not to grade counsel's performance. If it is easier to dispose of an ineffectiveness claim on the ground of lack of sufficient prejudice, which we expect will often be so, that course should be followed. Courts should strive to ensure that ineffectiveness claims not become so burdensome to defense counsel that the entire criminal justice system suffers as a result.

V

Application of the governing principles is not difficult in this case. The facts as described make clear that the conduct of respondent's counsel at and before respondent's sentencing proceeding cannot be found unreasonable. They also make clear that, even assuming the challenged conduct of counsel was unreasonable, respondent suffered insufficient prejudice to warrant setting aside his death sentence.

With respect to the performance component, the record shows that respondent's counsel made a strategic choice to argue for the extreme emotional distress mitigating circumstance and to rely as fully as possible on respondent's acceptance of responsibility for his crimes. Although counsel understandably felt hopeless about respondent's prospects, nothing in the record indicates that counsel's sense of hopelessness distorted his professional judgment. Counsel's strategy choice was well within the range of professionally reasonable judgments, and the decision not to seek more character or psychological evidence than was already in hand was likewise reasonable.

The trial judge's views on the importance of owning up to one's crimes were well known to counsel. The aggravating circumstances were utterly overwhelming. Trial counsel could reasonably surmise from his conversations with respondent that character and psychological evidence would be of little help. Respondent had already been able to mention at the plea colloquy the substance of what there was to know about his financial and emotional troubles. Restricting testimony on respondent's character to what had come in at the plea colloquy ensured that contrary character and psychological evidence and respondent's criminal history, which counsel had successfully moved to exclude, would not come in. On these facts, there can be little question, even without application of the presumption of adequate performance, that trial counsel's defense, though unsuccessful, was the result of reasonable professional judgment.

With respect to the prejudice component, the lack of merit of respondent's claim is even more stark. The evidence that respondent says his trial counsel should have offered at the sentencing hearing would barely have altered the sentencing profile presented to the sentencing judge. As the state courts and District Court found, at most this evidence shows that numerous people who knew respondent thought he was generally a good person and that a psychiatrist and a psychologist believed he was under considerable emotional stress that did not rise to the level of extreme disturbance. Given the overwhelming aggravating factors, there is no reasonable probability that the omitted evidence would have changed the conclusion that the aggravating circumstances outweighed the mitigating circumstances and, hence, the sentence imposed. Indeed, admission of the evidence respondent now offers might even have been harmful to his case: his "rap sheet" would probably have been admitted into evidence, and the psychological reports would have directly contradicted respondent's claim that the mitigating circumstance of extreme emotional disturbance applied to his case.

Failure to make the required showing of either deficient performance or sufficient prejudice defeats the ineffectiveness claim. Here there is a double failure. More generally, respondent has made no showing that the justice of his sentence was rendered unreliable by a breakdown in the adversary process caused by deficiencies in counsel's assistance. Respondent's sentencing proceeding was not fundamentally unfair.

We conclude, therefore, that the District Court properly declined to issue a writ of habeas corpus.

Justice MARSHALL, dissenting.

The Sixth and Fourteenth Amendments guarantee a person accused of a crime the right to the aid of a lawyer in preparing and presenting his defense.

It has long been settled that "the right to counsel is the right to the effective assistance of counsel."

My objection to the performance standard adopted by the Court is that it is so malleable that, in practice, it will either have no grip at all or will yield excessive variation in the manner in which the Sixth Amendment is interpreted and applied by different courts. To tell lawyers and the lower courts that counsel for a criminal defendant must behave "reasonably" and must act like "a reasonably competent attorney," is to tell them almost nothing. In essence, the majority has instructed judges called upon to assess claims of ineffective assistance of counsel to advert to their own intuitions regarding what constitutes "professional" representation, and has discouraged them from trying to develop more detailed standards governing the performance of defense counsel. In my view, the Court has thereby not only abdicated its own responsibility to interpret the Constitution, but also impaired the ability of the lower courts to exercise theirs.

I object to the prejudice standard adopted by the Court for two independent reasons. First, it is often very difficult to tell whether a defendant convicted after a trial in which he was ineffectively represented would have fared better if his lawyer had been competent. Seemingly impregnable cases can sometimes be dismantled by good defense counsel. On the basis of a cold record, it may be impossible for a reviewing court confidently to ascertain how the government's evidence and arguments would have stood up against rebuttal and cross-examination by a shrewd, well-prepared lawyer. The difficulties of estimating prejudice after the fact are exacerbated by the possibility that evidence of injury to the defendant may be missing from the record precisely because of the incompetence of defense counsel. In view of all these impediments to a fair evaluation of the probability that the outcome of a trial was affected by ineffectiveness of counsel, it seems to me senseless to impose on a defendant whose lawyer has been shown to have been incompetent the burden of demonstrating prejudice.

Second and more fundamentally, the assumption on which the Court's holding rests is that the only purpose of the constitutional guarantee of effective assistance of counsel is to reduce the chance that innocent persons will be convicted. In my view, the guarantee also functions to ensure that convictions are obtained only through fundamentally fair procedures. The majority contends that the Sixth Amendment is not violated when a manifestly guilty defendant is convicted after a trial in which he was represented by a manifestly ineffective attorney. I cannot agree. Every defendant is entitled to a trial in which his interests are vigorously and conscientiously advocated by an able lawyer. A proceeding in which the defendant does not receive meaningful assistance in meeting the forces of the State does not, in my opinion, constitute due process.

———————

The same day that the Court issued its decision in *Strickland*, it punctuated its decision by deciding Cronic v. United States, 466 U.S. 648 (1984). In *Cronic*, a young real estate lawyer had less than 30 days to prepare for his first criminal case (a mail fraud check kiting scheme) after the government had taken four and one-half years to prepare its prosecution. The defendant argued that his lawyer's lack of preparation time and inexperience gave rise to a presumption of prejudice. Writing for the Court, Justice Stevens rejected Cronic's argument:

> Neither the period of time that the Government spent investigating the case, nor the number of documents that its agents reviewed during that investigation, is necessarily relevant to the question whether a competent lawyer could prepare to defend the case in 25 days. The Government's task of finding and assembling admissible evidence that will carry its burden of proving guilt beyond a reasonable doubt is entirely different from the defendant's task in preparing to deny or rebut a criminal charge. . . .
>
> That conclusion is not undermined by the fact that respondent's lawyer was young, that his principal practice was in real estate, or that this was his first jury trial. Every experienced criminal defense attorney once tried his first criminal case. Moreover, a lawyer's experience with real estate transactions might be more useful in preparing to try a criminal case involving financial transactions than would prior experience in handling, for example, armed robbery prosecutions. . . .
>
> This case is not one in which the surrounding circumstances make it unlikely that the defendant could have received the effective assistance of counsel. . . . [On remand, respondent] can therefore make out a claim of ineffective assistance only by pointing to specific errors made by trial counsel.

In *Cronic*, the Court identified three circumstances under which prejudice may be presumed: (1) if there has been a complete denial of counsel, (2) "if counsel entirely fails to subject the prosecution's case to meaningful adversarial testing," or (3) when there is an actual conflict of interest for counsel.

1.   *Conflicts of Interest*

Before *Cronic*, the Supreme Court had held in Holloway v. Arkansas, 435 U.S. 475 (1978), that it violates a defendant's Sixth Amendment rights to force defense counsel to represent codefendants over counsel's timely objection. When there is a potential conflict of interest, the trial court should inquire regarding it and whether the defendant will still be able to receive effective assistance of counsel.

However, in Cuyler v. Sullivan, 446 U.S. 335 (1980), the Supreme Court held that a defendant can demonstrate a Sixth Amendment violation only by showing (1) defense counsel was actively representing conflicting interests, and (2) the conflict adversely affected counsel's performance for the defendant. In distinguishing its holding in Holloway v. Arkansas and rejecting Sullivan's claim that his privately retained counsel had a disqualifying conflict of interest because he represented all three defendants in their murder cases, the Court noted:

> In Holloway, a single public defender represented three defendants at the same trial. The trial court refused to consider the appointment of separate counsel despite the defense lawyer's timely and repeated assertions that the interests of his clients conflicted.
>
> Holloway requires state trial courts to investigate timely objections to multiple representation. But nothing in our precedents suggests that the Sixth Amendment requires state courts themselves to initiate inquiries into the propriety of multiple representation in every case. Defense counsel have an ethical obligation to avoid conflicting representations and to advise the court promptly when a conflict of interest arises during the course of trial.
>
> Nothing in the circumstances of this case indicates that the trial court had a duty to inquire whether there was a conflict of interest. The provision of separate trials for Sullivan and his codefendants significantly reduced the potential for a divergence in their interests. No participant in Sullivan's trial ever objected to the multiple representation. Counsel's opening argument for Sullivan outlined a defense compatible with the view that none of the defendants was connected with the murders. The opening argument also suggested that counsel was not afraid to call witnesses whose testimony might be needed at the trials of Sullivan's codefendants. Finally, counsel's critical decision to rest Sullivan's defense was on its face a reasonable tactical response to the weakness of the circumstantial evidence presented by the prosecutor.

As *Cuyler* makes clear, there is no per se rule of reversal when defense counsel has an actual or potential conflict of interest. Rather, the burden is on the defendant to demonstrate that defense counsel's conflicting interests negatively impacted counsel's performance at trial. For example, in Mickens v. Taylor, 535 U.S. 162 (2002), the Court held that there was no automatic claim of ineffective assistance of counsel even though defense counsel in that capital murder case had previously represented the murder victim.

Likewise, in Burger v. Kemp, 483 U.S. 776 (1987), the Court refused to find that the defendant's lawyer had an actual conflict of interest simply because his law partner represented Burger's codefendant. Burger argued that his lawyer's relationship with his codefendant's counsel prejudiced his case because Burger's lawyer did not claim that he was less culpable than his codefendant, but the Supreme Court found that the claim was mere speculation and that there was no actual conflict of interest that violated Burger's Sixth Amendment rights.

When there is a conflict of interest, the defendants may waive the right to conflict-free assistance of counsel if the waiver is knowing and intelligent. Holloway v. Arkansas, 435 U.S. at 483 n.5. However, the trial judge is not obliged to accept this waiver. The court still carries the responsibility of deciding whether the conflicted counsel can adequately represent the defendant's interests. *See* Wheat v. United States, 486 U.S. 153 (1988); *see also* Federal Rule of Criminal Procedure 44.

2. Complete Denial of Counsel

While the Court held in *Cronic* that prejudice may be presumed "if counsel entirely fails to subject the prosecution's case to meaningful adversarial testing," this exception is rarely recognized by the Court. For example, in Bell v. Cone, 535 U.S. 685 (2002), Cone argued that he was completely denied the assistance of counsel because his lawyer did not call any witnesses in mitigation of punishment at the penalty phase of his capital trial, although counsel did cross-examine some of the prosecution witnesses. The Court refused to find that counsel had "*entirely*" failed to test the prosecutor's case, and therefore, Cone needed to satisfy the prejudice standard of the *Strickland* test.

3. Strategic Decisions by Defense Counsel

Most claims of ineffective assistance of counsel are challenges to defense counsel's strategic decisions. Defense counsels have broad leeway in deciding on trial strategy. In *Strickland*, the Supreme Court cautioned against second-guessing defense counsels' decisions. Generally, it is very difficult for a defendant to succeed on a claim of ineffective assistance of counsel because an attorney's poor performance is excused if the evidence is otherwise strong in the case and the defendant, therefore, cannot satisfy the prejudice prong of *Strickland*'s ineffective assistance of counsel test. Courts have said that there is no per se rule of reversal even if defense counsel sleeps through portions of the trial. *See* Tippins v. Walker, 77 F.3d 682 (2d Cir. 1996) (in some cases, defense counsel's appearance of sleeping can be a tactical maneuver; however, in this case daily sleeping by counsel met *Cronic* standard of ineffective assistance of counsel).

However, are there any limits on the trial strategy a defense lawyer may choose without violating the Sixth Amendment? For example, what if defense counsel in a death penalty case concedes a defendant's guilt? Does that still meet *Strickland*'s standard for effective assistance of counsel?

FLORIDA v. NIXON

543 U.S. 175 (2004)

Justice GINSBURG delivered the opinion of the Court.

This capital case concerns defense counsel's strategic decision to concede, at the guilt phase of the trial, the defendant's commission of murder, and to concentrate the defense on establishing, at the penalty phase, cause for sparing the defendant's life. Any concession of that order, the Florida Supreme Court held, made without the defendant's express consent—however gruesome the crime and despite the strength of the evidence of guilt—automatically ranks as prejudicial ineffective assistance of counsel necessitating a new trial. We reverse the Florida Supreme Court's judgment.

Defense counsel undoubtedly has a duty to discuss potential strategies with the defendant. *See* Strickland v. Washington (1984). But when a defendant, informed by counsel, neither consents nor objects to the course counsel describes as the most promising means to avert a sentence of death, counsel is not automatically barred from pursuing that course. The reasonableness of counsel's performance, after consultation with the defendant yields no response, must be judged in accord with the inquiry generally applicable to ineffective-assistance-of-counsel claims: Did counsel's representation "f[a]ll below an objective standard of reasonableness"? The Florida Supreme Court erred in applying, instead, a presumption of deficient performance, as well as a presumption of prejudice; that latter presumption, we have instructed, is reserved for cases in which counsel fails meaningfully to oppose the prosecution's case. United States v. Cronic (1984). A presumption of prejudice is not in order based solely on a defendant's failure to provide express consent to a tenable strategy counsel has adequately disclosed to and discussed with the defendant.

I

On Monday, August 13, 1984, near a dirt road in the environs of Tallahassee, Florida, a passing motorist discovered Jeanne Bickner's charred body. Bickner had been tied to a tree and set on fire while still alive. Her left leg and arm, and most of her hair and skin, had been burned away. The next day, police found Bickner's car, abandoned on a Tallahassee street corner, on fire. Police arrested 23-year-old Joe Elton Nixon later that morning, after Nixon's brother informed the sheriff's office that Nixon had confessed to the murder.

Questioned by the police, Nixon described in graphic detail how he had kidnaped Bickner, then killed her. . . . The State gathered overwhelming evidence establishing that Nixon had committed the murder in the manner he described.

Nixon was indicted in Leon County, Florida, for first-degree murder, kidnaping, robbery, and arson. Assistant public defender Michael Corin, assigned to represent Nixon, filed a plea of not guilty, and deposed all of the State's potential witnesses. Corin concluded, given the strength of the evidence, that Nixon's guilt was not "subject to any reasonable dispute."[5] Corin thereupon commenced plea negotiations, hoping to persuade the prosecution to drop the death penalty in exchange for Nixon's guilty pleas to all charges. Negotiations broke down when the prosecutors indicated their unwillingness to recommend a sentence other than death.

---

5. Every court to consider this case, including the judge who presided over Nixon's trial, agreed with Corin's assessment of the evidence. [Footnote by the Court.]

Faced with the inevitability of going to trial on a capital charge, Corin turned his attention to the penalty phase, believing that the only way to save Nixon's life would be to present extensive mitigation evidence centering on Nixon's mental instability. Experienced in capital defense, . . . Corin concluded that the best strategy would be to concede guilt, thereby preserving his credibility in urging leniency during the penalty phase.

Corin attempted to explain this strategy to Nixon at least three times. Nixon was generally unresponsive during their discussions. He never verbally approved or protested Corin's proposed strategy. Overall, Nixon gave Corin very little, if any, assistance or direction in preparing the case. Corin eventually exercised his professional judgment to pursue the concession strategy.

When Nixon's trial began on July 15, 1985, his unresponsiveness deepened into disruptive and violent behavior. On the second day of jury selection, Nixon pulled off his clothing, demanded a black judge and lawyer, refused to be escorted into the courtroom, and threatened to force the guards to shoot him. When the judge examined Nixon on the record in a holding cell, Nixon stated he had no interest in the trial and threatened to misbehave if forced to attend. The judge ruled that Nixon had intelligently and voluntarily waived his right to be present at trial.

The guilt phase of the trial thus began in Nixon's absence. In his opening statement, Corin acknowledged Nixon's guilt and urged the jury to focus on the penalty phase:

> In this case, there won't be any question, none whatsoever, that my client, Joe Elton Nixon, caused Jeannie Bickner's death. . . . [T]hat fact will be proved to your satisfaction beyond any doubt.
>
> This case is about the death of Joe Elton Nixon and whether it should occur within the next few years by electrocution or maybe its natural expiration after a lifetime of confinement. . . .
>
> Now, in arriving at your verdict, in your penalty recommendation, for we will get that far, you are going to learn many facts . . . about Joe Elton Nixon. Some of those facts are going to be good. That may not seem clear to you at this time. But, and sadly, most of the things you learn of Joe Elton Nixon are not going to be good. But, I'm suggesting to you that when you have seen all the testimony, heard all the testimony and the evidence that has been shown, there are going to be reasons why you should recommend that his life be spared.

At the start of the penalty phase, Corin argued to the jury that "Joe Elton Nixon is not normal organically, intellectually, emotionally or educationally or in any other way." Corin presented the testimony of eight witnesses. Relatives and friends described Nixon's childhood emotional troubles and his erratic behavior in the days preceding the murder. A psychiatrist and a psychologist addressed Nixon's antisocial personality, his history of emotional instability and psychiatric care, his low IQ, and the possibility that at some point he suffered brain damage.

In his closing argument, Corin emphasized Nixon's youth, the psychiatric evidence, and the jury's discretion to consider any mitigating circumstances.

Corin urged that, if not sentenced to death, "Joe Elton Nixon would [n]ever be released from confinement." The death penalty, Corin maintained, was appropriate only for "intact human being[s]," and "Joe Elton Nixon is not one of those. He's never been one of those. He never will be one of those." Corin concluded: "You know, we're not around here all that long. And it's rare when we have the opportunity to give or take life. And you have that opportunity to give life. And I'm going to ask you to do that. Thank you." After deliberating for approximately three hours, the jury recommended that Nixon be sentenced to death.

We granted certiorari to resolve an important question of constitutional law, i.e., whether counsel's failure to obtain the defendant's express consent to a strategy of conceding guilt in a capital trial automatically renders counsel's performance deficient, and whether counsel's effectiveness should be evaluated under *Cronic* or *Strickland.*

II

An attorney undoubtedly has a duty to consult with the client regarding "important decisions," including questions of overarching defense strategy. That obligation, however, does not require counsel to obtain the defendant's consent to "every tactical decision." But certain decisions regarding the exercise or waiver of basic trial rights are of such moment that they cannot be made for the defendant by a surrogate. A defendant, this Court affirmed, has "the ultimate authority" to determine "whether to plead guilty, waive a jury, testify in his or her own behalf, or take an appeal." Concerning those decisions, an attorney must both consult with the defendant and obtain consent to the recommended course of action.

The Florida Supreme Court required Nixon's "affirmative, explicit acceptance" of Corin's strategy because it deemed Corin's statements to the jury "the functional equivalent of a guilty plea." We disagree with that assessment.

Corin was obliged to, and in fact several times did, explain his proposed trial strategy to Nixon. Given Nixon's constant resistance to answering inquiries put to him by counsel and court, Corin was not additionally required to gain express consent before conceding Nixon's guilt. The two evidentiary hearings conducted by the Florida trial court demonstrate beyond doubt that Corin fulfilled his duty of consultation by informing Nixon of counsel's proposed strategy and its potential benefits. Nixon's characteristic silence each time information was conveyed to him, in sum, did not suffice to render unreasonable Corin's decision to concede guilt and to home in, instead, on the life or death penalty issue.

On the record thus far developed, Corin's concession of Nixon's guilt does not rank as a "fail[ure] to function in any meaningful sense as the Government's adversary." Although such a concession in a run-of-the-mine trial might present a closer question, the gravity of the potential sentence in a capital trial and the proceeding's two-phase structure vitally affect counsel's strategic calculus. Attorneys representing capital defendants face daunting challenges in developing trial strategies, not least because the defendant's guilt is often clear. Prosecutors are more likely to seek the death penalty, and to refuse to accept a plea to a life sentence, when the evidence is overwhelming and the crime heinous. In such cases, "avoiding execution [may be] the best and only realistic result possible."

Renowned advocate Clarence Darrow, we note, famously employed a similar strategy as counsel for the youthful, cold-blooded killers Richard Loeb and Nathan Leopold. Imploring the judge to spare the boys' lives, Darrow declared: "I do not know how much salvage there is in these two boys. . . . I will be honest with this court as I have tried to be from the beginning. I know that these boys are not fit to be at large."

To summarize, in a capital case, counsel must consider in conjunction both the guilt and penalty phases in determining how best to proceed. When counsel informs the defendant of the strategy counsel believes to be in the defendant's best interest and the defendant is unresponsive, counsel's strategic choice is not impeded by any blanket rule demanding the defendant's explicit consent. Instead, if counsel's strategy, given the evidence bearing on the defendant's guilt, satisfies the *Strickland* standard, that is the end of the matter; no tenable claim of ineffective assistance would remain.

The Court has held firm to its decision not to require lawyers to follow specific guidelines in trying cases. However, in her opinion in Wiggins v. Smith, 539 U.S. 510 (2003), Justice O'Connor suggested that compliance with ABA Standards for Criminal Justice — especially those setting forth a lawyer's responsibility in investigating a case — may provide defense lawyers a safe harbor against claims of ineffective assistance of counsel. Kevin Wiggins was convicted of murder and sentenced to death. He argued that his Sixth Amendment right to counsel was violated because his lawyer failed to investigate his personal background, which would have provided mitigating evidence for his capital sentencing proceedings. If his lawyer had made the effort, he would have found that Wiggins had lived a nightmare as a child. He was abandoned by his mother, ended up in foster care where he was repeatedly raped and tortured, and ended up homeless with diminished mental capacities. In these extreme circumstances, the Supreme Court held that there was a reasonable probability that the sentencing jury would have returned a different verdict had it known of these facts.

In Rompilla v. Beard, 545 U.S. 374 (2005), the Supreme Court continued to focus on counsel's duty to adequately investigate a case before trial. It found that it was ineffective assistance of counsel in a capital case for defense counsel not to request defendant's file from prior cases that would have shown that he too suffered from mental health issues and childhood deprivations that could have been presented to the jury in mitigation of his sentence.

More recently, the Court reaffirmed the importance of having defense counsel adequately investigate a case before trial. In Porter v. McCollum, 558 U.S. 30 (2009), the Court held that it was ineffective assistance of counsel for defense counsel to fail to discover or present evidence during the penalty phase of Porter's murder trial that Porter had a long and distinguished military record, had been the victim of childhood abuse, and had impaired mental capacity. These cases emphasize that pretrial investigation is a critical aspect of defense counsel's responsibilities, especially in capital cases.

While the Court has repeatedly found that lack of investigation by defense counsel may be grounds for a Sixth Amendment challenge, the mere failure of defense counsel to comply with ABA Guidelines for the Appointment and Performance of Defense Counsel in Death Penalty Cases does not automatically establish a claim of ineffective assistance of counsel. Bobby v. Van Hook, 558 U.S. 4 (2009). After doing extensive investigation, it may be reasonable for defense counsel to decide not to seek out all possible evidence that could assist a defendant. Moreover, as Justice Alito expressed in his concurrence in Bobby v. Van Hook, some justices do not believe that the ABA guidelines have "special relevance in determining whether an attorney's performance meets the standard required by the Sixth Amendment."

Additionally, the right to counsel does not include the right to have counsel present any evidence the defendant wishes to admit. A defendant does not have the right to insist on counsel engaging in dishonest or unethical behavior for the defendant. In Nix v. Whiteside, 475 U.S. 157 (1986), the Court held that the defendant was not denied his right to counsel because he told the defendant that he would seek to withdraw if his client perjured himself on the witness stand. "[The] duty is limited to legitimate, lawful conduct compatible with the very nature of a trial as a search for truth. Although counsel must take all reasonable lawful means to attain the objectives of the client, counsel is precluded from taking steps or in any way assisting the client in presenting false evidence or otherwise violating the law." See also Disciplinary Rule 7-102(A)(4), (7).

4. Right to Retain Counsel

The right to counsel also does not entitle an indigent defendant to select his or her counsel (United States v. Allen, 789 F.2d 90 (1st Cir. 1986)), and it does not entitle a defendant to a "meaningful attorney-client relationship" (Morris v. Slappy, 461 U.S. 1 (1983)). Rather, the standards for a Sixth Amendment challenge to defense counsel are those set forth in *Strickland*.

A defendant who can afford to do so may retain counsel of his choosing. As long as that lawyer does not have an unwaivable conflict of interest or violate any of the other court rules, it is a per se error for the court to deny the defendant retained counsel of choice. United States v. Gonzales-Lopez,

548 U.S. 140 (2006).[6] Despite this right, the government may seek to forfeit illegal funds paid to retain a lawyer. "[T]here is a strong governmental interest in obtaining full recovery of all forfeitable assets, an interest that overrides any Sixth Amendment interest in permitting criminals to use assets adjudged forfeitable to pay for their defensel." Caplin & Drysdale v. United States, 491 U.S. 617 (1989).

5. Right to Retain Experts

In addition to the right to counsel, the defendant enjoys a limited due process right to the use of experts who will assist in the presentation of the defense. In Ake v. Oklahoma, 470 U.S. 68 (1985), the Supreme Court recognized an indigent defendant's right to a psychiatrist to assist with the defendant's insanity defense in a capital murder case. Justice Marshall wrote:

> This Court has long recognized that when a State brings its judicial power to bear on an indigent defendant in a criminal proceeding, it must take steps to assure that the defendant had a fair opportunity to present his defense. This elementary principle, grounded in significant part on the Fourteenth Amendment's due process guarantee of fundamental fairness, derives from the belief that justice cannot be equal where, simply as a result of his poverty, a defendant is denied the opportunity to participate meaningfully in a judicial proceeding in which his liberty is at stake.
>
> [A] criminal trial is fundamentally unfair if the State proceeds against an individual defendant without making certain that he has access to the raw materials integral to the building of an effective defense. Thus, while the Court has not held that a State must purchase for the indigent defendant all the assistance that his wealthier counterpart might buy, it has often reaffirmed that fundamental fairness entitles indigent defendants to "an equal opportunity to present their claims within the adversary system."
>
> Without the assistance of a psychiatrist . . . to help determine whether the insanity defense is viable . . . , the risk of an inaccurate resolution of sanity issues is extremely high. With such assistance, the defendant is fairly able to present at least enough information to the jury, in a meaningful manner, as to permit it to make a sensible determination.

Ake does not put defendants on equal footing with the prosecution, but it does provide a basis for requesting those "basic tools" necessary to present an effective defense, including access to investigators and expert witnesses. Although linked to a defendant's Sixth Amendment right to counsel, it is a

---

6. Moreover, it is a Sixth Amendment violation for the government to intrude on the attorney-client relationship. See Weatherford v. Bursey, 429 U.S. 545 (1977). The court considers four factors in determining whether the government has interfered with the right to counsel: (1) whether the government purposely intruded into the attorney-client relationship, (2) whether the government obtained any evidence it used at trial from the intrusion, (3) whether the prosecutor obtained any details about the defense's trial strategy from the intrusion, and (4) whether the information obtained was used in any other way to the substantial detriment of the defendant.

right that actually derives (like the right to counsel once did) from the Due Process clause.

E. RIGHT OF SELF-REPRESENTATION

Instead of being represented by counsel, can a defendant represent himself? The Sixth Amendment refers to the right to "assistance of counsel." Does that encompass the right of self-representation?

FARETTA v. CALIFORNIA
422 U.S. 806 (1975)

Justice STEWART delivered the opinion of the Court.

The Sixth and Fourteenth Amendments of our Constitution guarantee that a person brought to trial in any state or federal court must be afforded the right to the assistance of counsel before he can be validly convicted and punished by imprisonment. The question before us now is whether a defendant in a state criminal trial has a constitutional right to proceed without counsel when he voluntarily and intelligently elects to do so. Stated another way, the question is whether a State may constitutionally hale a person into its criminal courts and there force a lawyer upon him, even when he insists that he wants to conduct his own defense. It is not an easy question, but we have concluded that a State may not constitutionally do so.

I

Anthony Faretta was charged with grand theft. At the arraignment, the Superior Court Judge assigned to preside at the trial appointed the public defender to represent Faretta. Well before the date of trial, however, Faretta requested that he be permitted to represent himself. Questioning by the judge revealed that Faretta had once represented himself in a criminal pros-ecution, that he had a high school education, and that he did not want to be represented by the public defender because he believed that that office was "very loaded down with . . . a heavy case load." The judge responded that he believed Faretta was "making a mistake" and emphasized that in further proceedings Faretta would receive no special favors. Nevertheless, after establishing that Faretta wanted to represent himself and did not want a lawyer, the judge, in a "preliminary ruling," accepted Faretta's waiver of the assistance of counsel. The judge indicated, however, that he might reverse this ruling if it later appeared that Faretta was unable adequately to represent himself.

Several weeks thereafter, but still prior to trial, the judge sua sponte held a hearing to inquire into Faretta's ability to conduct his own defense, and questioned him specifically about both the hearsay rule and the state law governing the challenge of potential jurors.[7]

The California Court of Appeal affirmed the trial judge's ruling that Faretta had no federal or state constitutional right to represent himself and the California Supreme Court denied review. We granted certiorari.

7. The colloquy was as follows:

THE COURT: In the Faretta matter, I brought you back down here to do some reconsideration as to whether or not you should continue to represent yourself. How have you been getting along on your research?

THE DEFENDANT: Not bad, your Honor. Last night I put in the mail a 995 motion and it should be with the Clerk within the next day or two.

THE COURT: Have you been preparing yourself for the intricacies of the trial of the matter?

THE DEFENDANT: Well, your Honor, I was hoping that the case could possibly be disposed of on the 995.

Mrs. Ayers informed me yesterday that it was the Court's policy to hear the pretrial motions at the time of trial. If possible, your Honor, I would like a date set as soon as the Court deems adequate after they receive the motion, sometime before trial.

THE COURT: Let's see how you have been doing on your research. How many exceptions are there to the hearsay rule?

THE DEFENDANT: Well, the hearsay rule would, I guess, be called the best evidence rule, your Honor. And there are several exceptions in case law, but in actual statutory law, I don't feel there is none.

THE COURT: What are the challenges to the jury for cause?

THE DEFENDANT: Well, there is twelve peremptory challenges.

THE COURT: And how many for cause?

THE DEFENDANT: Well, as many as the Court deems valid.

THE COURT: And what are they? What are the grounds for challenging a juror for cause?

THE DEFENDANT: Well, numerous grounds to challenge a witness — I mean, a juror, your Honor, one being the juror is perhaps suffered, was a victim of the same type of offense, might be prejudiced toward the defendant. Any substantial ground that might make the juror prejudice[d] toward the defendant.

THE COURT: Anything else?

THE DEFENDANT: Well, a relative perhaps of the victim.

THE COURT: Have you taken a look at that code section to see what it is?

THE DEFENDANT: Challenge a juror?

THE COURT: Yes.

THE DEFENDANT: Yes, your Honor. I have done —

THE COURT: What is the code section?

THE DEFENDANT: On voir diring a jury, your Honor?

THE COURT: Yes.

THE DEFENDANT: I am not aware of the section right offhand.

THE COURT: What code is it in?

THE DEFENDANT: Well, the research I have done on challenging would be in Witkins Jurisprudence.

THE COURT: Have you looked at any of the codes to see where these various things are taken up?

THE DEFENDANT: No, your Honor, I haven't.

THE COURT: Have you looked in any of the California Codes with reference to trial procedure?

THE DEFENDANT: Yes, your Honor.

THE COURT: What codes?

THE DEFENDANT: I have done extensive research in the Penal Code, your Honor, and the Civil Code.

THE COURT: If you have done extensive research into it, then tell me about it.

THE DEFENDANT: On empaneling a jury, your Honor?

THE COURT: Yes.

THE DEFENDANT: Well, the District Attorney and the defendant, defense counsel, has both the right to 12 peremptory challenges of a jury. These 12 challenges are undisputable. Any reason that the defense or prosecution should feel that a juror would be inadequate to try the case or to rule on a case, they may then discharge that juror.

But if there is a valid challenge due to grounds of prejudice or some other grounds, then these aren't considered in the 12 peremptory challenges. There are numerous and the defendant, the defense and the prosecution both have the right to make any inquiry to the jury as to their feelings toward the case. [Footnote by the Court.]

II

In the federal courts, the right of self-representation has been protected by statute since the beginnings of our Nation. . . . With few exceptions, each of the several States also accords a defendant the right to represent himself in any criminal case.

III

This consensus is soundly premised. The right of self-representation finds support in the structure of the Sixth Amendment, as well as in the English and colonial jurisprudence from which the Amendment emerged.

The Sixth Amendment includes a compact statement of the rights necessary to a full defense:

> In all criminal prosecutions, the accused shall enjoy the right . . . to be informed of the nature and cause of the accusation; to be confronted with the witnesses against him; to have compulsory process for obtaining witnesses in his favor, and to have the Assistance of Counsel for his defence.

Because these rights are basic to our adversary system of criminal justice, they are part of the "due process of law" that is guaranteed by the Fourteenth Amendment to defendants in the criminal courts of the States.

The Sixth Amendment does not provide merely that a defense shall be made for the accused; it grants to the accused personally the right to make his defense. It is the accused, not counsel, who must be "informed of the nature and cause of the accusation," who must be "confronted with the witnesses against him," and who must be accorded "compulsory process for obtaining witnesses in his favor." Although not stated in the Amendment in so many words, the right to self-representation — to make one's own defense personally — is thus necessarily implied by the structure of the Amendment. The right to defend is given directly to the accused; for it is he who suffers the consequences if the defense fails.

The counsel provision supplements this design. It speaks of the "assistance" of counsel, and an assistant, however expert, is still an assistant. The language and spirit of the Sixth Amendment contemplate that counsel, like the other defense tools guaranteed by the Amendment, shall be an aid to a willing defendant — not an organ of the State interposed between an unwilling defendant and his right to defend himself personally. To thrust counsel upon the accused, against his considered wish, thus violates the logic of the Amendment. In such a case, counsel is not an assistant, but a master; and the right to make a defense is stripped of the personal character upon which the Amendment insists. . . . An unwanted counsel "represents" the defendant only through a tenuous and unacceptable legal fiction. Unless the accused has acquiesced in such representation, the defense presented is not the defense guaranteed him by the Constitution, for, in a very real sense, it is not his defense.

In the American Colonies the insistence upon a right of self-representation was, if anything, more fervent than in England.

The colonists brought with them an appreciation of the virtues of self-reliance and a traditional distrust of lawyers. When the Colonies were first settled, "the lawyer was synonymous with the cringing Attorneys-General and Solicitors-General of the Crown and the arbitrary Justices of the King's Court, all bent on the conviction of those who opposed the King's prerogatives, and twisting the law to secure convictions." This prejudice gained strength in the Colonies where "distrust of lawyers became an institution."

The right of self-representation was guaranteed in many colonial charters and declarations of rights. These early documents establish that the "right to counsel" meant to the colonists a right to choose between pleading through a lawyer and representing oneself.

[T]here is no evidence that the colonists and the Framers ever doubted the right of self-representation, or imagined that this right might be considered inferior to the right of assistance of counsel. To the contrary, the colonists and the Framers, as well as their English ancestors, always conceived of the right to counsel as an "assistance" for the accused, to be used at his option, in defending himself. The Framers selected in the Sixth Amendment a form of words that necessarily implies the right of self-representation. That conclusion is supported by centuries of consistent history.

IV

There can be no blinking the fact that the right of an accused to conduct his own defense seems to cut against the grain of this Court's decisions holding that the Constitution requires that no accused can be convicted and imprisoned unless he has been accorded the right to the assistance of counsel.

But it is one thing to hold that every defendant, rich or poor, has the right to the assistance of counsel, and quite another to say that a State may compel a defendant to accept a lawyer he does not want. The value of state-appointed counsel was not unappreciated by the Founders, yet the notion of compulsory counsel was utterly foreign to them. And whatever else may be said of those who wrote the Bill of Rights, surely there can be no doubt that they understood the inestimable worth of free choice.

It is undeniable that in most criminal prosecutions defendants could better defend with counsel's guidance than by their own unskilled efforts. But where the defendant will not voluntarily accept representation by counsel, the potential advantage of a lawyer's training and experience can be realized, if at all, only imperfectly. To force a lawyer on a defendant can only lead him to believe that the law contrives against him. Moreover, it is not inconceivable that in some rare instances, the defendant might in fact present his case more effectively by conducting his own defense. Personal liberties are not rooted in the law of averages. The right to defend is personal. The defendant, and not his lawyer or the State, will bear the personal consequences of a conviction. It is the defendant, therefore, who must be free personally to decide whether in his particular case counsel is to his advantage. And although he may conduct his own defense ultimately to his own detriment, his choice must be honored out of "that respect for the individual which is the lifeblood of the law."

V

When an accused manages his own defense, he relinquishes, as a purely factual matter, many of the traditional benefits associated with the right to counsel. For this reason, in order to represent himself, the accused must "knowingly and intelligently" forgo those relinquished benefits. Although a defendant need not himself have the skill and experience of a lawyer in order competently and intelligently to choose self-representation, he should be made aware of the dangers and disadvantages of self-representation, so that the record will establish that "he knows what he is doing and his choice is made with eyes open."

Here, weeks before trial, Faretta clearly and unequivocally declared to the trial judge that he wanted to represent himself and did not want counsel. The record affirmatively shows that Faretta was literate, competent, and understanding, and that he was voluntarily exercising his informed free will. The trial judge had warned Faretta that he thought it was a mistake not to accept the assistance of counsel, and that Faretta would be required to follow all the "ground rules" of trial procedure. We need make no assessment of how well or poorly Faretta had mastered the intricacies of the hearsay rule and the California code provisions that govern challenges of potential jurors on voir dire. For his technical legal knowledge, as such, was not relevant to an assessment of his knowing exercise of the right to defend himself.

In forcing Faretta, under these circumstances, to accept against his will a state-appointed public defender, the California courts deprived him of his constitutional right to conduct his own defense.

Chief Justice BURGER, with whom Justices BLACKMUN and REHNQUIST join, dissenting.

This case is another example of the judicial tendency to constitutionalize what is thought "good." That effort fails on its own terms here, because there is nothing desirable or useful in permitting every accused person, even the most uneducated and inexperienced, to insist upon conducting his own defense to criminal charges. Moreover, there is no constitutional basis for the Court's holding, and it can only add to the problems of an already malfunctioning criminal justice system. I therefore dissent.

I

The most striking feature of the Court's opinion is that it devotes so little discussion to the matter which it concedes is the core of the decision, that is, discerning an independent basis in the Constitution for the supposed right to represent oneself in a criminal trial. Its ultimate assertion that such a right is tucked between the lines of the Sixth Amendment is contradicted by the Amendment's language and its consistent judicial interpretation.

[T]his Court's decisions have consistently included the right to counsel as an integral part of the bundle making up the larger "right to a defense as we know it."

[It is not] accurate to suggest, as the Court seems to later in its opinion, that the quality of his representation at trial is a matter with which only the accused is legitimately concerned. Although we have adopted an adversary system of criminal justice, the prosecution is more than an ordinary litigant, and the trial judge is not simply an automaton who insures that technical rules are adhered to. Both are charged with the duty of insuring that justice, in the broadest sense of that term, is achieved in every criminal trial. That goal is ill-served, and the integrity of and public confidence in the system are undermined, when an easy conviction is obtained due to the defendant's ill-advised decision to waive counsel. . . . The system of criminal justice should not be available as an instrument of self-destruction.

In short, both the "spirit and the logic" of the Sixth Amendment are that every person accused of crime shall receive the fullest possible defense; in the vast majority of cases this command can be honored only by means of the expressly guaranteed right to counsel, and the trial judge is in the best position to determine whether the accused is capable of conducting his defense. True freedom of choice and society's interest in seeing that justice is achieved can be vindicated only if the trial court retains discretion to reject any attempted waiver of counsel and insist that the accused be tried according to the Constitution.

There is no way to reconcile the idea that the Sixth Amendment impliedly guaranteed the right of an accused to conduct his own defense with the contemporaneous action of the Congress in passing a statute explicitly giving that right. If the Sixth Amendment created a right to self-representation it was unnecessary for Congress to enact any statute on the subject at all.

IV

Society has the right to expect that, when courts find new rights implied in the Constitution, their potential effect upon the resources of our criminal justice system will be considered. However, such considerations are conspicuously absent from the Court's opinion in this case.

It hardly needs repeating that courts at all levels are already handicapped by the unsupplied demand for competent advocates, with the result that it often takes far longer to complete a given case than experienced counsel would require.

Justice BLACKMUN, with whom Chief Justice BURGER and Justice REHNQUIST join, dissenting.

Today the Court holds that the Sixth Amendment guarantees to every defendant in a state criminal trial the right to proceed without counsel whenever he elects to do so. I find no textual support for this conclusion in the language of the Sixth Amendment. I find the historical evidence relied upon by the Court to be unpersuasive, especially in light of the recent history of criminal procedure. Finally, I fear that the right to self-representation constitutionalized today frequently will cause procedural confusion without advancing any significant strategic interest of the defendant. I therefore dissent.

I

The starting point, of course, is the language of the Sixth Amendment:

> In all criminal prosecutions, the accused shall enjoy the right to a speedy and public trial, by an impartial jury of the State and district wherein the crime shall have been committed, which district shall have been previously ascertained by law, and to be informed of the nature and cause of the accusation; to be confronted with the witnesses against him; to have compulsory process for obtaining witnesses in his favor, and to have the Assistance of Counsel for his defence.

It is self-evident that the Amendment makes no direct reference to self-representation. Indeed, the Court concedes that the right to self-representation is "not stated in the Amendment in so many words."

Where then in the Sixth Amendment does one find this right to self-representation? According to the Court, it is "necessarily implied by the structure of the Amendment." Stated somewhat more succinctly, the Court reasons that because the accused has a personal right to "a defense as we know it," he necessarily has a right to make that defense personally. I disagree. Although I believe the specific guarantees of the Sixth Amendment are personal to the accused, I do not agree that the Sixth Amendment guarantees any particular procedural method of asserting those rights. If an accused has enjoyed a speedy trial by an impartial jury in which he was informed of the nature of the accusation, confronted with the witnesses against him, afforded the power of compulsory process, and represented effectively by competent counsel, I do not see that the Sixth Amendment requires more.

The Court seems to suggest that so long as the accused is willing to pay the consequences of his folly, there is no reason for not allowing a defendant the right to self-representation. That view ignores the established principle that the interest of the State in a criminal prosecution "is not that it shall win a case, but that justice shall be done." For my part, I do not believe that any amount of pro se pleading can cure the injury to society of an unjust result, but I do believe that a just result should prove to be an effective balm for almost any frustrated pro se defendant.

III

In conclusion, I note briefly the procedural problems that, I suspect, today's decision will visit upon trial courts in the future. Although the Court indicates that a pro se defendant necessarily waives any claim he might otherwise make of ineffective assistance of counsel, the opinion leaves open a host of other procedural questions. Must every defendant be advised of his right to proceed pro se? If so, when must that notice be given? Since the right to assistance of counsel and the right to self-representation are mutually exclusive, how is the waiver of each right to be measured? If a defendant has elected to exercise his right to proceed pro se, does he still have a constitutional right to assistance of standby counsel? How soon in the criminal proceeding must a defendant decide between proceeding by counsel or pro se? Must he be allowed to switch in midtrial? May a violation of the right to self-representation ever be harmless error? Must the trial court treat the pro se defendant differently than it would professional counsel? I assume that many of these questions will be answered with finality in due course. Many of them, however, such as the standards of waiver and the treatment of the pro se defendant, will haunt the trial of every defendant who elects to exercise his right to self-representation. The procedural problems spawned by an absolute right to self-representation will far outweigh whatever tactical advantage the defendant may feel he has gained by electing to represent himself.

If there is any truth to the old proverb that "one who is his own lawyer has a fool for a client," the Court by its opinion today now bestows a constitutional right on one to make a fool of himself.

In *Faretta*, the Court suggested that a court could appoint standby counsel over the defendant's objection. The Supreme Court upheld the appointment of standby counsel in McKaskle v. Wiggins, 465 U.S. 168 (1984), even though standby counsel openly argued with the defendant during trial. Most of their arguments took place outside of the presence of the jury. Ultimately, the Supreme Court upheld the appointment of standby counsel but warned that standby counsel cannot act in a manner that will "destroy the jury's perception that the defendant is representing himself." The Court further noted that there is no constitutional right to "hybrid counsel" — that is, appointment of counsel that allows the defendant to perform some of the "core functions" of the lawyer. Courts can insist that the defendant decide whether he wants to represent himself or have counsel appointed to represent him. Moreover, the defendant also does not have a right to be represented by a nonlawyer. *See* United States v. Turnbull, 888 F.2d 636 (9th Cir. 1989).

Special issues can arise when a potentially incompetent defendant seeks to represent himself. Recognizing the challenge that such cases pose for trial judges, the Supreme Court held in Indiana v. Edwards (2008) that courts may impose a heightened competency standard for a defendant who wants to represent himself at trial.

INDIANA v. EDWARDS

554 U.S. 164 (2008)

Justice BREYER delivered the opinion of the Court.

This case focuses upon a criminal defendant whom a state court found mentally competent to stand trial if represented by counsel but not mentally competent to conduct that trial himself. We must decide whether in these circumstances the Constitution forbids a State from insisting that the defendant proceed to trial with counsel, the State thereby denying the defendant the right to represent himself. We conclude that the Constitution does not forbid a State so to insist.

I

In July 1999 Ahmad Edwards, the respondent, tried to steal a pair of shoes from an Indiana department store. After he was discovered, he drew a gun, fired at a store security officer, and wounded a bystander. He was caught and then charged with attempted murder, battery with a deadly weapon, criminal recklessness, and theft. His mental condition subsequently became the subject of three competency proceedings and two self-representation requests, mostly before the same trial judge:

First Competency Hearing: August 2000. Five months after Edwards' arrest, his court-appointed counsel asked for a psychiatric evaluation. After hearing psychiatrist and neuropsychologist witnesses (in February 2000 and again in August 2000), the court found Edwards incompetent to stand trial, and committed him to Logansport State Hospital for evaluation and treatment.

Second Competency Hearing: March 2002. Seven months after his commitment, doctors found that Edwards' condition had improved to the point where he could stand trial. Several months later, however, but still before trial, Edwards' counsel asked for another psychiatric evaluation. In March 2002, the judge held a competency hearing, considered additional psychiatric evidence, and (in April) found that Edwards, while "suffer[ing] from mental illness," was "competent to assist his attorneys in his defense and stand trial for the charged crimes."

Third Competency Hearing: April 2003. Seven months later but still before trial, Edwards' counsel sought yet another psychiatric evaluation of his client. And, in April 2003, the court held yet another competency hearing. A testifying psychiatrist reported that Edwards could understand the charges against him, but he was "unable to cooperate with his attorney in his defense because of his schizophrenic illness"; "[h]is delusions and his marked difficulties in thinking make it impossible for him to cooperate with his attorney." In November 2003, the court concluded that Edwards was not then competent to stand trial and ordered his recommitment to the state hospital.

First Self-Representation Request and First Trial: June 2005. About eight months after his commitment, the hospital reported that Edwards' condition had again improved to the point that he had again become competent to stand trial. And almost one year after that Edwards' trial began. Just before trial, Edwards asked to represent himself. He also asked for a continuance, which, he said, he needed in order to proceed *pro se*. The court refused the continuance. Edwards then proceeded to trial represented by counsel. The jury convicted him of criminal recklessness and theft but failed to reach a verdict on the charges of attempted murder and battery.

Second Self-Representation Request and Second Trial: December 2005. The State decided to retry Edwards on the attempted murder and battery charges. Just before the retrial, Edwards again asked the court to permit him to represent himself. Referring to the lengthy record of psychiatric reports, the trial court noted that Edwards still suffered from schizophrenia and concluded that "[w]ith these findings, he's competent to stand trial but I'm not going to find he's competent to defend himself." The court denied Edwards' self-representation request. Edwards was represented by appointed counsel at his retrial. The jury convicted Edwards on both of the remaining counts.

II

Our examination of this Court's precedents convinces us that those precedents frame the question presented, but they do not answer it. *Dusky* defines the competency standard as including both (1) "whether" the defendant has "a rational as well as factual understanding of the proceedings against him" and (2) whether the defendant "has sufficient present ability *to consult with his lawyer* with a reasonable degree of rational understanding." [Neither *Dusky* nor any other prior case, including *Faretta*] considered the mental competency issue presented here, namely, the relation of the mental competence standard to the right of self-representation.

The sole case in which this Court considered mental competence and self-representation together, *Godinez* (1993), presents a question closer to that at issue here. The case focused upon a borderline-competent criminal defendant who had asked a state trial court to permit him to represent himself and to change his pleas from not guilty to guilty. This Court, reversing the Court of Appeals, "reject[ed] the notion that competence to plead guilty or to waive the right to counsel must be measured by a standard that is higher than (or even different from) the *Dusky* standard."

We concede that *Godinez* bears certain similarities with the present case. Both involve mental competence and self-representation. Both involve a defendant who wants to represent himself. Both involve a mental condition that falls in a gray area between *Dusky*'s minimal constitutional requirement that measures a defendant's ability to stand trial and a somewhat higher standard that measures mental fitness for another legal purpose.

We nonetheless conclude that *Godinez* does not answer the question before us now. *Godinez* defendant sought only to change his pleas to guilty, he did not seek to conduct trial proceedings, and his ability to conduct a defense at trial was expressly not at issue.

We now turn to the question presented. We assume that a criminal defendant has sufficient mental competence to stand trial (*i.e.*, the defendant meets *Dusky*'s standard) and that the defendant insists on representing himself during that trial. We ask whether the Constitution permits a State to limit that defendant's self-representation right by insisting upon representation by counsel at trial—on the ground that the defendant lacks the mental capacity to conduct his trial defense unless represented.

Several considerations taken together lead us to conclude that the answer to this question is yes. First, an instance in which a defendant who would choose to forgo counsel at trial presents a very different set of circumstances, which in our view, calls for a different standard.

Second, the nature of the problem before us cautions against the use of a single mental competency standard for deciding both (1) whether a defendant who is represented by counsel can proceed to trial and (2) whether a defendant who goes to trial must be permitted to represent himself. Mental illness itself is not a unitary concept. It varies in degree. It can vary over time. It interferes with an individual's functioning at different times in different ways. The history of this case illustrates the complexity of the problem. In certain instances an individual may well be able to satisfy *Dusky*'s mental competence standard, for he will be able to work with counsel at trial, yet at the same time he may be unable to carry out the basic tasks needed to present his own defense without the help of counsel.

Third, in our view, a right of self-representation at trial will not "affirm the dignity" of a defendant who lacks the mental capacity to conduct his defense without the assistance of counsel. To the contrary, given that defendant's uncertain mental state, the spectacle that could well result from his self-representation at trial is at least as likely to prove humiliating as ennobling. Moreover, insofar as a defendant's lack of capacity threatens an improper conviction or sentence, self-representation in that exceptional context undercuts the most basic of the Constitution's criminal law objectives, providing a fair trial.

Further, proceedings must not only be fair, they must "appear fair to all who observe them." An *amicus* brief reports one psychiatrist's reaction to having observed a patient (a patient who had satisfied *Dusky*) try to conduct his own defense: "[H]ow in the world can our legal system allow an insane man to defend himself?"

We consequently conclude that the Constitution permits judges to take realistic account of the particular defendant's mental capacities by asking whether a defendant who seeks to conduct his own defense at trial is mentally competent to do so. That is to say, the Constitution permits States to insist upon representation by counsel for those competent enough to stand trial under *Dusky* but who still suffer from severe mental illness to the point where they are not competent to conduct trial proceedings by themselves.

Indiana has also asked us to overrule *Faretta*. We decline to do so. We recognize that judges have sometimes expressed concern that *Faretta*, contrary to its intent, has led to trials that are unfair. But recent empirical research suggests that such instances are not common. See, *e.g.*, Hashimoto, *Defending the Right of Self-Representation: An Empirical Look at the Pro Se Felony Defendant*, 85 N. C. L. Rev. 423, 427, 447, 428 (2007) (noting that of the small number of defendants who chose to proceed *pro se*—"roughly 0.3% to 0.5%" of the total, state felony defendants in particular "appear to have achieved higher felony acquittal rates than their represented counterparts in that they were less likely to have been convicted of felonies").

For these reasons, the judgment of the Supreme Court of Indiana is vacated, and the case is remanded for further proceedings not inconsistent with this opinion.

Justice SCALIA, with whom Justice THOMAS joins, dissenting.

The Constitution guarantees a defendant who knowingly and voluntarily waives the right to counsel the right to proceed *pro se* at his trial. *Faretta v. California* (1975). A mentally ill defendant who knowingly and voluntarily elects to proceed *pro se* instead of through counsel receives a fair trial that comports with the Fourteenth Amendment. The Court today concludes that a State may nonetheless strip a mentally ill defendant of the right to represent himself when that would be fairer. In my view the Constitution does not permit a State to substitute its own perception of fairness for the defendant's right to make his own case before the jury—a specific right long understood as essential to a fair trial.

Over the course of what became two separate criminal trials, Edwards sought to act as his own lawyer. He filed a number of incoherent written pleadings with the judge on which the Court places emphasis, but he also filed several intelligible pleadings, such as a motion to dismiss counsel, a motion to dismiss charges under the Indiana speedy trial provision, and a motion seeking a trial transcript.

Edwards made arguments in the courtroom that were more coherent than his written pleadings. In seeking to represent himself at his first trial, Edwards complained in detail that the attorney representing him had not spent adequate time preparing and was not sharing legal materials for use in his defense. The trial judge concluded that Edwards had knowingly and voluntarily waived his right to counsel and proceeded to quiz Edwards about matters of state law. Edwards correctly answered questions about the meaning of *voir dire* and how it operated, and described the basic framework for admitting videotape evidence to trial, though he was unable to answer other questions, including questions about the topics covered by state evidentiary rules that the judge identified only by number. He persisted in his request to represent himself, but the judge denied the request because Edwards acknowledged he would need a continuance. Represented by counsel, he was convicted of criminal recklessness and theft, but the jury deadlocked on charges of attempted murder and battery.

At his second trial, Edwards again asked the judge to be allowed to proceed *pro se*. He explained that he and his attorney disagreed about which defense to present to the attempted murder charge.

The court again rejected Edwards' request to proceed *pro se*, and this time it did not have the justification that Edwards had sought a continuance. The court did not dispute that Edwards knowingly and intelligently waived his right to counsel, but stated it was "going to carve out a third exception" to the right of self-representation, and—without explaining precisely what abilities Edwards lacked—stated Edwards was "competent to stand trial but I'm not going to find he's competent to defend himself."

The Constitution guarantees to every criminal defendant the "right to proceed *without* counsel when he voluntarily and intelligently elects to do so." The right reflects "a nearly universal conviction, on the part of our people as well as our courts, that forcing a lawyer upon an unwilling defendant is contrary to his basic right to defend himself if he truly wants to do so."

When a defendant appreciates the risks of forgoing counsel and chooses to do so voluntarily, the Constitution protects his ability to present his own defense even when that harms his case. In fact waiving counsel "usually" does so. We have nonetheless said that the defendant's "choice must be honored out of 'that respect for the individual which is the lifeblood of the law.'" What the Constitution requires is not that a State's case be subject to the most rigorous adversarial testing possible—after all, it permits a defendant to eliminate *all* adversarial testing by pleading guilty. What the Constitution requires is that a defendant be given the right to challenge the State's case against him using the arguments *he* sees fit.

Although a competent defendant has a right to self-representation at trial, there is no such right on appeal. In Martinez v. Court of Appeal, 528 U.S. 152 (2000), the Court found that "the overriding state interest in the fair and efficient administration of justice" outweighed whatever interest in personal autonomy a defendant has after conviction.

F.   RIGHT OF COUNSEL FOR ENEMY COMBATANTS

Since September 11, 2001, the issue has arisen as to whether detainees designated as "enemy combatants" are entitled to the right to counsel. The executive branch has taken the position that enemy combatants have no such right. However, in Hamdi v. Rumsfeld, 542 U.S. 507 (2004), the Court held that "due process demands that a citizen held in the United States as an enemy combatant be given a meaningful opportunity to test the factual basis for that detention before a neutral decisionmaker." In her opinion, Justice O'Connor noted the integral role of counsel in whatever proceedings are formulated for enemy combatants, stating that Hamdi "unquestionably had the right to access to counsel in connection with the proceedings on remand."

CHAPTER
8

TRIAL

This chapter focuses on a defendant's rights at trial. The right to a fair trial is one of the most important rights in the American criminal justice system. As Alexis de Tocqueville noted in *Democracy in America*, trial by jury is more than just a judicial institution — "it is one of the forms of sovereignty of the people." The jury trial is one of the touchstones of the criminal justice system.

Although we speak of the defendant's right to a fair trial, a defendant is entitled to many rights at the trial stage of criminal proceedings. Thus, section A of this chapter begins by discussing the role of the jury, when a defendant is entitled to a jury trial, the composition of a jury, and the number of jurors needed to convict a defendant. Section B then focuses on how jurors are selected, including the voir dire and peremptory challenge procedures. Section C discusses additional issues regarding a defendant's right to a fair trial, including rulings on venue and pretrial publicity. Section D then reviews specific rules regarding the presentation of a case during trial, including the defendant's right of confrontation and right against self-incrimination. This section also discusses constitutional limits on a prosecutor's closing argument. Section E examines a defendant's right to present a defense. Finally, section F returns to the role of the jury and analyzes the burden of proof in criminal cases and the role of jury instructions.

A. TRIAL BY JURY

1. *Role of the Jury*

The right to a jury trial is so fundamental that it is mentioned twice in the Constitution. First, Article III, section 2, clause 3 provides that "[t]he trial of all Crimes, except in Cases of Impeachment, shall be by Jury." The Constitution addresses the right to a jury again in the Sixth Amendment, providing that "[i]n all criminal prosecutions, the accused shall enjoy the right to a speedy and public trial, by an impartial jury of the State and district wherein the crime shall have been committed."

The focus of the federal Constitution is on the defendant's right to a fair trial. However, as part of the movement to protect victims' rights, some states now guarantee the "People" the right to a fair and speedy trial.[1] Federal law also recognizes the government's right to a jury trial. Fed. R. Crim. P. 23(a)(2).

What is it about jury trials that make them so fundamental to the criminal justice process? The Supreme Court answered that question in Duncan v. Louisiana, in which it held that the right to a jury trial is so fundamental that it applies to the states.[2]

DUNCAN v. LOUISIANA
391 U.S. 145 (1968)

Justice WHITE delivered the opinion of the Court.

Appellant, Gary Duncan, was convicted of simple battery in the Twenty-fifth Judicial District Court of Louisiana. Under Louisiana law simple battery is a misdemeanor, punishable by a maximum of two years' imprisonment and a $300 fine. Appellant sought trial by jury, but because the Louisiana Constitution grants jury trials only in cases in which capital punishment or imprisonment at hard labor may be imposed, the trial judge denied the request. Appellant was convicted and sentenced to serve 60 days in the parish prison and pay a fine of $150.

Appellant was 19 years of age when tried. While driving on Highway 23 in Plaquemines Parish on October 18, 1966, he saw two younger cousins engaged in a conversation by the side of the road with four white boys. Knowing his cousins, Negroes who had recently transferred to a formerly all-white high school, had reported the occurrence of racial incidents at the school, Duncan stopped the car, got out, and approached the six boys. At trial the white boys and a white onlooker testified, as did appellant and his cousins. The testimony was in dispute on many points, but the witnesses agreed that appellant and the white boys spoke to each other, that appellant encouraged his cousins to break off the encounter and enter his car, and that appellant was about to enter the car himself for the purpose of driving away with his cousins. The whites testified that just before getting in the car appellant slapped Herman Landry, one of the white boys, on the elbow. The Negroes testified that appellant had not slapped Landry, but had merely touched him. The trial judge concluded that the State had proved beyond a reasonable doubt that Duncan had committed simple battery, and found him guilty.

---

1. *See, e.g.,* Cal. Const., Art. I, §29 ("In a criminal case, the people of the State of California have the right to due process of law and to a speedy and public trial.").

2. Chapter 1 discusses those portions of *Duncan* that expressly discuss the incorporation doctrine.

I

The claim before us is that the right to trial by jury guaranteed by the Sixth Amendment [is so fundamental to our system of justice, that it should be incorporated under the Fourteenth Amendment Due Process Clause and apply to the states]. The position of Louisiana, on the other hand, is that the Constitution imposes upon the States no duty to give a jury trial in any criminal case, regardless of the seriousness of the crime or the size of the punishment which may be imposed. Because we believe that trial by jury in criminal cases is fundamental to the American scheme of justice, we hold that the Fourteenth Amendment guarantees a right of jury trial in all criminal cases which—were they to be tried in a federal court—would come within the Sixth Amendment's guarantee. [W]e hold that the Constitution was violated when appellant's demand for jury trial was refused.

The history of trial by jury in criminal cases has been frequently told. It is sufficient for present purposes to say that by the time our Constitution was written, jury trial in criminal cases had been in existence in England for several centuries and carried impressive credentials traced by many to Magna Carta. . . . Jury trial came to America with English colonists, and received strong support from them. Royal interference with the jury trial was deeply resented.

Jury trial continues to receive strong support. The laws of every State guarantee a right to jury trial in serious criminal cases; no State has dispensed with it; nor are there significant movements underway to do so.

The guarantees of jury trial in the Federal and State Constitutions reflect a profound judgment about the way in which law should be enforced and justice administered. A right to jury trial is granted to criminal defendants in order to prevent oppression by the Government. Those who wrote our constitutions knew from history and experience that it was necessary to protect against unfounded criminal charges brought to eliminate enemies and against judges too responsive to the voice of higher authority. The framers of the constitutions strove to create an independent judiciary but insisted upon further protection against arbitrary action. Providing an accused with the right to be tried by a jury of his peers gave him an inestimable safeguard against the corrupt or overzealous prosecutor and against the compliant, biased, or eccentric judge. If the defendant preferred the common-sense judgment of a jury to the more tutored but perhaps less sympathetic reaction of the single judge, he was to have it. Beyond this, the jury trial provisions in the Federal and State Constitutions reflect a fundamental decision about the exercise of official power—a reluctance to entrust plenary powers over the life and liberty of the citizen to one judge or to a group of judges. Fear of unchecked power, so typical of our State and Federal Governments in other respects, found expression in the criminal law in this insistence upon community participation in the determination of guilt or innocence. The deep commitment of the Nation to the right of jury trial in serious criminal cases as a defense against arbitrary law enforcement qualifies for protection under the Due Process Clause of the Fourteenth Amendment, and must therefore be respected by the States.

Of course jury trial has "its weaknesses and the potential for misuse." We are aware of the long debate, especially in this century, among those who write about the administration of justice, as to the wisdom of permitting untrained laymen to determine the facts in civil and criminal proceedings. Although the debate has been intense, with powerful voices on either side, most of the controversy has centered on the jury in civil cases. Indeed, some of the severest critics of civil juries acknowledge that the arguments for criminal juries are much stronger. In addition, at the heart of the dispute have been express or implicit assertions that juries are incapable of adequately understanding evidence or determining issues of fact, and that they are unpredictable, quixotic, and little better than a roll of dice. Yet, the most recent and exhaustive study of the jury in criminal cases concluded that juries do understand the evidence and come to sound conclusions in most of the cases presented to them and that when juries differ with the result at which the judge would have arrived, it is usually because they are serving some of the very purposes for which they were created and for which they are now employed.

The State of Louisiana urges that holding that the Fourteenth Amendment assures a right to jury trial will cast doubt on the integrity of every trial conducted without a jury. Plainly, this is not the import of our holding. Our conclusion is that in the American States, as in the federal judicial system, a general grant of jury trial for serious offenses is a fundamental right, essential for preventing miscarriages of justice and for assuring that fair trials are provided for all defendants. We would not assert, however, that every criminal trial — or any particular trial — held before a judge alone is unfair or that a defendant may never be as fairly treated by a judge as he would be by a jury. Thus we hold no constitutional doubts about the practices, common in both federal and state courts, of accepting waivers of jury trial and prosecuting petty crimes without extending a right to jury trial. However, the fact is that in most places more trials for serious crimes are to juries than to a court alone; a great many defendants prefer the judgment of a jury to that of a court. Even where defendants are satisfied with bench trials, the right to a jury trial very likely serves its intended purpose of making judicial or prosecutorial unfairness less likely.

II

Louisiana's final contention is that even if it must grant jury trials in serious criminal cases, the conviction before us is valid and constitutional because here the petitioner was tried for simple battery and was sentenced to only 60 days in the parish prison. We are not persuaded. It is doubtless true that there is a category of petty crimes or offenses which is not subject to the Sixth Amendment jury trial provision and should not be subject to the Fourteenth Amendment jury trial requirement here applied to the States. Crimes carrying possible penalties up to six months do not require a jury trial if they otherwise qualify as petty offenses. But the penalty authorized for a particular crime is of major relevance in determining whether it is serious or not and may in itself, if severe enough, subject the trial to the mandates of the Sixth Amendment. The penalty authorized by the law of the locality may be taken "as a gauge of its social and ethical judgments," of the crime in question. In the case before us the Legislature of Louisiana has made simple battery a criminal offense punishable by imprisonment for up to two years and a fine. The question, then, is whether a crime carrying such a penalty is an offense which Louisiana may insist on trying without a jury.

We think not. So-called petty offenses were tried without juries both in England and in the Colonies and have always been held to be exempt from the otherwise comprehensive language of the Sixth Amendment's jury trial provisions. Of course the boundaries of the petty offense category have always been ill-defined, if not ambulatory. In the absence of an explicit constitutional provision, the definitional task necessarily falls on the courts.

In determining whether the length of the authorized prison term or the seriousness of other punishment is enough in itself to require a jury trial, we are counseled by the existing laws and practices in the Nation. In the federal system, petty offenses are defined as those punishable by no more than six months in prison and a $500 fine. In 49 of the 50 States crimes subject to trial without a jury, which occasionally include simple battery, are punishable by no more than one year in jail. Moreover, in the late 18th century in America crimes triable without a jury were for the most part punishable by no more than a six-month prison term, although there appear to have been exceptions to this rule. We need not, however, settle in this case the exact location of the line between petty offenses and serious crimes. It is sufficient for our purposes to hold that a crime punishable by two years in prison is, based on past and contemporary standards in this country, a serious crime and not a petty offense. Consequently, appellant was entitled to a jury trial and it was error to deny it.

The essential role of the jury is to decide whether the prosecution has proven each element of a crime beyond a reasonable doubt.[3] In doing so, jurors are expected to make credibility decisions and to decide what is "reasonable" for people in their community. They are not expected to be experts in the law. While jurors have a critical role in protecting defendants from the power of the government, the Supreme Court recognized, in Singer v. United States, 380 U.S. 24 (1965), that the government also has an interest in jury trials. Quoting the Court's earlier decision in Patton v. United States,

---

3. Section E analyzes the requirement that a case be proved beyond a reasonable doubt. Chapter 9 discusses in greater detail the role of jurors in making factual findings that will be used in sentencing and during the penalty phase of a capital case.

Chief Justice Warren wrote, "Not only must the right of the accused to a trial by a constitutional jury be jealously preserved, but the maintenance of the jury as a fact finding body in criminal cases is of such importance and has such a place in our traditions, that, before any waiver can become effective, the consent of government counsel and the sanction of the court must be had, in addition to the express and intelligent consent of the defendant." Accordingly, the Supreme Court upheld Federal Rule of Criminal Procedure 23(a), which requires both sides to agree before there can be a trial without a jury.

2. When Is There a Right to a Jury Trial?

The Court explained in *Duncan* that the defendant has the right to a jury trial in all but "petty" offenses. Although the *Duncan* Court did not expressly draw the line between serious and petty offenses, it suggested that, if the possible sentence for a crime is more than six months, the legislature in that jurisdiction has implicitly indicated that the offense is sufficiently serious to require the community's input through the use of juries.

In later cases, the Supreme Court affirmed that the line for the right to a jury trial should be drawn at six months. In Baldwin v. New York, 399 U.S. 66 (1970), the Court held that defendants charged with offenses carrying a maximum possible penalty of more than six months are entitled to a jury trial. In Blanton v. City of North Las Vegas, 489 U.S. 538 (1989), the Court was asked to decide whether other penalties, such as a fine and loss of driver's license, could be serious enough to indicate that the legislature considered the charged crime to be a "serious offense." While acknowledging that such circumstances might theoretically exist, Justice Marshall wrote for a unanimous Court that the Nevada penalties of a $1,000 maximum fine, community service, loss of driver's license, and maximum of six months in jail, were not enough to deem Blanton's driving-under-the-influence charge a "serious" offense.

Four years later, in United States v. Nachtigal, 507 U.S. 1 (1993) (per curiam), the Court cited *Blanton* in rejecting the argument that a man charged with driving under the influence in a national park faced a "serious" offense because the court could impose a $5,000 fine. As the Court emphasized, "it is a rare case where a legislature packs an offense it deems serious with onerous penalties that nonetheless do not puncture the 6-month incarceration line."

Most recently, in Lewis v. United States, 518 U.S. 322 (1996), the Court held that, even if a defendant is charged with multiple petty offenses, he is still not entitled to a jury trial. In *Lewis*, the defendant was charged with two misdemeanor counts of obstructing the mails. Each carried a maximum prison term of six months. However, if the sentences were ordered to run consecutively, Lewis would face one year in jail. Writing for the Court, Justice O'Connor noted that by setting the maximum authorized prison term at six months, the legislature categorized the offense of obstructing the mail as petty. The fact that the petitioner was charged with two counts of a petty offense does not revise the legislative judgment as to the gravity of that particular offense, nor does it transform the petty offense into a serious one, to which the jury-trial right would apply.

In a concurrence, Justice Kennedy attacked this reasoning, noting that "there is no limit to the length of the sentence a judge can impose on a defendant without entitling him to a jury, so long as the prosecutor carves up the charges into segments punishable by no more than six months apiece." Kennedy was willing to uphold Lewis's conviction but only because the trial judge had indicated that he would not sentence Lewis to more than six months even if he were convicted on both counts.

Thus, a firm line seems to have been drawn. Absent extraordinary circumstances, a defendant is entitled to a jury trial only if he faces a maximum of more than six months in prison on any one charge he faces.

3. Composition of the Jury

Television shows and movies frequently show juries of 12 persons.[4] But the Constitution does not specify how many persons must sit on a jury. The Supreme Court decided in Williams v. Florida whether there is a constitutional requirement regarding the number of jurors in criminal cases.

a. Number of Jurors

WILLIAMS v. FLORIDA
399 U.S. 78 (1970)

Justice WHITE delivered the opinion of the Court.

[Williams filed a pretrial motion to impanel a 12-man jury instead of the six-man jury provided by Florida law in all but capital cases. That motion was denied. Williams was convicted of robbery and was sentenced to life imprisonment. Part I of the Court's decision addressed a question regarding the state's rule that a defendant must give notice in advance of trial if he intends to claim an alibi defense. Part II of the decision discusses the right to a jury trial.]

II

In Duncan v. Louisiana (1968), we held that the Fourteenth Amendment guarantees a right to trial by jury in all criminal cases. The question in this

---

4. Among the most famous of these is *Twelve Angry Men* (1957), starring Henry Fonda.

case then is whether the constitutional guarantee of a trial by "jury" necessarily requires trial by exactly 12 persons, rather than some lesser number — in this case six. We hold that the 12-man panel is not a necessary ingredient of "trial by jury," and that respondent's refusal to impanel more than the six members provided for by Florida law did not violate petitioner's Sixth Amendment rights as applied to the States through the Fourteenth.

We had occasion in Duncan v. Louisiana to review briefly the oft-told history of the development of trial by jury in criminal cases. That history revealed a long tradition attaching great importance to the concept of relying on a body of one's peers to determine guilt or innocence as a safeguard against arbitrary law enforcement. That same history, however, affords little insight into the considerations that gradually led the size of that body to be generally fixed at 12. Some have suggested that the number 12 was fixed upon simply because that was the number of the presentment jury from the hundred, from which the petit jury developed. Other, less circular but more fanciful reasons for the number 12 have been given, and rest on little more than mystical or superstitious insights into the significance of "12." Lord Coke's explanation that the "number of twelve is much respected in holy writ, as 12 apostles, 12 stones, 12 tribes, etc.," is typical.[5] In short, while sometime in the 14th century the size of the jury at common law came to be fixed generally at 12, that particular feature of the jury system appears to have been a historical accident, unrelated to the great purposes which gave rise to the jury in the first place. The question before us is whether this accidental feature of the jury has been immutably codified into our Constitution.

While "the intent of the Framers" is often an elusive quarry, the relevant constitutional history casts considerable doubt on the easy assumption in our past decisions that if a given feature existed in a jury at common law in 1789, then it was necessarily preserved in the Constitution. The "very scanty history [of this provision] in the records of the Constitutional Convention" sheds little light either way on the intended correlation between Article III's "jury" and the features of the jury at common law.

The version that finally emerged from the Committee was the version that ultimately became the Sixth Amendment, ensuring an accused:

> the right to a speedy and public trial, by an impartial jury of the State and district wherein the crime shall have been committed, which district shall have been previously ascertained by law. . . .

---

5. In this connection it is interesting to note the following oath, required of the early 12-man jury:

> Hear this, ye Justices! that I will speak the truth of that which ye shall ask of me on the part of the king, and I will do faithfully to the best of my endeavour. So help me God, and these holy Apostles.

W. Forsyth, Trial by Jury 197 (1852). [Footnote by the Court.]

Gone were the provisions spelling out such common-law features of the jury as "unanimity," or "the accustomed requisites." And the "vicinage" requirement[6] itself had been replaced by wording that reflected a compromise between broad and narrow definitions of that term, and that left Congress the power to determine the actual size of the "vicinage" by its creation of judicial districts.

Three significant features may be observed in this sketch of the background of the Constitution's jury trial provisions. First, even though the vicinage requirement was as much a feature of the common-law jury as was the 12-man requirement, the mere reference to "trial by jury" in Article III was not interpreted to include that feature. . . . Second, provisions that would have explicitly tied the "jury" concept to the "accustomed requisites" of the time were eliminated. . . . Finally, contemporary legislative and constitutional provisions indicate that where Congress wanted to leave no doubt that it was incorporating existing common-law features of the jury system, it knew how to use express language to that effect.

We do not pretend to be able to divine precisely what the word "jury" imported to the Framers, the First Congress, or the States in 1789. It may well be that the usual expectation was that the jury would consist of 12, and that hence, the most likely conclusion to be drawn is simply that little thought was actually given to the specific question we face today. But there is absolutely no indication in "the intent of the Framers" of an explicit decision to equate the constitutional and common-law characteristics of the jury. Nothing in this history suggests, then, that we do violence to the letter of the Constitution by turning to other than purely historical considerations to determine which features of the jury system, as it existed at common law, were preserved in the Constitution. The relevant inquiry, as we see it, must be the function that the particular feature performs and its relation to the purposes of the jury trial. Measured by this standard, the 12-man requirement cannot be regarded as an indispensable component of the Sixth Amendment.

The purpose of the jury trial, as we noted in *Duncan*, is to prevent oppression by the Government. "Providing an accused with the right to be tried by a jury of his peers gave him an inestimable safeguard against the corrupt or overzealous prosecutor and against the compliant, biased, or eccentric judge." Given this purpose, the essential feature of a jury obviously lies in the interposition between the accused and his accuser of the commonsense judgment of a group of laymen, and in the community participation and shared responsibility that results from that group's determination of guilt or innocence. The performance of this role is not a function of the particular number of the body that makes up the jury. To be sure, the number should probably be large enough to promote group deliberation, free from outside attempts at intimidation, and to provide a fair possibility for obtaining a representative cross-section of the community. But we find little reason to

6. Technically, "vicinage" means neighborhood, and "vicinage of the jury" meant jury of the neighborhood or, in medieval England, jury of the county. [Footnote by the Court.]

think that these goals are in any meaningful sense less likely to be achieved when the jury numbers six, than when it numbers 12 — particularly if the requirement of unanimity is retained. And, certainly the reliability of the jury as a factfinder hardly seems likely to be a function of its size.

It might be suggested that the 12-man jury gives a defendant a greater advantage since he has more "chances" of finding a juror who will insist on acquittal and thus prevent conviction. But the advantage might just as easily belong to the State, which also needs only one juror out of twelve insisting on guilt to prevent acquittal. What few experiments have occurred — usually in the civil area — indicate that there is no discernible difference between the results reached by the two different-sized juries. In short, neither currently available evidence nor theory suggests that the 12-man jury is necessarily more advantageous to the defendant than a jury composed of fewer members.[7]

Similarly, while in theory the number of viewpoints represented on a randomly selected jury ought to increase as the size of the jury increases, in practice the difference between the 12-man and the six-man jury in terms of the cross-section of the community represented seems likely to be negligible. Even the 12-man jury cannot insure representation of every distinct voice in the community, particularly given the use of the peremptory challenge.

We conclude, in short, as we began: the fact that the jury at common law was composed of precisely 12 is a historical accident, unnecessary to effect the purposes of the jury system and wholly without significance "except to mystics." To read the Sixth Amendment as forever codifying a feature so incidental to the real purpose of the Amendment is to ascribe a blind formalism to the Framers which would require considerably more evidence than we have been able to discover in the history and language of the Constitution or in the reasoning of our past decisions. We do not mean to intimate that legislatures can never have good reasons for concluding that the 12-man jury is preferable to the smaller jury. Legislatures may well have their own views about the relative value of the larger and smaller juries, and may conclude that, wholly apart from the jury's primary function, it is desirable to spread the collective responsibility for the determination of guilt among the larger group. Our holding does no more than leave these considerations to Congress and the States, unrestrained by an interpretation of the Sixth Amendment that would forever dictate the precise number that can constitute a jury. Consistent with this holding, we conclude that petitioner's Sixth Amendment rights, as applied to the States through the Fourteenth

---

7. It is true, of course, that the "hung jury" might be thought to result in a minimal advantage for the defendant, who remains unconvicted and who enjoys the prospect that the prosecution will eventually be dropped if subsequent juries also "hang." Thus a 100-man jury would undoubtedly be more favorable for defendants than a 12-man jury. But when the comparison is between 12 and 6, the odds of continually "hanging" the jury seem slight, and the numerical difference in the number needed to convict seems unlikely to inure perceptibly to the advantage of either side. [Footnote by the Court.]

Amendment, were not violated by Florida's decision to provide a 6-man rather than a 12-man jury.

────────────

Not long after *Williams*, the Supreme Court had to decide whether the Constitution requires a minimum number of jurors in criminal cases to satisfy the defendant's right to a jury trial. A divided Court rendered its opinion on that issue.

BALLEW v. GEORGIA
435 U.S. 223 (1978)

Justice BLACKMUN announced the judgment of the Court and delivered an opinion in which Justice STEVENS joined.

This case presents the issue whether a state criminal trial to a jury of only five persons deprives the accused of the right to trial by jury guaranteed to him by the Sixth and Fourteenth Amendments. Our resolution of the issue requires an application of principles enunciated in Williams v. Florida (1970), where the use of a six-person jury in a state criminal trial was upheld against similar constitutional attack.

I

In November 1973 petitioner Claude Davis Ballew was the manager of the Paris Adult Theatre at 320 Peachtree Street, Atlanta, Ga. On November 9 two investigators from the Fulton County Solicitor General's office viewed at the theater a motion picture film entitled "Behind the Green Door." [P]etitioner was charged in a two-count misdemeanor accusation with "distributing obscene materials."

Petitioner was brought to trial in the Criminal Court of Fulton County. After a jury of 5 persons had been selected and sworn, petitioner moved that the court impanel a jury of 12 persons. That court, however, tried its misdemeanor cases before juries of five. Petitioner contended that for an obscenity trial, a jury of only five was constitutionally inadequate to assess the contemporary standards of the community. He also argued that the Sixth and Fourteenth Amendments required a jury of at least six members in criminal cases.

The motion for a 12-person jury was overruled, and the trial went on to its conclusion before the 5-person jury that had been impaneled. At the conclusion of the trial, the jury deliberated for 38 minutes and returned a verdict of guilty on both counts of the accusation.

In his petition for certiorari here, petitioner raised three issues: the unconstitutionality of the five-person jury; the constitutional sufficiency of the jury instructions on scienter and constructive, rather than actual, knowledge of the contents of the film; and obscenity vel non. We granted certiorari. Because we now hold that the five member jury does not satisfy the jury trial guarantee of the Sixth Amendment, as applied to the States through the Fourteenth, we do not reach the other issues.

II

In Williams v. Florida (1970), the Court reaffirmed that the "purpose of the jury trial, as we noted in *Duncan*, is to prevent oppression by the Government. 'Providing an accused with the right to be tried by a jury of his peers gave him an inestimable safeguard against the corrupt or overzealous prosecutor and against the compliant, biased, or eccentric judge.'" This purpose is attained by the participation of the community in determinations of guilt and by the application of the common sense of laymen who, as jurors, consider the case.

Williams held that these functions and this purpose could be fulfilled by a jury of six members. Although recognizing that by 1970 little empirical research had evaluated jury performance, the Court found no evidence that the reliability of jury verdicts diminished with six-member panels. Nor did the Court anticipate significant differences in result, including the frequency of "hung" juries. Because the reduction in size did not threaten exclusion of any particular class from jury roles, concern that the representative or cross-section character of the jury would suffer with a decrease to six members seemed "an unrealistic one." As a consequence, the six-person jury was held not to violate the Sixth and Fourteenth Amendments.

III

When the Court in *Williams* permitted the reduction in jury size — or, to put it another way, when it held that a jury of six was not unconstitutional — it expressly reserved ruling on the issue whether a number smaller than six passed constitutional scrutiny. The Court refused to speculate when this so-called "slippery slope" would become too steep. We face now, however, the two-fold question whether a further reduction in the size of the state criminal trial jury does make the grade too dangerous, that is, whether it inhibits the functioning of the jury as an institution to a significant degree, and, if so, whether any state interest counterbalances and justifies the disruption so as to preserve its constitutionality.

Williams v. Florida generated a quantity of scholarly work on jury size. These writings do not draw or identify a bright line below which the number of jurors would not be able to function as required by the standards enunciated in *Williams*. On the other hand, they raise significant questions about the wisdom and constitutionality of a reduction below six. We examine these concerns:

First, recent empirical data suggest that progressively smaller juries are less likely to foster effective group deliberation. At some point, this decline leads to inaccurate factfinding and incorrect application of the common sense of the community to the facts. Generally, a positive correlation exists between group size and the quality of both group performance and group productivity. The smaller the group, the less likely are members to make critical contributions necessary for the solution of a given problem. As juries decrease in size, then, they are less likely to have members who remember each of the important pieces of evidence or argument. Furthermore, the smaller the group, the less likely it is to overcome the biases of its members to obtain an accurate result.

Second, the data now raise doubts about the accuracy of the results achieved by smaller and smaller panels. Statistical studies suggest that the risk of convicting an innocent person rises as the size of the jury diminishes.

Third, the data suggest that the verdicts of jury deliberation in criminal cases will vary as juries become smaller, and that the variance amounts to an imbalance to the detriment of one side, the defense. [T]he number of hung juries would diminish as the panels decreased in size. Both studies emphasized that juries in criminal cases generally hang with only one, or more likely two, jurors remaining unconvinced of guilt. Also, group theory suggests that a person in the minority will adhere to his position more frequently when he has at least one other person supporting his argument.

Fourth, what has just been said about the presence of minority viewpoint as juries decrease in size foretells problems not only for jury decisionmaking, but also for the representation of minority groups in the community. The Court repeatedly has held that meaningful community participation cannot be attained with the exclusion of minorities or other identifiable groups from jury service. "It is part of the established tradition in the use of juries as instruments of public justice that the jury be a body truly representative of the community." The exclusion of elements of the community from participation "contravenes the very idea of a jury . . . composed of 'the peers or equals of the person whose rights it is selected or summoned to determine.'"

Fifth, several authors have identified in jury research methodological problems tending to mask differences in the operation of smaller and larger juries. Nationwide, however, these small percentages will represent a large number of cases. And it is with respect to those cases that the jury trial right has its greatest value. When the case is close, and the guilt or innocence of the defendant is not readily apparent, a properly functioning jury system will insure evaluation by the sense of the community and will also tend to insure accurate factfinding.

IV

While we adhere to, and reaffirm our holding in Williams v. Florida, these studies, most of which have been made since *Williams* was decided in 1970, lead us to conclude that the purpose and functioning of the jury in a criminal trial is seriously impaired, and to a constitutional degree, by a reduction in size to below six members. We readily admit that we do not pretend to discern a clear line between six members and five. But the assembled data raise substantial doubt about the reliability and appropriate representation of panels smaller than six. Because of the fundamental importance of the jury trial to the American system of criminal justice, any further reduction that promotes inaccurate and possibly biased decisionmaking, that causes untoward differences in verdicts, and that prevents juries from truly representing their communities, attains constitutional significance.

V

With the reduction in the number of jurors below six creating a substantial threat to Sixth and Fourteenth Amendment guarantees, we must consider whether any interest of the State justifies the reduction. We find no significant state advantage in reducing the number of jurors from six to five.

The States utilize juries of less than 12 primarily for administrative reasons. Savings in court time and in financial costs are claimed to justify the reductions. The financial benefits of the reduction from 12 to 6 are substantial; this is mainly because fewer jurors draw daily allowances as they hear cases. On the other hand, the asserted saving in judicial time is not so clear.

Petitioner, therefore, has established that his trial on criminal charges before a five-member jury deprived him of the right to trial by jury guaranteed by the Sixth and Fourteenth Amendments.

As with other aspects of jury trials, states can choose to provide defendants with more than the minimum number of six jurors required by the Supreme Court. Federal courts and most state courts provide jurors with the right to 12 jurors in a criminal case, but following *Williams* and *Ballew*, over 30 states permit fewer than 12 jurors in misdemeanor cases, and one state (Connecticut) allows 6 jurors for all noncapital trials.[8]

b.   Unanimity

A common myth about juries is that their verdicts must be unanimous. As it did in its decisions regarding the size of juries, the Supreme Court, in deciding whether jury verdicts must be unanimous, has focused on the role of jurors and how they can perform their responsibilities.

---

8. *See* State Court Organization (2004), Table 42.

APODACA v. OREGON

406 U.S. 404 (1972)

Justice WHITE announced the judgment of the Court and an opinion in which Chief Justice BURGER, Justice BLACKMUN, and Justice REHNQUIST joined.

[Oregon juries convicted three defendants of various serious crimes. The vote in the cases of Apodaca and Madden was 11-1, while the vote in Cooper's case was 10-2, the minimum requisite vote under Oregon law for sustaining a conviction. All three defendants claimed that a conviction rendered by a less-than-unanimous jury violates the right to trial by jury in criminal cases.]

Like the requirement that juries consist of 12 men, the requirement of unanimity arose during the Middle Ages and [became] an accepted feature of the common-law jury by the 18th century. But, as we observed in *Williams*, "the relevant constitutional history casts considerable doubt on the easy assumption . . . that if a given feature existed in a jury at common law in 1789, then it was necessarily preserved in the Constitution."

Our inquiry must focus upon the function served by the jury in contemporary society. As we said in *Duncan*, the purpose of trial by jury is to prevent oppression by the Government by providing a "safeguard against the corrupt or overzealous prosecutor and against the compliant, biased, or eccentric judge." "Given this purpose, the essential feature of a jury obviously lies in the interposition between the accused and his accuser of the commonsense judgment of a group of laymen." A requirement of unanimity, however, does not materially contribute to the exercise of this commonsense judgment. As we said in *Williams*, a jury will come to such a judgment as long as it consists of a group of laymen representative of a cross section of the community who have the duty and the opportunity to deliberate, free from outside attempts at intimidation, on the question of a defendant's guilt. In terms of this function we perceive no difference between juries required to act unanimously and those permitted to convict or acquit by votes of 10 to two or 11 to one. Requiring unanimity would obviously produce hung juries in some situations where nonunanimous juries will convict or acquit. But in either case, the interest of the defendant in having the judgment of his peers interposed between himself and the officers of the State who prosecute and judge him is equally well served.

Petitioners nevertheless argue that unanimity serves other purposes constitutionally essential to the continued operation of the jury system. Their principal contention is that a Sixth Amendment "jury trial" . . . should be held to require a unanimous jury verdict in order to give substance to the reasonable-doubt standard otherwise mandated by the Due Process Clause. *See* In re Winship (1970).

We are quite sure, however, that the Sixth Amendment itself has never been held to require proof beyond a reasonable doubt in criminal cases. The reasonable-doubt standard developed separately from both the jury trial and the unanimous verdict.[9] The reasonable-doubt argument is rooted, in effect, in due process and [is not linked to the Sixth Amendment jury requirements]. Petitioners also cite quite accurately a long line of decisions of this Court upholding the principle that the Fourteenth Amendment requires jury panels to reflect a cross section of the community. They then contend that unanimity is a necessary precondition for effective application of the cross-section requirement, because a rule permitting less than unanimous verdicts will make it possible for convictions to occur without the acquiescence of minority elements within the community.

There are two flaws in this argument. One is petitioners' assumption that every distinct voice in the community has a right to be represented on every jury and a right to prevent conviction of a defendant in any case. All that the Constitution forbids, however, is systematic exclusion of identifiable segments of the community from jury panels and from the juries ultimately drawn from those panels. No group, in short, has the right to block convictions; it has only the right to participate in the overall legal processes by which criminal guilt and innocence are determined.

We also cannot accept petitioners' second assumption — that minority groups, even when they are represented on a jury, will not adequately represent the viewpoint of those groups simply because they may be outvoted in the final result. They will be present during all deliberations, and their views will be heard. We cannot assume that the majority of the jury will refuse to weigh the evidence and reach a decision upon rational grounds, just as it must now do in order to obtain unanimous verdicts, or that a majority will deprive a man of his liberty on the basis of prejudice when a minority is presenting a reasonable argument in favor of acquittal. We simply find no proof for the notion that a majority will disregard its instructions and cast its votes for guilt or innocence based on prejudice rather than the evidence.

We accordingly [hold that nonunanimous jury verdicts are constitutional, at least as to 11-1 or 10-2 votes].

Justice BLACKMUN concurring.[10]

I join the Court's opinion and judgment in each of these cases. I add only the comment, which should be obvious and should not need saying, that in so doing I do not imply that I regard a State's split-verdict system as a wise one. My vote means only that I cannot conclude that the system is constitutionally offensive. Were I a legislator, I would disfavor it as a matter of policy. Our task here, however, is not to pursue and strike down what happens to impress us as undesirable legislative policy.

I do not hesitate to say, either, that a system employing a 7-5 standard, rather than a 9-3 or 75 percent minimum, would afford me great difficulty.

9. The requirement of proof beyond a reasonable doubt is discussed in section F of this chapter. [Footnote by casebook authors.]

10. The concurring and dissenting opinions were issued in the companion case of Johnson v. United States, in which the Court upheld a 9-3 verdict. [Footnote by casebook authors.]

As Mr. Justice White points out, "a substantial majority of the jury" are to be convinced. That is all that is before us in each of these cases.

Justice DOUGLAS, with whom Justice BRENNAN and Justice MARSHALL join, dissenting.

The plurality approves a procedure which diminishes the reliability of a jury. First, it eliminates the circumstances in which a minority of jurors (a) could have rationally persuaded the entire jury to acquit, or (b) while unable to persuade the majority to acquit, nonetheless could have convinced them to convict only on a lesser-included offense. Second, it permits prosecutors in Oregon and Louisiana to enjoy a conviction-acquittal ratio substantially greater than that ordinarily returned by unanimous juries.

The diminution of verdict reliability flows from the fact that nonunanimous juries need not debate and deliberate as fully as must unanimous juries. As soon as the requisite majority is attained, further consideration is not required either by Oregon or by Louisiana even though the dissident jurors might, if given the chance, be able to convince the majority.

It is said that there is no evidence that majority jurors will refuse to listen to dissenters whose votes are unneeded for conviction. Yet human experience teaches that polite and academic conversation is no substitute for the earnest and robust argument necessary to reach unanimity. [E]xperience shows that the less-than-unanimous jury overwhelmingly favors the States.

Moreover, even where an initial majority wins the dissent over to its side, the ultimate result in unanimous-jury States may nonetheless reflect the reservations of uncertain jurors. I refer to many compromise verdicts on lesser-included offenses and lesser sentences. Thus, even though a minority may not be forceful enough to carry the day, their doubts may nonetheless cause a majority to exercise caution.

The new rule also has an impact on cases in which a unanimous jury would have neither voted to acquit nor to convict, but would have deadlocked. Of these deadlocked juries, 56% contain either one, two, or three dissenters. In these latter cases, the majorities favor the prosecution 44% but the defendant only 12%. Thus, by eliminating these deadlocks, Louisiana wins 44 cases for every 12 that it loses. By eliminating the one-and-two-dissenting-juror cases, Oregon does even better, gaining 4.25 convictions for every acquittal. While the statutes on their face deceptively appear to be neutral, the use of the nonunanimous jury stacks the truth-determining process against the accused. Thus, we take one step more away from the accusatorial system that has been our proud boast.

The requirements of a unanimous jury verdict in criminal cases and proof beyond a reasonable doubt are so embedded in our constitutional law and touch so directly all the citizens and are such important barricades of liberty that if they are to be changed they should be introduced by constitutional amendment.

Suppose a jury begins with a substantial minority but then in the process of deliberation a sufficient number changes to reach the required 9:3 or 10:2

for a verdict. Is not there still a lingering doubt about that verdict? Is it not clear that the safeguard of unanimity operates in this context to make it far more likely that guilt is established beyond a reasonable doubt?

Today the Court approves a nine-to-three verdict. Would the Court relax the standard of reasonable doubt still further by resorting to eight-to-four verdicts, or even a majority rule? Is the next step the elimination of the presumption of innocence?

The vast restructuring of American law which is entailed in today's decisions is for political not for judicial action. Until the Constitution is rewritten, we have the present one to support and construe. It has served us well.

If a jury is unable to reach a verdict, it is referred to as a "hung jury." No matter how compelling the evidence might be, the trial judge may not direct a verdict of guilty. However, the judge may grant an acquittal for insufficient evidence.[11]

In the United States, jurors render "general verdicts" of "guilty" or "not guilty" of the charged offense. "Special verdicts" are verdicts that require jurors to answer specific questions regarding a case, such as which acts they found each defendant committed or whether particular property was used in a crime. They are occasionally used to guide the court in its sentencing or forfeiture decisions, but are generally disfavored as a way to guide jurors in their deliberative process.

Because jurors do not ordinarily need to explain their verdicts, jurors can engage in jury nullification and reject a case even though there appears to be sufficient evidence to support the verdict. *See* United States v. Dougherty, 473 F.2d 1113 (D.C. Cir. 1972) (recognizing jurors' power to nullify but rejecting request to instruct jurors of their right to nullify). Courts are reluctant to instruct jurors that they have the power to nullify, but some observers believe that jury nullification is a valid and important part of the right to a jury trial.

> It is not by chance that the jury has the power to issue an unreviewable general verdict of acquittal; it is a considered decision that the people should apply laws when criminal punishment is at stake to ensure that an individual does not lose her liberty unless it would be just in a particular case. . . . Trial by jury "gives protection against laws which the ordinary man may regard as harsh and oppressive" and provides "insurance that the criminal law will conform to the ordinary man's idea of what is fair and just."

Rachel E. Barkow, *Recharging the Jury: The Criminal Jury's Constitutional Role in an Era of Mandatory Sentencing*, 152 U. Pa. L. Rev. 33, 59 (2003).

Similarly, because jurors need not explain their verdicts, federal courts, as well as most state courts, accept inconsistent verdicts from the jury. It is

---

11. The circumstances in which the judge's acquittal bars retrial are discussed in Chapter 10 ("Double Jeopardy").

presumed that if jurors convict on some counts but acquit on others, their decision was the product of lenity. Dunn v. United States, 284 U.S. 390 (1932).

B. JURY COMPOSITION AND SELECTION

There is a two-step process for the selection of a jury. First, a pool of jurors, called the jury "venire," is summoned. Then, the "petit jury" is selected from the venire. The petit jury consists of those jurors who will actually hear the case.

Before the petit jury is selected, prospective jurors are questioned in a process called voir dire. Following voir dire, both the prosecution and defense have an opportunity to challenge jurors "for cause." For-cause challenges may be made on the basis that a particular juror cannot perform jury service, or has an actual bias. The parties also have an opportunity to exercise a limited number of "peremptory challenges." Unlike challenges for cause, peremptory challenges may be exercised for reasons unrelated to a juror's bias, although they may not be exercised in a discriminatory manner.

1. Selecting the Jury Venire

The Sixth Amendment guarantees an "impartial jury." The Supreme Court has repeatedly held, however, that a defendant does not have a right to a jury composed of particular groups. Rather, the Sixth Amendment prohibits the prosecution from systematically excluding certain cognizable groups in assembling the venire for jury selection.

TAYLOR v. LOUISIANA

419 U.S. 522 (1975)

Justice WHITE delivered the opinion of the Court.

When this case was tried, the Louisiana Constitution provided that a woman should not be selected for jury service unless she had previously filed a written declaration of her desire to be subject to jury service. The constitutionality of these provisions is the issue in this case.

I

Appellant, Billy J. Taylor, was indicted by the grand jury for aggravated kidnapping. On April 12, 1972, appellant moved the trial court to quash the petit jury venire. Appellant alleged that women were systematically excluded from the venire and that he would therefore be deprived of what he claimed to be his federal constitutional right to "a fair trial by jury of a representative segment of the community. . . ."

The [parties have stipulated] that 53% of the persons eligible for jury service in the parish were female, and that no more than 10% of the persons on the jury wheel were women. During the period from December 8, 1971, to November 3, 1972, 12 females were among the 1,800 persons drawn to fill petit jury venires in [that] Parish. In the present case, a venire totaling 175 persons was drawn for jury service beginning April 13, 1972. There were no females on the venire.

Appellant's motion to quash the venire was denied that same day. After being tried, convicted, and sentenced to death, appellant sought review.

II

The Louisiana jury-selection system does not disqualify women from jury service, but in operation its conceded systematic impact is that only a very few women, grossly disproportionate to the number of eligible women in the community, are called for jury service. In this case, no women were on the venire from which the petit jury was drawn. The issue we have, therefore, is whether a jury-selection system which operates to exclude from jury service an identifiable class of citizens constituting 53% of eligible jurors in the community comports with the Sixth and Fourteenth Amendments.

The State first insists that Taylor, a male, has no standing to object to the exclusion of women from his jury. But Taylor's claim is that he was constitutionally entitled to a jury drawn from a venire constituting a fair cross section of the community and that the jury that tried him was not such a jury by reason of the exclusion of women. Taylor was not a member of the excluded class; but there is no rule that claims such as Taylor presents may be made only by those defendants who are members of the group excluded from jury service.

III

The background against which this case must be decided includes our holding in Duncan v. Louisiana (1968), that the Sixth Amendment's provision for jury trial is made binding on the States by virtue of the Fourteenth Amendment. Our inquiry is whether the presence of a fair cross section of the community on venires, panels, or lists from which petit juries are drawn is essential to the fulfillment of the Sixth Amendment's guarantee of an impartial jury trial in criminal prosecutions.

The Court's prior cases are instructive. Both in the course of exercising its supervisory powers over trials in federal courts and in the constitutional context, the Court has unambiguously declared that the American concept of the jury trial contemplates a jury drawn from a fair cross section of the community. A unanimous Court stated in Smith v. Texas (1940), that "[it] is part of the established tradition in the use of juries as instruments of public justice that the jury be a body truly representative of the community." To exclude racial groups from jury service was said to be "at war with our basic concepts of a democratic society and a representative government." A state jury system that resulted in systematic exclusion of Negroes as jurors was therefore held to violate the Equal Protection Clause of the Fourteenth Amendment.

The unmistakable import of this Court's opinions is that the selection of a petit jury from a representative cross section of the community is an essential component of the Sixth Amendment right to a jury trial.

We accept the fair-cross-section requirement as fundamental to the jury trial guaranteed by the Sixth Amendment and are convinced that the requirement has solid foundation. The purpose of a jury is to guard against the exercise of arbitrary power — to make available the commonsense judgment of the community as a hedge against the overzealous or mistaken prosecutor and in preference to the professional or perhaps overconditioned or biased response of a judge. This prophylactic vehicle is not provided if the jury pool is made up of only special segments of the populace or if large, distinctive groups are excluded from the pool. Community participation in the administration of the criminal law, moreover, is not only consistent with our democratic heritage but is also critical to public confidence in the fairness of the criminal justice system. Restricting jury service to only special groups or excluding identifiable segments playing major roles in the community cannot be squared with the constitutional concept of jury trial. "Trial by jury presupposes a jury drawn from a pool broadly representative of the community as well as impartial in a specific case. . . . [The] broad representative character of the jury should be maintained, partly as assurance of a diffused impartiality and partly because sharing in the administration of justice is a phase of civic responsibility."

IV

We are also persuaded that the fair-cross-section requirement is violated by the systematic exclusion of women, who in the judicial district involved here amounted to 53% of the citizens eligible for jury service. This conclusion necessarily entails the judgment that women are sufficiently numerous and distinct from men and that if they are systematically eliminated from jury panels, the Sixth Amendment's fair-cross-section requirement cannot be satisfied. This very matter was debated in Ballard v. United States. The dissenting view that an all-male panel drawn from various groups in the community would be as truly representative as if women were included, was firmly rejected:

> The thought is that the factors which tend to influence the action of women are the same as those which influence the action of men — personality, background, economic status — and not sex. Yet it is not enough to say that women when sitting

as jurors neither act nor tend to act as a class. Men likewise do not act as a class. But, if the shoe were on the other foot, who would claim that a jury was truly representative of the community if all men were intentionally and systematically excluded from the panel? The truth is that the two sexes are not fungible; a community made up exclusively of one is different from a community composed of both; the subtle interplay of influence one on the other is among the imponderables. To insulate the courtroom from either may not in a given case make an iota of difference. Yet a flavor, a distinct quality is lost if either sex is excluded. The exclusion of one may indeed make the jury less representative of the community than would be true if an economic or racial group were excluded.

If the fair-cross-section rule is to govern the selection of juries, as we have concluded it must, women cannot be systematically excluded from jury panels from which petit juries are drawn. This conclusion is consistent with the current judgment of the country, now evidenced by legislative or constitutional provisions in every State and at the federal level qualifying women for jury service.

V

There remains the argument that women as a class serve a distinctive role in society and that jury service would so substantially interfere with that function that the State has ample justification for excluding women from service unless they volunteer, even though the result is that almost all jurors are men. The right to a proper jury cannot be overcome on merely rational grounds.[12] There must be weightier reasons if a distinctive class representing 53% of the eligible jurors is for all practical purposes to be excluded from jury service. No such basis has been tendered here.

The States are free to grant exemptions from jury service to individuals in case of special hardship or incapacity and to those engaged in particular occupations the uninterrupted performance of which is critical to the community's welfare. A system excluding all women, however, is a wholly different matter. It is untenable to suggest these days that it would be a special hardship for each and every woman to perform jury service or that society cannot spare any women from their present duties. This may be the case with many, and it may be burdensome to sort out those who should be exempted from those who should serve. But that task is performed in the case of men, and the administrative convenience in dealing with women as a class is insufficient justification for diluting the quality of community judgment represented by the jury in criminal trials.

---

12. Louisiana argued that women should be automatically exempt from jury service because they are the center of the home and family life. This argument had prevailed in the Court's prior decision in Hoyt v. Florida (1961). [Footnote by casebook authors.]

VI

Accepting as we do ... the view that the Sixth Amendment affords the defendant in a criminal trial the opportunity to have the jury drawn from venires representative of the community, we think it is no longer tenable to hold that women as a class may be excluded or given automatic exemptions based solely on sex if the consequence is that criminal jury venires are almost totally male. If it was ever the case that women were unqualified to sit on juries or were so situated that none of them should be required to perform jury service, that time has long since passed. If at one time it could be held that Sixth Amendment juries must be drawn from a fair cross section of the community but that this requirement permitted the almost total exclusion of women, this is not the case today. Communities differ at different times and places. What is a fair cross section at one time or place is not necessarily a fair cross section at another time or a different place. Nothing persuasive has been presented to us in this case suggesting that all-male venires in the parishes involved here are fairly representative of the local population otherwise eligible for jury service.

VII

It should also be emphasized that in holding that petit juries must be drawn from a source fairly representative of the community we impose no requirement that petit juries actually chosen must mirror the community and reflect the various distinctive groups in the population. Defendants are not entitled to a jury of any particular composition, but the jury wheels, pools of names, panels, or venires from which juries are drawn must not systematically exclude distinctive groups in the community and thereby fail to be reasonably representative thereof.

Justice REHNQUIST, dissenting.

The Court's opinion reverses a conviction without a suggestion, much less a showing, that the appellant has been unfairly treated or prejudiced in any way by the manner in which his jury was selected. In so doing, the Court invalidates a jury-selection system which it approved by a substantial majority only 13 years ago. I disagree with the Court and would affirm the judgment of the Supreme Court of Louisiana.

Challenges to jury venires are governed by the Sixth Amendment and may be raised by any defendant.[13] As set forth in *Taylor*, the jury pool must be

13. In Berghuis v. Smith, 129 S. Ct. 1382 (2010), the Supreme Court held that no clearly established federal law requires that a particular type of statistical method be used to determine whether there has been systematic exclusion of racial groups in the selection of jury pools.

drawn from a cross-section of the community. Cognizable groups may not be excluded unless there are compelling reasons. For example, the government may have compelling reasons to exclude convicted felons from the jury pool. However, the systematic exclusion of groups based on gender, race, and ethnicity is unconstitutional.

2. Selecting the Petit Jury

Once the jury pool is selected, the parties enter the second stage of the jury-selection process. The court or the parties will question individual jurors about their background, attitudes, experiences, and knowledge of the particular case.[14] When the defendant asks the court to inquire into potential jurors' possible racial biases, the court is required to do so if there is a reasonable possibility that racial prejudice may influence the jury. Moreover, where a defendant is charged with an interracial violent crime, the court must presume that the possibility of prejudice exists, and ask the jurors about their attitudes toward race. Mu'Min v. Virginia, 500 U.S. 415 (1991). The parties then have an opportunity to challenge individual prospective jurors.

There are two types of challenges: challenges for cause and peremptory challenges. A party may raise a challenge for cause when a juror does not meet statutory requirements for serving on a jury or has indicated that he or she cannot set aside personal opinions and render a fair verdict based on the evidence. By contrast, peremptory challenges allow the parties to excuse jurors whom they believe to be unfavorable to their side.

> The essential nature of the peremptory challenge is that it is one exercised without a reason stated, without inquiry, and without being subject to the court's control. While challenges for cause permit rejection of jurors on a narrowly specified, provable and legally cognizable basis of partiality, the peremptory permits rejection for a real or imagined partiality that is less easily designated or demonstrable.

Swain v. Alabama, 380 U.S. 202 (1965). Peremptory challenges are not constitutionally required, but they are a tradition in the American criminal justice system.

---

14. In death penalty cases, the Supreme Court has held that the jurors must be "death qualified." What that means is that jurors whose personal views on capital punishment will preclude them from voting in accordance with the court's instruction may be challenged for cause. In Witherspoon v. Witt, 391 U.S. 510, 522 (1968), the Supreme Court held that prosecutors could not use this requirement to excuse jurors because those prospective jurors have expressed some misgivings about the death penalty. Rather, as the Court subsequently held in Wainwright v. Witt, 469 U.S. 412, 423 (1985), jurors can be excused only if their views on capital punishment "would prevent or substantially impair the performance of [the juror's] duties . . . in accordance with his instructions and his oath." In Uttecht v. Brown, 127 S. Ct. 2218 (2007), the Court further held that courts should defer to the trial court in making this decision.

How much freedom do lawyers have in exercising peremptory challenges? Can they really be exercised for any reason? What if a party wants to excuse a juror because of her race or gender?

In Swain v. Alabama, the Supreme Court held that a defendant could raise an equal protection challenge to the prosecution's use of peremptory challenges but only if the defendant could prove that the prosecution, "in case after case, whatever the circumstances," removed jurors based on their race. This proof requirement was nearly impossible to meet. Thus, the Court revisited the issue in the landmark case of Batson v. Kentucky.

BATSON v. KENTUCKY
476 U.S. 79 (1986)

Justice POWELL delivered the opinion of the Court.

This case requires us to reexamine that portion of Swain v. Alabama (1965), concerning the evidentiary burden placed on a criminal defendant who claims that he has been denied equal protection through the State's use of peremptory challenges to exclude members of his race from the petit jury.

I

Petitioner, a black man, was indicted in Kentucky on charges of second-degree burglary and receipt of stolen goods. On the first day of trial, the judge conducted voir dire examination of the venire, excused certain jurors for cause, and permitted the parties to exercise peremptory challenges. The prosecutor used his peremptory challenges to strike all four black persons on the venire, and a jury composed only of white persons was selected. Defense counsel moved to discharge the jury before it was sworn on the ground that the prosecutor's removal of the black veniremen violated petitioner's rights under the Sixth and Fourteenth Amendments to a jury drawn from a cross section of the community, and under the Fourteenth Amendment to equal protection of the laws. Counsel requested a hearing on his motion. Without expressly ruling on the request for a hearing, the trial judge observed that the parties were entitled to use their peremptory challenges to "strike anybody they want to." The judge then denied petitioner's motion, reasoning that the cross-section requirement applies only to selection of the venire and not to selection of the petit jury itself.

The jury convicted petitioner on both counts.

II

In Swain v. Alabama, this Court recognized that a "State's purposeful or deliberate denial to Negroes on account of race of participation as jurors in the administration of justice violates the Equal Protection Clause." This principle has been "consistently and repeatedly" reaffirmed in numerous decisions of this Court. We reaffirm the principle today.[15]

More than a century ago, the Court decided that the State denies a black defendant equal protection of the laws when it puts him on trial before a jury from which members of his race have been purposefully excluded. Strauder v. West Virginia (1880). That decision laid the foundation for the Court's unceasing efforts to eradicate racial discrimination in the procedures used to select the venire from which individual jurors are drawn. In Strauder, the Court explained that the central concern of the recently ratified Fourteenth Amendment was to put an end to governmental discrimination on account of race. Exclusion of black citizens from service as jurors constitutes a primary example of the evil the Fourteenth Amendment was designed to cure.

In holding that racial discrimination in jury selection offends the Equal Protection Clause, the Court in Strauder recognized, however, that a defendant has no right to a "petit jury composed in whole or in part of persons of his own race." But the defendant does have the right to be tried by a jury whose members are selected pursuant to non-discriminatory criteria. The Equal Protection Clause guarantees the defendant that the State will not exclude members of his race from the jury venire on account of race, or on the false assumption that members of his race as a group are not qualified to serve as jurors.[16]

Purposeful racial discrimination in selection of the venire violates a defendant's right to equal protection because it denies him the protection that a trial by jury is intended to secure. "The very idea of a jury is a body . . . composed of the peers or equals of the person whose rights it is selected or summoned to determine; that is, of his neighbors, fellows, associates, persons having the same legal status in society as that which he holds." The petit jury has occupied a central position in our system of justice by safeguarding a person accused of crime against the arbitrary exercise of power by prosecutor or judge.

Racial discrimination in selection of jurors harms not only the accused whose life or liberty they are summoned to try. Competence to serve as a juror ultimately depends on an assessment of individual qualifications and

---

15. In this Court, petitioner has argued that the prosecutor's conduct violated his rights under the Sixth and Fourteenth Amendments to an impartial jury and to a jury drawn from a cross section of the community. Petitioner has framed his argument in these terms in an apparent effort to avoid inviting the Court directly to reconsider one of its own precedents. On the other hand, the State has insisted that petitioner is claiming a denial of equal protection and that we must reconsider Swain to find a constitutional violation on this record. We agree with the State that resolution of petitioner's claim properly turns on application of equal protection principles and express no view on the merits of any of petitioner's Sixth Amendment arguments. [Footnote by the Court.]

16. Similarly, though the Sixth Amendment guarantees that the petit jury will be selected from a pool of names representing a cross section of the community, Taylor v. Louisiana, 419 U.S. 522 (1975), we have never held that the Sixth Amendment requires that "petit juries actually chosen must mirror the community and reflect the various distinctive groups in the population," id., at 538. Indeed, it would be impossible to apply a concept of proportional representation to the petit jury in view of the heterogeneous nature of our society. [Footnote by the Court.]

ability impartially to consider evidence presented at a trial. A person's race simply "is unrelated to his fitness as a juror."

The harm from discriminatory jury selection extends beyond that inflicted on the defendant and the excluded juror to touch the entire community. Selection procedures that purposefully exclude black persons from juries undermine public confidence in the fairness of our system of justice.

B

In *Strauder*, the Court invalidated a state statute that provided that only white men could serve as jurors. We can be confident that no State now has such a law. The Constitution requires, however, that we look beyond the face of the statute defining juror qualifications and also consider challenged selection practices to afford "protection against action of the State through its administrative officers in effecting the prohibited discrimination."

Accordingly, the component of the jury selection process at issue here, the State's privilege to strike individual jurors through peremptory challenges, is subject to the commands of the Equal Protection Clause. Although a prosecutor ordinarily is entitled to exercise permitted peremptory challenges "for any reason at all, as long as that reason is related to his view concerning the outcome" of the case to be tried, the Equal Protection Clause forbids the prosecutor to challenge potential jurors solely on account of their race or on the assumption that black jurors as a group will be unable impartially to consider the State's case against a black defendant.

III

The principles announced in *Strauder* never have been questioned in any subsequent decision of this Court. Rather, the Court has been called upon repeatedly to review the application of those principles to particular facts.[17] A recurring question in these cases, as in any case alleging a violation of the Equal Protection Clause, was whether the defendant had met his burden of proving purposeful discrimination on the part of the State. That question also was at the heart of the portion of Swain v. Alabama we reexamine today.

Swain required the Court to decide, among other issues, whether a black defendant was denied equal protection by the State's exercise of peremptory challenges to exclude members of his race from the petit jury. The record in *Swain* showed that the prosecutor had used the State's peremptory challenges to strike the six black persons included on the petit jury venire. While rejecting the defendant's claim for failure to prove purposeful discrimination, the Court nonetheless indicated that the Equal Protection Clause placed some limits on the State's exercise of peremptory challenges.

The Court sought to accommodate the prosecutor's historical privilege of peremptory challenge free of judicial control, and the constitutional

---

17. We express no views on whether the Constitution imposes any limit on the exercise of peremptory challenges by defense counsel. [Footnote by the Court.]

prohibition on exclusion of persons from jury service on account of race. While the Constitution does not confer a right to peremptory challenges, those challenges traditionally have been viewed as one means of assuring the selection of a qualified and unbiased jury. To preserve the peremptory nature of the prosecutor's challenge, the Court in *Swain* declined to scrutinize his actions in a particular case by relying on a presumption that he properly exercised the State's challenges.

The Court went on to observe, however, that a State may not exercise its challenges in contravention of the Equal Protection Clause. It was impermissible for a prosecutor to use his challenges to exclude blacks from the jury "for reasons wholly unrelated to the outcome of the particular case on trial" or to deny to blacks "the same right and opportunity to participate in the administration of justice enjoyed by the white population." Accordingly, a black defendant could make out a prima facie case of purposeful discrimination on proof that the peremptory challenge system was "being perverted" in that manner. For example, an inference of purposeful discrimination would be raised on evidence that a prosecutor, "in case after case, whatever the circumstances, whatever the crime and whoever the defendant or the victim may be, is responsible for the removal of Negroes who have been selected as qualified jurors by the jury commissioners and who have survived challenges for cause, with the result that no Negroes ever serve on petit juries." Evidence offered by the defendant in *Swain* did not meet that standard. While the defendant showed that prosecutors in the jurisdiction had exercised their strikes to exclude blacks from the jury, he offered no proof of the circumstances under which prosecutors were responsible for striking black jurors beyond the facts of his own case.

A number of lower courts following the teaching of *Swain* reasoned that proof of repeated striking of blacks over a number of cases was necessary to establish a violation of the Equal Protection Clause. Since this interpretation of *Swain* has placed on defendants a crippling burden of proof, prosecutors' peremptory challenges are now largely immune from constitutional scrutiny. For reasons that follow, we reject this evidentiary formulation as inconsistent with standards that have been developed since *Swain* for assessing a prima facie case under the Equal Protection Clause.

B

Since the decision in *Swain*, we have explained that our cases concerning selection of the venire reflect the general equal protection principle that the "invidious quality" of governmental action claimed to be racially discriminatory "must ultimately be traced to a racially discriminatory purpose." As in any equal protection case, the "burden is, of course," on the defendant who alleges discriminatory selection of the venire "to prove the existence of purposeful discrimination." In deciding if the defendant has carried his burden of persuasion, a court must undertake "a sensitive inquiry into such circumstantial and direct evidence of intent as may be available."

[S]ince *Swain*, we have recognized that a black defendant alleging that members of his race have been impermissibly excluded from the venire may make out a prima facie case of purposeful discrimination by showing that the totality of the relevant facts gives rise to an inference of discriminatory purpose. Once the defendant makes the requisite showing, the burden shifts to the State to explain adequately the racial exclusion. The State cannot meet this burden on mere general assertions that its officials did not discriminate or that they properly performed their official duties. Rather, the State must demonstrate that "permissible racially neutral selection criteria and procedures have produced the monochromatic result."[18]

The showing necessary to establish a prima facie case of purposeful discrimination in selection of the venire may be discerned in this Court's decisions. The defendant initially must show that he is a member of a racial group capable of being singled out for differential treatment. In combination with that evidence, a defendant may then make a prima facie case by proving that in the particular jurisdiction members of his race have not been summoned for jury service over an extended period of time. Proof of systematic exclusion from the venire raises an inference of purposeful discrimination because the "result bespeaks discrimination."

Since the ultimate issue is whether the State has discriminated in selecting the defendant's venire, however, the defendant may establish a prima facie case "in other ways than by evidence of long-continued unexplained absence" of members of his race "from many panels."

Thus, since the decision in *Swain*, this Court has recognized that a defendant may make a prima facie showing of purposeful racial discrimination in selection of the venire by relying solely on the facts concerning its selection in his case.

C

The standards for assessing a prima facie case in the context of discriminatory selection of the venire have been fully articulated since *Swain*. These principles support our conclusion that a defendant may establish a prima facie case of purposeful discrimination in selection of the petit jury solely on evidence concerning the prosecutor's exercise of peremptory challenges at the defendant's trial. To establish such a case, the defendant first must show that he is a member of a cognizable racial group, and that the prosecutor has exercised peremptory challenges to remove from the venire members of the defendant's race. Second, the defendant is entitled to rely on the fact, as to which there can be no dispute, that peremptory challenges constitute a jury selection practice that permits "those to discriminate who are of a mind to discriminate." Finally, the defendant must show that these facts and any other relevant circumstances raise an inference that the prosecutor used that practice to exclude the veniremen from the petit jury on account of

---

18. Our decisions concerning "disparate treatment" under Title VII of the Civil Rights Act of 1964 have explained the operation of prima facie burden of proof rules. [Footnote by the Court.]

their race. This combination of factors in the empaneling of the petit jury, as in the selection of the venire, raises the necessary inference of purposeful discrimination.

In deciding whether the defendant has made the requisite showing, the trial court should consider all relevant circumstances. For example, a "pattern" of strikes against black jurors included in the particular venire might give rise to an inference of discrimination. Similarly, the prosecutor's questions and statements during voir dire examination and in exercising his challenges may support or refute an inference of discriminatory purpose. These examples are merely illustrative. We have confidence that trial judges, experienced in supervising voir dire, will be able to decide if the circumstances concerning the prosecutor's use of peremptory challenges creates a prima facie case of discrimination against black jurors.

Once the defendant makes a prima facie showing, the burden shifts to the State to come forward with a neutral explanation for challenging black jurors. Though this requirement imposes a limitation in some cases on the full peremptory character of the historic challenge, we emphasize that the prosecutor's explanation need not rise to the level justifying exercise of a challenge for cause. But the prosecutor may not rebut the defendant's prima facie case of discrimination by stating merely that he challenged jurors of the defendant's race on the assumption — or his intuitive judgment — that they would be partial to the defendant because of their shared race. The core guarantee of equal protection, ensuring citizens that their State will not discriminate on account of race, would be meaningless were we to approve the exclusion of jurors on the basis of such assumptions, which arise solely from the jurors' race. Nor may the prosecutor rebut the defendant's case merely by denying that he had a discriminatory motive or "[affirming] [his] good faith in making individual selections." If these general assertions were accepted as rebutting a defendant's prima facie case, the Equal Protection Clause "would be but a vain and illusory requirement." The prosecutor therefore must articulate a neutral explanation related to the particular case to be tried. The trial court then will have the duty to determine if the defendant has established purposeful discrimination.

IV

The State contends that our holding will eviscerate the fair trial values served by the peremptory challenge. Conceding that the Constitution does not guarantee a right to peremptory challenges and that *Swain* did state that their use ultimately is subject to the strictures of equal protection, the State argues that the privilege of unfettered exercise of the challenge is of vital importance to the criminal justice system.

While we recognize, of course, that the peremptory challenge occupies an important position in our trial procedures, we do not agree that our decision today will undermine the contribution the challenge generally makes to the administration of justice. The reality of practice, amply reflected in many state- and federal-court opinions, shows that the challenge may be, and unfortunately at times has been, used to discriminate against black jurors. By requiring trial courts to be sensitive to the racially discriminatory use of peremptory challenges, our decision enforces the mandate of equal protection and furthers the ends of justice. In view of the heterogeneous population of our Nation, public respect for our criminal justice system and the rule of law will be strengthened if we ensure that no citizen is disqualified from jury service because of his race.

Nor are we persuaded by the State's suggestion that our holding will create serious administrative difficulties. In those States applying a version of the evidentiary standard we recognize today, courts have not experienced serious administrative burdens and the peremptory challenge system has survived.

V

In this case, petitioner made a timely objection to the prosecutor's removal of all black persons on the venire. Because the trial court flatly rejected the objection without requiring the prosecutor to give an explanation for his action, we remand this case for further proceedings. If the trial court decides that the facts establish, prima facie, purposeful discrimination and the prosecutor does not come forward with a neutral explanation for his action, our precedents require that petitioner's conviction be reversed.[19]

It is so ordered.

Justice WHITE, concurring.

The Court overturns the principal holding in Swain v. Alabama (1965), that the Constitution does not require in any given case an inquiry into the prosecutor's reasons for using his peremptory challenges to strike blacks from the petit jury panel in the criminal trial of a black defendant and that in such a case it will be presumed that the prosecutor is acting for legitimate trial-related reasons. The Court now rules that such use of peremptory challenges in a given case may, but does not necessarily, raise an inference, which the prosecutor carries the burden of refuting, that his strikes were based on the belief that no black citizen could be a satisfactory juror or fairly try a black defendant.

I agree that, to this extent, *Swain* should be overruled. I do so because *Swain* itself indicated that the presumption of legitimacy with respect to the striking of black venire persons could be overcome by evidence that over a period of time the prosecution had consistently excluded blacks from petit juries. This should have warned prosecutors that using peremptories to exclude blacks on the assumption that no black juror could fairly judge a black defendant would violate the Equal Protection Clause.

19. To the extent that anything in Swain v. Alabama, 380 U.S. 202 (1965), is contrary to the principles we articulate today, that decision is overruled. [Footnote by the Court.]

It appears, however, that the practice of peremptorily eliminating blacks from petit juries in cases with black defendants remains widespread, so much so that I agree that an opportunity to inquire should be afforded when this occurs.

The Court emphasizes that using peremptory challenges to strike blacks does not end the inquiry; it is not unconstitutional, without more, to strike one or more blacks from the jury. The judge may not require the prosecutor to respond at all. If he does, the prosecutor, who in most cases has had a chance to voir dire the prospective jurors, will have an opportunity to give trial-related reasons for his strikes — some satisfactory ground other than the belief that black jurors should not be allowed to judge a black defendant.

Much litigation will be required to spell out the contours of the Court's equal protection holding today, and the significant effect it will have on the conduct of criminal trials cannot be gainsaid. But I agree with the Court that the time has come to rule as it has, and I join its opinion and judgment.

Justice MARSHALL, concurring.

I join Justice Powell's eloquent opinion for the Court, which takes a historic step toward eliminating the shameful practice of racial discrimination in the selection of juries. The Court's opinion cogently explains the pernicious nature of the racially discriminatory use of peremptory challenges, and the repugnancy of such discrimination to the Equal Protection Clause. The Court's opinion also ably demonstrates the inadequacy of any burden of proof for racially discriminatory use of peremptories that requires that "justice . . . sit supinely by" and be flouted in case after case before a remedy is available. I nonetheless write separately to express my views. The decision today will not end the racial discrimination that peremptories inject into the jury-selection process. That goal can be accomplished only by eliminating peremptory challenges entirely.

I

A little over a century ago, this Court invalidated a state statute providing that black citizens could not serve as jurors. Strauder v. West Virginia (1880). State officials then turned to somewhat more subtle ways of keeping blacks off jury venires.

Misuse of the peremptory challenge to exclude black jurors has become both common and flagrant. Black defendants rarely have been able to compile statistics showing the extent of that practice, but the few cases setting out such figures are instructive. *See* United States v. Carter (CA8 1975) (in the Western District of Missouri involving black defendants, prosecutors peremptorily challenged 81% of black jurors); McKinney v. Walker (SC 1974) (in Spartansburg County, South Carolina, prosecutors peremptorily challenged 82 percent of black jurors in cases involving black defendants). In 100 felony trials in Dallas County in 1983-1984, prosecutors peremptorily struck 405 out of 467 eligible black jurors; the chance of a qualified black sitting on a jury was 1 in 10, compared to 1 in 2 for a white.[20]

II

I wholeheartedly concur in the Court's conclusion that use of the peremptory challenge to remove blacks from juries, on the basis of their race, violates the Equal Protection Clause. I would go further, however, in fashioning a remedy adequate to eliminate that discrimination. Merely allowing defendants the opportunity to challenge the racially discriminatory use of peremptory challenges in individual cases will not end the illegitimate use of the peremptory challenge.

Evidentiary analysis . . . illustrate[s] the limitations of the approach. First, defendants cannot attack the discriminatory use of peremptory challenges at all unless the challenges are so flagrant as to establish a prima facie case. This means, in those States, that where only one or two black jurors survive the challenges for cause, the prosecutor need have no compunction about striking them from the jury because of their race. Prosecutors are left free to discriminate against blacks in jury selection provided that they hold that discrimination to an "acceptable" level.

Second, when a defendant can establish a prima facie case, trial courts face the difficult burden of assessing prosecutors' motives. Any prosecutor can easily assert facially neutral reasons for striking a juror, and trial courts are ill equipped to second-guess those reasons. How is the court to treat a prosecutor's statement that he struck a juror because the juror had a son about the same age as defendant, or seemed "uncommunicative," or "never cracked a smile" and, therefore "did not possess the sensitivities necessary to realistically look at the issues and decide the facts in this case." If such easily generated explanations are sufficient to discharge the prosecutor's obligation to justify his strikes on nonracial grounds, then the protection erected by the Court today may be illusory.

Nor is outright prevarication by prosecutors the only danger here. "[It] is even possible that an attorney may lie to himself in an effort to convince himself that his motives are legal." A prosecutor's own conscious or unconscious racism may lead him easily to the conclusion that a prospective black juror is "sullen," or "distant," a characterization that would not have come to his mind if a white juror had acted identically. A judge's own conscious or unconscious racism may lead him to accept such an explanation as well supported. [P]rosecutors' peremptories are based on their "seat-of-the-pants instincts" as to how particular jurors will vote. Yet "seat-of-the-pants instincts" may often be just another term for racial prejudice. Even if

---

20. An earlier jury-selection treatise circulated in the same county instructed prosecutors: "Do not take Jews, Negroes, Dagos, Mexicans or a member of any minority race on a jury, no matter how rich or how well educated." Quoted in Dallas Morning News, Mar. 9, 1986, p. 29, col. 1. [Footnote by the Court.]

all parties approach the Court's mandate with the best of conscious intentions, that mandate requires them to confront and overcome their own racism on all levels—a challenge I doubt all of them can meet. It is worth remembering that "114 years after the close of the War Between the States and nearly 100 years after *Strauder,* racial and other forms of discrimination still remain a fact of life, in the administration of justice as in our society as a whole."

III

The inherent potential of peremptory challenges to distort the jury process by permitting the exclusion of jurors on racial grounds should ideally lead the Court to ban them entirely from the criminal justice system.

Much ink has been spilled regarding the historic importance of defendants' peremptory challenges. But this Court has also repeatedly stated that the right of peremptory challenge is not of constitutional magnitude, and may be withheld altogether without impairing the constitutional guarantee of impartial jury and fair trial. The potential for racial prejudice, further, inheres in the defendant's challenge as well. If the prosecutor's peremptory challenge could be eliminated only at the cost of eliminating the defendant's challenge as well, I do not think that would be too great a price to pay.

I applaud the Court's holding that the racially discriminatory use of peremptory challenges violates the Equal Protection Clause, and I join the Court's opinion. However, only by banning peremptories entirely can such discrimination be ended.

Chief Justice BURGER, joined by Justice REHNQUIST, dissenting.

Today the Court sets aside the peremptory challenge, a procedure which has been part of the common law for many centuries and part of our jury system for nearly 200 years. It does so on the basis of a constitutional argument that was rejected, without a single dissent, in Swain v. Alabama (1965). What makes today's holding truly extraordinary is that it is based on a constitutional argument that the petitioner has expressly declined to raise, both in this Court and in the Supreme Court of Kentucky.

In the Kentucky Supreme Court, petitioner disclaimed specifically any reliance on the Equal Protection Clause of the Fourteenth Amendment, pressing instead only a claim based on the Sixth Amendment.

In reaching the equal protection issue despite petitioner's clear refusal to present it, the Court departs dramatically from its normal procedure without any explanation.

II

Because the Court nonetheless chooses to decide this case on the equal protection grounds not presented, it may be useful to discuss this issue as well. In *Swain,* Justice White traced the development of the peremptory challenge from the early days of the jury trial in England. Peremptory challenges have a venerable tradition in this country as well.

Instead of even considering the history or function of the peremptory challenge, the bulk of the Court's opinion is spent recounting the well-established principle that intentional exclusion of racial groups from jury venires is a violation of the Equal Protection Clause.

The Court never applies this conventional equal protection framework to the claims at hand, perhaps to avoid acknowledging that the state interest involved here has historically been regarded by this Court as substantial, if not compelling. Peremptory challenges have long been viewed as a means to achieve an impartial jury that will be sympathetic toward neither an accused nor witnesses for the State on the basis of some shared factor of race, religion, occupation, or other characteristic.

The Court also purports to express "no views on whether the Constitution imposes any limit on the exercise of peremptory challenges by defense counsel." But the clear and inescapable import of this novel holding will inevitably be to limit the use of this valuable tool to both prosecutors and defense attorneys alike. Once the Court has held that prosecutors are limited in their use of peremptory challenges, could we rationally hold that defendants are not?

Justice REHNQUIST, with whom Chief Justice BURGER, dissents.

In my view, there is simply nothing "unequal" about the State's using its peremptory challenges to strike blacks from the jury in cases involving black defendants, so long as such challenges are also used to exclude whites in cases involving white defendants, Hispanics in cases involving Hispanic defendants, Asians in cases involving Asian defendants, and so on. This case-specific use of peremptory challenges by the State does not single out blacks, or members of any other race for that matter, for discriminatory treatment. Such use of peremptories is at best based upon seat-of-the-pants instincts, which are undoubtedly crudely stereotypical and may in many cases be hopelessly mistaken. But as long as they are applied across-the-board to jurors of all races and nationalities, I do not see—and the Court most certainly has not explained—how their use violates the Equal Protection Clause.

———

Batson established a three-step process for challenging the alleged discriminatory use of peremptory challenges. First, the objecting party must establish a prima facie case of intentional racial discrimination. Then, the burden shifts to the other party to offer a race-neutral basis for its exercise of the challenges. Third, the trial court must evaluate the sincerity of the explanation and decide whether there really was a neutral reason for the exercise of the challenges. Each of these steps is discussed in more detail in the next section of this chapter.

3. *Applying* Batson

Batson left open many questions for the Court to answer:

1. Does the defendant need to be the same race as the excluded juror to have standing to raise the equal protection challenge?
2. Does the *Batson* ruling apply to civil cases?
3. Would the prohibition on discriminatory use of peremptory challenges apply to defense counsel?
4. Does *Batson* apply to other types of discrimination, such as gender and religious discrimination?
5. How exactly are *Batson* challenges raised and refuted, and what constitutes a neutral explanation for a peremptory challenge of a juror?

a. Standing to Raise *Batson* Challenges

The first question that the Supreme Court answered concerned standing to raise a *Batson* challenge. Five years after *Batson*, in Powers v. Ohio, 499 U.S. 400 (1991), a white defendant challenged the prosecutor's use of peremptory challenges to exclude African American jurors. The Supreme Court held that the defendant had standing to bring the excluded jurors' equal protection claim. Justice Kennedy noted that a defendant suffers a real injury when jurors are excluded because of their race:

> In the ordinary course, a litigant must assert his or her own legal rights and interests, and cannot rest a claim to relief on the legal rights or interests of third parties. . . .
> [However,] the discriminatory use of peremptory challenges by the prosecution causes a criminal defendant cognizable injury. . . . This is not because the individual jurors dismissed by the prosecution may have been predisposed to favor the defendant. . . . Rather, it is because racial discrimination in the selection of jurors "casts doubt on the integrity of the judicial process," and places the fairness of a criminal proceeding in doubt.

The Court recognized, moreover, that "[t]he purpose of the jury system is to impress upon the criminal defendant and the community as a whole that a verdict of conviction or acquittal is given in accordance with the law by persons who are fair. The verdict will not be accepted or understood in these terms if the jury is chosen by unlawful means at the outset." Finally, the Court recognized the defendant's standing to raise the jurors' equal protection challenge, reasoning that the jurors themselves would likely be unable to raise their own equal protection claim:

> The barriers to a suit by an excluded juror are daunting. Potential jurors are not parties to the jury selection process and have no opportunity to be heard at the time of their exclusion. . . . [I]t would be difficult for an individual juror to show a likelihood that discrimination against him at the *voir dire* stage will recur. And, there exist considerable practical barriers to suit by the excluded juror because of the small

financial stake involved and the economic burdens of litigation. The reality is that a juror dismissed because of race probably will leave the courtroom possessing little incentive to set in motion the arduous process needed to vindicate his own rights.

Following Powers v. Ohio, a litigant has third-party standing to object to the discriminatory use of peremptory challenges, even if the litigant is not the same race as the excluded juror.

b. *Batson* Challenges in Civil Cases

Immediately after Powers v. Ohio, the Supreme Court also decided whether the *Batson* rule applies to private litigants in civil cases, or is just a bar on government discrimination against jurors. In Edmonson v. Leesville Concrete Co., 500 U.S. 614 (1991), a black construction worker sued his company for negligence. When the company used two of its three peremptory challenges to remove black prospective jurors, the worker raised a *Batson* objection. The district court rejected the objection, holding that *Batson* did not apply in civil proceedings.

The Supreme Court reversed. Once again, Justice Kennedy wrote the majority opinion:

> Without the direct and indispensable participation of the judge, who beyond all question is a state actor, the peremptory challenge system would serve no purpose. By enforcing a discriminatory peremptory challenge, the court "has not only made itself a party to the [biased act], but has elected to place its power, property and prestige behind the [alleged] discrimination."

Thus, the *Batson* rule applies even in civil cases.

Chief Justice Rehnquist and Justices O'Connor and Scalia dissented. Writing for the dissent, Justice O'Connor objected that "not everything that happens in a courtroom is state action." The dissent argued that the government was not responsible for the acts of private individuals acting on behalf of private clients.

c. Discriminatory Use of Peremptory Challenges by the Defense

As you will recall, Chief Justice Burger in his dissent in *Batson* predicted that the Court's ruling would soon be applied to defense counsel. That prediction came true. In Georgia v. McCollum, 505 U.S. 42 (1992), two white defendants were charged with assaulting two black victims. The black community rallied around the victims. Before the trial, the prosecution moved to prohibit the defendants from using their peremptory challenges to strike black individuals from the jury. The state court rejected the challenge, holding that *Batson* applied only to prosecutors.

The Supreme Court reversed. Writing for the majority, Justice Blackmun identified the four issues the Court needed to decide in the case:

> In deciding whether the Constitution prohibits criminal defendants from exercising racially discriminatory peremptory challenges, we must answer four questions. First, whether a criminal defendant's exercise of peremptory challenges in a racially discriminatory manner inflicts the harms addressed by *Batson*. Second, whether the exercise of peremptory challenges by a criminal defendant constitutes state action. Third, whether prosecutors have standing to raise this constitutional challenge. And fourth, whether the constitutional rights of a criminal defendant nonetheless preclude the extension of our precedents to this case.

In addressing these issues, the Court first found that a defendant's exercise of racially discriminatory peremptory challenges does inflict the harms addressed by *Batson*: "Regardless of who invokes the discriminatory challenge, there can be no doubt that the harm is the same — in all cases, the juror is subjected to open and public racial discrimination."

Next, the Court relied on *Edmonson* to find that defense counsel's actions constitute state action: "[T]he defendant in a Georgia criminal case relies on [the state's jury selection system]. By enforcing a discriminatory peremptory challenge, the Court 'has . . . elected to place its power, property and prestige behind the [alleged] discrimination.'"

Third, the Court held that prosecutors have standing to raise an equal protection claim on behalf of the excused jurors. Relying on its decision in *Edmonson* once more, the Court stated:

> While third-party standing is a limited exception, the *Powers* Court recognized that a litigant may raise a claim on behalf of a third party if the litigant can demonstrate that he has suffered a concrete injury, that he has a close relation to the third party, and that there exists some hindrance to the third party's ability to protect its own interests. . . .
> . . . The State's relation to potential jurors in this case is closer than the relationships approved in *Powers* and *Edmonson*. As the representative of all its citizens, the State is the logical and proper party to assert the invasion of the constitutional rights of the excluded jurors in a criminal trial.

Finally, the Court rejected the defendants' argument that prohibiting their exercise of peremptory challenges would deny them a fair trial and the right to effective assistance of counsel: "This Court firmly has rejected the view that assumptions of partiality based on race provide a legitimate basis for disqualifying a person as an impartial juror."

Chief Justice Rehnquist concurred in the decision, but only because he felt obliged by what he believed was the Court's erroneous decision in *Edmonson*. Similarly, Justice Thomas wrote in his concurrence that he believed that the Court's *Edmonson* opinion precluded a different result in *McCollum*, but he expressed his "general dissatisfaction with [the Court's] continuing attempts to use the Constitution to regulate peremptory challenges." He warned that the Court's decision led it down a slippery slope: "Today, we decide only that white defendants may not strike black veniremen on the basis of race. Eventually, we will have to decide whether black defendants may strike white veniremen. Next will come the question whether defendants may exercise peremptories on the basis of sex."

Justice O'Connor dissented because she did not agree that criminal defendants and their lawyers could be considered government actors. She noted:

> What really seems to bother the Court is the prospect that leaving criminal defendants and their attorneys free to make racially motivated peremptory challenges will undermine the ideal of nondiscriminatory jury selection we espoused in *Batson*. The concept that the government alone must honor constitutional dictates, however, is a fundamental tenet of our legal order, not an obstacle to be circumvented. This is particularly so in the context of criminal trials, where we have held the prosecution to uniquely high standards of conduct.

Justice Scalia also dissented. Reiterating his argument that *Edmonson* was wrongly decided, he argued that "a bad decision should not be followed logically to its illogical conclusion." He warned that, "[i]n the interest of promoting the supposedly greater good of race relations in the society as a whole (make no mistake that that is what underlies all of this), we use the Constitution to destroy the ages-old right of criminal defendants to exercise peremptory challenges as they wish, to secure a jury that they consider fair."

d. *Batson* Challenges to Other Types of Discrimination

Batson focused on the exclusion of jurors on racial grounds. Its holding has been expanded, however, to other types of discrimination. Soon after *Batson*, the Court held that discrimination on the basis of ethnicity is also prohibited. In Hernandez v. New York, 400 U.S. 352 (1991), the Court held that Hispanics have a right not to be discriminated against in jury selection based on their ethnicity. Petitioner Dionisio Hernandez challenged the prosecution's use of peremptory challenges to excuse Hispanic jurors. While the Court recognized that such a use of peremptory challenges could be unconstitutional, it held that the prosecution offered a sufficient race-neutral explanation for its peremptory challenges. What was that explanation? The prosecutor argued that he excused the jurors because, as Spanish speakers, they might not follow the translations offered by the interpreters who would testify at trial. In response, Hernandez contended that Spanish-language ability bears a close relation to ethnicity and that, as a consequence, the exercise of a peremptory challenge on the ground that a Hispanic potential juror speaks Spanish violates the Equal Protection Clause. The Court, however, did not decide the issue because the prosecution argued that the jurors' demeanor during voir dire supported its argument that the jurors would not defer to the official translation of Spanish-language testimony.

In J.E.B. v. Alabama, 511 U.S. 127 (1994), the Supreme Court extended *Batson* to prohibit peremptory challenges based on gender. In a paternity and child-support case against the putative father, the state used nine of its ten jurors to strike males from the jury. The father objected on *Batson* grounds. Justice Blackmun, joined by Justices Stevens, O'Connor, Souter, and Ginsburg, held that *Batson*'s prohibition on the discriminatory use of peremptory challenges applies to all types of discrimination that receive heightened scrutiny, such as discriminating against prospective jurors on the basis of gender, race, and ethnicity. The Court held that such peremptory-challenge discrimination does not substantially further the state's legitimate interest in achieving a fair and impartial trial. The Court noted, however, that nevertheless,

> [o]ur conclusion that litigants may not strike potential jurors solely on the basis of gender does not imply the elimination of all peremptory challenges. . . . Parties still may remove jurors who they feel might be less acceptable than others on the panel; gender simply may not serve as a proxy for bias. Parties may also exercise their peremptory challenges to remove from the venire any group or class of individuals normally subject to "rational basis" review.[21]

Following J.E.B. v. Alabama, the Supreme Court has left it to lower courts to determine what other types of discrimination are prohibited by *Batson*. The Supreme Court has never held that the heightened scrutiny standard applies to challenges on the basis of religion, although prior to *J.E.B.*, the Supreme Court declined to review State v. Davis, 504 N.W.2d 767 (1994), a Minnesota Supreme Court decision that held that *Batson* does not prevent the exclusion of prospective jurors on religious affiliation grounds. Justices Thomas and Scalia dissented from the denial of review and argued that the case should have been remanded in light of the Court's decision in *J.E.B.* Justice Thomas wrote:

> [G]iven the Court's rationale in *J.E.B.*, no principled reason immediately appears for declining to apply *Batson* to any strike based on a classification that is accorded heightened scrutiny under the Equal Protection Clause. . . . In breaking the barrier between classifications that merit strict equal protection scrutiny and those that receive what we have termed "heightened" or "intermediate" scrutiny, *J.E.B.* would seem to have extended *Batson*'s equal protection analysis to all strikes based on the latter category of classifications—a category which presumably would include classifications based on religion.

Today, many states have enacted laws prohibiting discrimination in jury selection based on race, gender, religion, ethnicity, and even sexual orientation. *See, e.g.*, Cal. Code Civ. Proc. §231.5 (West 2007) ("A party may not use a

---

21. For example, challenging all persons who have had military experience would disproportionately affect men at this time, while challenging all persons employed as nurses would disproportionately affect women. Without a showing of pretext, however, these challenges may well not be unconstitutional, since they are not gender or race based. [Footnote by the Court.]

peremptory challenge to remove a prospective juror on the basis of an assumption that the prospective juror is biased merely because of his or her race, color, religion, sex, national origin, sexual orientation, or similar grounds"); N.Y. Civ. Rights Law §13 (McKinney 2007) ("No citizen of the state possessing all other qualifications which are or may be required or prescribed by law, shall be disqualified to serve as a grand or petit juror in any court of this state on account of race, creed, color, national origin or sex").

e. The Mechanics of Bringing *Batson* Challenges

As set forth by the Supreme Court in *Batson*, the burden is on the challenging party to make a prima facie showing of intentional discrimination during jury selection. Ordinarily, a party may meet this burden by demonstrating a pattern of challenges against a particular group of prospective jurors. However, in Johnson v. California, 545 U.S. 162 (2005), the Court held that an initial showing of intentional discrimination during jury selection need not establish that the prosecution's peremptory challenges were "more likely than not" based on group bias. Rather, Justice Kennedy wrote, "a prima facie case of discrimination can be made out by offering a wide variety of evidence, so long as the sum of the proffered facts gives 'rise to an inference of discriminatory purpose.'"

Once a prima facie case has been demonstrated, the burden shifts to the party exercising the peremptory challenge to provide a neutral explanation for its strikes. A peremptory challenge may be based on the juror's appearance and the manner in which the juror answers voir dire questions. And, as discussed in *Hernandez, supra,* a neutral explanation for excusing a juror may include something as simple as the contention that a juror of a certain ethnicity is not as likely to follow language translations in a case. In Purkett v. Elem, 514 U.S. 765 (1995), the Court, in a per curiam opinion, emphasized the minimal nature of establishing a neutral explanation for the exercise of a challenge. James Purkett, a black defendant, was accused of robbery. He objected to the prosecutor's use of peremptory challenges to strike two black men from the jury panel. The prosecutor explained that he struck the first juror because of his unkempt hair, mustache, and beard, and the second juror because he had been the victim of a prior robbery and might assume that the robbery charged against Purkett required similar circumstances. The Eighth Circuit found the prosecution's explanation for striking the first juror to be pretextual, but the U.S. Supreme Court overturned that finding. It held that while "implausible," "fantastic," "silly," or "superstitious" reasons might be pretextual, the prosecutor's explanation in this case satisfied *Batson* standards.

Finally, in the third step, the court must decide whether the proffered neutral explanation is merely a pretext for the discriminatory use of peremptory challenges. In Miller-El v. Dretke, 545 U.S. 231 (2005), the Court demonstrated the detailed examination that it and other courts might conduct to determine whether there has been a *Batson* violation. In *Miller-El*, Justice Souter, writing for the majority, stated that "[t]he whole of the *voir dire* testimony subject to consideration casts the prosecution's reasons for striking [a black juror] in an implausible light. Comparing [the excused black juror's] strike with the treatment of panel members who expressed similar views supports a conclusion that race was significant in determining who was challenged and who was not."

In *Miller-El*, the Court conducted an exhaustive comparison of the voir dire questions and answers of black and nonblack panel members. It found that the prosecution had challenged black jurors who had given answers nearly identical to those of white jurors. The Court also found that the prosecution had skewed its questions to black jurors so as to make it more likely that they would elicit answers that would make those jurors ineligible to sit on a death penalty case. Finally, the court pointed to an historic policy in that jurisdiction of excluding blacks from juries. In the end, the Court found that "[t]he prosecutors' chosen race-neutral reasons for the strikes do not hold up and are so far at odds with the evidence that pretext is the fair conclusion, indicating the very discrimination the explanations were meant to deny."

In his concurrence in *Miller-El*, Justice Breyer came around to the opinion offered by Justice Marshall in his concurrence in *Batson*: "The complexity of [the *Batson* test] reflects the difficulty of finding a legal test that will objectively measure the inherently subjective reasons that underline use of a peremptory challenge." Reasoning that, despite *Batson*, "the use of race- and gender-based stereotypes in the jury selection process seems better organized and more systematized than ever before," Justice Breyer, "[i]n light of [all] considerations . . . believe[d] it necessary to reconsider *Batson*'s test and the peremptory challenge system as a whole."

Since Miller-El v. Dretke, courts have looked to the entire record of jury selection to determine the validity of a proffered race-neutral reason for challenging a juror, as it did in Snyder v. Louisiana.

SNYDER v. LOUISIANA

552 U.S. 472 (2008)

Justice Alito delivered the opinion of the Court.

Petitioner Allen Snyder was convicted of first-degree murder in a Louisiana court and was sentenced to death. He asks us to review a decision of the Louisiana Supreme Court rejecting his claim that the prosecution exercised some of its peremptory jury challenges based on race, in violation of *Batson v. Kentucky (1986)*. We hold that the trial court committed clear error in its ruling on a *Batson* objection, and we therefore reverse.

The crime for which petitioner was convicted [of murdering his estranged wife].

Eighty-five prospective jurors were questioned as members of a panel. Thirty-six of these survived challenges for cause; 5 of the 36 were black;

and all 5 of the prospective black jurors were eliminated by the prosecution through the use of peremptory strikes. The jury found petitioner guilty of first-degree murder and determined that he should receive the death penalty.

Batson provides a three-step process for a trial court to use in adjudicating a claim that a peremptory challenge was based on race:

> First, a defendant must make a prima facie showing that a peremptory challenge has been exercised on the basis of race[; s]econd, if that showing has been made, the prosecution must offer a race-neutral basis for striking the juror in question[; and t]hird, in light of the parties' submissions, the trial court must determine whether the defendant has shown purposeful discrimination.

Miller-El v. Dretke (2005).

Petitioner centers his *Batson* claim on the prosecution's strikes of two black jurors, Jeffrey Brooks and Elaine Scott. Because we find that the trial court committed clear error in overruling petitioner's *Batson* objection with respect to Mr. Brooks, we have no need to consider petitioner's claim regarding Ms. Scott.

In *Miller-El* v. *Dretke*, the Court made it clear that in considering a *Batson* objection, or in reviewing a ruling claimed to be *Batson* error, all of the circumstances that bear upon the issue of racial animosity must be consulted. In this case, . . . the explanation given for the strike of Mr. Brooks is by itself unconvincing and suffices for the determination that there was *Batson* error.

When defense counsel made a *Batson* objection concerning the strike of Mr. Brooks, a college senior who was attempting to fulfill his student-teaching obligation, the prosecution offered two race-neutral reasons for the strike. The prosecutor explained:

> I thought about it last night. Number 1, the main reason is that he looked very nervous to me throughout the questioning. Number 2, he's one of the fellows that came up at the beginning [of *voir dire*] and said he was going to miss class. He's a student teacher. My main concern is for that reason, that being that he might, to go home quickly, come back with guilty of a lesser verdict so there wouldn't be a penalty phase. Those are my two reasons.

With respect to the first reason, deference is especially appropriate where a trial judge has made a finding that an attorney credibly relied on demeanor in exercising a strike. Here, however, the record does not show that the trial judge actually made a determination concerning Mr. Brooks' demeanor.

The second reason proffered for the strike of Mr. Brooks—his student-teaching obligation—fails even under the highly deferential standard of review that is applicable here. At the beginning of *voir dire*, when the trial court asked the members of the venire whether jury service or sequestration would pose an extreme hardship, Mr. Brooks was 1 of more than 50 members of the venire who expressed concern that jury service or sequestration would interfere with work, school, family, or other obligations.

When Mr. Brooks came forward, the following exchange took place:

MR. JEFFREY BROOKS: . . . I'm a student at Southern University, New Orleans. This is my last semester. My major requires me to student teach, and today I've already missed a half a day. That is part of my — it's required for me to graduate this semester.
[DEFENSE COUNSEL]:   Mr. Brooks, if you — how many days would you miss if you were sequestered on this jury? Do you teach every day?
MR. JEFFREY BROOKS: Five days a week.
[DEFENSE COUNSEL]:   Five days a week.
MR. JEFFREY BROOKS: And it's 8:30 through 3:00.
[DEFENSE COUNSEL]:   If you missed this week, is there any way that you could make it up this semester?
MR. JEFFREY BROOKS: Well, the first two weeks I observe, the remaining I begin teaching, so there is something I'm missing right now that will better me towards my teaching career.
[DEFENSE COUNSEL]:   Is there any way that you could make up the observed observation *[sic]* that you're missing today, at another time?
MR. JEFFREY BROOKS: It may be possible, I'm not sure.
[DEFENSE COUNSEL]:   Okay. So that —
THE COURT: Is there anyone we could call, like a Dean or anything, that we could speak to?
MR. JEFFREY BROOKS: Actually, I spoke to my Dean, Doctor Tillman, who's at the university probably right now.
THE COURT: All right.
MR. JEFFREY BROOKS: Would you like to speak to him?
THE COURT: Yeah.
MR. JEFFREY BROOKS: I don't have his card on me.
THE COURT: Why don't you give [a law clerk] his number, give [a law clerk] his name and we'll call him and we'll see what we can do.
(MR. JEFFREY BROOKS LEFT THE BENCH).

Shortly thereafter, the court again spoke with Mr. Brooks:

THE LAW CLERK: Jeffrey Brooks, the requirement for his teaching is a three hundred clock hour observation. Doctor Tillman at Southern University said that as long as it's just this week, he doesn't see that it would cause a problem with Mr. Brooks completing his observation time within this semester.
THE COURT: We talked to Doctor Tillman and he says he doesn't see a problem as long as it's just this week, you know, he'll work with you on it. Okay?
MR. JEFFREY BROOKS: Okay.

Once Mr. Brooks heard the law clerk's report about the conversation with Doctor Tillman, Mr. Brooks did not express any further concern about serving on the jury, and the prosecution did not choose to question him more deeply about this matter.

The prosecutor's second proffered reason for striking Mr. Brooks must be evaluated in light of these circumstances. The prosecutor claimed to be apprehensive that Mr. Brooks, in order to minimize the student-teaching hours missed during jury service, might have been motivated to find petitioner guilty, not of first-degree murder, but of a lesser included offense because this would obviate the need for a penalty phase proceeding. But this scenario was highly speculative. Even if Mr. Brooks had favored a quick resolution, that would not have necessarily led him to reject a finding of first-degree murder. If the majority of jurors had initially favored a finding of first-degree murder, Mr. Brooks' purported inclination might have led him to agree in order to speed the deliberations. Only if all or most of the other jurors had favored the lesser verdict would Mr. Brooks have been in a position to shorten the trial by favoring such a verdict.

The implausibility of this explanation is reinforced by the prosecutor's acceptance of white jurors who disclosed conflicting obligations that appear to have been at least as serious as Mr. Brooks'. We recognize that a retrospective comparison of jurors based on a cold appellate record may be very misleading when alleged similarities were not raised at trial. In that situation, an appellate court must be mindful that an exploration of the alleged similarities at the time of trial might have shown that the jurors in question were not really comparable. In this case, however, the shared characteristic, *i.e.*, concern about serving on the jury due to conflicting obligations, was thoroughly explored by the trial court when the relevant jurors asked to be excused for cause.

A comparison between Mr. Brooks and Roland Laws, a white juror, is particularly striking. During the initial stage of *voir dire*, Mr. Laws approached the court and offered strong reasons why serving on the sequestered jury would cause him hardship. Mr. Laws stated that he was "a self-employed general contractor," with "two houses that are nearing completion, one [with the occupants] . . . moving in this weekend." Mr. Laws also had demanding family obligations:

> [M]y wife just had a hysterectomy, so I'm running the kids back and forth to school, and we're not originally from here, so I have no family in the area, so between the two things, it's kind of bad timing for me.

Although these obligations seem substantially more pressing than Mr. Brooks', the prosecution questioned Mr. Laws and attempted to elicit assurances that he would be able to serve despite his work and family obligations. And the prosecution declined the opportunity to use a peremptory strike on Mr. Laws. If the prosecution had been sincerely concerned that Mr. Brooks would favor a lesser verdict than first-degree murder in order to shorten the trial, it is hard to see why the prosecution would not have had at least as much concern regarding Mr. Laws.

As previously noted, the question presented at the third stage of the *Batson* inquiry is "'whether the defendant has shown purposeful discrimination.'" The prosecution's proffer of this pretextual explanation naturally gives rise to an inference of discriminatory intent.

We therefore reverse the judgment.

Justice THOMAS, with whom Justice SCALIA joins, dissenting.

The Court's conclusion, however, reveals that it is only paying lipservice to the pivotal role of the trial court. The Court second-guesses the trial court's determinations in this case merely because the judge did not clarify which of the prosecutor's neutral bases for striking Mr. Brooks was dispositive.

The prosecution offered two neutral bases for striking Mr. Brooks: his nervous demeanor and his stated concern about missing class. The trial court, in rejecting defendant's *Batson* challenge, stated only "All right. I'm going to allow the challenge. I'm going to allow the challenge." Given the trial court's expertise in making credibility determinations and its firsthand knowledge of the *voir dire* exchanges, it is entirely proper to defer to its judgment. Accordingly, I would affirm the judgment below.

Although the Court has opened the door for greater scrutiny of the granting of possibly discriminatory peremptory challenges, it has not held that a judge's denial of a peremptory challenge — even if it was properly raised — requires automatic reversal. In Rivera v. Illinois, 556 U.S. 148 (2009), he Supreme Court held that if a judge erroneously seats a juror who could have been properly stricken by a peremptory challenge, the defendant is not entitled to reversal of the conviction if the record demonstrates that all of the seated jurors were actually qualified and unbiased.

RIVERA v. ILLINOIS
556 U.S. 148 (2009)

Justice GINSBURG delivered the opinion of the Court.

This case concerns the consequences of a state trial court's erroneous denial of a defendant's peremptory challenge to the seating of a juror in a criminal case. If all seated jurors are qualified and unbiased, does the *Due Process Clause of the Fourteenth Amendment* nonetheless require automatic reversal of the defendant's conviction?

Following a jury trial in an Illinois state court, defendant-petitioner Michael Rivera was convicted of first-degree murder and sentenced to a prison term of 85 years. On appeal, Rivera challenged the trial court's rejection of his peremptory challenge to venire member Deloris Gomez. Gomez sat on Rivera's jury and indeed served as the jury's foreperson. It is conceded that there was no basis to challenge Gomez for cause. She met the requirements for jury service, and Rivera does not contend that she was in fact biased against him. The Supreme Court of Illinois held that the peremptory challenge should have been allowed, but further held that the error was harmless and therefore did not warrant reversal of Rivera's conviction. We affirm the judgment of the Illinois Supreme Court.

The right to exercise peremptory challenges in state court is determined by state law. This Court has "long recognized" that "peremptory challenges are not of federal constitutional dimension." States may withhold peremptory challenges "altogether without impairing the constitutional guarantee of an impartial jury and a fair trial." Just as state law controls the existence and exercise of peremptory challenges, so state law determines the consequences of an erroneous denial of such a challenge. Accordingly, we have no cause to disturb the Illinois Supreme Court's determination that, in the circumstances Rivera's case presents, the trial court's error did not warrant reversal of his conviction.

I

Rivera was charged with first-degree murder in the Circuit Court of Cook County, Illinois. The State alleged that Rivera, who is Hispanic, shot and killed Marcus Lee, a 16-year-old African-American, after mistaking Lee for a member of a rival gang.

During jury selection, Rivera's counsel questioned prospective juror Deloris Gomez, a business office supervisor at Cook County Hospital's outpatient orthopedic clinic. Gomez stated that she sometimes interacted with patients during the check-in process and acknowledged that Cook County Hospital treats many gunshot victims. She maintained, however, that her work experience would not affect her ability to be impartial. After questioning Gomez, Rivera's counsel sought to use a peremptory challenge to excuse her. At that point in the jury's selection, Rivera had already used three peremptory challenges. Two of the three were exercised against women; one of the two women thus eliminated was African-American.

Rather than dismissing Gomez, the trial judge called counsel to chambers, where he expressed concern that the defense was discriminating against Gomez. Without specifying the type of discrimination he suspected or the reasons for his concern, the judge [indicated that he thought Gomez might be African American] and he directed Rivera's counsel to state his reasons for excusing Gomez. Counsel responded, first, that Gomez saw victims of violent crime on a daily basis. Dissatisfied with counsel's proffered reasons, the judge denied the challenge to Gomez, but agreed to allow counsel to question Gomez further.

Rivera's case proceeded to trial. The jury, with Gomez as its foreperson, found Rivera guilty of first-degree murder.

We granted certiorari to resolve an apparent conflict among state high courts over whether the erroneous denial of a peremptory challenge requires automatic reversal of a defendant's conviction as a matter of federal law.

II

The *Due Process Clause of the Fourteenth Amendment,* Rivera maintains, requires reversal whenever a criminal defendant's peremptory challenge is erroneously denied.

Rivera's arguments do not withstand scrutiny. If a defendant is tried before a qualified jury composed of individuals not challengeable for cause, the loss of a peremptory challenge due to a state court's good-faith error is not a matter of federal constitutional concern. Rather, it is a matter for the State to address under its own laws.

Because peremptory challenges are within the States' province to grant or withhold, the mistaken denial of a state-provided peremptory challenge does not, without more, violate the Federal Constitution.

The trial judge's refusal to excuse juror Gomez did not deprive Rivera of his constitutional right to a fair trial before an impartial jury. . . . Rivera received precisely what due process required: a fair trial before an impartial and properly instructed jury, which found him guilty of every element of the charged offense.

C. PRETRIAL PUBLICITY AND THE RIGHT TO A FAIR TRIAL

The Sixth Amendment guarantees defendants the right to a fair trial. Publicity, either before or after trial, may interfere with a defendant's right to an impartial jury. The court has the responsibility of ensuring the defendant a fair trial, but the court must also balance the defendant's rights against the First Amendment rights of the press. At what point does media coverage of a case cross the line and interfere with the defendant's right to a fair trial? What steps can the court take to ensure that the defendant will be judged by an impartial jury?

This section focuses on the standards for determining whether pretrial and trial publicity have interfered with the defendant's right to a fair trial. It then examines various mechanisms that courts have used to limit the impact of publicity on cases. These include, among other things, changes of venue, limiting access to courtroom proceedings, and gag orders. Finally, the section ends with a discussion of cameras in the courtroom.

1. When Does Pretrial Publicity Interfere with a Defendant's Right to a Fair Trial?

The Sixth Amendment does not guarantee a defendant the right to be tried by a jury that has heard nothing about the case. Rather, the focus is on whether the defendant has been prejudiced by pretrial publicity. The Supreme Court examined this principle in Irvin v. Dowd.

IRVIN v. DOWD
366 U.S. 717 (1961)

Justice CLARK delivered the opinion of the Court.

[The defendant brought a habeas corpus petition claiming that he did not receive a fair trial because pretrial publicity prejudiced the jurors.

The defendant was convicted of murder and sentenced to death in a state trial.]

The constitutional claim arises in this way. Six murders were committed in the vicinity of Evansville, Indiana, two in December 1954, and four in March 1955. The crimes, extensively covered by news media in the locality, aroused great excitement and indignation throughout the county and an adjoining rural county of approximately 30,000 inhabitants. The petitioner was arrested on April 8, 1955. Shortly thereafter, the Prosecutor of Vanderburgh County and Evansville police officials issued press releases, which were intensively publicized, stating that the petitioner had confessed to the six murders. The Grand Jury soon indicted the petitioner for the murder which resulted in his conviction. Counsel appointed to defend petitioner immediately sought a change of venue from Vanderburgh County, which was granted, but to adjoining Gibson County. Alleging that the widespread and inflammatory publicity had also highly prejudiced the inhabitants of Gibson County against the petitioner, counsel, on October 29, 1955, sought another change of venue, from Gibson County to a county sufficiently removed from the Evansville locality that a fair trial would not be prejudiced. The motion was denied, apparently because the pertinent Indiana statute allows only a single change of venue.

During the course of the voir dire examination, which lasted some four weeks, petitioner filed two more motions for a change of venue and eight motions for continuances. All were denied.

England, from whom the Western World has largely taken its concepts of individual liberty and of the dignity and worth of every man, has bequeathed to us safeguards for their preservation, the most priceless of which is that of trial by jury. This right has become as much American as it was once the most English. In essence, the right to jury trial guarantees to the criminally accused a fair trial by a panel of impartial, "indifferent" jurors. The failure to accord an accused a fair hearing violates even the minimal standards of due process.

It is not required, however, that the jurors be totally ignorant of the facts and issues involved. In these days of swift, widespread and diverse methods of communication, an important case can be expected to arouse the interest of the public in the vicinity, and scarcely any of those best qualified to serve as jurors will not have formed some impression or opinion as to the merits of the case. This is particularly true in criminal cases. To hold that the mere existence of any preconceived notion as to the guilt or innocence of an accused, without more, is sufficient to rebut the presumption of a prospective juror's impartiality would be to establish an impossible standard. It is sufficient if the juror can lay aside his impression or opinion and render a verdict based on the evidence presented in court.

Here the build-up of prejudice is clear and convincing. An examination of the then current community pattern of thought as indicated by the popular news media is singularly revealing. For example, petitioner's first motion for a change of venue from Gibson County alleged that the awaited trial of petitioner had become the cause celebre of this small community — so much so that curbstone opinions, not only as to petitioner's guilt but even as to what punishment he should receive, were solicited and recorded on the public streets by a roving reporter, and later were broadcast over the local stations. A reading of the 46 exhibits which petitioner attached to his motion indicates that a barrage of newspaper headlines, articles, cartoons and pictures was unleashed against him during the six or seven months preceding his trial. The motion further alleged that the newspapers in which the stories appeared were delivered regularly to approximately 95% of the dwellings in Gibson County and that, in addition, the Evansville radio and TV stations, which likewise blanketed that county, also carried extensive newscasts covering the same incidents. These stories revealed the details of his background, including a reference to crimes committed when a juvenile, his convictions for arson almost 20 years previously, for burglary and by a court-martial on AWOL charges during the war. He was accused of being a parole violator. The headlines announced his police line-up identification, that he faced a lie detector test, had been placed at the scene of the crime and that the six murders were solved but petitioner refused to confess. Finally, they announced his confession to the six murders and the fact of his indictment for four of them in Indiana. They reported petitioner's offer to plead guilty if promised a 99-year sentence, but also the determination, on the other hand, of the prosecutor to secure the death penalty, and that petitioner had confessed to 24 burglaries (the modus operandi of these robberies was compared to that of the murders and the similarity noted). One story dramatically relayed the promise of a sheriff to devote his life to securing petitioner's execution by the State of Kentucky, where petitioner is alleged to have committed one of the six murders, if Indiana failed to do so. Another characterized petitioner as remorseless and without conscience but also as having been found sane by a court-appointed panel of doctors. In many of the stories petitioner was described as the "confessed slayer of six," a parole violator and fraudulent-check artist. Petitioner's court-appointed counsel was quoted as having received "much criticism over being Irvin's counsel" and it was pointed out, by way of excusing the attorney, that he would be subject to disbarment should he refuse to represent Irvin. On the day before the trial the newspapers carried the story that Irvin had orally admitted the murder of Kerr (the victim in this case) as well as "the robbery-murder of Mrs. Mary Holland; the murder of Mrs. Wilhelmina Sailer in Posey County, and the slaughter of three members of the Duncan family in Henderson County, Ky."

It cannot be gainsaid that the force of this continued adverse publicity caused a sustained excitement and fostered a strong prejudice among the people of Gibson County. In fact, on the second day devoted to the selection of the jury, the newspapers reported that "strong feelings, often bitter and angry, rumbled to the surface," and that "the extent to which the multiple murders — three in one family — have aroused feelings throughout the area was emphasized Friday when 27 of the 35 prospective jurors questioned were excused for holding biased pretrial opinions. . . ." A few days later the feeling was described as "a pattern of deep and bitter prejudice against the former pipe-fitter." Spectator comments, as printed by the newspapers, were "my mind is made up"; "I think he is guilty"; and "he should be hanged."

Finally, and with remarkable understatement, the headlines reported that "impartial jurors are hard to find." The panel consisted of 430 persons. The court itself excused 268 of those on challenges for cause as having fixed opinions as to the guilt of petitioner; 103 were excused because of conscientious objection to the imposition of the death penalty; 20, the maximum allowed, were peremptorily challenged by petitioner and 10 by the State; 12 persons and two alternates were selected as jurors and the rest were excused on personal grounds, e.g., deafness, doctor's orders, etc. An examination of the 2,783-page voir dire record shows that 370 prospective jurors or almost 90% of those examined on the point (10 members of the panel were never asked whether or not they had any opinion) entertained some opinion as to guilt — ranging in intensity from mere suspicion to absolute certainty. A number admitted that, if they were in the accused's place in the dock and he in theirs on the jury with their opinions, they would not want him on a jury.

Here the "pattern of deep and bitter prejudice" shown to be present throughout the community was clearly reflected in the sum total of the voir dire examination of a majority of the jurors finally placed in the jury box. Eight out of the 12 thought petitioner was guilty. With such an opinion permeating their minds, it would be difficult to say that each could exclude this preconception of guilt from his deliberations. The influence that lurks in an opinion once formed is so persistent that it unconsciously fights detachment from the mental processes of the average man. Where one's life is at stake — and accounting for the frailties of human nature — we can only say that in the light of the circumstances here the finding of impartiality does not meet constitutional standards. Two-thirds of the jurors had an opinion that petitioner was guilty and were familiar with the material facts and circumstances involved, including the fact that other murders were attributed to him, some going so far as to say that it would take evidence to overcome their belief. One said that he "could not . . . give the defendant the benefit of the doubt that he is innocent." Another stated that he had a "somewhat" certain fixed opinion as to petitioner's guilt. No doubt each juror was sincere when he said that he would be fair and impartial to petitioner, but the psychological impact requiring such a declaration before one's fellows is often its father. Where so many, so many times, admitted prejudice, such a statement of impartiality can be given little weight. As one of the jurors put it, "You can't forget what you hear and see." With his life at stake, it is not requiring too much that petitioner be tried in an atmosphere undisturbed by so huge a wave of public passion and by a jury other than one in which two-thirds of the members admit, before hearing any testimony, to possessing a belief in his guilt.

Petitioner's detention and sentence of death pursuant to the void judgment is in violation of the Constitution.

Justice FRANKFURTER, concurring.

Of course I agree with the Court's opinion. But this is, unfortunately, not an isolated case that happened in Evansville, Indiana, nor an atypical miscarriage of justice due to anticipatory trial by newspapers instead of trial in court before a jury.

Not a Term passes without this Court being importuned to review conviction, had in States throughout the country, in which substantial claims are made that a jury trial has been distorted because of inflammatory newspaper accounts. Indeed such extraneous influences, in violation of the decencies guaranteed by our Constitution, are sometimes so powerful that an accused is forced, as a practical matter, to forego trial by jury. For one reason or another this Court does not undertake to review all such envenomed state prosecutions. But, again and again, such disregard of fundamental fairness is so flagrant that the Court is compelled . . . to reverse a conviction in which prejudicial newspaper intrusion has poisoned the outcome. This Court has not yet decided that the fair administration of criminal justice must be subordinated to another safeguard of our constitutional system—freedom of the press, properly conceived. The Court has not yet decided that, while convictions must be reversed and miscarriages of justice result because the minds of jurors or potential jurors were poisoned, the poisoner is constitutionally protected in plying his trade.

While the Court held in *Irvin* that extreme pretrial publicity may prejudice a defendant to the point where there has been a due process violation of his right to a fair trial, the Supreme Court has limited such challenges to extreme cases. The mere flooding of the airways with information about a case, especially in this Internet age, will not necessarily constitute a Sixth Amendment violation. It is difficult for defendants in even the most high-profile cases to raise Sixth Amendment challenges to their convictions.

SKILLING v. UNITED STATES

130 S. Ct. 2896 (2010)

Justice GINSBURG delivered the opinion of the Court.

In 2001, Enron Corporation, then the seventh highest-revenue-grossing company in America, crashed into bankruptcy. We consider in this opinion [whether pretrial publicity arising from the prosecution of Jeffrey Skilling, a long-time Enron executive, prevented] Skilling from obtaining a fair trial.

We conclude that Skilling's fair-trial argument fails; Skilling, we hold, did not establish that a presumption of juror prejudice arose or that actual bias infected the jury that tried him.

I

Founded in 1985, Enron Corporation grew from its headquarters in Houston, Texas, into one of the world's leading energy companies. Skilling launched his career there in 1990 when Kenneth Lay, the company's founder, hired him to head an Enron subsidiary. Skilling steadily rose through the corporation's ranks, serving as president and chief operating officer, and then as chief executive officer. On August 14, 2001, Skilling resigned from Enron.

Less than four months after Skilling's departure, Enron spiraled into bankruptcy. The Government's investigation uncovered an elaborate conspiracy to prop up Enron's short-run stock prices by overstating the company's financial well-being. In the years following Enron's bankruptcy, the Government prosecuted dozens of Enron employees who participated in the scheme. In time, the Government worked its way up the corporation's chain of command: On July 7, 2004, a grand jury indicted Skilling, Lay, and Richard Causey, Enron's former chief accounting officer.

In November 2004, Skilling moved to transfer the trial to another venue; he contended that hostility toward him in Houston, coupled with extensive pretrial publicity, had poisoned potential jurors. To support this assertion, Skilling, aided by media experts, submitted hundreds of news reports detailing Enron's downfall; he also presented affidavits from the experts he engaged portraying community attitudes in Houston in comparison to other potential venues.

The U.S. District Court for the Southern District of Texas . . . denied the venue-transfer motion. Despite "isolated incidents of intemperate commentary," the court observed, media coverage "ha[d] [mostly] been objective and unemotional," and the facts of the case were "neither heinous nor sensational."

In the months leading up to the trial, the District Court solicited from the parties questions the court might use to screen prospective jurors. The court converted Skilling's submission, with slight modifications, into a 77-question, 14-page document that asked prospective jurors about, *inter alia*, their sources of news and exposure to Enron-related publicity, beliefs concerning Enron and what caused its collapse, opinions regarding the defendants and their possible guilt or innocence, and relationships to the company and to anyone affected by its demise.

[During voir dire], the District Court first emphasized to the venire the importance of impartiality and explained the presumption of innocence and the Government's burden of proof. After questioning the venire as a group, the District Court brought prospective jurors one by one to the bench for individual examination. The court then permitted each side to pose follow-up questions.

Following a 4-month trial and nearly five days of deliberation, the jury found Skilling guilty of 19 counts, including the honest-services-fraud conspiracy charge, and not guilty of 9 insider-trading counts.

On appeal, Skilling raised a host of challenges to his convictions. He claimed there was a presumption of prejudice "stemming from . . . the large number of victims in Houston . . . [who] lost their jobs, and . . . saw their 401(k) accounts wiped out."

II

Pointing to "the community passion aroused by Enron's collapse and the vitriolic media treatment" aimed at him, Skilling argues that his trial "never should have proceeded in Houston." Skilling's fair-trial claim . . . raises two distinct questions. First, did the District Court err by failing to move the trial to a different venue based on a presumption of prejudice? Second, did actual prejudice contaminate Skilling's jury?

A

The Sixth Amendment secures to criminal defendants the right to trial by an impartial jury. By constitutional design, that trial occurs "in the State where the . . . Crimes . . . have been committed." Art. III, §2, cl. 3. The Constitution's place-of-trial prescriptions, however, do not impede transfer of the proceeding to a different district at the defendant's request if extraordinary local prejudice will prevent a fair trial — a "basic requirement of due process."

"The theory of our [trial] system is that the conclusions to be reached in a case will be induced only by evidence and argument in open court, and not by any outside influence, whether of private talk or public print." When does the publicity attending conduct charged as criminal dim prospects that the trier can judge a case, as due process requires, impartially, unswayed by outside influence? We begin our discussion by addressing . . . Rideau v. Louisiana (1963).

Wilbert Rideau robbed a bank in a small Louisiana town, kidnaped three bank employees, and killed one of them. Police interrogated Rideau in jail without counsel present and obtained his confession. Without informing Rideau, no less seeking his consent, the police filmed the interrogation. On three separate occasions shortly before the trial, a local television station broadcast the film to audiences ranging from 24,000 to 53,000 individuals. Rideau moved for a change of venue, arguing that he could not receive a fair trial in the parish where the crime occurred, which had a population of approximately 150,000 people. The trial court denied the motion, and a jury eventually convicted Rideau. The Supreme Court of Louisiana upheld the conviction.

We reversed. "What the people [in the community] saw on their television sets," we observed, "was Rideau, in jail, flanked by the sheriff and two state troopers, admitting in detail the commission of the robbery, kidnapping, and murder." "[T]o the tens of thousands of people who saw and heard it," we explained, the interrogation "in a very real sense *was* Rideau's trial — at which he pleaded guilty." We therefore "d[id] not hesitate to hold, without pausing to examine a particularized transcript of the *voir dire*," that "[t]he kangaroo court proceedings" trailing the televised confession violated due process.

We followed *Rideau*'s lead in two later cases in which media coverage manifestly tainted a criminal prosecution. In Estes v. Texas (1965), extensive publicity before trial swelled into excessive exposure during preliminary court proceedings as reporters and television crews overran the courtroom and "bombard[ed] . . . the community with the sights and sounds of" the pretrial hearing. The media's overzealous reporting efforts, we observed, "led to considerable disruption" and denied the "judicial serenity and calm to which [Billie Sol Estes] was entitled."

Similarly, in Sheppard v. Maxwell (1966), news reporters extensively covered the story of Sam Sheppard, who was accused of bludgeoning his pregnant wife to death. "[B]edlam reigned at the courthouse during the trial and newsmen took over practically the entire courtroom," thrusting jurors "into the role of celebrities." But Sheppard's case involved more than heated reporting pretrial: We upset the murder conviction because a "carnival atmosphere" pervaded the trial.

In each of these cases, we overturned a "conviction obtained in a trial atmosphere that [was] utterly corrupted by press coverage;" our decisions, however, "cannot be made to stand for the proposition that juror exposure to . . . news accounts of the crime . . . alone presumptively deprives the defendant of due process." Murphy v. Florida (1975). Prominence does not necessarily produce prejudice, and juror *impartiality*, we have reiterated, does not require *ignorance*. Irvin v. Dowd (1961). A presumption of prejudice, our decisions indicate, attends only the extreme case.

Relying on *Rideau, Estes,* and *Sheppard,* Skilling asserts that we need not pause to examine the screening questionnaires or the *voir dire* before declaring his jury's verdict void. We are not persuaded. Important differences separate Skilling's prosecution from those in which we have presumed juror prejudice.

First, we have emphasized in prior decisions the size and characteristics of the community in which the crime occurred. In *Rideau,* for example, we noted that the murder was committed in a parish of only 150,000 residents. Houston, in contrast, is the fourth most populous city in the Nation: At the time of Skilling's trial, more than 4.5 million individuals eligible for jury duty resided in the Houston area. Given this large, diverse pool of potential jurors, the suggestion that 12 impartial individuals could not be empaneled is hard to sustain.

Second, although news stories about Skilling were not kind, they contained no confession or other blatantly prejudicial information of the type readers or viewers could not reasonably be expected to shut from sight. Rideau's dramatically staged admission of guilt, for instance, was likely imprinted indelibly in the mind of anyone who watched it.

Third, unlike cases in which trial swiftly followed a widely reported crime, over four years elapsed between Enron's bankruptcy and Skilling's trial.

Although reporters covered Enron-related news throughout this period, the decibel level of media attention diminished somewhat in the years following Enron's collapse.

Finally, and of prime significance, Skilling's jury acquitted him of nine insider-trading counts. It would be odd for an appellate court to presume prejudice in a case in which jurors' actions run counter to that presumption.

Skilling's trial, in short, shares little in common with those in which we approved a presumption of juror prejudice.

B

We next consider whether actual prejudice infected Skilling's jury. *Voir dire*, Skilling asserts, did not adequately detect and defuse juror bias. We disagree with Skilling's characterization of the *voir dire* and the jurors selected through it.

Skilling deems the *voir dire* insufficient because, he argues, jury selection lasted "just five hours," "[m]ost of the court's questions were conclusory[,] high-level, and failed adequately to probe jurors' true feelings," and the court "consistently took prospective jurors at their word once they claimed they could be fair, no matter what other indications of bias were present." Our review of the record, however, yields a different appraisal.

[T]he District Court initially screened venire members by eliciting their responses to a comprehensive questionnaire drafted in large part by Skilling. That survey helped to identify prospective jurors excusable for cause and served as a springboard for further questions put to remaining members of the array. *Voir dire* thus was, in the court's words, the "culmination of a lengthy process."

The facts of *Irvin* are worlds apart from those presented here. Leslie Irvin stood accused of a brutal murder and robbery spree in a small rural community. In the months before Irvin's trial, "a barrage" of publicity was "unleashed against him," including reports of his confessions to the slayings and robberies. "[N]ewspapers in which the[se] stories appeared were delivered regularly to 95% of the dwellings in" the county where the trial occurred, which had a population of only 30,000; "radio and TV stations, which likewise blanketed that county, also carried extensive newscasts covering the same incidents."

In this case, news stories about Enron contained nothing resembling the horrifying information rife in reports about Irvin's rampage of robberies and murders. Of key importance, Houston shares little in common with the rural community in which Irvin's trial proceeded, and circulation figures for Houston media sources were far lower than the 95% saturation level recorded in *Irvin*.

Skilling also singles out several jurors in particular and contends they were openly biased. Skilling contends that Juror 11 — the only seated juror he challenged for cause — "expressed the most obvious bias." Juror 11 stated that "greed on Enron's part" triggered the company's bankruptcy and that corporate executives, driven by avarice, "walk a line that stretches sometimes the legality of something." But, as the Fifth Circuit accurately summarized, Juror 11 "had 'no idea' whether Skilling had 'crossed that line,' and he 'didn't say that' every CEO is probably a crook. He also asserted that he could be fair and require the government to prove its case, that he did not believe everything he read in the paper, that he did not 'get into the details' of the Enron coverage, that he did not watch television, and that Enron was 'old news.'"

In sum, Skilling failed to establish that a presumption of prejudice arose or that actual bias infected the jury that tried him. We therefore affirm the Fifth Circuit's ruling that Skilling received a fair trial.

Justice SOTOMAYOR, with whom Justice STEVENS and Justice BREYER join, concurring in part and dissenting in part.

I respectfully dissent from the Court's conclusion that Jeffrey Skilling received a fair trial before an impartial jury. Under our relevant precedents, the more intense the public's antipathy toward a defendant, the more careful a court must be to prevent that sentiment from tainting the jury. In this case, passions ran extremely high. The sudden collapse of Enron directly affected thousands of people in the Houston area and shocked the entire community. The accompanying barrage of local media coverage was massive in volume and often caustic in tone. As Enron's one-time CEO, Skilling was at the center of the storm. Even if these extraordinary circumstances did not constitutionally compel a change of venue, they required the District Court to conduct a thorough *voir dire* in which prospective jurors' attitudes about the case were closely scrutinized. The District Court's inquiry lacked the necessary thoroughness and left serious doubts about whether the jury empaneled to decide Skilling's case was capable of rendering an impartial decision based solely on the evidence presented in the courtroom. Accordingly, I would grant Skilling relief on his fair-trial claim.

Any doubt that the prevailing mindset in the Houston community remained overwhelmingly negative was dispelled by prospective jurors' responses to the written questionnaires. [M]ore than one-third of the prospective jurors either knew victims of Enron's collapse or were victims themselves, and two-thirds gave responses suggesting an antidefendant bias. In many instances their contempt for Skilling was palpable.

Given the extent of the antipathy evident both in the community at large and in the responses to the written questionnaire, it was critical for the District Court to take "strong measures" to ensure the selection of "an impartial jury free from outside influences." Perhaps because it had underestimated the public's antipathy toward Skilling, the District Court's 5-hour *voir dire* was manifestly insufficient to identify and remove biased jurors.

The court also rarely asked prospective jurors to describe personal interactions they may have had about the case, or to consider whether they might have difficulty avoiding discussion of the case with family, friends, or colleagues during the course of the lengthy trial. On the few occasions when prospective jurors were asked whether they would feel pressure from the public to convict, they acknowledged that it might be difficult to return home after delivering a not-guilty verdict.

The topics that the District Court did cover were addressed in cursory fashion. Most prospective jurors were asked just a few yes/no questions about their general exposure to media coverage and a handful of additional questions concerning any responses to the written questionnaire that suggested bias. In many instances, their answers were unenlightening.

Indeed, the District Court's anemic questioning did little to dispel similar doubts about the impartiality of numerous other seated jurors and alternates. In my estimation, more than half of those seated made written and oral comments suggesting active antipathy toward the defendants.

In sum, I cannot accept the majority's conclusion that *voir dire* gave the District Court "a sturdy foundation to assess fitness for jury service." Taken together, the District Court's failure to cover certain vital subjects, its superficial coverage of other topics, and its uncritical acceptance of assurances of impartiality leave me doubtful that Skilling's jury was indeed free from the deep-seated animosity that pervaded the community at large. "[R]egardless of the heinousness of the crime charged, the apparent guilt of the offender[,] or the station in life which he occupies," our system of justice demands trials that are fair in both appearance and fact. Because I do not believe Skilling's trial met this standard, I would grant him relief.

2. Remedies for Prejudicial Pretrial Publicity

Assuming there is substantial pretrial or trial publicity, what safeguards can the trial court employ to secure a defendant's right to a fair trial? The court has many available alternatives, including continuing the trial, sequestering the jury, conducting an intensive voir dire of the jury, giving cautionary jury instructions, or even changing venue.

In his concurrence in Irvin v. Dowd, *supra,* Justice Frankfurter suggested that something more may be needed, like putting restrictions on the "poisoner" (i.e., the media). In a series of decisions, the Supreme Court decided what restrictions can be placed on the media's coverage of criminal matters.

a. Closure of Courtrooms

Initially, the Supreme Court was open to the idea of allowing trial judges to exclude the press and public from pretrial hearings, such as motions to suppress. In Gannett Co. v. DePasquale, 443 U.S. 368 (1979), the Court upheld a trial judge's decision to close a suppression hearing from the media and the public. At the suppression hearing, the court was deciding whether to suppress the defendant's alleged confession and physical evidence in the case. Justice Stewart wrote for the Court:

Publicity concerning pretrial suppression hearings such as the one involved in the present case poses special risks of unfairness. The whole purpose of such hearings is to screen out unreliable or illegally obtained evidence and insure that this evidence does not become known to the jury. Publicity concerning the proceedings at a pretrial hearing, however, could influence public opinion against a defendant and inform potential jurors of inculpatory information wholly inadmissible at the actual trial.

The *Gannett* Court held that there is no Sixth Amendment right to attend a trial but left open the question of whether there is a First Amendment right of access. The Court did note, however, that if there is a First Amendment right, it must be balanced against the defendant's right to a fair trial.

The Supreme Court soon changed directions. In Richmond Newspapers, Inc. v. Virginia, 448 U.S. 555 (1980), the defendant had moved to close his murder trial from the public and reporters. Chief Justice Burger reversed the trial court's closure order. In a plurality decision, he wrote that "a presumption of openness inheres in the very nature of a criminal trial under our system of justice." Accordingly, the First Amendment provides a presumption that the press and public will have access to criminal trials and that this right can be compromised only if there is an overriding government interest set forth in findings by the court. Generally, courts must balance a defendant's right to a fair trial against the public's and the media's First Amendment right of access.

The issue then arose as to whether states may close courtrooms in cases involving sex offenses against minors. In Globe Newspaper Co. v. Superior Court, 457 U.S. 596 (1982), the Supreme Court struck down a Virginia statute that created a per se rule that the press and public must be excluded during the testimony of an underage victim in a sex crime case. In the majority's opinion, Justice Brennan wrote:

> The Court's recent decision in *Richmond Newspapers* firmly established for the first time that the press and general public have a constitutional right of access to criminal trials. Although there was no opinion of the Court in that case, seven Justices recognized that this right of access is embodied in the First Amendment, and applied to the States through the Fourteenth Amendment.
>
> Two features of the criminal justice system, emphasized in the various opinions in *Richmond Newspapers,* together serve to explain why a right of access to criminal trials in particular is properly afforded protection by the First Amendment. First, the criminal trial historically has been open to the press and general public. "[At] the time when our organic laws were adopted, criminal trials both here and in England had long been presumptively open." And since that time, the presumption of openness has remained secure. . . .
>
> Second, the right of access to criminal trials plays a particularly significant role in the functioning of the judicial process and the government as a whole. Public scrutiny of a criminal trial enhances the quality and safeguards the integrity of the factfinding process, with benefits to both the defendant and to society as a whole. Moreover, public access to the criminal trial fosters an appearance of fairness, thereby heightening public respect for the judicial process. And in the broadest terms, public access to criminal trials permits the public to participate in and

serve as a check upon the judicial process — an essential component in our structure of self-government. In sum, the institutional value of the open criminal trial is recognized in both logic and experience.

Although the right of access to criminal trials is of constitutional stature, it is not absolute. But the circumstances under which the press and public can be barred from a criminal trial are limited; the State's justification in denying access must be a weighty one. Where, as in the present case, the State attempts to deny the right of access in order to inhibit the disclosure of sensitive information, it must be shown that the denial is necessitated by a compelling governmental interest, and is narrowly tailored to serve that interest.

In rejecting the automatic closure rule, the Court noted in footnote 27 of the opinion that courts could decide on a case-by-case basis whether portions of a criminal trial should be closed:

> We emphasize that our holding is a narrow one: that a rule of mandatory closure respecting the testimony of minor sex victims is constitutionally infirm. In individual cases, and under appropriate circumstances, the First Amendment does not necessarily stand as a bar to the exclusion from the courtroom of the press and general public during the testimony of minor sex-offense victims. But a mandatory rule, requiring no particularized determinations in individual cases, is unconstitutional.

Even after *Globe*, courts continued to struggle with how to balance the defendant's right to a fair trial and the media's First Amendment right of access. In Press-Enterprise Co. v. Superior Court, 464 U.S. 501 (1984) (*Press-Enterprise I*), the Court struck down an order closing jury selection from the public and media. Emphasizing that the lower court must carefully weigh the media's right of access against the defendant's right to a fair trial, Chief Justice Burger wrote:

> Of course the right of an accused to fundamental fairness in the jury selection process is a compelling interest. But the California court's conclusion that Sixth Amendment and privacy interests were sufficient to warrant prolonged closure was unsupported by findings showing that an open proceeding in fact threatened those interests; hence it is not possible to conclude that closure was warranted. Even with findings adequate to support closure, the trial court's orders denying access to voir dire testimony failed to consider whether alternatives were available to protect the interests of the prospective jurors that the trial court's orders sought to guard. Absent consideration of alternatives to closure, the trial court could not constitutionally close the voir dire.

Two years later, in Press-Enterprise Co. v. Superior Court, 478 U.S. 1 (1986) (*Press Enterprise II*), the Court again upheld the media's right of access. This time, Chief Justice Burger wrote that the First Amendment right of access to criminal proceedings applies to preliminary hearings that have traditionally been open to the public, such as preliminary hearings. Two factors were key to the Court's decision: (1) a tradition of openness to the proceeding in question must exist and (2) the proceeding must be trial-like.

Thus, both the defendant and the press have the right to an open court-room. In Presley v. Georgia, 130 S. Ct. 721 (2010), the Supreme Court reaffirmed that a defendant's Sixth Amendment right to a public trial includes the right to an open voir dire process.

b.   Other Remedies

In lieu of closing proceedings, courts may look for alternative means to prevent pretrial and trial publicity from prejudicing the defendant's right to a fair trial. In Sheppard v. Maxwell, 384 U.S. 333 (1966), the Court criticized the trial judge for not considering the various means it had to control the media's coverage of Dr. Sam Sheppard's murder trial. It suggested that the court consider a wide range of remedies, from change of venue, to sequestration, to tighter control over the courtroom, to gag orders.

SHEPPARD v. MAXWELL
384 U.S. 333 (1966)

Justice CLARK delivered the opinion of the Court.

This federal habeas corpus application involves the question whether Sheppard was deprived of a fair trial in his state conviction for the second-degree murder of his wife because of the trial judge's failure to protect Sheppard sufficiently from the massive, pervasive and prejudicial publicity that attended his prosecution.

Marilyn Sheppard, petitioner's pregnant wife, was bludgeoned to death in the upstairs bedroom of their lakeshore home in Bay Village, Ohio, a suburb of Cleveland. On the day of the tragedy, July 4, 1954, Sheppard pieced together for several local officials the following story: He and his wife had entertained neighborhood friends, the Aherns, on the previous evening at their home. After dinner they watched television in the living room. Sheppard became drowsy and dozed off to sleep on a couch. Later, Marilyn partially awoke him saying that she was going to bed. The next thing he remembered was hearing his wife cry out in the early morning hours. He hurried upstairs and in the dim light from the hall saw a "form" standing next to his wife's bed. As he struggled with the "form" he was struck on the back of the neck and rendered unconscious. On regaining his senses he found himself on the floor next to his wife's bed. He rose, looked at her, took her pulse and "felt that she was gone."

From the outset officials focused suspicion on Sheppard. On July 7, the day of Marilyn Sheppard's funeral, a newspaper story appeared in which

Assistant County Attorney Mahon—later the chief prosecutor of Sheppard—sharply criticized the refusal of the Sheppard family to permit his immediate questioning. From there on headline stories repeatedly stressed Sheppard's lack of cooperation with the police and other officials.

Throughout this period the newspapers emphasized evidence that tended to incriminate Sheppard and pointed out discrepancies in his statements to authorities. At the same time, Sheppard made many public statements to the press and wrote feature articles asserting his innocence. During the inquest on July 26, a headline in large type stated: "Kerr [Captain of the Cleveland Police] Urges Sheppard's Arrest." In the story, Detective McArthur "disclosed that scientific tests at the Sheppard home have definitely established that the killer washed off a trail of blood from the murder bedroom to the downstairs section," a circumstance casting doubt on Sheppard's accounts of the murder. No such evidence was produced at trial. The newspapers also delved into Sheppard's personal life. Articles stressed his extramarital love affairs as a motive for the crime.

A front-page editorial on July 30 asked: "Why Isn't Sam Sheppard in Jail?" It was later titled "Quit Stalling—Bring Him In."

That night at 10 o'clock Sheppard was arrested at his father's home on a charge of murder. He was taken to the Bay Village City Hall where hundreds of people, newscasters, photographers and reporters were awaiting his arrival. He was immediately arraigned—having been denied a temporary delay to secure the presence of counsel—and bound over to the grand jury.

The publicity then grew in intensity until his indictment on August 17. There are five volumes filled with . . . clippings from each of the three Cleveland newspapers covering the period from the murder until Sheppard's conviction in December 1954.

With this background the case came on for trial two weeks before the November general election at which the chief prosecutor was a candidate for common pleas judge and the trial judge, Judge Blythin, was a candidate to succeed himself.

The courtroom in which the trial was held measured 26 by 48 feet. A long temporary table was set up inside the bar, in back of the single counsel table. It ran the width of the courtroom, parallel to the bar railing, with one end less than three feet from the jury box. Approximately 20 representatives of newspapers and wire services were assigned seats at this table by the court. Behind the bar railing there were four rows of benches. These seats were likewise assigned by the court for the entire trial. The first row was occupied by representatives of television and radio stations, and the second and third rows by reporters from out-of-town newspapers and magazines. One side of the last row, which accommodated 14 people, was assigned to Sheppard's family and the other to Marilyn's. The public was permitted to fill vacancies in this row on special passes only. Representatives of the news media also used all the rooms on the courtroom floor, including the room where cases were ordinarily called and assigned for trial. Private telephone lines and telegraphic equipment were installed in these rooms so that reports from the trial could be speeded to the papers. Station WSRS was permitted to set up broadcasting facilities on the third floor of the courthouse next door to the jury room, where the jury rested during recesses in the trial and deliberated. Newscasts were made from this room throughout the trial, and while the jury reached its verdict.

On the sidewalk and steps in front of the courthouse, television and newsreel cameras were occasionally used to take motion pictures of the participants in the trial, including the jury and the judge. Indeed, one television broadcast carried a staged interview of the judge as he entered the courthouse. In the corridors outside the courtroom there was a host of photographers and television personnel with flash cameras, portable lights and motion picture cameras. This group photographed the prospective jurors during selection of the jury. After the trial opened, the witnesses, counsel, and jurors were photographed and televised whenever they entered or left the courtroom. Sheppard was brought to the courtroom about 10 minutes before each session began; he was surrounded by reporters and extensively photographed for the newspapers and television.

All of these arrangements with the news media and their massive coverage of the trial continued during the entire nine weeks of the trial.

The jurors themselves were constantly exposed to the news media. Every juror, except one, testified at voir dire to reading about the case in the Cleveland papers or to having heard broadcasts about it. One newspaper ran pictures of the jurors at the Sheppard home when they went there to view the scene of the murder. Another paper featured the home life of an alternate juror. The day before the verdict was rendered — while the jurors were at lunch and sequestered by two bailiffs — the jury was separated into two groups to pose for photographs which appeared in the newspapers.

We now reach the conduct of the trial. [The Court described several flagrant episodes of media coverage and the jurors' exposure to this coverage.]

In light of this background, we believe that the arrangements made by the judge with the news media caused Sheppard to be deprived of that "judicial serenity and calm to which [he] was entitled." The fact is that bedlam reigned at the courthouse during the trial and newsmen took over practically the entire courtroom, hounding most of the participants in the trial, especially Sheppard.

The court's fundamental error is compounded by the holding that it lacked power to control the publicity about the trial. From the very inception of the proceedings the judge announced that neither he nor anyone else could restrict prejudicial news accounts. Since he viewed the news media as his target, the judge never considered other means that are often utilized to reduce the appearance of prejudicial material and to protect the jury from outside influence.

The carnival atmosphere at trial could easily have been avoided since the courtroom and courthouse premises are subject to the control of the court. Bearing in mind the massive pretrial publicity, the judge should have adopted stricter rules governing the use of the courtroom by newsmen, as Sheppard's counsel requested. The number of reporters in the courtroom itself could have been limited at the first sign that their presence would disrupt the trial. They certainly should not have been placed inside the bar. Furthermore, the judge should have more closely regulated the conduct of newsmen in the courtroom.

Secondly, the court should have insulated the witnesses. All of the newspapers and radio stations apparently interviewed prospective witnesses at will, and in many instances disclosed their testimony. Although the witnesses were barred from the courtroom during the trial the full verbatim testimony was available to them in the press. This completely nullified the judge's imposition of the rule.

Thirdly, the court should have made some effort to control the release of leads, information, and gossip to the press by police officers, witnesses, and the counsel for both sides. Much of the information thus disclosed was inaccurate, leading to groundless rumors and confusion.

[The judge should have sought] to alleviate this problem by imposing control over the statements made to the news media by counsel, witnesses, and especially the Coroner and police officers. The prosecution repeatedly made evidence available to the news media which was never offered in the trial.

Effective control of these sources—concededly within the court's power—might well have prevented the divulgence of inaccurate information, rumors, and accusations that made up much of the inflammatory publicity, at least after Sheppard's indictment.

More specifically, the trial court might well have proscribed extrajudicial statements by any lawyer, party, witness, or court official which divulged prejudicial matters, such as the refusal of Sheppard to submit to interrogation or take any lie detector tests; any statement made by Sheppard to officials; the identity of prospective witnesses or their probable testimony; any belief in guilt or innocence; or like statements concerning the merits of the case. In this manner, Sheppard's right to a trial free from outside interference would have been given added protection without corresponding curtailment of the news media. Had the judge, the other officers of the court, and the police placed the interest of justice first, the news media would have soon learned to be content with the task of reporting the case as it unfolded in the courtroom—not pieced together from extrajudicial statements.

Due process requires that the accused receive a trial by an impartial jury free from outside influences. Given the pervasiveness of modern communications and the difficulty of effacing prejudicial publicity from the minds of the jurors, the trial courts must take strong measures to ensure that the balance is never weighed against the accused. Of course, there is nothing that proscribes the press from reporting events that transpire in the courtroom. But where there is a reasonable likelihood that prejudicial news prior to trial will prevent a fair trial, the judge should continue the case until the threat abates, or transfer it to another county not so permeated with publicity. In addition, sequestration of the jury was something the judge should have raised sua sponte with counsel. If publicity during the proceedings threatens the fairness of the trial, a new trial should be ordered. But we must remember that reversals are but palliatives; the cure lies in those remedial measures that will prevent the prejudice at its inception. The courts must take such steps by rule and regulation that will protect their processes from prejudicial outside interferences.

Since the state trial judge did not fulfill his duty to protect Sheppard from the inherently prejudicial publicity which saturated the community and to control disruptive influences in the courtroom, we must reverse the denial of the habeas petition.

Sheppard was such an extreme case that it led the Supreme Court to reverse the defendant's conviction because of prejudicial pretrial and trial publicity. Nonetheless, even in that case, the Court still suggested that there are many steps a trial court can take to prevent publicity from impinging on a defendant's right to a fair trial.

In deciding what steps to take to prevent the defendant from being prejudiced by pretrial or trial publicity, it is critical that a court balance the First Amendment rights of the media against the defendant's right to a fair trial. As discussed by the Court in *Sheppard*, this balancing must be done through case-by-case analysis.

c.   Ethical Limitations on Lawyers' Extrajudicial Comments

What responsibilities do lawyers have to ensure that a trial is not adversely affected by pretrial and trial publicity? To what extent do lawyers possess a First Amendment right to speak out about their clients' cases, and what limitations may be placed on that right?

The American Bar Association, like state bar authorities throughout the country, has adopted ethical rules designed to limit a lawyer's comments to the press about a case. ABA Model Rule of Professional Conduct 3.6 provides:

> (a) A lawyer who is participating or has participated in the investigation or litigation of a matter shall not make an extrajudicial statement that the lawyer knows or reasonably should know will be disseminated by means of public communication and will have a substantial likelihood of materially prejudicing an adjudicative proceeding in the matter.
> (b) Notwithstanding paragraph (a), a lawyer may state:
> (1) the claim, offense or defense involved and, except when prohibited by law, the identity of the persons involved;
> (2) information contained in a public record;
> (3) that an investigation of a matter is in progress;
> (4) the scheduling or result of any step in litigation;

(5) a request for assistance in obtaining evidence and information necessary thereto;

(6) a warning of danger concerning the behavior of a person involved, when there is reason to believe that there exists the likelihood of substantial harm to an individual or to the public interest; and

(7) in a criminal case, in addition to subparagraphs (1) through (6):

(i)   the identity, residence, occupation and family status of the accused;

(ii) if the accused has not been apprehended, information necessary to aid in apprehension of that person;

(iii) the fact, time and place of arrest; and

(iv) the identity of investigating and arresting officers or agencies and the length of the investigation.

(c) Notwithstanding paragraph (a), a lawyer may make a statement that a reasonable lawyer would believe is required to protect a client from the substantial undue prejudicial effect of recent publicity not initiated by the lawyer or the lawyer's client. A statement made pursuant to this paragraph shall be limited to such information as is necessary to mitigate the recent adverse publicity.

In Gentile v. State Bar of Nevada, the Supreme Court considered whether ethical restrictions on a lawyer's speech are constitutional and under what conditions they can be enforced.

GENTILE v. STATE BAR OF NEVADA

501 U.S. 1030 (1991)

Justice KENNEDY announced the judgment of the Court.

Hours after his client was indicted on criminal charges, petitioner Gentile, who is a member of the Bar of the State of Nevada, held a press conference. [Gentile made a prepared statement, which was set forth in Appendix A to the court's opinion. In that statement, he accused the police of committing the crime that had been charged against his client.[22]]

Some six months later, the criminal case was tried to a jury and the client was acquitted on all counts. The State Bar of Nevada then filed a complaint against petitioner, alleging a violation of Nevada Supreme Court Rule 177, a rule governing pretrial publicity almost identical to ABA Model Rule of Professional Conduct 3.6. Rule 177(1) prohibits an attorney from making "an extrajudicial statement that a reasonable person would expect to be disseminated by means of public communication if the lawyer knows or

---

22. A brief excerpt from Gentile's press conference appears below. The complete statement is set forth in Appendix A of the Court's opinion.

MR. GENTILE: I want to start this off by saying in clear terms that I think that this indictment is a significant event in the history of the evolution of the sophistication of the City of Las Vegas, because things of this nature, of exactly this nature have happened in New York with the French connection case and in Miami with cases — at least two cases there — have happened in Chicago as well, but all three of those cities have been honest enough to indict the people who did it; the police department, crooked cops. [Footnote by casebook authors.]

reasonably should know that it will have a substantial likelihood of materially prejudicing an adjudicative proceeding." Rule 177(2) lists a number of statements that are "ordinarily . . . likely" to result in material prejudice. Rule 177(3) provides a safe harbor for the attorney, listing a number of statements that can be made without fear of discipline notwithstanding the other parts of the Rule.

Following a hearing, the Southern Nevada Disciplinary Board of the State Bar found that Gentile had made the statements in question and concluded that he violated Rule 177.

Nevada's application of Rule 177 in this case violates the First Amendment. Petitioner spoke at a time and in a manner that neither in law nor in fact created any threat of real prejudice to his client's right to a fair trial or to the State's interest in the enforcement of its criminal laws. Furthermore, the Rule's safe harbor provision, Rule 177(3), appears to permit the speech in question, and Nevada's decision to discipline petitioner in spite of that provision raises concerns of vagueness and selective enforcement.

The matter before us does not call into question the constitutionality of other States' prohibitions upon an attorney's speech that will have a "substantial likelihood of materially prejudicing an adjudicative proceeding," but is limited to Nevada's interpretation of that standard.

Model Rule 3.6's requirement of substantial likelihood of material prejudice is not necessarily flawed. Interpreted in a proper and narrow manner, for instance, to prevent an attorney of record from releasing information of grave prejudice on the eve of jury selection, the phrase substantial likelihood of material prejudice might punish only speech that creates a danger of imminent and substantial harm. A rule governing speech, even speech entitled to full constitutional protection, need not use the words "clear and present danger" in order to pass constitutional muster.

The record does not support the conclusion that petitioner knew or reasonably should have known his remarks created a substantial likelihood of material prejudice, if the Rule's terms are given any meaningful content. . . . [Gentile] did not blunder into a press conference, but acted with considerable deliberation.

An attorney's duties do not begin inside the courtroom door. He or she cannot ignore the practical implications of a legal proceeding for the client. Just as an attorney may recommend a plea bargain or civil settlement to avoid the adverse consequences of a possible loss after trial, so too an attorney may take reasonable steps to defend a client's reputation and reduce the adverse consequences of indictment, especially in the face of a prosecution deemed unjust or commenced with improper motives.

Petitioner was disciplined for statements to the effect that (1) the evidence demonstrated his client's innocence, (2) the likely thief was a police detective, Steve Scholl, and (3) the other victims were not credible, as most were drug dealers or convicted money launderers, all but one of whom had only accused Sanders in response to police pressure, in the process of "trying to work themselves out of something."

Much of the information provided by petitioner had been published in one form or another, obviating any potential for prejudice.

Petitioner's judgment that no likelihood of material prejudice would result from his comments was vindicated by events at trial.

The trial took place on schedule in August 1988, with no request by either party for a venue change or continuance. The jury was empaneled with no apparent difficulty. The trial judge questioned the jury venire about publicity. [N]ot a single juror indicated any recollection of petitioner or his press conference.

At trial, all material information disseminated during petitioner's press conference was admitted in evidence before the jury. The jury acquitted petitioner's client, and, as petitioner explained before the disciplinary board, "when the trial was over with and the man was acquitted the next week the foreman of the jury phoned me and said to me that if they would have had a verdict form before them with respect to the guilt of Steve Scholl they would have found the man proven guilty beyond a reasonable doubt."

There is no support for the conclusion that petitioner's statements created a likelihood of material prejudice, or indeed of any harm of sufficient magnitude or imminence to support a punishment for speech.

In *Gentile*, the Court upheld defense counsel's right to make his extrajudicial comments but noted that it would not violate counsel's First Amendment rights to limit speech that has a substantial likelihood of materially prejudicing a proceeding. Most remarks by counsel do not rise to that level. However, occasionally counsel will cross the line.

UNITED STATES v. CUTLER

58 F.3d 825 (2d Cir. 1995)

McLAUGHLIN, Circuit Judge:

The underworld exploits of John Gotti and the courtroom legerdemain of his attorney, Bruce Cutler, are now the stuff of legend. Cutler's last appearance on Gotti's behalf was in the United States District Court for the Eastern District of New York (I. Leo Glasser, Judge). Notwithstanding the court's pretrial admonition and orders to comply with Local Criminal Rule 7, Cutler spoke repeatedly and heatedly to the media on the merits of the government's case against his client.

Exasperated with Cutler, Judge Glasser issued an order to show cause why he should not be held in criminal contempt. Judge Glasser then recused himself, and the matter was reassigned. After a five-day bench trial, the district court found Cutler guilty of criminal contempt.

On appeal, Cutler argues that: (1) the orders and Local Rule 7 are unconstitutional; (2) the evidence, under the heightened standard applicable in First Amendment cases, does not support his contempt conviction; and (3) several aspects of his sentence were an abuse of discretion.

BACKGROUND

John Gotti was arrested on December 11, 1990, on racketeering charges. This marked the fourth time that the government tried to end Gotti's criminal career, the previous attempts having failed. The then-United States Attorney, Andrew Maloney, announced the indictment at a press conference, where he called Gotti a "murderer, not a folk hero" and boasted that this time the government's case, which included extensive wiretap evidence, was much stronger than in the prior trials.

Gotti's lawyer, Bruce Cutler, a member of the New York Bar, countered by calling the prosecutors "publicity-hungry" and on a vendetta to frame his client. He was quoted in New York's four major newspapers — the Daily News, Newsday, the New York Post, and the New York Times. He also gave an interview on Prime Time Live, a nationally-broadcast television show, where he emphatically denied that Gotti was a mob boss.

Cutler's and Maloney's comments seemed to be in tension with Local Rule 7, to phrase it charitably. That rule provides:

> It is the duty of the lawyer or law firm not to release or authorize the release of information or opinion which a reasonable person would expect to be disseminated by means of public communication, in connection with pending or imminent criminal litigation with which a lawyer or law firm is associated, if there is a reasonable likelihood that such dissemination will interfere with a fair trial or otherwise prejudice the due administration of justice. . . .

[The court admonished Cutler repeatedly to comply with the rule.] Undeterred, Cutler held a press conference outside the courthouse. He declaimed that the government had "thrown the Constitution out the window," mocked the government's witnesses as "bums," and erroneously described the government's tape recordings of wire-tapped conversations as the same ones used in earlier prosecutions. Cutler's performance at the press conference made the local news that night and the tabloids the next morning.

After four letters of complaint from the government about Cutler's extrajudicial statements, . . . Judge Glasser made clear he wanted no more comments to the press.

In the following week, stories about Gotti adorned the front pages of New York's dailies, together with excerpts from the transcripts of the wire-tapped conversations. In addition, television news programs obtained copies of the tapes of the conversations and repeatedly broadcast portions of them, allowing potential jurors to hear Gotti describe murders and other crimes.

Cutler countered with a media barrage of his own. The piece de resistance came on August 13, 1991, a mere month before the scheduled trial date. That day, Cutler appeared on a one-hour live television show called 9 Broadcast Plaza. His performance, aptly summarized by the district court, included the following:

> wherever Gotti lives, there is no problem with drugs and crime in the neighbor-hood; Gotti is not a danger to any community other than federal prosecutors; Gotti has "admirable qualities[,"] including being courageous, loyal, sincere, selfless and devoted to his family; Gotti is a "good man" and an "honorable man"; Gotti is not a "ruthless man"; Gotti is one of "the most compassionate men" Cutler knows; Gotti is "deadly against drugs"[;] . . . the prosecutors "are doing every-thing they can to destroy John Gotti" and are "dealing in vendettas[,"] "on a witch hunt[,"] and "framing people"; the Government "threw the Constitution out the window" and is on a "vendetta" against Gotti; the prosecution is an "example of McCarthyism"; Gotti was being persecuted "because of his lifestyle" and "friends"; the prosecutors want to "destroy" Gotti "because of his popularity" and because "he's deadly against drugs"; the "evidence is phony"; the "tapes are phony"[;] . . . the Government is "creating cases against individuals they target" by "giving freedom to drug dealers and murderers if they will sing the govern-ment's tune against the likes of John Gotti"; and . . . jurors realize that "the wit-nesses lie" and that "even the federal investigators lie" and that is why they vote "not guilty unabashedly."

Not surprisingly, the 9 Broadcast Plaza interview provoked yet another government letter complaining about Cutler. This time, Judge Glasser had had enough. He issued an order to show cause why Cutler should not be held in criminal contempt.

Cutler's contempt trial lasted five days. He did not contest the facts the government proffered. Moreover, he did not argue that he had no duty to comply with the orders and Local Rule 7. Instead, Cutler challenged the validity of the orders, arguing that Local Rule 7 was unconstitutional.

DISCUSSION

Cutler challenges the validity of the orders, contending that Local Rule 7 is unconstitutional. Local Rule 7 proscribes generally any statements by counsel that "a reasonable person would expect to be disseminated by means of public communication, in connection with pending or imminent criminal litigation . . . , if there is a reasonable likelihood that such dissem-ination will interfere with a fair trial or otherwise prejudice the due admin-istration of justice."

Cutler vastly understates the effect defense lawyers can have on prospec-tive jurors. As *Gentile* cautions, "lawyers' statements are likely to be received as especially authoritative" because "lawyers have special access to infor-mation through discovery and client communications." Indeed, *Gentile* affirmed the very portion of Nevada's pre-trial publicity rule that considered statements of the sort Cutler made as "ordinarily" likely to have a "substantial likelihood of materially prejudicing" a pending criminal proceeding.

We thus find that Cutler's comments were reasonably likely to prejudice the Gotti proceedings.

C. WILLFULNESS

We hold attorneys to a higher standard of conduct than we do lay persons. Cutler's persistent attempts to try Gotti's case in the media, despite Judge Glasser's repeated warnings, belie any notion that he did not intend these particular comments to prejudice the proceedings, or that he did not recklessly disregard the orders.

CONCLUSION

We have considered all of Cutler's arguments, and find them without merit. We recognize that Cutler did not singlehandedly generate the media circus that threatened the fairness of the final Gotti trial; federal prosecutors and law enforcement officials deserve their share of the blame. Moreover, we sympathize with the plight of a defense lawyer torn between his duties to act as an officer of the court and to zealously defend his client. Nonetheless, a lawyer, of all people, should know that in the face of a perceived injustice, one may not take the law into his own hands. Defendant did, and now he must pay the price.

In some quarters, doubtless, this affirmance will elicit thunderbolts that we are chilling effective advocacy. Obviously, that is neither our intention nor our result. The advocate is still entitled — indeed encouraged — to strike hard blows, but not unfair blows. Trial practice, whether criminal or civil, is not a contact sport. And, its tactics do not include eye-gouging or shin-kicking.

In this case, a conscientious trial judge tried mightily to limit the lawyers to press statements that were accurate and fair. The defendant's statements were dipped in venom and were deliberately couched to poison the well from which the jury would be selected. Such conduct goes beyond the pale, by any reasonable standard, and cannot be condoned under the rubric of "effective advocacy."

d. Prior Restraints

Although the Supreme Court has sanctioned many alternatives for controlling pretrial publicity, it has resisted authorizing prior restraints on the press except in the most extreme cases. This First Amendment limitation on the court's power to control the press was set forth in the following case.

NEBRASKA PRESS ASSOCIATION v. STUART

427 U.S. 539 (1976)

Chief Justice BURGER delivered the opinion of the Court.

The respondent State District Judge entered an order restraining the petitioners from publishing or broadcasting accounts of confessions or admissions made by the accused or facts "strongly implicative" of the accused in a widely reported murder of six persons. We granted certiorari to decide whether the entry of such an order on the showing made before the state court violated the constitutional guarantee of freedom of the press.

I

On the evening of October 18, 1975, local police found the six members of the Henry Kellie family murdered in their home in Sutherland, Neb., a town of about 850 people. Police released the description of a suspect, Erwin Charles Simants, to the reporters who had hastened to the scene of the crime. Simants was arrested and arraigned in Lincoln County Court the following morning, ending a tense night for this small rural community.

The crime immediately attracted widespread news coverage. Three days after the crime, the County Attorney and Simants' attorney joined in asking the County Court to enter a restrictive order relating to "matters that may or may not be publicly reported or disclosed to the public," because of the "mass coverage by news media" and the "reasonable likelihood of prejudicial news which would make difficult, if not impossible, the impaneling of an impartial jury and tend to prevent a fair trial." The County Court granted the prosecutor's motion for a restrictive order and entered it the next day. The order prohibited everyone in attendance from "releas[ing] or authoriz[ing] the release for public dissemination in any form or manner whatsoever any testimony given or evidence adduced."

Simants' preliminary hearing was held the same day, open to the public but subject to the order. The County Court bound over the defendant for trial to the State District Court. The charges, as amended to reflect the autopsy findings, were that Simants had committed the murders in the course of a sexual assault.

Petitioners — several press and broadcast associations, publishers, and individual reporters — [asked] that the restrictive order imposed by the County Court be vacated. The judge found "because of the nature of the crimes charged in the complaint that there is a clear and present danger that pre-trial publicity could impinge upon the defendant's right to a fair trial." The order . . . specifically prohibited petitioners from reporting five subjects, [including the contents of a confession Simants had made to law enforcement officers, which had been introduced in open court at arraignment, and testimony at the preliminary hearing.] It also prohibited reporting the exact nature of the restrictive order itself.

The Nebraska Supreme Court modified the District Court's order, [in an attempt] to accommodate the defendant's right to a fair trial and the petitioners' interest in reporting pre-trial events. The order as modified prohibited reporting of only three matters: (a) the existence and nature of any confessions or admissions made by the defendant to law enforcement officers, (b) any confessions or admissions made to any third parties, except members of the press, and (c) other facts "strongly implicative" of the accused.

We granted certiorari to address the important issues raised by the District Court order as modified by the Nebraska Supreme Court.

III

The problems presented by this case are almost as old as the Republic. Neither in the Constitution nor in contemporaneous writings do we find that the conflict between these two important rights was anticipated, yet it is inconceivable that the authors of the Constitution were unaware of the potential conflicts between the right to an unbiased jury and the guarantee of freedom of the press.

The trial of Aaron Burr in 1807 presented Mr. Chief Justice Marshall, presiding as a trial judge, with acute problems in selecting an unbiased jury. Few people in the area of Virginia from which jurors were drawn had not formed some opinions concerning Mr. Burr or the case.

The speed of communication and the pervasiveness of the modern news media have exacerbated these problems, however, as numerous appeals demonstrate. The trial of Bruno Hauptmann in a small New Jersey community for the abduction and murder of the Charles Lindberghs' infant child probably was the most widely covered trial up to that time, and the nature of the coverage produced widespread public reaction.

The excesses of press and radio and lack of responsibility of those in authority in the Hauptmann case and others of that era led to efforts to develop voluntary guidelines for courts, lawyers, press, and broadcasters.

In practice, of course, even the most ideal guidelines are subjected to powerful strains when a case such as Simants' arises, with reporters from many parts of the country on the scene.

IV

The Sixth Amendment guarantees "trial, by an impartial jury . . ." in federal criminal prosecutions.

In the overwhelming majority of criminal trials, pre-trial publicity presents few unmanageable threats to this important right. But when the case is a "sensational" one tensions develop between the right of the accused to trial by an impartial jury and the rights guaranteed others by the First Amendment.

Taken together, [prior] cases demonstrate that pre-trial publicity—even pervasive, adverse publicity—does not inevitably lead to an unfair trial. The capacity of the jury eventually impaneled to decide the case fairly is influenced by the tone and extent of the publicity. The trial judge has a major responsibility. What the judge says about a case, in or out of the courtroom, is likely to appear in newspapers and broadcasts. More important, the measures a judge takes or fails to take to mitigate the effects of pre-trial publicity—the measures described in *Sheppard*—may well determine whether the defendant receives a trial consistent with the requirements of due process.

The state trial judge in the case before us acted responsibly, out of a legitimate concern, in an effort to protect the defendant's right to a fair trial. What we must decide is not simply whether the Nebraska courts erred in seeing the possibility of real danger to the defendant's rights, but whether in the circumstances of this case the means employed were foreclosed by another provision of the Constitution.

V

The First Amendment provides that "Congress shall make no law . . . abridging the freedom . . . of the press."

In Near v. Minnesota ex rel. Olson (1931), the Court held invalid a Minnesota statute providing for the abatement as a public nuisance of any "malicious, scandalous and defamatory newspaper, magazine or other periodical."

Mr. Chief Justice Hughes, writing for the Court, noted . . . "[T]he main purpose of [the First Amendment] is 'to prevent all such previous restraints upon publications as had been practiced by other governments.'"

More recently in New York Times Co. v. United States (1971), the Government sought to enjoin the publication of excerpts from a massive, classified study of this Nation's involvement in the Vietnam conflict, going back to the end of the Second World War. The dispositive opinion of the Court simply concluded that the Government had not met its heavy burden of showing justification for the prior restraint.

The thread running through all these cases is that prior restraints on speech and publication are the most serious and the least tolerable infringement on First Amendment rights.

A prior restraint . . . has an immediate and irreversible sanction. If it can be said that a threat of criminal or civil sanctions after publication "chills" speech, prior restraint "freezes" it at least for the time.

The damage can be particularly great when the prior restraint falls upon the communication of news and commentary on current events. Truthful reports of public judicial proceedings have been afforded special protection against subsequent punishment.

The authors of the Bill of Rights did not undertake to assign priorities as between First Amendment and Sixth Amendment rights, ranking one as superior to the other. In this case, the petitioners would have us declare the right of an accused subordinate to their right to publish in all circumstances. But if the authors of these guarantees, fully aware of the potential conflicts between them, were unwilling or unable to resolve the issue by assigning to one priority over the other, it is not for us to rewrite the Constitution by undertaking what they declined to do. It is unnecessary, after nearly two centuries, to establish a priority applicable in all circumstances. Yet it is nonetheless clear that the barriers to prior restraint remain high unless we are to abandon what the Court has said for nearly a quarter of our national existence and implied throughout all of it.

VI

We turn now to the record in this case to determine whether, as Learned Hand put it, "the gravity of the 'evil,' discounted by its improbability, justifies such invasion of free speech as is necessary to avoid the danger."

Our review of the pre-trial record persuades us that the trial judge was justified in concluding that there would be intense and pervasive pre-trial publicity concerning this case. He could also reasonably conclude, based on common human experience, that publicity might impair the defendant's right to a fair trial. He did not purport to say more, for he found only "a clear and present danger that pre-trial publicity could impinge upon the defendant's right to a fair trial." His conclusion as to the impact of such publicity on prospective jurors was of necessity speculative, dealing as he was with factors unknown and unknowable.

B

We find little in the record that goes to another aspect of our task, determining whether measures short of an order restraining all publication would have insured the defendant a fair trial. Although the entry of the order might be read as a judicial determination that other measures would not suffice, the trial court made no express findings to that effect.

Most of the alternatives to prior restraint of publication in these circumstances were discussed with obvious approval in Sheppard v. Maxwell: (a) change of trial venue . . . (b) postponement of the trial to allow public attention to subside; (c) searching questioning of prospective jurors . . . (d) the use of emphatic and clear instructions on the sworn duty of each juror to decide the issues only on evidence presented in open court. Sequestration of jurors is, of course, always available.

We have therefore examined this record to determine the probable efficacy of the measures short of prior restraint on the press and speech. There is no finding that alternative measures would not have protected Simants' rights, and the Nebraska Supreme Court did no more than imply that such measures might not be adequate. Moreover, the record is lacking in evidence to support such a finding.

C

The Nebraska Supreme Court narrowed the scope of the restrictive order, and its opinion reflects awareness of the tensions between the need to protect the accused as fully as possible and the need to restrict publication as little as possible. The dilemma posed underscores how difficult it is for trial judges to predict what information will in fact undermine the impartiality of jurors, and the difficulty of drafting an order that will effectively keep prejudicial information from prospective jurors. When a restrictive order is sought, a court can anticipate only part of what will develop that may injure the accused. But information not so obviously prejudicial may emerge, and what may properly be published in these "gray zone" circumstances may not violate the restrictive order and yet be prejudicial.

Finally, we note that the events disclosed by the record took place in a community of 850 people. It is reasonable to assume that, without any news accounts being printed or broadcast, rumors would travel swiftly by word of mouth. One can only speculate on the accuracy of such reports, given the generative propensities of rumors; they could well be more damaging than reasonably accurate news accounts. But plainly a whole community cannot be restrained from discussing a subject intimately affecting life within it.

Given these practical problems, it is far from clear that prior restraint on publication would have protected Simants' rights.

E

The record demonstrates, as the Nebraska courts held, that there was indeed a risk that pretrial news accounts, true or false, would have some adverse impact on the attitudes of those who might be called as jurors. But on the record now before us it is not clear that further publicity, unchecked, would so distort the views of potential jurors that 12 could not be found who would, under proper instructions, fulfill their sworn duty to render a just verdict exclusively on the evidence presented in open court. We cannot say on this record that alternatives to a prior restraint on petitioners would not have sufficiently mitigated the adverse effects of pre-trial publicity so as to make prior restraint unnecessary. Nor can we conclude that the restraining order actually entered would serve its intended purpose.

Of necessity our holding is confined to the record before us. But our conclusion is not simply a result of assessing the adequacy of the showing made in this case; it results in part from the problems inherent in meeting the heavy burden of demonstrating, in advance of trial, that without prior restraint a fair trial will be denied. In this sense, the record now before us is illustrative rather than exceptional.

Our analysis ends as it began, with a confrontation between prior restraint imposed to protect one vital constitutional guarantee and the explicit command of another that the freedom to speak and publish shall not be abridged. We reaffirm that the guarantees of freedom of expression are not an absolute prohibition under all circumstances, but the barriers to prior restraint remain high and the presumption against its use continues intact.

Justice BRENNAN, with whom Justices STEWART and MARSHALL join, concurring in the judgment.

The question presented in this case is whether, consistently with the First Amendment, a court may enjoin the press, in advance of publication, from reporting or commenting on information acquired from public court proceedings, public court records, or other sources about pending judicial proceedings. The right to a fair trial by a jury of one's peers is unquestionably one of the most precious and sacred safeguards enshrined in the Bill of Rights. I would hold, however, that resort to prior restraints on the freedom of the press is a constitutionally impermissible method for enforcing that right; judges have at their disposal a broad spectrum of devices for ensuring that fundamental fairness is accorded the accused without necessitating so drastic an incursion on the equally fundamental and salutary constitutional mandate that discussion of public affairs in a free society cannot depend on the preliminary grace of judicial censors.

The Supreme Court has not yet decided on when, if ever, gag orders can be imposed on lawyers and trial participants. Lower courts remain split on the issue. *See* David D. Smthy III, *A New Framework for Analyzing Gag Orders Against Trial Witnesses*, 56 Baylor L. Rev. 89 (2004); Symposium, *The Sound of Silence: Reflections on the Use of the Gag Order*, 17 Loy. L.A. Ent. L.J. 304 (1997). Inevitably, the decision requires a balancing of the defendant's right to a fair trial against First Amendment rights of individuals and the press.

3. *Cameras in the Courtroom*

The Supreme Court has never held that there is a right to cameras in the courtroom, but it has also refused to overturn defendants' convictions merely because the proceedings were broadcast. Federal Rule of Criminal Procedure 53 provides that federal court proceedings may not be broadcast, although there have been experimental programs allowing broadcasts in some federal civil and appellate cases. By contrast, a majority of states now permit the broadcast of criminal proceedings. In these states, a trial court has discretion to determine whether and when to allow such broadcasts. In deciding how to exercise this discretion, a court will consider many factors, including the nature of the case; the parties' support of or opposition to the request; the privacy rights of the participants, witnesses, victims, and jurors; the effect of the coverage on the parties' ability to select a fair and unbiased jury; any ongoing needs of law enforcement; the need to maintain an orderly proceeding; and any other factors that may affect the right to a fair trial.[23]

---

23. *See, e.g.*, Cal. Rules of Court, R. 1.150 (2007).

In Chandler v. Florida, the Supreme Court addressed whether cameras in the courtroom constitute a per se violation of a defendant's fair trial right.

CHANDLER v. FLORIDA
449 U.S. 560 (1981)

Chief Justice BURGER delivered the opinion of the Court.

The question presented on this appeal is whether, consistent with constitutional guarantees, a state may provide for radio, television, and still photographic coverage of a criminal trial for public broadcast, notwithstanding the objection of the accused.

I

A

Over the past 50 years, some criminal cases characterized as "sensational" have been subjected to extensive coverage by news media, sometimes seriously interfering with the conduct of the proceedings and creating a setting wholly inappropriate for the administration of justice. Judges, lawyers, and others soon became concerned, and in 1937, after study, the American Bar Association House of Delegates adopted Judicial Canon 35, declaring that all photographic and broadcast coverage of courtroom proceedings should be prohibited. In 1952, the House of Delegates amended Canon 35 to proscribe television coverage as well. The Canon's proscription was reaffirmed in 1972 when the Code of Judicial Conduct replaced the Canons. A majority of the states, including Florida, adopted the substance of the ABA provision and its amendments.

[In 1975, Florida established a pilot program permitting electronic media to cover judicial proceedings without the consent of the proceeding's participants.]

Following [the pilot program], the Florida Supreme Court concluded "that on balance there [was] more to be gained than lost by permitting electronic media coverage of judicial proceedings subject to standards for such coverage." The Florida court was of the view that because of the significant effect of the courts on the day-to-day lives of the citizenry, it was essential that the people have confidence in the process. It felt that broadcast coverage of trials would contribute to wider public acceptance and understanding of decisions. Consequently, after revising the 1977 guidelines to reflect its evaluation of the pilot program, the Florida Supreme Court promulgated a revised Canon 3A (7). The Canon provides:

> Subject at all times to the authority of the presiding judge to (i) control the conduct of proceedings before the court, (ii) ensure decorum and prevent distractions, and (iii) ensure the fair administration of justice in the pending cause, electronic media and still photography coverage of public judicial proceedings in the appellate and trial courts of this state shall be allowed in accordance with

standards of conduct and technology promulgated by the Supreme Court of Florida.

In July 1977, appellants were charged with conspiracy to commit burglary, grand larceny, and possession of burglary tools. The counts covered breaking and entering a well-known Miami Beach restaurant.

The details of the alleged criminal conduct are not relevant to the issue before us, but several aspects of the case distinguish it from a routine burglary. At the time of their arrest, appellants were Miami Beach policemen. The State's principal witness was John Sion, an amateur radio operator who, by sheer chance, had overheard and recorded conversations between the appellants over their police walkie-talkie radios during the burglary. Not surprisingly, these novel factors attracted the attention of the media.

By pretrial motion, appellants sought to have . . . Canon 3A (7) declared unconstitutional on its face and as applied. The trial court denied relief.

After several additional fruitless attempts by the appellants to prevent electronic coverage of the trial, the jury was selected. At voir dire, the appellants' counsel asked each prospective juror whether he or she would be able to be "fair and impartial" despite the presence of a television camera during some, or all, of the trial. Each juror selected responded that such coverage would not affect his or her consideration in any way. A television camera recorded the voir dire.

A defense motion to sequester the jury because of the television coverage was denied by the trial judge. However, the court instructed the jury not to watch or read anything about the case in the media and suggested that jurors "avoid the local news and watch only the national news on television."

A television camera was in place for one entire afternoon, during which the State presented the testimony of . . . its chief witness. No camera was present for the presentation of any part of the case for the defense. The camera returned to cover closing arguments. Only 2 minutes and 55 seconds of the trial below were broadcast — and those depicted only the prosecution's side of the case.

The jury returned a guilty verdict on all counts. Appellants moved for a new trial, claiming that because of the television coverage, they had been denied a fair and impartial trial. No evidence of specific prejudice was tendered.

II

At the outset, it is important to note that in promulgating the revised Canon 3A (7), the Florida Supreme Court pointedly rejected any state or federal constitutional right of access on the part of photographers or the broadcast media to televise or electronically record and thereafter disseminate court proceedings.

The Florida Supreme Court predicated the revised Canon 3A (7) upon its supervisory authority over the Florida courts, and not upon any constitutional imperative.

This Court has no supervisory jurisdiction over state courts, and, in reviewing a state-court judgment, we are confined to evaluating it in relation to the Federal Constitution.

III

Appellants rely chiefly on Estes v. Texas (1965), and Chief Justice Warren's separate concurring opinion in that case. They argue that the televising of criminal trials is inherently a denial of due process, and they read *Estes* as announcing a per se constitutional rule to that effect.

If appellants' reading of *Estes* were correct, we would be obliged to apply that holding and reverse the judgment under review. [However, the six separate opinions in *Estes*, when examined carefully, do not represent a per se constitutional rule forbidding all electronic coverage.]

[In his concurring opinion in *Estes*, Justice Harlan noted what he perceived as the inherent dangers of televised trials:]

> In the context of a trial of intense public interest, there is certainly a strong possibility that the timid or reluctant witness, for whom a court appearance even at its traditional best is a harrowing affair, will become more timid or reluctant when he finds that he will also be appearing before a "hidden audience" of unknown but large dimensions. There is certainly a strong possibility that the "cocky" witness having a thirst for the limelight will become more "cocky" under the influence of television. And who can say that the juror who is gratified by having been chosen for a front-line case, an ambitious prosecutor, a publicity-minded defense attorney, and even a conscientious judge will not stray, albeit unconsciously, from doing what "comes naturally" into pluming themselves for a satisfactory television "performance"?

[But Justice Harlan also noted that there were "countervailing factors" and that broadcasting proceedings could have an "educational and information value to the public."]

Justice Harlan's opinion, upon which analysis of the constitutional holding of *Estes* turns, must be read as defining the scope of that holding; we conclude that *Estes* is not to be read as announcing a constitutional rule barring still photographic, radio, and television coverage in all cases and under all circumstances. It does not stand as an absolute ban on state experimentation with an evolving technology, which, in terms of modes of mass communication, was in its relative infancy in 1964, and is, even now, in a state of continuing change.

IV

Since we are satisfied that *Estes* did not announce a constitutional rule that all photographic or broadcast coverage of criminal trials is inherently a denial of due process, we turn to consideration, as a matter of first impression, of the appellants' suggestion that we now promulgate such a per se rule.

A

Any criminal case that generates a great deal of publicity presents some risks that the publicity may compromise the right of the defendant to a fair trial. Trial courts must be especially vigilant to guard against any impairment of the defendant's right to a verdict based solely upon the evidence and the relevant law. Over the years, courts have developed a range of curative devices to prevent publicity about a trial from infecting jury deliberations.

An absolute constitutional ban on broadcast coverage of trials cannot be justified simply because there is a danger that, in some cases, prejudicial broadcast accounts of pretrial and trial events may impair the ability of jurors to decide the issue of guilt or innocence uninfluenced by extraneous matter. The risk of juror prejudice in some cases does not justify an absolute ban on news coverage of trials by the printed media; so also the risk of such prejudice does not warrant an absolute constitutional ban on all broadcast coverage. A case attracts a high level of public attention because of its intrinsic interest to the public and the manner of reporting the event. The risk of juror prejudice is present in any publication of a trial, but the appropriate safeguard against such prejudice is the defendant's right to demonstrate that the media's coverage of his case—be it printed or broadcast—compromised the ability of the particular jury that heard the case to adjudicate fairly.

B

Not unimportant to the position asserted by Florida and other states is the change in television technology since 1962, when *Estes* was tried. [M]any of the negative factors found in *Estes*—cumbersome equipment, cables, distracting lighting, numerous camera technicians—are less substantial factors today than they were at that time.

It is also significant that safeguards have been built into the experimental programs in state courts, and into the Florida program, to avoid some of the most egregious problems envisioned by the six opinions in the *Estes* case. Florida admonishes its courts to take special pains to protect certain witnesses—for example, children, victims of sex crimes, some informants, and even the very timid witness or party—from the glare of publicity and the tensions of being "on camera."

Inherent in electronic coverage of a trial is the risk that the very awareness by the accused of the coverage and the contemplated broadcast may adversely affect the conduct of the participants and the fairness of the trial, yet leave no evidence of how the conduct or the trial's fairness was affected. Given this danger, it is significant that Florida requires that objections of the accused to coverage be heard and considered on the record by the trial court.

D

[A] defendant has the right on review to show that the media's coverage of his case—printed or broadcast—compromised the ability of the jury to judge him fairly. Alternatively, a defendant might show that broadcast coverage of his particular case had an adverse impact on the trial participants sufficient to constitute a denial of due process. Neither showing was made in this case.

To demonstrate prejudice in a specific case a defendant must show something more than juror awareness that the trial is such as to attract the attention of broadcasters. Murphy v. Florida (1975). No doubt the very presence of a camera in the courtroom made the jurors aware that the trial was thought to be of sufficient interest to the public to warrant coverage. Jurors, forbidden to watch all broadcasts, would have had no way of knowing that only fleeting seconds of the proceeding would be reproduced. But the appellants have not attempted to show with any specificity that the presence of cameras impaired the ability of the jurors to decide the case on only the evidence before them or that their trial was affected adversely by the impact on any of the participants of the presence of cameras and the prospect of broadcast.

[Defendants' convictions are affirmed.]

Currently, 48 out of 50 states have rules allowing, in some form or another, camera coverage of the courtroom. Forty-three of these states allow coverage at the trial level, and studies in 28 states show that television coverage in court proceedings has significant social and educational benefits. Although six federal districts and the Second and Ninth Circuit Courts of Appeals launched pilot programs in the 1990s for cameras in the courtroom, the federal courts still have not adopted such a rule opening their courts to broadcast.

The case for cameras in the courtroom suffered a setback in 1995 with the broadcast of the O.J. Simpson murder trial. Troubled by what they described as the "media circus," many judges exercised their discretion not to allow cameras in their courts. However, camera coverage of high-visibility trials has resumed and no conviction has been overturned because of the televising of a trial.

D.   TRIAL RIGHTS: DUE PROCESS, RIGHT OF CONFRONTATION, AND PRIVILEGE AGAINST SELF-INCRIMINATION

At trial, the defendant enjoys the Sixth Amendment right to a fair trial. To ensure that the defendant receives a fair trial, the defendant has the right to be present at trial, the right to confront witnesses, and the right to refuse to incriminate himself.

To enjoy these rights, a defendant must be competent to stand trial. The Supreme Court has held that the Due Process Clause prohibits the criminal prosecution of a defendant who is not competent to stand trial. Drope v. Missouri, 420 U.S. 162 (1975). Under Dusky v. United States, 362 U.S. 402 (1960), a defendant is competent to stand trial when he has "sufficient present ability to consult with his lawyer with a reasonable degree of rational understanding" and has a "rational as well as factual understanding of the proceedings against him."

Under certain circumstances, a state may medicate a defendant to make him competent to stand trial. In Sell v. United States, 539 U.S. 166 (2003), the Supreme Court applied a standard it had developed in the earlier case of Riggins v. Nevada, 504 U.S. 127 (1992). In general, the government may administer antipsychotic drugs to a mentally ill defendant facing serious criminal charges in order to render the defendant competent to stand trial but only if (1) treatment is medically appropriate; (2) it is substantially unlikely to have serious side effects that will undermine the fairness of the trial; and (3) there are important government interests in having the defendant medicated, such as that he poses a danger to himself or others.

Assuming a defendant is competent to stand trial, the defendant must be afforded each of the rights discussed in this section.

1. Right of Confrontation

The Sixth Amendment right of confrontation guarantees the defendant the right to confront witnesses at trial. Implicit in this right is the right of the defendant to be present at trial. This right can be limited, however, if the defendant acts in an obstreperous manner during trial.

a. Right to Be Present at Trial

ILLINOIS v. ALLEN
397 U.S. 337 (1970)

Justice BLACK delivered the opinion of the Court.

The Confrontation Clause of the Sixth Amendment to the United States Constitution provides that: "In all criminal prosecutions, the accused shall enjoy the right . . . to be confronted with the witnesses against him. . . ." One of the most basic of the rights guaranteed by the Confrontation Clause is the accused's right to be present in the courtroom at every stage of his trial. The question presented in this case is whether an accused can claim the benefit of this constitutional right to remain in the courtroom while at the same time he engages in speech and conduct which is so noisy, disorderly, and disruptive that it is exceedingly difficult or wholly impossible to carry on the trial.

The facts surrounding Allen's expulsion from the courtroom are set out in the Court of Appeals' opinion. [Allen acted as his own lawyer. He often argued with the judge in an abusive and disrespectful manner. Refusing to allow an appointed attorney to assist him, Allen finally stated to the judge: "When I go out for lunchtime, you're [the judge] going to be a corpse here." At that point he tore the file that his attorney had and threw the papers on the floor. The trial judge warned Allen, "One more outbreak of that sort and I'll remove you from the courtroom." This warning had no effect on Allen. After more abusive remarks by Allen, the trial judge ordered the trial to proceed in Allen's absence. Allen was removed from the courtroom. Although Allen was given a second chance, the court ordered him removed again from the courtroom when Allen made further outbursts. After this second removal, Allen remained out of the courtroom during the presentation of the state's case-in-chief, except that he was brought in on several occasions for purposes of identification. During one of these latter appearances, Allen responded to one of the judge's questions with vile and abusive language. After the prosecution's case had been presented, the trial judge reiterated his promise to Allen that he could return to the courtroom whenever he agreed to conduct himself properly. Allen gave some assurances of proper conduct and was permitted to be present through the remainder of the trial, principally his defense, which was conducted by his appointed counsel.]

It is essential to the proper administration of criminal justice that dignity, order, and decorum be the hallmarks of all court proceedings in our country. The flagrant disregard in the courtroom of elementary standards of proper conduct should not and cannot be tolerated. We believe trial judges confronted with disruptive, contumacious, stubbornly defiant defendants must be given sufficient discretion to meet the circumstances of each case. No one formula for maintaining the appropriate courtroom atmosphere will be best in all situations. We think there are at least three constitutionally permissible ways for a trial judge to handle an obstreperous defendant like Allen: (1) bind and gag him, thereby keeping him present; (2) cite him for contempt; (3) take him out of the courtroom until he promises to conduct himself properly.

I

Trying a defendant for a crime while he sits bound and gagged before the judge and jury would to an extent comply with that part of the Sixth Amendment's purposes that accords the defendant an opportunity to confront the witnesses at the trial. But even to contemplate such a technique, much less see it, arouses a feeling that no person should be tried while shackled and gagged except as a last resort. Not only is it possible that the sight of shackles and gags might have a significant effect on the jury's feelings about the defendant, but the use of this technique is itself something of an affront to the very dignity and decorum of judicial proceedings that the judge is seeking to uphold. Moreover, one of the defendant's primary advantages of being present at the trial, his ability to communicate with his counsel, is greatly reduced when the defendant is in a condition of total physical restraint. It is in part because of these inherent disadvantages and limitations in this method of dealing with disorderly defendants that we decline to hold with the Court of Appeals that a defendant cannot under any possible circumstances be deprived of his right to be present at trial. However, in some situations which we need not attempt to foresee, binding and gagging might possibly be the fairest and most reasonable way to handle a defendant who acts as Allen did here.

II

[C]riminal contempt has obvious limitations as a sanction when the defendant is charged with a crime so serious that a very severe sentence such as death or life imprisonment is likely to be imposed. In such a case the defendant might not be affected by a mere contempt sentence when he ultimately faces a far more serious sanction. Nevertheless, the contempt remedy should be borne in mind by a judge in the circumstances of this case.

III

The trial court in this case decided under the circumstances to remove the defendant from the courtroom and to continue his trial in his absence until and unless he promised to conduct himself in a manner befitting an American courtroom. As we said earlier, we find nothing unconstitutional about this procedure. Allen's behavior was clearly of such an extreme and aggravated nature as to justify either his removal from the courtroom or his total physical restraint. Prior to his removal he was repeatedly warned by the trial judge that he would be removed from the courtroom if he persisted in his unruly conduct. Allen was constantly informed that he could return to the trial when he would agree to conduct himself in an orderly manner. Under these circumstances we hold that Allen lost his right guaranteed by the Sixth and Fourteenth Amendments to be present throughout his trial.

Federal Rule of Criminal Procedure 43(a) provides that a defendant has the right to be present at trial and at other crucial stages of the criminal proceedings, including arraignment, plea, jury empanelment, return of the verdict, and sentencing. However, Rule 43(c) recognizes that a defendant may be tried *in absentia* if he engages in disruptive conduct or voluntarily absents himself after the trial starts.

As discussed in Illinois v. Allen, the defendant has the right to be present at trial but not the right to engage in unruly conduct. Courts may take security measures to safeguard their courts. These security measures may include the deployment of uniformed law enforcement officials (*see* Holbrook v. Flynn,

475 U.S. 560 (1986)), but the visible shackling of defendants raises serious due process concerns.

DECK v. MISSOURI
544 U.S. 622 (2005)

Justice BREYER delivered the opinion of the Court.

We here consider whether shackling a convicted offender during the penalty phase of a capital case violates the Federal Constitution. We hold that the Constitution forbids the use of visible shackles during the penalty phase, as it forbids their use during the guilt phase, unless that use is "justified by an essential state interest"—such as the interest in courtroom security—specific to the defendant on trial. Holbrook v. Flynn (1986); see also Illinois v. Allen (1970).

I

In July 1996, petitioner Carman Deck robbed, shot, and killed an elderly couple. In 1998, the State of Missouri tried Deck for the murders and the robbery. At trial, state authorities required Deck to wear leg braces that apparently were not visible to the jury. Deck was convicted and sentenced to death. The State Supreme Court upheld Deck's conviction but set aside the sentence. The State then held a new sentencing proceeding.

From the first day of the new proceeding, Deck was shackled with leg irons, handcuffs, and a belly chain. Deck's counsel objected to the shackles. The objection was overruled.

II

We first consider whether, as a general matter, the Constitution permits a State to use visible shackles routinely in the guilt phase of a criminal trial. The answer is clear: The law has long forbidden routine use of visible shackles during the guilt phase; it permits a State to shackle a criminal defendant only in the presence of a special need.

This rule has deep roots in the common law. In the 18th century, Blackstone wrote that a defendant "must be brought to the bar without irons, or any manner of shackles or bonds; unless there be evident danger of an escape."

American courts have traditionally followed Blackstone's "ancient" English rule, while making clear that "in extreme and exceptional cases, where the safe custody of the prisoner and the peace of the tribunal imperatively demand, the manacles may be retained."

More recently, this Court has suggested that a version of this rule forms part of the Fifth and Fourteenth Amendments' due process guarantee.

Thirty-five years ago, when considering the trial of an unusually obstreperous criminal defendant, the Court held that the Constitution sometimes permitted special measures, including physical restraints. *Allen* (1970).

Sixteen years later, the Court considered a special courtroom security arrangement that involved having uniformed security personnel sit in the first row of the courtroom's spectator section. The Court held that the Constitution allowed the arrangement, stating that the deployment of security personnel during trial is not "the sort of inherently prejudicial practice that, like shackling, should be permitted only where justified by an essential state interest specific to each trial." *Holbrook* (1986). *See also* Estelle v. Williams (1976) (making a defendant appear in prison garb poses such a threat to the "fairness of the factfinding process" that it must be justified by an "essential state policy").

Lower courts have disagreed about the specific procedural steps a trial court must take prior to shackling, about the amount and type of evidence needed to justify restraints, and about what forms of prejudice might warrant a new trial, but they have not questioned the basic principle. We now conclude that those statements identify a basic element of the "due process of law" protected by the Federal Constitution. Thus, the Fifth and Fourteenth Amendments prohibit the use of physical restraints visible to the jury absent a trial court determination, in the exercise of its discretion, that they are justified by a state interest specific to a particular trial. Such a determination may of course take into account the factors that courts have traditionally relied on in gauging potential security problems and the risk of escape at trial.

The considerations that militate against the routine use of visible shackles during the guilt phase of a criminal trial apply with like force to penalty proceedings in capital cases. This is obviously so in respect to the latter two considerations mentioned, securing a meaningful defense and maintaining dignified proceedings. It is less obviously so in respect to the first consideration mentioned, for the defendant's conviction means that the presumption of innocence no longer applies. Hence shackles do not undermine the jury's effort to apply that presumption.

Nonetheless, shackles at the penalty phase threaten related concerns. Although the jury is no longer deciding between guilt and innocence, it is deciding between life and death. That decision, given the "'severity'" and "'finality'" of the sanction, is no less important than the decision about guilt.

Justice THOMAS, with whom Justice SCALIA joins, dissenting.

Carman Deck was convicted of murdering and robbing an elderly couple. He stood before the sentencing jury not as an innocent man, but as a convicted double murderer and robber. Today this Court holds that Deck's due process rights were violated when he appeared at sentencing in leg irons, handcuffs, and a belly chain. The Court's holding defies common sense and all but ignores the serious security issues facing our courts. I therefore respectfully dissent.

b. Right to Confront Witnesses

The Sixth Amendment's Confrontation Clause provides to a criminal defendant the right to confront and cross-examine adverse witnesses. The Supreme Court has repeatedly recognized the importance of cross-examination. As the Court stated in Coy v. Iowa, 487 U.S. 1012, 1019 (1988), "[i]t is always more difficult to tell a lie about a person 'to his face' than 'behind his back.'"

Although defendants generally enjoy a right to face-to-face confrontation of witnesses, this right is not absolute. Unique circumstances in a case may require the court to take alternative measures to ensure the essence of the defendant's right of confrontation.

MARYLAND v. CRAIG
497 U.S. 836 (1990)

Justice O'CONNOR delivered the opinion of the Court.

This case requires us to decide whether the Confrontation Clause of the Sixth Amendment categorically prohibits a child witness in a child abuse case from testifying against a defendant at trial, outside the defendant's physical presence, by one-way closed circuit television.

I

In October 1986, a Howard County grand jury charged respondent, Sandra Ann Craig, with child abuse, first and second degree sexual offenses, perverted sexual practice, assault, and battery. The named victim in each count was a 6-year-old girl who had attended a kindergarten and prekindergarten center owned and operated by Craig.

In March 1987, before the case went to trial, the State sought to invoke a Maryland statutory procedure that permits a judge to receive, by one-way closed circuit television, the testimony of a child witness who is alleged to be a victim of child abuse. To invoke the procedure, the trial judge must first "determine that testimony by the child victim in the courtroom will result in the child suffering serious emotional distress such that the child cannot reasonably communicate." Once the procedure is invoked, the child witness, prosecutor, and defense counsel withdraw to a separate room; the judge, jury, and defendant remain in the courtroom. The child witness is then examined and cross-examined in the separate room, while a video monitor records and displays the witness' testimony to those in the courtroom. During this time the witness cannot see the defendant. The defendant remains in electronic communication with defense counsel, and objections may be made and ruled on as if the witness were testifying in the courtroom.

In support of its motion invoking the one-way closed circuit television procedure, the State presented expert testimony that the named victim, as well as a number of other children who were alleged to have been sexually abused by Craig, would suffer "serious emotional distress such that [they could not] reasonably communicate if required to testify in the courtroom."

Craig objected to the use of the procedure on Confrontation Clause grounds, but the trial court rejected that contention.

We granted certiorari to resolve the important Confrontation Clause issues raised by this case.

II

The Confrontation Clause of the Sixth Amendment, made applicable to the States through the Fourteenth Amendment, provides: "In all criminal prosecutions, the accused shall enjoy the right . . . to be confronted with the witnesses against him."

We observed in Coy v. Iowa (1988) that "the Confrontation Clause guarantees the defendant a face-to-face meeting with witnesses appearing before the trier of fact." This interpretation derives not only from the literal text of the Clause, but also from our understanding of its historical roots.

We have never held, however, that the Confrontation Clause guarantees criminal defendants the absolute right to a face-to-face meeting with witnesses against them at trial. Indeed, in Coy v. Iowa, we expressly "left for another day . . . the question whether any exceptions exist" to the "irreducible literal meaning of the Clause: 'a right to meet face to face all those who appear and give evidence at trial.'" The procedure challenged in *Coy* involved the placement of a screen that prevented two child witnesses in a child abuse case from seeing the defendant as they testified against him at trial. In holding that the use of this procedure violated the defendant's right to confront witnesses against him, we suggested that any exception to the right "would surely be allowed only when necessary to further an important public policy" — i.e., only upon a showing of something more than the generalized, "legislatively imposed presumption of trauma" underlying the statute at issue in that case. We concluded that "since there had been no individualized findings that these particular witnesses needed special protection, the judgment [in the case before us] could not be sustained by any conceivable exception." Because the trial court in this case made individualized findings that each of the child witnesses needed special protection, this case requires us to decide the question reserved in *Coy*.

The central concern of the Confrontation Clause is to ensure the reliability of the evidence against a criminal defendant by subjecting it to rigorous testing in the context of an adversary proceeding before the trier of fact.

[T]he right guaranteed by the Confrontation Clause includes not only a "personal examination," but also "(1) insures that the witness will give his statements under oath — thus impressing him with the seriousness of the matter and guarding against the lie by the possibility of a penalty for perjury; (2) forces the witness to submit to cross-examination, the 'greatest legal engine ever invented for the discovery of truth'; [and] (3) permits the jury that is to decide the defendant's fate to observe the demeanor of the witness in making his statement, thus aiding the jury in assessing his credibility."

The combined effect of these elements of confrontation — physical presence, oath, cross-examination, and observation of demeanor by the trier of fact — serves the purposes of the Confrontation Clause by ensuring that evidence admitted against an accused is reliable and subject to the rigorous adversarial testing that is the norm of Anglo-American criminal proceedings.

Although face-to-face confrontation forms "the core of the values furthered by the Confrontation Clause," we have nevertheless recognized that it is not the sine qua non of the confrontation right.

For this reason, we have never insisted on an actual face-to-face encounter at trial in every instance in which testimony is admitted against a defendant. Instead, we have repeatedly held that the Clause permits, where necessary, the admission of certain hearsay statements against a defendant despite the defendant's inability to confront the declarant at trial.

[A] literal reading of the Confrontation Clause would "abrogate virtually every hearsay exception, a result long rejected as unintended and too extreme." Given our hearsay cases, the word "confronted," as used in the Confrontation Clause, cannot simply mean face-to-face confrontation.

[O]ur precedents establish that "the Confrontation Clause reflects a preference for face-to-face confrontation at trial," a preference that "must occasionally give way to considerations of public policy and the necessities of the case."

III

Although we are mindful of the many subtle effects face-to-face confrontation may have on an adversary criminal proceeding, the presence of these other elements of confrontation — oath, cross-examination, and observation of the witness' demeanor — adequately ensures that the testimony is both reliable and subject to rigorous adversarial testing in a manner functionally equivalent to that accorded live, in-person testimony. These safeguards of reliability and adversariness render the use of such a procedure a far cry from the undisputed prohibition of the Confrontation Clause: trial by ex parte affidavit or inquisition.

We . . . conclude today that a State's interest in the physical and psychological well-being of child abuse victims may be sufficiently important to outweigh, at least in some cases, a defendant's right to face his or her accusers in court.

Justice SCALIA, with whom Justices BRENNAN, MARSHALL, and STEVENS join, dissenting.

The Sixth Amendment provides, with unmistakable clarity, that "in all criminal prosecutions, the accused shall enjoy the right . . . to be confronted with the witnesses against him." The purpose of enshrining this protection in the Constitution was to assure that none of the many policy interests from time to time pursued by statutory law could overcome a defendant's right to face his or her accusers in court.

Because the text of the Sixth Amendment is clear, and because the Constitution is meant to protect against, rather than conform to, current "widespread belief," I respectfully dissent.

[Justice Scalia discussed the problems that hearsay evidence poses to compliance with the Confrontation Clause—a subject he returned to in Crawford v. Washington (2004), discussed *infra*.]

The Court today has applied "interest-balancing" analysis where the text of the Constitution simply does not permit it. We are not free to conduct a cost-benefit analysis of clear and explicit constitutional guarantees, and then to adjust their meaning to comport with our findings. The Court has convincingly proved that the Maryland procedure serves a valid interest, and gives the defendant virtually everything the Confrontation Clause guarantees (everything, that is, except confrontation). I am persuaded, therefore, that the Maryland procedure is virtually constitutional. Since it is not, however, actually constitutional I would affirm the judgment of the Maryland Court of Appeals reversing the judgment of conviction.

As Justice Scalia previewed in his dissent in Maryland v. Craig, the Confrontation Clause has important implications with regard to the admissibility of hearsay. In Crawford v. Washington, 541 U.S. 36 (2004), the Supreme Court modified its approach to the admissibility of hearsay evidence.

CRAWFORD v. WASHINGTON
541 U.S. 36 (2004)

Justice SCALIA delivered the opinion of the Court.

Petitioner Michael Crawford stabbed a man who allegedly tried to rape his wife, Sylvia. At his trial, the State played for the jury Sylvia's tape-recorded statement to the police describing the stabbing, even though he had no opportunity for cross-examination. The Washington Supreme Court upheld petitioner's conviction after determining that Sylvia's statement was reliable. The question presented is whether this procedure complied with the Sixth Amendment's guarantee that, "[i]n all criminal prosecutions, the accused shall enjoy the right . . . to be confronted with the witnesses against him."

I

On August 5, 1999, Kenneth Lee was stabbed at his apartment. Police arrested petitioner later that night. After giving petitioner and his wife

Miranda warnings, detectives interrogated each of them twice. Petitioner eventually confessed that he and Sylvia had gone in search of Lee because he was upset over an earlier incident in which Lee had tried to rape her. The two had found Lee at his apartment, and a fight ensued in which Lee was stabbed in the torso and petitioner's hand was cut.

Sylvia generally corroborated petitioner's story about the events leading up to the fight.

The State charged petitioner with assault and attempted murder. At trial, he claimed self-defense. Sylvia did not testify because of the state marital privilege, which generally bars a spouse from testifying without the other spouse's consent. [T]he State sought to introduce Sylvia's tape-recorded statements to the police as evidence that the stabbing was not in self-defense.

Petitioner countered that, state law notwithstanding, admitting the evidence would violate his federal constitutional right to be "confronted with the witnesses against him."

We granted certiorari to determine whether the State's use of Sylvia's statement violated the Confrontation Clause.

II

The Sixth Amendment's Confrontation Clause provides that, "[i]n all criminal prosecutions, the accused shall enjoy the right . . . to be confronted with the witnesses against him." [Ohio v. Roberts] says that an unavailable witness's out-of-court statement may be admitted so long as it has adequate indicia of reliability — i.e., falls within a "firmly rooted hearsay exception" or bears "particularized guarantees of trustworthiness." Petitioner argues that this test strays from the original meaning of the Confrontation Clause and urges us to reconsider it.

A

The Constitution's text does not alone resolve this case. We must therefore turn to the historical background of the Clause to understand its meaning.

The right to confront one's accusers is a concept that dates back to Roman times. The founding generation's immediate source of the concept, however, was the common law. English common law has long differed from continental civil law in regard to the manner in which witnesses give testimony in criminal trials. The common-law tradition is one of live testimony in court subject to adversarial testing, while the civil law condones examination in private by judicial officers.

Nonetheless, England at times adopted elements of the civil-law practice. Justices of the peace or other officials examined suspects and witnesses before trial. These examinations were sometimes read in court in lieu of live testimony.

Pretrial examinations became routine under two statutes passed during the reign of Queen Mary in the 16th century. [For bail purposes], justices of the peace [would] examine suspects and witnesses in felony cases and

. . . certify the results to the court. It is doubtful that the original purpose of the examinations was to produce evidence admissible at trial. Whatever the original purpose, however, they came to be used as evidence in some cases.

The most notorious instances of civil-law examination occurred in the great political trials of the 16th and 17th centuries. One such was the 1603 trial of Sir Walter Raleigh for treason. Lord Cobham, Raleigh's alleged accomplice, had implicated him in an examination before the Privy Council and in a letter. At Raleigh's trial, these were read to the jury. Raleigh argued that Cobham had lied to save himself: "Cobham is absolutely in the King's mercy; to excuse me cannot avail him; by accusing me he may hope for favour." Suspecting that Cobham would recant, Raleigh demanded that the judges call him to appear. The judges refused and, despite Raleigh's protestations that he was being tried "by the Spanish Inquisition," the jury convicted, and Raleigh was sentenced to death.

B

Controversial examination practices were also used in the Colonies. Early in the 18th century, for example, the Virginia Council protested against the Governor for having "privately issued several commissions to examine witnesses against particular men ex parte," complaining that "the person accused is not admitted to be confronted with, or defend himself against his defamers."

Many declarations of rights adopted around the time of the Revolution guaranteed a right of confrontation.

III

This history supports two inferences about the meaning of the Sixth Amendment.

A

First, the principal evil at which the Confrontation Clause was directed was the civil-law mode of criminal procedure, and particularly its use of ex parte examinations as evidence against the accused. It was these practices that the Crown deployed in notorious treason cases like Raleigh's. The Sixth Amendment must be interpreted with this focus in mind.

The text of the Confrontation Clause . . . applies to "witnesses" against the accused — in other words, those who "bear testimony." "Testimony," in turn, is typically "[a] solemn declaration or affirmation made for the purpose of establishing or proving some fact."

Various formulations of this core class of "testimonial" statements exist: ". . . material such as affidavits, custodial examinations, prior testimony that the defendant was unable to cross-examine, or similar pretrial statements that declarants would reasonably expect to be used prosecutorially."

Statements taken by police officers in the course of interrogations are also testimonial under even a narrow standard. Police interrogations bear a striking resemblance to examinations by justices of the peace in England.

B

The historical record also supports a second proposition: that the Framers would not have allowed admission of testimonial statements of a witness who did not appear at trial unless he was unavailable to testify, and the defendant had had a prior opportunity for cross-examination. The text of the Sixth Amendment does not suggest any open-ended exceptions from the confrontation requirement to be developed by the courts. Rather, the "right . . . to be confronted with the witnesses against him," is most naturally read as a reference to the right of confrontation at common law, admitting only those exceptions established at the time of the founding.[24]

Where testimonial statements are involved, we do not think the Framers meant to leave the Sixth Amendment's protection to the vagaries of the rules of evidence, much less to amorphous notions of "reliability." To be sure, the Clause's ultimate goal is to ensure reliability of evidence, but it is a procedural rather than a substantive guarantee. It commands, not that evidence be reliable, but that reliability be assessed in a particular manner: by testing in the crucible of cross-examination. The Clause thus reflects a judgment, not only about the desirability of reliable evidence (a point on which there could be little dissent), but about how reliability can best be determined.

C

Where testimonial evidence is at issue . . . the Sixth Amendment demands what the common law required: unavailability and a prior opportunity for cross-examination. We leave for another day any effort to spell out a comprehensive definition of "testimonial." Whatever else the term covers, it applies at a minimum to prior testimony at a preliminary hearing, before a grand jury, or at a former trial; and to police interrogations. These are the modern practices with closest kinship to the abuses at which the Confrontation Clause was directed.

In this case, the State admitted Sylvia's testimonial statement against petitioner, despite the fact that he had no opportunity to cross-examine her. That alone is sufficient to make out a violation of the Sixth Amendment. *Roberts* notwithstanding, we decline to mine the record in search of indicia of reliability. Where testimonial statements are at issue, the only indicium of reliability sufficient to satisfy constitutional demands is the one the Constitution actually prescribes: confrontation.

---

24. For example, dying declarations had become accepted hearsay exceptions by the time the Confrontation Clause was adopted. *See* fn. 6 in original opinion. [Footnote by casebook authors.]

The Court's decision in *Crawford* rocked the world of evidence. Hearsay exceptions that were previously used routinely by trial courts could no longer be used simply because they met the prior Ohio v. Roberts standard of reliability. Many states had adopted statutes that allowed hearsay testimony for victims of sexual and domestic abuse. These statutes became unconstitutional under the new *Crawford* standard unless the victims had been subject to prior cross-examination and were unavailable at the time of trial.

Justice Scalia's opinion left it open for the lower courts to decide what constituted "testimonial" evidence subject to the new constitutional rule of confrontation. Would it include all statements to police officers? What about spontaneous statements by witnesses when they were not subject to interrogation? How about 911 calls for help?

In Davis v. Washington, 547 U.S. 813 (2006), the Court took the first step of trying to clarify the scope of *Crawford*. Again writing for the Court, Justice Scalia held that a 911 call identifying the defendant as the attacker was not necessarily "testimonial" if it related to an ongoing emergency. By contrast, statements made by the victim to the police at the crime scene were "testimonial" because they described past events. Courts continue to sort out whether other types of statements, such as statements to third persons (not the police) should also be subject to the new confrontation rules. *Crawford* has brought front and center the crucial nature of a defendant's Sixth Amendment right of confrontation. In Michigan v. Bryant (2010), the Court sought to clarify when statements to police officers would qualify as "testimonial hearsay" in violation of the Confrontation Clause.

MICHIGAN v. BRYANT

131 S. Ct. 1143 (2010)

Justice SOTOMAYOR delivered the opinion of the Court.

At respondent Richard Bryant's trial, the court admitted statements that the victim, Anthony Covington, made to police officers who discovered him mortally wounded in a gas station parking lot. A jury convicted Bryant of second-degree murder. We granted the State's petition for a writ of certiorari to consider whether the Confrontation Clause barred the admission at trial of Covington's statements to the police. We hold that the circumstances of the interaction between Covington and the police objectively indicate that the "primary purpose of the interrogation" was "to enable police assistance to meet an ongoing emergency." Therefore, Covington's identification and description of the shooter and the location of the shooting were not testimonial statements, and their admission at Bryant's trial did not violate the Confrontation Clause.

I

Around 3:25 A.M. on April 29, 2001, Detroit, Michigan police officers responded to a radio dispatch indicating that a man had been shot.

At the scene, they found the victim, Anthony Covington, lying on the ground next to his car in a gas station parking lot. Covington had a gunshot wound to his abdomen, appeared to be in great pain, and spoke with difficulty.

The police asked him "what had happened, who had shot him, and where the shooting had occurred." Covington stated that "Rick" shot him at around 3 A.M. He also indicated that he had a conversation with Bryant, whom he recognized based on his voice, through the back door of Bryant's house. Covington explained that when he turned to leave, he was shot through the door and then drove to the gas station, where police found him.

Covington's conversation with the police ended within 5 to 10 minutes when emergency medical services arrived. Covington was transported to a hospital and died within hours.

II

The Confrontation Clause of the Sixth Amendment states: "In all criminal prosecutions, the accused shall enjoy the right . . . to be confronted with the witnesses against him." In *Ohio v. Roberts* (1980), we explained that the confrontation right does not bar admission of statements of an unavailable witness if the statements "bea[r] adequate 'indicia of reliability.'"

Nearly a quarter century later, we decided *Crawford v. Washington*. [We] explained that "the principal evil at which the Confrontation Clause was directed was the civil-law mode of criminal procedure, and particularly its use of *ex parte* examinations as evidence against the accused." We noted that in England, pretrial examinations of suspects and witnesses by government officials "were sometimes read in court in lieu of live testimony." In light of this history, we emphasized the word "witnesses" in the Sixth Amendment, defining it as "those who 'bear testimony.'" We noted that "[a]n accuser who makes a formal statement to government officers bears testimony in a sense that a person who makes a casual remark to an acquaintance does not." We therefore limited the Confrontation Clause's reach to testimonial statements and held that in order for testimonial evidence to be admissible, the Sixth Amendment "demands what the common law required: unavailability and a prior opportunity for cross-examination." Although "leav[ing] for another day any effort to spell out a comprehensive definition of 'testimonial,'" *Crawford* noted that "at a minimum" it includes "prior testimony at a preliminary hearing, before a grand jury, or at a former trial; and . . . police interrogations."

In 2006, the Court in *Davis v. Washington* took a further step to "determine more precisely which police interrogations produce testimony" and therefore implicate a Confrontation Clause bar. We . . . made clear in *Davis* that not all those questioned by the police are witnesses and not all "interrogations by law enforcement officers," are subject to the Confrontation Clause. *Davis* and *Hammon* were both domestic violence cases. In *Davis*, Michelle McCottry made the statements at issue to a 911 operator during a domestic disturbance with Adrian Davis, her former boyfriend. McCottry told the operator, "'He's here jumpin' on me again,'" and, "'He's usin' his fists.'" In *Hammon*, decided along with *Davis*, police responded to a domestic disturbance call at the home of Amy and Hershel Hammon, where they found Amy alone on the front porch. She appeared "'somewhat frightened,'" but told them "'nothing was the matter.'" One officer remained in the kitchen with Hershel, while another officer talked to Amy in the living room about what had happened.

[W]e held that the statements at issue in *Davis* were nontestimonial and the statements in *Hammon* were testimonial. We distinguished the statements in *Davis* from the testimonial statements in *Crawford* on several grounds, including that the victim in *Davis* was "speaking about events *as they were actually happening*, rather than 'describ[ing] past events,'" that there was an ongoing emergency, that the "elicited statements were necessary to be able to *resolve* the present emergency," and that the statements were not formal. In *Hammon*, on the other hand, we held that, "[i]t is entirely clear from the circumstances that the interrogation was part of an investigation into possibly criminal past conduct." There was "no emergency in progress."

III

To determine whether the "primary purpose" of an interrogation is "to enable police assistance to meet an ongoing emergency," which would render the resulting statements nontestimonial, we objectively evaluate the circumstances in which the encounter occurs and the statements and actions of the parties.

The circumstances in which an encounter occurs — *e.g.*, at or near the scene of the crime versus at a police station, during an ongoing emergency or afterwards — are clearly matters of objective fact. The statements and actions of the parties must also be objectively evaluated. [T]he relevant inquiry is not the subjective or actual purpose of the individuals involved in a particular encounter, but rather the purpose that reasonable participants would have had, as ascertained from the individuals' statements and actions and the circumstances in which the encounter occurred.

In addition to the circumstances in which an encounter occurs, the statements and actions of both the declarant and interrogators provide objective evidence of the primary purpose of the interrogation. To give an extreme example, if the police say to a victim, "Tell us who did this to you so that we can arrest and prosecute them," the victim's response that "Rick did it," appears purely accusatory because by virtue of the phrasing of the question, the victim necessarily has prosecution in mind when she answers.

Victims are also likely to have mixed motives when they make statements to the police. A victim may want the attacker to be incapacitated temporarily. Objectively ascertaining the primary purpose of the interrogation by examining the statements and actions of all participants is also the approach most consistent with our past holdings.

IV

The existence of an emergency or the parties' perception that an emergency is ongoing is among the most important circumstances that courts must take into account in determining whether an interrogation is testimonial because statements made to assist police in addressing an ongoing emergency presumably lack the testimonial purpose that would subject them to the requirement of confrontation. As the context of this case brings into sharp relief, the existence and duration of an emergency depend on the type and scope of danger posed to the victim, the police, and the public.

[The first question by the officers to Covington was] "what happened?" The answer was either "I was shot" or "Rick shot me." The police did not know, and Covington did not tell them, whether the threat was limited to him.

An emergency does not last only for the time between when the assailant pulls the trigger and the bullet hits the victim. At no point during the questioning did either Covington or the police know the location of the shooter. In fact, Bryant was not at home by the time the police searched his house at approximately 5:30 A.M. At some point between 3 A.M. and 5:30 A.M., Bryant left his house. At bottom, there was an ongoing emergency here where an armed shooter, whose motive for and location after the shooting were unknown, had mortally wounded Covington within a few blocks and a few minutes of the location where the police found Covington.

Nothing in Covington's responses indicated to the police that, contrary to their expectation upon responding to a call reporting a shooting, there was no emergency or that a prior emergency had ended. Covington did indicate that he had been shot at another location about 25 minutes earlier, but he did not know the location of the shooter at the time the police arrived and, as far as we can tell from the record, he gave no indication that the shooter, having shot at him twice, would be satisfied that Covington was only wounded. In fact, Covington did not indicate any possible motive for the shooting, and thereby gave no reason to think that the shooter would not shoot again if he arrived on the scene.

Finally, we consider the informality of the situation and the interrogation. This situation is more similar, though not identical, to the informal, harried 911 call in *Davis* than to the structured, station-house interview in *Crawford*. The informality suggests that the interrogators' primary purpose was simply to address what they perceived to be an ongoing emergency, and the circumstances lacked any formality that would have alerted Covington to or focused him on the possible future prosecutorial use of his statements.

Because the circumstances of the encounter as well as the statements and actions of Covington and the police objectively indicate that the "primary purpose of the interrogation" was "to enable police assistance to meet an ongoing emergency," Covington's identification and description of the shooter and the location of the shooting were not testimonial hearsay. The Confrontation Clause did not bar their admission at Bryant's trial.

Justice THOMAS, concurring in the judgment.

I agree with the Court that the admission of Covington's out-of-court statements did not violate the Confrontation Clause, but I reach this conclusion because Covington's questioning by police lacked sufficient formality and solemnity for his statements to be considered "testimonial."

The police questioning was not "a formalized dialogue," did not result in "formalized testimonial materials" such as a deposition or affidavit, and bore no "indicia of solemnity."

Justice SCALIA, dissenting.

Today's tale — a story of five officers conducting successive examinations of a dying man with the primary purpose, not of obtaining and preserving his testimony regarding his killer, but of protecting him, them, and others from a murderer somewhere on the loose — is so transparently false that professing to believe it demeans this institution. Because I continue to adhere to the Confrontation Clause that the People adopted, as described in *Crawford v. Washington*, I dissent.

I

Looking to the declarant's purpose (as we should), this is an absurdly easy case. Roughly 25 minutes after Anthony Covington had been shot, Detroit police responded to a 911 call reporting that a gunshot victim had appeared at a neighborhood gas station. They quickly arrived at the scene, and in less than 10 minutes five different Detroit police officers questioned Covington about the shooting. Each asked him a similar battery of questions: "what happened" and when, "who shot the victim," and "where" did the shooting take place. After Covington would answer, they would ask follow-up questions, such as "how tall is" the shooter, "[h]ow much does he weigh," what is the exact address or physical description of the house where the shooting took place, and what chain of events led to the shooting. The battery relented when the paramedics arrived and began tending to Covington's wounds.

From Covington's perspective, his statements had little value except to ensure the arrest and eventual prosecution of Richard Bryant. He knew the "threatening situation," had ended six blocks away and 25 minutes earlier when he fled from Bryant's back porch. Even if Bryant had pursued him (unlikely), and after seeing that Covington had ended up at the gas station was unable to confront him there before the police arrived (doubly unlikely), it was entirely beyond imagination that Bryant would again open fire while Covington was surrounded by five armed police officers. And Covington knew the shooting was the work of a drug dealer, not a spree killer who might randomly threaten others.

Covington's knowledge that he had nothing to fear differs significantly from [the victim's] state of mind during her "frantic" statements to a 911 operator at issue in *Davis*. None of the officers asked Covington how he was doing, attempted more than superficially to assess the severity of his wounds, or attempted to administer first aid. They instead primarily asked questions with little, if any, relevance to Covington's dire situation. Police, paramedics, and doctors do not need to know the address where a shooting took place, the name of the shooter, or the shooter's height and weight to provide proper medical care. Underscoring that Covington understood the officers' investigative role, he interrupted their interrogation to ask "when is EMS coming?" When, in other words, would the focus shift to his medical needs rather than Bryant's crime?

The Court invents a world where an ongoing emergency exists whenever "an armed shooter, whose motive for and location after the shooting [are] unknown, . . . mortally wound[s]" one individual "within a few blocks and minutes of the location where the police" ultimately find that victim. Breathlessly, it worries that a shooter could leave the scene armed and ready to pull the trigger again. Nothing suggests the five officers in this case shared the Court's dystopian view of Detroit, where drug dealers hunt their shooting victim down and fire into a crowd of police officers to finish him off.

The Court's distorted view creates an expansive exception to the Confrontation Clause for violent crimes. This is a dangerous definition of emergency.

II

[T]oday's decision is not only a gross distortion of the facts. It is a gross distortion of the law — a revisionist narrative in which reliability continues to guide our Confrontation Clause jurisprudence, at least where emergencies and faux emergencies are concerned.

Justice GINSBURG, dissenting.

I agree with Justice Scalia that Covington's statements were testimonial and that "[t]he declarant's intent is what counts." I would add, however, . . . that in *Crawford*, this Court noted that, in the law we inherited from England, there was a well-established exception to the confrontation requirement: The cloak protecting the accused against admission of out-of-court testimonial statements was removed for dying declarations. Were the issue properly tendered here, I would take up the question whether the exception for dying declarations survives our recent Confrontation Clause decisions.

The Court has also been concerned about the defendant's right to confront witnesses when prosecutors seek to admit evidence through forensic expert reports or certificates of analysis. In Melendez-Diaz v. Massachusetts, 129 S. Ct. 2527 (2009), the Court held that the admission of forensic reports constituted "testimonial evidence" and was subject to the Confrontation Clause. Subsequently, in Bullcoming v. New Mexico, 129 S. Ct. 2705

(2011), the Court prohibited the introduction of a forensic laboratory report through a witness who did not sign the certification or perform the analysis. However, the Court recently held in Williams v. Illinois, 132 S. Ct. 2221 (2012), that experts can rely on forensic reports in reaching their opinions and refer to those reports in their testimony.

2. Privilege Against Self-Incrimination and Improper Closing Arguments

Another critical right at trial is the privilege against self-incrimination. The Fifth Amendment "protects a person . . . against being incriminated by his own compelled testimonial communications." That privilege affects law enforcement's ability to obtain statements and evidence from defendants. Yet the Fifth Amendment also plays a crucial role at trial. On the most basic level, the Fifth Amendment prohibits the state from calling the defendant to the witness stand and from compelling him to be a witness against himself. But does the Fifth Amendment also prevent the prosecution from asking jurors to draw adverse inferences from the fact that the defendant chose not to testify?

GRIFFIN v. CALIFORNIA
380 U.S. 609 (1965)

Justice DOUGLAS delivered the opinion of the Court.

Petitioner was convicted of murder in the first degree after a jury trial in a California court. He did not testify at the trial on the issue of guilt, though he did testify at the separate trial on the issue of penalty. The trial court instructed the jury on the issue of guilt, stating that a defendant has a constitutional right not to testify. But it told the jury:

> As to any evidence or facts against him which the defendant can reasonably be expected to deny or explain because of facts within his knowledge, if he does not testify or if, though he does testify, he fails to deny or explain such evidence, the jury may take that failure into consideration as tending to indicate the truth of such evidence and as indicating that among the inferences that may be reasonably drawn therefrom those unfavorable to the defendant are the more probable.

Petitioner had been seen with the deceased the evening of her death, the evidence placing him with her in the alley where her body was found. The prosecutor made much of the failure of petitioner to testify:

> The defendant certainly knows whether Essie Mae had this beat up appearance at the time he left her apartment and went down the alley with her.

What kind of a man is it that would want to have sex with a woman that beat up if she was beat up at the time he left?

He would know that. He would know how she got down the alley. He would know how the blood got on the bottom of the concrete steps. He would know how long he was with her in that box. He would know how her wig got off. He would know whether he beat her or mistreated her. He would know whether he walked away from that place cool as a cucumber when he saw Mr. Villasenor because he was conscious of his own guilt and wanted to get away from that damaged or injured woman.

These things he has not seen fit to take the stand and deny or explain.

And in the whole world, if anybody would know, this defendant would know.

Essie Mae is dead, she can't tell you her side of the story. The defendant won't.

The death penalty was imposed and the California Supreme Court affirmed. [W]e granted [certiorari] to consider whether comment on the failure to testify violated the Self-Incrimination Clause of the Fifth Amendment.

If this were a federal trial, reversible error would have been committed. Wilson v. United States so holds. It is said, however, that the *Wilson* decision rested not on the Fifth Amendment, but on an Act of Congress, now 18 U.S.C. §3481. The question remains whether, statute or not, the comment rule, approved by California, violates the Fifth Amendment.

We think it does.

It is not every one who can safely venture on the witness stand though entirely innocent of the charge against him. "Excessive timidity, nervousness when facing others and attempting to explain transactions of a suspicious character, and offences charged against him, will often confuse and embarrass him to such a degree as to increase rather than remove prejudices against him. It is not every one, however honest, who would, therefore, willingly be placed on the witness stand. The statute, in tenderness to the weakness of those who from the causes mentioned might refuse to ask to be a witness, particularly when they may have been in some degree compromised by their association with others, declares that the failure of the defendant in a criminal action to request to be a witness shall not create any presumption against him."

If the words "Fifth Amendment" are substituted for "act" and for "statute," the spirit of the Self-Incrimination Clause is reflected. For comment on the refusal to testify is a remnant of the "inquisitorial system of criminal justice." It is a penalty imposed by courts for exercising a constitutional privilege. It cuts down on the privilege by making its assertion costly. It is said, however, that the inference of guilt for failure to testify as to facts peculiarly within the accused's knowledge is in any event natural and irresistible, and that comment on the failure does not magnify that inference into a penalty for asserting a constitutional privilege. What the jury may infer, given no help from the court, is one thing. What it may infer when the court solemnizes the silence of the accused into evidence against him is quite another.

Justice STEWART, with whom Justice WHITE joins, dissenting.

The petitioner chose not to take the witness stand at his trial upon a charge of first-degree murder in a California court. Article I, §13, of the California Constitution establishes a defendant's privilege against self-incrimination and further provides:

> In any criminal case, whether the defendant testifies or not, his failure to explain or to deny by his testimony any evidence or facts in the case against him may be commented upon by the court and by counsel, and may be considered by the court or the jury.

We must determine whether the petitioner has been "compelled . . . to be a witness against himself." Compulsion is the focus of the inquiry. Certainly, if any compulsion be detected in the California procedure, it is of a dramatically different and less palpable nature than that involved in the procedures which historically gave rise to the Fifth Amendment guarantee. When a suspect was brought before the Court of High Commission or the Star Chamber, he was commanded to answer whatever was asked of him, and subjected to a far-reaching and deeply probing inquiry in an effort to ferret out some unknown and frequently unsuspected crime. He declined to answer on pain of incarceration, banishment, or mutilation. And if he spoke falsely, he was subject to further punishment. Faced with this formidable array of alternatives, his decision to speak was unquestionably coerced.

Those were the lurid realities which lay behind enactment of the Fifth Amendment, a far cry from the subject matter of the case before us. I think that the Court in this case stretches the concept of compulsion beyond all reasonable bounds, and that whatever compulsion may exist derives from the defendant's choice not to testify, not from any comment by court or counsel.

I think the California comment rule is not a coercive device which impairs the right against self-incrimination, but rather a means of articulating and bringing into the light of rational discussion a fact inescapably impressed on the jury's consciousness.

Although a defendant's assertion of his Fifth Amendment right cannot be used against him in a criminal case, it can be used against him in a related civil proceeding. *See* Baxter v. Palmigiano, 425 U.S. 308 (1976).

The Fifth Amendment privilege against self-incrimination includes the right to remain silent during the sentencing phase. Mitchell v. United States, 526 U.S. 314, 316 (1999). If a defendant chooses to testify at trial, the defendant may not choose to answer only some questions regarding her conduct but not others. Generally, by choosing to testify, the defendant waives his Fifth Amendment right against self-incrimination as to all questions regarding the subject matter of the case. *Id.*

In addition to prohibiting prosecutors from commenting on a defendant's exercise of the Fifth Amendment privilege against self-incrimination, the Court also has limited arguments designed simply to inflame the passions of the jury. The Court addressed the prosecutor's role and boundaries of proper closing arguments in Darden v. Wainwright. While there are limits on prosecutorial advocacy, prosecutorial misconduct does not necessarily result in a new trial.

DARDEN v. WAINWRIGHT
477 U.S. 168 (1986)

Justice POWELL delivered the opinion of the Court.

Petitioner was tried and found guilty of murder, robbery, and assault with intent to kill in the Circuit Court for Citrus County, Florida, in January 1974. [He was sentenced to death.]

Petitioner contends that the prosecution's closing argument at the guilt-innocence stage of the trial rendered his conviction fundamentally unfair and deprived the sentencing determination of the reliability that the Eighth Amendment requires.

The prosecutors' comments must be evaluated in light of the defense argument that preceded it, which blamed the Polk County Sheriff's Office for a lack of evidence, alluded to the death penalty, characterized the perpetrator of the crimes as an "animal," and contained counsel's personal opinion of the strength of the State's evidence.

The prosecutors then made their closing argument. That argument deserves the condemnation it has received from every court to review it, although no court has held that the argument rendered the trial unfair. Several comments attempted to place some of the blame for the crime on the Division of Corrections, because Darden was on weekend furlough from a prison sentence when the crime occurred. Some comments implied that the death penalty would be the only guarantee against a future similar act. Others incorporated the defense's use of the word "animal." Prosecutor McDaniel made several offensive comments reflecting an emotional reaction to the case.[25] These comments undoubtedly were improper. But . . . it "is not enough that the prosecutors' remarks were undesirable or even universally condemned." The relevant question is whether the prosecutors'

---

25. "He shouldn't be out of his cell unless he has a leash on him and a prison guard at the other end of that leash." *Id.,* at 16. "I wish [Mr. Turman] had had a shotgun in his hand when he walked in the back door and blown his [Darden's] face off. I wish that I could see him sitting here with no face, blown away by a shotgun." *Id.,* at 20. "I wish someone had walked in the back door and blown his head off at that point." *Ibid.* "He fired in the boy's back, number five, saving one. Didn't get a chance to use it. I wish he had used it on himself." *Id.,* at 28. "I wish he had been killed in the accident, but he wasn't. Again, we are unlucky that time." *Id.,* at 29. "[D]on't forget what he has done according to those witnesses, to make every attempt to change his appearance from September the 8th, 1973. The hair, the goatee, even the moustache and the weight. The only thing he hasn't done that I know of is cut his throat." *Id.,* at 31. [Footnote by the Court.]

comments "so infected the trial with unfairness as to make the resulting conviction a denial of due process."

Under this standard of review, we agree with the reasoning of every court to consider these comments that they did not deprive petitioner of a fair trial. The prosecutors' argument did not manipulate or misstate the evidence, nor did it implicate other specific rights of the accused such as the right to counsel or the right to remain silent. Much of the objectionable content was invited by or was responsive to the opening summation of the defense. As we explained in *United States v. Young* (1985), the idea of "invited response" is used not to excuse improper comments, but to determine their effect on the trial as a whole. The trial court instructed the jurors several times that their decision was to be made on the basis of the evidence alone, and that the arguments of counsel were not evidence. The weight of the evidence against petitioner was heavy; the "overwhelming eyewitness and circumstantial evidence to support a finding of guilt on all charges," reduced the likelihood that the jury's decision was influenced by argument. Finally, defense counsel made the tactical decision not to present any witness other than petitioner. This decision not only permitted them to give their summation prior to the prosecution's closing argument, but also gave them the opportunity to make a final rebuttal argument. Defense counsel were able to use the opportunity for rebuttal very effectively, turning much of the prosecutors' closing argument against them by placing many of the prosecutors' comments and actions in a light that was more likely to engender strong disapproval than result in inflamed passions against petitioner. For these reasons, we agree with the District Court below that "Darden's trial was not perfect — few are — but neither was it fundamentally unfair."

Justice BLACKMUN, with whom Justice BRENNAN, Justice MARSHALL, and Justice STEVENS join, dissenting.

Although the Constitution guarantees a criminal defendant only "a fair trial [and] not a perfect one," . . . this Court has stressed repeatedly in the decade since *Gregg v. Georgia* (1976), that the Eighth Amendment requires a heightened degree of reliability in any case where a State seeks to take the defendant's life. Today's opinion, however, reveals a Court willing to tolerate not only imperfection but a level of fairness and reliability so low it should make conscientious prosecutors cringe.

I

The following brief comparison of established standards of prosecutorial conduct with the prosecutors' behavior in this case merely illustrates, but hardly exhausts, the scope of the misconduct involved:

1. "A lawyer shall not . . . state a personal opinion as to . . . the credibility of a witness . . . or the guilt or innocence of an accused." Model Rules of Professional Conduct, Rule 3.4(e) (1984). Yet one prosecutor, White, stated: "I am convinced, as convinced as I know I am standing before you today, that

Willie Jasper Darden is a murderer, that he murdered Mr. Turman, that he robbed Mrs. Turman and that he shot to kill Phillip Arnold. I will be convinced of that the rest of my life."

2. "The prosecutor should refrain from argument which would divert the jury from its duty to decide the case on the evidence, by injecting issues broader than the guilt or innocence of the accused under the controlling law, or by making predictions of the consequences of the jury's verdict." ABA Standards for Criminal Justice 3-5.8(d) (2d ed. 1980). Yet McDaniel's argument was filled with references to Darden's status as a prisoner on furlough who "shouldn't be out of his cell unless he has a leash on him."

3. "The prosecutor should not use arguments calculated to inflame the passions or prejudices of the jury." ABA Standards for Criminal Justice 3-5.8(c) (2d ed. 1980). Yet McDaniel repeatedly expressed a wish "that I could see [Darden] sitting here with no face, blown away by a shotgun."

The misconduct here was not "slight or confined to a single instance, but . . . was pronounced and persistent, with a probable cumulative effect upon the jury which cannot be disregarded as inconsequential." *Berger v. United States* (1935).

E. DEFENDANT'S RIGHT TO PRESENT A DEFENSE

In an effort to ensure that a defendant has a fair trial, the Supreme Court has held in a series of decisions that evidentiary and procedural obstacles should not impair a defendant's ability to present a defense. In Chambers v. Mississippi (1973), the Court held that due process required that the defendant be allowed to present evidence that another individual committed the murder for which he was charged, notwithstanding the fact that the proffered evidence violated applicable evidentiary rules.

CHAMBERS v. MISSISSIPPI
410 U.S. 284 (1973)

Justice POWELL delivered the opinion of the Court.

Petitioner, Leon Chambers, was tried by a jury in a Mississippi trial court and convicted of murdering a policeman. The jury assessed punishment at life imprisonment. The events that led to petitioner's prosecution for murder occurred in the small town of Woodville in southern Mississippi. On Saturday evening, June 14, 1969, two Woodville policemen, James Forman and Aaron "Sonny" Liberty, entered a local bar and pool hall to execute a warrant for the arrest of a youth named C. C. Jackson. Jackson resisted and a hostile crowd of some 50 or 60 persons gathered. The officers' first attempt to handcuff Jackson was frustrated when 20 or 25 men in the crowd intervened and wrestled him free. Three deputy sheriffs arrived shortly thereafter and the officers again attempted to make their arrest. Once more, the officers were attacked by the onlookers and during the commotion five or six pistol shots were fired. Before Liberty died, he turned around and fired both barrels of his riot gun into an alley in the area from which the shots appeared to have come. Liberty hit one of the men in the crowd in the back of the head and neck as he ran down the alley. That man was Leon Chambers. Chambers was subsequently charged with Liberty's murder. He pleaded not guilty and has asserted his innocence throughout.

The story of Leon Chambers is intertwined with the story of another man, Gable McDonald. McDonald was in the crowd on the evening of Liberty's death. [McDonald gave a sworn confession to Chambers' attorney] that he shot Officer Liberty. He also stated that he had already told a friend of his, James Williams, that he shot Liberty. He said that he used his own pistol, a nine-shot .22-caliber revolver, which he had discarded shortly after the shooting. In response to questions from Chambers' attorneys, McDonald affirmed that his confession was voluntary and that no one had compelled him to come to them. Once the confession had been transcribed, signed, and witnessed, McDonald was turned over to the local police authorities and was placed in jail.

One month later, at a preliminary hearing, McDonald repudiated his prior sworn confession. He testified that [a friend] had persuaded him to confess that he shot Liberty. He claimed that this person had promised that he would not go to jail and that he would share in the proceeds of a lawsuit that Chambers would bring against the town of Woodville.

Chambers' case came on for trial in October of the next year. At trial, he endeavored to develop two grounds of defense. He first attempted to show that he did not shoot Liberty. Petitioner's second defense was that Gable McDonald had shot Officer Liberty. He was only partially successful, however, in his efforts to bring before the jury the testimony supporting this defense. Chambers endeavored to show the jury that McDonald had repeatedly confessed to the crime. In large measure, he was thwarted in his attempt to present this portion of his defense by the strict application of certain Mississippi rules of evidence. Chambers asserts that the application of these evidentiary rules rendered his trial fundamentally unfair and deprived him of due process of law.

II

At trial, after the State failed to put McDonald on the stand, Chambers called McDonald, laid a predicate for the introduction of his sworn out-of-court confession, had it admitted into evidence, and read it to the jury. The State, upon cross-examination, elicited from McDonald the fact that he had repudiated his prior confession. At the conclusion of the State's cross-examination, Chambers renewed his motion to examine McDonald as an adverse witness. The trial court denied the motion.

Defeated in his attempt to challenge directly McDonald's renunciation of his prior confession, Chambers sought to introduce the testimony of the three witnesses to whom McDonald had admitted that he shot the officer. The State objected to the admission of this testimony on the ground that it was hearsay. The trial court sustained the objection.

III

The right of an accused in a criminal trial to due process is, in essence, the right to a fair opportunity to defend against the State's accusations. The rights to confront and cross-examine witnesses and to call witnesses in one's own behalf have long been recognized as essential to due process.

Both of these elements of a fair trial are implicated in the present case.

Chambers was denied an opportunity to subject McDonald's damning repudiation and alibi to cross-examination. He was not allowed to test the witness' recollection, to probe into the details of his alibi, or to "sift" his conscience so that the jury might judge for itself whether McDonald's testimony was worthy of belief.

We need not decide, however, whether this error alone would occasion reversal since Chambers' claimed denial of due process rests on the ultimate impact of that error when viewed in conjunction with the trial court's refusal to permit him to call other witnesses. The trial court refused to allow him to introduce the testimony of [witnesses] who would have testified to the statements purportedly made by McDonald, on three separate occasions shortly after the crime, naming himself as the murderer.

The hearsay rule, which has long been recognized and respected by virtually every State, is based on experience and grounded in the notion that untrustworthy evidence should not be presented to the triers of fact.

The hearsay statements involved in this case were originally made and subsequently offered at trial under circumstances that provided considerable assurance of their reliability. First, each of McDonald's confessions was made spontaneously to a close acquaintance shortly after the murder had occurred. Second, each one was corroborated by some other evidence in the case-McDonald's sworn confession, the testimony of an eyewitness to the shooting, the testimony that McDonald was seen with a gun immediately after the shooting, and proof of his prior ownership of a .22-caliber revolver and subsequent purchase of a new weapon. The sheer number of independent confessions provided additional corroboration for each. Third, whatever may be the parameters of the penal-interest rationale, each confession here was in a very real sense self-incriminatory and unquestionably against interest. McDonald stood to benefit nothing by disclosing his role in the shooting to any of his three friends and he must have been aware of the possibility that disclosure would lead to criminal prosecution. Finally, if there was any question about the truthfulness of the extrajudicial statements, McDonald was present in the courtroom and was under oath.

He could have been cross-examined by the State, and his demeanor and responses weighed by the jury.

Few rights are more fundamental than that of an accused to present witnesses in his own defense. Although perhaps no rule of evidence has been more respected or more frequently applied in jury trials than that applicable to the exclusion of hearsay, exceptions tailored to allow the introduction of evidence which in fact is likely to be trustworthy have long existed. The testimony rejected by the trial court here bore persuasive assurances of trustworthiness and thus was well within the basic rationale of the exception for declarations against interest. That testimony also was critical to Chambers' defense. In these circumstances, where constitutional rights directly affecting the ascertainment of guilt are implicated, the hearsay rule may not be applied mechanistically to defeat the ends of justice.

We conclude that the exclusion of this critical evidence, coupled with the State's refusal to permit Chambers to cross-examine McDonald, denied him a trial in accord with traditional and fundamental standards of due process. In reaching this judgment, we establish no new principles of constitutional law.

More than 30 years later, the Supreme Court again focused on a defendant's right to present evidence that a third party was responsible for the charged offense.

HOLMES v. SOUTH CAROLINA

547 U.S. 319 (2006)

Justice ALITO delivered the opinion of the Court.

This case presents the question whether a criminal defendant's federal constitutional rights are violated by an evidence rule under which the defendant may not introduce proof of third-party guilt if the prosecution has introduced forensic evidence that, if believed, strongly supports a guilty verdict.

I

On the morning of December 31, 1989, 86-year-old Mary Stewart was beaten, raped, and robbed in her home. She later died of complications stemming from her injuries. Petitioner was convicted by a South Carolina jury of murder, first-degree criminal sexual conduct, first-degree burglary, and robbery, and he was sentenced to death. Upon state postconviction review, however, petitioner was granted a new trial.

At the second trial, the prosecution relied heavily on the following forensic evidence:

> (1) [Petitioner's] palm print was found just above the door knob on the interior side of the front door of the victim's house; (2) fibers consistent with a black sweatshirt owned by [petitioner] were found on the victim's bed sheets; (3) matching blue fibers were found on the victim's pink nightgown and on [petitioner's] blue jeans; (4) microscopically consistent fibers were found on the pink nightgown and on [petitioner's] underwear; (5) [petitioner's] underwear contained a mixture of DNA from two individuals, and 99.99% of the population other than [petitioner] and the victim were excluded as contributors to that mixture; and (6) [petitioner's] tank top was found to contain a mixture of [petitioner's] blood and the victim's blood.

In addition, the prosecution introduced evidence that petitioner had been seen near Stewart's home within an hour of the time when, according to the prosecution's evidence, the attack took place.

As a major part of his defense, petitioner attempted to undermine the State's forensic evidence by suggesting that it had been contaminated and that certain law enforcement officers had engaged in a plot to frame him. Petitioner's expert witnesses criticized the procedures used by the police in handling the fiber and DNA evidence and in collecting the fingerprint evidence. Another defense expert provided testimony that petitioner cited as supporting his claim that the palm print had been planted by the police.

Petitioner also sought to introduce proof that another man, Jimmy McCaw White, had attacked Stewart. At a pretrial hearing, petitioner proffered several witnesses who placed White in the victim's neighborhood on the morning of the assault, as well as four other witnesses who testified that White had either acknowledged that petitioner was "'innocent'" or had actually admitted to committing the crimes. One witness recounted that when he asked White about the "word . . . on the street" that White was responsible for Stewart's murder, White "put his head down and he raised his head back up and he said, well, you know I like older women." According to this witness, White added that "he did what they say he did" and that he had "no regrets about it at all." Another witness, who had been incarcerated with White, testified that White had admitted to assaulting Stewart, that a police officer had asked the witness to testify falsely against petitioner, and that employees of the prosecutor's office, while soliciting the witness' cooperation, had spoken of manufacturing evidence against petitioner. White testified at the pretrial hearing and denied making the incriminating statements. He also provided an alibi for the time of the crime, but another witness refuted his alibi.

The trial court excluded petitioner's third-party guilt evidence citing [a South Carolina case] which held that such evidence is admissible if it "'raise[s] a reasonable inference or presumption as to [the defendant's] own innocence'" but is not admissible if it merely "'cast[s] a bare suspicion upon another'" or "'raise[s] a conjectural inference as to the commission of the crime by another.'"

II

"[S]tate and federal rulemakers have broad latitude under the Constitution to establish rules excluding evidence from criminal trials." This latitude, however, has limits. "Whether rooted directly in the Due Process Clause of the Fourteenth Amendment or in the Compulsory Process or Confrontation Clauses of the Sixth Amendment, the Constitution guarantees criminal defendants 'a meaningful opportunity to present a complete defense.'" This right is abridged by evidence rules that "infring[e] upon a weighty interest of the accused" and are "'arbitrary' or 'disproportionate to the purposes they are designed to serve.'"

This Court's cases contain several illustrations of "arbitrary" rules, *i.e.,* rules that excluded important defense evidence but that did not serve any legitimate interests. In *Washington v. Texas* (1967), state statutes barred a person who had been charged as a participant in a crime from testifying in defense of another alleged participant unless the witness had been acquitted. As a result, when the defendant in *Washington* was tried for murder, he was precluded from calling as a witness a person who had been charged and previously convicted of committing the same murder.

A similar constitutional violation occurred in *Chambers v. Mississipi* (1973). A murder defendant called as a witness a man named McDonald, who had previously confessed to the murder. When McDonald repudiated the confession on the stand, the defendant was denied permission to examine McDonald as an adverse witness based on the State's "'voucher' rule," which barred parties from impeaching their own witnesses. In addition, because the state hearsay rule did not include an exception for statements against penal interest, the defendant was not permitted to introduce evidence that McDonald had made self-incriminating statements to three other persons.

Another arbitrary rule was held unconstitutional in *Crane v. Kentucky* (1986). There, the defendant was prevented from attempting to show at trial that his confession was unreliable because of the circumstances under which it was obtained.

In *Rock v. Arkansas* (1987), this Court held that a rule prohibiting hypnotically refreshed testimony was unconstitutional because "[w]holesale inadmissibility of a defendant's testimony is an arbitrary restriction on the right to testify in the absence of clear evidence by the State repudiating the validity of all post-hypnosis recollections."

While the Constitution thus prohibits the exclusion of defense evidence under rules that serve no legitimate purpose or that are disproportionate to the ends that they are asserted to promote, well-established rules of evidence permit trial judges to exclude evidence if its probative value is outweighed by certain other factors such as unfair prejudice, confusion of the issues, or potential to mislead the jury.

[The South Carolina Supreme Court had previously] adopted and applied a rule [that] "evidence offered by accused as to the commission of the crime by another person must be limited to such facts as are inconsistent with his own guilt; evidence which can have (no) other effect than to cast a bare suspicion upon another, or to raise a conjectural inference as to the commission of the crime by another, is not admissible." Under this rule, the trial judge does not focus on the probative value or the potential adverse effects of admitting the defense evidence of third-party guilt. Instead, the critical inquiry concerns the strength of the prosecution's case: If the prosecution's case is strong enough, the evidence of third-party guilt is excluded even if that evidence, if viewed independently, would have great probative value and even if it would not pose an undue risk of harassment, prejudice, or confusion of the issues.

Interpreted in this way, the rule applied by the State Supreme Court does not rationally serve the end that [it was] designed to promote, *i.e.*, to focus the trial on the central issues by excluding evidence that has only a very weak logical connection to the central issues.

[B]y evaluating the strength of only one party's evidence, no logical conclusion can be reached regarding the strength of contrary evidence offered by the other side to rebut or cast doubt. Because the rule applied by the State Supreme Court in this case did not heed this point, the rule is "arbitrary" in the sense that it does not rationally serve the end that the evidentiary rule and other similar third-party guilt rules were designed to further. It follows that the rule applied in this case by the State Supreme Court violates a criminal defendant's right to have "'a meaningful opportunity to present a complete defense.'"

––––––––––––––––

Just as a defendant's right of fair trial may be violated by unfair limitations on a defendant's opportunity to present a defense, the prosecution may also violate a defendant's right to a fair trial by misconduct in its presentation. Specifically, the Court has held that prosecutors must not go beyond the bounds of zealous advocacy and make closing arguments that appeal merely to jurors' passions and not the evidence in the case. As Justice Sutherland stated in Berger v. United States (1935), prosecutors "may strike hard blows, [but they are] not at liberty to strike foul ones."

Notwithstanding this rule, the Court will not automatically reverse a conviction merely because a prosecutor uses improper language at trial. The question is whether those comments, in context and with curative actions taken by the court, deprived the defendant of a fair trial.

F. ROLE OF THE JURY AND PROOF BEYOND A REASONABLE DOUBT

The last issue to be addressed in this chapter is the role of the jury. In a criminal case, the primary role of the jury is to decide whether the government has proved every element of each crime charged beyond a reasonable doubt. This requirement is inherent in the defendant's rights to a jury trial and due process.

IN RE WINSHIP

397 U.S. 358 (1970)

Justice BRENNAN delivered the opinion of the Court.

This case presents the single, narrow question whether proof beyond a reasonable doubt is among the "essentials of due process and fair treatment" required during the adjudicatory stage when a juvenile is charged with an act which would constitute a crime if committed by an adult.

[Samuel Winship, a 12-year-old boy, was charged with stealing $112 from a woman's pocketbook. Had he been charged as an adult, the prosecution would have had to prove his guilt beyond a reasonable doubt. In the juvenile proceedings, however, the judge relied on a New York law that allowed Winship to be found to be a delinquent based on "a preponderance of the evidence."]

The requirement that guilt of a criminal charge be established by proof beyond a reasonable doubt dates at least from our early years as a Nation. The "demand for a higher degree of persuasion in criminal cases was recurrently expressed from ancient times, [though] its crystallization into the formula 'beyond a reasonable doubt' seems to have occurred as late as 1798. It is now accepted in common law jurisdictions as the measure of persuasion by which the prosecution must convince the trier of all the essential elements of guilt."

Expressions in many opinions of this Court indicate that it has long been assumed that proof of a criminal charge beyond a reasonable doubt is constitutionally required. Mr. Justice Frankfurter stated that "it is the duty of the Government to establish . . . guilt beyond a reasonable doubt. This notion — basic in our law and rightly one of the boasts of a free society — is a requirement and a safeguard of due process of law in the historic, procedural content of 'due process.'"

The reasonable-doubt standard plays a vital role in the American scheme of criminal procedure. It is a prime instrument for reducing the risk of convictions resting on factual error. The standard provides concrete substance for the presumption of innocence — that bedrock "axiomatic and elementary" principle whose "enforcement lies at the foundation of the administration of our criminal law."

The requirement of proof beyond a reasonable doubt has this vital role in our criminal procedure for cogent reasons. The accused during a criminal prosecution has at stake interests of immense importance, both because of the possibility that he may lose his liberty upon conviction and because of the certainty that he would be stigmatized by the conviction. Accordingly, a society that values the good name and freedom of every individual should not condemn a man for commission of a crime when there is reasonable doubt about his guilt. As we [have previously] said: "There is always in litigation a margin of error, representing error in factfinding, which both parties must take into account. Where one party has at stake an interest of transcending value—as a criminal defendant his liberty—this margin of error is reduced as to him by the process of placing on the other party the burden of . . . persuading the factfinder at the conclusion of the trial of his guilt beyond a reasonable doubt. Due process commands that no man shall lose his liberty unless the Government has borne the burden of . . . convincing the factfinder of his guilt." To this end, the reasonable-doubt standard is indispensable, for it "impresses on the trier of fact the necessity of reaching a subjective state of certitude of the facts in issue."

Moreover, use of the reasonable-doubt standard is indispensable to command the respect and confidence of the community in applications of the criminal law. It is critical that the moral force of the criminal law not be diluted by a standard of proof that leaves people in doubt whether innocent men are being condemned. It is also important in our free society that every individual going about his ordinary affairs have confidence that his government cannot adjudge him guilty of a criminal offense without convincing a proper factfinder of his guilt with utmost certainty.

Lest there remain any doubt about the constitutional stature of the reasonable-doubt standard, we explicitly hold that the Due Process Clause protects the accused against conviction except upon proof beyond a reasonable doubt of every fact necessary to constitute the crime with which he is charged.

II

We turn to the question whether juveniles, like adults, are constitutionally entitled to proof beyond a reasonable doubt when they are charged with violation of a criminal law. The same considerations that demand extreme caution in factfinding to protect the innocent adult apply as well to the innocent child.

Justice HARLAN, concurring.

No one, I daresay, would contend that state juvenile court trials are subject to no federal constitutional limitations. Differences have existed, however, among the members of this Court as to what constitutional protections do apply.

The present case draws in question the validity of a New York statute that permits a determination of juvenile delinquency, founded on a charge of criminal conduct, to be made on a standard of proof that is less rigorous than that which would obtain had the accused been tried for the same conduct in an ordinary criminal case. While I am in full agreement that this statutory provision offends the requirement of fundamental fairness embodied in the Due Process Clause of the Fourteenth Amendment, I am constrained to add something.

The standard of proof influences the relative frequency of these two types of erroneous outcomes. If, for example, the standard of proof for a criminal trial were a preponderance of the evidence rather than proof beyond a reasonable doubt, there would be a smaller risk of factual errors that result in freeing guilty persons, but a far greater risk of factual errors that result in convicting the innocent. Because the standard of proof affects the comparative frequency of these two types of erroneous outcomes, the choice of the standard to be applied in a particular kind of litigation should, in a rational world, reflect an assessment of the comparative social disutility of each.

When one makes such an assessment, the reason for different standards of proof in civil as opposed to criminal litigation becomes apparent. In a civil suit between two private parties for money damages, for example, we view it as no more serious in general for there to be an erroneous verdict in the defendant's favor than for there to be an erroneous verdict in the plaintiff's favor. A preponderance of the evidence standard therefore seems peculiarly appropriate for, as explained most sensibly, it simply requires the trier of fact "to believe that the existence of a fact is more probable than its nonexistence before [he] may find in favor of the party who has the burden to persuade the [judge] of the fact's existence."

In a criminal case, on the other hand, we do not view the social disutility of convicting an innocent man as equivalent to the disutility of acquitting someone who is guilty.

In this context, I view the requirement of proof beyond a reasonable doubt in a criminal case as bottomed on a fundamental value determination of our society that it is far worse to convict an innocent man than to let a guilty man go free.

Because of the requirement that each element of a crime be proved beyond a reasonable doubt,[26] it is improper for a court to instruct jurors that they must presume certain facts based on evidence they have received at trial. For example, in Sandstrom v. Montana, 442 U.S. 510, 517 (1979), the Court struck down an instruction that told jurors to presume that a person who commits an act intends the consequences of that act.[27] *See also*

26. The Supreme Court has never defined "beyond a reasonable doubt," other than to state that it does not require that there be a "grave uncertainty," or that the jurors have a "moral certainty" of the defendant's guilt. *See* Cage v. Louisiana, 498 U.S. 39 (1990).

27. In *Sandstrom,* the Court invalidated a jury instruction that provided, "The acts of a person of sound mind and discretion are presumed to be the product of the person's will, but the

Leary v. United States, 395 U.S. 6, 52-53 (1969) (holding that it is improper to instruct jurors that they should presume from a defendant's possession of narcotics that the defendant knew they were illegally imported). Courts may, however, give jurors instructions that allow the jurors to make permissible presumptions, but that do not require them to do so.

Shifting the burden to the defense to prove affirmative defenses also does not violate the defendant's right of due process. For example, in Patterson v. New York, 432 U.S. 197 (1977), the Court upheld a New York law that shifted the burden to the defense to prove extreme emotional disturbance by a preponderance of the evidence once the prosecution had proved an intentional homicide. If the defense could make such a showing, a murder charge could be reduced to a manslaughter conviction. *Compare* Mullaney v. Wilbur, 421 U.S. 684 (1975) (Maine law placed burden on prosecution to prove absence of heat of passion or sudden provocation, and burden could not be shifted to the defendant).

Once the jury finds a defendant guilty beyond a reasonable doubt, reviewing courts will not second guess that decision as long as the jury verdict was based on sufficient evidence. In Virginia v. Jackson, 443 U.S. 307 (1979), the Supreme Court held that the presumption of innocence applies at the trial stage but not upon review.

> The relevant question [on review] is whether, after viewing the evidence in the light most favorable to the prosecution, any rational trier of fact could have found the essential elements of the crime beyond a reasonable doubt. This familiar standard gives full play to the responsibility of the trier of fact fairly to resolve conflicts in the testimony, to weigh the evidence, and to draw reasonable inferences from basic facts to ultimate facts. Once a defendant has been found guilty of the crime charged, the factfinder's role as weigher of the evidence is preserved through a legal conclusion that upon judicial review all of the evidence is to be considered in the light most favorable to the prosecution. The criterion thus impinges upon "jury" discretion only to the extent necessary to guarantee the fundamental protection of due process of law.

Jackson, supra at 319.

In Apprendi v. New Jersey, 530 U.S. 466 (2000), the Court addressed whether a fact that is used as a sentencing enhancement must also be proved to the jury beyond a reasonable doubt, or whether the judge can make the finding based on a lower standard at the time of sentencing. As discussed in greater detail in Chapter 9, the Court started a revolution in sentencing with its decision. *Apprendi* requires that the jury find beyond a reasonable doubt not only those facts that prove the defendant's guilt but also those facts that would enhance the defendant's sentence beyond the ordinary statutory maximum.

---

presumption may be rebutted. A person of sound mind and discretion is presumed to intend the natural and probable consequences of his acts but his presumption may be rebutted."

CHAPTER
9

SENTENCING

A. INTRODUCTION

For most defendants, sentencing is the most important part of the criminal justice process. Whether the defendant has pled guilty or the case has gone to trial, sentencing will determine the defendant's fate. Likewise, sentencing is a crucial stage for the victim, because the sentence imposed will reflect society's assessment of the amount of punishment the defendant deserves.

Sentencing serves multiple objectives. It is designed to punish the defendant for his actions, deter the defendant and others from committing future offenses, protect society from the defendant, and change the defendant's behavior. These sentencing goals are reflected in the traditional purposes of punishment: retribution, deterrence, incapacitation, and rehabilitation. But there is no magic formula that courts can use to determine whether a sentence type and length will accomplish these sentencing goals. Indeed, other factors may influence the sentence imposed in a particular case, such as the prosecution's need to secure cooperation from the defendant to prosecute codefendants.

The standard feature of sentencing schemes is the court's power to sentence defendants to particular periods of incarceration. For short sentences, a defendant may be incarcerated in local jail facilities. For longer sentences, a defendant will ordinarily serve time in a state or federal prison facility. When a defendant is released from incarceration, he may remain under the supervision of corrections officials. In states that have parole boards, a defendant may be released prior to serving the full term of incarceration and will subsequently be supervised by a parole officer for a period of time. If a defendant violates a condition of *parole*, he may be forced to return to prison. There is no parole board under the federal sentencing system. Thus, federal defendants are subject to *supervised release* after being released from prison. Like parole, supervised release ordinarily places restrictions on a defendant's activities. If the defendant violates these restrictions, he will be returned to custody.[1]

For less serious crimes, a defendant may be placed on probation in lieu of a term, or after a short period, of custody. Probation typically carries with it restrictions on the defendant's behavior. It can even carry a condition such as house arrest. If the defendant violates probation, the court may order him to serve a longer period of time in custody. Under creative sentencing schemes, judges may use probationary sentences to reform the defendant's behavior by imposing unusual conditions. For example, a court may require a defendant to visit a victim's grave or write an apology letter to the victim's family. Most courts, however, limit probation conditions to work, education, and rehabilitation requirements imposed on the defendant. Conditions that unduly impede a defendant's exercise of his First Amendment rights, such as prohibitions on the sale of a defendant's book regarding his crime, are unconstitutional.[2]

The central feature of sentencing is the court's power to incarcerate a defendant. Over the years, courts have employed various types of sentencing schemes. The two primary sentencing schemes are indeterminate sentencing and determinate sentencing. As discussed in section B, indeterminate sentencing typically affords broad discretion to judges in imposing sentences. Determinate sentencing schemes tend to limit court discretion by setting guidelines and mandatory sentences that courts must follow. In Apprendi v. New Jersey, 530 U.S. 466 (2000), the Supreme Court made dramatic changes to the manner in which determinate sentencing schemes may be implemented by state and federal judges. Accordingly, section B also addresses the "*Apprendi* revolution" and its impact on sentencing procedures.

Section C addresses the Eighth Amendment limits on sentencing. This section focuses on the Supreme Court's approach to determining when a sentence constitutes "cruel and unusual punishment." It also examines when fines imposed as part of a sentence are considered "excessive fines" under the Eighth Amendment.

Finally, there are special rules for cases that involve the ultimate sanction — the death penalty. Section D discusses death penalty cases and

---

1. In determining whether a defendant has violated probation or parole, the court must comply with due process standards and allow the defendant to challenge the alleged grounds of violation. *See* Morrissey v. Brewer, 408 U.S. 471 (1972).

2. *See* Simon & Schuster, Inc. v. Members of New York State Crime Victims Board, 502 U.S. 105 (1991) (invalidating New York's "Son of Sam" law because it was a content-based statute that prohibited defendants from engaging in particular types of expression). Although some states require that defendants pay restitution to victims, states cannot prohibit defendants from authoring works regarding their crimes.

the procedures used to determine whether capital punishment should be imposed. It also addresses the constitutionality of different methods of executing defendants, including lethal injection.

Sentencing is the responsibility of the court, but each jurisdiction has procedures to ensure that both sides have an opportunity to address the court before sentencing. Likewise, the court may receive input from probation officers, victims, and members of the public. In the end, it is the responsibility of the court to balance the interests of all parties and to impose a fair and just sentence. This goal must be accomplished within the realities of today's world — a world where prisons are already overcrowded and limited resources are available to incarcerate additional defendants.[3] Thus, like many aspects of the criminal justice system, sentencing is imperfect and constantly changing.

B. INDETERMINATE VERSUS DETERMINATE SENTENCING

The two primary models of sentencing are indeterminate and determinate sentencing, but each model may be implemented slightly differently depending on the jurisdiction.

1. Indeterminate Sentencing

In indeterminate sentencing schemes, judges typically have broad discretion in imposing sentences. The sentencing judge will impose a sentence anywhere from probation to the maximum authorized sentence. If a defendant is sentenced to incarceration, a parole board later determines when the defendant will be released. Prior to 1987 and the adoption of the Federal Sentencing Guidelines, federal courts used an indeterminate sentencing scheme. Federal judges could impose a sentence anywhere between probation to the maximum statutory sentence for a crime. As a result, indeterminate sentencing led to large disparities in sentencing. One judge would issue a sentence of probation for an offense

---

3. Currently, approximately 1.6 million Americans are in state or federal prison, and nearly every jurisdiction suffers from a shortage of incarceration facilities. *See* U.S. Department of Justice, Office of Justice Programs, Bureau of Justice Statistics Bulletin: Key Facts at a Glance (2011).

See also Bureau of Justice Statistics, *Prisoners in 2011*, December 2012, http://bjs.gov/index.cfm?ty=pbdetail&iid=4559; U.S. Department of Justice, Office of Justice Programs, Bureau of Justice Statistics Bulletin: Prisoners in 2005, at 7-8 & tables 8-9 (stating that, collectively, state prisons operated at 99 percent of their highest capacity measures since 2005).

while another judge might impose the maximum sentence for the same offense.

Indeterminate sentencing can give great discretion to the court to fashion a sentence. Its advantages are that it allows the judge and parole supervising authority to tailor a sentence for a particular defendant. The downsides include disparities in sentencing and less control over judges who might be too lenient or too tough in the eyes of others.

Since 1984, the trend has been away from indeterminate sentencing. Following Congress's lead in its adoption of sentencing guidelines for federal courts, state courts around the nation have moved toward determinate sentencing schemes.[4]

2. *Determinate Sentencing*

Determinate sentencing eliminates the role of a parole board. The sentence imposed by the court is the sentence the defendant will serve, absent time credited for a defendant's good behavior in prison. Sentences are set by the legislature and depend to a great extent on the charge brought by the prosecution. As such, determinate sentencing tends to limit judicial discretion in sentencing.

Historically, determinate sentencing has often been adopted as a way to rectify perceived disparities in sentencing. For example, the Sentencing Reform Act of 1984 established the U.S. Sentencing Commission to create a set of guidelines to limit judges' discretion in sentencing. Calculating sentences under the Federal Sentencing Guidelines is a multistep process. The court must determine the base offense level for a particular defendant's crime, consider aggravating and mitigating factors that will affect the offense level, consider the impact of multiple offenses, and examine any other relevant characteristics, such as the defendant's role in the crime and the impact on victims. Then, the court must calculate the defendant's criminal history level. Ultimately, the court will determine the indices that it will apply to the sentencing grid. The point at which these indices meet indicates the range, in months, within which the judge's sentence must fall, unless the judge engages in other findings supporting a departure from the Sentencing Guidelines.

---

4. *See* Blakely v. Washington, 542 U.S. 296, 323 (2004).

United States Sentencing Guidelines Sentencing Table (Effective November 1, 2010)
(in months of imprisonment)

Offense Level	Criminal History Category (Criminal History Points)					
	I (0 or 1)	II (2 or 3)	III (4, 5, 6)	IV (7, 8, 9)	V (10, 11, 12)	VI (13 or more)
1	0-6	0-6	0-6	0-6	0-6	0-6
2	0-6	0-6	0-6	0-6	0-6	1-7
3	0-6	0-6	0-6	0-6	2-8	3-9
4	0-6	0-6	0-6	2-8	4-10	6-12
5	0-6	0-6	1-7	4-10	6-12	9-15
6	0-6	1-7	2-8	6-12	9-15	12-18
7	0-6	2-8	4-10	8-14	12-18	15-21
8	0-6	4-10	6-12	10-16	15-21	18-24
9	4-10	6-12	8-14	12-18	18-24	21-27
10	6-12	8-14	10-16	15-21	21-27	24-30
11	8-14	10-16	12-18	18-24	24-30	27-33
12	10-16	12-18	15-21	21-27	27-33	30-37
13	12-18	15-21	18-24	24-30	30-37	33-41
14	15-21	18-24	21-27	27-33	33-41	37-46
15	18-24	21-27	24-30	30-37	37-46	41-51
16	21-27	24-30	27-33	33-41	41-51	46-57
17	24-30	27-33	30-37	37-46	46-57	51-63
18	27-33	30-37	33-41	41-51	51-63	57-71
19	30-37	33-41	37-46	46-57	57-71	63-78
20	33-41	37-46	41-51	51-63	63-78	70-87
21	37-46	41-51	46-57	57-71	70-87	77-96
22	41-51	46-57	51-63	63-78	77-96	84-105
23	46-57	51-63	57-71	70-87	84-105	92-115
24	51-63	57-71	63-78	77-96	92-115	100-125
25	57-71	63-78	70-87	84-105	100-125	110-137
26	63-78	70-87	78-97	92-115	110-137	120-150
27	70-87	78-97	87-108	100-125	120-150	130-162
28	78-97	87-108	97-121	110-137	130-162	140-175
29	87-108	97-121	108-135	121-151	140-175	151-188
30	97-121	108-135	121-151	135-168	151-188	168-210
31	108-135	121-151	135-168	151-188	168-210	188-235
32	121-151	135-168	151-188	168-210	188-235	210-262
33	135-168	151-188	168-210	188-235	210-262	235-293
34	151-188	168-210	188-235	210-262	235-293	262-327
35	168-210	188-235	210-262	235-293	262-327	292-365
36	188-235	210-262	235-293	262-327	292-365	324-405
37	210-262	235-293	262-327	292-365	324-405	360-life
38	235-293	262-327	292-365	324-405	360-life	360-life
39	262-327	292-365	324-405	360-life	360-life	360-life
40	292-365	324-405	360-life	360-life	360-life	360-life
41	324-405	360-life	360-life	360-life	360-life	360-life
42	360-life	360-life	360-life	360-life	360-life	360-life
43	life	life	life	life	life	life

Zones: Zone A (levels 1–8 region), Zone B, Zone C, Zone D as marked on the table.

Application Notes

The Offense Level (1-43) forms the vertical axis of the Sentencing Table. The Criminal History Category (I-VI) forms the horizontal axis of the Table. The intersection of the Offense Level and Criminal History Category displays the Guideline Range in months of imprisonment. "Life" means life imprisonment.

Determining the Sentence

To use the above grid, a judge must first determine the base term for a particular crime. For example, the crime of bank robbery has a base offense level of 30. The court must then examine the specific offense characteristics of defendant's crime. If, for example, a person was injured during the robbery, the offense level is increased by at least 2 levels. The defendant now faces an offense level of 32. If the loss was more than $10,000, but less than $50,000, another level is added to the offense, placing defendant's crime now at a level of 33.

Next, it is time to look at the defendant's role in the offense. If the defendant was the leader of the robbery gang, another 4 levels are added, putting the total level now at a 37. If the defendant then tries to obstruct justice by intimidating potential witnesses, another 2 levels would be added, making the new total 39. In the end, the defendant may end up with an adjusted offense level. Assuming there are not multiple counts which need to be considered, the defendant's total adjusted offense level is 39.

After the court decides on the adjusted offense level, it must examine the defendant's criminal history to determine defendant's horizontal matrix for the sentencing chart. If, for example, the defendant has at least one adult prior felony conviction in the past ten years, the defendant may be at a Level II for criminal history.

Assuming there are no other adjustments for defendant accepting responsibility for his acts, or reasons to depart from the guidelines for reasons not considered by the Sentencing Commission or assistance to the government, defendant's sentence will be listed at the intersection of an offense level of 39 and a Criminal History of Level II. As shown on the chart, defendant would face 292-365 months in prison.

Supporters of determinate sentencing argue that it provides more consistency and predictability in sentencing. Opponents, however, reject the formulaic and rigid approach of determinate sentencing, arguing that it does a poor job of actually assessing how deserving of punishment a defendant is.

From 1987 to 2005, the federal courts were required to impose sentences under the Federal Sentencing Guidelines. Many states also had sentencing protocols that limited courts' power to impose a sentence based on certain findings that were made at sentencing. For example, in California, sentencing laws provided for a presumptive mid-term sentence, but the sentencing court could impose a higher sentence if it found facts that constituted aggravating factors in the case. Likewise, the sentencing court could pick a lower term if it made the appropriate findings. Other states followed schemes that prescribed statutory maximum sentences for certain crimes that courts were required to follow, unless they found certain enhancements that would allow them to impose a higher sentence.

3. Mandatory Minimum Sentences

Mandatory minimum sentences are another way in which legislatures restrict judges' discretion at sentencing. Supporters argue that mandatory minimums are necessary to reflect the gravity of a crime and to ensure that defendants who have committed certain types of crimes receive similar sentences.

Mandatory minimum sentences can apply to a variety of crimes. For example, federal law dictates mandatory minimum sentences for defendants who possess certain amounts of narcotics (21 U.S.C. §841), use a firearm during the commission of a crime (18 U.S.C. §924(c)), or distribute child pornography (18 U.S.C. §2252(b)(1)). Legislatures may also impose mandatory minimum sentences for recidivists. For example, under three strikes laws, a defendant convicted of a third qualifying offense may face a mandatory minimum sentence of 15 years of incarceration for an offense that might otherwise qualify for a minimal prison term.

Mandatory minimum sentences are controversial because, as Supreme Court Justice Stephen Breyer stated, "Statutory minimums generally deny the judge the legal power to depart downward, no matter how unusual the special circumstances that call for leniency. . . . [These statutes] tend to transfer sentencing power to prosecutors, who can determine sentences through the charges they decide to bring." Harris v. United States, 536 U.S. 545 (2002) (Breyer, J., concurring).

Concerned about the impact of mandatory minimum sentences, the Supreme Court is requiring that the key aspects of crimes triggering mandatory minimum sentences be treated as elements of the crime and not just sentencing factors determined by the sentencing court. *See* United States v. O'Brien, 130 S. Ct. 2169 (2010).

4. Apprendi *and Its Progeny*

In 2000, the Supreme Court examined the constitutionality of sentencing schemes that require sentencing judges to increase a defendant's sentence based on facts never pleaded or proved to a jury but rather found by the court. In Apprendi v. New Jersey, the Court held that such sentencing schemes violate defendants' right to due process.

APPRENDI v. NEW JERSEY

530 U.S. 466 (2000)

Justice STEVENS delivered the opinion of the Court.

[A] New Jersey statute classifies the possession of a firearm for an unlawful purpose as a "second-degree" offense. Such an offense is punishable by imprisonment for "between five years and 10 years." A separate statute, described by that State's Supreme Court as a "hate crime" law, provides for an "extended term" of imprisonment if the trial judge finds, by a preponderance of the evidence, that "the defendant in committing the crime acted with a purpose to intimidate an individual or group of individuals because of race, color, gender, handicap, religion, sexual orientation or ethnicity." The extended term authorized by the hate crime law for second-degree offenses is imprisonment for "between 10 and 20 years."

The question presented is whether the Due Process Clause of the Fourteenth Amendment requires that a factual determination authorizing an increase in the maximum prison sentence for an offense from 10 to 20 years be made by a jury on the basis of proof beyond a reasonable doubt.

I

At 2:04 A.M. on December 22, 1994, petitioner Charles C. Apprendi, Jr., fired several .22-caliber bullets into the home of an African-American family that had recently moved into a previously all-white neighborhood in Vineland, New Jersey. Apprendi was promptly arrested and, at 3:05 A.M., admitted that he was the shooter. After further questioning, at 6:04 A.M., he made a statement—which he later retracted—that even though he did not know the occupants of the house personally, "because they are black in color he does not want them in the neighborhood."

A New Jersey grand jury returned a 23-count indictment charging Apprendi with four first-degree, eight second-degree, six third-degree, and five fourth-degree offenses. The charges alleged shootings on four different dates, as well as the unlawful possession of various weapons. None of the counts referred to the hate crime statute, and none alleged that Apprendi acted with a racially biased purpose.

The parties entered into a plea agreement, pursuant to which Apprendi pleaded guilty to two counts (3 and 18) of second-degree possession of a firearm for an unlawful purpose, and one count (22) of the third-degree offense of unlawful possession of an antipersonnel bomb; the prosecutor dismissed the other 20 counts. Under state law, a second-degree offense carries a penalty range of 5 to 10 years, a third-degree offense carries a penalty range of between 3 and 5 years. As part of the plea agreement, however, the State reserved the right to request the court to impose a higher "enhanced" sentence on count 18 (which was based on the December 22 shooting) on the ground that that offense was committed with a biased purpose. Apprendi, correspondingly, reserved the right to challenge the hate crime sentence enhancement on the ground that it violates the United States Constitution.

After the trial judge accepted the three guilty pleas, the prosecutor filed a formal motion for an extended term. The trial judge thereafter held an evidentiary hearing on the issue of Apprendi's "purpose" for the shooting on December 22. Apprendi adduced evidence from a psychologist and from seven character witnesses who testified that he did not have a reputation for racial bias. He also took the stand himself, explaining that the incident was an unintended consequence of overindulgence in alcohol, denying that he was in any way biased against African-Americans, and denying that his statement to the police had been accurately described. The judge, however, found the police officer's testimony credible, and concluded that the evidence supported a finding "that the crime was motivated by racial bias." Having found "by a preponderance of the evidence" that Apprendi's actions were taken "with a purpose to intimidate" as provided by the statute, the trial judge held that the hate crime enhancement applied. Rejecting Apprendi's constitutional challenge to the statute, the judge sentenced him to a 12-year term of imprisonment on count 18, and to shorter concurrent sentences on the other two counts.

Apprendi appealed, arguing . . . that the Due Process Clause of the United States Constitution requires that the finding of bias upon which his hate crime sentence was based must be proved to a jury beyond a reasonable doubt, In re Winship (1970).

II

At stake in this case are constitutional protections of surpassing importance: the proscription of any deprivation of liberty without "due process of law," and the guarantee that "in all criminal prosecutions, the accused shall enjoy the right to a speedy and public trial, by an impartial jury." Taken together, these rights indisputably entitle a criminal defendant to "a jury determination that [he] is guilty of every element of the crime with which he is charged, beyond a reasonable doubt."

Any possible distinction between an "element" of a felony offense and a "sentencing factor" was unknown to the practice of criminal indictment, trial by jury, and judgment by court as it existed during the years surrounding our Nation's founding. As a general rule, criminal proceedings were submitted to a jury after being initiated by an indictment containing "all the facts and circumstances which constitute the offence, . . . stated with such certainty and precision, that the defendant . . . may be enabled to determine the species of offence they constitute, in order that he may prepare his defence accordingly . . . and that there may be no doubt as to the judgment which should be given, if the defendant be convicted."

The historic link between verdict and judgment and the consistent limitation on judges' discretion to operate within the limits of the legal penalties provided highlight the novelty of a legislative scheme that removes the jury from the determination of a fact that, if found, exposes the criminal defendant to a penalty exceeding the maximum he would receive if punished according to the facts reflected in the jury verdict alone.

IV

It was in McMillan v. Pennsylvania (1986), that this Court, for the first time, coined the term "sentencing factor" to refer to a fact that was not found by a jury but that could affect the sentence imposed by the judge. That case involved a challenge to the State's Mandatory Minimum Sentencing Act. According to its provisions, anyone convicted of certain felonies would be subject to a mandatory minimum penalty of five years imprisonment if the judge found, by a preponderance of the evidence, that the person "visibly possessed a firearm" in the course of committing one of the specified felonies. Articulating for the first time, and then applying, a multifactor set of criteria for determining whether the *Winship* protections applied to bar such a system, we concluded that the Pennsylvania statute did not run afoul of our previous admonitions against relieving the State of its burden of proving guilt, or tailoring the mere form of a criminal statute solely to avoid *Winship*'s strictures.

We did not, however, there budge from the position that (1) constitutional limits exist to States' authority to define away facts necessary to constitute a criminal offense, and (2) that a state scheme that keeps from the jury facts that "expose [defendants] to greater or additional punishment," may raise serious constitutional concern.

Finally, . . . Almendarez-Torres v. United States (1998), represents at best an exceptional departure from the historic practice that we have described. In that case, . . . we concluded that sentencing him to a term higher than that attached to the offense alleged in the indictment did not violate the strictures of *Winship* . . . [b]ecause Almendarez-Torres had admitted the three earlier convictions for aggravated felonies.

Even though it is arguable that *Almendarez-Torres* was incorrectly decided, Apprendi does not contest the decision's validity and we need not revisit it for purposes of our decision today to treat the case as a narrow exception to the general rule we recalled at the outset. Given its unique facts, it surely does not warrant rejection of the otherwise uniform course of decision during the entire history of our jurisprudence.

In sum, our reexamination of our cases in this area, and of the history upon which they rely, confirms the opinion that we expressed in *Jones.* Other than the fact of a prior conviction, any fact that increases the penalty for a crime beyond the prescribed statutory maximum must be submitted to a jury, and proved beyond a reasonable doubt.

V

The New Jersey statutory scheme that Apprendi asks us to invalidate allows a jury to convict a defendant of a second-degree offense based on its finding beyond a reasonable doubt that he unlawfully possessed a prohibited weapon; after a subsequent and separate proceeding, it then allows a judge to impose punishment identical to that New Jersey provides for crimes of the first degree based upon the judge's finding, by a preponderance of the evidence, that the defendant's "purpose" for unlawfully possessing the weapon was "to intimidate" his victim on the basis of a particular characteristic the victim possessed. In light of the constitutional rule explained above, and all of the cases supporting it, this practice cannot stand.

New Jersey's reliance on *Almendarez-Torres* is . . . unavailing. The reasons supporting an exception from the general rule for the statute construed in that case do not apply to the New Jersey statute. Whereas recidivism [which was the issue in *Almendarez-Torres*] "does not relate to the commission of the offense" itself, New Jersey's biased purpose inquiry goes precisely to what happened in the "commission of the offense." Moreover, there is a vast difference between accepting the validity of a prior judgment of conviction entered in a proceeding in which the defendant had the right to a jury trial and the right to require the prosecutor to prove guilt beyond a reasonable doubt, and allowing the judge to find the required fact under a lesser standard of proof.

The New Jersey procedure challenged in this case is an unacceptable departure from the jury tradition that is an indispensable part of our criminal justice system. Accordingly, the judgment of the Supreme Court of New Jersey is reversed, and the case is remanded for further proceedings not inconsistent with this opinion.

Justice SCALIA, concurring.

I feel the need to say a few words in response to Justice Breyer's dissent. It sketches an admirably fair and efficient scheme of criminal justice designed for a society that is prepared to leave criminal justice to the State. The founders of the American Republic were not prepared to leave it to the State, which is why the jury-trial guarantee was one of the least controversial provisions of the Bill of Rights. It has never been efficient; but it has always been free.

What ultimately demolishes the case for the dissenters is that they are unable to say what the right to trial by jury does guarantee if, as they assert, it does not guarantee — what it has been assumed to guarantee throughout our history — the right to have a jury determine those facts that determine the maximum sentence the law allows. They provide no coherent alternative.

Justice THOMAS, with whom Justice SCALIA joins as to Parts I and II, concurring.

I write separately to explain my view that the Constitution requires a broader rule than the Court adopts.

This case turns on the seemingly simple question of what constitutes a "crime" . . . that is, which facts are the "elements" or "ingredients" of a crime.

Sentencing enhancements may be new creatures, but the question that they create for courts is not. Courts have long had to consider which facts are elements in order to determine the sufficiency of an accusation (usually an indictment). The answer that courts have provided regarding the accusation tells us what an element is, and it is then a simple matter to apply that answer to whatever constitutional right may be at issue in a case — here, *Winship* and the right to trial by jury. A long line of essentially uniform authority addressing accusations, and stretching from the earliest reported cases after the founding until well into the 20th century, establishes that the original understanding of which facts are elements was even broader than the rule that the Court adopts today.

This authority establishes that a "crime" includes every fact that is by law a basis for imposing or increasing punishment (in contrast with a fact that mitigates punishment). Thus, if the legislature defines some core crime and then provides for increasing the punishment of that crime upon a finding of some aggravating fact—of whatever sort, including the fact of a prior conviction—the core crime and the aggravating fact together constitute an aggravated crime, just as much as grand larceny is an aggravated form of petit larceny. The aggravating fact is an element of the aggravated crime. Similarly, if the legislature, rather than creating grades of crimes, has provided for setting the punishment of a crime based on some fact—such as a fine that is proportional to the value of stolen goods—that fact is also an element.

Justice O'CONNOR, with whom Chief Justice REHNQUIST, Justice KENNEDY, and Justice BREYER join, dissenting.

Our Court has long recognized that not every fact that bears on a defendant's punishment need be charged in an indictment, submitted to a jury, and proved by the government beyond a reasonable doubt. Rather, we have held that the "legislature's definition of the elements of the offense is usually dispositive." Although we have recognized that "there are obviously constitutional limits beyond which the States may not go in this regard," and that "in certain limited circumstances *Winship*'s reasonable-doubt requirement applies to facts not formally identified as elements of the offense charged," *McMillan*, we have proceeded with caution before deciding that a certain fact must be treated as an offense element despite the legislature's choice not to characterize it as such.

In one bold stroke the Court today casts aside our traditional cautious approach and instead embraces a universal and seemingly bright-line rule limiting the power of Congress and state legislatures to define criminal offenses and the sentences that follow from convictions thereunder. The Court states: "Other than the fact of a prior conviction, any fact that increases the penalty for a crime beyond the prescribed statutory maximum must be submitted to a jury, and proved beyond a reasonable doubt."

Because I do not believe that the Court's "increase in the maximum penalty" rule is required by the Constitution, I would evaluate New Jersey's sentence-enhancement statute, by analyzing the factors we have examined in past cases. *See, e.g., Almendarez-Torres; McMillan*. First, the New Jersey statute does not shift the burden of proof on an essential ingredient of the offense by presuming that ingredient upon proof of other elements of the offense. Second, the magnitude of the New Jersey sentence enhancement, as applied in petitioner's case, is constitutionally permissible. Under New Jersey law, the weapons possession offense to which petitioner pleaded guilty carries a sentence range of 5 to 10 years' imprisonment. The fact that petitioner, in committing that offense, acted with a purpose to intimidate because of race exposed him to a higher sentence range of 10 to 20 years' imprisonment. The 10-year increase in the maximum penalty to which petitioner was exposed falls well within the range we have found permissible. *See Almendarez-Torres* (approving 18-year enhancement). Third, the New Jersey statute gives no impression of having been enacted to evade the constitutional requirements that attach when a State makes a fact an element of the charged offense. For example, New Jersey did not take what had previously been an element of the weapons possession offense and transform it into a sentencing factor. *See McMillan.*

In sum, New Jersey "simply took one factor that has always been considered by sentencing courts to bear on punishment" — a defendant's motive for committing the criminal offense — "and dictated the precise weight to be given that factor" when the motive is to intimidate a person because of race.

On the basis of our prior precedent, then, I would hold that the New Jersey sentence-enhancement statute is constitutional, and affirm the judgment of the Supreme Court of New Jersey.

Justice BREYER, with whom Chief Justice REHNQUIST, joins, dissenting.

The majority holds that the Constitution contains the following requirement: "any fact [other than recidivism] that increases the penalty for a crime beyond the prescribed statutory maximum must be submitted to a jury, and proved beyond a reasonable doubt." This rule would seem to promote a procedural ideal — that of juries, not judges, determining the existence of those facts upon which increased punishment turns. But the real world of criminal justice cannot hope to meet any such ideal. It can function only with the help of procedural compromises, particularly in respect to sentencing. And those compromises, which are themselves necessary for the fair functioning of the criminal justice system, preclude implementation of the procedural model that today's decision reflects. At the very least, the impractical nature of the requirement that the majority now recognizes supports the proposition that the Constitution was not intended to embody it.

In modern times the law has left it to the sentencing judge to find those facts which (within broad sentencing limits set by the legislature) determine the sentence of a convicted offender.

There are many manner-related differences in respect to criminal behavior. Empirical data collected by the Sentencing Commission makes clear that, before the Guidelines, judges who exercised discretion within broad legislatively determined sentencing limits (say, a range of 0 to 20 years) would impose very different sentences upon offenders engaged in the same basic criminal conduct, depending, for example, upon the amount of drugs distributed (in respect to drug crimes), the amount of money taken (in respect to robbery, theft, or fraud), the presence or use of a weapon, injury to a victim, the vulnerability of a victim, the offender's role in the offense, recidivism, and many other offense-related or offender-related factors. The majority does not deny that judges have exercised, and, constitutionally speaking, may exercise sentencing discretion in this way.

[I]t is important for present purposes to understand why judges, rather than juries, traditionally have determined the presence or absence of such sentence-affecting facts in any given case. And it is important to realize that the reason is not a theoretical one, but a practical one. There are, to put it simply, far too many potentially relevant sentencing factors to permit submission of all (or even many) of them to a jury.

A sentencing system in which judges have discretion to find sentencing-related factors is a workable system and one that has long been thought consistent with the Constitution.

———————

Apprendi requires that all facts increasing a defendant's sentence beyond the offense's statutory maximum be pleaded and proved to a jury beyond a reasonable doubt. It preserves, however, *Almendarez-Torres*'s exception for increased sentences based on the defendant's commission of prior offenses. Two years after *Apprendi* was decided, the Court, in Harris v. United States, 536 U.S. 545 (2002), clarified that the *Apprendi* rule does not apply to facts that trigger a mandatory minimum sentence. Justice Kennedy, writing for the Court, held that a sentencing judge can find those facts necessary to trigger a mandatory minimum sentencing provision. That same year, the Court, in Ring v. Arizona, 536 U.S. 584 (2002), held that Arizona's capital sentencing statute was unconstitutional because it allowed judges to find whether factors justifying imposition of the death penalty exist.

In 2004, the Court considered how *Apprendi* affects state sentencing schemes that allow sentences to be enhanced based on judicial findings in guideline sentencing schemes. Continuing the *Apprendi* movement, the Supreme Court held that *Apprendi* applies when a factual finding triggers a sentence beyond the standard sentencing range.

BLAKELY v. WASHINGTON
542 U.S. 296 (2004)

Justice SCALIA delivered the opinion of the Court.

Petitioner Ralph Howard Blakely, Jr., pleaded guilty to the kidnaping of his estranged wife. The facts admitted in his plea, standing alone, supported a maximum sentence of 53 months. Pursuant to state law, the court imposed an "exceptional" sentence of 90 months after making a judicial determination that he had acted with "deliberate cruelty." We consider whether this violated petitioner's Sixth Amendment right to trial by jury.

I

Petitioner married his wife Yolanda in 1973. He was evidently a difficult man to live with, having been diagnosed at various times with psychological and personality disorders including paranoid schizophrenia. His wife ultimately filed for divorce. In 1998, he abducted her from their orchard home in Grant County, Washington, binding her with duct tape and forcing her at knife-point into a wooden box in the bed of his pickup truck. In the process, he implored her to dismiss the divorce suit and related trust proceedings.

When the couple's 13-year-old son Ralphy returned home from school, petitioner ordered him to follow in another car, threatening to harm Yolanda with a shotgun if he did not do so. Ralphy escaped and sought help when they stopped at a gas station, but petitioner continued on with Yolanda to a friend's house in Montana. He was finally arrested after the friend called the police.

The State charged petitioner with first-degree kidnaping. Upon reaching a plea agreement, however, it reduced the charge to second-degree kidnaping involving domestic violence and use of a firearm. Petitioner entered a guilty plea admitting the elements of second-degree kidnaping and the domestic-violence and firearm allegations, but no other relevant facts.

The case then proceeded to sentencing. In Washington, second-degree kidnaping is a class B felony. State law provides that "no person convicted of a [class B] felony shall be punished by confinement . . . exceeding . . . a term of ten years." Other provisions of state law, however, further limit the range of sentences a judge may impose. Washington's Sentencing Reform Act specifies, for petitioner's offense of second-degree kidnaping with a firearm, a "standard range" of 49 to 53 months. A judge may impose a sentence above the standard range if he finds "substantial and compelling reasons justifying an exceptional sentence." The Act lists aggravating factors that justify such a departure, which it recites to be illustrative rather than exhaustive. When a judge imposes an exceptional sentence, he must set forth findings of fact and conclusions of law supporting it.

Pursuant to the plea agreement, the State recommended a sentence within the standard range of 49 to 53 months. After hearing Yolanda's description of the kidnaping, however, the judge rejected the State's recommendation and imposed an exceptional sentence of 90 months—37 months beyond the standard maximum. He justified the sentence on the ground that petitioner had acted with "deliberate cruelty," a statutorily enumerated ground for departure in domestic-violence cases.

Faced with an unexpected increase of more than three years in his sentence, petitioner objected. The judge accordingly conducted a 3-day bench hearing featuring testimony from petitioner, Yolanda, Ralphy, a police officer, and medical experts. After the hearing, he issued 32 findings of fact, concluding:

> The defendant's motivation to commit kidnapping was complex, contributed to by
> his mental condition and personality disorders, the pressures of the divorce

litigation, the impending trust litigation trial and anger over his troubled inter-personal relationships with his spouse and children.

The defendant's methods were more homogeneous than his motive. He used stealth and surprise, and took advantage of the victim's isolation. He immediately employed physical violence, restrained the victim with tape, and threatened her with injury and death to herself and others. He immediately coerced the victim into providing information by the threatening application of a knife. He violated a subsisting restraining order.

The judge adhered to his initial determination of deliberate cruelty. Petitioner appealed, arguing that this sentencing procedure deprived him of his federal constitutional right to have a jury determine beyond a reasonable doubt all facts legally essential to his sentence. The State Court of Appeals affirmed. The Washington Supreme Court denied discretionary review. We granted certiorari.

II

This case requires us to apply the rule we expressed in Apprendi v. New Jersey (2000): "Other than the fact of a prior conviction, any fact that increases the penalty for a crime beyond the prescribed statutory maximum must be submitted to a jury, and proved beyond a reasonable doubt." This rule reflects two longstanding tenets of common-law criminal jurisprudence: that the "truth of every accusation" against a defendant "should afterwards be confirmed by the unanimous suffrage of twelve of his equals and neighbours," 4 W. Blackstone, Commentaries on the Laws of England 343 (1769), and that "an accusation which lacks any particular fact which the law makes essential to the punishment is . . . no accusation within the requirements of the common law, and it is no accusation in reason," 1 J. Bishop, Criminal Procedure §87, p. 55 (2d ed. 1872). These principles have been acknowledged by courts and treatises since the earliest days of graduated sentencing. . . .

In this case, petitioner was sentenced to more than three years above the 53-month statutory maximum of the standard range because he had acted with "deliberate cruelty." The facts supporting that finding were neither admitted by petitioner nor found by a jury. The State nevertheless contends that there was no Apprendi violation because the relevant "statutory maximum" is not 53 months, but the 10-year maximum for class B felonies. It observes that no exceptional sentence may exceed that limit. Our precedents make clear, however, that the "statutory maximum" for Apprendi purposes is the maximum sentence a judge may impose solely on the basis of the facts reflected in the jury verdict or admitted by the defendant. In other words, the relevant "statutory maximum" is not the maximum sentence a judge may impose after finding additional facts, but the maximum he may impose without any additional findings. When a judge inflicts punishment that the jury's verdict alone does not allow, the jury has not found all the facts "which the law makes essential to the punishment," and the judge exceeds his proper authority.

The judge in this case could not have imposed the exceptional 90-month sentence solely on the basis of the facts admitted in the guilty plea. Those facts alone were insufficient. . . .

Because the State's sentencing procedure did not comply with the Sixth Amendment, petitioner's sentence is invalid.

III

Our commitment to *Apprendi* in this context reflects not just respect for longstanding precedent, but the need to give intelligible content to the right of jury trial. That right is no mere procedural formality, but a fundamental reservation of power in our constitutional structure. Just as suffrage ensures the people's ultimate control in the legislative and executive branches, jury trial is meant to ensure their control in the judiciary.

IV

By reversing the judgment below, we are not, as the State would have it, "finding determinate sentencing schemes unconstitutional." This case is not about whether determinate sentencing is constitutional, only about how it can be implemented in a way that respects the Sixth Amendment.

Ultimately, our decision cannot turn on whether or to what degree trial by jury impairs the efficiency or fairness of criminal justice. One can certainly argue that both these values would be better served by leaving justice entirely in the hands of professionals; many nations of the world, particularly those following civil-law traditions, take just that course. There is not one shred of doubt, however, about the Framers' paradigm for criminal justice: not the civil-law ideal of administrative perfection, but the common-law ideal of limited state power accomplished by strict division of authority between judge and jury. As *Apprendi* held, every defendant has the right to insist that the prosecutor prove to a jury all facts legally essential to the punishment. Under the dissenters' alternative, he has no such right. That should be the end of the matter.

Petitioner was sentenced to prison for more than three years beyond what the law allowed for the crime to which he confessed, on the basis of a disputed finding that he had acted with "deliberate cruelty." The Framers would not have thought it too much to demand that, before depriving a man of three more years of his liberty, the State should suffer the modest inconvenience of submitting its accusation to "the unanimous suffrage of twelve of his equals and neighbours," 4 Blackstone, Commentaries, at 343, rather than a lone employee of the State.

The judgment of the Washington Court of Appeals is reversed, and the case is remanded for further proceedings not inconsistent with this opinion.

Justice O'CONNOR, with whom Justice BREYER joins, and with whom Chief Justice REHNQUIST and Justice KENNEDY join as to all but Part IV-B, dissenting.

The legacy of today's opinion, whether intended or not, will be the consolidation of sentencing power in the State and Federal Judiciaries. The Court says to Congress and state legislatures: If you want to constrain the sentencing discretion of judges and bring some uniformity to sentencing, it will cost you — dearly. Congress and States, faced with the burdens imposed by the extension of *Apprendi* to the present context, will either trim or eliminate altogether their Sentencing Guidelines schemes and, with them, 20 years of sentencing reform. The "effect" of today's decision will be greater judicial discretion and less uniformity in sentencing. Because I find it implausible that the Framers would have considered such a result to be required by the Due Process Clause or the Sixth Amendment, and because the practical consequences of today's decision may be disastrous, I respectfully dissent.

I

One need look no further than the history leading up to and following the enactment of Washington's guidelines scheme to appreciate the damage that today's decision will cause. Prior to 1981, Washington, like most other States and the Federal Government, employed an indeterminate sentencing scheme. Sentencing judges, in conjunction with parole boards, had virtually unfettered discretion to sentence defendants to prison terms falling anywhere within the statutory range, including probation — i.e., no jail sentence at all.

This system of unguided discretion inevitably resulted in severe disparities in sentences received and served by defendants committing the same offense and having similar criminal histories.

To counteract these trends, the state legislature passed the Sentencing Reform Act of 1981. The Act had the laudable purposes of "making the criminal justice system accountable to the public," and "ensur[ing] that the punishment for a criminal offense is proportionate to the seriousness of the offense . . . [and] commensurate with the punishment imposed on others committing similar offenses." The Act neither increased any of the statutory sentencing ranges for the three types of felonies, nor reclassified any substantive offenses. It merely placed meaningful constraints on discretion to sentence offenders within the statutory ranges, and eliminated parole. There is thus no evidence that the legislature was attempting to manipulate the statutory elements of criminal offenses or to circumvent the procedural protections of the Bill of Rights. Rather, lawmakers were trying to bring some much-needed uniformity, transparency, and accountability to an otherwise "'labyrinthine' sentencing and corrections system that 'lacked any principle except unguided discretion.'"

II

Far from disregarding principles of due process and the jury trial right, as the majority today suggests, Washington's reform has served them. Before passage of the Act, a defendant charged with second degree kidnaping, like petitioner, had no idea whether he would receive a 10-year sentence or probation. The ultimate sentencing determination could turn as much on the idiosyncrasies of a particular judge as on the specifics of the defendant's crime or background. A defendant did not know what facts, if any, about his offense or his history would be considered relevant by the sentencing judge or by the parole board. After passage of the Act, a defendant charged with second degree kidnaping knows what his presumptive sentence will be; he has a good idea of the types of factors that a sentencing judge can and will consider when deciding whether to sentence him outside that range; he is guaranteed meaningful appellate review to protect against an arbitrary sentence. Criminal defendants still face the same statutory maximum sentences, but they now at least know, much more than before, the real consequences of their actions.

Washington's move to a system of guided discretion has served equal protection principles as well. Over the past 20 years, there has been a substantial reduction in racial disparity in sentencing across the State.

The majority does not, because it cannot, disagree that determinate sentencing schemes, like Washington's, serve important constitutional values. Thus, the majority says: "this case is not about whether determinate sentencing is constitutional, only about how it can be implemented in a way that respects the Sixth Amendment." But extension of *Apprendi* to the present context will impose significant costs on a legislature's determination that a particular fact, not historically an element, warrants a higher sentence. While not a constitutional prohibition on guidelines schemes, the majority's decision today exacts a substantial constitutional tax.

IV

The consequences of today's decision will be as far reaching as they are disturbing. Washington's sentencing system is by no means unique. Numerous other States have enacted guidelines systems, as has the Federal Government. Today's decision casts constitutional doubt over them all and, in so doing, threatens an untold number of criminal judgments. Every sentence imposed under such guidelines in cases currently pending on direct appeal is in jeopardy. And, despite the fact that we hold in Schriro v. Summerlin that *Ring* (and a fortiori *Apprendi*) does not apply retroactively on habeas review, all criminal sentences imposed under the federal and state guidelines since *Apprendi* was decided in 2000 arguably remain open to collateral attack.

The practical consequences for trial courts, starting today, will be equally unsettling: How are courts to mete out guidelines sentences? Do courts apply the guidelines as to mitigating factors, but not as to aggravating factors? Do they jettison the guidelines altogether? The Court ignores the havoc it is about to wreak on trial courts across the country.

What I have feared most has now come to pass: Over 20 years of sentencing reform are all but lost, and tens of thousands of criminal judgments are in jeopardy. I respectfully dissent.

Justice KENNEDY, with whom Justice BREYER joins, dissenting.

The majority opinion does considerable damage to our laws and to the administration of the criminal justice system for all the reasons well stated in Justice O'Connor's dissent, plus one more: The Court, in my respectful submission, disregards the fundamental principle under our constitutional system that different branches of government "converse with each other on matters of vital common interest."

Sentencing guidelines are a prime example of this collaborative process. Dissatisfied with the wide disparity in sentencing, participants in the criminal justice system, including judges, pressed for legislative reforms. In response, legislators drew from these participants' shared experiences and enacted measures to correct the problems.

[T]he Constitution does not prohibit the dynamic and fruitful dialogue between the judicial and legislative branches of government that has marked sentencing reform on both the state and the federal levels for more than 20 years. I dissent.

Justice BREYER, with whom Justice O'CONNOR joins, dissenting.

The majority ignores the adverse consequences inherent in its conclusion. As a result of the majority's rule, sentencing must now take one of three forms, each of which risks either impracticality, unfairness, or harm to the jury trial right the majority purports to strengthen.

A first option for legislators is to create a simple, pure or nearly pure "charge offense" or "determinate" sentencing system. In such a system, an indictment would charge a few facts which, taken together, constitute a crime, such as robbery. Robbery would carry a single sentence, say, five years' imprisonment. And every person convicted of robbery would receive that sentence—just as, centuries ago, everyone convicted of almost any serious crime was sentenced to death.

Such a system assures uniformity, but at intolerable costs. First, simple determinate sentencing systems impose identical punishments on people who committed their crimes in very different ways. When dramatically different conduct ends up being punished the same way, an injustice has taken place. Simple determinate sentencing has the virtue of treating like cases alike, but it simultaneously fails to treat different cases differently.

Second, in a world of statutorily fixed mandatory sentences for many crimes, determinate sentencing gives tremendous power to prosecutors to manipulate sentences through their choice of charges. Prosecutors can simply charge, or threaten to charge, defendants with crimes bearing higher mandatory sentences. Defendants, knowing that they will not have a chance to argue for a lower sentence in front of a judge, may plead to charges that they might otherwise contest. Considering that most criminal cases do not go to trial and resolution by plea bargaining is the norm, the rule of *Apprendi*, to the extent it results in a return to determinate sentencing, threatens serious unfairness.

A second option for legislators is to return to a system of indeterminate sentencing. Under indeterminate systems, the length of the sentence is entirely or almost entirely within the discretion of the judge or of the parole board, which typically has broad power to decide when to release a prisoner.

When such systems were in vogue, they were criticized, and rightly so, for producing unfair disparities, including race-based disparities, in the punishment of similarly situated defendants. The length of time a person spent in prison appeared to depend on "what the judge ate for breakfast" on the day of sentencing, on which judge you got, or on other factors that should not have made a difference to the length of the sentence. And under such a system, the judge could vary the sentence greatly based upon his findings about how the defendant had committed the crime — findings that might not have been made by a "preponderance of the evidence," much less "beyond a reasonable doubt."

Returning to such a system would diminish the "'reason'" the majority claims it is trying to uphold. It also would do little to "ensure [the] control" of what the majority calls "the peopl[e,]" i.e., the jury, "in the judiciary," since "the people" would only decide the defendant's guilt, a finding with no effect on the duration of the sentence. While "the judge's authority to sentence" would formally derive from the jury's verdict, the jury would exercise little or no control over the sentence itself.

A third option is that which the Court seems to believe legislators will in fact take. That is the option of retaining structured schemes that attempt to punish similar conduct similarly and different conduct differently, but modifying them to conform to *Apprendi*'s dictates. Judges would be able to depart downward from presumptive sentences upon finding that mitigating factors were present, but would not be able to depart upward unless the prosecutor charged the aggravating fact to a jury and proved it beyond a reasonable doubt. It is therefore worth exploring how this option could work in practice, as well as the assumptions on which it depends.

This option can be implemented in one of two ways. The first way would be for legislatures to subdivide each crime into a list of complex crimes, each of which would be defined to include commonly found sentencing factors such as drug quantity, type of victim, presence of violence, degree of injury, use of gun, and so on.

This possibility is, of course, merely a highly calibrated form of the "pure charge" system . . . [a]nd it suffers from some of the same defects. The prosecutor, through control of the precise charge, controls the punishment, thereby marching the sentencing system directly away from, not toward, one important guideline goal: rough uniformity of punishment for those who engage in roughly the same real criminal conduct.

The second way to make sentencing guidelines *Apprendi*-compliant would be to require at least two juries for each defendant whenever aggravating facts are present: one jury to determine guilt of the crime charged, and an additional jury to try the disputed facts that, if found, would aggravate the sentence. Our experience with bifurcated trials in the capital punishment context suggests that requiring them for run-of-the-mill sentences would be costly, both in money and in judicial time and resources.

Efforts to tie real punishment to real conduct are not new. They are embodied in well-established pre-guidelines sentencing practices — practices under which a judge, looking at a presentence report, would seek to tailor the sentence in significant part to fit the criminal conduct in which the offender actually engaged.

In these and other ways, the two-jury system would work a radical change in pre-existing criminal law. It is not surprising that this Court has never previously suggested that the Constitution — outside the unique context of the death penalty — might require bifurcated jury-based sentencing. And it is the impediment the Court's holding poses to legislative efforts to achieve that greater systematic fairness that casts doubt on its constitutional validity.

Is there a fourth option? Perhaps. Congress and state legislatures might, for example, rewrite their criminal codes, attaching astronomically high sentences to each crime, followed by long lists of mitigating facts, which, for the most part, would consist of the absence of aggravating facts.

Taken together these three sets of considerations, concerning consequences, concerning history, concerning institutional reliance, leave me where I was in *Apprendi*, i.e., convinced that the Court is wrong. Until now, I would have thought the Court might have limited *Apprendi* so that its underlying principle would not undo sentencing reform efforts. Today's case dispels that illusion.

Although the individual justices remained divided on the wisdom and applicability of *Apprendi*, the case continued to have a dramatic impact on sentencing schemes throughout the country. *Blakely* led to the invalidation and revision of state sentencing schemes. Next in the line of fire were the Federal Sentencing Guidelines.

The Sentencing Guidelines establish base sentencing levels for offenses and require courts to enhance those sentences based on facts found by the sentencing judges, not juries. In United States v. Booker, the Supreme Court examined whether the federal sentencing scheme also ran afoul of defendants' right to be sentenced only on those facts (other than a prior conviction) that have been pleaded and proved to a jury. In a deeply divided decision, Justice Stevens delivered the opinion of the Court, in part, concluding that the Sixth Amendment, as construed in *Blakely*, applies to the Federal Sentencing Guidelines. Justice Breyer delivered the opinion of the

Court regarding the appropriate remedy that should be administered given that the Sentencing Guidelines, as enacted, did not comply with *Apprendi*'s requirements. Justice Ginsburg was the only justice in the majority in both opinions. She voted with Justice Stevens's majority opinion in finding that the principles of *Apprendi* apply to the Federal Sentencing Guidelines, but she joined Justice Breyer holding that the remedy is to make the guidelines advisory and not mandatory.

UNITED STATES v. BOOKER

543 U.S. 220 (2005)

STEVENS, J., delivered the opinion of the Court in part, in which SCALIA, SOUTER, THOMAS, and GINSBURG, JJ., joined.

The question presented . . . is whether an application of the Federal Sentencing Guidelines violated the Sixth Amendment. We hold that [the lower] courts correctly concluded that the Sixth Amendment as construed in *Blakely* does apply to the Sentencing Guidelines. In a separate opinion authored by Justice Breyer, the Court concludes that in light of this holding, two provisions of the Sentencing Reform Act of 1984 (SRA) that have the effect of making the Guidelines mandatory must be invalidated in order to allow the statute to operate in a manner consistent with congressional intent.

I

Respondent Booker was charged with possession with intent to distribute at least 50 grams of cocaine base (crack). Having heard evidence that he had 92.5 grams in his duffel bag, the jury found him guilty of violating 21 U.S.C. §841(a)(1). That statute prescribes a minimum sentence of 10 years in prison and a maximum sentence of life for that offense.

Based upon Booker's criminal history and the quantity of drugs found by the jury, the Sentencing Guidelines required the District Court Judge to select a "base" sentence of not less than 210 nor more than 262 months in prison. The judge, however, held a post-trial sentencing proceeding and concluded by a preponderance of the evidence that Booker had possessed an additional 566 grams of crack and that he was guilty of obstructing justice. Those findings mandated that the judge select a sentence between 360 months and life imprisonment; the judge imposed a sentence at the low end of the range. Thus, instead of the sentence of 21 years and 10 months that the judge could have imposed on the basis of the facts proved to the jury beyond a reasonable doubt, Booker received a 30-year sentence.

[T]he Government asks us to determine whether our *Apprendi* line of cases applies to the Sentencing Guidelines, and if so, what portions of the Guidelines remain in effect.

II

It has been settled throughout our history that the Constitution protects every criminal defendant "against conviction except upon proof beyond a reasonable doubt of every fact necessary to constitute the crime with which he is charged." It is equally clear that the "Constitution gives a criminal defendant the right to demand that a jury find him guilty of all the elements of the crime with which he is charged." These basic precepts, firmly rooted in the common law, have provided the basis for recent decisions interpreting modern criminal statutes and sentencing procedures.

In Apprendi v. New Jersey (2000), [t]his Court set aside the enhanced sentence. We held: "Other than the fact of a prior conviction, any fact that increases the penalty for a crime beyond the prescribed statutory maximum must be submitted to a jury, and proved beyond a reasonable doubt." The fact that New Jersey labeled the hate crime a "sentence enhancement" rather than a separate criminal act was irrelevant for constitutional purposes.

In Blakely v. Washington (2004), we dealt with a determinate sentencing scheme similar to the Federal Sentencing Guidelines. The application of Washington's sentencing scheme violated the defendant's right to have the jury find the existence of "'any particular fact'" that the law makes essential to his punishment. That right is implicated whenever a judge seeks to impose a sentence that is not solely based on "facts reflected in the jury verdict or admitted by the defendant."

As the dissenting opinions in *Blakely* recognized, there is no distinction of constitutional significance between the Federal Sentencing Guidelines and the Washington procedures at issue in that case. This conclusion rests on the premise, common to both systems, that the relevant sentencing rules are mandatory and impose binding requirements on all sentencing judges.

If the Guidelines as currently written could be read as merely advisory provisions that recommended, rather than required, the selection of particular sentences in response to differing sets of facts, their use would not implicate the Sixth Amendment.

The Guidelines as written, however, are not advisory; they are mandatory and binding on all judges.

The availability of a departure in specified circumstances does not avoid the constitutional issue, just as it did not in *Blakely* itself. The Guidelines permit departures from the prescribed sentencing range in cases in which the judge "finds that there exists an aggravating or mitigating circumstance of a kind, or to a degree, not adequately taken into consideration by the Sentencing Commission in formulating the guidelines that should result in a sentence different from that described." At first glance, one might believe that the ability of a district judge to depart from the Guidelines means that she is bound only by the statutory maximum. Were this the case, there would be no *Apprendi* problem. Importantly, however, departures are not available in every case, and in fact are unavailable in most. In most cases, as a matter of law, the Commission will have adequately taken all relevant factors into account, and no departure will be legally permissible. In those instances, the judge is bound to impose a sentence within the Guidelines range. It was for this reason that we rejected a similar argument in *Blakely*, holding that although the Washington statute allowed the judge to impose a sentence outside the sentencing range for "'substantial and compelling reasons,'" that exception was not available for Blakely himself.

It is quite true that once determinate sentencing had fallen from favor, American judges commonly determined facts justifying a choice of a heavier sentence on account of the manner in which particular defendants acted. In 1986, however, our own cases first recognized a new trend in the legislative regulation of sentencing when we considered the significance of facts selected by legislatures that not only authorized, or even mandated, heavier sentences than would otherwise have been imposed, but increased the range of sentences possible for the underlying crime. Provisions for such enhancements of the permissible sentencing range reflected growing and wholly justified legislative concern about the proliferation and variety of drug crimes and their frequent identification with firearms offences.

The effect of the increasing emphasis on facts that enhanced sentencing ranges, however, was to increase the judge's power and diminish that of the jury. It became the judge, not the jury, who determined the upper limits of sentencing, and the facts determined were not required to be raised before trial or proved by more than a preponderance.

As the enhancements became greater, the jury's finding of the underlying crime became less significant. The new sentencing practice forced the Court to address the question how the right of jury trial could be preserved, in a meaningful way guaranteeing that the jury would still stand between the individual and the power of the government under the new sentencing regime.

All of the foregoing support our conclusion that our holding in *Blakely* applies to the Sentencing Guidelines. We recognize . . . that in some cases jury factfinding may impair the most expedient and efficient sentencing of defendants. But the interest in fairness and reliability protected by the right to a jury trial — a common-law right that defendants enjoyed for centuries and that is now enshrined in the Sixth Amendment — has always outweighed the interest in concluding trials swiftly.

Justice BREYER delivered the opinion of the Court in part.[5]

The first question that the Government has presented in these cases is the following: "Whether the Sixth Amendment is violated by the imposition of an enhanced sentence under the United States Sentencing Guidelines based

---

5. The Chief Justice, Justice O'Connor, Justice Kennedy, and Justice Ginsburg join this opinion. [Footnote by the Court.]

on the sentencing judge's determination of a fact (other than a prior conviction) that was not found by the jury or admitted by the defendant." The Court, in an opinion by Justice Stevens, answers this question in the affirmative.

We here turn to the second question presented, a question that concerns the remedy. We answer the remedial question by looking to legislative intent.

One approach, that of Justice Stevens' dissent, would retain the Sentencing Act (and the Guidelines) as written, but would engraft onto the existing system today's Sixth Amendment "jury trial" requirement. The addition would change the Guidelines by preventing the sentencing court from increasing a sentence on the basis of a fact that the jury did not find (or that the offender did not admit).

The other approach, which we now adopt, would (through severance and excision of two provisions) make the Guidelines system advisory while maintaining a strong connection between the sentence imposed and the offender's real conduct — a connection important to the increased uniformity of sentencing that Congress intended its Guidelines system to achieve.

Several considerations convince us that, were the Court's constitutional requirement added onto the Sentencing Act as currently written, the requirement would so transform the scheme that Congress created that Congress likely would not have intended the Act as so modified to stand.

[T]he sentencing statutes, read to include the Court's Sixth Amendment requirement, would create a system far more complex than Congress could have intended.

Application of these criteria indicates that we must sever and excise two specific statutory provisions: the provision that requires sentencing courts to impose a sentence within the applicable Guidelines range (in the absence of circumstances that justify a departure), and the provision that sets forth standards of review on appeal, including de novo review of departures from the applicable Guidelines range. With these two sections excised, the remainder of the Act satisfies the Court's constitutional requirements.

The remainder of the Act "function[s] independently." Without the "mandatory" provision, the Act nonetheless requires judges to take account of the Guidelines together with other sentencing goals.

In our view, it is more consistent with Congress' likely intent in enacting the Sentencing Reform Act (1) to preserve important elements of that system while severing and excising two provisions than (2) to maintain all provisions of the Act and engraft today's constitutional requirement onto that statutory scheme.

Ours, of course, is not the last word: The ball now lies in Congress' court. The National Legislature is equipped to devise and install, long term, the sentencing system, compatible with the Constitution, that Congress judges best for the federal system of justice.

Booker marked the end of mandatory Federal Sentencing Guidelines. Post-*Booker*, such guidelines are only advisory. The Supreme Court and lower courts continue to struggle over what it means for the Sentencing Guidelines to be advisory and not mandatory. In *Booker*, the Court held that the sentence must be "reasonable." However, the Court then slowly articulated the standards to determine whether a sentence is reasonable. In Rita v. United States, 551 U.S. 338 (2007), the Supreme Court began by holding that sentences falling within the advisory guidelines are presumptively reasonable.

Then, in Gall v. United States, 552 U.S. 38 (2007), the Supreme Court has held in an opinion authored by Justice Stevens that appellate courts must give great deference to the sentencing court's decision to impose a sentence outside the range of the guidelines. When deciding to depart from the guidelines range, a trial court need not show "extraordinary" circumstances or employ a rigid mathematical approach. Rather, after correctly calculating the applicable guidelines range, the sentencing court should base its sentence on all of the relevant factors in the case (as set forth in 18 U.S.C. §3553(a)) and determine whether it wants to deviate from the guidelines and, if so, by how much. In reviewing the sentencing court's determination for reasonableness, the appellate court must first ensure that the sentencing court made no significant procedural errors and then consider the sentence under an abuse-of-discretion standard. Using this approach, the Supreme Court held that it was reasonable for the sentencing judge to depart from a guidelines sentence of 30 to 37 months for Brian Gall to a sentence of probation. Gall was a college student who voluntarily withdrew from a conspiracy to distribute the drug ecstasy, turned his life around, and pled guilty.

In a companion case, Kimbrough v. United States, 552 U.S. 85 (2007), the Supreme Court held that a sentencing judge may depart from the Sentencing Guidelines if he or she disagrees with the guidelines' approach of imposing significantly higher sentences for the possession of crack cocaine. As Justice Ginsburg noted in her opinion, the 100-to-1 ratio imposed for the possession of crack rather than powder cocaine "fails to meet the sentencing objectives set forth by Congress." The crack/powder sentencing differential "fosters disrespect for and lack of confidence in the criminal justice system" and has had a significant impact on the sentencing of black offenders. Derrick Kimbrough was facing a guidelines sentence of 19 to 22.5 years in prison for possessing more than 50 grams of crack cocaine. Had he possessed the equivalent amount of powder cocaine, his guidelines range would have been 8 to 9 years. The trial judge found that a sentence of 15 years in prison was "clearly long enough" to accomplish the goals of sentencing set forth in §3553(a).

Federal sentencing today is governed by the sentencing judge's evaluation of a sentence under 18 U.S.C. §3553(a). It provides that a federal offender's sentence should be based on:

> (1) the nature and circumstances of the offense and the history of the defendant;

(2) the need for the sentence imposed —

   (A) to reflect the seriousness of the offense, to promote respect for the law, and to provide just punishment for the offense;

   (B) to afford adequate deterrence to criminal conduct;

   (C) to protect the public from future crimes of the defendant;

   (D) to provide the defendant with needed educational or vocational training, medical care, or other correctional treatment in the most effective manner;

(3) the kinds of sentences available;

(4) [the applicable sentencing guidelines];

(5) any pertinent policy statement . . . ;

(6) the need to avoid unwarranted sentence disparities . . . ; and

(7) the need to provide restitution to any victims of the offense.

Great deference is given to the sentencing court as long as the judge complies with the terms of 18 U.S.C. §3553a. The appellate courts can strike down a sentence for being too excessive. However, unless the government cross-appeals, the appellate court cannot increase a sentence even if it believes that it was plainly wrong. In Greenlaw v. United States, 564 U.S. 237 (2008), the Court held that it was up to the parties to frame the issues on appeal and the court will not "sally forth each day looking for wrongs to right." By reaching this result, the Supreme Court made it less risky for defendants to appeal their federal sentences.

As for state determinative sentencing laws, the Court has also made it clear that sentencing schemes that allow trial judges to impose sentences in a higher sentencing category than supported by a jury's verdict or a defendant's guilty plea are invalid under *Apprendi* and *Blakely*, regardless of how those categories are structured. For instance, in Cunningham v. California, 549 U.S. 270 (2007), the Supreme Court struck down California's determinative sentencing scheme.

In recent years, the Court limited the impact of *Apprendi* by holding that its ruling does not extend to judges deciding facts that will determine whether a defendant receives a consecutive or concurrent sentence. In Oregon v. Ice (2009), Justice Ginsburg, writing for a 5-4 majority, held that the historical practice of having judges decide whether sentences will be consecutive or concurrent does not violate the Sixth Amendment.

Yet the Court still remains very committed to *Apprendi*. In 2012, the Court held in Southern Union Co. v. United States, 132 S. Ct. 2344 (2012), that *Apprendi* applies to the imposition of criminal fines. Except in petty offenses, a jury must find the predicate facts to support the imposition of criminal fines.

Overall, the *Apprendi* revolution has had a dramatic impact on state and federal sentencing laws. The sentencing pendulum has swung back toward indeterminate sentencing schemes that give broader discretion to sentencing judges and thus do not require jury determinations regarding the facts that the court uses to make some of its sentencing decisions.

C.   EIGHTH AMENDMENT: WHEN DOES A SENTENCE CONSTITUTE CRUEL AND UNUSUAL PUNISHMENT?

In addition to statutory limits on sentences and the Sixth Amendment requirements of *Apprendi* and its progeny, the Eighth Amendment prohibits "cruel and unusual punishment" and "excessive fines." The standard for what constitutes cruel and unusual punishment is one of proportionality. Instead of looking at the manner in which punishment is imposed, as some justices would favor, the current approach to determining whether a sentence constitutes cruel and unusual punishment involves determining whether the sentence "fits the crime." The Supreme Court developed this standard in two cases: Rummell v. Estelle, 445 U.S. 263 (1980), and Solem v. Helm, 463 U.S. 277 (1983).

In Rummell v. Estelle, the defendant was sentenced, under the state's recidivist statute, to life imprisonment with the possibility of parole in 12 years for his third felony: obtaining $120.75 by false pretenses. Rummell's two prior felony convictions involved fraudulent use of a credit card to obtain $80 and passing a forged check in the amount of $28.36. The Supreme Court, in a decision authored by Justice Rehnquist, held that Rummell's sentence did not amount to cruel and unusual punishment.

Three years later, the Court reexamined the issue in Solem v. Helm and articulated its standard for determining whether a sentence constitutes cruel and unusual punishment.

1.   Determining When a Sentence Is Proportional

SOLEM v. HELM
463 U.S. 277 (1983)

Justice POWELL delivered the opinion of the Court.

The issue presented is whether the Eighth Amendment proscribes a life sentence without possibility of parole for a seventh nonviolent felony.

I

By 1975 the State of South Dakota had convicted respondent Jerry Helm of six nonviolent felonies. In 1964, 1966, and 1969 Helm was convicted of third-degree burglary. In 1972 he was convicted of obtaining money under false pretenses. In 1973 he was convicted of grand larceny. And in 1975 he was convicted of third-offense driving while intoxicated. The record contains no details about the circumstances of any of these offenses, except that they were all nonviolent, none was a crime against a person, and alcohol was a contributing factor in each case.

In 1979 Helm was charged with uttering a "no account" check for $100. Ordinarily the maximum punishment for uttering a "no account" check would have been five years' imprisonment in the state penitentiary and a $5,000 fine. As a result of his criminal record, however, Helm was subject to South Dakota's recidivist statute: "When a defendant has been convicted of at least three prior convictions in addition to the principal felony, the sentence for the principal felony shall be enhanced to the sentence for a Class 1 felony."

The maximum penalty for a "Class 1 felony" was life imprisonment in the state penitentiary and a $25,000 fine. The Governor is authorized to pardon prisoners, or to commute their sentences, S. D. Const., Art. IV, §3, but no other relief from sentence is available even to a rehabilitated prisoner.

Immediately after accepting Helm's guilty plea, the South Dakota Circuit Court sentenced Helm to life imprisonment. The Court of Appeals examined the nature of Helm's offenses, the nature of his sentence, and the sentence he could have received in other States for the same offense. It concluded, on the basis of this examination, that Helm's sentence was "grossly disproportionate to the nature of the offense."

We granted certiorari to consider the Eighth Amendment question presented by this case.

II

The Eighth Amendment declares: "Excessive bail shall not be required, nor excessive fines imposed, nor cruel and unusual punishments inflicted." The final clause prohibits not only barbaric punishments, but also sentences that are disproportionate to the crime committed.

A

The principle that a punishment should be proportionate to the crime is deeply rooted and frequently repeated in common-law jurisprudence. In 1215 three chapters of Magna Carta were devoted to the rule that "amercements" [fines] may not be excessive. When prison sentences became the normal criminal sanctions, the common law recognized that these, too, must be proportional.

When the Framers of the Eighth Amendment adopted the language of the English Bill of Rights, they also adopted the English principle of proportionality.

B

The constitutional principle of proportionality has been recognized explicitly in this Court for almost a century. In the leading case of Weems v. United States (1910), the defendant had been convicted of falsifying a public document and sentenced to 15 years [of] hard labor in chains and permanent civil disabilities. The Court noted that "it is a precept of justice that punishment for crime should be graduated and proportioned to offense," and held that the sentence violated the Eighth Amendment.

Most recently, the Court has applied the principle of proportionality to hold capital punishment excessive in certain circumstances. Enmund v. Florida (1982) (death penalty excessive for felony murder when defendant did not take life, attempt to take life, or intend that a life be taken or that lethal force be used).

III

A

When sentences are reviewed under the Eighth Amendment, courts should be guided by objective factors that our cases have recognized. First, we look to the gravity of the offense and the harshness of the penalty.

Second, it may be helpful to compare the sentences imposed on other criminals in the same jurisdiction. If more serious crimes are subject to the same penalty, or to less serious penalties, that is some indication that the punishment at issue may be excessive.

Third, courts may find it useful to compare the sentences imposed for commission of the same crime in other jurisdictions.

In sum, a court's proportionality analysis under the Eighth Amendment should be guided by objective criteria, including (i) the gravity of the offense and the harshness of the penalty; (ii) the sentences imposed on other criminals in the same jurisdiction; and (iii) the sentences imposed for commission of the same crime in other jurisdictions.

IV

It remains to apply the analytical framework established by our prior decisions to the case before us.

A

Helm's crime was "one of the most passive felonies a person could commit. It involved neither violence nor threat of violence to any person. The $100 face value of Helm's "no account" check was not trivial, but neither was it a large amount. One hundred dollars was less than half the amount South Dakota required for a felonious theft. It is easy to see why such a crime is viewed by society as among the less serious offenses.

Helm, of course, was not charged simply with uttering a "no account" check, but also with being a habitual offender. And a State is justified in punishing a recidivist more severely than it punishes a first offender. Helm's status, however, cannot be considered in the abstract. His prior offenses, although classified as felonies, were all relatively minor. All were nonviolent and none was a crime against a person.

Helm's present sentence is life imprisonment without possibility of parole. Barring executive clemency, Helm will spend the rest of his life in the state penitentiary. This sentence is far more severe than the life sentence we considered in Rummel v. Estelle. Rummel was likely to have been eligible for parole within 12 years of his initial confinement, a fact on which the Court relied heavily. Helm's sentence is the most severe punishment that the State could have imposed on any criminal for any crime. Only capital punishment, a penalty not authorized in South Dakota when Helm was sentenced, exceeds it.

We next consider the sentences that could be imposed on other criminals in the same jurisdiction. When Helm was sentenced, a South Dakota court was required to impose a life sentence for murder, and was authorized to impose a life sentence for treason, first-degree manslaughter, first-degree arson, and kidnaping, No other crime was punishable so severely on the first offense.

Finally, we compare the sentences imposed for commission of the same crime in other jurisdictions. The Court of Appeals found that "Helm could have received a life sentence without parole for his offense in only one other state, Nevada." At the very least, therefore, it is clear that Helm could not have received such a severe sentence in 48 of the 50 States. But even under Nevada law, a life sentence without possibility of parole is merely authorized in these circumstances. We are not advised that any defendant such as Helm, whose prior offenses were so minor, actually has received the maximum penalty in Nevada. It appears that Helm was treated more severely than he would have been in any other State.

B

The State argues that the present case is essentially the same as Rummel v. Estelle, for the possibility of parole in that case is matched by the possibility of executive clemency here. The State reasons that the Governor could commute Helm's sentence to a term of years. We conclude, however, that the South Dakota commutation system is fundamentally different from the parole system that was before us in *Rummel*.

As a matter of law, parole and commutation are different concepts, despite some surface similarities. Parole is a regular part of the rehabilitative process. Assuming good behavior, it is the normal expectation in the vast majority of cases. The law generally specifies when a prisoner will be eligible to be considered for parole, and details the standards and procedures applicable at that time. Thus it is possible to predict, at least to some extent, when parole might be granted. Commutation, on the other hand, is an ad hoc exercise of executive clemency.

The possibility of commutation is nothing more than a hope for "an ad hoc exercise of clemency." It is little different from the possibility of executive clemency that exists in every case in which a defendant challenges his sentence under the Eighth Amendment. Recognition of such a bare possibility would make judicial review under the Eighth Amendment meaningless.

V

The Constitution requires us to examine Helm's sentence to determine if it is proportionate to his crime. Applying objective criteria, we find that Helm has received the penultimate sentence for relatively minor criminal conduct. He has been treated more harshly than other criminals in the State who have committed more serious crimes. He has been treated more harshly than he would have been in any other jurisdiction, with the possible exception of a single State. We conclude that his sentence is significantly disproportionate to his crime, and is therefore prohibited by the Eighth Amendment.

Chief Justice BURGER, with whom Justice WHITE, Justice REHNQUIST, and Justice O'CONNOR join, dissenting.

The controlling law governing this case is crystal clear, but today the Court blithely discards any concept of stare decisis, trespasses gravely on the authority of the states, and distorts the concept of proportionality of punishment by tearing it from its moorings in capital cases. Only three Terms ago, we held in Rummel v. Estelle (1980), that a life sentence imposed after only a third nonviolent felony conviction did not constitute cruel and unusual punishment under the Eighth Amendment. Today, the Court ignores its recent precedent and holds that a life sentence imposed after a seventh felony conviction constitutes cruel and unusual punishment under the Eighth Amendment. Moreover, I reject the fiction that all Helm's crimes were innocuous or nonviolent. Among his felonies were three burglaries and a third conviction for drunken driving. By comparison Rummel was a relatively "model citizen." Although today's holding cannot rationally be reconciled with *Rummel,* the Court does not purport to overrule *Rummel.* I therefore dissent.

Although historians and scholars have disagreed about the Framers' original intentions, the more common view seems to be that the Framers viewed the Cruel and Unusual Punishments Clause as prohibiting the kind of torture meted out during the reign of the Stuarts. Moreover, it is clear that until 1892, over 100 years after the ratification of the Bill of Rights, not a single Justice of this Court even asserted the doctrine adopted for the first time by the Court today. The prevailing view up to now has been that the Eighth Amendment reaches only the mode of punishment and not the length of a sentence of imprisonment. In light of this history, it is disingenuous for the Court blandly to assert that "[the] constitutional principle of proportionality has been recognized explicitly in this Court for almost a century."

This Court has applied a proportionality test only in extraordinary cases, *Weems* being one example and the line of capital cases another. Today's conclusion by five Justices that they are able to say that one offense has less "gravity" than another is nothing other than a bald substitution of individual subjective moral values for those of the legislature.

By asserting the power to review sentences of imprisonment for excessiveness the Court launches into uncharted and unchartable waters. Today it holds that a sentence of life imprisonment, without the possibility of parole, is excessive punishment for a seventh allegedly "nonviolent" felony. How about the eighth "nonviolent" felony? The ninth? The twelfth? Suppose one offense was a simple assault? Or selling liquor to a minor? Or statutory rape? Or price fixing? The permutations are endless and the Court's opinion is bankrupt of realistic guiding principles.

There is a real risk that this holding will flood the appellate courts with cases in which equally arbitrary lines must be drawn.

Indeed, Chief Justice Burger was not far off the mark. Soon after Solem v. Helm, appellate courts became flooded with claims of cruel and unusual punishment. Therefore, it was not surprising when a few years later, the Supreme Court revisited the issue of proportionality review in Harmelin v. Michigan, 501 U.S. 957 (1991).

In *Harmelin*, the Court sought to limit the effects of proportionality review. Justice Scalia, joined by Chief Justice Rehnquist, would have taken the dramatic step of overturning *Solem* and holding, based on Justice Scalia's detailed review of history, that the Eighth Amendment does not require proportionality review. Justice Scalia wrote that Eighth Amendment challenges should be limited to attacks on the mode of punishment: "Throughout the 19th century, state courts interpreting state constitutional provisions with identical or more expansive wording (i.e., 'cruel or unusual') concluded that these provisions did not proscribe disproportionality but only certain modes of punishment." *Id.* at 983. Justice Scalia gave examples of cruel and unusual punishments that would be proscribed, noting in particular the "vicious punishments for treason decreed in the Bloody Assizes (drawing and quartering, burning of women felons, beheading, disembowling, etc.)." Lengthy imprisonment, however, would not be covered.

Justice Kennedy, joined by Justices O'Connor and Souter, wrote the controlling concurrence in the case. On the basis of stare decisis, Justice Kennedy held that the Supreme Court's 80-year jurisprudence of proportionality should govern the outcome of the case. He did not believe, however, that Harmelin's sentence — mandatory life imprisonment without the possibility of parole — was disproportional given the nature of his crime: possessing 672 grams of cocaine. Even though Harmelin had never been convicted for a prior offense, Justice Kennedy held that Harmelin's sentence should be upheld.

Setting forth his view of the Eighth Amendment proportionality review, Justice Kennedy identified four principles that should govern: First, deference should be given to legislatures as to the appropriate sentence for specific crimes. Second, the Eighth Amendment "does not mandate adoption of any one penological theory." Third, "marked divergences both in underlying theories of sentencing and in the length of prescribed prison terms are the inevitable, often beneficial, result of the federal structure." Finally, proportionality review "should be informed by 'objective factors to the maximum possible extent.'"

With these considerations in mind, Justice Kennedy held that a life sentence for Harmelin's offense was not disproportionate:

> Petitioner was convicted of possession of more than 650 grams (over 1.5 pounds) of cocaine. This amount of pure cocaine has a potential yield of between 32,500 and 65,000 doses. From any standpoint, this crime falls in a different category from the relatively minor, nonviolent crime at issue in *Solem*. Petitioner's suggestion that his crime was nonviolent and victimless is false to the point of absurdity. To the contrary, petitioner's crime threatened to cause grave harm to society.
>
> The severity of petitioner's crime brings his sentence within the constitutional boundaries established by our prior decisions.

Justice Kennedy also wrote that although Harmelin's sentence may have been harsh in comparison to sentences imposed by other jurisdictions for similar crimes,

> intrajurisdictional and interjurisdictional analyses are appropriate only in the rare case in which a threshold comparison of the crime committed and the sentence imposed leads to an inference of gross disproportionality. . . . In light of the gravity of petitioner's offense, a comparison of his crime with his sentence does not give rise to an inference of gross disproportionality, and comparative analysis of his sentence with others in Michigan and across the Nation need not be performed.

Finally, Justice Kennedy wrote that the mandatory nature of Harmelin's sentence did not affect its constitutionality:

> It is beyond question that the legislature "has the power to define criminal punishments without giving the courts any sentencing discretion." Since the beginning of the Republic, Congress and the States have enacted mandatory sentencing schemes. To set aside petitioner's mandatory sentence would require rejection not of the judgment of a single jurist, as in *Solem*, but rather the collective wisdom of the Michigan Legislature and, as a consequence, the Michigan citizenry.[6]

---

6. Justice Kennedy added:

> In asserting the constitutionality of this mandatory sentence, I offer no judgment on its wisdom. Mandatory sentencing schemes can be criticized for depriving judges of the power to exercise individual discretion when remorse and acknowledgment of guilt, or other extenuating facts, present what might seem a compelling case for departure from the maximum. On the other hand, broad and unreviewed discretion exercised by sentencing judges leads to the perception that no clear standards are being applied, and that the rule of law is imperiled by sentences imposed for no discernible reason other than the subjective reactions of the sentencing judge. The debate illustrates that, as noted at the outset, arguments for and against particular sentencing schemes are for legislatures to resolve.

Justices White, Blackmun, and Stevens dissented. First, they contested Justice Scalia's contention that the words "cruel and unusual punishment" apply only to the mode of punishment and do not authorize a proportionality review. They then applied the *Solem* factors and held that, notwithstanding the gravity of Harmelin's offense, his sentence was disproportionate to the offense.

2. Proportionality and Three Strikes Laws

The trend in many states has been to adopt "three strikes" laws that impose particularly long sentences on repeat offenders. For example, California has adopted a "Three Strikes and You're Out" law that requires the court to impose a prison term of 25 years to life on any offender convicted of any felony who has two prior "serious" or "violent" offenses. As constructed, the law has permitted a defendant who had prior felonies for burglary and drug use to be sentenced to 50 years to life for stealing children's videos worth approximately $150 from a Kmart store. *See* Lockyer v. Andrade, 538 U.S. 63 (2003).

In the next case, the Supreme Court applied the *Rummel-Solem-Harmelin* line of cases to determine whether three strikes sentences are constitutional.

EWING v. CALIFORNIA
538 U.S. 11 (2003)

Justice O'CONNOR announced the judgment of the Court and delivered an opinion in which Chief Justice REHNQUIST and Justice KENNEDY join.

In this case, we decide whether the Eighth Amendment prohibits the State of California from sentencing a repeat felon to a prison term of 25 years to life under the State's "Three Strikes and You're Out" law.

I

A

California's three strikes law reflects a shift in the State's sentencing policies toward incapacitating and deterring repeat offenders who threaten the public safety. The law was designed "to ensure longer prison sentences and greater punishment for those who commit a felony and have been previously convicted of serious and/or violent felony offenses."

Between 1993 and 1995, 24 States and the Federal Government enacted three strikes laws. Though the three strikes laws vary from State to State, they share a common goal of protecting the public safety by providing lengthy prison terms for habitual felons.

B

When a defendant is convicted of a felony, and he has previously been convicted of one or more prior felonies defined as "serious" or "violent" in Cal. Penal Code Ann. §§667.5 and 1192.7, sentencing is conducted pursuant to the three strikes law. Prior convictions must be alleged in the charging document, and the defendant has a right to a jury determination that the prosecution has proved the prior convictions beyond a reasonable doubt.

If the defendant has one prior "serious" or "violent" felony conviction, he must be sentenced to "twice the term otherwise provided as punishment for the current felony conviction." If the defendant has two or more prior "serious" or "violent" felony convictions, he must receive "an indeterminate term of life imprisonment." Defendants sentenced to life under the three strikes law become eligible for parole on a date calculated by reference to a "minimum term," which is the greater of (a) three times the term otherwise provided for the current conviction, (b) 25 years, or (c) the term determined by the court pursuant to §1170 for the underlying conviction, including any enhancements.

Under California law, certain offenses may be classified as either felonies or misdemeanors. These crimes are known as "wobblers." Some crimes that would otherwise be misdemeanors become "wobblers" because of the defendant's prior record. For example, petty theft, a misdemeanor, becomes a "wobbler" when the defendant has previously served a prison term for committing specified theft-related crimes. Other crimes, such as grand theft, are "wobblers" regardless of the defendant's prior record. Both types of "wobblers" are triggering offenses under the three strikes law only when they are treated as felonies. Under California law, a "wobbler" is presumptively a felony and "remains a felony except when the discretion is actually exercised" to make the crime a misdemeanor.

In California, prosecutors may exercise their discretion to charge a "wobbler" as either a felony or a misdemeanor. Likewise, California trial courts have discretion to reduce a "wobbler" charged as a felony to a misdemeanor either before preliminary examination or at sentencing to avoid imposing a three strikes sentence.

California trial courts can also vacate allegations of prior "serious" or "violent" felony convictions, either on motion by the prosecution or sua sponte. In ruling whether to vacate allegations of prior felony convictions, courts consider whether, "in light of the nature and circumstances of [the defendant's] present felonies and prior serious and/or violent felony convictions, and the particulars of his background, character, and prospects, the defendant may be deemed outside the [three strikes'] scheme's spirit, in whole or in part." Thus, trial courts may avoid imposing a three strikes sentence in two ways: first, by reducing "wobblers" to misdemeanors (which do not qualify as triggering offenses), and second, by vacating allegations of prior "serious" or "violent" felony convictions.

C

On parole from a 9-year prison term, petitioner Gary Ewing walked into the pro shop of the El Segundo Golf Course in Los Angeles County on March 12, 2000. He walked out with three golf clubs, priced at $399 apiece, concealed in his pants leg. A shop employee, whose suspicions were aroused when he observed Ewing limp out of the pro shop, telephoned the police. The police apprehended Ewing in the parking lot.

Ewing is no stranger to the criminal justice system. In 1984, at the age of 22, he pleaded guilty to theft. The court sentenced him to six months in jail (suspended), three years' probation, and a $300 fine. In 1988, he was convicted of felony grand theft auto and sentenced to one year in jail and three years' probation. After Ewing completed probation, however, the sentencing court reduced the crime to a misdemeanor, permitted Ewing to withdraw his guilty plea, and dismissed the case. In 1990, he was convicted of petty theft with a prior and sentenced to 60 days in the county jail and three years' probation. In 1992, Ewing was convicted of battery and sentenced to 30 days in the county jail and two years' summary probation. One month later, he was convicted of theft and sentenced to 10 days in the county jail and 12 months' probation. In January 1993, Ewing was convicted of burglary and sentenced to 60 days in the county jail and one year's summary probation. In February 1993, he was convicted of possessing drug paraphernalia and sentenced to six months in the county jail and three years' probation. In July 1993, he was convicted of appropriating lost property and sentenced to 10 days in the county jail and two years' summary probation. In September 1993, he was convicted of unlawfully possessing a firearm and trespassing and sentenced to 30 days in the county jail and one year's probation.

In October and November 1993, Ewing committed three burglaries and one robbery at a Long Beach, California, apartment complex over a 5-week period. He awakened one of his victims, asleep on her living room sofa, as he tried to disconnect her video cassette recorder from the television in that room. When she screamed, Ewing ran out the front door. On another occasion, Ewing accosted a victim in the mailroom of the apartment complex. Ewing claimed to have a gun and ordered the victim to hand over his wallet. When the victim resisted, Ewing produced a knife and forced the victim back to the apartment itself. While Ewing rifled through the bedroom, the victim fled the apartment screaming for help. Ewing absconded with the victim's money and credit cards.

On December 9, 1993, Ewing was arrested on the premises of the apartment complex for trespassing and lying to a police officer. The knife used in the robbery and a glass cocaine pipe were later found in the back seat of the patrol car used to transport Ewing to the police station. A jury convicted Ewing of first-degree robbery and three counts of residential burglary. Sentenced to nine years and eight months in prison, Ewing was paroled in 1999.

Only 10 months later, Ewing stole the golf clubs at issue in this case. He was charged with, and ultimately convicted of, one count of felony grand theft of personal property in excess of $400. As required by the three strikes law, the prosecutor formally alleged, and the trial court later found, that Ewing had been convicted previously of four serious or violent felonies for the three burglaries and the robbery in the Long Beach apartment complex.

At the sentencing hearing, Ewing asked the court to reduce the conviction for grand theft, a "wobbler" under California law, to a misdemeanor so as to avoid a three strikes sentence. Ewing also asked the trial court to exercise its discretion to dismiss the allegations of some or all of his prior serious or violent felony convictions, again for purposes of avoiding a three strikes sentence.

In the end, the trial judge determined that the grand theft should remain a felony. The court also ruled that the four prior strikes for the three burglaries and the robbery in Long Beach should stand. As a newly convicted felon with two or more "serious" or "violent" felony convictions in his past, Ewing was sentenced under the three strikes law to 25 years to life.

II

A

The Eighth Amendment, which forbids cruel and unusual punishments, contains a "narrow proportionality principle" that "applies to noncapital sentences." Harmelin v. Michigan (1991) (Kennedy, J., concurring in part and concurring in judgment). We have most recently addressed the proportionality principle as applied to terms of years in a series of cases beginning with Rummel v. Estelle. [Justice O'Connor then reviewed Rummel v. Estelle, Solem v. Helm, and Justice Kennedy's controlling opinion in *Harmelin*.]

The proportionality principles in our cases distilled in Justice Kennedy's concurrence guide our application of the Eighth Amendment in the new context that we are called upon to consider.

B

For many years, most States have had laws providing for enhanced sentencing of repeat offenders. Yet between 1993 and 1995, three strikes laws effected a sea change in criminal sentencing throughout the Nation. These laws responded to widespread public concerns about crime by targeting the class of offenders who pose the greatest threat to public safety: career criminals.

Throughout the States, legislatures enacting three strikes laws made a deliberate policy choice that individuals who have repeatedly engaged in serious or violent criminal behavior, and whose conduct has not been deterred by more conventional approaches to punishment, must be isolated from society in order to protect the public safety.

When the California Legislature enacted the three strikes law, it made a judgment that protecting the public safety requires incapacitating criminals who have already been convicted of at least one serious or violent crime. Nothing in the Eighth Amendment prohibits California from making that choice.

California's justification is no pretext. Recidivism is a serious public safety concern in California and throughout the Nation. According to a recent report, approximately 67 percent of former inmates released from state prisons were charged with at least one "serious" new crime within three years of their release.

The State's interest in deterring crime also lends some support to the three strikes law. We have long viewed both incapacitation and deterrence as rationales for recidivism statutes: "[A] recidivist statute['s] . . . primary goals are to deter repeat offenders and, at some point in the life of one who repeatedly commits criminal offenses serious enough to be punished as felonies, to segregate that person from the rest of society for an extended period of time." *Rummel.* Four years after the passage of California's three strikes law, the recidivism rate of parolees returned to prison for the commission of a new crime dropped by nearly 25 percent.

To be sure, California's three strikes law has sparked controversy. Critics have doubted the law's wisdom, cost-efficiency, and effectiveness in reaching its goals. This criticism is appropriately directed at the legislature, which has primary responsibility for making the difficult policy choices that underlie any criminal sentencing scheme. We do not sit as a "superlegislature" to second-guess these policy choices. It is enough that the State of California has a reasonable basis for believing that dramatically enhanced sentences for habitual felons "advances the goals of [its] criminal justice system in any substantial way."

III

Against this backdrop, we consider Ewing's claim that his three strikes sentence of 25 years to life is unconstitutionally disproportionate to his offense of "shoplifting three golf clubs." We first address the gravity of the offense compared to the harshness of the penalty. At the threshold, we note that Ewing incorrectly frames the issue. The gravity of his offense was not merely "shoplifting three golf clubs." Rather, Ewing was convicted of felony grand theft for stealing nearly $1,200 worth of merchandise after previously having been convicted of at least two "violent" or "serious" felonies.

In weighing the gravity of Ewing's offense, we must place on the scales not only his current felony, but also his long history of felony recidivism. Any other approach would fail to accord proper deference to the policy judgments that find expression in the legislature's choice of sanctions. In imposing a three strikes sentence, the State's interest is not merely punishing the offense of conviction, or the "triggering" offense: "It is in addition the interest . . . in dealing in a harsher manner with those who by repeated criminal acts have shown that they are simply incapable of conforming to the norms of society as established by its criminal law."

Ewing's sentence is justified by the State's public-safety interest in incapacitating and deterring recidivist felons, and amply supported by his own long, serious criminal record.

We hold that Ewing's sentence of 25 years to life in prison, imposed for the offense of felony grand theft under the three strikes law, is not grossly disproportionate and therefore does not violate the Eighth Amendment's prohibition on cruel and unusual punishments.

Justice SCALIA, concurring in the judgment.

In my concurring opinion in Harmelin v. Michigan (1991), I concluded that the Eighth Amendment's prohibition of "cruel and unusual punishments" was aimed at excluding only certain modes of punishment, and was not a "guarantee against disproportionate sentences." Out of respect for the principle of stare decisis, I might nonetheless accept the contrary holding of Solem v. Helm that the Eighth Amendment contains a narrow proportionality principle — if I felt I could intelligently apply it. This case demonstrates why I cannot.

Proportionality — the notion that the punishment should fit the crime — is inherently a concept tied to the penological goal of retribution. "It becomes difficult even to speak intelligently of 'proportionality,' once deterrence and rehabilitation are given significant weight," — not to mention giving weight to the purpose of California's three strikes law: incapacitation. In the present case, the game is up once the plurality has acknowledged that "the Constitution does not mandate adoption of any one penological theory," and that a "sentence can have a variety of justifications, such as incapacitation, deterrence, retribution, or rehabilitation." That acknowledgment having been made, it no longer suffices merely to assess "the gravity of the offense compared to the harshness of the penalty;" that classic description of the proportionality principle (alone and in itself quite resistant to policy-free, legal analysis) now becomes merely the "first" step of the inquiry. Having completed that step (by a discussion which, in all fairness, does not convincingly establish that 25-years-to-life is a "proportionate" punishment for stealing three golf clubs), the plurality must then add an analysis to show that "Ewing's sentence is justified by the State's public-safety interest in incapacitating and deterring recidivist felons."

Which indeed it is — though why that has anything to do with the principle of proportionality is a mystery. Perhaps the plurality should revise its terminology, so that what it reads into the Eighth Amendment is not the unstated proposition that all punishment should be reasonably proportionate to the gravity of the offense, but rather the unstated proposition that all punishment should reasonably pursue the multiple purposes of the criminal law. That formulation would make it clearer than ever, of course, that the plurality is not applying law but evaluating policy.

Justice THOMAS, concurring in the judgment.

I agree with Justice Scalia's view that the proportionality test announced in Solem v. Helm is incapable of judicial application. Even were *Solem's* test perfectly clear, however, I would not feel compelled by stare decisis to apply it. In my view, the Cruel and Unusual Punishments Clause of the Eighth Amendment contains no proportionality principle.

Justice STEVENS, with whom Justices SOUTER, GINSBURG, and BREYER join, dissenting.

"The Eighth Amendment succinctly prohibits 'excessive' sanctions." . . . The absence of a black-letter rule does not disable judges from exercising their discretion in construing the outer limits on sentencing authority that the Eighth Amendment imposes.

Throughout most of the Nation's history—before guideline sentencing became so prevalent—federal and state trial judges imposed specific sentences pursuant to grants of authority that gave them uncabined discretion within broad ranges. It was not unheard of for a statute to authorize a sentence ranging from one year to life, for example. In exercising their discretion, sentencing judges wisely employed a proportionality principle that took into account all of the justifications for punishment—namely, deterrence, incapacitation, retribution and rehabilitation. Likewise, I think it clear that the Eighth Amendment's prohibition of "cruel and unusual punishments" expresses a broad and basic proportionality principle that takes into account all of the justifications for penal sanctions. It is this broad proportionality principle that would preclude reliance on any of the justifications for punishment to support, for example, a life sentence for overtime parking.

Justice BREYER, with whom Justice STEVENS, Justice SOUTER, and Justice GINSBURG join, dissenting.

The constitutional question is whether the "three strikes" sentence imposed by California upon repeat-offender Gary Ewing is "grossly disproportionate" to his crime. The sentence amounts to a real prison term of at least 25 years. The sentence-triggering criminal conduct consists of the theft of three golf clubs priced at a total of $1,197. The offender has a criminal history that includes four felony convictions arising out of three separate burglaries (one armed). In Solem v. Helm, the Court found grossly disproportionate a somewhat longer sentence imposed on a recidivist offender for triggering criminal conduct that was somewhat less severe. In my view, the differences are not determinative, and the Court should reach the same ultimate conclusion here.

Ewing's sentence on its face imposes one of the most severe punishments available upon a recidivist who subsequently engaged in one of the less serious forms of criminal conduct. I do not deny the seriousness of shoplifting, which an amicus curiae tells us costs retailers in the range of $30 billion annually. But consider that conduct in terms of the factors that this Court mentioned in *Solem*—the "harm caused or threatened to the victim or society," the "absolute magnitude of the crime," and the offender's "culpability." In respect to all three criteria, the sentence-triggering behavior here ranks well toward the bottom of the criminal conduct scale.

In a companion case to *Ewing*, Lockyer v. Andrade, 538 U.S. 63 (2003), the Supreme Court denied habeas corpus relief to a criminal defendant who received a sentence of 50 years to life in prison for stealing $153 worth of videotapes from a Kmart store. He received the sentence under California's three strikes law even though he had never committed a violent crime. The Supreme Court, in a 5-4 decision, denied habeas relief on the ground that there was not clearly established law that the sentence was disproportionate.

As *Ewing* and *Andrade* demonstrate, although it is theoretically possible for a defendant sentenced under a three strikes law to claim an Eighth Amendment violation, the task will be very difficult because of the great deference the Court gives to the legislature's determination that a recidivist must face harsh punishment.

3. *Juveniles and Sentencing*

The Eighth Amendment proportionality test is ordinarily a case-by-case analysis. However, in addressing standards for sentencing juveniles, the Court has set forth per se rules striking down certain juvenile sentences as grossly disproportionate. In recognizing that juveniles should not be judged by the same standards as adults, the Court held in Graham v. Florida, 130 S. Ct. 2011 (2010), that it is per se unconstitutional to impose on a juvenile offender the sentence of life without the possibility of parole (LWOP) for non-homicide offenses. In Miller v. Alabama, 132 S. Ct. 2455 (2012), the Court recognized that mandatory LWOP sentences for juveniles, even those convicted of homicide offenses, also violate the Eighth Amendment.

GRAHAM v. FLORIDA

130 S. Ct. 2011 (2010)

Justice KENNEDY delivered the opinion of the Court.

The issue before the Court is whether the Constitution permits a juvenile offender to be sentenced to life in prison without parole for a nonhomicide crime.

I

Petitioner is Terrance Jamar Graham. He was born on January 6, 1987. Graham's parents were addicted to crack cocaine, and their drug use persisted in his early years. Graham was diagnosed with attention deficit hyperactivity disorder in elementary school. He began drinking alcohol and using tobacco at age 9 and smoked marijuana at age 13.

In July 2003, when Graham was age 16, he and three other school-age youths attempted to rob a barbeque restaurant in Jacksonville, Florida. Graham's masked accomplice twice struck the restaurant manager in the back of the head with a metal bar. The restaurant manager required stitches for his head injury. No money was taken.

Graham was arrested for the robbery attempt [and tried as an adult and pled guilty. He was sentenced to a 3-year term of probation, requiring him to spend the first 12 months of his probation in the county jail. He was released on June 25, 2004.]

Less than 6 months later, on the night of December 2, 2004, Graham again was arrested. Graham participated in a home invasion robbery. [He and his two accomplices forcibly entered the home of Carlos Rodriguez and held a pistol to Rodriguez's chest. For the next 30 minutes, the three ransacked the home searching for money.]

The State further alleged that Graham [and his cohorts] later the same evening, attempted a second robbery. When detectives interviewed Graham, he denied involvement in the crimes [and denied knowing his codefendants]. The night that Graham allegedly committed the robbery, he was 34 days short of his 18th birthday.

The trial court held a sentencing hearing. The State recommended that Graham receive 30 years on the armed burglary count and 15 years on the attempted armed robbery count.

After hearing Graham's testimony, the trial court explained the sentence it was about to pronounce:

> Mr. Graham, as I look back on your case, yours is really candidly a sad situation. You had, as far as I can tell, you have quite a family structure. You had a lot of people who wanted to try and help you get your life turned around including the court system, and you had a judge who took the step to try and give you direction through his probation order to give you a chance to get back onto track. And at the time you seemed through your letters that that is exactly what you wanted to do. And I don't know why it is that you threw your life away. I don't know why.
>
> But you did, and that is what is so sad about this today is that you have actually been given a chance to get through this, the original charge, which were very serious charges to begin with. . . . The attempted robbery with a weapon was a very serious charge. . . .
>
> [I]n a very short period of time you were back before the Court on a violation of this probation, and then here you are two years later standing before me, literally—facing a life sentence as to count 1 and up to 15 years as to count 2.
>
> And I don't understand why you would be given such a great opportunity to do something with your life and why you would throw it away. The only thing that I can

rationalize is that you decided that this is how you were going to lead your life and that there is nothing that we can do for you. And as the state pointed out, that this is an escalating pattern of criminal conduct on your part and that we can't help you any further. We can't do anything to deter you. This is the way you are going to lead your life, and I don't know why you are going to. You've made that decision. I have no idea. But, evidently, that is what you decided to do.

So then it becomes a focus, if I can't do anything to help you, if I can't do anything to get you back on the right path, then I have to start focusing on the community and trying to protect the community from your actions. And, unfortunately, that is where we are today is I don't see where I can do anything to help you any further. You've evidently decided this is the direction you're going to take in life, and it's unfortunate that you made that choice.

I have reviewed the statute. I don't see where any further juvenile sanctions would be appropriate. I don't see where any youthful offender sanctions would be appropriate. Given your escalating pattern of criminal conduct, it is apparent to the Court that you have decided that this is the way you are going to live your life and that the only thing I can do now is to try and protect the community from your actions.

The trial court . . . sentenced him to the maximum sentence authorized by law on each charge: life imprisonment for the armed burglary and 15 years for the attempted armed robbery. Because Florida has abolished its parole system, a life sentence gives a defendant no possibility of release unless he is granted executive clemency.

II

The Eighth Amendment states: "Excessive bail shall not be required, nor excessive fines imposed, nor cruel and unusual punishments inflicted." The Cruel and Unusual Punishments Clause prohibits the imposition of inherently barbaric punishments under all circumstances. "[P]unishments of torture," for example, "are forbidden."

For the most part, however, the Court's precedents consider punishments challenged not as inherently barbaric but as disproportionate to the crime. The concept of proportionality is central to the Eighth Amendment. Embodied in the Constitution's ban on cruel and unusual punishments is the "precept of justice that punishment for crime should be graduated and proportioned to [the] offense."

The Court's cases addressing the proportionality of sentences fall within two general classifications. The first involves challenges to the length of term-of-years sentences given all the circumstances in a particular case. The second comprises cases in which the Court implements the proportionality standard by certain categorical restrictions on the death penalty.

In the first classification the Court considers all of the circumstances of the case to determine whether the sentence is unconstitutionally excessive. Under this approach, the Court has held unconstitutional a life without parole sentence for the defendant's seventh nonviolent felony, the crime of passing a worthless check. Solem v. Helm (1983).

The second classification of cases has used categorical rules to define Eighth Amendment standards. With respect to the nature of the offense, the Court has concluded that capital punishment is impermissible for non-homicide crimes against individuals. In cases turning on the characteristics of the offender, the Court has adopted categorical rules prohibiting the death penalty for defendants who committed their crimes before the age of 18, Roper v. Simmons (2005), or whose intellectual functioning is in a low range, Atkins v. Virginia (2002).

III

The analysis begins with objective indicia of national consensus. Six jurisdictions do not allow life without parole sentences for any juvenile offenders. Seven jurisdictions permit life without parole for juvenile offenders, but only for homicide crimes. Thirty-seven States as well as the District of Columbia permit sentences of life without parole for a juvenile nonhomicide offender in some circumstances. Federal law also allows for the possibility of life without parole for offenders as young as 13. Relying on this metric, the State and its amici argue that there is no national consensus against the sentencing practice at issue.

This argument is incomplete and unavailing. "There are measures of consensus other than legislation." Actual sentencing practices are an important part of the Court's inquiry into consensus. [O]nly 12 jurisdictions nationwide in fact impose life without parole sentences on juvenile nonhomicide offenders — and most of those impose the sentence quite rarely — while 26 States as well as the District of Columbia do not impose them despite apparent statutory authorization.

Roper established that because juveniles have lessened culpability they are less deserving of the most severe punishments. As compared to adults, juveniles have a "'lack of maturity and an underdeveloped sense of responsibility'" they "are more vulnerable or susceptible to negative influences and outside pressures, including peer pressure"; and their characters are "not as well formed." A juvenile is not absolved of responsibility for his actions, but his transgression "is not as morally reprehensible as that of an adult."

[A] life without parole sentence for a juvenile defendant . . . "means denial of hope; it means that good behavior and character improvement are immaterial; it means that whatever the future might hold in store for the mind and spirit of [the convict], he will remain in prison for the rest of his days."

Life without parole is an especially harsh punishment for a juvenile. Under this sentence a juvenile offender will on average serve more years and a greater percentage of his life in prison than an adult offender. A 16-year-old and a 75-year-old each sentenced to life without parole receive the same punishment in name only. This reality cannot be ignored.

The penological justifications for the sentencing practice are also relevant to the analysis. With respect to life without parole for juvenile nonhomicide offenders, none of the goals of penal sanctions that have been recognized as legitimate — retribution, deterrence, incapacitation, and rehabilitation, provides an adequate justification.

Retribution is a legitimate reason to punish, but it cannot support the sentence at issue here. Society is entitled to impose severe sanctions on a juvenile nonhomicide offender to express its condemnation of the crime and to seek restoration of the moral imbalance caused by the offense. But "[t]he heart of the retribution rationale is that a criminal sentence must be directly related to the personal culpability of the criminal offender." [R]etribution does not justify imposing the second most severe penalty on the less culpable juvenile nonhomicide offender.

Deterrence does not suffice to justify the sentence either. Roper noted that "the same characteristics that render juveniles less culpable than adults suggest . . . that juveniles will be less susceptible to deterrence." Because juveniles' "lack of maturity and underdeveloped sense of responsibility . . . often result in impetuous and ill-considered actions and decisions," they are less likely to take a possible punishment into consideration when making decisions.

Incapacitation, a third legitimate reason for imprisonment, does not justify the life without parole sentence in question here. To justify life without parole on the assumption that the juvenile offender forever will be a danger to society requires the sentencer to make a judgment that the juvenile is incorrigible. The characteristics of juveniles make that judgment questionable. "It is difficult even for expert psychologists to differentiate between the juvenile offender whose crime reflects unfortunate yet transient immaturity, and the rare juvenile offender whose crime reflects irreparable corruption."

Finally there is rehabilitation, a penological goal that forms the basis of parole systems. A sentence of life imprisonment without parole, however, cannot be justified by the goal of rehabilitation. The penalty forswears altogether the rehabilitative ideal. By denying the defendant the right to reenter the community, the State makes an irrevocable judgment about that person's value and place in society.

In sum, penological theory is not adequate to justify life without parole for juvenile nonhomicide offenders. This Court now holds that for a juvenile offender who did not commit homicide the Eighth Amendment forbids the sentence of life without parole.

A State is not required to guarantee eventual freedom to a juvenile offender convicted of a nonhomicide crime. What the State must do, however, is give defendants like Graham some meaningful opportunity to obtain release based on demonstrated maturity and rehabilitation. Those who commit truly horrifying crimes as juveniles may turn out to be irredeemable, and thus deserving of incarceration for the duration of their lives. The Eighth Amendment does not foreclose the possibility that persons convicted of nonhomicide crimes committed before adulthood will remain behind bars for life. It does forbid States from making the judgment at the outset that those offenders never will be fit to reenter society.

Terrance Graham's sentence guarantees he will die in prison without any meaningful opportunity to obtain release, no matter what he might do to demonstrate that the bad acts he committed as a teenager are not representative of his true character, even if he spends the next half century attempting to atone for his crimes and learn from his mistakes. The State has denied him any chance to later demonstrate that he is fit to rejoin society based solely on a nonhomicide crime that he committed while he was a child in the eyes of the law. This the Eighth Amendment does not permit.

There is support for our conclusion in the fact that, in continuing to impose life without parole sentences on juveniles who did not commit homicide, the United States adheres to a sentencing practice rejected the world over. The United States is the only Nation that imposes life without parole sentences on juvenile nonhomicide offenders.

The Constitution prohibits the imposition of a life without parole sentence on a juvenile offender who did not commit homicide.

Justice STEVENS, with whom Justice GINSBURG and Justice SOTOMAYOR join, concurring.

Society changes. Knowledge accumulates. We learn, sometimes, from our mistakes. Punishments that did not seem cruel and unusual at one time may, in the light of reason and experience, be found cruel and unusual at a later time; unless we are to abandon the moral commitment embodied in the Eighth Amendment, proportionality review must never become effectively obsolete.

Chief Justice ROBERTS, concurring in the judgment.

I agree with the Court that Terrance Graham's sentence of life without parole violates the Eighth Amendment's prohibition on "cruel and unusual punishments." Unlike the majority, however, I see no need to invent a new constitutional rule of dubious provenance in reaching that conclusion. Instead, my analysis is based on an application of this Court's precedents.

Graham's case arises at the intersection of two lines of Eighth Amendment precedent. The first consists of decisions holding that the Cruel and Unusual Punishments Clause embraces a "narrow proportionality principle" that we apply, on a case-by-case basis, when asked to review noncapital sentences. Today, the Court views Roper as providing the basis for a new categorical rule that juveniles may never receive a sentence of life without parole for nonhomicide crimes. I disagree. Treating juvenile life sentences as analogous to capital punishment is at odds with our longstanding view that "the death penalty is different from other punishments in kind rather than degree."

Applying the "narrow proportionality" framework to the particular facts of this case, I conclude that Graham's sentence of life without parole violates the Eighth Amendment. There is no question that the crime for which Graham received his life sentence . . . is "a serious crime deserving serious punishment." But [his] crimes are certainly less serious than other crimes, such as murder or rape. Both intrajurisdictional and interjurisdictional comparisons of Graham's sentence confirm the threshold inference of disproportionality.

So much for Graham. But what about Milagro Cunningham, a 17-year-old who beat and raped an 8-year-old girl before leaving her to die under 197 pounds of rock in a recycling bin in a remote landfill? Or Nathan Walker and Jakaris Taylor, the Florida juveniles who together with their friends gang-raped a woman and forced her to perform oral sex on her 12-year-old son? The fact that Graham cannot be sentenced to life without parole for his conduct says nothing whatever about these offenders, or others like them who commit nonhomicide crimes far more reprehensible than the conduct at issue here. The Court uses Graham's case as a vehicle to proclaim a new constitutional rule—applicable well beyond the particular facts of Graham's case—that a sentence of life without parole imposed on any juvenile for any nonhomicide offense is unconstitutional. This categorical conclusion is as unnecessary as it is unwise.

Justice THOMAS, with whom Justice SCALIA joins, and with whom Justice ALITO joins as to Parts I and III, dissenting.

The Court holds today that it is "grossly disproportionate" and hence unconstitutional for any judge or jury to impose a sentence of life without parole on an offender less than 18 years old, unless he has committed a homicide. [T]the Court insists that the standards of American society have evolved such that the Constitution now requires its prohibition.

The news of this evolution will, I think, come as a surprise to the American people. Congress, the District of Columbia, and 37 States allow judges and juries to consider this sentencing practice in juvenile nonhomicide cases, and those judges and juries have decided to use it in the very worst cases they have encountered.

I am unwilling to assume that we, as members of this Court, are any more capable of making such moral judgments than our fellow citizens. Nothing in our training as judges qualifies us for that task, and nothing in Article III gives us that authority.

I agree with Justice Stevens that "[w]e learn, sometimes, from our mistakes." Perhaps one day the Court will learn from this one.

MILLER v. ALABAMA

132 S. Ct. 2455 (2012)

Justice KAGAN delivered the opinion of the Court.

The two 14-year-old offenders in these cases were convicted of murder and sentenced to life imprisonment without the possibility of parole. In neither case did the sentencing authority have any discretion to impose a different punishment. State law mandated that each juvenile die in prison even if a judge or jury would have thought that his youth and its attendant characteristics, along with the nature of his crime, made a lesser sentence (for example, life *with* the possibility of parole) more appropriate. Such a scheme prevents those meting out punishment from considering a juvenile's "lessened culpability" and greater "capacity for change," Graham v. Florida (2010), and runs afoul of our cases' requirement of individualized sentencing for defendants facing the most serious penalties. We therefore hold that mandatory life without parole for those under the age of 18 at the time of their crimes violates the Eighth Amendment's prohibition on "cruel and unusual punishments."

I

A

In November 1999, petitioner Kuntrell Jackson, then 14 years old, and two other boys decided to rob a video store. En route to the store, Jackson learned that one of the boys, Derrick Shields, was carrying a sawed-off shotgun in his coat sleeve. Jackson decided to stay outside when the two other boys entered the store. Inside, Shields pointed the gun at the store clerk, Laurie Troup, and demanded that she "give up the money." Troup refused. When Troup threatened to call the police, Shields shot and killed her. The three boys fled empty-handed.

Arkansas law gives prosecutors discretion to charge 14-year-olds as adults when they are alleged to have committed certain serious offenses. The prosecutor here exercised that authority by charging Jackson with capital felony murder and aggravated robbery. A jury later convicted Jackson of both crimes. Noting that "in view of [the] verdict, there's only one possible punishment," the judge sentenced Jackson to life without parole.

B

Like Jackson, petitioner Evan Miller was 14 years old at the time of his crime. Miller had by then been in and out of foster care because his mother suffered from alcoholism and drug addiction and his stepfather abused him. Miller, too, regularly used drugs and alcohol; and he had attempted suicide four times, the first when he was six years old.

One night in 2003, Miller was at home with a friend, Colby Smith, when a neighbor, Cole Cannon, came to make a drug deal with Miller's mother. The two boys followed Cannon back to his trailer, where all three smoked marijuana and played drinking games. When Cannon passed out, Miller stole his wallet, splitting about $300 with Smith. Miller then tried to put the wallet back in Cannon's pocket, but Cannon awoke and grabbed Miller by the throat. Smith hit Cannon with a nearby baseball bat, and once released, Miller grabbed the bat and repeatedly struck Cannon with it. Miller placed a sheet over Cannon's head, told him "'I am God, I've come to take your life,'" and delivered one more blow. The boys then retreated to Miller's trailer, but soon decided to return to Cannon's to cover up evidence of their crime. Once there, they lit two fires. Cannon eventually died from his injuries and smoke inhalation.

Alabama law . . . allowed the District Attorney to seek removal of the case to adult court. The State accordingly charged Miller as an adult with murder in the course of arson. That crime (like capital murder in Arkansas) carries a mandatory minimum punishment of life without parole.

We granted certiorari in both cases and now reverse.

II

To start with the first set of cases: *Roper* and *Graham* establish that children are constitutionally different from adults for purposes of sentencing. Because juveniles have diminished culpability and greater prospects for reform, we explained, "they are less deserving of the most severe punishments." Those cases relied on three significant gaps between juveniles and adults. First, children have a "'lack of maturity and an underdeveloped sense of responsibility,'" leading to recklessness, impulsivity, and heedless risk-taking. Second, children "are more vulnerable . . . to negative influences and outside pressures," including from their family and peers; they have limited "contro[l] over their own environment" and lack the ability to extricate themselves from horrific, crime-producing settings. And third, a child's character is not as "well formed" as an adult's; his traits are "less fixed" and his actions less likely to be "evidence of irretrievabl[e] deprav[ity]."

Graham concluded from this analysis that life-without-parole sentences, like capital punishment, may violate the Eighth Amendment when imposed on children. To be sure, *Graham*'s flat ban on life without parole applied only to nonhomicide crimes, and the Court took care to distinguish those offenses from murder, based on both moral culpability and consequential harm. But none of what it said about children — about their distinctive (and transitory) mental traits and environmental vulnerabilities — is crime-specific.

[T]he mandatory penalty schemes at issue here prevent the sentencer from taking account of these central considerations. By removing youth from the balance — by subjecting a juvenile to the same life-without-parole sentence applicable to an adult — these laws prohibit a sentencing authority from assessing whether the law's harshest term of imprisonment proportionately punishes a juvenile offender. That contravenes *Graham*'s (and also *Roper*'s) foundational principle: that imposition of a State's most severe penalties on juvenile offenders cannot proceed as though they were not children.

Both cases before us illustrate the problem. Take Jackson's first. As noted earlier, Jackson did not fire the bullet that killed Laurie Troup. Both his mother and his grandmother had previously shot other individuals. At the least, a sentencer should look at such facts before depriving a 14-year-old of any prospect of release from prison.

That is true also in Miller's case. No one can doubt that he and Smith committed a vicious murder. But they did it when high on drugs and alcohol consumed with the adult victim. And if ever a pathological background might have contributed to a 14-year-old's commission of a crime, it is here. Miller's stepfather physically abused him; his alcoholic and drug-addicted mother neglected him; he had been in and out of foster care as a result; and he had tried to kill himself four times, the first when he should have been in kindergarten. That Miller deserved severe punishment for killing Cole Cannon is beyond question. But once again, a sentencer needed to examine all these circumstances before concluding that life without any possibility of parole was the appropriate penalty.

We therefore hold that the Eighth Amendment forbids a sentencing scheme that mandates life in prison without possibility of parole for juvenile offenders.

Chief Justice ROBERTS, with whom Justice SCALIA, Justice THOMAS, and Justice ALITO join, dissenting.

Determining the appropriate sentence for a teenager convicted of murder presents grave and challenging questions of morality and social policy. Our role, however, is to apply the law, not to answer such questions. The pertinent law here is the Eighth Amendment to the Constitution, which prohibits "cruel and unusual punishments." Today, the Court invokes that Amendment to ban a punishment that the Court does not itself characterize as unusual, and that could not plausibly be described as such. I therefore dissent.

The parties agree that nearly 2,500 prisoners are presently serving life sentences without the possibility of parole for murders they committed before the age of 18. The Court accepts that over 2,000 of those prisoners received that sentence because it was mandated by a legislature. Put simply, if a 17-year-old is convicted of deliberately murdering an innocent victim, it is not "unusual" for the murderer to receive a mandatory sentence of life without parole. That reality should preclude finding that mandatory life imprisonment for juvenile killers violates the Eighth Amendment.

In this case, there is little doubt about the direction of society's evolution: For most of the 20th century, American sentencing practices emphasized rehabilitation of the offender and the availability of parole. But by the 1980's, outcry against repeat offenders, broad disaffection with the rehabilitative model, and other factors led many legislatures to reduce or eliminate the possibility of parole, imposing longer sentences in order to punish criminals and prevent them from committing more crimes. Statutes establishing life without parole sentences in particular became more common in the past quarter century. And the parties agree that most States have changed their laws relatively recently to expose teenage murderers to mandatory life without parole.

[T]he Court's holding does not follow from *Roper* and *Graham.* Those cases undoubtedly stand for the proposition that teenagers are less mature, less responsible, and less fixed in their ways than adults—not that a Supreme Court case was needed to establish that. What they do not stand for, and do not even suggest, is that legislators—who also know that teenagers are different from adults—may not require life without parole for juveniles who commit the worst types of murder.

Justice THOMAS, with whom Justice SCALIA joins, dissenting.

As I have previously explained, "the Cruel and Unusual Punishments Clause was originally understood as prohibiting torturous *methods* of punishment—specifically methods akin to those that had been considered cruel and unusual at the time the Bill of Rights was adopted." The clause does not contain a "proportionality principle."

The legislatures of Arkansas and Alabama, like those of 27 other jurisdictions, *ante*, at 19-20, have determined that all offenders convicted of specified homicide offenses, whether juveniles or not, deserve a sentence of life in prison without the possibility of parole. Nothing in our Constitution authorizes this Court to supplant that choice.

Justice ALITO, with whom Justice SCALIA joins, dissenting.

The Court long ago abandoned the original meaning of the Eighth Amendment, holding instead that the prohibition of "cruel and unusual punishment" embodies the "evolving standards of decency that mark the progress of a maturing society." Both the provenance and philosophical basis for this standard were problematic from the start.

The two (carefully selected) cases before us concern very young defendants. But no one should be confused by the particulars of the two cases before us. The category of murderers that the Court delicately calls "children" (murderers under the age of 18) consists overwhelmingly of young men who are fast approaching the legal age of adulthood.

Seventeen-year-olds commit a significant number of murders every year, and some of these crimes are incredibly brutal. Many of these murderers are at least as mature as the average 18-year-old. Congress and the legislatures of 43 States have concluded that at least some of these murderers should be sentenced to prison without parole, and 28 States and the Federal Government have decided that for some of these offenders life without parole should be mandatory. The majority of this Court now overrules these legislative judgments.

4. Excessive Fines and Forfeitures

In addition to prohibiting "cruel and unusual punishment," the Eighth Amendment also bars the imposition of "excessive fines." The Court uses a proportionality approach similar to that used in cases involving cruel and unusual punishment to determine whether a fine or forfeiture is excessive.

UNITED STATES v. BAJAKAJIAN

524 U.S. 321 (1998)

Justice THOMAS delivered the opinion of the Court.

Respondent Hosep Bajakajian attempted to leave the United States without reporting, as required by federal law, that he was transporting more than $10,000 in currency. Federal law also provides that a person convicted of willfully violating this reporting requirement shall forfeit to the government "any property . . . involved in such offense." The question in this case is whether forfeiture of the entire $357,144 that respondent failed to declare would violate the Excessive Fines Clause of the Eighth Amendment. We hold that it would, because full forfeiture of respondent's currency would be grossly disproportional to the gravity of his offense.

I

On June 9, 1994, respondent, his wife, and his two daughters were waiting at Los Angeles International Airport to board a flight to Italy; their final destination was Cyprus. Using dogs trained to detect currency by its smell, customs inspectors discovered some $230,000 in cash in the Bajakajians' checked baggage. A customs inspector approached respondent and his wife and told them that they were required to report all money in excess of $10,000 in their possession or in their baggage. Respondent said that he had $8,000 and that his wife had another $7,000, but that the family had no additional currency to declare. A search of their carry-on bags, purse, and wallet revealed more cash; in all, customs inspectors found $357,144. The currency was seized and respondent was taken into custody.

A federal grand jury indicted respondent on three counts. Count One charged him with failing to report that he was transporting more than $10,000 outside the United States, and with doing so "willfully," in violation of §5322(a). Count Two charged him with making a false material statement to the United States Customs Service, in violation of 18 U.S.C. §1001. Count Three sought forfeiture of the $357,144 pursuant to 18 U.S.C. §982(a)(1), which provides:

"The court, in imposing sentence on a person convicted of an offense in violation of section . . . 5316, . . . shall order that the person forfeit to the United States any property, real or personal, involved in such offense, or any property traceable to such property." 18 U.S.C. §982(a)(1).

Respondent pleaded guilty to the failure to report in Count One; the Government agreed to dismiss the false statement charge in Count Two; and respondent elected to have a bench trial on the forfeiture in Count Three. After the bench trial, the District Court found that the entire $357,144 was subject to forfeiture because it was "involved in" the offense.

Although §982(a)(1) directs sentencing courts to impose full forfeiture, the District Court concluded that such forfeiture would be "extraordinarily harsh" and "grossly disproportionate to the offense in question," and that it would therefore violate the Excessive Fines Clause. The court instead ordered forfeiture of $15,000, in addition to a sentence of three years of probation and a fine of $5,000 — the maximum fine under the Sentencing Guidelines — because the court believed that the maximum Guidelines fine was "too little" and that a $15,000 forfeiture would "make up for what I think a reasonable fine should be."

The United States appealed, seeking full forfeiture of respondent's currency.

II

The Eighth Amendment provides: "Excessive bail shall not be required, nor excessive fines imposed, nor cruel and unusual punishments inflicted." This Court has had little occasion to interpret, and has never actually applied, the Excessive Fines Clause. We have, however, explained that at the time the Constitution was adopted, "the word 'fine' was understood to mean a payment to a sovereign as punishment for some offense." The Excessive Fines Clause thus "limits the government's power to extract payments, whether in cash or in kind, 'as punishment for some offense.'" Forfeitures — payments in kind — are thus "fines" if they constitute punishment for an offense.

We have little trouble concluding that the forfeiture of currency ordered by §982(a)(1) constitutes punishment. The statute directs a court to order forfeiture as an additional sanction when "imposing sentence on a person convicted of" a willful violation of §5316's reporting requirement.

The United States . . . argues that the forfeiture mandated by §982(a)(1) is constitutional because it falls within a class of historic forfeitures of property tainted by crime. In so doing, the Government relies upon a series of cases involving traditional civil in rem forfeitures that are inapposite because such forfeitures were historically considered nonpunitive.

The theory behind such forfeitures was the fiction that the action was directed against "guilty property," rather than against the offender himself.[7] Historically, the conduct of the property owner was irrelevant; indeed, the owner of forfeited property could be entirely innocent of any crime.

Traditional in rem forfeitures were thus not considered punishment against the individual for an offense. Because they were viewed as nonpunitive, such forfeitures traditionally were considered to occupy a place outside the domain of the Excessive Fines Clause. Recognizing the nonpunitive character of such proceedings, we have held that the Double Jeopardy Clause does not bar the institution of a civil, in rem forfeiture action after the criminal conviction of the defendant.

---

7. The "guilty property" theory behind in rem forfeiture can be traced to the Bible, which describes property being sacrificed to God as a means of atoning for an offense. See Exodus 21:28. In medieval Europe and at common law, this concept evolved into the law of deodand, in which offending property was condemned and confiscated by the church or the Crown in remediation for the harm it had caused. [Footnote by the Court.]

The forfeiture in this case does not bear any of the hallmarks of traditional civil in rem forfeitures. The Government has not proceeded against the currency itself, but has instead sought and obtained a criminal conviction of respondent personally. The forfeiture serves no remedial purpose, is designed to punish the offender, and cannot be imposed upon innocent owners.

III

Because the forfeiture of respondent's currency constitutes punishment and is thus a "fine" within the meaning of the Excessive Fines Clause, we now turn to the question of whether it is "excessive."

A

The touchstone of the constitutional inquiry under the Excessive Fines Clause is the principle of proportionality: The amount of the forfeiture must bear some relationship to the gravity of the offense that it is designed to punish. Until today, however, we have not articulated a standard for determining whether a punitive forfeiture is constitutionally excessive. We now hold that a punitive forfeiture violates the Excessive Fines Clause if it is grossly disproportional to the gravity of a defendant's offense.

The constitutional question that we address, however, is just how proportional to a criminal offense a fine must be, and the text of the Excessive Fines Clause does not answer it. Nor does its history.

We must therefore rely on other considerations in deriving a constitutional excessiveness standard, and there are two that we find particularly relevant. The first, which we have emphasized in our cases interpreting the Cruel and Unusual Punishments Clause, is that judgments about the appropriate punishment for an offense belong in the first instance to the legislature. The second is that any judicial determination regarding the gravity of a particular criminal offense will be inherently imprecise.

In applying this standard, the district courts in the first instance, and the courts of appeals, reviewing the proportionality determination must compare the amount of the forfeiture to the gravity of the defendant's offense. If the amount of the forfeiture is grossly disproportional to the gravity of the defendant's offense, it is unconstitutional.

B

Under this standard, the forfeiture of respondent's entire $357,144 would violate the Excessive Fines Clause. Respondent's crime was solely a reporting offense. It was permissible to transport the currency out of the country so long as he reported it. Section 982(a)(1) orders currency to be forfeited for a "willful" violation of the reporting requirement. Thus, the essence of respondent's crime is a willful failure to report the removal of currency from the United States. Furthermore, as the District Court found, respondent's violation was unrelated to any other illegal activities. The money was the proceeds of legal activity and was to be used to repay a lawful debt. Whatever his other vices, respondent does not fit into the class of persons for whom the statute was principally designed: He is not a money launderer, a drug trafficker, or a tax evader.

The harm that respondent caused was also minimal. Failure to report his currency affected only one party, the Government, and in a relatively minor way. There was no fraud on the United States, and respondent caused no loss to the public fisc. Had his crime gone undetected, the Government would have been deprived only of the information that $357,144 had left the country.

Comparing the gravity of respondent's crime with the $357,144 forfeiture the Government seeks, we conclude that such a forfeiture would be grossly disproportional to the gravity of his offense. It is larger than the $5,000 fine imposed by the District Court by many orders of magnitude, and it bears no articulable correlation to any injury suffered by the Government.

Justice KENNEDY, with whom Chief Justice REHNQUIST, Justice O'CONNOR, and Justice SCALIA join, dissenting.

For the first time in its history, the Court strikes down a fine as excessive under the Eighth Amendment. The decision is disturbing both for its specific holding and for the broader upheaval it foreshadows. At issue is a fine Congress fixed in the amount of the currency respondent sought to smuggle or to transport without reporting. If a fine calibrated with this accuracy fails the Court's test, its decision portends serious disruption of a vast range of statutory fines.

The crime of smuggling or failing to report cash is more serious than the Court is willing to acknowledge. The drug trade, money laundering, and tax evasion all depend in part on smuggled and unreported cash.

In my view, forfeiture of all the unreported currency is sustainable whenever a willful violation is proven.

D. THE DEATH PENALTY

There is one penalty that is unique in the criminal justice system: the death penalty. Currently, 32 states have laws authorizing the imposition of the death penalty, although defendants continue to challenge its use. The Supreme Court has never held that capital punishment is per se unconstitutional under the Eighth Amendment's prohibition of cruel and unusual punishment. Rather, it has focused on the fairness of the procedures used to impose the death penalty and whether those procedures ensure that the punishment is proportionate to the crime.

Subsection 1 of this section discusses the constitutionality of the death penalty under the Eighth Amendment. Subsection 2 then analyzes what standards must be used to ensure that it is not "cruel and unusual punishment" and complies with due process. Subsection 3 examines recent limitations put on the death penalty, including prohibitions on its use against mentally retarded defendants and minors. The subsection also examines the future of the death penalty and the nature of current challenges to today's primary method of execution — lethal injection.

The death penalty remains one of the most controversial issues of the criminal justice system. Public polls show support for the penalty, but this support can vary depending on how the question is presented.[8] There are also continuing concerns about the fairness of its application and whether it has a disproportionate impact on minorities and the poor.[9] Finally, with the advent of DNA science, there is growing evidence that defendants have been wrongfully convicted and executed.[10]

Concerns about the death penalty are not new. As the following cases detail, the Supreme Court's approach sought to address these and other concerns by adjudging the procedures for death penalty cases, rather than striking down capital punishment as per se unconstitutional.

1. Is the Death Penalty Unconstitutional?

In a 5-4 decision, the Supreme Court held in Furman v. Georgia that capital punishment, as then administered, violated the Eighth Amendment's prohibition of cruel and unusual punishment. However, the Court's per curiam opinion made no attempt to set forth a majority approach, and each of the justices filed separate concurring or dissenting opinions. Only two of the justices — Brennan and Marshall — concluded that all capital punishment was per se unconstitutional. The other three concurring justices — Douglas, White, and Stewart — focused their objections on the implementation of the death penalty. Justice Douglas stressed the potential for discriminatory enforcement of the death penalty. Justices White and Stewart focused on the arbitrary manner in which the punishment was imposed in the particular cases the Court was reviewing. The dissenters, in turn, challenged the majority's position as an unwarranted intrusion into the legislative process.

FURMAN v. GEORGIA
408 U.S. 238 (1972)

PER CURIAM.

[Petitioners were convicted of murder or rape and sentenced to death.] Certiorari was granted limited to the following question: "Does the

---

8. In a 2006 poll by ABC News/Washington Post, 65 percent of the American public favors the death penalty, and 32 percent oppose it. However, when asked, "Which punishment to you prefer for people who commit murder: the death penalty or life in prison without parole?" 50 percent support the death penalty, and 46 percent support life without parole. The remaining persons are undecided.

9. See Corinna Barrett Lain, Deciding Death, 57 Duke L.J. 1, *3 (2007).

10. Recent estimates have been as high as one out of every seven defendants executed being wrongfully convicted. See Jean Coleman Blackerby, Life After Death Row: Preventing Wrongful Capital Convictions and Restoring Innocence After Exoneration, 56 Vand. L. Rev. 1179 (2003).

imposition and carrying out of the death penalty in [these cases] constitute cruel and unusual punishment in violation of the Eighth and Fourteenth Amendments?" The Court holds that the imposition and carrying out of the death penalty in these cases constitute cruel and unusual punishment in violation of the Eighth and Fourteenth Amendments. The judgment in each case is therefore reversed insofar as it leaves undisturbed the death sentence imposed, and the cases are remanded for further proceedings.

Justice BRENNAN, concurring.

The question presented in these cases is whether death is today a punishment for crime that is "cruel and unusual" and consequently, by virtue of the Eighth and Fourteenth Amendments, beyond the power of the State to inflict.

I

[W]e cannot now know exactly what the Framers thought "cruel and unusual punishments" were. Certainly they intended to ban torturous punishments. . . . [F]or instance, the . . . "punishments of torture," which the Court labeled "atrocities," were cases where the criminal "was embowelled alive, beheaded, and quartered," and cases "of public dissection . . . and burning alive."

II

Ours would indeed be a simple task were we required merely to measure a challenged punishment against those that history has long condemned. [However,] we know, therefore, that the Clause "must draw its meaning from the evolving standards of decency that mark the progress of a maturing society."

The primary principle is that a punishment must not be so severe as to be degrading to the dignity of human beings. . . . In determining whether a punishment comports with human dignity, we are aided . . . by a . . . principle inherent in the Clause — that the State must not arbitrarily inflict a severe punishment . . . that it does not inflict upon others. Indeed, the very words "cruel and unusual punishments" imply condemnation of the arbitrary infliction of severe punishments.

[Also, a] severe punishment must not be unacceptable to contemporary society. Rejection by society, of course, is a strong indication that a severe punishment does not comport with human dignity.

The final principle inherent in the Clause is that a severe punishment must not be excessive.

There are, then, four principles by which we may determine whether a particular punishment is "cruel and unusual." If a punishment is unusually severe, if there is a strong probability that it is inflicted arbitrarily, if it is substantially rejected by contemporary society, and if there is no reason to believe that it serves any penal purpose more effectively than some less severe punishment, then the continued infliction of that punishment violates the command of the Clause that the State may not inflict inhuman and uncivilized punishment upon those convicted of crimes.

III

Under these principles and this test, death is today a "cruel and unusual" punishment.

Death is truly an awesome punishment. The calculated killing of a human being by the State involves, by its very nature, a denial of the executed person's humanity. . . . In comparison to all other punishments today, then, the deliberate extinguishment of human life by the State is uniquely degrading to human dignity. I therefore turn to the second principle — that the State may not arbitrarily inflict an unusually severe punishment.

There has been a steady decline in the infliction of this punishment in every decade since the 1930's, the earliest period for which accurate statistics are available. In the 1930's, executions averaged 167 per year; in the 1940's, the average was 128; in the 1950's, it was 72; and in the years 1960-1962, it was 48. There has been a total of 46 executions since then, 36 of them in 1963-1964. Yet our population and the number of capital crimes committed have increased greatly over the past four decades. The contemporary rarity of the infliction of this punishment is thus the end result of a long-continued decline.

When a country of over 200 million people inflicts an unusually severe punishment no more than 50 times a year, the inference is strong that the punishment is not being regularly and fairly applied.

When the punishment of death is inflicted in a trivial number of the cases in which it is legally available, the conclusion is virtually inescapable that it is being inflicted arbitrarily. Indeed, it smacks of little more than a lottery system.

[Third], the progressive decline in, and the current rarity of, the infliction of death demonstrate that our society seriously questions the appropriateness of this punishment today.

The final principle to be considered is that an unusually severe and degrading punishment may not be excessive in view of the purposes for which it is inflicted.

The States' primary claim is that death is a necessary punishment because it prevents the commission of capital crimes more effectively than any less severe punishment. The sufficient answer to this is that if a criminal convicted of a capital crime poses a danger to society, effective administration of the State's pardon and parole laws can delay or deny his release from prison, and techniques of isolation can eliminate or minimize the danger while he remains confined.

The more significant argument is that the threat of death prevents the commission of capital crimes because it deters potential criminals who would not be deterred by the threat of imprisonment. The argument is not based upon evidence that the threat of death is a superior deterrent.

There is, however, another aspect to the argument that the punishment of death is necessary for the protection of society. The infliction of death, the States urge, serves to manifest the community's outrage at the commission of the crime. It is, they say, a concrete public expression of moral indignation that inculcates respect for the law and helps assure a more peaceful community.

When the overwhelming number of criminals who commit capital crimes go to prison, it cannot be concluded that death serves the purpose of retribution more effectively than imprisonment. The asserted public belief that murderers and rapists deserve to die is flatly inconsistent with the execution of a random few.

In sum, the punishment of death is inconsistent with all four principles: Death is an unusually severe and degrading punishment; there is a strong probability that it is inflicted arbitrarily; its rejection by contemporary society is virtually total; and there is no reason to believe that it serves any penal purpose more effectively than the less severe punishment of imprisonment. The function of these principles is to enable a court to determine whether a punishment comports with human dignity. Death, quite simply, does not.

Justice MARSHALL, concurring.

The criminal acts with which we are confronted are ugly, vicious, reprehensible acts. Their sheer brutality cannot and should not be minimized. But, we are not called upon to condone the penalized conduct; we are asked only to examine the penalty imposed on each of the petitioners and to determine whether or not it violates the Eighth Amendment.

Perhaps the most important principle in analyzing "cruel and unusual" punishment questions is one that is reiterated again and again in the prior opinions of the Court: i.e., the cruel and unusual language "must draw its meaning from the evolving standards of decency that mark the progress of a maturing society." Thus, a penalty that was permissible at one time in our Nation's history is not necessarily permissible today.

At the present time, 41 States, the District of Columbia, and other federal jurisdictions authorize the death penalty for at least one crime. . . . The [history of the death penalty in America] demonstrates that capital punishment was carried from Europe to America but, once here, was tempered considerably. At times in our history, strong abolitionist movements have existed. But, they have never been completely successful, as no more than one-quarter of the States of the Union have, at any one time, abolished the death penalty. They have had partial success, however, especially in reducing the number of capital crimes, replacing mandatory death sentences with jury discretion, and developing more humane methods of conducting executions.

I cannot believe that at this stage in our history, the American people would ever knowingly support purposeless vengeance. I believe that the great mass of citizens would conclude on the basis of the material already considered that the death penalty is immoral and therefore unconstitutional.

I believe that the following facts would serve to convince even the most hesitant of citizens to condemn death as a sanction: capital punishment is imposed discriminatorily against certain identifiable classes of people; there is evidence that innocent people have been executed before their innocence can be proved; and the death penalty wreaks havoc with our entire criminal justice system.

"[I]t is usually the poor, the illiterate, the underprivileged, the member of the minority group — the man who, because he is without means, and is defended by a court-appointed attorney — who becomes society's sacrificial lamb. . . ." There is also overwhelming evidence that the death penalty is employed against men and not women.

Assuming knowledge of all the facts presently available regarding capital punishment, the average citizen would, in my opinion, find it shocking to his conscience and sense of justice.

At a time in our history when the streets of the Nation's cities inspire fear and despair, rather than pride and hope, it is difficult to maintain objectivity and concern for our fellow citizens. But, the measure of a country's greatness is its ability to retain compassion in time of crisis. No nation in the recorded history of man has a greater tradition of revering justice and fair treatment for all its citizens in times of turmoil, confusion, and tension than ours. This is a country which stands tallest in troubled times, a country that clings to fundamental principles, cherishes its constitutional heritage, and rejects simple solutions that compromise the values that lie at the roots of our democratic system.

In striking down capital punishment, this Court does not malign our system of government. On the contrary, it pays homage to it. Only in a free society could right triumph in difficult times, and could civilization record its magnificent advancement. In recognizing the humanity of our fellow beings, we pay ourselves the highest tribute. We achieve "a major milestone in the long road up from barbarism" and join the approximately 70 other jurisdictions in the world which celebrate their regard for civilization and humanity by shunning capital punishment.

Justice STEWART, concurring.

The penalty of death differs from all other forms of criminal punishment, not in degree but in kind. It is unique in its total irrevocability. It is unique in its rejection of rehabilitation of the convict as a basic purpose of criminal justice. And it is unique, finally, in its absolute renunciation of all that is embodied in our concept of humanity.

For these and other reasons, at least two of my Brothers have concluded that the infliction of the death penalty is constitutionally impermissible in all circumstances under the Eighth and Fourteenth Amendments. Their case is a strong one. But I find it unnecessary to reach the ultimate question they would decide.

The constitutionality of capital punishment in the abstract is not . . . before us in these cases. . . . Instead, the death sentences now before us are the product of a legal system that brings them, I believe, within the very core of the Eighth Amendment's guarantee against cruel and unusual punishments, a guarantee applicable against the States through the Fourteenth Amendment. In the first place, it is clear that these sentences are "cruel" in the sense that they excessively go beyond, not in degree but in kind, the punishments that the state legislatures have determined to be necessary. In the second place, it is equally clear that these sentences are "unusual" in the sense that the penalty of death is infrequently imposed for murder, and that its imposition for rape is extraordinarily rare.

These death sentences are cruel and unusual in the same way that being struck by lightning is cruel and unusual. For, of all the people convicted of rapes and murders in 1967 and 1968, many just as reprehensible as these, the petitioners are among a capriciously selected random handful upon whom the sentence of death has in fact been imposed. . . . I simply conclude that the Eighth and Fourteenth Amendments cannot tolerate the infliction of a sentence of death under legal systems that permit this unique penalty to be so wantonly and so freakishly imposed.

Justice DOUGLAS, concurring.

It would seem to be incontestable that the death penalty inflicted on one defendant is "unusual" if it discriminates against him by reason of his race, religion, wealth, social position, or class, or if it is imposed under a procedure that gives room for the play of such prejudices.

The words "cruel and unusual" certainly include penalties that are barbaric. But the words, at least when read in light of the English proscription against selective and irregular use of penalties, suggest that it is "cruel and unusual" to apply the death penalty — or any other penalty — selectively to minorities whose numbers are few, who are outcasts of society, and who are unpopular. . . .

There is increasing recognition of the fact that the basic theme of equal protection is implicit in "cruel and unusual" punishments. "A penalty . . . should be considered 'unusually' imposed if it is administered arbitrarily or discriminatorily." The President's Commission on Law Enforcement and Administration of Justice recently concluded: "Finally there is evidence that the imposition of the death sentence and the exercise of dispensing power by the courts and the executive follow discriminatory patterns. The death sentence is disproportionately imposed and carried out on the poor, the Negro, and the members of unpopular groups."

A study of capital cases in Texas from 1924 to 1968 reached the following conclusions:

> Application of the death penalty is unequal: most of those executed were poor, young, and ignorant.
>
> Seventy-five of the 460 cases involved co-defendants, who, under Texas law, were given separate trials. In several instances where a white and a Negro were co-defendants, the white was sentenced to life imprisonment or a term of years, and the Negro was given the death penalty.
>
> Another ethnic disparity is found in the type of sentence imposed for rape. The Negro convicted of rape is far more likely to get the death penalty than a term sentence, whereas whites and Latins are far more likely to get a term sentence than the death penalty.

Former Attorney General Ramsey Clark has said, "It is the poor, the sick, the ignorant, the powerless and the hated who are executed." One searches our chronicles in vain for the execution of any member of the affluent strata of this society. The Leopolds and Loebs are given prison terms, not sentenced to death.

Those who wrote the Eighth Amendment knew what price their forebears had paid for a system based, not on equal justice, but on discrimination. In those days the target was not the blacks or the poor, but the dissenters, those who opposed absolutism in government, who struggled for a parliamentary regime, and who opposed governments' recurring efforts to foist a particular religion on the people. But the tool of capital punishment was used with vengeance against the opposition and those unpopular with the regime. One cannot read this history without realizing that the desire for equality was reflected in the ban against "cruel and unusual punishments" contained in the Eighth Amendment.

In a Nation committed to equal protection of the laws there is no permissible "caste" aspect of law enforcement. Yet we know that the discretion of judges and juries in imposing the death penalty enables the penalty to be selectively applied, feeding prejudices against the accused if he is poor and despised, and lacking political clout, or if he is a member of a suspect or unpopular minority, and saving those who by social position may be in a more protected position.

The high service rendered by the "cruel and unusual" punishment clause of the Eighth Amendment is to require legislatures to write penal laws that are evenhanded, nonselective, and nonarbitrary, and to require judges to see to it that general laws are not applied sparsely, selectively, and spottily to unpopular groups.

Justice WHITE, concurring.

In joining the Court's judgments, therefore, I do not at all intimate that the death penalty is unconstitutional per se or that there is no system of capital punishment that would comport with the Eighth Amendment.

It is . . . my judgment that this point has been reached with respect to capital punishment as it is presently administered under the statutes involved in these cases. I cannot avoid the conclusion that as the statutes before us are now administered, the penalty is so infrequently imposed that the threat of execution is too attenuated to be of substantial service to criminal justice.

Chief Justice BURGER, with whom Justices BLACKMUN, POWELL, and REHNQUIST join, dissenting.

At the outset it is important to note that only two members of the Court, Mr. Justice Brennan and Mr. Justice Marshall, have concluded that the Eighth Amendment prohibits capital punishment for all crimes and under all circumstances. Mr. Justice Douglas has also determined that the death penalty contravenes the Eighth Amendment, although I do not read his opinion as necessarily requiring final abolition of the penalty. For the reasons set forth, I conclude that the constitutional prohibition against "cruel and unusual punishments" cannot be construed to bar the imposition of the punishment of death.

If we were possessed of legislative power, I would either join with Mr. Justice Brennan and Mr. Justice Marshall or, at the very least, restrict the use of capital punishment to a small category of the most heinous crimes. Our constitutional inquiry, however, must be divorced from personal feelings as to the morality and efficacy of the death penalty, and be confined to the meaning and applicability of the uncertain language of the Eighth Amendment.

Counsel for petitioners properly concede that capital punishment was not impermissibly cruel at the time of the adoption of the Eighth Amendment. Not only do the records of the debates indicate that the Founding Fathers were limited in their concern to the prevention of torture, but it is also clear from the language of the Constitution itself that there was no thought whatever of the elimination of capital punishment.

In the 181 years since the enactment of the Eighth Amendment, not a single decision of this Court has cast the slightest shadow of a doubt on the constitutionality of capital punishment. . . . The Court's quiescence in this area can be attributed to the fact that in a democratic society legislatures, not courts, are constituted to respond to the will and consequently the moral values of the people.

There are no obvious indications that capital punishment offends the conscience of society to such a degree that our traditional deference to the legislative judgment must be abandoned. It is not a punishment such as burning at the stake that everyone would ineffably find to be repugnant to all civilized standards. Nor is it a punishment so roundly condemned that only a few aberrant legislatures have retained it on the statute books. Capital punishment is authorized by statute in 40 States, the District of Columbia, and in the federal courts for the commission of certain crimes.

One conceivable source of evidence that legislatures have abdicated their essentially barometric role with respect to community values would be public opinion polls, of which there have been many in the past decade addressed to the question of capital punishment. Without assessing the reliability of such polls, or intimating that any judicial reliance could ever be placed on them, it need only be noted that the reported results have shown nothing approximating the universal condemnation of capital punishment that might lead us to suspect that the legislatures in general have lost touch with current social values.[11]

The selectivity of juries in imposing the punishment of death is properly viewed as a refinement on, rather than a repudiation of, the statutory authorization for that penalty. The rate of imposition of death sentences falls far short of providing the requisite unambiguous evidence that the legislatures of 40 States and the Congress have turned their backs on current or evolving standards of decency in continuing to make the death penalty available.

Capital punishment has also been attacked as violative of the Eighth Amendment on the ground that it is not needed to achieve legitimate penal aims and is thus "unnecessarily cruel." As a pure policy matter, this approach has much to recommend it, but it seeks to give a dimension to the Eighth Amendment that it was never intended to have and promotes a line of inquiry that this Court has never before pursued.

Two of the several aims of punishment are generally associated with capital punishment — retribution and deterrence. It is argued that retribution can be discounted because that, after all, is what the Eighth Amendment seeks to eliminate. There is no authority suggesting that the Eighth Amendment was intended to purge the law of its retributive elements. . . . Furthermore, responsible legal thinkers of widely varying persuasions have debated the sociological and philosophical aspects of the retribution question for generations, neither side being able to convince the other.

The less esoteric but no less controversial question is whether the death penalty acts as a superior deterrent. Those favoring abolition find no evidence that it does. Those favoring retention start from the intuitive notion that capital punishment should act as the most effective deterrent and note that there is no convincing evidence that it does not. Escape from this empirical stalemate is sought by placing the burden of proof on the States and concluding that they have failed to demonstrate that capital punishment is a more effective deterrent than life imprisonment. Comparative deterrence is not a matter that lends itself to precise measurement; to shift the burden to the States is to provide an illusory solution to an enormously complex problem. If it were proper to put the States to the test of demonstrating the deterrent value of capital punishment, we could just as well ask them to prove the need for life imprisonment or any other punishment.

Since there is no majority of the Court on the ultimate issue presented in these cases, the future of capital punishment in this country has been left in an uncertain limbo. Rather than providing a final and unambiguous answer on the basic constitutional question, the collective impact of the majority's

---

11. A 1966 poll indicated that 42% of those polled favored capital punishment while 47% opposed it, and 11% had no opinion. A 1969 poll found 51% in favor, 40% opposed, and 9% with no opinion. [Footnote by the Court.]

ruling is to demand an undetermined measure of change from the various state legislatures and the Congress.

Justice BLACKMUN, dissenting.

I join the respective opinions of [the dissenters] and add only the following, somewhat personal, comments.

Cases such as these provide for me an excruciating agony of the spirit. . . . Were I a legislator, I would vote against the death penalty for the policy reasons argued by counsel for the respective petitioners and expressed and adopted in the several opinions filed by the Justices who vote to reverse these judgments.

Having lived for many years in a State[12] that does not have the death penalty, that effectively abolished it in 1911, and that carried out its last execution on February 13, 1906, capital punishment had never been a part of life for me. In my State, it just did not exist. So far as I can determine, the State, purely from a statistical deterrence point of view, was neither the worse nor the better for its abolition, for, as the concurring opinions observe, the statistics prove little, if anything.

I do not sit on these cases, however, as a legislator, responsive, at least in part, to the will of constituents. Our task here, as must so frequently be emphasized and re-emphasized, is to pass upon the constitutionality of legislation that has been enacted and that is challenged. This is the sole task for judges. We should not allow our personal preferences as to the wisdom of legislative and congressional action, or our distaste for such action, to guide our judicial decision in cases such as these.

Justice POWELL, with whom Chief Justice BURGER, Justice BLACKMUN, and Justice REHNQUIST join, dissenting.

Although the central theme of petitioners' presentations in these cases is that the imposition of the death penalty is per se unconstitutional, only two of today's opinions explicitly conclude that so sweeping a determination is mandated by the Constitution. Both Mr. Justice Brennan and Mr. Justice Marshall call for the abolition of all existing state and federal capital punishment statutes. They intimate as well that no capital statute could be devised in the future that might comport with the Eighth Amendment.

The Constitution itself poses the first obstacle to petitioners' argument that capital punishment is per se unconstitutional. The relevant provisions are the Fifth, Eighth, and Fourteenth Amendments. The first of these provides in part:

"No person shall be held to answer for a capital, or otherwise infamous crime, unless on a presentment or indictment of a Grand Jury . . . ; nor shall any person be subject for the same offence to be twice put in jeopardy of life

---

12. Minn. Stat. §609.10 (1971). [Footnote by the Court.]

or limb; . . . nor be deprived of life, liberty, or property, without due process of law. . . ."

The Eighth Amendment, adopted at the same time as the Fifth, proscribes "cruel and unusual" punishments. [W]hatever punishments the Framers of the Constitution may have intended to prohibit under the "cruel and unusual" language, there cannot be the slightest doubt that they intended no absolute bar on the Government's authority to impose the death penalty.

On virtually every occasion that any opinion has touched on the question of the constitutionality of the death penalty, it has been asserted affirmatively, or tacitly assumed, that the Constitution does not prohibit the penalty. No Justice of the Court, until today, has dissented from this consistent reading of the Constitution.

One must conclude, contrary to petitioners' submission, that the indicators most likely to reflect the public's view — legislative bodies, state referenda and the juries which have the actual responsibility — do not support the contention that evolving standards of decency require total abolition of capital punishment. Indeed, the weight of the evidence indicates that the public generally has not accepted either the morality or the social merit of the views so passionately advocated by the articulate spokesmen for abolition. But however one may assess the amorphous ebb and flow of public opinion generally on this volatile issue, this type of inquiry lies at the periphery — not the core — of the judicial process in constitutional cases. The assessment of popular opinion is essentially a legislative, not a judicial, function.

Petitioners seek to salvage their thesis by arguing that the infrequency and discriminatory nature of the actual resort to the ultimate penalty tend to diffuse public opposition. We are told that the penalty is imposed exclusively on uninfluential minorities — "the poor and powerless, personally ugly and socially unacceptable."

Certainly the claim is justified that this criminal sanction falls more heavily on the relatively impoverished and underprivileged elements of society. The "have-nots" in every society always have been subject to greater pressure to commit crimes and to fewer constraints than their more affluent fellow citizens. This is, indeed, a tragic byproduct of social and economic deprivation, but it is not an argument of constitutional proportions under the Eighth or Fourteenth Amendment.

2. Standards for Constitutional Implementation of the Death Penalty

Because a clear majority in *Furman* neither rejected the death penalty nor approved of its current implementation, the Court left it up to the states to adopt procedures that would satisfy the Court's concerns. State legislatures then slowly enacted legislation to create guidelines as to who would be subjected to capital punishment. By 1976, 35 states had enacted new capital punishment legislation. Some of these states adopted mandatory death penalty provisions so that capital punishment would not be imposed in an arbitrary manner. Others opted for sentencing schemes that provided for separate penalty phases in death penalty cases. In these bifurcated trials, the jury first must convict the defendant of a qualifying death-penalty offense and then consider whether specified aggravating circumstances outweigh mitigating circumstances that militate against imposing capital punishment.

In Woodson v. North Carolina, 428 U.S. 280 (1976), the Supreme Court struck down mandatory death sentences for any first-degree murders. The Court held that mandatory capital punishment is inconsistent with contemporary standards of decency and fails to provide standards to guide the jury. The Court also wrote that mandatory capital punishment undermines respect for the dignity of the individual, a requirement under the Eighth Amendment.

Accordingly, the states and Congress were left with implementing capital punishment systems that allowed jurors to weigh the aggravating circumstances of a capital defendant's case against the mitigating factors. This approach was upheld by the Supreme Court in Gregg v. Georgia, 428 U.S. 153 (1976). In its split decision in *Gregg*, the Court held that the death penalty is not disproportionate if a jury properly considers factors that make the defendant deserving of the most severe punishment.

> [C]apital punishment is an expression of society's moral outrage at particularly offensive conduct. This function may be unappealing to many, but it is essential in an ordered society that asks its citizens to rely on legal processes rather than self-help to vindicate their wrongs.

Id. at 183. After acknowledging the role of retribution in sentencing, Justice Stewart wrote:

> There is no question that death as a punishment is unique in its severity and irrevocability. When a defendant's life is at stake, the Court has been particularly sensitive to insure that every safeguard is observed. But we are concerned here only with the imposition of capital punishment for the crime of murder, and when a life has been taken deliberately by the offender, we cannot say that the punishment is invariably disproportionate to the crime. It is an extreme sanction, suitable to the most extreme of crimes. . . .
>
> *Furman* mandates that where discretion is afforded a sentencing body on a matter so grave as the determination of whether a human life should be taken or spared, that discretion must be suitably directed and limited so as to minimize the risk of wholly arbitrary and capricious action. . . .
>
> The basic concern of *Furman* centered on those defendants who were being condemned to death capriciously and arbitrarily. Under the procedures before the Court in that case, sentencing authorities were not directed to give attention to the nature or circumstances of the crime committed or to the character or record of the defendant. Left unguided, juries imposed the death sentence in a way that could only be called freakish. The new Georgia sentencing procedures, by contrast, focus the jury's attention on the particularized nature of the crime and the particularized characteristics of the individual defendant. While the jury is permitted

to consider any aggravating or mitigating circumstances, it must find and identify at least one statutory aggravating factor before it may impose a penalty of death. In this way the jury's discretion is channeled. No longer can a jury wantonly and freakishly impose the death sentence; it is always circumscribed by the legislative guidelines. In addition, the review function of the Supreme Court of Georgia affords additional assurance that the concerns that prompted our decision in *Furman* are not present to any significant degree in the Georgia procedure applied here.

Id. at 187-189.

Since 1976, the Supreme Court has sought to fine-tune administration of the death penalty. For example, in Coker v. Georgia, 433 U.S. 584 (1977), the Court held that the death penalty is "grossly disproportionate and excessive punishment for the crime of rape and is therefore forbidden by the Eighth Amendment." In 2008, the Supreme Court further held that the death penalty is disproportionate for child rapes as well. Kennedy v. Louisiana, 554 U.S. 407 (2008).

In Enmund v. Florida, 458 U.S. 782 (1982), the Court held that the death penalty must be proportionate not only to the crime committed but also to the defendant's role in that crime. Thus, while the death penalty may be imposed in certain felony-murder cases, it is disproportionate punishment to impose the death penalty on someone who "does not himself kill, attempt to kill, or intend that a killing take place or that lethal force will be employed." In Tison v. Arizona, 481 U.S. 137 (1987), the Court held that the death penalty may be imposed in felony-murder cases in which the defendant demonstrates a "reckless disregard for human life" and plays a major role in the crime.

Attacks on the death penalty have continued, but the Supreme Court has steadfastly refused to strike it down as per se unconstitutional, even when presented with statistical studies that demonstrate that it is applied disproportionately based on the race of the defendant and victim. In McCleskey v. Kemp, 481 U.S. 279 (1987), the Court rejected a claim that the death penalty is unconstitutional because a black defendant who kills a white victim is 4.3 times more likely to receive a death sentence as a defendant charged with killing blacks.

Since *Furman*, the Supreme Court has attempted to set standards that will ensure that the death penalty is administered in a fashion consistent with the Constitution. Yet its task has not been an easy one. Almost every year, the Court is faced with some type of challenge to capital punishment — with respect to its scope or application, habeas corpus review procedures, or standards for effective assistance of counsel. Because of the challenges that inhere in the construction of a constitutional system of capital punishment, one of the justices who originally agreed in *Furman* that the death penalty was not per se unconstitutional abandoned hopes of implementing it in a constitutional manner. In his dissent to the denial of certiorari in Callins v. Collins, 510 U.S. 1141 (1994), Justice Blackmun wrote:

On February 23, 1994, at approximately 1:00 A.M., Bruce Edwin Callins will be executed by the State of Texas. Intravenous tubes attached to his arms will carry the instrument of death, a toxic fluid designed specifically for the purpose of killing human beings. The witnesses, standing a few feet away, will behold Callins, no longer a defendant, an appellant, or a petitioner, but a man, strapped to a gurney, and seconds away from extinction.

Within days, or perhaps hours, the memory of Callins will begin to fade. The wheels of justice will churn again, and somewhere, another jury or another judge will have the unenviable task of determining whether some human being is to live or die. We hope, of course, that the defendant whose life is at risk will be represented by competent counsel — someone who is inspired by the awareness that a less-than-vigorous defense truly could have fatal consequences for the defendant. We hope that the attorney will investigate all aspects of the case, follow all evidentiary and procedural rules, and appear before a judge who is still committed to the protection of defendants' rights — even now, as the prospect of meaningful judicial oversight has diminished. In the same vein, we hope that the prosecution, in urging the penalty of death, will have exercised its discretion wisely, free from bias, prejudice, or political motive, and will be humbled, rather than emboldened, by the awesome authority conferred by the State.

But even if we can feel confident that these actors will fulfill their roles to the best of their human ability, our collective conscience will remain uneasy. Twenty years have passed since this Court declared that the death penalty must be imposed fairly, and with reasonable consistency, or not at all, *see* Furman v. Georgia (1972), and, despite the effort of the States and courts to devise legal formulas and procedural rules to meet this daunting challenge, the death penalty remains fraught with arbitrariness, discrimination, caprice, and mistake. This is not to say that the problems with the death penalty today are identical to those that were present 20 years ago. Rather, the problems that were pursued down one hole with procedural rules and verbal formulas have come to the surface somewhere else, just as virulent and pernicious as they were in their original form. Experience has taught us that the constitutional goal of eliminating arbitrariness and discrimination from the administration of death can never be achieved without compromising an equally essential component of fundamental fairness — individualized sentencing.

From this day forward, I no longer shall tinker with the machinery of death. For more than 20 years I have endeavored — indeed, I have struggled — along with a majority of this Court, to develop procedural and substantive rules that would lend more than the mere appearance of fairness to the death penalty endeavor. Rather than continue to coddle the Court's delusion that the desired level of fairness has been achieved and the need for regulation eviscerated, I feel morally and intellectually obligated simply to concede that the death penalty experiment has failed. It is virtually self-evident to me now that no combination of procedural rules or substantive regulations ever can save the death penalty from its inherent constitutional deficiencies.

Perhaps one day this Court will develop procedural rules or verbal formulas that actually will provide consistency, fairness, and reliability in a capital-sentencing scheme. I am not optimistic that such a day will come. I am more optimistic, though, that this Court eventually will conclude that the effort to eliminate arbitrariness while preserving fairness "in the infliction of [death] is so plainly doomed to failure that it — and the death penalty — must be abandoned altogether." I may not live to see that day, but I have faith that eventually it will arrive.

3. Recent Limits on the Scope of the Death Penalty

The Supreme Court has not held that the death penalty is unconstitutional, but in this new century, it has decided three cases that have resulted in limiting its scope. In Atkins v. Virginia, 536 U.S. 304 (2002), the Court held that the Eighth Amendment prohibits the execution of mentally retarded persons.[13] In Roper v. Simmons, 543 U.S. 551 (2005), the Court struck down death sentences imposed on persons who were younger than 18 years of age when they committed their capital crimes. In Kennedy v. Louisiana, 554 U.S. 407 (2008), the Court struck down the death penalty for non-homicide crimes such as child rape.

a. Prohibition of the Death Penalty for Mentally Retarded Defendants

ATKINS v. VIRGINIA
536 U.S. 304 (2002)

Justice STEVENS delivered the opinion of the Court.

Those mentally retarded persons who meet the law's requirements for criminal responsibility should be tried and punished when they commit crimes. Because of their disabilities in areas of reasoning, judgment, and control of their impulses, however, they do not act with the level of moral culpability that characterizes the most serious adult criminal conduct. Moreover, their impairments can jeopardize the reliability and fairness of capital proceedings against mentally retarded defendants. Presumably for these reasons, in the [last] 13 years, the American public, legislators, scholars, and judges have deliberated over the question whether the death penalty should ever be imposed on a mentally retarded criminal. The consensus reflected in those deliberations informs our answer to the question presented by this case: whether such executions are "cruel and unusual punishments" prohibited by the Eighth Amendment to the Federal Constitution.

I

Petitioner, Daryl Renard Atkins, was convicted of abduction, armed robbery, and capital murder, and sentenced to death. At approximately midnight on August 16, 1996, Atkins and William Jones, armed with a semiautomatic handgun, abducted Eric Nesbitt, robbed him of the money on his person,

---

13. Previously, in Ford v. Wainwright, 477 U.S. 399 (1986), the Supreme Court had found that the execution of persons who become insane while awaiting execution violates the Eighth Amendment.

drove him to an automated teller machine in his pickup truck where cameras recorded their withdrawal of additional cash, then took him to an isolated location where he was shot eight times and killed.

Jones and Atkins both testified in the guilt phase of Atkins' trial.[14] Each confirmed most of the details in the other's account of the incident, with the important exception that each stated that the other had actually shot and killed Nesbitt. Jones' testimony, which was both more coherent and credible than Atkins', was obviously credited by the jury and was sufficient to establish Atkins' guilt. At the penalty phase of the trial, the State introduced victim impact evidence and proved two aggravating circumstances: future dangerousness and "vileness of the offense." To prove future dangerousness, the State relied on Atkins' prior felony convictions as well as the testimony of four victims of earlier robberies and assaults. To prove the second aggravator, the prosecution relied upon the trial record, including pictures of the deceased's body and the autopsy report.

In the penalty phase, the defense relied on one witness, Dr. Evan Nelson, a forensic psychologist who had evaluated Atkins before trial and concluded that he was "mildly mentally retarded." His conclusion was based on interviews with people who knew Atkins, a review of school and court records, and the administration of a standard intelligence test which indicated that Atkins had a full scale IQ of 59.

The jury sentenced Atkins to death, but the Virginia Supreme Court ordered a second sentencing hearing because the trial court had used a misleading verdict form. At the resentencing, Dr. Nelson again testified. The State presented an expert rebuttal witness, Dr. Stanton Samenow, who expressed the opinion that Atkins was not mentally retarded, but rather was of "average intelligence, at least," and diagnosable as having antisocial personality disorder. The jury again sentenced Atkins to death.

The Supreme Court of Virginia affirmed the imposition of the death penalty. Atkins did not argue before the Virginia Supreme Court that his sentence was disproportionate to penalties imposed for similar crimes in Virginia, but he did contend "that he is mentally retarded and thus cannot be sentenced to death." The Court was "not willing to commute Atkins' sentence of death to life imprisonment merely because of his IQ score."

Justice Hassell and Justice Koontz dissented. They rejected Dr. Samenow's opinion that Atkins possesses average intelligence as "incredulous as a matter of law," and concluded that "the imposition of the sentence of death upon a criminal defendant who has the mental age of a child between the ages of 9 and 12 is excessive." In their opinion, "it is indefensible to conclude that individuals who are mentally retarded are not to some degree less culpable for their criminal acts. By definition, such individuals

14. Initially, both Jones and Atkins were indicted for capital murder. The prosecution ultimately permitted Jones to plead guilty to first-degree murder in exchange for his testimony against Atkins. As a result of the plea, Jones became ineligible to receive the death penalty. [Footnote by the Court.]

have substantial limitations not shared by the general population. A moral and civilized society diminishes itself if its system of justice does not afford recognition and consideration of those limitations in a meaningful way."

Because of the gravity of the concerns expressed by the dissenters, and in light of the dramatic shift in the state legislative landscape that has occurred in the past 13 years, we granted certiorari to revisit the issue that we first addressed in the *Penry* case.

II

The Eighth Amendment succinctly prohibits "excessive" sanctions. It provides: "Excessive bail shall not be required, nor excessive fines imposed, nor cruel and unusual punishments inflicted." In *Weems v. United States* (1910), we held that a punishment of 12 years jailed in irons at hard and painful labor for the crime of falsifying records was excessive. We explained "that it is a precept of justice that punishment for crime should be graduated and proportioned to the offense." We have repeatedly applied this proportionality precept in later cases interpreting the Eighth Amendment. *See* Harmelin v. Michigan (1991).

A claim that punishment is excessive is judged not by the standards that prevailed in 1685 when Lord Jeffreys presided over the "Bloody Assizes" or when the Bill of Rights was adopted, but rather by those that currently prevail.

Proportionality review under those evolving standards should be informed by "objective factors to the maximum possible extent." We have pinpointed that the "clearest and most reliable objective evidence of contemporary values is the legislation enacted by the country's legislatures." Relying in part on such legislative evidence, we have held that death is an impermissibly excessive punishment for the rape of an adult woman, Coker v. Georgia (1977), or for a defendant who neither took life, attempted to take life, nor intended to take life, Enmund v. Florida (1982).

Guided by our approach in these cases, we shall first review the judgment of legislatures that have addressed the suitability of imposing the death penalty on the mentally retarded and then consider reasons for agreeing or disagreeing with their judgment.

III

The parties have not called our attention to any state legislative consideration of the suitability of imposing the death penalty on mentally retarded offenders prior to 1986. In that year, the public reaction to the execution of a mentally retarded murderer in Georgia, apparently led to the enactment of the first state statute prohibiting such executions. In 1988, when Congress enacted legislation reinstating the federal death penalty, it expressly provided that a "sentence of death shall not be carried out upon a person who is mentally retarded." In 1989, Maryland enacted a similar prohibition. It was in that year that we decided *Penry*, and concluded that those two state enactments, "even when added to the 14 States that have rejected capital punishment completely, do not provide sufficient evidence at present of a national consensus."

Much has changed since then. Responding to the national attention received by the Bowden execution and our decision in *Penry*, state legislatures across the country began to address the issue. In 1990 Kentucky and Tennessee enacted statutes similar to those in Georgia and Maryland, as did New Mexico in 1991, and Arkansas, Colorado, Washington, Indiana, and Kansas in 1993 and 1994. In 1995, when New York reinstated its death penalty, it emulated the Federal Government by expressly exempting the mentally retarded. Nebraska followed suit in 1998. [I]n 2000 and 2001 six more States — South Dakota, Arizona, Connecticut, Florida, Missouri, and North Carolina—joined the procession. The Texas Legislature unanimously adopted a similar bill, and bills have passed at least one house in other States, including Virginia and Nevada.

It is not so much the number of these States that is significant, but the consistency of the direction of change. Given the well-known fact that anti-crime legislation is far more popular than legislation providing protections for persons guilty of violent crime, the large number of States prohibiting the execution of mentally retarded persons (and the complete absence of States passing legislation reinstating the power to conduct such executions) provides powerful evidence that today our society views mentally retarded offenders as categorically less culpable than the average criminal. The evidence carries even greater force when it is noted that the legislatures that have addressed the issue have voted overwhelmingly in favor of the prohibition. Moreover, even in those States that allow the execution of mentally retarded offenders, the practice is uncommon. And it appears that even among those States that regularly execute offenders and that have no prohibition with regard to the mentally retarded, only five have executed offenders possessing a known IQ less than 70. The practice, therefore, has become truly unusual, and it is fair to say that a national consensus has developed against it.

To the extent there is serious disagreement about the execution of mentally retarded offenders, it is in determining which offenders are in fact retarded. As was our approach in Ford v. Wainwright, with regard to insanity, "we leave to the States the task of developing appropriate ways to enforce the constitutional restriction upon its execution of sentences."

IV

This consensus unquestionably reflects widespread judgment about the relative culpability of mentally retarded offenders, and the relationship between mental retardation and the penological purposes served by the death penalty. Additionally, it suggests that some characteristics of mental retardation undermine the strength of the procedural protections that our capital jurisprudence steadfastly guards.

[There are] two reasons consistent with the legislative consensus that the mentally retarded should be categorically excluded from execution. First, there is a serious question as to whether either justification that we have recognized as a basis for the death penalty applies to mentally retarded offenders. Gregg v. Georgia (1976), identified "retribution and deterrence of capital crimes by prospective offenders" as the social purposes served by the death penalty. Unless the imposition of the death penalty on a mentally retarded person "measurably contributes to one or both of these goals, it 'is nothing more than the purposeless and needless imposition of pain and suffering,' and hence an unconstitutional punishment."

With respect to retribution — the interest in seeing that the offender gets his "just deserts" — the severity of the appropriate punishment necessarily depends on the culpability of the offender. If the culpability of the average murderer is insufficient to justify the most extreme sanction available to the State, the lesser culpability of the mentally retarded offender surely does not merit that form of retribution.

With respect to deterrence — the interest in preventing capital crimes by prospective offenders — "it seems likely that 'capital punishment can serve as a deterrent only when murder is the result of premeditation and deliberation.'" Exempting the mentally retarded from that punishment will not affect the "cold calculus that precedes the decision" of other potential murderers. The theory of deterrence in capital sentencing is predicated upon the notion that the increased severity of the punishment will inhibit criminal actors from carrying out murderous conduct. Yet it is the same cognitive and behavioral impairments that make these defendants less morally culpable — for example, the diminished ability to understand and process information, to learn from experience, to engage in logical reasoning, or to control impulses — that also make it less likely that they can process the information of the possibility of execution as a penalty and, as a result, control their conduct based upon that information.

The reduced capacity of mentally retarded offenders provides a second justification for a categorical rule making such offenders ineligible for the death penalty. The risk "that the death penalty will be imposed in spite of factors which may call for a less severe penalty" is enhanced, not only by the possibility of false confessions, but also by the lesser ability of mentally retarded defendants to make a persuasive showing of mitigation in the face of prosecutorial evidence of one or more aggravating factors. Mentally retarded defendants may be less able to give meaningful assistance to their counsel and are typically poor witnesses, and their demeanor may create an unwarranted impression of lack of remorse for their crimes. Mentally retarded defendants in the aggregate face a special risk of wrongful execution.

Our independent evaluation of the issue reveals no reason to disagree with the judgment of "the legislatures that have recently addressed the matter" and concluded that death is not a suitable punishment for a mentally retarded criminal. We are not persuaded that the execution of mentally retarded criminals will measurably advance the deterrent or the retributive purpose of the death penalty. Construing and applying the Eighth Amendment in the light of our "evolving standards of decency," we therefore conclude that such punishment is excessive and that the Constitution "places a substantive restriction on the State's power to take the life" of a mentally retarded offender.

Justice SCALIA, with whom Chief Justice REHNQUIST and Justice THOMAS join, dissenting.

Today's decision is the pinnacle of our Eighth Amendment death-is-different jurisprudence. Not only does it, like all of that jurisprudence, find no support in the text or history of the Eighth Amendment; it does not even have support in current social attitudes regarding the conditions that render an otherwise just death penalty inappropriate. Seldom has an opinion of this Court rested so obviously upon nothing but the personal views of its members.

I

I begin with a brief restatement of facts that are abridged by the Court but important to understanding this case. After spending the day drinking alcohol and smoking marijuana, petitioner Daryl Renard Atkins and a partner in crime drove to a convenience store, intending to rob a customer. Their victim was Eric Nesbitt, an airman from Langley Air Force Base, whom they abducted, drove to a nearby automated teller machine, and forced to withdraw $200. They then drove him to a deserted area, ignoring his pleas to leave him unharmed. According to the co-conspirator, whose testimony the jury evidently credited, Atkins ordered Nesbitt out of the vehicle and, after he had taken only a few steps, shot him one, two, three, four, five, six, seven, eight times in the thorax, chest, abdomen, arms, and legs.

The jury convicted Atkins of capital murder. At resentencing, the jury heard extensive evidence of petitioner's alleged mental retardation. A psychologist testified that petitioner was mildly mentally retarded with an IQ of 59, that he was a "slow learner," who showed a "lack of success in pretty much every domain of his life," and that he had an "impaired" capacity to appreciate the criminality of his conduct and to conform his conduct to the law, *id.* Petitioner's family members offered additional evidence in support of his mental retardation claim.

The jury also heard testimony about petitioner's 16 prior felony convictions for robbery, attempted robbery, abduction, use of a firearm, and maiming. *Id.* The victims of these offenses provided graphic depictions of petitioner's violent tendencies: The jury sentenced petitioner to death.

II

As the foregoing history demonstrates, petitioner's mental retardation was a central issue at sentencing. The jury concluded, however, that his alleged retardation was not a compelling reason to exempt him from the death penalty in light of the brutality of his crime and his long demonstrated propensity for violence.

Under our Eighth Amendment jurisprudence, a punishment is "cruel and unusual" if it falls within one of two categories: "those modes or acts of punishment that had been considered cruel and unusual at the time that the Bill of Rights was adopted," and modes of punishment that are inconsistent with modern "standards of decency," as evinced by objective indicia, the most important of which is "legislation enacted by the country's legislatures."

The Court makes no pretense that execution of the mildly mentally retarded would have been considered "cruel and unusual" in 1791.

The Court is left to argue, therefore, that execution of the mildly retarded is inconsistent with the "evolving standards of decency that mark the progress of a maturing society." Before today, our opinions consistently emphasized that Eighth Amendment judgments regarding the existence of social "standards" "should be informed by objective factors to the maximum possible extent" and "should not be, or appear to be, merely the subjective views of individual Justices."

The Court pays lipservice to these precedents as it miraculously extracts a "national consensus" forbidding execution of the mentally retarded from the fact that 18 States — less than half (47%) of the 38 States that permit capital punishment (for whom the issue exists) — have very recently enacted legislation barring execution of the mentally retarded.

How is it possible that agreement among 47% of the death penalty jurisdictions amounts to "consensus"?

Moreover, a major factor that the Court entirely disregards is that the legislation of all 18 States it relies on is still in its infancy. The oldest of the statutes is only 14 years old. It is "myopic to base sweeping constitutional principles upon the narrow experience of [a few] years."

The Court attempts to bolster its embarrassingly feeble evidence of "consensus" with the following: "It is not so much the number of these States that is significant, but the consistency of the direction of change." But in what other direction could we possibly see change? Given that 14 years ago all the death penalty statutes included the mentally retarded, any change (except precipitate undoing of what had just been done) was bound to be in the one direction the Court finds significant enough to overcome the lack of real consensus.

Even less compelling (if possible) is the Court's argument that evidence of "national consensus" is to be found in the infrequency with which retarded persons are executed in States that do not bar their execution. To begin with, what the Court takes as true is in fact quite doubtful. It is not at all clear that execution of the mentally retarded is "uncommon," ibid., as even the sources cited by the Court suggests. If, however, execution of the mentally retarded is "uncommon," then surely the explanation is that mental retardation is a constitutionally mandated mitigating factor at sentencing.

But the Prize for the Court's Most Feeble Effort to fabricate "national consensus" must go to its appeal (deservedly relegated to a footnote) to the views of assorted professional and religious organizations, members of the so-called "world community," and respondents to opinion polls. I agree with the Chief Justice that the views of professional and religious organizations and the results of opinion polls are irrelevant. Where there is not first a settled consensus among our own people, the views of other nations, however enlightened the Justices of this Court may think them to be, cannot be imposed upon Americans through the Constitution.

III

Beyond the empty talk of a "national consensus," the Court gives us a brief glimpse of what really underlies today's decision: "The Constitution," the Court says, "contemplates that in the end *our own judgment* will be brought to bear on the question of the acceptability of the death penalty under the Eighth Amendment." The arrogance of this assumption of power takes one's breath away.

The genuinely operative portion of the opinion, then, is the Court's statement of the reasons why it agrees with the contrived consensus it has found, that the "diminished capacities" of the mentally retarded render the death penalty excessive.

Proceeding from these faulty assumptions, the Court gives two reasons why the death penalty is an excessive punishment for all mentally retarded offenders. First, the "diminished capacities" of the mentally retarded raise a "serious question" whether their execution contributes to the "social purposes" of the death penalty, viz., retribution and deterrence. Retribution is not advanced, the argument goes, because the mentally retarded are no more culpable than the average murderer, whom we have already held lacks sufficient culpability to warrant the death penalty. Who says so? Is there an established correlation between mental acuity and the ability to conform one's conduct to the law in such a rudimentary matter as murder? Are the mentally retarded really more disposed (and hence more likely) to commit willfully cruel and serious crime than others? In my experience, the opposite is true: being childlike generally suggests innocence rather than brutality.

Assuming, however, that there is a direct connection between diminished intelligence and the inability to refrain from murder, what scientific analysis can possibly show that a mildly retarded individual who commits an exquisite torture-killing is "no more culpable" than the "average" murderer in a holdup-gone-wrong or a domestic dispute? Or a moderately retarded individual who commits a series of 20 exquisite torture-killings? Surely culpability, and deservedness of the most severe retribution, depends not merely (if at all) upon the mental capacity of the criminal (above the level where he is able to distinguish right from wrong) but also upon the depravity of the crime — which is precisely why this sort of question has traditionally been thought answerable not by a categorical rule of the sort the Court today imposes upon all trials, but rather by the sentencer's weighing of the circumstances (both degree of retardation and depravity of crime) in the particular case. The fact that juries continue to sentence mentally retarded offenders to death for extreme crimes shows that society's moral outrage sometimes demands execution of retarded offenders.

As for the other social purpose of the death penalty that the Court discusses, deterrence: That is not advanced, the Court tells us, because the mentally retarded are "less likely" than their non-retarded counterparts to "process the information of the possibility of execution as a penalty and . . . control their conduct based upon that information." But surely the deterrent effect of a penalty is adequately vindicated if it successfully deters many, but not all, of the target class. In other words, the supposed fact that some retarded criminals cannot fully appreciate the death penalty has nothing to do with the deterrence rationale, but is simply an echo of the arguments denying a retribution rationale, discussed and rejected above.

The Court throws one last factor into its grab bag of reasons why execution of the retarded is "excessive" in all cases: Mentally retarded offenders "face a special risk of wrongful execution" because they are less able "to make a persuasive showing of mitigation," "to give meaningful assistance to their counsel," and to be effective witnesses. "Special risk" is pretty flabby language (even flabbier than "less likely") — and I suppose a similar "special risk" could be said to exist for just plain stupid people, inarticulate people, even ugly people. If this unsupported claim has any substance to it (which I doubt) it might support a due process claim in all criminal prosecutions of the mentally retarded; but it is hard to see how it has anything to do with an Eighth Amendment claim that execution of the mentally retarded is cruel and unusual. We have never before held it to be cruel and unusual punishment to impose a sentence in violation of some other constitutional imperative.

Today's opinion adds one more to the long list of substantive and procedural requirements impeding imposition of the death penalty imposed under this Court's assumed power to invent a death-is-different jurisprudence. None of those requirements existed when the Eighth Amendment was adopted, and some of them were not even supported by current moral consensus. They include prohibition of the death penalty for "ordinary" murder, for rape of an adult woman, and for felony murder absent a showing that the defendant possessed a sufficiently culpable state of mind; prohibition of the death penalty for any person under the age of 16 at the time of the crime, prohibition of the death penalty as the mandatory punishment for any crime, requirement that the sentencer not be given unguided discretion, a requirement that the sentencer be empowered to take into account all mitigating circumstances, and a requirement that the accused receive a judicial evaluation of his claim of insanity before the sentence can be executed. There is something to be said for popular abolition of the death penalty; there is nothing to be said for its incremental abolition by this Court.

This newest invention promises to be more effective than any of the others in turning the process of capital trial into a game.

Chief Justice REHNQUIST, with whom Justices SCALIA and THOMAS join, dissenting.

I agree with Justice Scalia that the Court's assessment of the current legislative judgment regarding the execution of defendants like petitioner more resembles a post hoc rationalization for the majority's subjectively preferred result rather than any objective effort to ascertain the content of an evolving standard of decency. I write separately, however, to call attention to the defects in the Court's decision to place weight on foreign laws, the views of professional and religious organizations, and opinion polls in reaching its conclusion.

In making determinations about whether a punishment is "cruel and unusual" under the evolving standards of decency embraced by the Eighth Amendment, we have emphasized that legislation is the "clearest and most reliable objective evidence of contemporary values." The reason we ascribe primacy to legislative enactments follows from the constitutional role legislatures play in expressing policy of a State.

Our opinions have also recognized that data concerning the actions of sentencing juries, though entitled to less weight than legislative judgments, "is a significant and reliable index of contemporary values," because of the jury's intimate involvement in the case and its function of "maintaining a link between contemporary community values and the penal system."

In my view, these two sources — the work product of legislatures and sentencing jury determinations — ought to be the sole indicators by which courts ascertain the contemporary American conceptions of decency for purposes of the Eighth Amendment. They are the only objective indicia of contemporary values firmly supported by our precedents.

To further buttress its appraisal of contemporary societal values, the Court marshals public opinion poll results and evidence that several professional organizations and religious groups have adopted official positions opposing the imposition of the death penalty upon mentally retarded offenders. In my view, none should be accorded any weight on the Eight Amendment scale when the elected representatives of a State's populace have not deemed them persuasive enough to prompt legislative action.

Even if I were to accept the legitimacy of the Court's decision to reach beyond the product of legislatures and practices of sentencing juries to discern a national standard of decency, I would take issue with the blind-faith credence it accords the opinion polls brought to our attention. An extensive body of social science literature describes how methodological and other errors can affect the reliability and validity of estimates about the opinions and attitudes of a population derived from various sampling techniques.

b. Prohibition of the Death Penalty for Crimes Committed by Minors

Three years later, in Roper v. Simmons, the Supreme Court again took steps to limit the scope of the death penalty. This time, the Court examined whether the imposition of the death penalty on persons who were younger than 18 years of age when they committed crimes violates the Eighth Amendment.

ROPER v. SIMMONS

543 U.S. 551 (2005)

Justice KENNEDY delivered the opinion of the Court.

This case requires us to address, for the second time in a decade and a half, whether it is permissible under the Eighth and Fourteenth Amendments to the Constitution of the United States to execute a juvenile offender who was older than 15 but younger than 18 when he committed a capital crime. In Stanford v. Kentucky (1989), a divided Court rejected the proposition that the Constitution bars capital punishment for juvenile offenders in this age group. We reconsider the question.

I

At the age of 17, when he was still a junior in high school, Christopher Simmons, the respondent here, committed murder. About nine months later, after he had turned 18, he was tried and sentenced to death. There is little doubt that Simmons was the instigator of the crime. Before its commission Simmons said he wanted to murder someone. In chilling, callous terms he talked about his plan, discussing it for the most part with two friends, Charles Benjamin and John Tessmer, then aged 15 and 16 respectively. Simmons proposed to commit burglary and murder by breaking and entering, tying up a victim, and throwing the victim off a bridge. Simmons assured his friends they could "get away with it" because they were minors.

The three met at about 2 A.M. on the night of the murder, but Tessmer left before the other two set out. (The State later charged Tessmer with conspiracy, but dropped the charge in exchange for his testimony against Simmons.) Simmons and Benjamin entered the home of the victim, Shirley Crook, after reaching through an open window and unlocking the back door. Simmons turned on a hallway light. Awakened, Mrs. Crook called out, "Who's there?" In response Simmons entered Mrs. Crook's bedroom, where he recognized her from a previous car accident involving them both. Simmons later admitted this confirmed his resolve to murder her.

Using duct tape to cover her eyes and mouth and bind her hands, the two perpetrators put Mrs. Crook in her minivan and drove to a state park. They reinforced the bindings, covered her head with a towel, and walked her to a railroad trestle spanning the Meramec River. There they tied her hands and feet together with electrical wire, wrapped her whole face in duct tape and threw her from the bridge, drowning her in the waters below.

By the afternoon of September 9, Steven Crook had returned home from an overnight trip, found his bedroom in disarray, and reported his wife missing. On the same afternoon fishermen recovered the victim's body from the river. Simmons, meanwhile, was bragging about the killing, telling friends he had killed a woman "because the bitch seen my face."

The next day, after receiving information of Simmons' involvement, police arrested him at his high school and took him to the police station in Fenton, Missouri. They read him his *Miranda* rights. Simmons waived his right to an attorney and agreed to answer questions. After less than two hours of interrogation, Simmons confessed to the murder and agreed to perform a videotaped reenactment at the crime scene.

The State charged Simmons with burglary, kidnaping, stealing, and murder in the first degree. As Simmons was 17 at the time of the crime, he was outside the criminal jurisdiction of Missouri's juvenile court system. He was tried as an adult. At trial the State introduced Simmons' confession and the videotaped reenactment of the crime, along with testimony that Simmons discussed the crime in advance and bragged about it later. The defense called no witnesses in the guilt phase. The jury having returned a verdict of murder, the trial proceeded to the penalty phase.

The State sought the death penalty. As aggravating factors, the State submitted that the murder was committed for the purpose of receiving money; was committed for the purpose of avoiding, interfering with, or preventing lawful arrest of the defendant; and involved depravity of mind and was outrageously and wantonly vile, horrible, and inhuman. The State called Shirley Crook's husband, daughter, and two sisters, who presented moving evidence of the devastation her death had brought to their lives.

In mitigation Simmons' attorneys first called an officer of the Missouri juvenile justice system, who testified that Simmons had no prior convictions and that no previous charges had been filed against him. Simmons' mother, father, two younger half brothers, a neighbor, and a friend took the stand to tell the jurors of the close relationships they had formed with Simmons and to plead for mercy on his behalf. Simmons' mother, in particular, testified to the responsibility Simmons demonstrated in taking care of his two younger half brothers and of his grandmother and to his capacity to show love for them.

During closing arguments, both the prosecutor and defense counsel addressed Simmons' age, which the trial judge had instructed the jurors they could consider as a mitigating factor. Defense counsel reminded the jurors that juveniles of Simmons' age cannot drink, serve on juries, or even see certain movies, because "the legislatures have wisely decided that individuals of a certain age aren't responsible enough." Defense counsel argued that Simmons' age should make "a huge difference to [the jurors] in deciding just exactly what sort of punishment to make." In rebuttal, the prosecutor gave the following response: "Age, he says. Think about age. Seventeen years old. Isn't that scary? Doesn't that scare you? Mitigating? Quite the contrary I submit. Quite the contrary."

The jury recommended the death penalty after finding the State had proved each of the three aggravating factors submitted to it. Accepting the jury's recommendation, the trial judge imposed the death penalty.

Simmons obtained new counsel, who moved in the trial court to set aside the conviction and sentence. One argument was that Simmons had received ineffective assistance at trial. To support this contention, the new counsel called as witnesses Simmons' trial attorney, Simmons' friends and neighbors, and clinical psychologists who had evaluated him.

Part of the submission was that Simmons was "very immature," "very impulsive," and "very susceptible to being manipulated or influenced." The experts testified about Simmons' background including a difficult home environment and dramatic changes in behavior, accompanied by poor school performance in adolescence. Simmons was absent from home for long periods, spending time using alcohol and drugs with other teenagers or young adults. The contention by Simmons' postconviction counsel was that these matters should have been established in the sentencing proceeding.

The trial court found no constitutional violation by reason of ineffective assistance of counsel and denied the motion for postconviction relief.

After these proceedings in Simmons' case had run their course, this Court held that the Eighth and Fourteenth Amendments prohibit the execution of a mentally retarded person. Atkins v. Virginia (2002). Simmons filed a new petition for state postconviction relief, arguing that the reasoning of *Atkins* established that the Constitution prohibits the execution of a juvenile who was under 18 when the crime was committed.

The Missouri Supreme Court agreed. State ex rel. Simmons v. Roper, 112 S.W.3d 397 (2003) (en banc). It held that since *Stanford,* "a national consensus has developed against the execution of juvenile offenders, as demonstrated by the fact that eighteen states now bar such executions for juveniles, that twelve other states bar executions altogether, that no state has lowered its age of execution below 18 since *Stanford,* that five states have legislatively or by case law raised or established the minimum age at 18, and that the imposition of the juvenile death penalty has become truly unusual over the last decade." On this reasoning it set aside Simmons' death sentence and resentenced him to "life imprisonment without eligibility for probation, parole, or release except by act of the Governor."

We granted certiorari and now affirm.

II

The Eighth Amendment provides: "Excessive bail shall not be required, nor excessive fines imposed, nor cruel and unusual punishments inflicted." As the Court explained in *Atkins*, the Eighth Amendment guarantees individuals the right not to be subjected to excessive sanctions. The right flows from the basic "precept of justice that punishment for crime should be graduated and proportioned to [the] offense." By protecting even those convicted of heinous crimes, the Eighth Amendment reaffirms the duty of the government to respect the dignity of all persons.

The prohibition against "cruel and unusual punishments," like other expansive language in the Constitution, must be interpreted according to its text, by considering history, tradition, and precedent, and with due regard for its purpose and function in the constitutional design. To implement this framework we have established the propriety and affirmed the necessity of referring to "the evolving standards of decency that mark the progress of a maturing society" to determine which punishments are so disproportionate as to be cruel and unusual.

In Thompson v. Oklahoma (1988), a plurality of the Court determined that our standards of decency do not permit the execution of any offender under the age of 16 at the time of the crime. The plurality opinion explained that no death penalty State that had given express consideration to a minimum age for the death penalty had set the age lower than 16. The plurality also observed that "[t]he conclusion that it would offend civilized standards of decency to execute a person who was less than 16 years old at the time of his or her offense is consistent with the views that have been expressed by respected professional organizations, by other nations that share our Anglo-American heritage, and by the leading members of the Western European community." The opinion further noted that juries imposed the death penalty on offenders under 16 with exceeding rarity; the last execution of an offender for a crime committed under the age of 16 had been carried out in 1948, 40 years prior.

Bringing its independent judgment to bear on the permissibility of the death penalty for a 15-year-old offender, the *Thompson* plurality stressed that "[t]he reasons why juveniles are not trusted with the privileges and responsibilities of an adult also explain why their irresponsible conduct is not as morally reprehensible as that of an adult." According to the plurality, the lesser culpability of offenders under 16 made the death penalty inappropriate as a form of retribution, while the low likelihood that offenders under 16 engaged in "the kind of cost-benefit analysis that attaches any weight to the possibility of execution" made the death penalty ineffective as a means of deterrence.

The next year, in Stanford v. Kentucky (1989), the Court, over a dissenting opinion joined by four Justices, referred to contemporary standards of decency in this country and concluded the Eighth and Fourteenth Amendments did not proscribe the execution of juvenile offenders over 15 but under 18. The Court noted that 22 of the 37 death penalty States permitted the death penalty for 16-year-old offenders, and, among these 37 States, 25 permitted it for 17-year-old offenders. These numbers, in the Court's view, indicated there was no national consensus "sufficient to label a particular punishment cruel and unusual."

The same day the Court decided *Stanford*, it held that the Eighth Amendment did not mandate a categorical exemption from the death penalty for the mentally retarded. Penry v. Lynaug (1989). In reaching this conclusion it stressed that only two States had enacted laws banning the imposition of the death penalty on a mentally retarded person convicted of a capital offense.

Three Terms ago the subject was reconsidered in *Atkins*. We held that standards of decency have evolved since *Penry* and now demonstrate that the execution of the mentally retarded is cruel and unusual punishment.

Just as the *Atkins* Court reconsidered the issue decided in *Penry*, we now reconsider the issue decided in *Stanford*. The beginning point is a review of objective indicia of consensus, as expressed in particular by the enactments of legislatures that have addressed the question. These data give us essential instruction. We then must determine, in the exercise of our own independent judgment, whether the death penalty is a disproportionate punishment for juveniles.

III

A

The evidence of national consensus against the death penalty for juveniles is similar, and in some respects parallel, to the evidence *Atkins* held sufficient to demonstrate a national consensus against the death penalty for the mentally retarded. When *Atkins* was decided, 30 States prohibited the death penalty for the mentally retarded. This number comprised 12 that had abandoned the death penalty altogether, and 18 that maintained it but excluded the mentally retarded from its reach. By a similar calculation in this case, 30 States prohibit the juvenile death penalty, comprising 12 that have rejected the death penalty altogether and 18 that maintain it but, by express provision or judicial interpretation, exclude juveniles from its reach.

There is, to be sure, at least one difference between the evidence of consensus in *Atkins* and in this case. Impressive in *Atkins* was the rate of abolition of the death penalty for the mentally retarded. Sixteen States that permitted the execution of the mentally retarded at the time of *Penry* had prohibited the practice by the time we heard *Atkins*. By contrast, the rate of change in reducing the incidence of the juvenile death penalty, or in taking specific steps to abolish it, has been slower. Five States that allowed the juvenile death penalty at the time of *Stanford* have abandoned it in the intervening 15 years—four through legislative enactments and one through judicial decision.

Though less dramatic than the change from *Penry* to *Atkins* we still consider the change from *Stanford* to this case to be significant. As noted in *Atkins*, with respect to the States that had abandoned the death penalty for the mentally retarded since *Penry*, "[i]t is not so much the number of these States that is significant, but the consistency of the direction of change." The number of States that have abandoned capital punishment for juvenile offenders since *Stanford* is smaller than the number of States that abandoned capital punishment for the mentally retarded after *Penry*; yet we think the same consistency of direction of change has been demonstrated. Since *Stanford*, no State that previously prohibited capital punishment for juveniles has reinstated it. This fact, coupled with the trend toward abolition of the juvenile death penalty, carries special force in light of the general popularity of anticrime legislation. Any difference between this case and *Atkins* with respect to the pace of abolition is thus counterbalanced by the consistent direction of the change.

B

A majority of States have rejected the imposition of the death penalty on juvenile offenders under 18, and we now hold this is required by the Eighth Amendment.

Three general differences between juveniles under 18 and adults demonstrate that juvenile offenders cannot with reliability be classified among the worst offenders. First, as any parent knows and as the scientific and sociological studies respondent and his amici cite tend to confirm, "[a] lack of maturity and an underdeveloped sense of responsibility are found in youth more often than in adults and are more understandable among the young. These qualities often result in impetuous and ill-considered actions and decisions." It has been noted that "adolescents are overrepresented statistically in virtually every category of reckless behavior." In recognition of the comparative immaturity and irresponsibility of juveniles, almost every State prohibits those under 18 years of age from voting, serving on juries, or marrying without parental consent.

The second area of difference is that juveniles are more vulnerable or susceptible to negative influences and outside pressures, including peer pressure. This is explained in part by the prevailing circumstance that juveniles have less control, or less experience with control, over their own environment.

The third broad difference is that the character of a juvenile is not as well formed as that of an adult. The personality traits of juveniles are more transitory, less fixed.

These differences render suspect any conclusion that a juvenile falls among the worst offenders. From a moral standpoint it would be misguided to equate the failings of a minor with those of an adult, for a greater possibility exists that a minor's character deficiencies will be reformed.

As for deterrence, it is unclear whether the death penalty has a significant or even measurable deterrent effect on juveniles, as counsel for petitioner acknowledged at oral argument. Here, however, the absence of evidence of deterrent effect is of special concern because the same characteristics that render juveniles less culpable than adults suggest as well that juveniles will be less susceptible to deterrence. In particular, as the plurality observed in *Thompson*, "[t]he likelihood that the teenage offender has made the kind of cost-benefit analysis that attaches any weight to the possibility of execution is so remote as to be virtually nonexistent." To the extent the juvenile death penalty might have residual deterrent effect, it is worth noting that the punishment of life imprisonment without the possibility of parole is itself a severe sanction, in particular for a young person.

The differences between juvenile and adult offenders are too marked and well understood to risk allowing a youthful person to receive the death penalty despite insufficient culpability. An unacceptable likelihood exists that the brutality or cold-blooded nature of any particular crime would over-power mitigating arguments based on youth as a matter of course, even where the juvenile offender's objective immaturity, vulnerability, and lack of true depravity should require a sentence less severe than death. In some cases a defendant's youth may even be counted against him. In this very case, as we noted above, the prosecutor argued Simmons' youth was aggravating rather than mitigating.

Drawing the line at 18 years of age is subject, of course, to the objections always raised against categorical rules. The qualities that distinguish juve-niles from adults do not disappear when an individual turns 18. By the same token, some under 18 have already attained a level of maturity some adults will never reach. For the reasons we have discussed, however, a line must be drawn. The age of 18 is the point where society draws the line for many purposes between childhood and adulthood. It is, we conclude, the age at which the line for death eligibility ought to rest.

IV

Our determination that the death penalty is disproportionate punishment for offenders under 18 finds confirmation in the stark reality that the United States is the only country in the world that continues to give official sanction to the juvenile death penalty. This reality does not become controlling, for the task of interpreting the Eighth Amendment remains our responsibility. Yet at least from the time of the Court's decision in *Trop*, the Court has referred to the laws of other countries and to international authorities as instructive for its interpretation of the Eighth Amendment's prohibition of "cruel and unusual punishments."

As respondent and a number of amici emphasize, Article 37 of the United Nations Convention on the Rights of the Child, which every country in the world has ratified save for the United States and Somalia, contains an express prohibition on capital punishment for crimes committed by juveniles under 18. No ratifying country has entered a reservation to the provision prohibit-ing the execution of juvenile offenders.

Respondent and his amici have submitted, and petitioner does not con-test, that only seven countries other than the United States have executed juvenile offenders since 1990: Iran, Pakistan, Saudi Arabia, Yemen, Nigeria, the Democratic Republic of Congo, and China. Since then each of these countries has either abolished capital punishment for juveniles or made public disavowal of the practice. In sum, it is fair to say that the United States now stands alone in a world that has turned its face against the juvenile death penalty.

It is proper that we acknowledge the overwhelming weight of international opinion against the juvenile death penalty, resting in large part on the understanding that the instability and emotional imbalance of young people may often be a factor in the crime. The opinion of the world community, while not controlling our outcome, does provide respected and significant confirmation for our own conclusions.

The Eighth and Fourteenth Amendments forbid imposition of the death penalty on offenders who were under the age of 18 when their crimes were committed.

Justice O'CONNOR, dissenting.

The Court's decision today establishes a categorical rule forbidding the execution of any offender for any crime committed before his 18th birthday, no matter how deliberate, wanton, or cruel the offense. Neither the objective evidence of contemporary societal values, nor the Court's moral proportionality analysis, nor the two in tandem suffice to justify this ruling.

Although the Court finds support for its decision in the fact that a majority of the States now disallow capital punishment of 17-year-old offenders, it refrains from asserting that its holding is compelled by a genuine national consensus. Indeed, the evidence before us fails to demonstrate conclusively that any such consensus has emerged in the brief period since we upheld the constitutionality of this practice in Stanford v. Kentucky (1989).

Instead, the rule decreed by the Court rests, ultimately, on its independent moral judgment that death is a disproportionately severe punishment for any 17-year-old offender. I do not subscribe to this judgment. Adolescents as a class are undoubtedly less mature, and therefore less culpable for their misconduct, than adults. But the Court has adduced no evidence impeaching the seemingly reasonable conclusion reached by many state legislatures: that at least some 17-year-old murderers are sufficiently mature to deserve the death penalty in an appropriate case. Nor has it been shown that capital sentencing juries are incapable of accurately assessing a youthful defendant's maturity or of giving due weight to the mitigating characteristics associated with youth.

On this record—and especially in light of the fact that so little has changed since our recent decision in *Stanford*—I would not substitute our judgment about the moral propriety of capital punishment for 17-year-old murderers for the judgments of the Nation's legislatures. Rather, I would demand a clearer showing that our society truly has set its face against this practice before reading the Eighth Amendment categorically to forbid it.

Because I do not believe that a genuine national consensus against the juvenile death penalty has yet developed, and because I do not believe the Court's moral proportionality argument justifies a categorical, age-based constitutional rule, I can assign no such confirmatory role to the international consensus described by the Court. In short, the evidence of an international consensus does not alter my determination that the Eighth Amendment does not, at this time, forbid capital punishment of 17-year-old murderers in all cases.

Nevertheless, I disagree with Justice Scalia's contention that foreign and international law have no place in our Eighth Amendment jurisprudence. Over the course of nearly half a century, the Court has consistently referred to foreign and international law as relevant to its assessment of evolving standards of decency. This inquiry reflects the special character of the Eighth Amendment, which, as the Court has long held, draws its meaning directly from the maturing values of civilized society. Obviously, American law is distinctive in many respects, not least where the specific provisions of our Constitution and the history of its exposition so dictate. But this Nation's evolving understanding of human dignity certainly is neither wholly isolated from, nor inherently at odds with, the values prevailing in other countries. At least, the existence of an international consensus of this nature can serve to confirm the reasonableness of a consonant and genuine American consensus. The instant case presents no such domestic consensus, however, and the recent emergence of an otherwise global consensus does not alter that basic fact.

Justice SCALIA, with whom THE CHIEF JUSTICE and Justice THOMAS join, dissenting.

In urging approval of a constitution that gave life-tenured judges the power to nullify laws enacted by the people's representatives, Alexander Hamilton assured the citizens of New York that there was little risk in this, since "[t]he judiciary . . . ha[s] neither FORCE nor WILL but merely judgment." But Hamilton had in mind a traditional judiciary, "bound down by strict rules and precedents which serve to define and point out their duty in every particular case that comes before them." Bound down, indeed. What a mockery today's opinion makes of Hamilton's expectation, announcing the Court's conclusion that the meaning of our Constitution has changed over the past 15 years — not, mind you, that this Court's decision 15 years ago was wrong, but that the Constitution has changed. The Court reaches this implausible result by purporting to advert, not to the original meaning of the Eighth Amendment, but to "the evolving standards of decency." It then finds, on the flimsiest of grounds, that a national consensus which could not be perceived in our people's laws barely 15 years ago now solidly exists. Worse still, the Court says in so many words that what our people's laws say about the issue does not, in the last analysis, matter: "[I]n the end our own judgment will be brought to bear on the question of the acceptability of the death penalty under the Eighth Amendment." The Court thus proclaims itself sole arbiter of our Nation's moral standards—and in the course of discharging that awesome responsibility purports to take guidance from the views of foreign courts and legislatures. Because I do not believe that the meaning of our Eighth Amendment, any more than the meaning of other provisions of our Constitution, should be determined by the subjective views of five Members of this Court and like-minded foreigners, I dissent.

Today's opinion provides a perfect example of why judges are ill equipped to make the type of legislative judgments the Court insists on making here. To support its opinion that States should be prohibited from imposing the death penalty on anyone who committed murder before age 18, the Court looks to scientific and sociological studies, picking and choosing those that support its position. It never explains why those particular studies are methodologically sound; none was ever entered into evidence or tested in an adversarial proceeding.

In other words, all the Court has done today, to borrow from another context, is to look over the heads of the crowd and pick out its friends.

Though the views of our own citizens are essentially irrelevant to the Court's decision today, the views of other countries and the so-called international community take center stage. [T]he basic premise of the Court's argument—that American law should conform to the laws of the rest of the world—ought to be rejected out of hand. In fact the Court itself does not believe it. In many significant respects the laws of most other countries differ from our law—including not only such explicit provisions of our Constitution as the right to jury trial and grand jury indictment, but even many interpretations of the Constitution prescribed by this Court itself. The Court-pronounced exclusionary rule, for example, is distinctively American.

The Court has been oblivious to the views of other countries when deciding how to interpret our Constitution's requirement that "Congress shall make no law respecting an establishment of religion. . . ." And let us not forget the Court's abortion jurisprudence, which makes us one of only six countries that allow abortion on demand until the point of viability.

Foreign sources are cited today, not to underscore our "fidelity" to the Constitution, our "pride in its origins," and "our own [American] heritage." To the contrary, they are cited to set aside the centuries-old American practice—a practice still engaged in by a large majority of the relevant States—of letting a jury of 12 citizens decide whether, in the particular case, youth should be the basis for withholding the death penalty. What these foreign sources "affirm," rather than repudiate, is the Justices' own notion of how the world ought to be, and their diktat that it shall be so henceforth in America.

———————————

The Court's reliance on foreign law in *Roper* sparked controversy over the proper role of foreign law in American criminal law. Originalists, such as

Justice Scalia, maintain that reliance on foreign law is inconsistent with the unique tradition and values of American law.[15] As he stated, "We don't have the same moral and legal framework as the rest of the world, and never have." The practice of considering foreign law invites judges to cherry-pick from foreign laws so they can reach the conclusions they have already formed. As a result, they use foreign law to impose their own moral judgments on the populace.

By contrast, Justice Breyer and those who support the transnationalist approach to constitutional interpretation argue that "consideration of foreign law permits a natural process of judicial dialogue that is inescapable in the modern world."[16] They also argue that relying on foreign laws, such as those in Great Britain, makes sense given our common reliance on common law in the development of our legal practices. Given the history of American laws, transnationalists, including Justice Kennedy in *Roper*, argue that common values transcend national borders.

c. Prohibition of the Death Penalty for Non-Homicide Offenses

In Kennedy v. Louisiana, 554 U.S. 407 (2008), the Court took another step to limit the death penalty by holding that its application to a non-homicide offense, such as child rape, violates the Eighth Amendment.

KENNEDY v. LOUISIANA
554 U.S. 407 (2008)

Justice KENNEDY delivered the opinion of the Court.

Patrick Kennedy, the petitioner here, seeks to set aside his death sentence under the Eighth Amendment. He was charged by the respondent, the State of Louisiana, with the aggravated rape of his then-8-year-old stepdaughter. This case presents the question whether the Constitution bars respondent from imposing the death penalty for the rape of a child where the crime did not result, and was not intended to result, in death of the victim. We hold the Eighth Amendment prohibits the death penalty for this offense. The Louisiana statute is unconstitutional.

Petitioner's crime was one that cannot be recounted in these pages in a way sufficient to capture in full the hurt and horror inflicted on his victim or to convey the revulsion society, and the jury that represents it, sought to express by sentencing petitioner to death. [The Court then described the

---

15. *See A Conversation Between U.S. Supreme Court Justices*, 3 Intl. J. Const. L. 519, 525 (2005) (including a transcript of a debate between Justices Antonin Scalia and Stephen Breyer held at the American University Washington College of Law on January 13, 2005).

16. Daniel J. Frank, *Constitutional Interpretation Revisited: The Effects of a Delicate Supreme Court Balance on the Inclusion of Foreign Law in American Jurisprudence*, 92 Iowa L. Rev. 1037, 1046 (2007).

horrific rape of the child. Kennedy was convicted of aggravated rape of the child and sentenced to death.]

The Eighth Amendment, applicable to the States through the Fourteenth Amendment, provides that "[e]xcessive bail shall not be required, nor excessive fines imposed, nor cruel and unusual punishments inflicted." The Amendment "draw[s] its meaning from the evolving standards of decency that mark the progress of a maturing society."

In 1925, 18 States, the District of Columbia, and the Federal Government had statutes that authorized the death penalty for the rape of a child or an adult. See *Coker* (1977) (plurality opinion). Between 1930 and 1964, 455 people were executed for those crimes. To our knowledge the last individual executed for the rape of a child was Ronald Wolfe in 1964.

In 1972, *Furman* invalidated most of the state statutes authorizing the death penalty for the crime of rape; and in *Furman*'s aftermath only six States reenacted their capital rape provisions. Three States — Georgia, North Carolina, and Louisiana — did so with respect to all rape offenses. Three States — Florida, Mississippi, and Tennessee — did so with respect only to child rape.

Louisiana reintroduced the death penalty for rape of a child in 1995. Five States have since followed Louisiana's lead: Georgia, Montana, Oklahoma, South Carolina, and Texas. By contrast, 44 States have not made child rape a capital offense. As for federal law, Congress in the Federal Death Penalty Act of 1994 expanded the number of federal crimes for which the death penalty is a permissible sentence, including certain nonhomicide offenses; but it did not do the same for child rape or abuse.

The evidence of a national consensus with respect to the death penalty for child rapists, as with respect to juveniles, mentally retarded offenders, and vicarious felony murderers, shows divided opinion but, on balance, an opinion against it.

Louisiana is the only State since 1964 that has sentenced an individual to death for the crime of child rape; and petitioner and Richard Davis, who was convicted and sentenced to death for the aggravated rape of a 5-year-old child by a Louisiana jury in December 2007 are the only two individuals now on death row in the United States for a nonhomicide offense.

Our concern here is limited to crimes against individual persons. We do not address, for example, crimes defining and punishing treason, espionage, terrorism, and drug kingpin activity, which are offenses against the State. As it relates to crimes against individuals, though, the death penalty should not be expanded to instances where the victim's life was not taken.

It is not at all evident that the child rape victim's hurt is lessened when the law permits the death of the perpetrator. There are . . . serious systemic concerns in prosecuting the crime of child rape that are relevant to the constitutionality of making it a capital offense. The problem of unreliable, induced, and even imagined child testimony means there is a "special risk of wrongful execution" in some child rape cases.

In addition, by in effect making the punishment for child rape and murder equivalent, a State that punishes child rape by death may remove a strong incentive for the rapist not to kill the victim.

The rule of evolving standards of decency . . . means that resort to the penalty must be reserved for the worst of crimes and limited in its instances of application. Difficulties in administering the penalty to ensure against its arbitrary and capricious application require adherence to a rule reserving its use, at this stage of evolving standards and in cases of crimes against individuals, for crimes that take the life of the victim.

Justice ALITO, with whom THE CHIEF JUSTICE, Justice SCALIA, and Justice THOMAS join, dissenting.

The Court today holds that the Eighth Amendment categorically prohibits the imposition of the death penalty for the crime of raping a child. This is so, according to the Court, no matter how young the child, no matter how many times the child is raped, no matter how many children the perpetrator rapes, no matter how sadistic the crime, no matter how much physical or psychological trauma is inflicted, and no matter how heinous the perpetrator's prior criminal record may be.

The rape of any victim inflicts great injury, and "[s]ome victims are so grievously injured physically or psychologically that life *is* beyond repair." It has been estimated that as many as 40% of 7- to 13-year-old sexual assault victims are considered "seriously disturbed." The harm that is caused to the victims and to society at large by the worst child rapists is grave. It is the judgment of the Louisiana lawmakers and those in an increasing number of other States that these harms justify the death penalty. The Court provides no cogent explanation why this legislative judgment should be overridden. Conclusory references to "decency," "moderation," "restraint," "full progress," and "moral judgment" are not enough.

d. Method of Execution

Defendants may also challenge the method of execution as violating the prohibition against cruel and unusual punishment. The prevailing method of execution today is lethal injection. Defendants have challenged the three-drug protocol as inhumane. However, in a plurality decision in 2008, the Supreme Court held that the three-drug protocol for lethal injection, if properly administered, does not violate the Eighth Amendment. In his concurrence, Justice Stevens takes the opportunity to summarize the arguments for moving beyond the question of the constitutionality of our methods of execution to whether the death penalty should be retained.

BAZE v. REES
553 U.S. 35 (2008)

Chief Justice ROBERTS announced the judgment of the Court and delivered an opinion, in which Justice KENNEDY and Justice ALITO join.

Like 35 other States and the Federal Government, Kentucky has chosen to impose capital punishment for certain crimes. As is true with respect to each of these States and the Federal Government, Kentucky has altered its method of execution over time to more humane means of carrying out the sentence. That progress has led to the use of lethal injection by every jurisdiction that imposes the death penalty.

Petitioners in this case — each convicted of double homicide — acknowledge that the lethal injection procedure, if applied as intended, will result in a humane death. They nevertheless contend that the lethal injection protocol is unconstitutional under the Eighth Amendment's ban on "cruel and unusual punishments," because of the risk that the protocol's terms might not be properly followed, resulting in significant pain.

The trial court held extensive hearings and entered detailed Findings of Fact and Conclusions of Law. It recognized that "[t]here are no methods of legal execution that are satisfactory to those who oppose the death penalty on moral, religious, or societal grounds," but concluded that Kentucky's procedure "complies with the constitutional requirements against cruel and unusual punishment." We too agree that petitioners have not carried their burden of showing that the risk of pain from maladministration of a concededly humane lethal injection protocol, and the failure to adopt untried and untested alternatives, constitute cruel and unusual punishment.

I

By the middle of the 19th century, "hanging was the 'nearly universal form of execution' in the United States." By 1915, 11 other States had followed suit, motivated by the "well-grounded belief that electrocution is less painful and more humane than hanging."

Electrocution remained the predominant mode of execution for nearly a century, although several methods, including hanging, firing squad, and lethal gas were in use at one time. Following the 9-year hiatus in executions that ended with our decision in *Gregg v. Georgia* (1976), however, state legislatures began responding to public calls to reexamine electrocution as a means of assuring a humane death. In 1977, legislators in Oklahoma, after consulting with the head of the anesthesiology department at the University of Oklahoma College of Medicine, introduced the first bill proposing lethal injection as the State's method of execution. A total of 36 States have now adopted lethal injection as the exclusive or primary means of implementing the death penalty, making it by far the most prevalent method of execution in the United States. It is also the method used by the Federal Government.

Of these 36 States, at least 30 (including Kentucky) use the same combination of three drugs in their lethal injection protocols. The first drug, sodium thiopental (also known as Pentathol), is a fast-acting barbiturate sedative that induces a deep, comalike unconsciousness when given in the amounts used for lethal injection. The second drug, pancuronium bromide (also known as Pavulon), is a paralytic agent that inhibits all muscular-skeletal movements and, by paralyzing the diaphragm, stops respiration. Potassium chloride, the third drug, interferes with the electrical signals that stimulate the contractions of the heart, inducing cardiac arrest. The proper administration of the first drug ensures that the prisoner does not experience any pain associated with the paralysis and cardiac arrest caused by the second and third drugs.

Kentucky replaced electrocution with lethal injection in 1998. The Kentucky statute does not specify the drugs or categories of drugs to be used during an execution, instead mandating that "every death sentence shall be executed by continuous intravenous injection of a substance or combination of substances sufficient to cause death."

Shortly after the adoption of lethal injection, officials working for the Kentucky Department of Corrections set about developing a written protocol for execution. Kentucky's protocol called for the injection of 2 grams of sodium thiopental, 50 milligrams of pancuronium bromide, and 240 milli-equivalents of potassium chloride. In 2004, as a result of this litigation, the department chose to increase the amount of sodium thiopental from 2 grams to 3 grams. Between injections, members of the execution team flush the intravenous (IV) lines with 25 milligrams of saline to prevent clogging of the lines by precipitates that may form when residual sodium thiopental comes into contact with pancuronium bromide. The protocol reserves responsibility for inserting the IV catheters to qualified personnel having at least one year of professional experience. Currently, Kentucky uses a certified phlebotomist and an emergency medical technician (EMT) to perform the venipunctures necessary for the catheters. They have up to one hour to establish both primary and secondary peripheral intravenous sites in the arm, hand, leg, or foot of the inmate. Other personnel are responsible for mixing the solutions containing the three drugs and loading them into syringes.

Kentucky's execution facilities consist of the execution chamber, a control room separated by a one-way window, and a witness room. The warden and deputy warden remain in the execution chamber with the prisoner, who is strapped to a gurney. The execution team administers the drugs remotely from the control room through five feet of IV tubing. If, as determined by the warden and deputy warden through visual inspection, the prisoner is not unconscious within 60 seconds following the delivery of the sodium thiopental to the primary IV site, a new 3-gram dose of thiopental is administered to the secondary site before injecting the pancuronium and potassium chloride. In addition to assuring that the first dose of thiopental is successfully administered, the warden and deputy warden also watch for any problems with the IV catheters and tubing.

A physician is present to assist in any effort to revive the prisoner in the event of a last-minute stay of execution. By statute, however, the physician is prohibited from participating in the "conduct of an execution," except to certify the cause of death. An electrocardiogram (EKG) verifies the death of the prisoner. Only one Kentucky prisoner, Eddie Lee Harper, has been executed since the Commonwealth adopted lethal injection. There were no reported problems at Harper's execution.

II

The Eighth Amendment to the Constitution, applicable to the States through the Due Process Clause of the Fourteenth Amendment, provides that "[e]xcessive bail shall not be required, nor excessive fines imposed, nor cruel and unusual punishments inflicted." We begin with the principle, settled by *Gregg*, that capital punishment is constitutional. It necessarily follows that there must be a means of carrying it out. Some risk of pain is inherent in any method of execution—no matter how humane—if only from the prospect of error in following the required procedure. It is clear, then, that the Constitution does not demand the avoidance of all risk of pain in carrying out executions. Petitioners do not claim that it does. Rather, they contend that the Eighth Amendment prohibits procedures that create an "unnecessary risk" of pain.

Kentucky responds that this "unnecessary risk" standard is tantamount to a requirement that States adopt the "least risk" alternative in carrying out an execution, a standard the Commonwealth contends will cast recurring constitutional doubt on any procedure adopted by the States. Instead, Kentucky urges the Court to approve the "substantial risk" test used by the courts below.

A

This Court has never invalidated a State's chosen procedure for carrying out a sentence of death as the infliction of cruel and unusual punishment. In *Wilkerson v. Utah* (1879), we upheld a sentence to death by firing squad imposed by a territorial court, rejecting the argument that such a sentence constituted cruel and unusual punishment. We noted there the difficulty of "defin[ing] with exactness the extent of the constitutional provision which provides that cruel and unusual punishments shall not be inflicted." Rather than undertake such an effort, the *Wilkerson* Court simply noted that "it is safe to affirm that punishments of torture . . . and all others in the same line of unnecessary cruelty, are forbidden" by the Eighth Amendment. By way of example, the Court cited cases from England in which "terror, pain, or disgrace were sometimes superadded" to the sentence, such as where the condemned was "embowelled alive, beheaded, and quartered," or instances of "public dissection in murder, and burning alive."

We observed that "[p]unishments are cruel when they involve torture or a lingering death; but the punishment of death is not cruel within the meaning of that word as used in the Constitution. It implies there something inhuman and barbarous, something more than the mere extinguishment of life."

B

Petitioners do not claim that lethal injection or the proper administration of the particular protocol adopted by Kentucky by themselves constitute the cruel or wanton infliction of pain. Quite the contrary, they concede that "if performed properly," an execution carried out under Kentucky's procedures would be "humane and constitutional." Instead, petitioners claim that there is a significant risk that the procedures will *not* be properly followed — in particular, that the sodium thiopental will not be properly administered to achieve its intended effect — resulting in severe pain when the other chemicals are administered.

Simply because an execution method may result in pain, either by accident or as an inescapable consequence of death, does not establish the sort of "objectively intolerable risk of harm" that qualifies as cruel and unusual. In *Louisiana ex rel. Francis v. Reswebe* (1947), a plurality of the Court upheld a second attempt at executing a prisoner by electrocution after a mechanical malfunction had interfered with the first attempt. The principal opinion noted that "[a]ccidents happen for which no man is to blame," and concluded that such "an accident, with no suggestion of malevolence."

C

Much of petitioners' case rests on the contention that they have identified a significant risk of harm that can be eliminated by adopting alternative procedures, such as a one-drug protocol that dispenses with the use of pancuronium and potassium chloride, and additional monitoring by trained personnel to ensure that the first dose of sodium thiopental has been adequately delivered. Given what our cases have said about the nature of the risk of harm that is actionable under the Eighth Amendment, a condemned prisoner cannot successfully challenge a State's method of execution merely by showing a slightly or marginally safer alternative.

Instead, the proffered alternatives must effectively address a "substantial risk of serious harm." To qualify, the alternative procedure must be feasible, readily implemented, and in fact significantly reduce a substantial risk of severe pain. If a State refuses to adopt such an alternative in the face of these documented advantages, without a legitimate penological justification for adhering to its current method of execution, then a State's refusal to change its method can be viewed as "cruel and unusual" under the Eighth Amendment.

III

In applying these standards to the facts of this case, we note at the outset that it is difficult to regard a practice as "objectively intolerable" when it is in fact widely tolerated. No State uses or has ever used the alternative one-drug protocol belatedly urged by petitioners.

We agree with the state trial court and State Supreme Court that petitioners have not shown that the risk of an inadequate dose of the first drug is substantial. And we reject the argument that the Eighth Amendment requires Kentucky to adopt the untested alternative procedures petitioners have identified.

The broad framework of the Eighth Amendment has accommodated . . . progress toward more humane methods of execution, and our approval of a particular method in the past has not precluded legislatures from taking the steps they deem appropriate, in light of new developments, to ensure humane capital punishment. There is no reason to suppose that today's decision will be any different.

The judgment below concluding that Kentucky's procedure is consistent with the Eighth Amendment is, accordingly, affirmed.

Justice ALITO, concurring.

The issue presented in this case — the constitutionality of a *method* of execution — should be kept separate from the controversial issue of the death penalty itself. If the Court wishes to reexamine the latter issue, it should do so directly, as Justice Stevens now suggests. The Court should not produce a *de facto* ban on capital punishment by adopting method-of-execution rules that lead to litigation gridlock.

Justice STEVENS, concurring in the judgment.

When we granted certiorari in this case, I assumed that our decision would bring the debate about lethal injection as a method of execution to a close. It now seems clear that it will not. The question whether a similar three-drug protocol may be used in other States remains open, and may well be answered differently in a future case on the basis of a more complete record. Instead of ending the controversy, I am now convinced that this case will generate debate not only about the constitutionality of the three-drug protocol, and specifically about the justification for the use of the paralytic agent, pancuronium bromide, but also about the justification for the death penalty itself.

I

Because it masks any outward sign of distress, pancuronium bromide creates a risk that the inmate will suffer excruciating pain before death occurs. There is a general understanding among veterinarians that the risk of pain is sufficiently serious that the use of the drug should be proscribed when an animal's life is being terminated. As a result of this understanding among knowledgeable professionals, several States — including Kentucky — have enacted legislation prohibiting use of the drug in animal euthanasia. It is unseemly — to say the least — that Kentucky may well kill petitioners using a drug that it would not permit to be used on their pets.

Use of pancuronium bromide is particularly disturbing because — as the trial court specifically found in this case — it serves "no therapeutic purpose." The drug's primary use is to prevent involuntary muscle movements, and its secondary use is to stop respiration. In my view, neither of these purposes is sufficient to justify the risk inherent in the use of the drug.

The plurality believes that preventing involuntary movement is a legitimate justification for using pancuronium bromide because "[t]he Commonwealth has an interest in preserving the dignity of the procedure, especially where convulsions or seizures could be misperceived as signs of consciousness or distress." This is a woefully inadequate justification. Whatever minimal interest there may be in ensuring that a condemned inmate dies a dignified death, and that witnesses to the execution are not made uncomfortable by an incorrect belief (which could easily be corrected) that the inmate is in pain, is vastly outweighed by the risk that the inmate is actually experiencing excruciating pain that no one can detect.

In my view, therefore, States wishing to decrease the risk that future litigation will delay executions or invalidate their protocols would do well to reconsider their continued use of pancuronium bromide.

II

The thoughtful opinions written by The Chief Justice and by Justice Ginsburg have persuaded me that current decisions by state legislatures, by the Congress of the United States, and by this Court to retain the death penalty as a part of our law are the product of habit and inattention rather than an acceptable deliberative process that weighs the costs and risks of administering that penalty against its identifiable benefits, and rest in part on a faulty assumption about the retributive force of the death penalty.

In *Gregg v. Georgia* (1976), we explained that unless a criminal sanction serves a legitimate penological function, it constitutes "gratuitous infliction of suffering" in violation of the Eighth Amendment. While incapacitation may have been a legitimate rationale in 1976, the recent rise in statutes providing for life imprisonment without the possibility of parole demonstrates that incapacitation is neither a necessary nor a sufficient justification for the death penalty. Moreover, a recent poll indicates that support for the death penalty drops significantly when life without the possibility of parole is presented as an alternative option.

The legitimacy of deterrence as an acceptable justification for the death penalty is also questionable, at best. Despite 30 years of empirical research in the area, there remains no reliable statistical evidence that capital punishment in fact deters potential offenders. In the absence of such evidence, deterrence cannot serve as a sufficient penological justification for this uniquely severe and irrevocable punishment.

We are left, then, with retribution as the primary rationale for imposing the death penalty. And indeed, it is the retribution rationale that animates much of the remaining enthusiasm for the death penalty. [O]ur society has moved away from public and painful retribution towards ever more humane forms of punishment. In an attempt to bring executions in line with our evolving standards of decency, we have adopted increasingly less painful methods of execution, and then declared previous methods barbaric and archaic. But by requiring that an execution be relatively painless, we necessarily protect the inmate from enduring any punishment that is comparable to the suffering inflicted on his victim. This trend, while appropriate and required by the Eighth Amendment's prohibition on cruel and unusual punishment, actually undermines the very premise on which public approval of the retribution rationale is based.

Full recognition of the diminishing force of the principal rationales for retaining the death penalty should lead this Court and legislatures to reexamine the question recently posed by Professor Salinas, a former Texas prosecutor and judge: "The time for a dispassionate, impartial comparison of the enormous costs that death penalty litigation imposes on society with the benefits that it produces has surely arrived."

III

Our decisions in 1976 upholding the constitutionality of the death penalty relied heavily on our belief that adequate procedures were in place that would avoid the danger of discriminatory application. Ironically, however, more recent cases have endorsed procedures that provide less protections to capital defendants than to ordinary offenders. Of special concern to me are rules that deprive the defendant of a trial by jurors representing a fair cross section of the community. Litigation involving both challenges for cause and peremptory challenges has persuaded me that the process of obtaining a "death qualified jury" is really a procedure that has the purpose and effect of obtaining a jury that is biased in favor of conviction.

Another serious concern is that the risk of error in capital cases may be greater than in other cases because the facts are often so disturbing that the interest in making sure the crime does not go unpunished may overcome residual doubt concerning the identity of the offender.

A third significant concern is the risk of discriminatory application of the death penalty. While that risk has been dramatically reduced, the Court has allowed it to continue to play an unacceptable role in capital cases.

Finally, given the real risk of error in this class of cases, the irrevocable nature of the consequences is of decisive importance to me. Whether or not any innocent defendants have actually been executed, abundant evidence accumulated in recent years has resulted in the exoneration of an unacceptable number of defendants found guilty of capital offenses. The risk of executing innocent defendants can be entirely eliminated by treating any penalty more severe than life imprisonment without the possibility of parole as constitutionally excessive.

In sum, I have relied on my own experience in reaching the conclusion that the imposition of the death penalty represents "the pointless and needless extinction of life with only marginal contributions to any discernible social or public purposes. A penalty with such negligible returns to the State [is] patently excessive and cruel and unusual punishment violative of the Eighth Amendment."

IV

The conclusion that I have reached with regard to the constitutionality of the death penalty itself makes my decision in this case particularly difficult. It does not, however, justify a refusal to respect precedents that remain a part of our law. This Court has held that the death penalty is constitutional, and has established a framework for evaluating the constitutionality of particular methods of execution. Under those precedents, I am persuaded that the evidence adduced by petitioners fails to prove that Kentucky's lethal injection protocol violates the Eighth Amendment. Accordingly, I join the Court's judgment.

Justice SCALIA, with whom Justice THOMAS joins, concurring in the judgment.

I write separately to provide what I think is needed response to Justice Stevens' separate opinion.

According to Justice Stevens, the death penalty promotes none of the purposes of criminal punishment because it neither prevents more crimes than alternative measures nor serves a retributive purpose.

These conclusions are not supported by the available data. According to a "leading national study," "each execution prevents some eighteen murders, on average." "But even if Justice Stevens' assertion about the deterrent value of the death penalty were correct, the death penalty would yet be constitutional (as he concedes) if it served the appropriate purpose of retribution. The decision that capital punishment may be the appropriate sanction in extreme cases is an expression of the community's belief that certain crimes are themselves so grievous an affront to humanity that the only adequate response may be the penalty of death.

Justice Stevens' final refuge in his cost-benefit analysis is a familiar one: There is a risk that an innocent person might be convicted and sentenced to death. That rationale, however, supports not Justice Stevens' conclusion that the death penalty is unconstitutional, but the more sweeping proposition that any conviction in a case in which facts are disturbing is suspect—including, of course, convictions resulting in life without parole in those States that do not have capital punishment.

But of all Justice Stevens' criticisms of the death penalty, the hardest to take is his bemoaning of "the enormous costs that death penalty litigation imposes on society," including the "burden on the courts and the lack of finality for victim's families." Those costs, those burdens, and that lack of finality are in large measure the creation of Justice Stevens and other Justices opposed to the death penalty.

Justice THOMAS, with whom Justice SCALIA joins, concurring in the judgment.

Although I agree that petitioners have failed to establish that Kentucky's lethal injection protocol violates the Eighth Amendment, I write separately because I cannot subscribe to the plurality opinion's formulation of the governing standard. As I understand it, that opinion would hold that a method of execution violates the Eighth Amendment if it poses a substantial risk of severe pain that could be significantly reduced by adopting readily available alternative procedures. This standard — along with petitioners' proposed "unnecessary risk" standard and the dissent's "untoward risk" standard, — finds no support in the original understanding of the Cruel and Unusual Punishments Clause. Because, in my view, a method of execution violates the Eighth Amendment only if it is deliberately designed to inflict pain, I concur only in the judgment.

Justice BREYER, concurring in the judgment.

In respect to *how* a court should review such a claim, I agree with Justice Ginsburg. She highlights the relevant question, whether the method creates an untoward, readily avoidable risk of inflicting severe and unnecessary suffering. [However], I cannot find, either in the record in this case or in the literature on the subject, sufficient evidence that Kentucky's execution method poses the "significant and unnecessary risk of inflicting severe pain" that petitioners assert.

Justice GINSBURG, with whom Justice SOUTER joins, dissenting.

The constitutionality of Kentucky's protocol therefore turns on whether inmates are adequately anesthetized by the first drug in the protocol, sodium thiopental. Kentucky's system is constitutional, the plurality states, because "petitioners have not shown that the risk of an inadequate dose of the first drug is substantial." I would not dispose of the case so swiftly given the character of the risk at stake. Kentucky's protocol lacks basic safeguards used by other States to confirm that an inmate is unconscious before injection of the second and third drugs. I would vacate and remand with instructions to consider whether Kentucky's omission of those safeguards poses an untoward, readily avoidable risk of inflicting severe and unnecessary pain.

CHAPTER
10

DOUBLE JEOPARDY

The Double Jeopardy Clause of the Fifth Amendment states that "[n]o person shall . . . be subject for the same offence to be twice put in jeopardy of life or limb." U.S. Const. Amend. V. In Benton v. Maryland, 395 U.S. 784 (1969), the Supreme Court held that this right applies to the states as well. The Double Jeopardy Clause provides three separate protections: "It protects against a second prosecution for the same offense after acquittal. It protects against a second prosecution for the same offense after conviction. And it protects against multiple punishment for the same offense." North Carolina v. Pearce, 395 U.S. 711, 717 (1969).

The double jeopardy rule dates back to common law. At common law, a defendant could plead *autrefois acquit, autrefois convict,* and pardon, which meant that the defendant had been previously acquitted, convicted, or pardoned for the same offense. These pleas, if upheld, would bar the defendant from being retried.

Today, there continue to be strong policy reasons supporting the Double Jeopardy Clause. As stated by the Court in Green v. United States, 355 U.S. 184, 187-188 (1957):

> The underlying idea [for the rule] is that the State with all its resources and power should not be allowed to make repeated attempts to convict an individual for an alleged offense, thereby subjecting him to embarrassment, expense and ordeal and compelling him to live in a continuing state of anxiety and insecurity, as well as enhancing the possibility that even though he is innocent, he may be found guilty.

In its simplest application, the Double Jeopardy Clause prohibits the prosecution from trying a defendant, getting an acquittal, appealing the acquittal, and then retrying the defendant. However, there are many other scenarios in which the Double Jeopardy Clause may apply. This chapter will focus on the wide range of rules that apply when a defendant claims a violation of the Double Jeopardy Clause. Section B focuses on the basics: (1) What types of proceedings does the Double Jeopardy Clause cover? (2) When is an offense the "same offense"? (3) When does jeopardy attach? Section C then focuses on the effect of an acquittal or conviction on future prosecutions if the defendant goes to trial. Section D discusses common exceptions to the double jeopardy rule, including the permissibility of retrials after mistrials and the dual sovereignty doctrine. Section E examines whether a defendant's actions may result in multiple charges and cumulative punishments. Finally, section F looks at the related doctrine of collateral estoppel and discusses how it affects future prosecutions like the Double Jeopardy Clause.

Before jumping into the basics, it is worth examining the Court's explanation of the history and policy reasons behind the double jeopardy rule.

A. INTRODUCTION

UNITED STATES v. SCOTT

437 U.S. 82 (1978)

Justice Rehnquist delivered the opinion of the Court.

On March 5, 1975, respondent, a member of the police force in Muskegon, Mich., was charged in a three-count indictment with distribution of various narcotics. Both before his trial in the United States District Court for the Western District of Michigan, and twice during the trial, respondent moved to dismiss the two counts of the indictment . . . on the ground that his defense had been prejudiced by preindictment delay. At the close of all the evidence, the court granted respondent's motion. Although the court did not explain its reasons for dismissing the second count, it explicitly concluded that respondent had "presented sufficient proof of prejudice with respect to Count I."

The Government sought to appeal the dismissals of the first two counts.

I

The problem presented by this case could not have arisen during the first century of this Court's existence. The Court has long taken the view that the United States has no right of appeal in a criminal case, absent explicit statutory authority. Such authority was not provided until the enactment of the Criminal Appeals Act, Act of Mar. 2, 1907. In 1971, however, Congress adopted the current language of the Act, permitting Government appeals from any decision dismissing an indictment, "except that no appeal shall lie where the double jeopardy clause of the United States Constitution prohibits further prosecution." 18 U.S.C. §3731.

In our first encounter with the new statute, we concluded that "Congress intended to remove all statutory barriers to Government appeals and to allow appeals whenever the Constitution would permit." United States v. Wilson (1975). Since up to that point Government appeals had been subject to statutory restrictions independent of the Double Jeopardy Clause, our previous cases construing the statute proved to be of little assistance in determining when the Double Jeopardy Clause of the Fifth Amendment would prohibit further prosecution. A detailed canvass of the history of the double jeopardy principles in English and American law led us to conclude that the Double Jeopardy Clause was primarily "directed at the threat of multiple prosecutions," and posed no bar to Government appeals "where those appeals would not require a new trial."

II

The origin and history of the Double Jeopardy Clause are hardly a matter of dispute. The constitutional provision had its origin in the three common-law pleas of *autrefois acquit, autrefois convict,* and pardon. These three pleas prevented the retrial of a person who had previously been acquitted, convicted, or pardoned for the same offense. As this Court has described the purpose underlying the prohibition against double jeopardy:

> The underlying idea, one that is deeply ingrained in at least the Anglo-American system of jurisprudence, is that the State with all its resources and power should not be allowed to make repeated attempts to convict an individual for an alleged offense, thereby subjecting him to embarrassment, expense and ordeal and compelling him to live in a continuing state of anxiety and insecurity, as well as enhancing the possibility that even though innocent he may be found guilty.

These historical purposes are necessarily general in nature, and their application has come to abound in often subtle distinctions which cannot by any means all be traced to the original three common-law pleas referred to above.

Part of the difficulty arises from the development of other protections for criminal defendants in the years since the adoption of the Bill of Rights. At the time the Fifth Amendment was adopted, its principles were easily applied, since most criminal prosecutions proceeded to final judgment, and neither the United States nor the defendant had any right to appeal an adverse verdict. The verdict in such a case was unquestionably final, and could be raised in bar against any further prosecution for the same offense. [However, today there are numerous rulings that a trial judge may make that can lead to dismissal of a case, such as motions for preindictment delay and suppression of evidence, that the prosecution may seek to appeal.]

III

Although the primary purpose of the Double Jeopardy Clause was to protect the integrity of a final judgment, the Court has also developed a body of law guarding the separate but related interest of a defendant in avoiding multiple prosecutions even where no final determination of guilt or innocence has been made.

In the present case, the District Court's dismissal of the first count of the indictment was based upon a claim of preindictment delay and not on the court's conclusion that the Government had not produced sufficient evidence to establish the guilt of the defendant.

IV

Our [earlier decisions were] based upon our perceptions of the underlying purposes of the Double Jeopardy Clause:

> The underlying idea, one that is deeply ingrained in at least the Anglo-American system of jurisprudence, is that the State with all its resources and power should not be allowed to make repeated attempts to convict an individual for an alleged offense, thereby subjecting him to embarrassment, expense and ordeal and compelling him to live in a continuing state of anxiety and insecurity. . . .

It is quite true that the Government with all its resources and power should not be allowed to make repeated attempts to convict an individual for an alleged offense. . . . But that situation is obviously a far cry from the present case, where the Government was quite willing to continue with its production of evidence to show the defendant guilty before the jury first empaneled to try him, but the defendant elected to seek termination of the trial on grounds unrelated to guilt or innocence. This is scarcely a picture of an all-powerful state relentlessly pursuing a defendant who had either been found not guilty or who had at least insisted on having the issue of guilt submitted to the first trier of fact. It is instead a picture of a defendant who chooses to avoid conviction and imprisonment, not because of his assertion that the Government has failed to make out a case against him, but because of a legal claim that the Government's case against him must fail even though it might satisfy the trier of fact that he was guilty beyond a reasonable doubt.

We have previously noted that "the trial judge's characterization of his own action cannot control the classification of the action." Rather, a defendant is acquitted only when "the ruling of the judge, whatever its label, actually represents a resolution [in the defendant's favor], correct or not, of some or all of the factual elements of the offense charged."

We think that in a case such as this the defendant, by deliberately choosing to seek termination of the proceedings against him on a basis unrelated to factual guilt or innocence of the offense of which he is accused, suffers no injury cognizable under the Double Jeopardy Clause if the Government is permitted to appeal from such a ruling of the trial court in favor of the defendant. [W]e conclude that the Double Jeopardy Clause, which guards against Government oppression, does not relieve a defendant from the consequences of his voluntary choice.

Here, "the lessons of experience" indicate that Government appeals from midtrial dismissals requested by the defendant would significantly advance the public interest in assuring that each defendant shall be subject to a just judgment on the merits of his case, without "enhancing the possibility that even though innocent he may be found guilty."

B.   THE BASICS

1.   *What Is a Criminal Offense?*

By its terms, the Fifth Amendment applies only to multiple prosecutions and punishments of a defendant for the same offense. However, it does not bar a defendant from facing both criminal and civil sanctions for the same act. For example, if a defendant drives recklessly and kills another person, that defendant may face both criminal prosecution and a civil suit. Similarly, in the famous murder case of O.J. Simpson, the victims' families were able to sue and win a multimillion-dollar judgment against Simpson after he was acquitted of murder because the failure to prove murder beyond a reasonable doubt in the criminal case did not bar the victims' families from proving by a preponderance of the evidence in a civil case that Simpson was liable for the wrongful deaths.

Sometimes it is not readily apparent whether a defendant is facing multiple criminal sanctions, or civil penalties that are not subject to the double jeopardy prohibition. In Hudson v. United States, the Supreme Court set forth the approach to determine whether a sanction is civil or criminal for double jeopardy purposes.

HUDSON v. UNITED STATES

522 U.S. 93 (1997)

Chief Justice REHNQUIST delivered the opinion of the Court.

The Government administratively imposed monetary penalties and occupational debarment on petitioners for violation of federal banking statutes, and later criminally indicted them for essentially the same conduct. We hold that the Double Jeopardy Clause of the Fifth Amendment is not a bar to the later criminal prosecution because the administrative proceedings were civil, not criminal. Our reasons for so holding in large part disavow the method of analysis used in United States v. Halper (1989), and reaffirm the previously established rule exemplified in United States v. Ward (1980).

During the early and mid-1980's, petitioner John Hudson [and his copetitioners] used their bank positions to arrange a series of loans to third parties, in violation of various federal banking statutes and regulations. According to the Office of the Comptroller of the Currency [OCC], those loans, while nominally made to third parties, were in reality made to Hudson in order to enable him to redeem bank stock that he had pledged as collateral on defaulted loans.

[Hudson] resolved the OCC proceedings against [him] by . . . entering into a "Stipulation and Consent Order" [that] provided [he] would pay [an] assessment[] of $16,500 [and that he would agree] not to "participate in any manner" in the affairs of any banking institution without the written authorization of the OCC.

[Thereafter, Hudson was] indicted in the Western District of Oklahoma in a 22-count indictment on charges of conspiracy, misapplication of bank funds, and making false bank entries. The violations charged in the indictment rested on the same lending transactions that formed the basis for the prior administrative actions brought by OCC. [Hudson] moved to dismiss the indictment on double jeopardy grounds.

The Double Jeopardy Clause provides that no "person [shall] be subject for the same offence to be twice put in jeopardy of life or limb." We have long recognized that the Double Jeopardy Clause does not prohibit the imposition of any additional sanction that could, "'in common parlance,'" described as punishment. The Clause protects only against the imposition of multiple criminal punishments for the same offense.

Whether a particular punishment is criminal or civil is, at least initially, a matter of statutory construction. A court must first ask whether the legislature, "in establishing the penalizing mechanism, indicated either expressly or impliedly a preference for one label or the other." Even in those cases where the legislature "has indicated an intention to establish a civil penalty, we have inquired further whether the statutory scheme was so punitive either in purpose or effect," as to "transform what was clearly intended as a civil remedy into a criminal penalty."

In making this latter determination, the factors listed in Kennedy v. Mendoza-Martinez (1963) provide useful guideposts, including: (1) "whether the sanction involves an affirmative disability or restraint"; (2) "whether it has historically been regarded as a punishment"; (3) "whether it comes into play only on a finding of scienter"; (4) "whether its operation will promote the traditional aims of punishment—retribution and deterrence"; (5) "whether the behavior to which it applies is already a crime"; (6) "whether an alternative purpose to which it may rationally be connected is assignable for it"; and (7) "whether it appears excessive in relation to the alternative purpose assigned." It is important to note, however, that "these factors must be considered in relation to the statute on its face," and "only the clearest proof" will suffice to override legislative intent and transform what has been denominated a civil remedy into a criminal penalty, *Ward, supra,* at 249.

Our opinion in United States v. Halper marked the first time we applied the Double Jeopardy Clause to a sanction without first determining that it was criminal in nature. In that case, Irwin Halper was convicted of violating the criminal false claims statute based on his submission of 65 inflated Medicare claims each of which overcharged the Government by $9. He was sentenced to two years' imprisonment and fined $5,000. The Government then brought an action against Halper under the civil False Claims Act. The remedial provisions of the False Claims Act provided that a violation of the Act rendered one "liable to the United States Government for a civil penalty of $2,000, an amount equal to 2 times the amount of damages the Government sustains because of the act of that person, and costs of the civil action." Given Halper's 65 separate violations of the Act, he appeared to be liable for a penalty of $130,000, despite the fact he actually defrauded the Government of less than $600. However, the District Court concluded that a penalty of this magnitude would violate the Double Jeopardy Clause in light of Halper's previous criminal conviction. While explicitly recognizing that the statutory damages provision of the Act "was not itself a criminal punishment," the District Court nonetheless concluded that application of the full penalty to Halper would constitute a second "punishment" in violation of the Double Jeopardy Clause.

On direct appeal, this Court affirmed. As the *Halper* Court saw it, the imposition of "punishment" of any kind was subject to double jeopardy constraints, and whether a sanction constituted "punishment" depended primarily on whether it served the traditional "goals of punishment," namely "retribution and deterrence." Any sanction that was so "overwhelmingly disproportionate" to the injury caused that it could not "fairly be said solely to serve [the] remedial purpose" of compensating the government for its loss, was thought to be explainable only as "serving either retributive or deterrent purposes."

The analysis applied by the *Halper* Court deviated from our traditional double jeopardy doctrine in two key respects. First, the *Halper* Court bypassed the threshold question: whether the successive punishment at issue is a "criminal" punishment. Instead, it focused on whether the sanction, regardless of whether it was civil or criminal, was so grossly disproportionate to the harm caused as to constitute "punishment." In so doing, the Court elevated a single *Kennedy* factor — whether the sanction appeared excessive in relation to its nonpunitive purposes — to dispositive status. But as we emphasized in *Kennedy* itself, no one factor should be considered controlling as they "may often point in differing directions." The second significant departure in *Halper* was the Court's decision to "assess the character of the actual sanctions imposed," rather than, as *Kennedy* demanded, evaluating the "statute on its face" to determine whether it provided for what amounted to a criminal sanction.

We believe that *Halper*'s deviation from longstanding double jeopardy principles was ill considered. As subsequent cases have demonstrated, *Halper*'s test for determining whether a particular sanction is "punitive," and thus subject to the strictures of the Double Jeopardy Clause, has proved unworkable. We have since recognized that all civil penalties have some deterrent effect. If a sanction must be "solely" remedial (i.e., entirely non-deterrent) to avoid implicating the Double Jeopardy Clause, then no civil penalties are beyond the scope of the Clause. Under *Halper*'s method of analysis, a court must also look at the "sanction actually imposed" to determine whether the Double Jeopardy Clause is implicated. Thus, it will not be possible to determine whether the Double Jeopardy Clause is violated until a defendant has proceeded through a trial to judgment. But in those cases where the civil proceeding follows the criminal proceeding, this approach flies in the face of the notion that the Double Jeopardy Clause forbids the government from even "attempting a second time to punish criminally."

Finally, it should be noted that some of the ills at which *Halper* was directed are addressed by other constitutional provisions. The Due Process and Equal Protection Clauses already protect individuals from sanctions which are downright irrational. The Eighth Amendment protects against excessive civil fines, including forfeitures.

Applying traditional double jeopardy principles to the facts of this case, it is clear that the criminal prosecution of these petitioners would not violate the Double Jeopardy Clause. It is evident that Congress intended the OCC money penalties and debarment sanctions imposed to be civil in nature.

Turning to the second stage of the *Ward* test, we find that there is little evidence, much less the clearest proof that we require, suggesting that either OCC money penalties or debarment sanctions are "so punitive in form and effect as to render them criminal despite Congress' intent to the contrary." First, neither money penalties nor debarment have historically been viewed as punishment.

Second, the sanctions imposed do not involve an "affirmative disability or restraint," as that term is normally understood. While petitioners have been prohibited from further participating in the banking industry, this is "certainly nothing approaching the 'infamous punishment' of imprisonment." Third, neither sanction comes into play "only" on a finding of scienter. The provisions under which the money penalties were imposed, allow for the assessment of a penalty against any person "who violates" any of the underlying banking statutes, without regard to the violator's state of mind.

Fourth, the conduct for which OCC sanctions are imposed may also be criminal (and in this case formed the basis for petitioners' indictments). This fact is insufficient to render the money penalties and debarment sanctions criminally punitive, particularly in the double jeopardy context.

Finally, we recognize that the imposition of both money penalties and debarment sanctions will deter others from emulating petitioners' conduct, a traditional goal of criminal punishment. But the mere presence of this purpose is insufficient to render a sanction criminal, as deterrence "may serve civil as well as criminal goals."

In sum, there simply is very little showing, to say nothing of the "clearest proof" required by *Ward*, that OCC money penalties and debarment sanctions are criminal. The Double Jeopardy Clause is therefore no obstacle to their trial on the pending indictments, and it may proceed.

Affirmed.

As the Court made clear in *Hudson*, "only the clearest proof will suffice to override legislative intent and transform what has been denominated a civil remedy into a criminal penalty." Thus, there generally is no bar to a defendant facing both a criminal and civil (and even administrative) action for the same conduct. The Double Jeopardy Clause also does not apply to private proceedings, even if punitive damages are awarded, United States v. Halper, 490 U.S. 435, 451 (1989), or to disciplinary, parole, probation, or bond revocation hearings. It does apply, however, to juvenile delinquent proceedings if the defendant faces a loss of liberty. Breed v. Jones, 421 U.S. 519, 529 (1975).

2. What Is the "Same Offense"?

Assuming that the defendant is charged with two criminal offenses, the prohibition on double jeopardy applies only if the defendant is prosecuted twice for the "*same offense.*" In other words, a single criminal act can lead to multiple charges; a double jeopardy violation occurs only if the defendant is retried for the same offense.

There are two possible approaches to determining whether two charges constitute the same offense. One approach is to determine whether both charges arose from the "same conduct" by the defendant. The other approach is to determine whether both offenses require proof of the "same elements."

For most of the last 80 years, the Supreme Court has adopted the "same elements" test, which the Court established in Blockburger v. United States.

BLOCKBURGER v. UNITED STATES
284 U.S. 299 (1932)

Justice SUTHERLAND delivered the opinion of the Court.

The petitioner was charged with violating provisions of the Harrison Narcotic Act: The indictment contained five counts. The jury returned a verdict against petitioner upon the second, third and fifth counts only. Each of these counts charged a sale of morphine hydrochloride to the same purchaser. The second count charged a sale on a specified day of ten grains of the drug not in or from the original stamped package; the third count charged a sale on the following day of eight grains of the drug not in or from the original stamped package; the fifth count charged the latter sale also as having been made not in pursuance of a written order of the purchaser as required by the statute. The court sentenced petitioner to five years imprisonment and a fine of $2,000 upon each count, the terms of imprisonment to run consecutively; and this judgment was affirmed on appeal.

The principal contentions here made by petitioner are as follows: (1) that, upon the facts, the two sales charged in the second and third counts as having been made to the same person, constitute a single offense; and (2) that the sale charged in the third count as having been made not from the original stamped package, and the same sale charged in the fifth count as having been made not in pursuance of a written order of the purchaser, constitute but one offense for which only a single penalty lawfully may be imposed.

One. The sales charged in the second and third counts, although made to the same person, were distinct and separate sales made at different times. It appears from the evidence that shortly after delivery of the drug which was the subject of the first sale, the purchaser paid for an additional quantity, which was delivered the next day. But the first sale had been consummated, and the payment for the additional drug, however closely following, was the initiation of a separate and distinct sale completed by its delivery.

In the present case, the first transaction, resulting in a sale, had come to an end. The next sale was not the result of the original impulse, but of a fresh one — that is to say, of a new bargain.

Two. Section 1 of the Narcotic Act creates the offense of selling any of the forbidden drugs except in or from the original stamped package; and §2 creates the offense of selling any of such drugs not in pursuance of a written order of the person to whom the drug is sold. Thus, upon the face of the statute, two distinct offenses are created. Here there was but one sale, and the question is whether, both sections being violated by the same act, the accused committed two offenses or only one.

Each of the offenses created requires proof of a different element. The applicable rule is that where the same act or transaction constitutes a violation of two distinct statutory provisions, the test to be applied to determine whether there are two offenses or only one, is whether each provision requires proof of a fact which the other does not. "A single act may be an offense against two statutes; and if each statute requires proof of an additional fact which the other does not, an acquittal or conviction under either statute does not exempt the defendant from prosecution and punishment under the other." Applying the test, we must conclude that here, although both sections were violated by the one sale, two offenses were committed.

Judgment affirmed.

For a short period of time, the Supreme Court adopted the "same conduct" test for determining whether crimes were the same offense for double jeopardy purposes. In Grady v. Corbin, 495 U.S. 508 (1990), a five-justice majority, led by Justice Brennan, wrote that "the Double Jeopardy Clause bars a subsequent prosecution if, to establish an essential element of an offense charged in that prosecution, the government will prove conduct that constitutes an offense for which the defendant has already been prosecuted." Thus, Corbin, who had pleaded guilty to traffic tickets arising out of his arrest for drunk driving, successfully argued that he could not be reindicted for manslaughter because the government's proof for the manslaughter charges would include the evidence used to charge him with the misdemeanor drunk driving citations. Under the *Blockburger* test, Corbin would not have prevailed because the crime of manslaughter required elements not required by the drunk driving charges. Justice Brennan wrote, however, that the Double Jeopardy Clause should nonetheless bar Corbin's re-prosecution because the charges arose from the same conduct.

The holding in Grady v. Corbin did not last long. Three years later, in United States v. Dixon, 509 U.S. 688 (1993), in an opinion written by Justice Scalia, the Court returned to the *Blockburger* "same elements" test. Thus, to determine whether a defendant is not being charged with the same offense, the Court must analyze each charge to see if its elements require proof of an additional fact that the other does not. Offenses are considered separate offenses even if there is substantial overlap in the proof required for each offense. For example, drunk driving and manslaughter are two separate offenses because (1) drunk driving requires proof that the defendant was intoxicated, but manslaughter does not; and (2) manslaughter requires proof that the defendant caused a death, but drunk driving does not.

Under the *Blockburger* test, double jeopardy bars successive prosecutions for greater- and lesser-included offenses if all of the elements of the lesser offense are included in the elements for the greater offense. In that situation, the prosecution is not entitled to "two bites at the apple." For instance, if a defendant is charged with murder and is acquitted, the government cannot retry him for manslaughter because manslaughter is a lesser-included offense of murder.

3.   *When Does Jeopardy Attach?*

The Double Jeopardy Clause bars a second prosecution for the same offense only if jeopardy attached in the original proceeding. Ex parte Lange, 85 U.S. (18 Wall.) 163, 168-169 (1873). As a general rule, jeopardy attaches when a defendant's trial begins. In a jury trial, jeopardy attaches when the jury is impaneled and sworn. In a bench trial, jeopardy attaches when the judge begins to hear evidence. It is only at these times that a defendant faces the risk of being found guilty of an offense. Crist v. Bretz, 437 U.S. 28 (1978).

Given these rules, not every dismissal of a criminal case will bar retrying the defendant. Cases that are dismissed before the trial begins may be appealed by the prosecution because jeopardy has not attached. However, once the trial has begun and jeopardy has attached, the prosecution cannot move to dismiss and then seek to retry the defendant.

C.   NO RETRIAL FOLLOWING CONVICTION OR ACQUITTAL

Both acquittals and convictions may bar a defendant's retrial for the same offense. Unless the defendant seeks a retrial by, for example, moving for a mistrial or appealing a conviction, the prosecution will only have "one bite at the apple." The Double Jeopardy Clause is designed to protect a defendant not just from double convictions but from repeated prosecutions.

1.   No Retrial After Acquittal

The Double Jeopardy Clause bars retrying a defendant for an offense after the defendant has been acquitted of that offense. An acquittal can arise in several ways: (1) the jury may return a verdict of not guilty; (2) the trial judge may find, before the jury has an opportunity to decide the case, that there is insufficient evidence for a conviction; or (3) the appellate court may find that a conviction was not supported by sufficient evidence.

The clearest case of double jeopardy is when a defendant has been acquitted of an offense, even if that acquittal resulted from a trial court's erroneous interpretation of the indictment. Justice Marshall, writing for the Court in Sanabria v. United States, 437 U.S. 54 (1978) explained:

> The Government's real quarrel is with the judgment of acquittal. While the numbers evidence was erroneously excluded, the judgment of acquittal produced thereby is final and unreviewable. [T]he Double Jeopardy Clause [does not permit] the Government to obtain relief from all of the adverse rulings — most of which result from defense motions — that lead to the termination of a criminal trial in the defendant's favor. To hold that a defendant waives his double jeopardy protection whenever a trial court error in his favor on a midtrial motion leads to an acquittal would undercut the adversary assumption on which our system of criminal justice rests and would vitiate one of the fundamental rights established by the Fifth Amendment.

The prohibition on retrying a defendant after an acquittal also applies when the appellate court finds that there was insufficient evidence to support a conviction. The appellate court's finding of insufficient evidence is equivalent to an acquittal.

BURKS v. UNITED STATES
437 U.S. 1 (1978)

Chief Justice BURGER delivered the opinion of the Court.

We granted certiorari to resolve the question of whether an accused may be subjected to a second trial when conviction in a prior trial was reversed by an appellate court solely for lack of sufficient evidence to sustain the jury's verdict.

I

Petitioner Burks was tried in the United States District Court for the crime of robbing a federally insured bank by use of a dangerous weapon, a violation of 18 U.S.C. §2113 (d). Burks' principal defense was insanity.

Before the case was submitted to the jury, the court denied a motion for a judgment of acquittal. The jury found Burks guilty as charged. Thereafter, he filed a timely motion for a new trial, maintaining, among other things, that "[the] evidence was insufficient to support the verdict." The motion was denied by the District Court, which concluded that petitioner's challenge to the sufficiency of the evidence was "utterly without merit."[1]

On appeal petitioner narrowed the issues by admitting the affirmative factual elements of the charge against him, leaving only his claim concerning criminal responsibility to be resolved. With respect to this point, the Court of Appeals agreed with petitioner's claim that the evidence was insufficient to support the verdict and reversed his conviction. The court began by noting that "the government has the burden of proving sanity [beyond a reasonable doubt] once a prima facie defense of insanity has been raised." Petitioner had met his obligation, the court indicated, by presenting "the specific testimony of three experts with unchallenged credentials." [E]ven when viewed in the light most favorable to the Government, [the United States] did not "effectively [rebut]" petitioner's proof with respect to insanity and criminal responsibility.

At this point, the Court of Appeals, rather than terminating the case against petitioner, remanded to the District Court "for a determination of whether a directed verdict of acquittal should be entered or a new trial ordered."

[W]e are squarely presented with the question of whether a defendant may be tried a second time when a reviewing court has determined that in a prior trial the evidence was insufficient to sustain the verdict of the jury.

It is unquestionably true that the Court of Appeals' decision "[represented] a resolution, correct or not, of some or all of the factual elements of the offense charged." United States v. Martin Linen Supply Co. (1977). By deciding that the Government had failed to come forward with sufficient proof of petitioner's capacity to be responsible for criminal acts, that court was clearly saying that Burks' criminal culpability had not been established. If the District Court had so held in the first instance, as the reviewing court said it should have done, a judgment of acquittal would have been entered and, of course, petitioner could not be retried for the same offense.

The Double Jeopardy Clause forbids a second trial for the purpose of affording the prosecution another opportunity to supply evidence which it failed to muster in the first proceeding. This is central to the objective of the prohibition against successive trials. The Clause does not allow "the State . . . to make repeated attempts to convict an individual for an alleged offense," since "[the] constitutional prohibition against 'double jeopardy' was designed to protect an individual from being subjected to the hazards of trial and possible conviction more than once for an alleged offense."

---

1. Petitioner did not file a post-trial motion for judgment of acquittal, which he was entitled to do under *Fed. Rule Crim. Proc. 29 (c)*. [Footnote by the Court.]

Various rationales have been advanced to support the policy of allowing retrial to correct trial error, but in our view the most reasonable justification is: "It would be a high price indeed for society to pay were every accused granted immunity from punishment because of any defect sufficient to constitute reversible error in the proceedings leading to conviction."

In short, reversal for trial error, as distinguished from evidentiary insufficiency, does not constitute a decision to the effect that the government has failed to prove its case. As such, it implies nothing with respect to the guilt or innocence of the defendant. Rather, it is a determination that a defendant has been convicted through a judicial process which is defective in some fundamental respect, *e.g.*, incorrect receipt or rejection of evidence, incorrect instructions, or prosecutorial misconduct. When this occurs, the accused has a strong interest in obtaining a fair readjudication of his guilt free from error, just as society maintains a valid concern for insuring that the guilty are punished.

The same cannot be said when a defendant's conviction has been overturned due to a failure of proof at trial, in which case the prosecution cannot complain of prejudice, for it has been given one fair opportunity to offer whatever proof it could assemble. Moreover, such an appellate reversal means that the government's case was so lacking that it should not have even been *submitted* to the jury. Since we necessarily afford absolute finality to a jury's *verdict* of acquittal — no matter how erroneous its decision — it is difficult to conceive how society has any greater interest in retrying a defendant when, on review, it is decided as a matter of law that the jury could not properly have returned a verdict of guilty.[2]

The importance of a reversal on grounds of evidentiary insufficiency for purposes of inquiry under the Double Jeopardy Clause is underscored by the fact that a federal court's role in deciding whether a case should be considered by the jury is quite limited. Even the trial court, which has heard the testimony of witnesses firsthand, is not to weigh the evidence or assess the credibility of witnesses when it judges the merits of a motion for acquittal. The prevailing rule has long been that a district judge is to submit a case to the jury if the evidence and inferences therefrom most favorable to the prosecution would warrant the jury's finding the defendant guilty beyond a reasonable doubt. Obviously a federal appellate court applies no higher a standard; rather, it must sustain the verdict if there is substantial evidence, viewed in the light most favorable to the Government, to uphold the jury's decision. See Glasser v. United States (1942). While this is not the appropriate occasion to re-examine in detail the standards for appellate reversal on grounds of insufficient evidence, it is apparent that such a decision will be confined to cases where the prosecution's failure is clear. Given the requirements for entry of a judgment of acquittal, the purposes of the Clause

---

2. In holding the evidence insufficient to sustain guilt, an appellate court determines that the prosecution has failed to prove guilt beyond a reasonable doubt. See American Tobacco Co. v. United States (1946). [Footnote by the Court.]

would be negated were we to afford the government an opportunity for the proverbial "second bite at the apple."

———————————

The Double Jeopardy Clause bars the prosecution from appealing an acquittal even if the acquittal was based on juror misconduct or jury nullification.[3] A mid-trial ruling by the court dismissing a charge for insufficient evidence is the equivalent of an acquittal unless the judge reserves the right to reconsider the ruling or state law indicates that such judgments are not final until the end of trial. Smith v. Massachusetts, 543 U.S. 462 (2005). As Justice Scalia explained in that case, a mid-trial ruling might influence a defendant's decision as to what evidence to present in the defense case, thereby making the Double Jeopardy Clause guarantee "a potential snare for those who reasonably rely upon it."

It is only when the defendant will not face another trial that the prosecution can appeal the dismissal of a case. Thus, the prosecution can appeal the pretrial dismissal of a case or the judge's acquittal of a defendant *after* the jury has returned a guilty verdict. 28 U.S.C. §3731. In the first situation, the defendant has not yet been subject to jeopardy because the case was dismissed before trial. In the second situation, if the appellate court reverses the trial court's ruling, the defendant will not be subject to a retrial, but the jury's verdict will just be reinstated. In neither case will there be a double jeopardy violation.

2.   *No Retrial After Conviction*

The Double Jeopardy Clause also bars retrying a defendant for the same offense unless (1) the defendant is granted a retrial after a successful appeal, (2) or the trial judge grants a motion for acquittal after the jury has already convicted the defendant. In the latter situation, if the appellate court disagrees with the judge's post-conviction acquittal, there will be no need for a retrial. The jury's original conviction of the defendant can simply be reinstated and the defendant will not face an actual retrial for the same offense. *See, e.g.*, United States v. Guadagna, 183 F.3d 122, 129 (2d Cir. 1999).

As for retrial following a successful appeal, if a defendant chooses to challenge the fairness of the procedures in his first trial and seek a new trial with correct procedures, he is bound by that choice and retrial is permitted. United States v. Ball, 163 U.S. 662 (1896) ("[W]here the accused successfully seeks review of a conviction, there is no double jeopardy upon a new trial").

———————————

3. Some commentators challenge this rule and have advocated for a change in the rules that would allow limited government appeals of acquittals. *See* Anne Bowen Poulin, *Double Jeopardy and Judicial Accountability: When Is an Acquittal Not an Acquittal?*, 27 Ariz. St. L.J. 953 (1995).

D. EXCEPTIONS TO THE DOUBLE JEOPARDY RULE

1. *Retrial After Mistrials*

Just as a defendant's appeal will not bar a retrial if the appellate court reverses for unfair trial procedures, a mistrial will not necessarily bar a retrial either. The Supreme Court has held that if there is "manifest necessity" for declaring a mistrial, retrial is not prohibited. United States v. Perez, 22 U.S. (9 Wheat) 579, 580 (1824). The key question, of course, is whether something constitutes a "manifest necessity."

a. Retrial After Mistrial for Hung Jury

In *Perez*, the Court held that granting a mistrial when a jury cannot reach a verdict constitutes "manifest necessity" and that retrying the defendant is not barred in this situation. Although the defendant has already faced one trial, if "public justice" is served by granting the mistrial, the Double Jeopardy Clause does not prohibit retrying the defendant.

UNITED STATES v. SANFORD
429 U.S. 14 (1976)

PER CURIAM.

Respondents were indicted for illegal game hunting in Yellowstone National Park. A jury trial resulted in a hung jury, and the District Court declared a mistrial. Four months later, while the Government was preparing to retry them, respondents moved to dismiss the indictment. [The district court dismissed the indictment and the government appealed. The appellate court upheld the dismissal and the prosecution filed a petition for certiorari.]

In ruling against the government, the Court of Appeals stated:

> Here appellees have undergone trial. There is no question but that jeopardy has attached. That being so, and since the proceedings in the district court have ended in appellees' favor and the consequences of a reversal in favor of the Government would be that appellees must be tried again, we conclude that they would, on retrial, be placed twice in jeopardy.

We agree with the Court of Appeals that jeopardy attached at the time of the empaneling of the jury for the first trial of respondents. But we do not agree with that court's conclusion that by reason of the sequence of events in the District Court the Government would be barred by the Double Jeopardy Clause from retrying respondents. The trial of respondents on the indictment terminated, not in their favor, but in a mistrial declared, sua sponte, by the District Court. Where the trial is terminated in this manner, the classical test for determining whether the defendants may be retried without violating the Double Jeopardy Clause is stated in Mr. Justice Story's opinion for this Court in United States v. Perez (1824):

> We are of opinion, that the facts constitute no legal bar to a future trial. The prisoner has not been convicted or acquitted, and may again be put upon his defence. We think, that in all cases of this nature, the law has invested courts of justice with the authority to discharge a jury from giving any verdict, whenever, in their opinion, taking all the circumstances into consideration, there is a manifest necessity for the act, or the ends of public justice would otherwise be defeated.

The Government's right to retry the defendant, after a mistrial, in the face of his claim of double jeopardy is generally governed by the test laid down in *Perez, supra*. The situation of a hung jury presented here is precisely the situation that was presented in *Perez, supra*, and therefore the Double Jeopardy Clause does not bar retrial of these respondents on the indictment which had been returned against them.[4]

The District Court's dismissal of the indictment occurred several months after the first trial had ended in a mistrial, but before the retrial of respondents had begun. This case is, therefore, governed by United States v. Serfass in which we held that a pretrial order of the District Court dismissing an indictment charging refusal to submit to induction into the Armed Forces was appealable under 18 U.S.C. §3731. The dismissal in this case, like that in *Serfass*, was prior to a trial that the Government had a right to prosecute and that the defendant was required to defend. Since in such cases a trial following the Government's successful appeal of a dismissal is not barred by double jeopardy, an appeal from the dismissal is authorized by 18 U.S.C. §3731.

[The Court of Appeals' judgment was reversed.]

The Court further explained the rationale for the rule that a hung jury does not bar retrial in Richardson v. United States, 468 U.S. 317 (1984). Writing for the majority, Justice Rehnquist explained:

> [Richardson] asserts that if the Government failed to introduce sufficient evidence to establish his guilt beyond a reasonable doubt at his first trial, he may not be tried again following a declaration of a mistrial because of a hung jury. While petitioner bases this contention on Burks v. United States (1978), we do not agree that *Burks* resulted in the sweeping change in the law of double jeopardy which petitioner would have us hold. In *Burks* we held that once a

---

4. If the mistrial is declared at the behest of the defendant, the manifest necessity test does not apply. See United States v. Dinitz, 424 U.S. 600 (1976). [Footnote by the Court.]

defendant obtained an unreversed appellate ruling that the Government had failed to introduce sufficient evidence to convict him at trial, a second trial was barred by the Double Jeopardy Clause.

The Court in *Burks* did not deal with the situation in which a trial court declares a mistrial because of a jury's inability to agree on a verdict.

The case law dealing with the application of the prohibition against placing a defendant twice in jeopardy following a mistrial because of a hung jury has its own sources and logic. It has been established for 160 years, since the opinion of Justice Story in United States v. Perez (1824) that a failure of the jury to agree on a verdict was an instance of "manifest necessity" which permitted a trial judge to terminate the first trial and retry the defendant, because "the ends of public justice would otherwise be defeated." [W]e have constantly adhered to the rule that a retrial following a "hung jury" does not violate the Double Jeopardy Clause. Explaining our reasons for this conclusion in Arizona v. Washington (1978), we said:

> [Without] exception, the courts have held that the trial judge may discharge a genuinely deadlocked jury and require the defendant to submit to a second trial. This rule accords recognition to society's interest in giving the prosecution one complete opportunity to convict those who have violated its laws.

Thirty-five years ago we said in Wade v. Hunter (1949):

> The double-jeopardy provision of the Fifth Amendment, however, does not mean that every time a defendant is put to trial before a competent tribunal he is entitled to go free if the trial fails to end in a final judgment. Such a rule would create an insuperable obstacle to the administration of justice in many cases in which there is no semblance of the type of oppressive practices at which the double-jeopardy prohibition is aimed. There may be unforeseeable circumstances that arise during a trial making its completion impossible, such as the failure of a jury to agree on a verdict. In such event the purpose of law to protect society from those guilty of crimes frequently would be frustrated by denying courts power to put the defendant to trial again. . . . What has been said is enough to show that a defendant's valued right to have his trial completed by a particular tribunal must in some instances be subordinated to the public's interest in fair trials designed to end in just judgments.

The Government, like the defendant, is entitled to resolution of the case by verdict from the jury, and jeopardy does not terminate when the jury is discharged because it is unable to agree. Regardless of the sufficiency of the evidence at petitioner's first trial, he has no valid double jeopardy claim to prevent his retrial.

b. Retrials After Other Mistrials

Mistrials can also occur because developments during trial make it difficult, if not impossible, to afford a fair trial. Generally, if the defendant requests a mistrial, retrial is permitted unless the government has acted in bad faith. If the prosecutor or judge goads the defendant into seeking a mistrial, retrial may be barred. The same year the Court decided *Sanford, supra,* it decided another double jeopardy case that addresses whether mistrials caused by the government necessarily bar retrial. In United States v. Dinitz, the defendant was the one who sought a mistrial.

UNITED STATES v. DINITZ

424 U.S. 600 (1976)

Justice STEWART delivered the opinion of the Court.

The question in this case is whether the Double Jeopardy Clause of the Fifth Amendment was violated by the retrial of the respondent after his original trial had ended in a mistrial granted at his request.

I

The respondent, Nathan Dinitz, [was charged with narcotics offenses]. Five days before the trial was scheduled to begin, [Dinitz retained a new] lawyer, Maurice Wagner, to conduct his defense. Wagner had not been admitted to practice [in that court], but on the first day of the trial the court permitted him to appear pro hac vice.

The jury was selected and sworn, and opening statements by counsel began. The prosecutor's opening statement briefly outlined the testimony that he expected an undercover agent to give. Wagner then began his opening statement for the defense. After introducing himself and his co-counsel, Wagner turned to the case against the respondent. [In opening statements, Wagner gave improper personal opinions regarding the prosecution's key witness and case. The prosecutor objected. The judge then warned Wagner that he did not approve of his behavior and cautioned Wagner that he did not want to have to remind him again about the purpose of the opening statement.

Following this initial incident, the trial judge found it necessary twice again to remind Wagner of the purpose of the opening statement and to instruct him to relate "the facts that you expect the evidence to show, the admissible evidence." Wagner continued to make improper arguments.

The judge then asked original defense counsel if he was prepared to proceed with the trial.] The judge then set forth three alternative courses that might be followed — (1) a stay or recess pending application to the Court of Appeals to review the propriety of expelling Wagner, (2) continuation of the trial with prior counsel, or (3) a declaration of a mistrial which would permit the respondent to obtain other counsel. Following a short recess, Meldon moved for a mistrial, stating that, after "full consideration of the situation and an explanation of the alternatives before him, [the respondent] feels that he would move for a mistrial and that this would be in his best interest." The Government prosecutor did not oppose the motion. The judge thereupon declared a mistrial, expressing his belief that such a course would serve the interest of justice.

Before his second trial, the respondent[5] moved to dismiss the indictment on the ground that a retrial would violate the Double Jeopardy Clause of the

___

5. The respondent was a third-year law student at the time of his arrest. [Footnote by the Court.]

Constitution. This motion was denied. The appellate court took the view that the trial judge's exclusion of Wagner and his questioning of Meldon had left the respondent no choice but to move for a mistrial. On that basis, the court concluded that the respondent's request for a mistrial should be ignored and the case should be treated as though the trial judge had declared a mistrial over the objection of the defendant. So viewing the case, the court held that the Double Jeopardy Clause barred the second trial of the respondent, because there had been no manifest necessity requiring the expulsion of Wagner. We granted certiorari.

II

The Double Jeopardy Clause of the Fifth Amendment protects a defendant in a criminal proceeding against multiple punishments or repeated prosecutions for the same offense. Underlying this constitutional safeguard is the belief that "the State with all its resources and power should not be allowed to make repeated attempts to convict an individual for an alleged offense, thereby subjecting him to embarrassment, expense and ordeal and compelling him to live in a continuing state of anxiety and insecurity, as well as enhancing the possibility that even though innocent he may be found guilty."

Since Mr. Justice Story's 1824 opinion for the Court in United States v. Perez, this Court has held that the question whether under the Double Jeopardy Clause there can be a new trial after a mistrial has been declared without the defendant's request or consent depends on whether "there is a manifest necessity for the [mistrial], or the ends of public justice would otherwise be defeated." Different considerations obtain, however, when the mistrial has been declared at the defendant's request. The reasons for the distinction were discussed in the plurality opinion in the *Jorn* case: If that right to go to a particular tribunal is valued, it is because, independent of the threat of bad-faith conduct by judge or prosecutor, the defendant has a significant interest in the decision whether or not to take the case from the jury when circumstances occur which might be thought to warrant a declaration of mistrial. Thus, where circumstances develop not attributable to prosecutorial or judicial overreaching, a motion by the defendant for mistrial is ordinarily assumed to remove any barrier to reprosecution, even if the defendant's motion is necessitated by prosecutorial or judicial error. In the absence of such a motion, the *Perez* doctrine of manifest necessity stands as a command to trial judges not to foreclose the defendant's option until a scrupulous exercise of judicial discretion leads to the conclusion that the ends of public justice would not be served by a continuation of the proceedings.

The distinction between mistrials declared by the court sua sponte and mistrials granted at the defendant's request or with his consent is wholly consistent with the protections of the Double Jeopardy Clause. Even when judicial or prosecutorial error prejudices a defendant's prospects of securing an acquittal, he may nonetheless desire "to go to the first jury and, perhaps, end the dispute then and there with an acquittal." Our prior decisions recognize the defendant's right to pursue this course in the absence of circumstances of manifest necessity requiring a sua sponte judicial declaration of mistrial. But it is evident that when judicial or prosecutorial error seriously prejudices a defendant, he may have little interest in completing the trial and obtaining a verdict from the first jury. The defendant may reasonably conclude that a continuation of the tainted proceeding would result in a conviction followed by a lengthy appeal and, if a reversal is secured, by a second prosecution. In such circumstances, a defendant's mistrial request has objectives not unlike the interests served by the Double Jeopardy Clause — the avoidance of the anxiety, expense, and delay occasioned by multiple prosecutions.

The Court of Appeals viewed the doctrine that permits a retrial following a mistrial sought by the defendant as resting on a waiver theory. The court concluded, therefore, that "something more substantial than a Hobson's choice" is required before a defendant can "be said to have relinquished voluntarily his right to proceed before the first jury." The court thus held that no waiver could be imputed to the respondent because the trial judge's action in excluding Wagner left the respondent with "no choice but to move for or accept a mistrial." But traditional waiver concepts have little relevance where the defendant must determine whether or not to request or consent to a mistrial in response to judicial or prosecutorial error. In such circumstances, the defendant generally does face a "Hobson's choice" between giving up his first jury and continuing a trial tainted by prejudicial judicial or prosecutorial error. The important consideration, for purposes of the Double Jeopardy Clause, is that the defendant retain[ed] primary control over the course to be followed in the event of such error.

The Double Jeopardy Clause does protect a defendant against governmental actions intended to provoke mistrial requests and thereby to subject defendants to the substantial burdens imposed by multiple prosecutions. It bars retrials where "bad-faith conduct by judge or prosecutor," threatens the "[harassment] of an accused by successive prosecutions or declaration of a mistrial so as to afford the prosecution a more favorable opportunity to convict" the defendant.

But here the trial judge's banishment of Wagner from the proceedings was not done in bad faith in order to goad the respondent into requesting a mistrial or to prejudice his prospects for an acquittal. As the Court of Appeals noted, Wagner "was guilty of improper conduct" during his opening statement which "may have justified disciplinary action." Even accepting the appellate court's conclusion that the trial judge overreacted in expelling Wagner from the courtroom, the court did not suggest, the respondent has not contended, and the record does not show that the judge's action was motivated by bad faith or undertaken to harass or prejudice the respondent.

Under these circumstances we hold that the Court of Appeals erred in finding that the retrial violated the respondent's constitutional right not to be twice put in jeopardy.

Chief Justice BURGER, concurring.

A trial judge is under a duty, in order to protect the integrity of the trial, to take prompt and affirmative action to stop such professional misconduct. Here the misconduct of the attorney, Wagner, was not only unprofessional per se but contemptuous in that he defied the court's explicit order.

Far from "overreacting" to the misconduct of Wagner, in my view, the trial judge exercised great restraint in not citing Wagner for contempt then and there.

Justice BRENNAN, with whom Justice MARSHALL joins, dissenting.

The Court's premise is that the mistrial was directed at respondent's request or with his consent. [F]or purposes of double jeopardy analysis, it was not, but rather that "the trial judge's response to the conduct of defense counsel deprived Dinitz's motion for a mistrial of its necessary consensual character." Therefore the rule that "a motion by the defendant for mistrial is ordinarily assumed to remove any barrier to reprosecution" is inapplicable.

The most likely scenario in which a mistrial will bar retrial is when the prosecution engages in misconduct. However, even prosecutorial misconduct does not guarantee that a defendant's double jeopardy rights will prohibit retrial.

OREGON v. KENNEDY
456 U.S. 667 (1982)

Justice REHNQUIST delivered the opinion of the Court.

The Oregon Court of Appeals decided that the Double Jeopardy Clause of the Fifth Amendment to the United States Constitution barred respondent's retrial after his first trial ended in a mistrial granted on his own motion. The Court of Appeals concluded that retrial was barred because the prosecutorial misconduct that occasioned the mistrial in the first instance amounted to "overreaching." Because that court took an overly expansive view of the application of the Double Jeopardy Clause following a mistrial resulting from the defendant's own motion, we reverse its judgment.

I

Respondent was charged with the theft of an oriental rug. During his first trial, the State called an expert witness on the subject of Middle Eastern rugs to testify as to the value and the identity of the rug in question. On cross-examination, respondent's attorney apparently attempted to establish bias on the part of the expert witness by asking him whether he had filed a criminal complaint against respondent. The witness eventually acknowledged this fact, but explained that no action had been taken on his complaint. On redirect examination, the prosecutor sought to elicit the reasons why the witness had filed a complaint against respondent, but the trial court sustained a series of objections to this line of inquiry. The following colloquy then ensued:

Prosecutor: Have you ever done business with the Kennedys?
Witness: No, I have not.
Prosecutor: Is that because he is a crook?

The trial court then granted respondent's motion for a mistrial.

When the State later sought to retry respondent, he moved to dismiss the charges because of double jeopardy. After a hearing at which the prosecutor testified, the trial court found as a fact that "it was not the intention of the prosecutor in this case to cause a mistrial." On the basis of this finding, the trial court held that double jeopardy principles did not bar retrial, and respondent was then tried and convicted.

Respondent then successfully appealed to the Oregon Court of Appeals, which sustained his double jeopardy claim. That court set out what it considered to be the governing principles in this kind of case:

> The general rule is said to be that the double jeopardy clause does not bar reprosecution, ". . . where circumstances develop not attributable to prosecutorial or judicial overreaching, . . . even if defendant's motion is necessitated by a prosecutorial error." United States v. Jorn (1971). However, retrial is barred where the error that prompted the mistrial is intended to provoke a mistrial or is "motivated by bad faith or undertaken to harass or prejudice" the defendant. United States v. Dinitz (1976).

The Court of Appeals accepted the trial court's finding that it was not the intent of the prosecutor to cause a mistrial. Nevertheless, the court held that retrial was barred because the prosecutor's conduct in this case constituted what it viewed as "overreaching." Although the prosecutor intended to rehabilitate the witness, the Court of Appeals expressed the view that the question was in fact "a direct personal attack on the general character of the defendant." This personal attack left respondent with a "Hobson's choice — either to accept a necessarily prejudiced jury, or to move for a mistrial and face the process of being retried at a later time."

II

The Double Jeopardy Clause of the Fifth Amendment protects a criminal defendant from repeated prosecutions for the same offense. As a part of this protection against multiple prosecutions, the Double Jeopardy Clause affords a criminal defendant a "valued right to have his trial completed by a particular tribunal." Wade v. Hunter (1949). The Double Jeopardy Clause, however, does not offer a guarantee to the defendant that the State will vindicate its societal interest in the enforcement of the criminal laws in one proceeding. If the law were otherwise, "the purpose of law to protect society from those guilty of crimes frequently would be frustrated by denying courts power to put the defendant to trial again."

Where the trial is terminated over the objection of the defendant, the classical test for lifting the double jeopardy bar to a second trial is the "manifest necessity" standard first enunciated in United States v. Perez. *Perez* dealt with the most common form of "manifest necessity": a mistrial declared by the judge following the jury's declaration that it was unable to reach a verdict. The "manifest necessity" standard provides sufficient protection to the defendant's interests in having his case finally decided by the jury first selected while at the same time maintaining "the public's interest in fair trials designed to end in just judgments."

But in the case of a mistrial declared at the behest of the defendant, quite different principles come into play. Here the defendant himself has elected to terminate the proceedings against him, and the "manifest necessity" standard has no place in the application of the Double Jeopardy Clause.

Our cases, however, have indicated that even where the defendant moves for a mistrial, there is a narrow exception to the rule that the Double Jeopardy Clause is no bar to retrial. The circumstances under which respondent's first trial was terminated require us to delineate the bounds of that exception more fully than we have in previous cases.

Since one of the principal threads making up the protection embodied in the Double Jeopardy Clause is the right of the defendant to have his trial completed before the first jury empaneled to try him, it may be wondered as a matter of original inquiry why the defendant's election to terminate the first trial by his own motion should not be deemed a renunciation of that right for all purposes. We have recognized, however, that there would be great difficulty in applying such a rule where the prosecutor's actions giving rise to the motion for mistrial were done "in order to goad the [defendant] into requesting a mistrial." In such a case, the defendant's valued right to complete his trial before the first jury would be a hollow shell if the inevitable motion for mistrial were held to prevent a later invocation of the bar of double jeopardy in all circumstances. But the precise phrasing of the circumstances which will allow a defendant to interpose the defense of double jeopardy to a second prosecution where the first has terminated on his own motion for a mistrial have been stated with less than crystal clarity in our cases which deal with this area of the law.

Every act on the part of a rational prosecutor during a trial is designed to "prejudice" the defendant by placing before the judge or jury evidence leading to a finding of his guilt. Given the complexity of the rules of evidence, it will be a rare trial of any complexity in which some proffered evidence by the prosecutor or by the defendant's attorney will not be found objectionable by the trial court. Most such objections are undoubtedly curable by simply refusing to allow the proffered evidence to be admitted, or in the case of a particular line of inquiry taken by counsel with a witness, by an admonition to desist from a particular line of inquiry.

More serious infractions on the part of the prosecutor may provoke a motion for mistrial on the part of the defendant, and may in the view of the trial court warrant the granting of such a motion. The "overreaching" standard applied by the court below and urged today, however, would add another classification of prosecutorial error, one requiring dismissal of the indictment, but without supplying any standard by which to assess that error.

By contrast, a standard that examines the intent of the prosecutor, though certainly not entirely free from practical difficulties, is a manageable standard to apply. It merely calls for the court to make a finding of fact. Inferring the existence or nonexistence of intent from objective facts and circumstances is a familiar process in our criminal justice system. When it is remembered that resolution of double jeopardy questions by state trial courts are reviewable not only within the state court system, but in the federal court system on habeas corpus as well, the desirability of an easily applied principle is apparent.

Prosecutorial conduct that might be viewed as harassment or overreaching, even if sufficient to justify a mistrial on defendant's motion, therefore, does not bar retrial absent intent on the part of the prosecutor to subvert the protections afforded by the Double Jeopardy Clause. Only where the governmental conduct in question is intended to "goad" the defendant into moving for a mistrial may a defendant raise the bar of double jeopardy to a second trial after having succeeded in aborting the first on his own motion.

Were we to embrace the broad and somewhat amorphous standard adopted by the Oregon Court of Appeals, we are not sure that criminal defendants as a class would be aided. Knowing that the granting of the defendant's motion for mistrial would all but inevitably bring with it an attempt to bar a second trial on grounds of double jeopardy, the judge presiding over the first trial might well be more loath to grant a defendant's motion for mistrial.

Justice POWELL, concurring.

I join the Court's opinion holding that the intention of a prosecutor determines whether his conduct, viewed by the defendant and the court as justifying a mistrial, bars a retrial of the defendant under the Double Jeopardy Clause. Because "subjective" intent often may be unknowable, I emphasize that a court—in considering a double jeopardy motion—should rely primarily upon the objective facts and circumstances of the particular case.

In the present case the mistrial arose from the prosecutor's conduct in pursuing a line of redirect examination of a key witness. The Oregon Court of Appeals identified a single question as constituting "overreaching" so

serious as to bar a retrial. Yet, there are few vigorously contested lawsuits —
whether criminal or civil — in which improper questions are not asked. Our
system is adversarial and vigorous advocacy is encouraged.

Nevertheless, this would have been a close case for me if there had been
substantial factual evidence of intent beyond the question itself. Here,
however, other relevant facts and circumstances strongly support the view
that prosecutorial intent to cause a mistrial was absent. First, there was no
sequence of overreaching prior to the single prejudicial question. Moreover,
it is evident from a colloquy between counsel and the court, out of the
presence of the jury, that the prosecutor not only resisted, but also was
surprised by, the defendant's motion for a mistrial. Finally, at the hearing
on respondent's double jeopardy motion, the prosecutor testified — and the
trial found as a fact and the appellate court agreed — that there was no
"'intention . . . to cause a mistrial.'"

In view of these circumstances, the Double Jeopardy Clause provides no
bar to retrial.

2.   *Dual Sovereignty*

The dual sovereignty doctrine is another exception to the double jeopardy
rule. The doctrine allows two different sovereigns to prosecute the defendant for the same crime, because each sovereign has a separate and legitimate interest in prosecuting the defendant. Thus, for example, state and
federal authorities can prosecute a defendant for the same crime. This occurred in the famous 1993 case of four white police officers who beat black
motorist, Rodney King. The officers were acquitted in a state prosecution,
precipitating devastating riots in Los Angeles. Soon thereafter, federal
authorities charged the officers with civil rights violations based on the
same beating incidents. The officers were retried in federal court, and two
of them were convicted.[6]

The rationale for the dual sovereignty doctrine is set forth in the next case.

BARTKUS v. ILLINOIS

359 U.S. 121 (1959)

Justice FRANKFURTER delivered the opinion of the Court.

Petitioner was tried in the Federal District Court for the Northern District
of Illinois on December 18, 1953, for robbery of a federally insured savings
and loan association, the General Savings and Loan Association of Cicero,
Illinois, in violation of 18 U.S.C. §2113. The case was tried to a jury and

---

6. For more details regarding the state and federal prosecutions, *see* Laurie L. Levenson, *The
Future of State and Federal Civil Rights Prosecutions: The Lessons of the Rodney King Trial,* 41 UCLA L. Rev.
509 (1994).

resulted in an acquittal. On January 8, 1954, an Illinois grand jury indicted Bartkus. The facts recited in the Illinois indictment were substantially identical to those contained in the prior federal indictment. The Illinois indictment charged that these facts constituted a violation of Illinois Revised Statutes, 1951, c. 38, §501, a robbery statute. Bartkus was tried and convicted in the Criminal Court of Cook County and was sentenced to life imprisonment under the Illinois Habitual Criminal Statute.

The Illinois trial court considered and rejected petitioner's plea of autrefois acquit. We granted certiorari because the petition raised a substantial question concerning the application of the Fourteenth Amendment.[7]

The state and federal prosecutions were separately conducted. It is true that the agent of the Federal Bureau of Investigation who had conducted the investigation on behalf of the Federal Government turned over to the Illinois prosecuting officials all the evidence he had gathered against the petitioner. Concededly, some of that evidence had been gathered after acquittal in the federal court. The only other connection between the two trials is to be found in a suggestion that the federal sentencing of the accomplices who testified against petitioner in both trials was purposely continued by the federal court until after they testified in the state trial. The record establishes that the prosecution was undertaken by state prosecuting officials within their discretionary responsibility and on the basis of evidence that conduct contrary to the penal code of Illinois had occurred within their jurisdiction. It establishes also that federal officials acted in cooperation with state authorities, as is the conventional practice between the two sets of prosecutors throughout the country. It does not support the claim that the State of Illinois in bringing its prosecution was merely a tool of the federal authorities, who thereby avoided the prohibition of the Fifth Amendment against a retrial of a federal prosecution after an acquittal. It does not sustain a conclusion that the state prosecution was a sham and a cover for a federal prosecution, and thereby in essential fact another federal prosecution.

[The convictions were affirmed.]

On the same day as it decided *Bartkus*, the Supreme Court decided the companion case of Abbate v. United States, 359 U.S. 187 (1959). Whereas *Bartkus* held that states could prosecute the same crime following a federal prosecution, *Abbate* held that federal authorities could prosecute the same crime after a state prosecution. Justice Brennan wrote:

> Every citizen of the United States is also a citizen of a State or territory. He may be said to owe allegiance to two sovereigns, and may be liable to punishment for an

7. The case was decided under the Fourteenth Amendment because the Fifth Amendment double jeopardy right had not yet been incorporated to the states. The Double Jeopardy Clause was subsequently incorporated to the states. Missouri v. Hunter, 459 U.S. 359 (1983); Benton v. Maryland, 395 U.S. 784 (1969). [Footnote by casebook authors.]

infraction of the laws of either. The same act may be an offence or transgression of the laws of both.

That either or both may (if they see fit) punish such an offender, cannot be doubted.

Id. at 195.

The dual sovereignty doctrine allows state and federal governments to try a defendant for the same offense, two different states to try a defendant for the same offense, Heath v. Alabama, 474 U.S. 82, 88 (1985), and the United States and a foreign government to try a defendant for the same offense, United States v. Villanueva, 408 F.3d 193, 201 (5th Cir. 2005). Local governments, however, are not considered to be separate sovereigns for double jeopardy purposes and cannot try a defendant for the same offense. Waller v. Florida, 397 U.S. 387, 394-395 (1970). Cities and states are not considered to be "separate sovereigns."

The dual sovereignty doctrine has two limitations. First, as suggested in *Bartkus*, if both sovereigns are working together in a way that would make a second prosecution a "sham" prosecution, the dual sovereignty doctrine does not apply. *Bartkus*, 359 U.S. 122-124. Second, the Department of Justice has an internal policy, known as the "Petite policy,"[8] that authorizes federal prosecutors to bring a successive prosecution only when there are compelling reasons to do so and there is approval from the Assistant U.S. Attorney General. The policy, however, does not confer on a defendant the right to seek dismissal of an indictment for alleged violations of the federal authorities' protocol.

Dual prosecutions of defendants by state and federal authorities have occurred in several recent high-profile cases, including the state and federal prosecutions of the officers accused of beating black motorist Rodney King, and the state and federal prosecutions of Terry Nichols, who was accused of being a coconspirator in the bombing of the Murrah Federal Building in Oklahoma City. Yet the practice is not without controversy.

> The protection against double jeopardy, known as non bis in idem in the international context, is part of the "universal law of nations." There are at least fifty countries that provide protection from multiple prosecutions. Accordingly, the fact that the doctrine exists internationally in both the laws of foreign countries and treaties demonstrates its strong establishment in international criminal law. Because most nations view protection against multiple prosecutions as a fundamental right, double jeopardy appears as a stipulation in human rights treaties. For example, Article 14(7) of the International Covenant of Civil and Political Rights contains a general provision of double jeopardy which states "no one shall be liable to be tried or punished again for an offense for which he has already been finally convicted or acquitted in accordance with the law and penalty of each country."

---

8. *See Dual and Successive Federal Prosecution Policy,* Department of Justice Manual 9-2.031 (2005). The "Petite policy" is named after the Supreme Court's decision in Petite v. United States, 361 U.S. 529 (1960) (per curiam).

Eric M. Cranman, *The Dual Sovereign Exception to Double Jeopardy: A Champion of Justice or a Violation of a Fundamental Right*, 14 Emory Int'l L. Rev. 1641, 1645-1646 (2000). With the dual sovereignty exception, defendants cannot expect the finality associated with the double jeopardy rule and it gives the prosecution the opportunity to try a case, learn from its mistakes, and try the defendant again.

States are free to reject the dual sovereignty exception and many have done so. A majority of states prohibit a state prosecution that follows a federal prosecution for the same act or transaction. *See* Adam H. Kurland, Successive Criminal Prosecutions: The Dual Sovereignty to Double Jeopardy in State and Federal Courts (2001).

E. MULTIPLE CHARGES AND CUMULATIVE PUNISHMENTS

The Double Jeopardy Clause does not bar a defendant from being charged with multiple crimes arising from the same act or transaction. Because the primary purpose of the Double Jeopardy Clause is to protect against multiple trials, a legislature may constitutionally provide for multiple punishments even when the charges arise from one activity by the defendant. Missouri v. Hunter, 459 U.S. 359 (1983). The legislative intent to impose cumulative punishment must be clearly established. United States v. Universal C.I.T. Credit Corp., 344 U.S. 218, 221 (1952).

If the legislative intent does not demonstrate that the defendant may be subject to multiple punishments, or if one charge is the lesser-included offense of the other charge, the Double Jeopardy Clause bars multiple punishments.

RUTLEDGE v. UNITED STATES

517 U.S. 292 (1996)

Justice STEVENS delivered the opinion of the Court.

A jury found petitioner guilty of participating in a conspiracy to distribute controlled substances in violation of 21 U.S.C. §846, and of conducting a continuing criminal enterprise (CCE) in violation of §848. The "in concert" element of his CCE offense was based on the same agreement as the §846 conspiracy. The question presented is whether it was therefore improper for the District Court to sentence him to concurrent life sentences on the two counts.

I

Petitioner organized and supervised a criminal enterprise that distributed cocaine in Warren County, Illinois, from 1988 until December 1990, when he was arrested by federal agents. He was charged with several offenses, of which only Count One, the CCE charge, and Count Two, the conspiracy charge, are relevant to the issue before us.

Count One alleged that during the period between early 1988 and late 1990, petitioner violated §848 by engaging in a CCE that consisted of a series of unlawful acts involving the distribution of cocaine. The count alleged that these actions were undertaken "in concert with at least five (5) other persons," that petitioner supervised those other persons, and that he obtained substantial income from the continuing series of violations.

Count Two separately alleged that during the same period, petitioner violated 21 U.S.C. §846 by conspiring with four codefendants and others to engage in the unlawful distribution of cocaine.

[A] jury found petitioner guilty on all counts. The trial court entered judgment of conviction on both Count One and Count Two and imposed a sentence of life imprisonment without possible release on each count, the sentences to be served concurrently.

On appeal, petitioner contended in a pro se supplemental brief that even though the life sentences were concurrent, entering both convictions and sentences impermissibly punished him twice for the same offense. The Court of Appeals for the Seventh Circuit accepted the premise of his argument, namely, that the conspiracy charge was a lesser included offense of the CCE charge. The Court of Appeals nonetheless affirmed his convictions and sentences.

The decision of the Seventh Circuit is at odds with the practice of other Circuits. Most federal courts that have confronted the question hold that only one judgment should be entered when a defendant is found guilty on both a CCE count and a conspiracy count based on the same agreements. The Second and Third Circuits have adopted an intermediate position, allowing judgment to be entered on both counts but permitting only one sentence rather than the concurrent sentences allowed in the Seventh Circuit. We granted certiorari to resolve the conflict.

II

Courts may not "prescrib[e] greater punishment than the legislature intended." Missouri v. Hunter (1983). In accord with principles rooted in common law and constitutional jurisprudence, we presume that "where two statutory provisions proscribe the 'same offense,'" a legislature does not intend to impose two punishments for that offense.

For over half a century we have determined whether a defendant has been punished twice for the "same offense" by applying the rule set forth in Blockburger v. United States (1932). If "the same act or transaction constitutes a violation of two distinct statutory provisions, the test to be applied to determine whether there are two offenses or only one, is whether each provision requires proof of a fact which the other does not." In subsequent applications of the test, we have often concluded that two different statutes define the "same offense," typically because one is a lesser included offense of the other.

In this case it is perfectly clear that the CCE offense requires proof of a number of elements that need not be established in a conspiracy case. The *Blockburger* test requires us to consider whether the converse is also true — whether the §846 conspiracy offense requires proof of any element that is not a part of the CCE offense. That question could be answered affirmatively only by assuming that while the §846 conspiracy requires proof of an actual agreement among the parties, the "in concert" element of the CCE offense might be satisfied by something less.

[T]he Courts of Appeals have also consistently rejected the Government's interpretation of the "in concert" language of §848; they have concluded, without exception, that conspiracy is a lesser included offense of CCE. [We also] hold that this element of the CCE offense requires proof of a conspiracy that would also violate §846. Because §846 does not require proof of any fact that is not also a part of the CCE offense, a straightforward application of the *Blockburger* test leads to the conclusion that conspiracy as defined in §846 does not define a different offense from the CCE offense defined in §848. Furthermore, since the latter offense is the more serious of the two, and because only one of its elements is necessary to prove a §846 conspiracy, it is appropriate to characterize §846 as a lesser included offense of §848.

III

The Government contends that even if conspiracy is a lesser included offense of CCE, the resulting presumption against multiple punishments does not invalidate either of petitioner's convictions. The second conviction, the Government first argues, may not amount to a punishment at all.

We begin by noting that 18 U.S.C. §3013 requires a federal district court to impose a $50 special assessment for every conviction, and that such an assessment was imposed on both convictions in this case. As long as §3013 stands, a second conviction will amount to a second punishment.

[Moreover,] "[t]he second conviction, whose concomitant sentence is served concurrently, does not evaporate simply because of the concurrence of the sentence. The separate conviction, apart from the concurrent sentence, has potential adverse collateral consequences that may not be ignored. For example, the presence of two convictions on the record may delay the defendant's eligibility for parole or result in an increased sentence under a recidivist statute for a future offense. Moreover, the second conviction may be used to impeach the defendant's credibility and certainly carries the societal stigma accompanying any criminal conviction. Thus, the second conviction, even if it results in no greater sentence, is an impermissible punishment."

IV

The Government further argues that even if the second conviction amounts to punishment, the presumption against allowing multiple punishments for the same crime may be overcome if Congress clearly indicates that it intended to allow courts to impose them.

The Government finds support for its position in this Court's judgment in *Jeffers* because that judgment allowed convictions under both §§846 and 848 to stand. Those convictions, however, had been entered in separate trials and our review only addressed the conviction under §848.[9]

VI

A guilty verdict on a §848 charge necessarily includes a finding that the defendant also participated in a conspiracy violative of §846; conspiracy is therefore a lesser included offense of CCE. Because the Government's arguments have not persuaded us otherwise, we adhere to the presumption that Congress intended to authorize only one punishment. Accordingly, "one of [petitioner's] convictions, as well as its concurrent sentence, is unauthorized punishment for a separate offense" and must be vacated.

The judgment of the Court of Appeals is reversed, and the case is remanded for further proceedings consistent with this opinion.

As noted in *Rutledge*, the test to determine whether one charge is a lesser-included offense of the other is the *Blockburger* test, discussed in section B of this chapter. If a defendant is convicted of separate offenses, multiple punishments are permitted as long as the legislative intent supports a finding that cumulative punishments may be imposed.

F.   COLLATERAL ESTOPPEL

The Double Jeopardy Clause includes within it the concept of collateral estoppel. This means that if an issue of ultimate fact has been determined by a valid and final judgment, it cannot be relitigated in a future case. Consider, for example, a defendant who is charged with robbing two victims. In trial number one, the jurors acquit the defendant of robbing victim one

---

9. The Government suggests that convictions are authorized for both §§846 and 848 because they are different sections of the United States Code. This does not rise to the level of the clear statement necessary for us to conclude that despite the identity of the statutory elements, Congress intended to allow multiple punishments. After all, we concluded in *Ball* that the statutes at issue did not authorize separate convictions, and they were even more distant in the Code. If anything, the proximity of §§846 and 848 indicates that Congress understood them to be directed to similar, rather than separate, evils. [Footnote by the Court.]

because there is a reasonable doubt as to whether he was the robber. The government cannot prosecute the defendant for robbery of the other victim, because there has already been a finding that he was not the robber. The Supreme Court explained this concept in the key case of Ashe v. Swenson.

ASHE v. SWENSON
397 U.S. 436 (1970)

Justice STEWART delivered the opinion of the Court.

The question in this case is whether the State of Missouri violated [the guarantee against double jeopardy] when it prosecuted the petitioner a second time for armed robbery in the circumstances here presented.

Sometime in the early hours of the morning of January 10, 1960, six men were engaged in a poker game in the basement of the home of John Gladson at Lee's Summit, Missouri. Suddenly three or four masked men, armed with a shotgun and pistols, broke into the basement and robbed each of the poker players of money and various articles of personal property. The robbers — and it has never been clear whether there were three or four of them — then fled in a car belonging to one of the victims of the robbery. Shortly thereafter the stolen car was discovered in a field, and later that morning three men were arrested by a state trooper while they were walking on a highway not far from where the abandoned car had been found. The petitioner was arrested by another officer some distance away.

The four were subsequently charged with seven separate offenses — the armed robbery of each of the six poker players and the theft of the car. In May 1960 the petitioner went to trial on the charge of robbing Donald Knight, one of the participants in the poker game. At the trial the State called Knight and three of his fellow poker players as prosecution witnesses. Each of them described the circumstances of the holdup and itemized his own individual losses. The proof that an armed robbery had occurred and that personal property had been taken from Knight as well as from each of the others was unassailable. The testimony of the four victims in this regard was consistent both internally and with that of the others. But the State's evidence that the petitioner had been one of the robbers was weak. Two of the witnesses thought that there had been only three robbers altogether, and could not identify the petitioner as one of them. Another of the victims, who was the petitioner's uncle by marriage, said that at the "patrol station" he had positively identified each of the other three men accused of the holdup, but could say only that the petitioner's voice "sounded very much like" that of one of the robbers. The fourth participant in the poker game did identify the petitioner, but only by his "size and height, and his actions."

The cross-examination of these witnesses was brief, and it was aimed primarily at exposing the weakness of their identification testimony. Defense counsel made no attempt to question their testimony regarding the holdup itself or their claims as to their losses. Knight testified without contradiction that the robbers had stolen from him his watch, $250 in cash, and about $500 in checks. His billfold, which had been found by the police in the possession of one of the three other men accused of the robbery, was admitted in evidence. The defense offered no testimony and waived final argument.

The trial judge instructed the jury that if it found that the petitioner was one of the participants in the armed robbery, the theft of "any money" from Knight would sustain a conviction. He also instructed the jury that if the petitioner was one of the robbers, he was guilty under the law even if he had not personally robbed Knight. The jury—though not instructed to elaborate upon its verdict—found the petitioner "not guilty due to insufficient evidence."

Six weeks later the petitioner was brought to trial again, this time for the robbery of another participant in the poker game, a man named Roberts. The petitioner filed a motion to dismiss, based on his previous acquittal. The motion was overruled, and the second trial began. The witnesses were for the most part the same, though this time their testimony was substantially stronger on the issue of the petitioner's identity.

The case went to the jury on instructions virtually identical to those given at the first trial. This time the jury found the petitioner guilty, and he was sentenced to a 35-year term in the state penitentiary.

The petitioner then brought the present habeas corpus proceeding . . . claiming that the second prosecution had violated his right not to be twice put in jeopardy.

The question is [whether collateral estoppel is a part of the Fifth Amendment's guarantee against double jeopardy].

"Collateral estoppel" is an awkward phrase, but it stands for an extremely important principle in our adversary system of justice. It means simply that when an issue of ultimate fact has once been determined by a valid and final judgment, that issue cannot again be litigated between the same parties in any future lawsuit.

The federal decisions have made clear that the rule of collateral estoppel in criminal cases is not to be applied with the hypertechnical and archaic approach of a 19th century pleading book, but with realism and rationality. Where a previous judgment of acquittal was based upon a general verdict, as is usually the case, this approach requires a court to "examine the record of a prior proceeding, taking into account the pleadings, evidence, charge, and other relevant matter, and conclude whether a rational jury could have grounded its verdict upon an issue other than that which the defendant seeks to foreclose from consideration." The inquiry "must be set in a practical frame and viewed with an eye to all the circumstances of the proceedings." Any test more technically restrictive would, of course, simply amount to a rejection of the rule of collateral estoppel in criminal proceedings, at least in every case where the first judgment was based upon a general verdict of acquittal.

Straightforward application of the federal rule to the present case can lead to but one conclusion. For the record is utterly devoid of any indication that the first jury could rationally have found that an armed robbery had not occurred, or that Knight had not been a victim of that robbery. The single rationally conceivable issue in dispute before the jury was whether the petitioner had been one of the robbers. And the jury by its verdict found that he had not. The federal rule of law, therefore, would make a second prosecution for the robbery of Roberts wholly impermissible.

The question is not whether Missouri could validly charge the petitioner with six separate offenses for the robbery of the six poker players. It is not whether he could have received a total of six punishments if he had been convicted in a single trial of robbing the six victims. It is simply whether, after a jury determined by its verdict that the petitioner was not one of the robbers, the State could constitutionally hale him before a new jury to litigate that issue again.

In this case the State in its brief has frankly conceded that following the petitioner's acquittal, it treated the first trial as no more than a dry run for the second prosecution: "No doubt the prosecutor felt the state had a provable case on the first charge and, when he lost, he did what every good attorney would do — he refined his presentation in light of the turn of events at the first trial." But this is precisely what the constitutional guarantee forbids.

The judgment is reversed.

Chief Justice BURGER, dissenting.

The Fifth Amendment to the Constitution of the United States provides in part: "nor shall any person be subject for the same offence to be twice put in jeopardy of life or limb. . . ." Nothing in the language or gloss previously placed on this provision of the Fifth Amendment remotely justifies the treatment that the Court today accords to the collateral-estoppel doctrine. Nothing in the purpose of the authors of the Constitution commands or even justifies what the Court decides today; this is truly a case of expanding a sound basic principle beyond the bounds — or needs — of its rational and legitimate objectives to preclude harassment of an accused.

The majority rests its holding in part on a series of cases beginning with United States v. Oppenheimer (1916), which did not involve constitutional double jeopardy but applied collateral estoppel as developed in civil litigation to federal criminal prosecutions as a matter of this Court's supervisory power over the federal court system. The Court now finds the federal collateral estoppel rule to be an "ingredient" of the Fifth Amendment guarantee against double jeopardy and applies it to the States through the Fourteenth Amendment; this is an ingredient that eluded judges and justices for nearly two centuries.

The collateral-estoppel concept — originally a product only of civil litigation — is a strange mutant as it is transformed to control this criminal case. In civil cases the doctrine was justified as conserving judicial resources as well as those of the parties to the actions and additionally as providing the finality needed to plan for the future. It ordinarily applies to parties on each side of the litigation who have the same interest as or who are identical with the parties in the initial litigation. Here the complainant in the second trial is not the same as in the first even though the State is a party in both cases. Very properly, in criminal cases, finality and conservation of private, public, and judicial resources are lesser values than in civil litigation. Also, courts that have applied the collateral-estoppel concept to criminal actions would certainly not apply it to both parties, as is true in civil cases, i.e., here, if Ashe had been convicted at the first trial, presumably no court would then hold that he was thereby foreclosed from litigating the identification issue at the second trial.

Perhaps, then, it comes as no surprise to find that the only expressed rationale for the majority's decision is that Ashe has "run the gantlet" once before. This is not a doctrine of the law or legal reasoning but a colorful and graphic phrase, which, as used originally in an opinion of the Court written by Mr. Justice Black, was intended to mean something entirely different. The full phrase is "run the gantlet once on that charge. . . ." [I]t is to be found in Green v. United States (1957), where no question of multiple crimes against multiple victims was involved. Green, having been found guilty of second-degree murder on a charge of first degree, secured a new trial. This Court held nothing more than that Green, once put in jeopardy — once having "run the gantlet . . . on that charge" — of first-degree murder, could not be compelled to defend against that charge again on retrial.

Today's step in this area of constitutional law ought not be taken on no more basis than casual reliance on the "gantlet" phrase lifted out of the context in which it was originally used. This is decision by slogan.

In Ashe v. Swenson, the Court established that double jeopardy barred retrial of issues that were necessarily decided in a prior case. In Yeager v. United States (2009), a slim majority of justices held that an acquittal on some counts may preclude a retrial on those issues even if the initial jury did not reach a verdict on other counts.

YEAGER v. UNITED STATES

557 U.S. 110 (2009)

Justice STEVENS delivered the opinion of the Court.

The question presented in this case is whether an apparent inconsistency between a jury's verdict of acquittal on some counts and its failure to return a verdict on other counts affects the preclusive force of the acquittals under the Double Jeopardy Clause of the Fifth Amendment. We hold that it does not.

[Petitioner F. Scott Yeager served as an officer for a division of Enron Corporation (Enron). Yeager allegedly made false and misleading statements about the value of one of Enron's projects, causing the price of Enron stock to rise dramatically. The petitioner sold stock shares that he had received as part of his compensation and made $19 million in personal profit. As it happened, the project turned out to be worthless.

Yeager was charged in a 126-count Fifth Superseding Indictment with (1) conspiracy to commit securities and wire fraud, (2) securities fraud, (3) wire fraud, (4) insider trading, and (5) money laundering. The government's theory of prosecution was that petitioner — acting in concert with other Enron executives — purposefully deceived the public about the project in order to inflate the value of Enron's stock and, ultimately, enrich himself.]

The trial lasted 13 weeks. After four days of deliberations, the jury notified the court that it had reached agreement on some counts but had deadlocked on others. The jury acquitted petitioner on the fraud counts but failed to reach a verdict on the insider trading counts. The court entered judgment on the acquittals and declared a mistrial on the hung counts.

[Thereafter], the Government obtained a new indictment against petitioner. This "Eighth Superseding Indictment" recharged petitioner with some, but not all, of the insider trading counts on which the jury had previously hung. Petitioner moved to dismiss all counts in the new indictment on the ground that the acquittals on the fraud counts precluded the Government from retrying him on the insider trading counts. He argued that the jury's acquittals had necessarily decided that he did not possess material, nonpublic information about the performance of the project and its value to Enron. In petitioner's view, because reprosecution for insider trading would require the Government to prove that critical fact, the issue-preclusion component of the Double Jeopardy Clause barred a second trial of that issue and mandated dismissal of all of the insider trading counts.

The Double Jeopardy Clause of the Fifth Amendment provides: "[N]or shall any person be subject for the same offence to be twice put in jeopardy of life or limb."

Our cases have recognized that the Clause embodies two vitally important interests. The first is the "deeply ingrained" principle that "the State with all its resources and power should not be allowed to make repeated attempts to convict an individual for an alleged offense, thereby subjecting him to embarrassment, expense and ordeal and compelling him to live in a continuing state of anxiety and insecurity, as well as enhancing the possibility that even though innocent he may be found guilty." The second interest is the preservation of "the finality of judgments."

The first interest is implicated whenever the State seeks a second trial after its first attempt to obtain a conviction results in a mistrial because the jury has failed to reach a verdict. While the case before us involves a mistrial on the insider trading counts, the question presented cannot be resolved by asking whether the Government should be given one complete opportunity to convict petitioner on those charges. Rather, the case turns on the second interest at the core of the Clause. We must determine whether the interest in preserving the finality of the jury's judgment on the fraud counts, including the jury's finding that petitioner did not possess insider information, bars a retrial on the insider trading counts.

In *Ashe*, we squarely held that the Double Jeopardy Clause precludes the Government from relitigating any issue that was necessarily decided by a jury's acquittal in a prior trial. [In this case], the Court of Appeals reasoned that the hung counts must be considered to determine what issues the jury decided in the first trial. Viewed in isolation, the court explained, the acquittals on the fraud charges would preclude retrial because they appeared to support petitioner's argument that the jury decided he lacked insider information. Viewed alongside the hung counts, however, the acquittals appeared less decisive.

The Court of Appeals' issue-preclusion analysis was in error. A hung count is not a "relevant" part of the "record of [the] prior proceeding." Because a jury speaks only through its verdict, its failure to reach a verdict cannot — by negative implication — yield a piece of information that helps put together the trial puzzle. A mistried count is therefore nothing like the other forms of record material that *Ashe* suggested should be part of the preclusion inquiry. A host of reasons — sharp disagreement, confusion about the issues, exhaustion after a long trial, to name but a few — could work alone or in tandem to cause a jury to hang. To ascribe meaning to a hung count would presume an ability to identify which factor was at play in the jury room. But that is not reasoned analysis; it is guesswork.

To identify what a jury necessarily determined at trial, courts should scrutinize a jury's decisions, not its failures to decide. Thus, if the possession of insider information was a critical issue of ultimate fact in all of the charges against petitioner, a jury verdict that necessarily decided that issue in his favor protects him from prosecution for any charge for which that is an essential element.

[W]e decline to engage in a fact-intensive analysis of the voluminous record [to determine the basis for the acquittal]. If it chooses, the Court of Appeals may revisit its factual analysis in light of the Government's arguments before this Court.

CHAPTER
11

HABEAS CORPUS

A. INTRODUCTION

After a person has been convicted of a crime and exhausted all appeals, he or she may file a petition for a writ of habeas corpus in federal court. Habeas petitions are commonly filed by inmates while they are in prison. Although there are difficult procedural issues for petitioners to navigate, there is no right to counsel to assist in the filing of habeas corpus petitions. This chapter discusses in detail the procedural hurdles for habeas corpus petitions, as well as the limitation on the types of claims that may be made through habeas corpus petitions.

A person convicted in a state court proceeding generally may secure federal court review of the state court's judgments and proceedings only by first exhausting all available appeals within the state system. Federal district courts lack the authority to hear appeals from state judicial systems. Under federal law, a person who claims to be held in custody by a state government in violation of the Constitution, treaties, or laws of the United States may file a civil lawsuit in federal court seeking a writ of habeas corpus. Technically, federal court consideration of the habeas corpus petition is not considered a direct review of the state court decision; rather, the petition constitutes a separate civil suit filed in federal court and is termed *collateral relief.* If the federal court grants a writ of habeas corpus, it may order the release of a state prisoner who is held by the state in violation of federal law. Federal courts may also hear habeas petitions of federal prisoners pursuant to 28 U.S.C. §2255.

The writ of habeas corpus has its origins in English law.[1] Blackstone referred to habeas corpus as "the most celebrated writ in English law."[2] Recognizing its importance, the Framers of the Constitution provided that "[t]he Privilege of the Writ of Habeas Corpus shall not be suspended,

---

Portions of the text in this chapter are taken from Erwin Chemerinsky, *Federal Jurisdiction* Ch. 15 (6th ed. 2012).

1. For an excellent history of habeas corpus, *see* W. Duker, *A Constitutional History of Habeas Corpus* (1980).

2. 3 *Blackstone's Commentaries* 129 (1791).

unless when in Cases of Rebellion or Invasion the public Safety may require it."[3] Under the Judiciary Act of 1789, habeas corpus was available to prisoners who claimed that they were held in custody by the *federal* government in violation of the Constitution, treaties, or laws of the United States.[4] After the Civil War, at a time of great distrust in the ability and willingness of state courts to protect federal rights, Congress provided habeas corpus relief to state prisoners if they were held "in custody in violation of the Constitution or laws or treaties of the United States."[5]

The writ of habeas corpus protects individuals against arbitrary and wrongful imprisonment. It is not surprising, therefore, that habeas corpus long has been viewed as the "great writ of liberty."[6] At the same time, however, the availability of federal court relief pursuant to the writ of habeas corpus remains enormously controversial. Conservatives feel that habeas corpus is a vehicle that guilty criminals often use to escape their convictions and their sentences.[7] But liberals see the writ as an essential protection of constitutional rights — ensuring that individuals are not held in custody in violation of those rights.[8] The writ of habeas corpus also is controversial because it is a source of direct confrontation between federal district courts and state judiciaries. The power of a single federal judge to overturn a decision affirmed by an entire state court system is troubling to many.[9] A reflection of this ideological split is that in 1996, the Republican-controlled Congress enacted the Antiterrorism and Effective Death Penalty Act, which substantially changed the law of habeas corpus and, in many ways, restricted its availability.[10] Yet the controversy over habeas corpus must be put in perspective. Statistics indicate that less than 1 percent of state prisoners who file habeas corpus petitions ultimately prevail.[11]

In recent years, there has been a major debate over whether federal courts should be able to exercise habeas corpus over those who are detained as part of the war on terrorism, especially those held in Guantánamo Bay, Cuba.[12] In Rasul v. Bush, the Supreme Court held that federal courts have jurisdiction to hear habeas petitions by those detained in Guantánamo.[13] Congress responded by enacting the Detainee Treatment Act, which held that those

---

3. U.S. Const. art. I, §9, cl. 2.

4. Judiciary Act of 1789, ch. 20, 1 Stat. 73.

5. 28 U.S.C. §2254.

6. Duker, *supra* note 1, at 3.

7. *See, e.g.,* Henry J. Friendly, *Is Innocence Irrelevant? Collateral Attack on Criminal Judgments,* 38 U. Chi. L. Rev. 142 (1970) (arguing that habeas corpus should be available only where there is a colorable showing of a defendant's innocence).

8. *See, e.g.,* Stephen A. Saltzburg, *Habeas Corpus: The Supreme Court and the Congress,* 44 Ohio St. L.J. 367 (1983) (habeas corpus is symbolic of the ideal that no person should be convicted in violation of the fundamental law of the land).

9. *See, e.g.,* Engle v. Isaac, 456 U.S. 107, 126 (1982).

10. Pub. L. No. 104-132, April 24, 1996.

11. John Blume, *AEDPA: The "Hype" and the "Bite,"* 91 Cornell L. Rev. 259, 284 (2006).

12. This is discussed in detail in section D below.

13. 542 U.S. 466 (2004).

held in Guantánamo shall not have access to federal courts via a writ of habeas corpus; they must go through military commissions and then seek review in the District of Columbia Circuit.[14] In Hamdan v. Rumsfeld, the Supreme Court held that this provision applies only prospectively, not retroactively to those petitions that already were pending in federal court at the time that the law was enacted.[15] In the fall of 2006, Congress responded by enacting the Military Commissions Act of 2006, which makes clear that the restrictions on habeas corpus in the Detainee Treatment Act apply retroactively.[16] In Boumediene v. Bush, the Supreme Court declared this unconstitutional as an impermissible suspension of the writ of habeas corpus.[17]

These events reflect a deep disagreement over whether federal courts, via habeas corpus, should be available to those held as enemy combatants. The Bush administration and Congress saw habeas corpus review as inconsistent with the war on terrorism. But the Supreme Court viewed habeas corpus review as essential to make sure that no one is detained indefinitely without meaningful due process.

Because of the divergence of views concerning habeas corpus for prisoners and for detainees, it is hardly surprising that the law concerning habeas corpus availability has been particularly volatile. No area of federal jurisdiction has changed more dramatically in the last 25 years than habeas corpus. As discussed below, the Court has imposed substantial new obstacles to habeas relief, including generally preventing successive habeas petitions[18] and preventing the use of habeas corpus to develop new rules of constitutional law.[19] Even more dramatically, the Antiterrorism and Effective Death Penalty Act substantially changed many aspects of the law of habeas corpus, including creating a statute of limitations for filing petitions, precluding successive petitions except in very limited circumstances and only with the approval of a United States Court of Appeals, and narrowing the scope of federal court review.[20] In addition, as mentioned above, twice Congress enacted statutes precluding habeas corpus by those held as enemy combatants.

This chapter is divided into three major sections. First, section B considers the major issues that must be addressed in order for a federal court to grant habeas corpus review. Second, section C summarizes key procedural issues in habeas corpus litigation. Finally, section D looks at habeas corpus for those held as enemy combatants as part of the war on terrorism.

14. 119 Stat. 2739, codified at 10 U.S.C. §801.
15. 548 U.S. 557 (2006).
16. Pub. L. No. 109-366, 120 Stat. 2600 (2006).
17. 553 U.S. 723 (2008).
18. McCleskey v. Zant, 499 U.S. 467 (1991), discussed below.
19. Teague v. Lane, 489 U.S. 288 (1989), discussed below.
20. Antiterrorism and Effective Death Penalty Act of 1996, Pub. L. No. 104-132, 110 Stat. 1214.

B.   THE ISSUES THAT MUST BE ADDRESSED IN ORDER FOR A FEDERAL COURT TO GRANT HABEAS CORPUS RELIEF

Federal statutes and Supreme Court interpretation of them have created a number of hurdles that must be overcome in order for a federal court to grant a habeas corpus petition. Although the order of the questions is somewhat arbitrary, a federal court considering a habeas petition must address all of the following issues:

1. Is the habeas petition time barred? The Antiterrorism and Effective Death Penalty Act has created strict time limits for when a habeas petition must be filed. If the petition is untimely, it must be dismissed.
2. Is it a first habeas petition by the individual or is it a successive petition (a second, third, fourth, etc. petition)? If it is a successive petition, it must be dismissed unless the federal court of appeals approves its filing based on finding that the case meets stringent requirements for successive petitions.
3. Has there been exhaustion of state procedures for all claims presented in the habeas petition? If there has not been exhaustion for all claims, then the entire petition must be dismissed.
4. Does the petition rely on an already established rule of criminal procedure, or does it seek recognition of a new rule? If it seeks the recognition of a new rule, the petition must be dismissed unless it is an extraordinary rule that applies retroactively.
5. Is it a claim that can be heard on habeas corpus? Generally, individuals are allowed to relitigate their constitutional claims on habeas, but there is a notable exception: Fourth Amendment claims by state prisoners generally cannot be raised on habeas corpus as long as there was a full and fair hearing in state court.
6. Has there been a procedural default in the sense of a failure to follow the required procedures of the forum, state or federal, in which the person was convicted? For example, were the claims raised in the habeas petition properly raised at trial, or were they defaulted for failure to raise them? If a claim was procedurally defaulted, it must be dismissed unless there is either a showing of good cause for the failure and prejudice to not being heard on habeas or a showing of likely actual innocence.
7. If the claim is heard, can the federal court hold an evidentiary hearing, or is it limited to the record that was in the state court?
8. Can the federal court provide habeas corpus relief? For example, under the provisions of the Antiterrorism and Effective Death Penalty Act, a federal court may grant habeas corpus relief only if the state court decision is contrary to or an unreasonable application of law clearly established by the Supreme Court.

These eight questions might be thought of as filters, with each question causing a significant number of habeas petitions to be dismissed. Relatively few make it to the last question, and even fewer are granted. This section is organized around these eight questions. These are not the only requirements for habeas corpus. Others are discussed in section C below, such as the requirement that a person be in custody. But these issues certainly are the focus of most habeas corpus litigation in the United States.

1. Is the Petition Time Barred?

Until 1996, the federal statutes concerning habeas corpus review did not prescribe any time limit within which petitions must be filed.[21] The habeas corpus rules that went into effect in 1977 provided that a petition may be dismissed if the state is prejudiced by a delay in the filing of the petition, "unless the petitioner shows that it is based on grounds of which he could not have had knowledge by the exercise of reasonable diligence before the circumstances prejudicial to the state occurred."[22]

The Antiterrorism and Effective Death Penalty Act, enacted in 1996, imposes a one-year statute of limitations on the filing of habeas petitions. Section 101 of the act provides, "A 1-year period of limitation shall apply to an application for a writ of habeas corpus by a person in custody pursuant to the judgment of a state court."[23] Section 101 also states that "[t]he time during which a properly filed application for state post-conviction or other collateral review with respect to the pertinent judgment or claim is pending shall not be counted toward any period of limitation under this subsection."[24]

The act also provides that in capital cases a six-month statute of limitations applies if it is determined that a state has established an adequate system for providing attorneys for post-conviction proceedings.[25] To this point, only Arizona has been found to have created such a system and thus be entitled to invoke the shorter statute of limitations.[26] In Calderon v. Ashmus, the Supreme Court unanimously dismissed as nonjusticiable a request for a

---

21. *See, e.g.*, United States v. Smith, 331 U.S. 469, 475 (1947). Indeed, prior to the act's going into effect, the Court ruled that there was no time limit on first habeas petitions, and they could be filed even on the day of execution. Lonchar v. Thomas, 517 U.S. 314 (1996).

22. 28 U.S.C. §2254, Rule 9(a).

23. 28 U.S.C. §2244.

24. *Id.*

25. The act states that the shorter statute of limitations applies "if a State establishes by statute, rules of its court of last resort, or by another agency authorized by state law, a mechanism for the appointment, compensation, and payment of reasonable litigation expenses of competent counsel in State post-conviction proceedings brought by indigent prisoners whose capital convictions and sentences have been upheld on direct appeal to the court of last resort in the State or have otherwise become final for State law purposes." 28 U.S.C. §2261.

26. For an argument that states are unlikely to choose to comply and thus trigger the shorter statute of limitations in habeas cases, *see* John Blume, *AEDPA: The "Hype" and the "Bite,"* 91 Cornell L. Rev. 259 (2006).

declaratory judgment by death-row inmates that California was not in compliance with the act.[27] *Calderon* means that inmates cannot seek a system-wide
determination of whether a state is in compliance with the act; rather, in
each case, the issue must be raised and litigated.

The crucial issue in habeas litigation frequently is whether there was tolling of the statute of limitations. One key aspect of this is whether there is
tolling while a habeas petition is pending in federal court. If a state prisoner
files a habeas corpus petition in federal court that is then dismissed, is the
time that it was pending counted toward the statute of limitations for the
habeas petition? The Supreme Court addressed this in Duncan v. Walker,
533 U.S. 167 (2001). Justice O'Connor, writing for the Court, held that the
statutory language in the act provided that the statute of limitations was
tolled while a prisoner was seeking collateral relief in state court under
state law but not while a habeas petition was pending in federal court.[28]

Justice O'Connor wrote:

> To begin with, Congress placed the word "State" before "post-conviction or other
> collateral review" without specifically naming any kind of "Federal" review. The
> essence of respondent's position is that Congress used the phrase "other collateral
> review" to incorporate federal habeas petitions into the class of applications for
> review that toll the limitation period. But a comparison of the text of §2244(d)(2)
> with the language of other AEDPA provisions supplies strong evidence that, had
> Congress intended to include federal habeas petitions within the scope of
> §2244(d)(2), Congress would have mentioned "Federal" review expressly. In
> several other portions of AEDPA, Congress specifically used both the words
> "State" and "Federal" to denote state and federal proceedings. For example, 28
> U.S.C. §2254(i) provides: "The ineffectiveness or incompetence of counsel during
> Federal or State collateral post-conviction proceedings shall not be a ground for
> relief in a proceeding arising under section 2254."
>
> Section 2244(d)(2), by contrast, employs the word "State," but not the word
> "Federal," as a modifier for "review." It is well settled that "[w]here Congress
> includes particular language in one section of a statute but omits it in another
> section of the same Act, it is generally presumed that Congress acts intentionally
> and purposely in the disparate inclusion or exclusion." We find no likely expla-
> nation for Congress' omission of the word "Federal" in §2244(d)(2) other than
> that Congress did not intend properly filed applications for federal review to toll
> the limitation period. It would be anomalous, to say the least, for Congress to usher
> in federal review under the generic rubric of "other collateral review" in a statutory
> provision that refers expressly to "State" review, while denominating expressly
> both "State" and "Federal" proceedings in other parts of the same statute. The
> anomaly is underscored by the fact that the words "State" and "Federal" are likely
> to be of no small import when Congress drafts a statute that governs federal
> collateral review of state court judgments.

27. 523 U.S. 740 (1998).

28. Also, in Lawrence v. Florida, 549 U.S. 327 (2007), the Court considered whether there is
tolling — that is, whether the statute of limitations clock stops running — while a petition for a writ
of certiorari is pending in the Supreme Court seeking review of a state court's denial of relief in
collateral proceedings. In other words, while a state habeas corpus petition is pending, there is
tolling of the statute of limitations; does that include the time while certiorari is being sought in the
Supreme Court of the state court's decision? The Supreme Court, 5-4, held that there was not
tolling.

Justice Stevens, in an opinion concurring and concurring in the judgment, expressed concern that the majority's holding could lead to tremendous unfairness. Imagine a state prisoner who files an immediate habeas petition in federal court after completion of the state proceedings, but the federal court waits 13 months before dismissing the petition for failure to adequately exhaust state remedies. The entire year of the statute of limitations has expired because there is no tolling while the case was pending in federal court. Justice Stevens explained:

> This possibility is not purely theoretical. A Justice Department study indicates that 63% of all habeas petitions are dismissed, and 57% of those are dismissed for failure to exhaust state remedies. And it can take courts a significant amount of time to dispose of even those petitions that are not addressed on the merits; on the average, district courts took 268 days to dismiss petitions on procedural grounds. Thus, if the words "other collateral review" do not include federal collateral review, a large group of federal habeas petitioners, seeking to return to federal court after subsequent state-court rejection of an unexhausted claim, may find their claims time barred. Moreover, because district courts vary substantially in the time they take to rule on habeas petitions, two identically situated prisoners can receive opposite results. If Prisoner A and Prisoner B file mixed petitions in different district courts six months before the federal limitations period expires, and the court takes three months to dismiss Prisoner A's petition, but seven months to dismiss Prisoner B's petition, Prisoner A will be able to return to federal court after exhausting state remedies, but Prisoner B — due to no fault of his own — may not.

Justice Stevens suggested that the solution would be to allow federal courts to use equitable tolling to preserve the ability of the habeas petitioner to have access to the federal court. He wrote:

> [N]either the Court's narrow holding, nor anything in the text or legislative history of AEDPA, precludes a federal court from deeming the limitations period tolled for such a petition as a matter of equity. The Court's opinion does not address a federal court's ability to toll the limitations period apart from §2244(d)(2). Furthermore, a federal court might very well conclude that tolling is appropriate based on the reasonable belief that Congress could not have intended to bar federal habeas review for petitioners who invoke the court's jurisdiction within the 1-year interval prescribed by AEDPA.

In Holland v. Florida, the Supreme Court held that equitable tolling, as suggested by Justice Stevens, is permissible.

<u>HOLLAND v. FLORIDA</u>

130 S. Ct. 2549 (2010)

Justice BREYER delivered the opinion of the Court.

We here decide that the timeliness provision in the federal habeas corpus statute is subject to equitable tolling. See Antiterrorism and Effective Death

Penalty Act of 1996 (AEDPA). We also consider its application in this case. In the Court of Appeals' view, when a petitioner seeks to excuse a late filing on the basis of his attorney's unprofessional conduct, that conduct, even if it is "negligent" or "grossly negligent," cannot "rise to the level of egregious attorney misconduct" that would warrant equitable tolling unless the petitioner offers "proof of bad faith, dishonesty, divided loyalty, mental impairment or so forth." In our view, this standard is too rigid.

I

AEDPA states that "[a] 1-year period of limitation shall apply to an application for a writ of habeas corpus by a person in custody pursuant to the judgment of a State court." It also says that "[t]he time during which a properly filed application for State post-conviction . . . review" is "pending shall not be counted" against the 1-year period.

On January 19, 2006, Albert Holland filed a *pro se* habeas corpus petition in the Federal District Court for the Southern District of Florida. Both Holland (the petitioner) and the State of Florida (the respondent) agree that, unless equitably tolled, the statutory limitations period applicable to Holland's petition expired approximately five weeks before the petition was filed. Holland asked the District Court to toll the limitations period for equitable reasons. We shall set forth in some detail the record facts that underlie Holland's claim.

In 1997, Holland was convicted of first-degree murder and sentenced to death. The Florida Supreme Court affirmed that judgment. On *October 1, 2001*, this Court denied Holland's petition for certiorari. And on that date — the date that our denial of the petition ended further direct review of Holland's conviction — the 1-year AEDPA limitations clock began to run.

Thirty-seven days later, on *November 7, 2001*, Florida appointed attorney Bradley Collins to represent Holland in all state and federal postconviction proceedings. By *September 19, 2002* — 316 days after his appointment and 12 days before the 1-year AEDPA limitations period expired — Collins, acting on Holland's behalf, filed a motion for postconviction relief in the state trial court. That filing automatically stopped the running of the AEDPA limitations period, with, as we have said, 12 days left on the clock.

For the next three years, Holland's petition remained pending in the state courts. During that time, Holland wrote Collins letters asking him to make certain that all of his claims would be preserved for any subsequent federal habeas corpus review. Collins wrote back, stating, "I would like to reassure you that we are aware of state-time limitations and federal exhaustion requirements." He also said that he would "presen[t] . . . to the . . . federal courts" any of Holland's claims that the state courts denied.

In mid-May 2003 the state trial court denied Holland relief, and Collins appealed that denial to the Florida Supreme Court. Almost two years later, in February 2005, the Florida Supreme Court heard oral argument in the case. But during that 2-year period, relations between Collins and Holland began to break down. Indeed, between April 2003 and January 2006, Collins communicated with Holland only three times — each time by letter.

Holland, unhappy with this lack of communication, twice wrote to the Florida Supreme Court, asking it to remove Collins from his case. In the second letter, filed on June 17, 2004, he said that he and Collins had experienced "a complete breakdown in communication." The State responded that Holland could not file any *pro se* papers with the court while he was represented by counsel, including papers seeking new counsel. The Florida Supreme Court agreed and denied Holland's requests.

Collins argued Holland's appeal before the Florida Supreme Court on February 10, 2005. Shortly thereafter, Holland wrote to Collins emphasizing the importance of filing a timely petition for habeas corpus in federal court once the Florida Supreme Court issued its ruling.

Five months later, in November 2005, the Florida Supreme Court affirmed the lower court decision denying Holland relief. Three weeks after that, on *December 1, 2005*, the court issued its mandate, making its decision final. At that point, the AEDPA federal habeas clock again began to tick — with 12 days left on the 1-year meter. Twelve days later, on December 13, 2005, Holland's AEDPA time limit expired.

Four weeks after the AEDPA time limit expired, on January 9, 2006, Holland, still unaware of the Florida Supreme Court ruling issued in his case two months earlier, wrote Collins [again].

Nine days later, on January 18, 2006, Holland, working in the prison library, learned for the first time that the Florida Supreme Court had issued a final determination in his case and that its mandate had issued — five weeks prior. He immediately wrote out his own *pro se* federal habeas petition and mailed it to the Federal District Court for the Southern District of Florida the next day.

After considering the briefs, the Federal District Court held that the facts did not warrant equitable tolling and that consequently Holland's petition was untimely. On appeal, the Eleventh Circuit agreed with the District Court that Holland's habeas petition was untimely.

II

We have not decided whether AEDPA's statutory limitations period may be tolled for equitable reasons. Now, like all 11 Courts of Appeals that have considered the question, we hold that §2244(d) is subject to equitable tolling in appropriate cases.

We base our conclusion on the following considerations. First, the AEDPA "statute of limitations defense . . . is not 'jurisdictional.'" It does not set forth "an inflexible rule requiring dismissal whenever" its "clock has run." We have previously made clear that a nonjurisdictional federal statute of limitations is normally subject to a "rebuttable presumption" in *favor* "of equitable tolling."

In the case of AEDPA, the presumption's strength is reinforced by the fact that "'equitable principles'" have traditionally "'governed'" the substantive law of habeas corpus, for we will "not construe a statute to displace courts' traditional equitable authority absent the 'clearest command.'"

[F]inally, we disagree with respondent that equitable tolling undermines AEDPA's basic purposes. We recognize that AEDPA seeks to eliminate delays in the federal habeas review process. But AEDPA seeks to do so without undermining basic habeas corpus principles and while seeking to harmonize the new statute with prior law, under which a petition's timeliness was always determined under equitable principles. When Congress codified new rules governing this previously judicially managed area of law, it did so without losing sight of the fact that the "writ of habeas corpus plays a vital role in protecting constitutional rights." It did not seek to end every possible delay at all costs. The importance of the Great Writ, the only writ explicitly protected by the Constitution, Art. I, §9, cl. 2, along with congressional efforts to harmonize the new statute with prior law, counsels hesitancy before interpreting AEDPA's statutory silence as indicating a congressional intent to close courthouse doors that a strong equitable claim would ordinarily keep open.

III

We have previously made clear that a "petitioner" is "entitled to equitable tolling" only if he shows "(1) that he has been pursuing his rights diligently, and (2) that some extraordinary circumstance stood in his way" and prevented timely filing. In this case, the "extraordinary circumstances" at issue involve an attorney's failure to satisfy professional standards of care. The Court of Appeals held that, where that is so, even attorney conduct that is "grossly negligent" can never warrant tolling absent "bad faith, dishonesty, divided loyalty, mental impairment or so forth on the lawyer's part." But in our view, the Court of Appeals' standard is too rigid.

We have said that courts of equity "must be governed by rules and precedents no less than the courts of law." But we have also made clear that often the "exercise of a court's equity powers . . . must be made on a case-by-case basis." In emphasizing the need for "flexibility," for avoiding "mechanical rules," we have followed a tradition in which courts of equity have sought to "relieve hardships which, from time to time, arise from a hard and fast adherence" to more absolute legal rules, which, if strictly applied, threaten the "evils of archaic rigidity." The "flexibility" inherent in "equitable procedure" enables courts "to meet new situations [that] demand equitable intervention, and to accord all the relief necessary to correct . . . particular injustices." Taken together, these cases recognize that courts of equity can and do draw upon decisions made in other similar cases for guidance. Such courts exercise judgment in light of prior precedent, but with awareness of the fact that specific circumstances, often hard to predict in advance, could warrant special treatment in an appropriate case.

In short, no pre-existing rule of law or precedent demands a rule like the one set forth by the Eleventh Circuit in this case. That rule is difficult to reconcile with more general equitable principles in that it fails to recognize that, at least sometimes, professional misconduct that fails to meet the Eleventh Circuit's standard could nonetheless amount to egregious behavior and create an extraordinary circumstance that warrants equitable tolling. And, given the long history of judicial application of equitable tolling, courts can easily find precedents that can guide their judgments. Several lower courts have specifically held that unprofessional attorney conduct may, in certain circumstances, prove "egregious" and can be "extraordinary" even though the conduct in question may not satisfy the Eleventh Circuit's rule.

We have previously held that "a garden variety claim of excusable neglect," such as a simple "miscalculation" that leads a lawyer to miss a filing deadline, does not warrant equitable tolling. But the case before us does not involve, and we are not considering, a "garden variety claim" of attorney negligence. Rather, the facts of this case present far more serious instances of attorney misconduct. And, as we have said, although the circumstances of a case must be "extraordinary" before equitable tolling can be applied, we hold that such circumstances are not limited to those that satisfy the test that the Court of Appeals used in this case.

IV

The record facts that we have set forth in Part I of this opinion suggest that this case may well be an "extraordinary" instance in which petitioner's attorney's conduct constituted far more than "garden variety" or "excusable neglect." Here, Collins failed to file Holland's federal petition on time despite Holland's many letters that repeatedly emphasized the importance of his doing so. Collins apparently did not do the research necessary to find out the proper filing date, despite Holland's letters that went so far as to identify the applicable legal rules. Collins failed to inform Holland in a timely manner about the crucial fact that the Florida Supreme Court had decided his case, again despite Holland's many pleas for that information. And Collins failed to communicate with his client over a period of years, despite various pleas from Holland that Collins respond to his letters. And in this case, the failures seriously prejudiced a client who thereby lost what was likely his single opportunity for federal habeas review of the lawfulness of his imprisonment and of his death sentence.

We do not state our conclusion in absolute form, however, because more proceedings may be necessary. And we also recognize the prudence, when faced with an "equitable, often fact-intensive" inquiry, of allowing the lower courts "to undertake it in the first instance." Thus, because we conclude that the District Court's determination must be set aside, we leave it to the Court of Appeals to determine whether the facts in this record entitle Holland to equitable tolling, or whether further proceedings, including an evidentiary hearing, might indicate that respondent should prevail.

Justice ALITO, concurring in part and concurring in the judgment.

Although I agree that the Court of Appeals applied the *wrong* standard, I think that the majority does not do enough to explain the *right* standard.

It is of course true that equitable tolling requires "extraordinary circumstances," but that conclusory formulation does not provide much guidance to lower courts charged with reviewing the many habeas petitions filed every year. I therefore write separately to set forth my understanding of the principles governing the availability of equitable tolling in cases involving attorney misconduct.

"Generally, a litigant seeking equitable tolling bears the burden of establishing two elements: (1) that he has been pursuing his rights diligently, and (2) that some extraordinary circumstance stood in his way." The dispute in this case concerns whether and when attorney misconduct amounts to an "extraordinary circumstance" that stands in a petitioner's way and prevents the petitioner from filing a timely petition. I agree with the majority that it is not practical to attempt to provide an exhaustive compilation of the kinds of situations in which attorney misconduct may provide a basis for equitable tolling. In my view, however, it is useful to note that several broad principles may be distilled from this Court's precedents.

First, our prior cases make it abundantly clear that attorney negligence is not an extraordinary circumstance warranting equitable tolling. Second, the mere fact that a missed deadline involves "gross negligence" on the part of counsel does not by itself establish an extraordinary circumstance. [T]he principal rationale for disallowing equitable tolling based on ordinary attorney miscalculation is that the error of an attorney is constructively attributable to the client and thus is not a circumstance beyond the litigant's control. That rationale plainly applies regardless whether the attorney error in question involves ordinary or gross negligence.

Allowing equitable tolling in cases involving *gross* rather than *ordinary* attorney negligence would not only fail to make sense in light of our prior cases; it would also be impractical in the extreme. Missing the statute of limitations will generally, if not always, amount to negligence, and it has been aptly said that gross negligence is ordinary negligence with a vituperative epithet added. Therefore, if gross negligence may be enough for equitable tolling, there will be a basis for arguing that tolling is appropriate in almost every counseled case involving a missed deadline. This would not just impose a severe burden on the district courts; it would also make the availability of tolling turn on the highly artificial distinction between gross and ordinary negligence. That line would be hard to administer, would needlessly consume scarce judicial resources, and would almost certainly yield inconsistent and often unsatisfying results.

Finally, it is worth noting that a rule that distinguishes between ordinary and gross attorney negligence for purposes of the equitable tolling analysis would have demonstrably "inequitable" consequences. For example, it is hard to see why a habeas petitioner should be effectively penalized just because his counsel was negligent rather than grossly negligent, or why the State should be penalized just because petitioner's counsel was grossly negligent rather than moderately negligent. Regardless of how one characterizes counsel's deficient performance in such cases, the petitioner is not personally at fault for the untimely filing, attorney error is a but-for cause of the late filing, and the governmental interest in enforcing the statutory limitations period is the same.

Although attorney negligence, however styled, does not provide a basis for equitable tolling, the AEDPA statute of limitations may be tolled if the missed deadline results from attorney misconduct that is not constructively attributable to the petitioner. In this case, petitioner alleges facts that amount to such misconduct. In particular, he alleges that his attorney essentially "abandoned" him, as evidenced by counsel's near-total failure to communicate with petitioner or to respond to petitioner's many inquiries and requests over a period of several years.

If true, petitioner's allegations would suffice to establish extraordinary circumstances beyond his control. Common sense dictates that a litigant cannot be held constructively responsible for the conduct of an attorney who is not operating as his agent in any meaningful sense of that word. That is particularly so if the litigant's reasonable efforts to terminate the attorney's representation have been thwarted by forces wholly beyond the petitioner's control. The Court of Appeals apparently did not consider petitioner's abandonment argument or assess whether the State improperly prevented petitioner from either obtaining new representation or assuming the responsibility of representing himself. Accordingly, I agree with the majority that the appropriate disposition is to reverse and remand so that the lower courts may apply the correct standard to the facts alleged here.

Justice SCALIA, with whom Justice THOMAS joins, dissenting.

The Antiterrorism and Effective Death Penalty Act of 1996 (AEDPA), establishes a 1-year limitations period for state prisoners to seek federal habeas relief, subject to several specific exceptions. 28 U.S.C. §2244(d). In my view §2244(d) leaves no room for equitable exceptions, and Holland could not qualify even if it did.

I

If §2244(d) merely created a limitations period for federal habeas applicants, I agree that applying equitable tolling would be appropriate.

But §2244(d) does much more than that, establishing a detailed scheme regarding the filing deadline that addresses an array of contingencies.

The question, therefore, is not whether §2244(d)'s time bar is subject to tolling, but whether it is consistent with §2244(d) for federal courts to toll the time bar for *additional* reasons beyond those Congress included.

In my view it is not. It is fair enough to infer, when a statute of limitations says nothing about equitable tolling, that Congress did not displace the default rule. But when Congress has *codified* that default rule and specified the instances where it applies, we have no warrant to extend it to other cases. Unless the Court believes §2244(d) contains an implicit, across-the-board exception that subsumes (and thus renders unnecessary) §2244(d)(1)(B)-(D) and (d)(2), it must rely on the untenable assumption that when Congress enumerated the events that toll the limitations period — with no indication the list is merely illustrative — it implicitly authorized courts to add others as they see fit. We should assume the opposite: that by specifying situations in which an equitable principle applies to a specific requirement, Congress has displaced courts' discretion to develop ad hoc exceptions.

II

Even if §2244(d) left room for equitable tolling in some situations, tolling surely should not excuse the delay here. Where equitable tolling is available, we have held that a litigant is entitled to it only if he has diligently pursued his rights and — the requirement relevant here — if "'some extraordinary circumstance stood in his way.'" Because the attorney is the litigant's agent, the attorney's acts (or failures to act) within the scope of the representation are treated as those of his client, and thus such acts (or failures to act) are necessarily not extraordinary circumstances.

To be sure, the rule that an attorney's acts and oversights are attributable to the client is relaxed where the client has a constitutional right to effective assistance of counsel. Where a State is constitutionally obliged to provide an attorney but fails to provide an effective one, the attorney's failures that fall below the standard set forth in *Strickland v. Washington* (1984), are chargeable to the State, not to the prisoner. But where the client has no right to counsel — which in habeas proceedings he does not — the rule holding him responsible for his attorney's acts applies with full force. Thus, when a state habeas petitioner's appeal is filed too late because of attorney error, the petitioner is out of luck — no less than if he had proceeded *pro se* and neglected to file the appeal himself.

Congress could, of course, have included errors by state-appointed habeas counsel as a basis for delaying the limitations period, but it did not. Nor was that an oversight: Section 2244(d)(1)(B) expressly allows tolling for state-created impediments that prevent a prisoner from filing his application, but *only if* the impediment violates the Constitution or federal law.

The Court's impulse to intervene when a litigant's lawyer has made mistakes is understandable; the temptation to tinker with technical rules to achieve what appears a just result is often strong, especially when the client faces a capital sentence. But the Constitution does not empower federal courts to rewrite, in the name of equity, rules that Congress has made. Endowing unelected judges with that power is irreconcilable with our system, for it "would literally place the whole rights and property of the community under the arbitrary will of the judge," arming him with "a despotic and sovereign authority." The danger is doubled when we disregard our own precedent, leaving only our own consciences to constrain our discretion. Because both the statute and *stare decisis* foreclose Holland's claim, I respectfully dissent.

Another mechanism for preventing injustice from the lack of tolling discussed by some of the justices in Duncan v. Walker is "stay and abeyance" — federal courts keep the case on their docket, stay the proceedings, and allow the petitioner to return to exhaust state court proceedings. When they are completed, the petitioner then can resume the federal court habeas proceedings without needing to be concerned about the statute of limitations. However, subsequent to Duncan v. Walker, in Rhines v. Weber, 544 U.S. 269 (2005), the Supreme Court held that stay and abeyance should be used only in exceptional circumstances. The Court, in an opinion by Justice O'Connor, concluded that "[d]istrict courts do ordinarily have authority to issue stays, where such a stay would be a proper exercise of discretion. AEDPA does not deprive district courts of that authority."

But the Court then went on to declare:

[S]tay and abeyance should be available only in limited circumstances. Because granting a stay effectively excuses a petitioner's failure to present his claims first to the state courts, stay and abeyance is only appropriate when the district court determines there was good cause for the petitioner's failure to exhaust his claims first in state court. Moreover, even if a petitioner had good cause for that failure, the district court would abuse its discretion if it were to grant him a stay when his unexhausted claims are plainly meritless. Even where stay and abeyance is appropriate, the district court's discretion in structuring the stay is limited by the timeliness concerns reflected in AEDPA. A mixed petition should not be stayed indefinitely. Without time limits, petitioners could frustrate AEDPA's goal of finality by dragging out indefinitely their federal habeas review. Thus, district courts should place reasonable time limits on a petitioner's trip to state court and back. And if a petitioner engages in abusive litigation tactics or intentional delay, the district court should not grant him a stay at all.

Still, it is crucial to note that Rhines v. Weber does expressly authorize the stay and abeyance procedure. Indeed, the Court concluded its opinion by declaring:

On the other hand, it likely would be an abuse of discretion for a district court to deny a stay and to dismiss a mixed petition if the petitioner had good cause for his failure to exhaust, his unexhausted claims are potentially meritorious, and there is no indication that the petitioner engaged in intentionally dilatory litigation tactics. In such circumstances, the district court should stay, rather than dismiss, the mixed petition.

2. Is It a First or a Successive Habeas Corpus Petition?

One of the most important changes in habeas corpus law in the 1990s was the imposition, by both the Supreme Court and Congress, of strict bans on successive habeas corpus petitions. As originally drafted, the habeas corpus statutes did not bar individuals from filing repeated petitions presenting the same claims. In the 1948 revisions of the habeas corpus laws, a provision was added excusing a federal court from ruling on a petition when the matter contained in it already had been presented and decided in a prior petition. Specifically, §2244(a) provided that a judge need not entertain a petition for a writ of habeas corpus when the legality of the detention "has been determined by a judge or court of the United States on a prior application for a writ of habeas corpus and the petition presents no new ground not theretofore presented and determined, and the judge or court is satisfied that the ends of justice will not be served by such inquiry."

In McCleskey v. Zant, 499 U.S. 467 (1991), the Supreme Court held that an individual who has previously filed a habeas corpus petition challenging a conviction may file a subsequent petition presenting a new issue only if the individual can show cause and prejudice from the earlier omission of the issue. A criminal defendant, who had been sentenced to death, learned after the filing of his first habeas corpus petition that there had been an informant in his cell. The defendant then filed a second habeas corpus petition arguing that the government's coaching and use of the informant violated Massiah v. United States, 377 U.S. 201 (1964), which held that the government may not, in the absence of counsel, deliberately elicit statements from a person under indictment.

The Supreme Court held that the defendant could not raise the issue in the second habeas petition. The Court explained that the doctrines of abuse of the writ and procedural default implicate "nearly identical concerns flowing from the significant costs of federal habeas corpus review." Thus, the Court concluded that "[w]e have held that a procedural default will be excused only upon a showing of cause and prejudice. . . . We now hold that the same standard applies to determine if there has been an abuse of the writ through inexcusable neglect." The majority concluded that in this case, the petitioner knew enough without the wrongly withheld information that he should have pursued his *Massiah* claim in his earlier habeas petition.

Justice Marshall, joined by Justices Blackmun and Stevens, strongly criticized the decision. Justice Marshall, in dissent, wrote that "[t]oday's decision departs drastically from the norms that inform the proper judicial function. Without even the most casual admission that it is discarding long-standing legal principles, the Court radically redefines the content of the abuse of the writ doctrine." The dissent objected especially to precluding a second habeas petition that was based on information that was not available when the first was filed, precisely because the government wrongly had withheld the information from the defendant.

McCleskey never has been overruled, but from a practical perspective it has been superseded by the ever stricter restrictions on successive petitions contained in the Antiterrorism and Effective Death Penalty Act. Under AEDPA, an individual may file a successive petition only if he or she first obtains permission from the United States Court of Appeals. The act states, "Before a second or successive application permitted by the section is filed in the district court, the applicant shall move in the appropriate court of appeals for an order authorizing the district court to consider the application." 28 U.S.C. §2244(3)(A).

Moreover, the act provides that "[t]he grant or denial of an authorization by a court of appeals to file a second or successive application shall not be appealable and shall not be the subject of a petition for rehearing or for a writ of certiorari." In Felker v. Turpin, 518 U.S. 651 (1996), the Supreme Court upheld the constitutionality of this preclusion of its ability to review court of appeals decisions denying successive petitions. The Court explained that its review was not completely foreclosed because the Court retained the ability to grant habeas corpus petitions in its original jurisdiction. The Court also stressed the broad authority of Congress to control the procedures concerning habeas corpus. Chief Justice Rehnquist, writing for the Court, said, "[W]e have long recognized that the power to award the writ, by any of the courts of the United States must be found in the written law, and we have likewise recognized that judgments about the proper scope of the writ are normally for Congress to make." The Court thus rejected the claim that the restrictions on successive petitions amounted to an unconstitutional suspension of the writ of habeas corpus.

Under the act, a court of appeals may allow a successive petition only in two circumstances. First, a successive petition may be allowed if "the applicant shows that the claim relies on a new rule of constitutional law, made retroactive to cases on collateral review by the Supreme Court that was previously unavailable." Alternatively, the petition may be permitted if "the factual predicate for the claim could not have been discovered previously through the exercise of due diligence and the facts underlying the claim, if proven and viewed in light of the evidence as a whole, would be sufficient to establish by clear and convincing evidence that, but for the constitutional error, no reasonable factfinder would have found the applicant guilty of the underlying offense."

In Tyler v. Cain, below, the Court considered whether a federal court may grant a habeas petition by finding that a Supreme Court decision applies retroactively or whether it requires that the Supreme Court, itself, deem that the rule applies retroactively. In other words, under a prior Supreme Court decision, a conviction was clearly unconstitutional. But could the federal district court and court of appeals provide habeas relief by finding that it was a decision that should be applied retroactively, or did it require an express declaration by the Supreme Court that its decision applied retroactively?

TYLER v. CAIN

533 U.S. 656 (2001)

Justice THOMAS delivered the opinion of the Court.

Under Cage v. Louisiana (1990), a jury instruction is unconstitutional if there is a reasonable likelihood that the jury understood the instruction to allow conviction without proof beyond a reasonable doubt. In this case, we must decide whether this rule was "made retroactive to cases on collateral review by the Supreme Court." 28 U.S.C. §2244(b)(2)(A). We hold that it was not.

I

During a fight with his estranged girlfriend in March 1975, petitioner Melvin Tyler shot and killed their 20-day-old daughter. A jury found Tyler guilty of second-degree murder, and his conviction was affirmed on appeal. After sentencing, Tyler assiduously sought postconviction relief. By 1986, he had filed five state petitions, all of which were denied. He next filed a federal habeas petition, which was unsuccessful as well. After this Court's decision in *Cage*, Tyler continued his efforts. Because the jury instruction defining reasonable doubt at Tyler's trial was substantively identical to the instruction condemned in *Cage*, Tyler filed a sixth state postconviction petition, this time raising a *Cage* claim. The State District Court denied relief, and the Louisiana Supreme Court affirmed.

In early 1997, Tyler returned to federal court. Seeking to pursue his *Cage* claim, Tyler moved the United States Court of Appeals for the Fifth Circuit for permission to file a second habeas corpus application, as required by the Antiterrorism and Effective Death Penalty Act of 1996 (AEDPA). The Court of Appeals recognized that it could not grant the motion unless Tyler made "a prima facie showing," §2244(b)(3)(C), that his "claim relies on a new rule of constitutional law, made retroactive to cases on collateral review by the Supreme Court, that was previously unavailable," §2244(b)(2)(A). Finding that Tyler had made the requisite prima facie showing, the Court of Appeals granted the motion, thereby allowing Tyler to file a habeas petition in District Court.

II

AEDPA greatly restricts the power of federal courts to award relief to state prisoners who file second or successive habeas corpus applications. If the prisoner asserts a claim that he has already presented in a previous federal habeas petition, the claim must be dismissed in all cases. §2244(b)(1). And if the prisoner asserts a claim that was not presented in a previous petition, the claim must be dismissed unless it falls within one of two narrow exceptions. One of these exceptions is for claims predicated on newly discovered facts that call into question the accuracy of a guilty verdict. §2244(b)(2)(B). The other is for certain claims relying on new rules of constitutional law. §2244(b)(2)(A).

It is the latter exception that concerns us today. Specifically, §2244(b)(2)(A) covers claims that "rel[y] on a new rule of constitutional law, made retroactive to cases on collateral review by the Supreme Court, that was previously unavailable." This provision establishes three prerequisites to obtaining relief in a second or successive petition: First, the rule on which the claim relies must be a "new rule" of constitutional law; second, the rule must have been "made retroactive to cases on collateral review by the Supreme Court"; and third, the claim must have been "previously unavailable." In this case, the parties ask us to interpret only the second requirement; respondent does not dispute that Cage created a "new rule" that was "previously unavailable." Based on the plain meaning of the text read as a whole, we conclude that "made" means "held" and, thus, the requirement is satisfied only if this Court has held that the new rule is retroactively applicable to cases on collateral review.

A

As commonly defined, "made" has several alternative meanings, none of which is entirely free from ambiguity. See, e.g., Webster's Ninth New Collegiate Dictionary 718-719 (1991) (defining "to make" as "to cause to happen," "to cause to exist, occur or appear," "to lay out and construct," and "to cause to act in a certain way"). Out of context, it may thus be unclear which meaning should apply in §2244(b)(2)(A), and how the term should be understood. We do not, however, construe the meaning of statutory terms in a vacuum. Rather, we interpret the words "in their context and with a view to their place in the overall statutory scheme." In §2244(b)(2)(A), the word "made" falls within a clause that reads as follows: "[A] new rule of constitutional law, made retroactive to cases on collateral review by the Supreme Court." Quite significantly, under this provision, the Supreme Court is the only entity that can "ma[k]e" a new rule retroactive. The new rule becomes retroactive, not by the decisions of the lower court or by the combined action of the Supreme Court and the lower courts, but simply by the action of the Supreme Court.

The only way the Supreme Court can, by itself, "lay out and construct" a rule's retroactive effect, or "cause" that effect "to exist, occur, or appear," is through a holding. The Supreme Court does not "ma[k]e" a rule retroactive when it merely establishes principles of retroactivity and leaves the application of those principles to lower courts. In such an event, any legal conclusion that is derived from the principles is developed by the lower court (or perhaps by a combination of courts), not by the Supreme Court. We thus conclude that a new rule is not "made retroactive to cases on collateral review" unless the Supreme Court holds it to be retroactive.

B

Because "made" means "held" for purposes of §2244(b)(2)(A), it is clear that the *Cage* rule has not been "made retroactive to cases on collateral review by the Supreme Court." *Cage* itself does not hold that it is retroactive. The only holding in *Cage* is that the particular jury instruction violated the Due Process Clause.

Finally, Tyler suggests that, if *Cage* has not been made retroactive to cases on collateral review, we should make it retroactive today. We disagree. Because Tyler's habeas application was his second, the District Court was required to dismiss it unless Tyler showed that this Court already had made *Cage* retroactive. §2244(b)(4) ("A district court shall dismiss any claim presented in a second or successive application that the court of appeals has authorized to be filed unless the applicant shows that the claim satisfies the requirements of this section"). We cannot decide today whether *Cage* is retroactive to cases on collateral review, because that decision would not help Tyler in this case. Any statement on *Cage*'s retroactivity would be dictum, so we decline to comment further on the issue.

Justice O'CONNOR, concurring.

I join the Court's opinion and write separately to explain more fully the circumstances in which a new rule is "made retroactive to cases on collateral review by the Supreme Court." 28 U.S.C. §2244(b)(2)(A).

It is only through the holdings of this Court, as opposed to this Court's dicta and as opposed to the decisions of any other court, that a new rule is "made retroactive . . . by the Supreme Court" within the meaning of §2244(b)(2)(A). The clearest instance, of course, in which we can be said to have "made" a new rule retroactive is where we expressly have held the new rule to be retroactive in a case on collateral review and applied the rule to that case. But, as the Court recognizes, a single case that expressly holds a rule to be retroactive is not a sine qua non for the satisfaction of this statutory provision. This Court instead may "ma[k]e" a new rule retroactive through multiple holdings that logically dictate the retroactivity of the new rule.

The relationship between the conclusion that a new rule is retroactive and the holdings that "ma[k]e" this rule retroactive, however, must be strictly logical — i.e., the holdings must dictate the conclusion and not merely provide principles from which one may conclude that the rule applies retroactively. As the Court observes, "[t]he Supreme Court does not 'ma[k]e' a rule retroactive when it merely establishes principles of retroactivity and leaves the application of those principles to lower courts." The Court instead can be said to have "made" a rule retroactive within the meaning of §2244(b)(2)(A) only where the Court's holdings logically permit no other conclusion than that the rule is retroactive.

Justice BREYER, with whom Justice STEVENS, Justice SOUTER, and Justice GINSBURG join, dissenting.

In Cage v. Louisiana (1990), this Court held that a certain jury instruction violated the Constitution because it inaccurately defined "reasonable doubt," thereby permitting a jury to convict "based on a degree of proof below that required by the Due Process Clause." Here we must decide whether this Court has "made" *Cage* "retroactive to cases on collateral review." I believe that it has.

Insofar as the majority means to suggest that a rule may be sufficiently "new" that it does not apply retroactively but not "new enough" to qualify for the watershed exception, I note only that the cases establishing this exception suggest no such requirement. Rather than focus on the "degree of newness" of a new rule, these decisions emphasize that watershed rules are those that form part of the fundamental requirements of due process.

[T]he most likely consequence of the majority's holding is further procedural complexity. After today's opinion, the only way in which this Court can make a rule such as *Cage*'s retroactive is to repeat its reasoning in a case triggered by a prisoner's filing a first habeas petition (a "second or successive" petition itself being barred by the provision here at issue) or in some other case that presents the issue in a posture that allows such language to have the status of a "holding." Then, after the Court takes the case and says that it meant what it previously said, prisoners could file "second or successive" petitions to take advantage of the now-clearly-made-applicable new rule. We will be required to restate the obvious, case by case, even when we have explicitly said, but not "held," that a new rule is retroactive.

Even this complex route will remain open only if the relevant statute of limitations is interpreted to permit its 1-year filing period to run from the time that this Court has "made" a new rule retroactive, not from the time it initially recognized that new right. See 28 U.S.C. §2244(d)(1)(C) (limitations period runs from "the date on which the constitutional right asserted was initially recognized by the Supreme Court, if the right has been newly recognized by the Supreme Court and made retroactively applicable to cases on collateral review"). Otherwise, the Court's approach will generate not only complexity, along with its attendant risk of confusion, but also serious additional unfairness.

I do not understand the basis for the Court's approach. I fear its consequences. For these reasons, with respect, I dissent.

In Panetti v. Quarterman, 551 U.S. 930 (2007), the Supreme Court considered whether a person facing execution could bring a successive habeas corpus petition on the grounds of mental incompetence to be executed. As Justice Kennedy, who wrote for the majority, explained:

> [T]he Eighth Amendment prohibits a State from carrying out a sentence of death upon a prisoner who is insane. Ford v. Wainwright (1986). The prohibition applies despite a prisoner's earlier competency to be held responsible for committing a crime and to be tried for it. Prior findings of competency do not foreclose a prisoner from proving he is incompetent to be executed because of his present mental condition. Under *Ford*, once a prisoner makes the requisite preliminary showing that his current mental state would bar his execution, the Eighth Amendment, applicable to the States under the Due Process Clause of the Fourteenth Amendment, entitles him to an adjudication to determine his condition.

The Court, by a 5-4 margin, concluded that the bar on successive habeas petitions does not apply to those challenging competence to be executed.

> We conclude, that Congress did not intend the provisions of AEDPA addressing "second or successive" petitions to govern a filing in the unusual posture presented here: a §2254 application raising a *Ford*-based incompetency claim filed as soon as that claim is ripe.

Our conclusion is confirmed when we consider AEDPA's purposes. The statute's design is to "further the principles of comity, finality, and federalism." These purposes, and the practical effects of our holdings, should be considered when interpreting AEDPA. This is particularly so when petitioners "run the risk" under the proposed interpretation of "forever losing their opportunity for any federal review of their unexhausted claims." An empty formality requiring prisoners to file unripe *Ford* claims neither respects the limited legal resources available to the States nor encourages the exhaustion of state remedies. Instructing prisoners to file premature claims, particularly when many of these claims will not be colorable even at a later date, does not conserve judicial resources, "reduc[e] piecemeal litigation," or "streamlin[e] federal habeas proceedings." And last-minute filings that are frivolous and designed to delay executions can be dismissed in the regular course. The requirement of a threshold preliminary showing, for instance, will, as a general matter, be imposed before a stay is granted or the action is allowed to proceed.

There is, in addition, no argument that petitioner's actions constituted an abuse of the writ, as that concept is explained in our cases. To the contrary, we have confirmed that claims of incompetency to be executed remain unripe at early stages of the proceedings.

In the usual case, a petition filed second in time and not otherwise permitted by the terms of §2244 will not survive AEDPA's "second or successive" bar. There are, however, exceptions. We are hesitant to construe a statute, implemented to further the principles of comity, finality, and federalism, in a manner that would require unripe (and, often, factually unsupported) claims to be raised as a mere formality, to the benefit of no party.

The statutory bar on "second or successive" applications does not apply to a *Ford* claim brought in an application filed when the claim is first ripe. Petitioner's habeas application was properly filed, and the District Court had jurisdiction to adjudicate his claim.

Justice Thomas, writing for the four dissenters, stressed that the statutory language creates no exception for successive petitions based on incompetency to be executed. He wrote:

This case should be simple. Panetti brings a claim under Ford v. Wainwright (1986), that he is incompetent to be executed. Presented for the first time in Panetti's second federal habeas application, this claim undisputedly does not meet the statutory requirements for filing a "second or successive" habeas application. As such, Panetti's habeas application must be dismissed. Ignoring this clear statutory mandate, the Court bends over backwards to allow Panetti to bring his *Ford* claim despite no evidence that his condition has worsened — or even changed — since 1995.

The Antiterrorism and Effective Death Penalty Act of 1996 (AEDPA) requires applicants to receive permission from the court of appeals prior to filing second or successive federal habeas applications. 28 U.S.C. §2244(b)(3). Even if permission is sought, AEDPA requires courts to decline such requests in all but two narrow circumstances. §2244(b)(3)(C); §2244(b)(2). Panetti raised his *Ford* claim for the first time in his second federal habeas application, but he admits that he did not seek authorization from the Court of Appeals and that his claim does not satisfy either of the statutory exceptions. Accordingly, §2244(b) requires dismissal of Panetti's second habeas corpus application.

Requiring that *Ford* claims be included in an initial habeas application would have the added benefit of putting a State on notice that a prisoner intends to challenge his or her competency to be executed. In any event, regardless of whether the Court's concern is justified, judicial economy considerations cannot override AEDPA's plain meaning. Remaining faithful to AEDPA's mandate, I would dismiss Panetti's application as second or successive.

Most recently, the Court considered whether it was an impermissible successive petition if a prisoner prevailed on a first habeas petition, was accorded a new trial, and then sought to file a habeas petition relative to challenge the conviction or sentence from that proceeding. The Court held that this was not a successive petition, and thus the restrictive rules of AEDPA did not apply.

MAGWOOD v. PATTERSON

130 S. Ct. 2788 (2010)

Justice THOMAS delivered the opinion of the Court.

Petitioner Billy Joe Magwood was sentenced to death for murdering a sheriff. After the Alabama courts denied relief on direct appeal and in post-conviction proceedings, Magwood filed an application for a writ of habeas corpus in Federal District Court, challenging both his conviction and his sentence. The District Court conditionally granted the writ as to the sentence, mandating that Magwood either be released or resentenced. The state trial court conducted a new sentencing hearing and again sentenced Magwood to death. Magwood filed an application for a writ of habeas corpus in federal court challenging this new sentence. The District Court once again conditionally granted the writ, finding constitutional defects in the new sentence. The Court of Appeals for the Eleventh Circuit reversed, holding in relevant part that Magwood's challenge to his new death sentence was an unreviewable "second or successive" challenge under 28 U.S.C. §2244(b) because he could have mounted the same challenge to his original death sentence. We granted certiorari, and now reverse. Because Magwood's habeas application challenges a new judgment for the first time, it is not "second or successive" under §2244(b).

I

After a conviction for a drug offense, Magwood served several years in the Coffee County Jail in Elba, Alabama, under the watch of Sheriff C.F. "Neil" Grantham. During his incarceration, Magwood, who had a long history of mental illness, became convinced that Grantham had imprisoned him without cause, and vowed to get even upon his release. Magwood followed through on his threat. On the morning of March 1, 1979, shortly after his release, he parked outside the jail and awaited the sheriff's arrival. When Grantham exited his car, Magwood shot him and fled the scene.

The prosecution asked the jury to find Magwood guilty of aggravated murder as charged in the indictment, and sought the death penalty.

Magwood pleaded not guilty by reason of insanity; however, the jury found him guilty of capital murder and imposed the sentence of death based on the aggravation charged in the indictment. In accordance with Alabama law, the trial court reviewed the basis for the jury's decision. Weighing the aggravation against the mitigating factors, the court approved the sentence of death. The Alabama courts affirmed.

Eight days before his scheduled execution, Magwood filed an application for a writ of habeas corpus under 28 U.S.C. §2254, and the District Court granted a stay of execution. After briefing by the parties, the District Court upheld Magwood's conviction but vacated his sentence and conditionally granted the writ based on the trial court's failure to find statutory mitigating circumstances relating to Magwood's mental state.

In response to the conditional writ, the state trial court held a new sentencing proceeding in September 1986. This time, the judge found that Magwood's mental state, as well as his age and lack of criminal history, qualified as statutory mitigating circumstances. As before, the court found that Magwood's capital felony included sufficient aggravation to render him death eligible. The Alabama courts affirmed, and this Court denied certiorari.

In April 1997, Magwood sought leave to file a second or successive application for a writ of habeas corpus challenging his 1981 judgment of conviction. The Court of Appeals denied his request. He simultaneously filed a petition for a writ of habeas corpus challenging his new death sentence, which the District Court conditionally granted. In that petition, Magwood again argued that his sentence was unconstitutional because he did not have fair warning at the time of his offense that his conduct would be sufficient to warrant a death sentence under Alabama law, and that his attorney rendered ineffective assistance during the resentencing proceeding.

We granted certiorari to determine whether Magwood's application challenging his 1986 death sentence, imposed as part of resentencing in response to a conditional writ from the District Court, is subject to the constraints that §2244(b) imposes on the review of "second or successive" habeas applications.

II

This case turns on the meaning of the phrase "second or successive" in §2244(b). More specifically, it turns on when a claim should be deemed to arise in a "second or successive habeas corpus application." If an application is "second or successive," the petitioner must obtain leave from the Court of Appeals before filing it with the district court. The district court must dismiss any claim presented in an authorized second or successive application unless the applicant shows that the claim satisfies certain statutory requirements. Thus, if Magwood's application was "second or successive," the District Court should have dismissed it in its entirety because he failed to obtain the requisite authorization from the Court of Appeals. If, however, Magwood's application was not second or successive, it was not subject to §2244(b) at all, and his fair-warning claim was reviewable (absent procedural default).

The State contends that although §2244(b), as amended by AEDPA, applies the phrase "second or successive" to "application[s]," it "is a claim-focused statute," and "[c]laims, not applications, are barred by §2244(b)." According to the State, the phrase should be read to reflect a principle that "a prisoner is entitled to one, but only one, full and fair opportunity to wage a collateral attack." The State asserts that under this "one opportunity" rule, Magwood's fair-warning claim was successive because he had an opportunity to raise it in his first application, but did not do so.

Magwood, in contrast, reads §2244(b) to apply only to a "second or successive" application challenging the same state-court *judgment*. According to Magwood, his 1986 resentencing led to a new judgment, and his first application challenging that new judgment cannot be "second or successive" such that §2244(b) would apply. We agree.

We begin with the text. Although Congress did not define the phrase "second or successive," as used to modify "habeas corpus application under section 2254," it is well settled that the phrase does not simply "refe[r] to all §2254 applications filed second or successively in time."

We have described the phrase "second or successive" as a "term of art." To determine its meaning, we look first to the statutory context. The limitations imposed by §2244(b) apply only to a "habeas corpus application under §2254," that is, an "application for a writ of habeas corpus on behalf of a person in custody pursuant to *the judgment* of a State court." The reference to a state-court judgment in §2254(b) is significant because the term "application" cannot be defined in a vacuum. A §2254 petitioner is applying for something: His petition "seeks *invalidation* (in whole or in part) *of the judgment* authorizing the prisoner's confinement." If his petition results in a district court's granting of the writ, "the State may seek a *new* judgment (through a new trial or a new sentencing proceeding)." Thus, both §2254(b)'s text and the relief it provides indicate that the phrase "second or successive" must be interpreted with respect to the judgment challenged.

III

Appearing to recognize that Magwood has the stronger textual argument, the State argues that we should rule based on the statutory purpose. According to the State, a "one opportunity" rule is consistent with the statutory text, and better reflects AEDPA's purpose of preventing piecemeal litigation and gamesmanship.

We are not persuaded. AEDPA uses the phrase "second or successive" to modify "application." The State reads the phrase to modify "claims." We cannot replace the actual text with speculation as to Congress' intent.

The State's reading leads to a second, more fundamental error. Under the State's "one opportunity" rule, the phrase "second or successive" would apply to any claim that the petitioner had a full and fair opportunity to raise in a prior application. And the phrase "second or successive" would *not* apply to a claim that the petitioner did *not* have a full and fair opportunity to raise previously.

This is Magwood's *first* application challenging that intervening judgment. The errors he alleges are *new*. It is obvious to us—and the State does not dispute—that his claim of ineffective assistance at resentencing turns upon new errors. But, according to the State, his fair-warning claim does not, because the state court made the same mistake before. We disagree. An error made a second time is still a new error. That is especially clear here, where the state court conducted a full resentencing and reviewed the aggravating evidence afresh.

For these reasons, we conclude that Magwood's first application challenging his new sentence under the 1986 judgment is not "second or successive" under §2244(b). The Court of Appeals erred by reading §2244(b) to bar review of the fair-warning claim Magwood presented in that application. We do not address whether the fair-warning claim is procedurally defaulted. Nor do we address Magwood's contention that the Court of Appeals erred in rejecting his ineffective-assistance claim by not addressing whether his attorney should have objected under federal law.

Justice KENNEDY, with whom the CHIEF JUSTICE, Justice GINSBURG, and Justice ALITO join, dissenting.

The Court today decides that a state prisoner who succeeds in his first federal habeas petition on a discrete sentencing claim may later file a second petition raising numerous previously unraised claims, even if that petition is an abuse of the writ of habeas corpus. The Court, in my respectful submission, reaches this conclusion by misreading precedents on the meaning of the phrase "second or successive" in the Antiterrorism and Effective Death Penalty Act of 1996 (AEDPA). The Court then rewrites AEDPA's text but refuses to grapple with the logical consequences of its own editorial judgment. The design and purpose of AEDPA is to avoid abuses of the writ of habeas corpus, in recognition of the potential for the writ's intrusive effect on state criminal justice systems. But today's opinion, with considerable irony, is not only a step back from AEDPA protection for States but also a step back even from abuse-of-the-writ principles that were in place before AEDPA. So this respectful dissent becomes necessary.

I

Absent two exceptions that are inapplicable here, the relevant statutory provision in AEDPA provides: "A claim presented in a second or successive habeas corpus application under section 2254 that was not presented in a prior application shall be dismissed. . . ."

The question before the Court is whether petitioner Billy Joe Magwood filed "a second or successive" application by raising a claim in his second habeas petition that he had available and yet failed to raise in his first petition. The term "second or successive" is a habeas "term of art." It incorporates the pre-AEDPA abuse-of-the-writ doctrine. Under that rule, to determine whether an application is "second or successive," a court must look to the substance of the claim the application raises and decide whether the petitioner had a full and fair opportunity to raise the claim in the prior application. Applying this analytical framework puts applications into one of three categories.

First, if the petitioner had a full and fair opportunity to raise the claim in the prior application, a second-in-time application that seeks to raise the same claim is barred as "second or successive." This is consistent with pre-AEDPA cases applying the abuse-of-the-writ doctrine and the bar on "second or successive" applications.

Second, if the petitioner had no fair opportunity to raise the claim in the prior application, a subsequent application raising that claim is not "second or successive," and §2244(b)(2)'s bar does not apply. This can occur where the claim was not yet ripe at the time of the first petition, or where the alleged violation occurred only after the denial of the first petition, such as the State's failure to grant the prisoner parole as required by state law. And to respond to the Court's concern, if the applicant in his second petition raises a claim that he raised in his first petition but the District Court left unaddressed at its own discretion, the second application would not be "second or successive." Reraising a previously unaddressed claim is not abusive by any definition.

Third, a "mixed petition"—raising both abusive and nonabusive claims—would be "second or successive." In that circumstance the petitioner would have to obtain authorization from the court of appeals to proceed with the nonabusive claims. After the court of appeals makes its determination, a district court may consider nonabusive claims that the petitioner had no fair opportunity to present in his first petition and dismiss the abusive claims.

The above principles apply to a situation, like the present one, where the petitioner in his first habeas proceeding succeeds in obtaining a conditional grant of relief, which allows the state court to correct an error that occurred at the original sentencing. Assume, as alleged here, that in correcting the error in a new sentencing proceeding, the state court duplicates a different mistake that also occurred at the first sentencing. The second application is "second or successive" with respect to that claim because the alleged error "could and should have" been raised in the first petition. Put another way, under abuse-of-the-writ principles, a petitioner loses his right to challenge the error by not raising a claim at the first opportunity after his claim becomes ripe. On the other hand, if the petitioner raises a claim in his second habeas petition that could not have been raised in the earlier petition—perhaps because the error occurred for the first time during resentencing—then the application raising the claim is not "second or successive" and §2244(b)(2)'s bar does not apply.

Although the above-cited authorities are adequate to show that the application in this case is "second or successive," it must be noted that no previous case from this Court has dealt with the precise sequence of events here: A petitioner attempts to bring a previously unraised claim after a second resentencing proceeding that followed a grant of federal habeas relief. The conclusion that such an application is barred as "second or successive" unless the claim was previously unavailable is consistent with the approach of every court of appeals that has considered the issue, although some of those cases highlight subtleties that are not relevant under abuse-of-the-writ principles.

In the present case the Court should conclude that Magwood has filed a "second or successive habeas corpus application." In 1983, he filed a first federal habeas petition raising nine claims, including that the trial court improperly failed to consider two mitigating factors when it imposed Magwood's death sentence. The District Court granted Magwood's petition and ordered relief only on the mitigating factor claim. The state trial court then held a new sentencing proceeding, in which it considered all of the mitigating factors and reimposed the death penalty. In 1997, Magwood brought a second habeas petition, this time raising an argument that could have been, but was not, raised in his first petition. The argument was that he was not eligible for the death penalty because he did not have fair notice that his crime rendered him death eligible. There is no reason that Magwood could not have raised the identical argument in his first habeas petition. Because Magwood had a full and fair opportunity to adjudicate his death-eligibility claim in his first petition in 1983, his 1997 petition raising this claim is barred as "second or successive."

II

The Court reaches the opposite result by creating an ill-defined exception to the "second or successive" application bar. The Court concludes that because AEDPA refers to "second or successive" applications rather than "second or successive" claims, the nature of the claims raised in the second application is irrelevant. This is incorrect. [D]eciding whether an application itself is "second or successive" requires looking to the nature of the claim that the application raises to determine whether the petitioner had a full and fair opportunity to raise that claim in his earlier petition.

Failing to consider the nature of the claim when deciding whether an application is barred as "second or successive" raises other difficulties. Consider a second-in-time habeas petition challenging an alleged violation that occurred entirely after the denial of the first petition; for example, a failure to grant a prisoner parole at the time promised him by state law or the unlawful withdrawal of good-time credits. Under the Court's rule, it would appear that a habeas application challenging those alleged violations would be barred as "second or successive" because it would be a second-in-time application challenging custody pursuant to the same judgment. That result would be inconsistent with abuse-of-the-writ principles and might work a suspension of the writ of habeas corpus.

Having unmoored the phrase "second or successive" from its textual and historical underpinnings, the Court creates a new puzzle for itself: If the nature of the claim is not what makes an application "second or successive," then to what should a court look?

The Court's approach disregards AEDPA's "'principles of comity, finality, and federalism.'" Under the Court's newly created exception to the "second or successive" application bar, a defendant who succeeds on even the most minor and discrete issue relating to his sentencing would be able to raise 25 or 50 new sentencing claims in his second habeas petition, all based on arguments he failed to raise in his first petition. "[I]f reexamination of [a] convictio[n] in the first round of habeas offends federalism and comity, the offense increases when a State must defend its conviction in a second or subsequent habeas proceeding on grounds not even raised in the first petition."

The Court's novel exception would also allow the once-successful petitioner to reraise every argument against a sentence that was rejected by the federal courts during the first round of federal habeas review. Because traditional res judicata principles do not apply to federal habeas proceedings, this would force federal courts to address twice (or thrice, or more) the same claims of error. The State and the victims would have to bear anew the "significant costs of federal habeas corpus review," all because the petitioner previously succeeded on a wholly different, discrete, and possibly unrelated claim.

The Court's suggestion that "[i]t will not take a court long to dispose of such claims where the court has already analyzed the legal issues," misses the point. This reassurance will be cold comfort to overworked state district attorneys, who will now have to waste time and resources writing briefs analyzing dozens of claims that should be barred by abuse-of-the-writ principles. It is difficult to motivate even the most dedicated professionals to do their best work, day after day, when they have to deal with the dispiriting task of responding to previously rejected or otherwise abusive claims. But that is exactly what the Court is mandating, under a statute that was designed to require just the opposite result. If the analysis in this dissent is sound it is to be hoped that the States will document the ill effects of the Court's opinion so that its costs and deficiencies are better understood if this issue, or a related one, can again come before the Court.

The Court's new exception will apply not only to death penalty cases like the present one, where the newly raised claim appears arguably meritorious. It will apply to all federal habeas petitions following a prior successful petition, most of which will not be in death cases and where the abusive claims the Court now permits will wholly lack merit. And, in this vein, it is striking that the Court's decision means that States subject to federal habeas review henceforth receive less recognition of a finality interest than the Federal Government does on direct review of federal criminal convictions.

The Court's approach also turns AEDPA's bar against "second or successive" applications into a one-way ratchet that favors habeas petitioners. Had Magwood been unsuccessful in his first petition, all agree that claims then available, but not raised, would be barred. But because he prevailed in his attack on one part of his sentencing proceeding the first time around, the Court rules that he is free, postsentencing, to pursue claims on federal habeas review that might have been raised earlier. The Court is mistaken in concluding that Congress, in enacting a statute aimed at placing new restrictions on successive petitions, would have intended this irrational result.

Magwood had every chance to raise his death-eligibility claim in his first habeas petition. He has abused the writ by raising this claim for the first time in his second petition. His application is therefore "second or successive." I would affirm the judgment of the Court of Appeals.

3.   Has There Been Exhaustion of All of the Claims Raised in the Habeas Petition?

An extremely important limitation on the power of federal courts to hear habeas corpus petitions is the requirement that petitioners in state custody exhaust all available state court procedures prior to seeking federal court review. One study of habeas corpus in federal courts in Massachusetts found that over half of all habeas petitions were dismissed for failure to exhaust state remedies.[29] Because the Supreme Court has made the exhaustion requirement even more stringent since this study was completed, it is quite likely that a large number of habeas petitions will continue to be dismissed for failure to exhaust state remedies. Some studies suggest that between 30 and 50 percent of habeas petitions are dismissed for failure to exhaust.[30]

The exhaustion requirement originally was created by the Supreme Court, although now it is embodied in the habeas statutes. The original statutes authorizing habeas corpus review for state prisoners did not require exhaustion of state court proceedings prior to federal habeas corpus review. However, in Ex parte Royall, 117 U.S. 241 (1886), the Court held that because of comity considerations and deference to state courts, federal courts should not entertain a claim in a habeas corpus petition until after the state courts have had an opportunity to hear the matter. Royall had been indicted under two state statutes and sought habeas corpus review to have the statutes declared unconstitutional.

---

29. David L. Shapiro, *Federal Habeas Corpus: A Study in Massachusetts*, 87 Harv. L. Rev. 321, 333-334 (1973).

30. *See* Richard H. Fallon, Jr., Daniel J. Meltzer & David L. Shapiro, *2002 Supplement to Hart & Wechsler's The Federal Courts and the Federal System* 218 (2002).

The Supreme Court upheld the lower court's refusal to hear the habeas corpus petition. The Court stated that habeas corpus jurisdiction "should be exercised in light of the relations existing under our system of government, between judicial tribunals of the Union and of the States, and in recognition of the fact that the public good requires that those relations be not disturbed by unnecessary conflict between courts equally bound to guard and protect rights secured by the Constitution."

In 1948, the habeas corpus statutes were revised and among the changes was the inclusion of specific language requiring that individuals challenging state custody exhaust state court remedies. Specifically, 28 U.S.C. §2254(b) provides:

> An application for a writ of habeas corpus on behalf of a person in custody pursuant to the judgment of a State court shall not be granted unless it appears that (A) the applicant has exhausted remedies available in the courts of the State; or (B)(i) there is an absence of available State corrective process or (ii) circumstances exist that render such process ineffective to protect the rights of the applicant.

The exhaustion requirement prevents federal courts from interfering with ongoing state criminal prosecutions. If there were no exhaustion requirement, then a person contending that he or she was being prosecuted under an unconstitutional statute could halt the state court litigation by filing a habeas corpus petition in federal court. But the Supreme Court has emphasized that considerations of equity and comity prevent federal courts from enjoining or otherwise interfering with pending state criminal proceedings.[31] Thus, the exhaustion requirement for federal court habeas corpus review allows state courts to interpret and enforce state criminal laws. Federal court review is delayed until the state has had a full chance to correct any errors in its law or procedures.

In analyzing the exhaustion requirement, three questions are crucial: What state court procedures must be used? What must be presented to state courts? When are petitions deemed sufficient to meet the exhaustion requirement? Each question is considered in turn.

First, the petitioner must pursue all available state court remedies; that is, exhaustion of state proceedings is incomplete as long as there remains an available state court proceeding that might provide the relief sought by the petitioner. This means that a habeas corpus petition may be brought if potential state remedies once existed but are no longer available. For example, exhaustion has occurred if the time limit for direct appeal has expired such that no state remedies are available at the time of the filing of the habeas petition.[32] However, the failure to use available state procedures likely will prevent federal habeas corpus relief, not because of exhaustion problems but rather, as discussed below, because state procedural

---

31. *See, e.g.*, Younger v. Harris, 401 U.S. 37 (1971) (federal courts may not enjoin pending state court criminal prosecutions).

32. Fay v. Noia, 372 U.S. 391 (1963).

defaults bar federal habeas corpus relief unless there is good "cause" for the omission and "prejudice" to the denial of review. The Supreme Court has ruled that a failure to include claims in a petition for discretionary review before a state's highest court is a procedural default that precludes raising those claims on habeas corpus.

A state prisoner need not seek United States Supreme Court review of the state court's decision in order to present a federal court habeas petition.[33] Nor is habeas corpus precluded when a state prisoner seeks Supreme Court review of the state court ruling via a writ of certiorari and the Supreme Court declines to hear the case.[34] Of course, if the Supreme Court hears and decides the case, the Court's decision is determinative and must be followed in subsequent habeas corpus proceedings.

A state prisoner need not use state procedures for collateral review, such as state court habeas corpus mechanisms, as long as the issues have been presented and decided by the state courts on direct appeal. The Court explained that it "is not necessary . . . for the prisoner to ask the state for collateral relief, based on the same evidence and issues already decided by direct review."[35] However, a petitioner must use available state court collateral review procedures for issues not raised on direct appeal.[36] Conversely, a petitioner need not present a matter on direct appeal to the state courts, even if direct appeals are still available, if the issue already was raised and decided by the state court in a collateral proceeding. In other words, once an issue is raised and litigated in state court it need not be presented again even when additional state proceedings are possible.

Section 2254(b) excuses the failure to use state procedures if "circumstances render such process ineffective to protect the rights of the prisoner." The Court has interpreted this clause as creating an exception to the exhaustion requirement "only if there is no opportunity to obtain redress in state court or if the corrective process is so clearly deficient as to render futile any effort to obtain relief."[37]

A second major issue concerning exhaustion of state remedies involves what must be presented to the state courts in order for the exhaustion requirement to be deemed fulfilled. The Supreme Court has held that the "federal claim must be fairly presented to the state courts."[38] That is, the same matter raised in the federal court habeas corpus petition must have been presented to the state court or the matter will be dismissed for the failure to exhaust if state proceedings remain available where the issue can be raised. Federal courts use state court records to determine whether the

---

33. Lawrence v. Florida, 127 S. Ct. 1079, 1083 (2007); Fay v. Noia, 372 U.S. 391, 435 (1963).

34. *See, e.g.,* Brown v. Allen, 344 U.S. 443, 450 (1953).

35. Brown v. Allen, 344 U.S. 443, 447 (1953); *see also* Roberts v. LaVallee, 389 U.S. 40, 42-43 (1967).

36. *See, e.g.,* Wade v. Mayo, 334 U.S. 672, 677-678 (1948).

37. Duckworth v. Serrano, 454 U.S. 1, 3 (1981).

38. Picard v. Connor, 404 U.S. 270, 275 (1971); *see also* Anderson v. Harless, 459 U.S. 4 (1982).

petitioner raised the same issue in state court that is now presented in the habeas proceeding.

However, the exhaustion requirement is deemed to have been met when the habeas petitioner supplements the evidence presented in state court but does not raise a new issue. In Vasquez v. Hillery, 474 U.S. 254 (1986), the Supreme Court permitted a habeas corpus petitioner to present additional statistical evidence proving discrimination in the selection of the grand jury. The Court explained that it had "never held that presentation of additional facts to the district court, pursuant to that court's directions, evades the exhaustion requirement when the prisoner has presented the substance of his claim to the state courts." In other words, exhaustion will not present a problem to the defendant who is supplementing the evidence for a claim already presented to the state court and is not raising a new issue. However, there certainly will be cases in which it is a fine line between what constitutes a new issue as opposed to merely new evidence.[39]

Finally, there is the issue of what the petition must contain in order to meet the exhaustion requirement. The Supreme Court, in Rose v. Lundy, considered how a federal court should handle a habeas petition that includes some claims that have been exhausted in state court and some in which there has not been exhaustion.

ROSE v. LUNDY
455 U.S. 509 (1982)

Justice O'CONNOR delivered the opinion of the Court, except as to Part III-C.

In this case we consider whether the exhaustion rule in 28 U.S.C. §§2254(b), (c) requires a federal district court to dismiss a petition for a writ of habeas corpus containing any claims that have not been exhausted in the state courts. Because a rule requiring exhaustion of all claims furthers the purposes underlying the habeas statute, we hold that a district court must dismiss such "mixed petitions," leaving the prisoner with the choice of returning to state court to exhaust his claims or of amending or resubmitting the habeas petition to present only exhausted claims to the district court.

I

Following a jury trial, respondent Noah Lundy was convicted on charges of rape and crime against nature, and sentenced to the Tennessee State Penitentiary. After the Tennessee Court of Criminal Appeals affirmed the convictions and the Tennessee Supreme Court denied review, the respondent

---

39. It should be noted that issues must be presented to the state courts even when it is clear that the state law or procedures are unconstitutional. Duckworth v. Serrano, 454 U.S. 1, 4 (1981). Thus, there is no exception to the exhaustion requirement for patently unconstitutional state statutes.

filed an unsuccessful petition for post-conviction relief in the Knox County Criminal Court.

The respondent subsequently filed a petition in Federal District Court for a writ of habeas corpus under 28 U.S.C. §2254, alleging four grounds for relief: (1) that he had been denied the right to confrontation because the trial court limited the defense counsel's questioning of the victim; (2) that he had been denied the right to a fair trial because the prosecuting attorney stated that the respondent had a violent character; (3) that he had been denied the right to a fair trial because the prosecutor improperly remarked in his closing argument that the State's evidence was uncontradicted; and (4) that the trial judge improperly instructed the jury that every witness is presumed to swear the truth. After reviewing the state court records, however, the District Court concluded that it could not consider claims three and four "in the constitutional framework" because the respondent had not exhausted his state remedies for those grounds. The court nevertheless stated that "in assessing the atmosphere of the cause taken as a whole these items may be referred to collaterally." In short, the District Court considered several instances of prosecutorial misconduct never challenged in the state trial or appellate courts, or even raised in the respondent's habeas petition.

The Sixth Circuit affirmed the judgment of the District Court, concluding in an unreported order that the court properly found that the respondent's constitutional rights had been "seriously impaired by the improper limitation of his counsel's cross-examination of the prosecutrix and by the prosecutorial misconduct." The court specifically rejected the State's argument that the District Court should have dismissed the petition because it included both exhausted and unexhausted claims.

II

The petitioner urges this Court to apply a "total exhaustion" rule requiring district courts to dismiss every habeas corpus petition that contains both exhausted and unexhausted claims. The petitioner argues at length that such a rule furthers the policy of comity underlying the exhaustion doctrine because it gives the state courts the first opportunity to correct federal constitutional errors and minimizes federal interference and disruption of state judicial proceedings. The petitioner also believes that uniform adherence to a total exhaustion rule reduces the amount of piecemeal habeas litigation.

Under the petitioner's approach, a district court would dismiss a petition containing both exhausted and unexhausted claims, giving the prisoner the choice of returning to state court to litigate his unexhausted claims, or of proceeding with only his exhausted claims in federal court. The petitioner believes that a prisoner would be reluctant to choose the latter route since a district court could, in appropriate circumstances under Habeas Corpus Rule 9(b), dismiss subsequent federal habeas petitions as an abuse of the writ. In other words, if the prisoner amended the petition to delete the unexhausted claims or immediately refiled in federal court a petition alleging only his exhausted claims, he could lose the opportunity to litigate his presently unexhausted claims in federal court.

In order to evaluate the merits of the petitioner's arguments, we turn to the habeas statute, its legislative history, and the policies underlying the exhaustion doctrine.

III

A

The exhaustion doctrine existed long before its codification by Congress in 1948. In Ex parte Royall (1886), this Court wrote that as a matter of comity, federal courts should not consider a claim in a habeas corpus petition until after the state courts have had an opportunity to act. Subsequent cases refined the principle that state remedies must be exhausted except in unusual circumstances. None of these cases, however, specifically applied the exhaustion doctrine to habeas petitions containing both exhausted and unexhausted claims.

In 1948, Congress codified the exhaustion doctrine in 28 U.S.C. §2254. Section 2254, however, does not directly address the problem of mixed petitions. To be sure, the provision states that a remedy is not exhausted if there exists a state procedure to raise "the question presented," but we believe this phrase to be too ambiguous to sustain the conclusion that Congress intended to either permit or prohibit review of mixed petitions. Because the legislative history of §2254, as well as the pre-1948 cases, contains no reference to the problem of mixed petitions, in all likelihood Congress never thought of the problem. Consequently, we must analyze the policies underlying the statutory provision to determine its proper scope.

B

The exhaustion doctrine is principally designed to protect the state courts' role in the enforcement of federal law and prevent disruption of state judicial proceedings. Under our federal system, the federal and state "courts [are] equally bound to guard and protect rights secured by the Constitution." Because "it would be unseemly in our dual system of government for a federal district court to upset a state court conviction without an opportunity to the state courts to correct a constitutional violation," federal courts apply the doctrine of comity, which "teaches that one court should defer action on causes properly within its jurisdiction until the courts of another sovereignty with concurrent powers, and already cognizant of the litigation, have had an opportunity to pass upon the matter."

A rigorously enforced total exhaustion rule will encourage state prisoners to seek full relief first from the state courts, thus giving those courts the first opportunity to review all claims of constitutional error. As the number of prisoners who exhaust all of their federal claims increases, state courts may become increasingly familiar with and hospitable toward federal constitutional issues. Equally as important, federal claims that have been fully exhausted in state courts will more often be accompanied by a complete factual record to aid the federal courts in their review.

The facts of the present case underscore the need for a rule encouraging exhaustion of all federal claims. In his opinion, the District Court Judge wrote that "there is such mixture of violations that one cannot be separated from and considered independently of the others." Because the two unexhausted claims for relief were intertwined with the exhausted ones, the judge apparently considered all of the claims in ruling on the petition. Requiring dismissal of petitions containing both exhausted and unexhausted claims will relieve the district courts of the difficult if not impossible task of deciding when claims are related, and will reduce the temptation to consider unexhausted claims.

Rather than increasing the burden on federal courts, strict enforcement of the exhaustion requirement will encourage habeas petitioners to exhaust all of their claims in state court and to present the federal court with a single habeas petition. To the extent that the exhaustion requirement reduces piecemeal litigation, both the courts and the prisoners should benefit, for as a result the district court will be more likely to review all of the prisoner's claims in a single proceeding, thus providing for a more focused and thorough review.

C

The prisoner's principal interest, of course, is in obtaining speedy federal relief on his claims. A total exhaustion rule will not impair that interest since he can always amend the petition to delete the unexhausted claims, rather than returning to state court to exhaust all of his claims. By invoking this procedure, however, the prisoner would risk forfeiting consideration of his unexhausted claims in federal court.[40]

IV

In sum, because a total exhaustion rule promotes comity and does not unreasonably impair the prisoner's right to relief, we hold that a district court must dismiss habeas petitions containing both unexhausted and exhausted claims.

Justice BLACKMUN, concurring in the judgment.
The important issue before the Court in this case is whether the conservative "total exhaustion" rule is required by 28 U.S.C. §§2254(b)

---

40. Subsequent to Rose v. Lundy, the Antiterrorism and Effective Death Penalty Act was adopted, which greatly limits successive habeas corpus petitions. This is discussed above. [Footnote by casebook authors.]

and (c), or whether a district court may review the exhausted claims of a mixed petition is the proper interpretation of the statute.

I do not dispute the value of comity when it is applicable and productive of harmony between state and federal courts, nor do I deny the principle of exhaustion that §§2254(b) and (c) so clearly embrace. What troubles me is that the "total exhaustion" rule, now adopted by this Court, can be read into the statute, as the Court concedes, only by sheer force; that it operates as a trap for the uneducated and indigent pro se prisoner-applicant; that it delays the resolution of claims that are not frivolous; and that it tends to increase, rather than to alleviate, the caseload burdens on both state and federal courts. To use the old expression, the Court's ruling seems to me to "throw the baby out with the bath water."

Although purporting to rely on the policies upon which the exhaustion requirement is based, the Court uses that doctrine as "a blunderbuss to shatter the attempt at litigation of constitutional claims without regard to the purposes that underlie the doctrine and that called it into existence." Those purposes do not require the result the Court reaches; in fact, they support the approach taken by the Court of Appeals in this case and call for dismissal of only the unexhausted claims of a mixed habeas petition. Moreover, to the extent that the Court's ruling today has any impact whatsoever on the workings of federal habeas, it will alter, I fear, the litigation techniques of very few habeas petitioners.

The Court correctly observes, that neither the language nor the legislative history of the exhaustion provisions of §§2254(b) and (c) mandates dismissal of a habeas petition containing both exhausted and unexhausted claims. Nor does precedent dictate the result reached here.

The Court fails to note, moreover, that prisoners are not compelled to utilize every available state procedure in order to satisfy the exhaustion requirement. Although this Court's precedents do not address specifically the appropriate treatment of mixed habeas petitions, they plainly suggest that state courts need not inevitably be given every opportunity to safeguard a prisoner's constitutional rights and to provide him relief before a federal court may entertain his habeas petition.

In reversing the judgment of the Sixth Circuit, the Court focuses, as it must, on the purposes the exhaustion doctrine is intended to serve. I do not dispute the importance of the exhaustion requirement or the validity of the policies on which it is based. But I cannot agree that those concerns will be sacrificed by permitting district courts to consider exhausted habeas claims.

The first interest relied on by the Court involves an offshoot of the doctrine of federal-state comity. The Court hopes to preserve the state courts' role in protecting constitutional rights, as well as to afford those courts an opportunity to correct constitutional errors and — somewhat patronizingly — to "become increasingly familiar with and hospitable toward federal constitutional issues." My proposal, however, is not inconsistent with the Court's concern for comity: indeed, the state courts have occasion to rule first on every constitutional challenge, and have ample opportunity to correct any such error, before it is considered by a federal court on habeas.

In some respects, the Court's ruling appears more destructive than solicitous of federal-state comity. Remitting a habeas petitioner to state court to exhaust a patently frivolous claim before the federal court may consider a serious, exhausted ground for relief hardly demonstrates respect for the state courts. The state judiciary's time and resources are then spent rejecting the obviously meritless unexhausted claim, which doubtless will receive little or no attention in the subsequent federal proceeding that focuses on the substantial exhausted claim. I can "conceive of no reason why the State would wish to burden its judicial calendar with a narrow issue the resolution of which is predetermined by established federal principles."

A pending state proceeding involving claims not included in the prisoner's federal habeas petition will be mooted only if the federal court grants the applicant relief. Even in those cases, though, the state courts will be saved the trouble of undertaking the useless exercise of ruling on unexhausted claims that are unnecessary to the disposition of the case.

The second set of interests relied upon by the Court involves those of federal judicial administration — ensuring that a §2254 petition is accompanied by a complete factual record to facilitate review and relieving the district courts of the responsibility for determining when exhausted and unexhausted claims are interrelated. If a prisoner has presented a particular challenge in the state courts, however, the habeas court will have before it the complete factual record relating to that claim. And the Court's Draconian approach is hardly necessary to relieve district courts of the obligation to consider exhausted grounds for relief when the prisoner also has advanced interrelated claims not yet reviewed by the state courts. When the district court believes, on the facts of the case before it, that the record is inadequate or that full consideration of the exhausted claims is impossible, it has always been free to dismiss the entire habeas petition pending resolution of unexhausted claims in the state courts. Certainly, it makes sense to commit these decisions to the discretion of the lower federal courts, which will be familiar with the specific factual context of each case.

The federal courts that have addressed the issue of interrelatedness have had no difficulty distinguishing related from unrelated habeas claims. Mixed habeas petitions have been dismissed in toto when "the issues before the federal court logically depend for their relevance upon resolution of an unexhausted issue," or when consideration of the exhausted claim "would necessarily be affected . . ." by the unexhausted claim. Thus, some of the factors to be considered in determining whether a prisoner's grounds for collateral relief are interrelated are whether the claims are based on the same constitutional right or factual issue, and whether they require an understanding of the totality of the circumstances and therefore necessitate examination of the entire record.

The Court's interest in efficient administration of the federal courts therefore does not require dismissal of mixed habeas petitions. In fact, that concern militates against the approach taken by the Court today. In order to comply with the Court's ruling, a federal court now will have to review the record in a §2254 proceeding at least summarily in order to determine whether all claims have been exhausted. In many cases a decision on the merits will involve only negligible additional effort. And in other cases the court may not realize that one of a number of claims is unexhausted until after substantial work has been done. If the district court must nevertheless dismiss the entire petition until all grounds for relief have been exhausted, the prisoner will likely return to federal court eventually, thereby necessitating duplicative examination of the record and consideration of the exhausted claims — perhaps by another district judge. Moreover, when the §2254 petition does find its way back to federal court, the record on the exhausted grounds for relief may well be state and resolution of the merits more difficult.

The interest of the prisoner and of society in "preserv[ing] the writ of habeas corpus as a 'swift and imperative remedy in all cases of illegal restraint or confinement,'" is the final policy consideration to be weighed in the balance. Compelling the habeas petitioner to repeat his journey through the entire state and federal legal process before receiving a ruling on his exhausted claims obviously entails substantial delay. And if the prisoner must choose between undergoing that delay and forfeiting unexhausted claims, society is likewise forced to sacrifice either the swiftness of habeas or its availability to remedy all unconstitutional imprisonments. Dismissing only unexhausted grounds for habeas relief, while ruling on the merits of all unrelated exhausted claims, will diminish neither the promptness nor the efficacy of the remedy and, at the same time, will serve the state and federal interests described by the Court.

I therefore would remand the case, directing that the courts below dismiss respondent's unexhausted claims and examine those that have been properly presented to the state courts in order to determine whether they are interrelated with the unexhausted grounds and, if not, whether they warrant collateral relief.

Justice BRENNAN, with whom Justice MARSHALL joins, concurring in part and dissenting in part.

I agree with the Court's holding that the exhaustion requirement of 28 U.S.C. §§2254(b), (c) obliges a federal district court to dismiss, without consideration on the merits, a habeas corpus petition from a state prisoner when that petition contains claims that have not been exhausted in the state courts, "leaving the prisoner with the choice of returning to state court to exhaust his claims or of amending or resubmitting the habeas petition to present only exhausted claims to the district court." But I disagree with the plurality's view, that a habeas petitioner must "risk forfeiting consideration of his unexhausted claims in federal court" if he "decides to proceed only with his exhausted claims and deliberately sets aside his unexhausted claims" in the face of the district court's refusal to consider his "mixed" petition.

Justice STEVENS, dissenting.

This case raises important questions about the authority of federal judges. In my opinion claims of constitutional error are not fungible. There are at least four types. The one most frequently encountered is a claim that attaches a constitutional label to a set of facts that does not disclose a violation of any constitutional right. In my opinion, each of the four claims asserted in this case falls in that category. The second class includes constitutional violations that are not of sufficient import in a particular case to justify reversal even on direct appeal, when the evidence is still fresh and a fair retrial could be promptly conducted. A third category includes errors that are important enough to require reversal on direct appeal but do not reveal the kind of fundamental unfairness to the accused that will support a collateral attack on a final judgment. The fourth category includes those errors that are so fundamental that they infect the validity of the underlying judgment itself, or the integrity of the process by which that judgment was obtained. This category cannot be defined precisely; concepts of "fundamental fairness" are not frozen in time. But the kind of error that falls in this category is best illustrated by recalling the classic grounds for the issuance of a writ of habeas corpus — that the proceeding was dominated by mob violence; that the prosecutor knowingly made use of perjured testimony; or that the conviction was based on a confession extorted from the defendant by brutal methods. Errors of this kind justify collateral relief no matter how long a judgment may have been final and even though they may not have been preserved properly in the original trial.

In this case, I think it is clear that neither the exhausted claims nor the unexhausted claims describe any error demonstrating that respondent's trial was fundamentally unfair. Since his lawyer found insufficient merit in the two unexhausted claims to object to the error at trial or to raise the claims on direct appeal, I would expect that the Tennessee courts will consider them to have been waived as a matter of state law; thereafter, they undoubtedly will not support federal relief. This case is thus destined to return to the Federal District Court and the Court of Appeals where, it is safe to predict, those courts will once again come to the conclusion that the writ should issue. The additional procedure that the Court requires before considering the merits will be totally unproductive.

If my appraisal of respondent's exhausted claims is incorrect — if the trial actually was fundamentally unfair to the respondent — postponing relief until another round of review in the state and federal judicial systems has been completed is truly outrageous. The unnecessary delay will make it more difficult for the prosecutor to obtain a conviction on retrial if respondent is in fact guilty; if he is innocent, requiring him to languish in jail because he made a pleading error is callous indeed.

There are some situations in which a district judge should refuse to entertain a mixed petition until all of the prisoner's claims have been exhausted. If the unexhausted claim appears to involve error of the most serious kind and if it is reasonably clear that the exhausted claims do not, addressing the merits of the exhausted claims will merely delay the ultimate disposition of the case. Or if an evidentiary hearing is necessary to decide the merits of both the exhausted and unexhausted claims, a procedure that enables all fact questions to be resolved in the same hearing should be followed. I therefore would allow district judges to exercise discretion to determine whether the presence of an unexhausted claim in a habeas corpus application makes it inappropriate to consider the merits of a properly pleaded exhausted claim. The inflexible, mechanical rule the Court adopts today arbitrarily denies district judges the kind of authority they need to administer their calendars effectively.

In recent years federal judges at times have lost sight of the true office of the great writ of habeas corpus. It is quite unlike the common-law writ of error that enabled a higher court to correct errors committed by a nisi prius tribunal in the trial of civil or criminal cases by ordering further proceedings whenever trial error was detected. The writ of habeas corpus is a fundamental guarantee of liberty.

Procedural regularity is a matter of fundamental importance in the administration of justice. But procedural niceties that merely complicate and delay the resolution of disputes are another matter. In my opinion the federal habeas corpus statute should be construed to protect the former and, whenever possible, to avoid the latter.

4. Does the Petition Rely on Existing Rules or Seek Recognition of a New Rule of Constitutional Law?

Teague v. Lane, below, is one of the Supreme Court's most important habeas corpus decisions in decades in that it substantially limits the ability of federal courts to hear constitutional claims raised in habeas corpus petitions. Until *Teague*, the Supreme Court considered habeas corpus petitions alleging constitutional violations, even when they asked the Court to recognize a new constitutional right that would not be applied retroactively to other cases. When the Court articulated a new right it benefitted the habeas petitioner and future criminal defendants. The Court subsequently would decide, in another case, whether it was to be applied retroactively to others. But in *Teague*, the Supreme Court ruled that retroactivity must be determined first; federal courts may not hear habeas petitions asking the Court to recognize new rights unless such rights would be retroactively applied in all cases.

TEAGUE v. LANE
489 U.S. 288 (1989)

Justice O'CONNOR announced the judgment of the Court and delivered the opinion of the Court with respect to Parts I, II, and III, and an opinion with respect to Parts IV and V, in which THE CHIEF JUSTICE, Justice SCALIA, and Justice KENNEDY join.

In Taylor v. Louisiana (1975), this Court held that the Sixth Amendment required that the jury venire be drawn from a fair cross section of the community. The Court stated, however, that "in holding that petit juries must be drawn from a source fairly representative of the community we impose no requirement that petit juries actually chosen must mirror the community and reflect the various distinctive groups in the population. Defendants are not entitled to a jury of any particular composition." The principal question presented in this case is whether the Sixth Amendment's fair cross section requirement should now be extended to the petit jury. Because we adopt Justice Harlan's approach to retroactivity for cases on collateral review, we leave the resolution of that question for another day.

I

Petitioner, a black man, was convicted by an all-white Illinois jury of three counts of attempted murder, two counts of armed robbery, and one count of aggravated battery. During jury selection for petitioner's trial, the prosecutor used all 10 of his peremptory challenges to exclude blacks. Petitioner's counsel used one of his 10 peremptory challenges to exclude a black woman who was married to a police officer. After the prosecutor had struck six blacks, petitioner's counsel moved for a mistrial. The trial court denied the motion. When the prosecutor struck four more blacks, petitioner's counsel again moved for a mistrial, arguing that petitioner was "entitled to a jury of his peers." The prosecutor defended the challenges by stating that he was trying to achieve a balance of men and women on the jury. The trial court denied the motion, reasoning that the jury "appear[ed] to be a fair [one]."

On appeal, petitioner argued that the prosecutor's use of peremptory challenges denied him the right to be tried by a jury that was representative of the community. The Illinois Appellate Court rejected petitioner's fair cross section claim. The Illinois Supreme Court denied leave to appeal, and we denied certiorari.

Petitioner then filed a petition for a writ of habeas corpus in the United States District Court for the Northern District of Illinois. Petitioner repeated his fair cross section claim, and argued that the opinions of several Justices concurring in, or dissenting from, the denial of certiorari in McCray v. New York (1983), had invited a reexamination of Swain v. Alabama, (1965), which prohibited States from purposefully and systematically denying blacks the opportunity to serve on juries. He also argued, for the first time, that under *Swain* a prosecutor could be questioned about his use of peremptory challenges once he volunteered an explanation. The District Court, though sympathetic to petitioner's arguments, held that it was bound by *Swain* and Circuit precedent. On appeal, petitioner repeated his fair cross section claim and his *McCray* argument. A panel of the Court of Appeals agreed with petitioner that the Sixth Amendment's fair cross section requirement applied to the petit jury and held that petitioner had made out a prima facie case of discrimination. A majority of the judges on the Court of Appeals voted to rehear the case en banc, and the panel opinion was vacated. Rehearing was postponed until after our decision in Batson v. Kentucky, (1986), which overruled a portion of *Swain*. After *Batson* was decided, the Court of Appeals held that petitioner could not benefit from the rule in that case because [we] had held that *Batson* would not be applied retroactively to cases on collateral review.

II

Petitioner's first contention is that he should receive the benefit of our decision in *Batson* even though his conviction became final before *Batson* was decided. Before addressing petitioner's argument, we think it helpful to explain how *Batson* modified *Swain*. *Swain* held that a "State's purposeful or deliberate denial" to blacks of an opportunity to serve as jurors solely on account of race violates the Equal Protection Clause of the Fourteenth Amendment. In order to establish a prima facie case of discrimination under *Swain*, a defendant had to demonstrate that the peremptory challenge system had been "perverted." A defendant could raise an inference of purposeful discrimination if he showed that the prosecutor in the county where the trial was held "in case after case, whatever the circumstances, whatever the crime and whoever the defendant or the victim may be," has been responsible for the removal of qualified blacks who had survived challenges for cause, with the result that no blacks ever served on petit juries.

In *Batson*, the Court overruled that portion of *Swain* setting forth the evidentiary showing necessary to make out a prima facie case of racial discrimination under the Equal Protection Clause. The Court held that a defendant can establish a prima facie case by showing that he is a "member of a cognizable racial group," that the prosecutor exercised "peremptory challenges to remove from the venire members of the defendant's race," and that those "facts and any other relevant circumstances raise an inference that the prosecutor used that practice to exclude the veniremen from the petit jury on account of their race." Once the defendant makes out a prima facie case of discrimination, the burden shifts to the prosecutor "to come forward with a neutral explanation for challenging black jurors."

[T]he Court concluded that the rule announced in *Batson* should not be applied retroactively on collateral review of convictions that became final before *Batson* was announced. The Court defined final to mean a case "'where the judgment of conviction was rendered, the availability of appeal exhausted, and the time for petition for certiorari had elapsed before our decision in' *Batson*. . . ."

Petitioner's conviction became final 2 1/2 years prior to *Batson*, thus depriving petitioner of any benefit from the rule announced in that case.

[III]

Petitioner's final contention is that the Sixth Amendment's fair cross section requirement applies to the petit jury. As we noted at the outset, *Taylor* expressly stated that the fair cross section requirement does not apply to the petit jury. Petitioner nevertheless contends that the ratio decidendi of *Taylor* cannot be limited to the jury venire, and he urges adoption of a new rule. Because we hold that the rule urged by petitioner should not be applied retroactively to cases on collateral review, we decline to address petitioner's contention.

A

In the past, the Court has, without discussion, often applied a new constitutional rule of criminal procedure to the defendant in the case announcing the new rule, and has confronted the question of retroactivity later when a different defendant sought the benefit of that rule.

The question of retroactivity with regard to petitioner's fair cross section claim has been raised only in an amicus brief. *See* Brief for Criminal Justice Legal Foundation as Amicus Curiae. Nevertheless, that question is not foreign to the parties, who have addressed retroactivity with respect to petitioner's *Batson* claim. In our view, the question "whether a decision [announcing a new rule should] be given prospective or retroactive effect should be faced at the time of [that] decision." Retroactivity is properly treated as a threshold question, for, once a new rule is applied to the defendant in the case announcing the rule, evenhanded justice requires that it be applied retroactively to all who are similarly situated. Thus, before deciding whether the fair cross section requirement should be extended to the petit jury, we should ask whether such a rule would be applied retroactively to the case at issue. This retroactivity determination would normally entail application of the *Linkletter* standard, but we believe that our approach to retroactivity for cases on collateral review requires modification.

It is admittedly often difficult to determine when a case announces a new rule, and we do not attempt to define the spectrum of what may or may not constitute a new rule for retroactivity purposes. In general, however, a case announces a new rule when it breaks new ground or imposes a new obligation on the States or the Federal Government. To put it differently, a case announces a new rule if the result was not dictated by precedent existing at the time the defendant's conviction became final.

B

Justice Harlan believed that new rules generally should not be applied retroactively to cases on collateral review. He argued that retroactivity for cases on collateral review could "be responsibly [determined] only by focusing, in the first instance, on the nature, function, and scope of the adjudicatory process in which such cases arise. The relevant frame of reference, in other words, is not the purpose of the new rule whose benefit the [defendant] seeks, but instead the purposes for which the writ of habeas corpus is made available." With regard to the nature of habeas corpus, Justice Harlan wrote:

> Habeas corpus always has been a collateral remedy, providing an avenue for upsetting judgments that have become otherwise final. It is not designed as a substitute for direct review. The interest in leaving concluded litigation in a state of repose, that is, reducing the controversy to a final judgment not subject to further judicial revision, may quite legitimately be found by those responsible for defining the scope of the writ to outweigh in some, many, or most instances the competing interest in readjudicating convictions according to all legal standards in effect when a habeas petition is filed.

Given the "broad scope of constitutional issues cognizable on habeas," Justice Harlan argued that it is "sounder, in adjudicating habeas petitions, generally to apply the law prevailing at the time a conviction became final than it is to seek to dispose of [habeas] cases on the basis of intervening changes in constitutional interpretation." Justice Harlan identified only two exceptions to his general rule of nonretroactivity for cases on collateral review. First, a new rule should be applied retroactively if it places "certain kinds of primary, private individual conduct beyond the power of the criminal law-making authority to proscribe." Second, a new rule should be applied retroactively if it requires the observance of "those procedures that . . . are 'implicit in the concept of ordered liberty.'"

We agree with Justice Harlan's description of the function of habeas corpus. "[T]he Court never has defined the scope of the writ simply by reference to a perceived need to assure that an individual accused of crime is afforded a trial free of constitutional error." Rather, we have recognized that interests of comity and finality must also be considered in determining the proper scope of habeas review. These underlying considerations of finality find significant and compelling parallels in the criminal context.

Application of constitutional rules not in existence at the time a conviction became final seriously undermines the principle of finality which is essential to the operation of our criminal justice system. Without finality, the criminal law is deprived of much of its deterrent effect. The fact that life and liberty are at stake in criminal prosecutions "shows only that 'conventional notions of finality' should not have as much place in criminal as in civil litigation, not that they should have none."

We find these criticisms to be persuasive, and we now adopt Justice Harlan's view of retroactivity for cases on collateral review. Unless they fall within an exception to the general rule, new constitutional rules of criminal procedure will not be applicable to those cases which have become final before the new rules are announced.

V

Petitioner's conviction became final in 1983. As a result, the rule petitioner urges would not be applicable to this case, which is on collateral review, unless it would fall within an exception.

The first exception suggested by Justice Harlan — that a new rule should be applied retroactively if it places "certain kinds of primary, private individual conduct beyond the power of the criminal law-making authority to proscribe," — is not relevant here. Application of the fair cross section requirement to the petit jury would not accord constitutional protection to any primary activity whatsoever.

The second exception suggested by Justice Harlan — that a new rule should be applied retroactively if it requires the observance of "those procedures that . . . are 'implicit in the concept of ordered liberty,'" — we apply with a modification. The language used by Justice Harlan in *Mackey* leaves no doubt that he meant the second exception to be reserved for watershed rules of criminal procedure:

> We therefore hold that, implicit in the retroactivity approach we adopt today, is the principle that habeas corpus cannot be used as a vehicle to create new constitutional rules of criminal procedure unless those rules would be applied retroactively to all defendants on collateral review through one of the two exceptions we have articulated. Because a decision extending the fair cross section requirement to the petit jury would not be applied retroactively to cases on collateral review under the approach we adopt today, we do not address petitioner's claim.

Justice STEVENS, with whom Justice BLACKMUN joins, concurring in part and concurring in the judgment.

When a criminal defendant claims that a procedural error tainted his conviction, an appellate court often decides whether error occurred before deciding whether that error requires reversal or should be classified as harmless. I would follow a parallel approach in cases raising novel questions of constitutional law on collateral review, first determining whether the trial process violated any of the petitioner's constitutional rights and then deciding whether the petitioner is entitled to relief. If error occurred, factors relating to retroactivity — most importantly, the magnitude of unfairness — should be examined before granting the petitioner relief. Proceeding in reverse, a plurality of the Court today declares that a new rule should not apply retroactively without ever deciding whether there is such a rule.

Justice BRENNAN, with whom Justice MARSHALL joins, dissenting.

Today a plurality of this Court, without benefit of briefing and oral argument, adopts a novel threshold test for federal review of state criminal convictions on habeas corpus. It does so without regard for — indeed, without even mentioning — our contrary decisions over the past 35 years delineating the broad scope of habeas relief. The plurality further appears oblivious to the importance we have consistently accorded the principle of stare decisis in nonconstitutional cases. Out of an exaggerated concern for treating similarly situated habeas petitioners the same, the plurality would for the first time preclude the federal courts from considering on collateral review a vast range of important constitutional challenges; where those challenges have merit, it would bar the vindication of personal constitutional rights and deny society a check against further violations until the same claim is presented on direct review. In my view, the plurality's "blind adherence to the principle of treating like cases alike" amounts to "letting the tail wag the dog" when it stymies the resolution of substantial and unheralded constitutional questions. Because I cannot acquiesce in this unprecedented curtailment of the reach of the Great Writ, particularly in the absence of any discussion of these momentous changes by the parties or the lower courts, I dissent.

Unfortunately, the plurality turns its back on established case law and would erect a formidable new barrier to relief. Any time a federal habeas petitioner's claim, if successful, would result in the announcement of a new rule of law, the plurality says, it may only be adjudicated if that rule would "plac[e] 'certain kinds of primary, private individual conduct beyond the power of the criminal law-making authority to proscribe.'" Equally disturbing, in my view, is the plurality's infidelity to the doctrine of stare decisis. The plurality does not so much as mention stare decisis. Indeed, from the plurality's exposition of its new rule, one might infer that its novel fabrication will work no great change in the availability of federal collateral review of state convictions. Nothing could be further from the truth. Although the plurality declines to "define the spectrum of what may or may not constitute a new rule for retroactivity purposes," it does say that generally "a case announces a new rule when it breaks new ground or imposes a new obligation on the States or the Federal Government." Otherwise phrased, "a case announces a new rule if the result was not dictated by precedent existing at the time the defendant's conviction became final." This account is extremely broad. Few decisions on appeal or collateral review are "dictated" by what came before. Most such cases involve a question of law that is at least debatable, permitting a rational judge to resolve the case in more than one way. Virtually no case that prompts a dissent on the relevant legal point, for example, could be said to be "dictated" by prior decisions. By the plurality's test, therefore, a great many cases could only be heard on habeas if the rule urged by the petitioner fell within one of the two exceptions the plurality has sketched. Those exceptions, however, are narrow. Rules that place "'certain kinds of primary, private individual conduct beyond the power of the criminal law-making authority to proscribe,'" are rare. And rules that would require "new procedures without which the likelihood of an accurate conviction is seriously diminished," are not appreciably more common. The plurality admits, in fact, that it "believe[s] it unlikely that many such components of basic due process have yet to emerge." The plurality's approach today can thus be expected to contract substantially the Great Writ's sweep.

[There are an] abundance and variety of habeas cases we have decided in recent years that could never have been adjudicated had the plurality's new rule been in effect.

Teague applies whenever the habeas petition seeks recognition of a "new right." The Court broadly defined what is a "new" right, thus limiting the constitutional claims that can be presented to a federal court on habeas corpus. The Court said that a case announces a new rule "when it breaks new ground or imposes a new obligation on the States or Federal government. . . . [A] case announces new rule if the result was not dictated by precedent existing at the time the defendant's conviction became final."

If the petitioner is seeking a new right, the question then becomes whether it would apply retroactively. Because very few criminal procedure rights have retroactive application, the effect will be to prevent habeas petitions from preventing claims except as to rights that have been previously established. The Court recognized only two situations in which rights have retroactive effect. One is where the new rules place "certain kinds of primary, private individual conduct beyond the power of the criminal law-making authority to proscribe." The other is a new rule that adopts a procedure that is "implicit in the concept of ordered liberty." The latter, the Court emphasized, is "reserved for watershed rules of criminal procedure."

The reluctance of the Court to find criminal procedure rights to be retroactive is illustrated by its recent decision in Schriro v. Summerlin, 542 U.S. 348 (2004). In Ring v. Arizona, 536 U.S. 584 (2002), the Supreme Court held that it is for the jury to decide whether there are sufficient aggravating circumstances to warrant the imposition of the death penalty. In other words, it was deemed unconstitutional for states to allow the judge, on his or her own, to decide whether to impose a death sentence. The issue in Schriro v. Summerlin is whether *Ring* should apply retroactively to those who were sentenced to death before it was decided. The Court, in a 5-4 decision, held that *Ring* does not apply retroactively — that it neither puts matters beyond the reach of the criminal law nor is a watershed rule of criminal procedure. The result is that individuals who were sentenced through an unconstitutional procedure could be put to death.

The Supreme Court again considered when a criminal procedure rule applies retroactively in Whorton v. Bockting, 549 U.S. 406 (2007). In Crawford v. Washington, 541 U.S. 36 (2004), the Supreme Court significantly changed the law under the Confrontation Clause of the Sixth Amendment as to when prosecutors may use statements against a criminal defendant when the declarant is unavailable. Previously, a prosecutor could use such statements as long as they were reliable. In *Crawford*, the Supreme Court held that "testimonial" statements could not be used against a criminal defendant when the declarant was unavailable even though they were deemed reliable.

The issue in Whorton v. Bockting is whether *Crawford* applies retroactively. The Supreme Court unanimously held that it does not. Justice Alito, writing for the Court, explained:

> In *Teague* and subsequent cases, we have laid out the framework to be used in determining whether a rule announced in one of our opinions should be applied retroactively to judgments in criminal cases that are already final on direct review.

Under the *Teague* framework, an old rule applies both on direct and collateral review, but a new rule is generally applicable only to cases that are still on direct review.

A new rule applies retroactively in a collateral proceeding only if (1) the rule is substantive or (2) the rule is a "watershed rul[e] of criminal procedure" implicating the fundamental fairness and accuracy of the criminal proceeding.

Because *Crawford* announced a "new rule" and because it is clear and undisputed that the rule is procedural and not substantive, that rule cannot be applied in this collateral attack on respondent's conviction unless it is a "watershed rul[e] of criminal procedure" implicating the fundamental fairness and accuracy of the criminal proceeding. This exception is "extremely narrow." We have observed that it is "unlikely" that any such rules "ha[ve] yet to emerge." And in the years since *Teague*, we have rejected every claim that a new rule satisfied the requirements for watershed status.

In order to qualify as watershed, a new rule must meet two requirements. First, the rule must be necessary to prevent "an impermissibly large risk of an inaccurate conviction." Second, the rule must alter our understanding of the bedrock procedural elements essential to the fairness of a proceeding.

The *Crawford* rule does not satisfy the first requirement relating to an impermissibly large risk of an inaccurate conviction. To be sure, the *Crawford* rule reflects the Framers' preferred mechanism (cross-examination) for ensuring that inaccurate out-of-court testimonial statements are not used to convict an accused. But in order for a new rule to meet the accuracy requirement at issue here, "[i]t is . . . not enough . . . to say that [the] rule is aimed at improving the accuracy of trial," or that the rule is directed toward the enhancement of reliability and accuracy in some sense. Instead, the question is whether the new rule remedied "an impermissibly large risk" of an inaccurate conviction.

The *Crawford* rule also did not "alter our understanding of the bedrock procedural elements essential to the fairness of a proceeding." [I]n order to meet this requirement, a new rule must itself constitute a previously unrecognized bedrock procedural element that is essential to the fairness of a proceeding. In applying this requirement, we again have looked to the example of *Gideon* [v. Wainwright], and "we have not hesitated to hold that less sweeping and fundamental rules" do not qualify.

In this case, it is apparent that the rule announced in *Crawford*, while certainly important, is not in the same category with *Gideon*. *Gideon* effected a profound and "sweeping" change. The *Crawford* rule simply lacks the "primacy" and "centrality" of the *Gideon* rule, and does not qualify as a rule that "alter[ed] our understanding of the bedrock procedural elements essential to the fairness of a proceeding."

In sum, we hold that *Crawford* announced a "new rule" of criminal procedure and that this rule does not fall within the *Teague* exception for watershed rules.

The bottom line is that it is highly unlikely that any criminal procedure rule will be found to apply retroactively. Therefore, habeas corpus petitions cannot assert "new rules" but must rely solely on existing rights.

5.   Is It an Issue That Can Be Raised on Habeas Corpus?

The principles of res judicata and collateral estoppel generally preclude a party from relitigating a matter already presented to a court and decided on. Brown v. Allen, 344 U.S. 443 (1953), created an important exception to

collateral estoppel and res judicata for habeas petitions. The Supreme
Court, in an opinion by Justice Frankfurter, held that a constitutional
claim may be raised on habeas even though it had been raised, fully litigated,
and decided in state court. Justice Frankfurter observed that "even the highest State courts" had failed to give adequate protection to federal constitutional rights. Because the *Brown* Court believed that habeas corpus exists
to remedy state court disregard of violations of defendant's rights, the Court
established that a state prisoner should have the chance to have a hearing in federal court on federal constitutional claims.

In fact, the Warren Court so valued the importance of the opportunity to
relitigate constitutional issues to ensure correct decisions that it held that a
prisoner convicted by a *federal* court also may raise issues on habeas that had
been presented and decided at trial.[41] The Court concluded that "[t]he
provision of federal collateral remedies rests . . . fundamentally upon a recognition that adequate protection of constitutional rights . . . requires the
continuing availability of a mechanism for relief."

There is one major exception to Brown v. Allen. In Stone v. Powell, the
Supreme Court held that claims that a state court improperly failed to
exclude evidence as being the product of an illegal search or seizure
could not be relitigated on habeas corpus if the state court provided a full
and fair opportunity for a hearing.

STONE v. POWELL
428 U.S. 465 (1976)

Justice POWELL delivered the opinion of the Court.

Respondents in these cases were convicted of criminal offenses in state
courts, and their convictions were affirmed on appeal. The prosecution in
each case relied upon evidence obtained by searches and seizures alleged by
respondents to have been unlawful. Each respondent subsequently sought
relief in a Federal District Court by filing a petition for a writ of federal
habeas corpus. The question presented is whether a federal court should
consider, in ruling on a petition for habeas corpus relief filed by a state
prisoner, a claim that evidence obtained by an unconstitutional search or
seizure was introduced at his trial, when he has previously been afforded an
opportunity for full and fair litigation of his claim in the state courts. The
issue is of considerable importance to the administration of criminal justice.

I

In the landmark decision in Brown v. Allen (1953), the scope of the writ was
expanded. In that case and its companion case, Daniels v. Allen, prisoners

---

41. Kaufman v. United States, 394 U.S. 217 (1969).

applied for federal habeas corpus relief claiming that the trial courts had erred in failing to quash their indictments due to alleged discrimination in the selection of grand jurors and in ruling certain confessions admissible. In *Brown*, the highest court of the State had rejected these claims on direct appeal, and this Court had denied certiorari. Despite the apparent adequacy of the state corrective process, the Court reviewed the denial of the writ of habeas corpus and held that Brown was entitled to a full reconsideration of these constitutional claims, including, if appropriate, a hearing in the Federal District Court.

During the period in which the substantive scope of the writ was expanded, the Court did not consider whether exceptions to full review might exist with respect to particular categories of constitutional claims. Prior to the Court's decision in Kaufman v. United States (1969), however, a substantial majority of the Federal Courts of Appeals had concluded that collateral review of search-and-seizure claims was inappropriate on motions filed by federal prisoners under 28 U.S.C. §2255, the modern post conviction procedure available to federal prisoners in lieu of habeas corpus. The primary rationale advanced in support of those decisions was that Fourth Amendment violations are different in kind from denials of Fifth or Sixth Amendment rights in that claims of illegal search and seizure do not "impugn the integrity of the fact-finding process or challenge evidence as inherently unreliable; rather, the exclusion of illegally seized evidence is simply a prophylactic device intended generally to deter Fourth Amendment violations by law enforcement officers."

Kaufman rejected this rationale and held that search-and-seizure claims are cognizable in §2255 proceedings. The Court noted that "the federal habeas remedy extends to state prisoners alleging that unconstitutionally obtained evidence was admitted against them at trial."

The discussion in *Kaufman* of the scope of federal habeas corpus rests on the view that the effectuation of the Fourth Amendment, as applied to the States through the Fourteenth Amendment, requires the granting of habeas corpus relief when a prisoner has been convicted in state court on the basis of evidence obtained in an illegal search or seizure since those Amendments were held in Mapp v. Ohio (1961), to require exclusion of such evidence at trial and reversal of conviction upon direct review. Until these cases we have not had occasion fully to consider the validity of this view. Upon examination, we conclude, in light of the nature and purpose of the Fourth Amendment exclusionary rule, that this view is unjustified. We hold, therefore, that where the State has provided an opportunity for full and fair litigation of a Fourth Amendment claim, the Constitution does not require that a state prisoner be granted federal habeas corpus relief on the ground that evidence obtained in an unconstitutional search or seizure was introduced at his trial.

III

The Fourth Amendment assures the "right of the people to be secure in their persons, houses, papers, and effects, against unreasonable searches and seizures." The Amendment was primarily a reaction to the evils associated with the use of the general warrant in England and the writs of assistance in the Colonies, and was intended to protect the "sanctity of a man's home and the privacies of life" from searches under unchecked general authority.

The exclusionary rule was a judicially created means of effectuating the rights secured by the Fourth Amendment. Prior to the Court's decisions in Weeks v. United States (1914), and Gouled v. United States (1921), there existed no barrier to the introduction in criminal trials of evidence obtained in violation of the Amendment. In *Weeks*, the Court held that the defendant could petition before trial for the return of property secured through an illegal search or seizure conducted by federal authorities. In *Gouled*, the Court held broadly that such evidence could not be introduced in a federal prosecution.

Decisions prior to *Mapp* [v. Ohio (1961)] advanced two principal reasons for application of the rule in federal trials. The Court in the context of its special supervisory role over the lower federal courts, referred to the "imperative of judicial integrity," suggesting that exclusion of illegally seized evidence prevents contamination of the judicial process. The *Mapp* majority justified the application of the rule to the States on several grounds, but relied principally upon the belief that exclusion would deter future unlawful police conduct.

Although our decisions often have alluded to the "imperative of judicial integrity," they demonstrate the limited role of this justification in the determination whether to apply the rule in a particular context. Logically extended this justification would require that courts exclude unconstitutionally seized evidence despite lack of objection by the defendant, or even over his assent. It also would require abandonment of the standing limitations on who may object to the introduction of unconstitutionally seized evidence, and retreat from the proposition that judicial proceedings need not abate when the defendant's person is unconstitutionally seized. Similarly, the interest in promoting judicial integrity does not prevent the use of illegally seized evidence in grand jury proceedings. Nor does it require that the trial court exclude such evidence from use for impeachment of a defendant, even though its introduction is certain to result in conviction in some cases.

The teaching of these cases is clear. While courts, of course, must ever be concerned with preserving the integrity of the judicial process, this concern has limited force as a justification for the exclusion of highly probative evidence. The force of this justification becomes minimal where federal habeas corpus relief is sought by a prisoner who previously has been afforded the opportunity for full and fair consideration of his search-and-seizure claim at trial and on direct review.

The primary justification for the exclusionary rule then is the deterrence of police conduct that violates Fourth Amendment rights. Post-*Mapp* decisions have established that the rule is not a personal constitutional right. It is not calculated to redress the injury to the privacy of the victim of the search or seizure, for any "[r]eparation comes too late." Instead, "the rule is a judicially created remedy designed to safeguard Fourth Amendment rights generally through its deterrent effect. . . ."

IV

We turn now to the specific question presented by these cases. Respondents allege violations of Fourth Amendment rights guaranteed them through the Fourteenth Amendment. The question is whether state prisoners who have been afforded the opportunity for full and fair consideration of their reliance upon the exclusionary rule with respect to seized evidence by the state courts at trial and on direct review may invoke their claim again on federal habeas corpus review. The answer is to be found by weighing the utility of the exclusionary rule against the costs of extending it to collateral review of Fourth Amendment claims.

The costs of applying the exclusionary rule even at trial and on direct review are well known: the focus of the trial, and the attention of the participants therein, are diverted from the ultimate question of guilt or innocence that should be the central concern in a criminal proceeding. Moreover, the physical evidence sought to be excluded is typically reliable and often the most probative information bearing on the guilt or innocence of the defendant.

Application of the rule thus deflects the truthfinding process and often frees the guilty. The disparity in particular cases between the error committed by the police officer and the windfall afforded a guilty defendant by application of the rule is contrary to the idea of proportionality that is essential to the concept of justice. Thus, although the rule is thought to deter unlawful police activity in part through the nurturing of respect for Fourth Amendment values, if applied indiscriminately it may well have the opposite effect of generating disrespect for the law and administration of justice. These long-recognized costs of the rule persist when a criminal conviction is sought to be overturned on collateral review on the ground that a search-and-seizure claim was erroneously rejected by two or more tiers of state courts.

We nevertheless afford broad habeas corpus relief, recognizing the need in a free society for an additional safeguard against compelling an innocent man to suffer an unconstitutional loss of liberty. The Court in Fay v. Noia (1963), described habeas corpus as a remedy for "whatever society deems to be intolerable restraints," and recognized that those to whom the writ should be granted "are persons whom society has grievously wronged." But in the case of a typical Fourth Amendment claim, asserted on collateral attack, a convicted defendant is usually asking society to redetermine an issue that has no bearing on the basic justice of his incarceration.

Evidence obtained by police officers in violation of the Fourth Amendment is excluded at trial in the hope that the frequency of future violations will decrease. Despite the absence of supportive empirical evidence, we have assumed that the immediate effect of exclusion will be to discourage law enforcement officials from violating the Fourth Amendment by removing the incentive to disregard it. More importantly, over the long term, this demonstration that our society attaches serious consequences to violation of constitutional rights is thought to encourage those who formulate law enforcement policies, and the officers who implement them, to incorporate Fourth Amendment ideals into their value system.

We adhere to the view that these considerations support the implementation of the exclusionary rule at trial and its enforcement on direct appeal of state-court convictions. But the additional contribution, if any, of the consideration of search-and-seizure claims of state prisoners on collateral review is small in relation to the costs. To be sure, each case in which such claim is considered may add marginally to an awareness of the values protected by the Fourth Amendment. There is no reason to believe, however, that the overall educative effect of the exclusionary rule would be appreciably diminished if search-and-seizure claims could not be raised in federal habeas corpus review of state convictions. Nor is there reason to assume that any specific disincentive already created by the risk of exclusion of evidence at trial or the reversal of convictions on direct review would be enhanced if there were the further risk that a conviction obtained in state court and affirmed on direct review might be overturned in collateral proceedings often occurring years after the incarceration of the defendant. The view that the deterrence of Fourth Amendment violations would be furthered rests on the dubious assumption that law enforcement authorities would fear that federal habeas review might reveal flaws in a search or seizure that went undetected at trial and on appeal.[42] Even if one rationally could assume that some additional incremental deterrent effect would be presented in isolated cases, the resulting advance of the legitimate goal of furthering Fourth Amendment rights would be outweighed by the acknowledged costs to other values vital to a rational system of criminal justice.

In sum, we conclude that where the State has provided an opportunity for full and fair litigation of a Fourth Amendment claim, a state prisoner may

---

42. The policy arguments that respondents marshal in support of the view that federal habeas corpus review is necessary to effectuate the Fourth Amendment stem from a basic mistrust of the state courts as fair and competent forums for the adjudication of federal constitutional rights. The argument is that state courts cannot be trusted to effectuate Fourth Amendment values through fair application of the rule, and the oversight jurisdiction of this Court on certiorari is an inadequate safeguard. The principal rationale for this view emphasizes the broad differences in the respective institutional settings within which federal judges and state judges operate. Despite differences in institutional environment and the unsympathetic attitude to federal constitutional claims of some state judges in years past, we are unwilling to assume that there now exists a general lack of appropriate sensitivity to constitutional rights in the trial and appellate courts of the several States. State courts, like federal courts, have a constitutional obligation to safeguard personal liberties and to uphold federal law. Moreover, the argument that federal judges are more expert in applying federal constitutional law is especially unpersuasive in the context of search-and-seizure claims, since they are dealt with on a daily basis by trial level judges in both systems. In sum, there is "no intrinsic reason why the fact that a man is a federal judge should make him more competent, or conscientious, or learned with respect to the [consideration of Fourth Amendment claims] than his neighbor in the state courthouse." [Footnote by the Court.]

not be granted federal habeas corpus relief on the ground that evidence obtained in an unconstitutional search or seizure was introduced at his trial. In this context the contribution of the exclusionary rule, if any, to the effectuation of the Fourth Amendment is minimal, and the substantial societal costs of application of the rule persist with special force.

With all respect, the hyperbole of the dissenting opinion is misdirected. Our decision today is not concerned with the scope of the habeas corpus statute as authority for litigating constitutional claims generally. We do reaffirm that the exclusionary rule is a judicially created remedy rather than a personal constitutional right, and we emphasize the minimal utility of the rule when sought to be applied to Fourth Amendment claims in a habeas corpus proceeding. In sum, we hold only that a federal court need not apply the exclusionary rule on habeas review of a Fourth Amendment claim absent a showing that the state prisoner was denied an opportunity for a full and fair litigation of that claim at trial and on direct review. Our decision does not mean that the federal court lacks jurisdiction over such a claim, but only that the application of the rule is limited to cases in which there has been both such a showing and a Fourth Amendment violation.

Justice BRENNAN, with whom Justice MARSHALL concurs, dissenting.

The Court today holds "that where the State has provided an opportunity for full and fair litigation of a Fourth Amendment claim, a state prisoner may not be granted federal habeas corpus relief on the ground that evidence obtained in an unconstitutional search or seizure was introduced at his trial." To be sure, my Brethren are hostile to the continued vitality of the exclusionary rule as part and parcel of the Fourth Amendment's prohibition of unreasonable searches and seizures. Today's holding portends substantial evisceration of federal habeas corpus jurisdiction, and I dissent.

The Court's opinion does not specify the particular basis on which it denies federal habeas jurisdiction over claims of Fourth Amendment violations brought by state prisoners.

Much of the Court's analysis implies that respondents are not entitled to habeas relief because they are not being unconstitutionally detained. Although purportedly adhering to the principle that the Fourth and Fourteenth Amendments "require exclusion" of evidence seized in violation of their commands, the Court informs us that there has merely been a "view" in our cases that "the effectuation of the Fourth Amendment . . . requires the granting of habeas corpus relief when a prisoner has been convicted in state court on the basis of evidence obtained in an illegal search or seizure. . . ." Applying a "balancing test," the Court then concludes that this "view" is unjustified and that the policies of the Fourth Amendment would not be implemented if claims to the benefits of the exclusionary rule were cognizable in collateral attacks on state-court convictions.

Understandably the Court must purport to cast its holding in constitutional terms, because that avoids a direct confrontation with the incontrovertible facts that the habeas statutes have heretofore always been construed to grant jurisdiction to entertain Fourth Amendment claims of both state and federal prisoners, that Fourth Amendment principles have been applied in decisions on the merits in numerous cases on collateral review of final convictions, and that Congress has legislatively accepted our interpretation of congressional intent as to the necessary scope and function of habeas relief. Indeed, the Court reaches its result without explicitly overruling any of our plethora of precedents inconsistent with that result or even discussing principles of stare decisis. Rather, the Court asserts, in essence, that the Justices joining those prior decisions or reaching the merits of Fourth Amendment claims simply overlooked the obvious constitutional dimension to the problem in adhering to the "view" that granting collateral relief when state courts erroneously decide Fourth Amendment issues would effectuate the principles underlying that Amendment.

But, shorn of the rhetoric of "interest balancing" used to obscure what is at stake in this case, it is evident that today's attempt to rest the decision on the Constitution must fail so long as Mapp v. Ohio remains undisturbed.

Under *Mapp*, as a matter of federal constitutional law, a state court must exclude evidence from the trial of an individual whose Fourth and Fourteenth Amendment rights were violated by a search or seizure that directly or indirectly resulted in the acquisition of that evidence. When a state court admits such evidence, it has committed a Constitutional error, and unless that error is harmless under federal standards, it follows ineluctably that the defendant has been placed "in custody in violation of the Constitution" within the comprehension of 28 U.S.C. §2254. In short, it escapes me as to what logic can support the assertion that the defendant's unconstitutional confinement obtains during the process of direct review, no matter how long that process takes, but that the unconstitutionality then suddenly dissipates at the moment the claim is asserted in a collateral attack on the conviction.

The only conceivable rationale upon which the Court's "constitutional" thesis might rest is the statement that "the [exclusionary] rule is not a personal constitutional right. . . . Instead, 'the rule is a judicially created remedy designed to safeguard Fourth Amendment rights generally through its deterrent effect.'" [I]n light of contrary decisions establishing the role of the exclusionary rule, the premise that an individual has no constitutional right to have unconstitutionally seized evidence excluded from all use by the government [has no basis]. [But] I need not dispute that point here. For today's holding is not logically defensible. However, the Court reinterprets *Mapp*, and whatever the rationale now attributed to *Mapp*'s holding or the purpose ascribed to the exclusionary rule, the prevailing constitutional rule is that unconstitutionally seized evidence cannot be admitted in the criminal trial of a person whose federal constitutional rights were violated by the search or seizure. The erroneous admission of such evidence is a violation of the Federal Constitution — *Mapp* inexorably means at least this much, or there would be no basis for applying the exclusionary rule in state criminal proceedings — and an accused against whom such evidence is admitted has been convicted in derogation of rights mandated by, and is "in custody in violation," of the Constitution of the United States. Indeed, since state courts violate the strictures of the Federal Constitution by admitting such evidence, then even if federal habeas review did not directly effectuate Fourth Amendment values, a proposition I deny, that review would nevertheless serve to effectuate what is concededly a constitutional principle concerning admissibility of evidence at trial.

The Court's arguments respecting the cost/benefit analysis of applying the exclusionary rule on collateral attack also have no merit. For all of the "costs" of applying the exclusionary rule on habeas should already have been incurred at the trial or on direct review if the state court had not misapplied federal constitutional principles. As such, these "costs" were evaluated and deemed to be outweighed when the exclusionary rule was fashioned. The only proper question on habeas is whether federal courts, acting under congressional directive to have the last say as to enforcement of federal constitutional principles, are to permit the States free enjoyment of the fruits of a conviction which by definition were only obtained through violations of the Constitution as interpreted in *Mapp*. And as to the question whether any "educative" function is served by such habeas review, today's decision will certainly provide a lesson that, tragically for an individual's constitutional rights, will not be lost on state courts.

Therefore, the real ground of today's decision — a ground that is particularly troubling in light of its portent for habeas jurisdiction generally — is the Court's novel reinterpretation of the habeas statutes; this would read the statutes as requiring the district courts routinely to deny habeas relief to prisoners "in custody in violation of the Constitution or laws . . . of the United States" as a matter of judicial "discretion" — a "discretion" judicially manufactured today contrary to the express statutory language — because such claims are "different in kind" from other constitutional violations in that they "do not 'impugn the integrity of the fact-finding process,'" and because application of such constitutional strictures "often frees the guilty." Much in the Court's opinion suggests that a construction of the habeas statutes to deny relief for non-"guilt-related" constitutional violations, based on this Court's vague notions of comity and federalism, is the actual premise for today's decision, and although the Court attempts to bury its underlying premises in footnotes, those premises mark this case as a harbinger of future eviscerations of the habeas statutes that plainly does violence to congressional power to frame the statutory contours of habeas jurisdiction. For we are told that "[r]esort to habeas corpus, especially for purposes other than to assure that no innocent person suffers an unconstitutional loss of liberty, results in serious intrusions on values important to our system of government," including waste of judicial resources, lack of finality of criminal convictions, friction between the federal and state judiciaries, and incursions on "federalism." We are told that federal determination of Fourth Amendment claims merely involves "an issue that has no bearing on the basic justice of [the defendant's] incarceration," and that "the ultimate question [in the criminal process should invariably be] guilt or innocence." We are told that the "policy arguments" of respondents to the effect that federal courts must be the ultimate arbiters of federal constitutional rights, and that our certiorari jurisdiction is inadequate to perform this task, "stem from a basic mistrust of the state courts as fair and competent forums for the adjudication of federal constitutional rights"; the Court, however, finds itself "unwilling to assume that there now exists a general lack of appropriate sensitivity to constitutional rights in the trial and appellate courts of the several States," and asserts that it is "unpersuaded" by "the argument that federal judges are more expert in applying federal constitutional law" because "there is 'no intrinsic reason why the fact that a man is a federal judge should make him more competent, or conscientious, or learned with respect to the [consideration of Fourth Amendment claims] than his neighbor in the state courthouse.'" Finally, we are provided a revisionist history of the genesis and growth of federal habeas corpus jurisdiction. If today's decision were only that erroneous state-court resolution of Fourth Amendment claims did not render the defendant's resultant confinement "in violation of the Constitution," these pronouncements would have been wholly irrelevant and unnecessary. I am therefore justified in apprehending that the groundwork is being laid today for a drastic withdrawal of federal habeas jurisdiction, if not for all grounds of alleged unconstitutional detention, then at least for claims—for example, of double jeopardy, entrapment, self-incrimination, *Miranda* violations, and use of invalid identification procedures—that this Court later decides are not "guilt related."

At least since Brown v. Allen, detention emanating from judicial proceedings in which constitutional rights were denied has been deemed "contrary to fundamental law," and all constitutional claims have thus been cognizable on federal habeas corpus. There is no foundation in the language or history of the habeas statutes for discriminating between types of constitutional transgressions, and efforts to relegate certain categories of claims to the status of "second-class rights" by excluding them from that jurisdiction have been repulsed. Today's opinion, however, marks the triumph of those who have sought to establish a hierarchy of constitutional rights, and to deny for all practical purposes a federal forum for review of those rights that this Court deems less worthy or important. Without even paying the slightest deference to principles of stare decisis or acknowledging Congress' failure for two decades to alter the habeas statutes in light of our interpretation of congressional intent to render all federal constitutional contentions cognizable on habeas, the Court today rewrites Congress' jurisdictional statutes as heretofore construed and bars access to federal courts by state prisoners with constitutional claims distasteful to a majority of my Brethren. But even ignoring principles of stare decisis dictating that Congress is the appropriate vehicle for embarking on such a fundamental shift in the jurisdiction of the federal courts, I can find no adequate justification elucidated by the Court for concluding that habeas relief for all federal constitutional claims is no longer compelled under the reasoning of *Brown*, *Fay*, and *Kaufman*.

For a time it appeared that *Stone* might represent a first step to overruling Brown v. Allen and thus would prevent relitigation of constitutional claims on habeas corpus. After all, if the legislative history of the habeas corpus statutes is read as preventing relitigation, or if state courts are generally equal to federal courts in their protection of constitutional rights, relitigation appears unnecessary. However, the Supreme Court has not extended *Stone* to other constitutional rights or further limited the application of Brown v. Allen.

In Rose v. Mitchell, 443 U.S. 545 (1979), the Supreme Court held that habeas petitioners could challenge the racial composition of grand juries even when the claim had been litigated and rejected in the state court. Although on the merits the Court found that there was no discrimination, the Court emphasized the availability of habeas corpus review to determine the issue. The Court, in an opinion by Justice Blackmun, said that federal habeas review was "necessary to ensure that constitutional defects in the state judiciary's grand jury selection procedure are not overlooked by the very judges who operate that system." Thus the Court concluded that a claim of discrimination in grand jury selection is not rendered harmless by a subsequent determination of guilt beyond a reasonable doubt by a petit jury and that *Stone* did not apply to foreclose federal court habeas review.

Likewise, the Supreme Court held that the constitutionality of jury instructions concerning the standard of proof to be applied could be challenged on habeas corpus even though the issue had been presented and decided at trial. In Jackson v. Virginia, 443 U.S. 307 (1979), the Court held that habeas corpus review is available for a petitioner who claims that "no rational trier of fact" could have concluded that the state presented sufficient evidence to establish each element of the crime beyond a reasonable doubt. The Court expressly stated that this contention could be relitigated on habeas corpus even though it had been rejected by the state courts.

In Kimmelman v. Morrison, 477 U.S. 365 (1986), the Supreme Court held that a Sixth Amendment claim of ineffective assistance of counsel could be relitigated on habeas corpus, even where the attorney's error was a failure to raise Fourth Amendment objections to the introduction of evidence. In *Kimmelman*, the defendant was convicted of rape largely on the basis of evidence obtained in an allegedly illegal search. The defendant sought habeas corpus relief both on the grounds that illegally seized evidence was admitted and that the defense attorney's failure to object to the introduction of the evidence constituted ineffective assistance of counsel.

The Supreme Court held that although Stone v. Powell barred litigating the Fourth Amendment claim on habeas corpus, the Sixth Amendment issue of ineffective assistance of counsel could be relitigated in federal court. The

Court, in an opinion by Justice Brennan, observed that "[t]he right to counsel is a fundamental right of criminal defendants; it assures the fairness, and thus the legitimacy of our adversary process." As such the Court concluded that "while respondent's defaulted Fourth Amendment claim is one element of proof of his Sixth Amendment claim, the two claims have separate identities and reflect different constitutional values."

Most recently and most importantly, in Withrow v. Williams, 507 U.S. 680 (1993), the Court refused to extend Stone v. Powell to *Miranda* claims. Justice Souter, writing for the Court, declared, "Today we hold that *Stone*'s restriction on the exercise of federal habeas jurisdiction does not extend to a state prisoner's claim that his conviction rests on statements obtained in violation of the safeguards mandated by Miranda v. Arizona (1966)."

The decision provided the occasion for the majority and dissenting justices to express very different views about *Miranda* and its constitutional status. Justice Souter, writing for the majority, stated:

> We have made it clear that *Stone*'s limitation on federal habeas relief was not jurisdictional in nature, but rested on prudential concerns counseling against the application of the Fourth Amendment exclusionary rule on collateral review. We simply concluded in *Stone* that the costs of applying the exclusionary rule on collateral review outweighed any potential advantage to be gained by applying it there.
>
> Petitioner, supported by the United States as amicus curiae, argues that *Miranda*'s safeguards are not constitutional in character, but merely "prophylactic," and that in consequence habeas review should not extend to a claim that a state conviction rests on statements obtained in the absence of those safeguards. We accept petitioner's premise for purposes of this case, but not her conclusion.
>
> The *Miranda* Court did of course caution that the Constitution requires no "particular solution for the inherent compulsions of the interrogation process," and left it open to a State to meet its burden by adopting "other procedures . . . at least as effective in apprising accused persons" of their rights. The Court indeed acknowledged that, in barring introduction of a statement obtained without the required warnings, *Miranda* might exclude a confession that we would not condemn as "involuntary in traditional terms," and for this reason we have sometimes called the *Miranda* safeguards "prophylactic" in nature. Calling the *Miranda* safeguards "prophylactic," however, is a far cry from putting *Miranda* on all fours with *Mapp*, or from rendering *Miranda* subject to *Stone*.
>
> As we explained in *Stone*, the *Mapp* rule "is not a personal constitutional right," but serves to deter future constitutional violations; although it mitigates the juridical consequences of invading the defendant's privacy, the exclusion of evidence at trial can do nothing to remedy the completed and wholly extrajudicial Fourth Amendment violation. Nor can the *Mapp* rule be thought to enhance the soundness of the criminal process by improving the reliability of evidence introduced at trial. Quite the contrary, as we explained in *Stone*, the evidence excluded under *Mapp* "is typically reliable and often the most probative information bearing on the guilt or innocence of the defendant."
>
> *Miranda* differs from *Mapp* in both respects. "Prophylactic" though it may be, in protecting a defendant's Fifth Amendment privilege against self-incrimination, *Miranda* safeguards "a fundamental trial right." The privilege embodies "principles of humanity and civil liberty, which had been secured in the mother country only after years of struggle," and reflects "many of our fundamental values and

most noble aspirations: . . . our preference for an accusatorial rather than an inquisitorial system of criminal justice"; our fear that self-incriminating statements will be elicited by inhumane treatment and abuses; our sense of fair play which dictates "a fair state-individual balance by requiring the government to leave the individual alone until good cause is shown for disturbing him and by requiring the government in its contest with the individual to shoulder the entire load"; our respect for the inviolability of the human personality and of the right of each individual "to a private enclave where he may lead a private life"; our distrust of self-deprecatory statements; and our realization that the privilege, while sometimes "a shelter to the guilty," is often "a protection to the innocent."

Nor does the Fifth Amendment "trial right" protected by *Miranda* serve some value necessarily divorced from the correct ascertainment of guilt. "[A] system of criminal law enforcement which comes to depend on the confession will, in the long run, be less reliable and more subject to abuses than a system relying on independent investigation." By bracing against "the possibility of unreliable statements in every instance of in-custody interrogation," *Miranda* serves to guard against "the use of unreliable statements at trial."

Finally, and most importantly, eliminating review of *Miranda* claims would not significantly benefit the federal courts in their exercise of habeas jurisdiction, or advance the cause of federalism in any substantial way. As one amicus concedes, eliminating habeas review of *Miranda* issues would not prevent a state prisoner from simply converting his barred *Miranda* claim into a due process claim that his conviction rested on an involuntary confession. Indeed, although counsel could provide us with no empirical basis for projecting the consequence of adopting petitioner's position, it seems reasonable to suppose that virtually all *Miranda* claims would simply be recast in this way.

If that is so, the federal courts would certainly not have heard the last of *Miranda* on collateral review. Under the due process approach, as we have already seen, courts look to the totality of circumstances to determine whether a confession was voluntary. Those potential circumstances include not only the crucial element of police coercion, the length of the interrogation, its location, the defendant's maturity, education, physical condition, and mental health. They also include the failure of police to advise the defendant of his rights to remain silent and to have counsel present during custodial interrogation. We could lock the front door against *Miranda*, but not the back.

We thus fail to see how abdicating *Miranda*'s bright-line (or, at least, brighter-line) rules in favor of an exhaustive totality-of-circumstances approach on habeas would do much of anything to lighten the burdens placed on busy federal courts. We likewise fail to see how purporting to eliminate *Miranda* issues from federal habeas would go very far to relieve such tensions as *Miranda* may now raise between the two judicial systems. Relegation of habeas petitioners to straight involuntariness claims would not likely reduce the amount of litigation, and each such claim would in any event present a legal question requiring an independent federal determination on habeas.

But four justices would have extended *Stone* to *Miranda* claims. Justice O'Connor, with whom the chief justice joined, dissented and expressed a very different view of *Miranda*. She wrote:

Today the Court permits the federal courts to overturn on habeas the conviction of a double murderer, not on the basis of an inexorable constitutional or statutory command, but because it believes the result desirable from the standpoint of equity and judicial administration. Because the principles that inform our habeas jurisprudence — finality, federalism, and fairness — counsel decisively against the result the Court reaches, I respectfully dissent from this holding.

Today we face the question whether Stone v. Powell should extend to bar claims on habeas that alleged violations of the prophylactic rule of Miranda v. Arizona (1966). Continuing the tradition of caution in this area, the Court answers that question in the negative. This time I must disagree. In my view, the "prudential concerns," that inform our habeas jurisprudence counsel the exclusion of *Miranda* claims just as strongly as they did the exclusionary rule claims at issue in *Stone* itself.

I continue to believe that these same considerations apply to *Miranda* claims with equal, if not greater, force. Like the suppression of the fruits of an illegal search or seizure, the exclusion of statements obtained in violation of *Miranda* is not constitutionally required. This Court repeatedly has held that *Miranda*'s warning requirement is not a dictate of the Fifth Amendment itself, but a prophylactic rule. Because *Miranda* "sweeps more broadly than the Fifth Amendment itself," it excludes some confessions even though the Constitution would not. Indeed, "in the individual case, *Miranda*'s preventive medicine [often] provides a remedy even to the defendant who has suffered no identifiable constitutional harm."

Miranda's overbreadth, of course, is not without justification. The exclusion of unwarned statements provides a strong incentive for the police to adopt "procedural safeguards," against the exaction of compelled or involuntary statements. It also promotes institutional respect for constitutional values. But, like the exclusionary rule for illegally seized evidence, *Miranda*'s prophylactic rule does so at a substantial cost. Unlike involuntary or compelled statements — which are of dubious reliability and are therefore inadmissible for any purpose — confessions obtained in violation of *Miranda* are not necessarily untrustworthy. In fact, because voluntary statements are "trustworthy" even when obtained without proper warnings, their suppression actually impairs the pursuit of truth by concealing probative information from the trier of fact.

When the case is on direct review, that damage to the truth-seeking function is deemed an acceptable sacrifice for the deterrence and respect for constitutional values that the *Miranda* rule brings. But once a case is on collateral review, the balance between the costs and benefits shifts; the interests of federalism, finality, and fairness compel *Miranda*'s exclusion from habeas. The benefit of enforcing *Miranda* through habeas is marginal at best. To the extent *Miranda* ensures the exclusion of involuntary statements, that task can be performed more accurately by adjudicating the voluntariness question directly. And, to the extent exclusion of voluntary but unwarned confessions serves a deterrent function, "[t]he awarding of habeas relief years after conviction will often strike like lightning, and it is absurd to think that this added possibility . . . will have any appreciable effect on police training or behavior."

Despite its meager benefits, the relitigation of *Miranda* claims on habeas imposes substantial costs. Just like the application of the exclusionary rule, application of *Miranda*'s prophylactic rule on habeas consumes scarce judicial resources on an issue unrelated to guilt or innocence. No less than the exclusionary rule, it undercuts finality. It creates tension between the state and federal courts. And it upsets the division of responsibilities that underlies our federal system. But most troubling of all, *Miranda*'s application on habeas sometimes precludes the just application of law altogether. The order excluding the statement will often be issued "years after trial, when a new trial may be a practical impossibility." Whether the Court admits it or not, the grim result of applying *Miranda* on habeas will be, time and time again, "the release of an admittedly guilty individual who may pose a continuing threat to society."

Any rule that so demonstrably renders truth and society "the loser," "bear[s] a heavy burden of justification, and must be carefully limited to the circumstances in which it will pay its way by deterring official lawlessness." That burden is heavier still on collateral review. In light of the meager deterrent benefit it brings and the tremendous costs it imposes, in my view application of *Miranda*'s prophylactic rule on habeas "falls short" of justification.

As the Court emphasizes today, *Miranda*'s prophylactic rule is now 27 years old; the police and the state courts have indeed grown accustomed to it. But it is precisely because the rule is well accepted that there is little further benefit to enforcing it on habeas. We can depend on law enforcement officials to administer warnings in the first instance and the state courts to provide a remedy when law enforcement officers err. None of the Court's asserted justifications for enforcing Miranda's prophylactic rule through habeas — neither reverence for the Fifth Amendment nor the concerns of reliability, efficiency, and federalism — counsel in favor of the Court's chosen course. Indeed, in my view they cut in precisely the opposite direction. The Court may reconsider its decision when presented with empirical data. But I see little reason for such a costly delay. Logic and experience are at our disposal now. And they amply demonstrate that applying *Miranda*'s prophylactic rule on habeas does not increase the amount of justice dispensed; it only increases the frequency with which the admittedly guilty go free. In my view, *Miranda* imposes such grave costs and produces so little benefit on habeas that its continued application is neither tolerable nor justified.

Justice Scalia also wrote a dissent, with which Justice Thomas joined, in which he said:

In my view, both the Court and Justice O'Connor disregard the most powerful equitable consideration: that Williams has already had full and fair opportunity to litigate this claim. He had the opportunity to raise it in the Michigan trial court; he did so and lost. He had the opportunity to seek review of the trial court's judgment in the Michigan Court of Appeals; he did so and lost. Finally, he had the opportunity to seek discretionary review of that Court of Appeals judgment in both the Michigan Supreme Court and this Court; he did so and review was denied. The question at this stage is whether, given all that, a federal habeas court should now reopen the issue and adjudicate the *Miranda* claim anew. The answer seems to me obvious: it should not. That would be the course followed by a federal habeas court reviewing a federal conviction; it mocks our federal system to accord state convictions less respect.

So, at least for now, the only constitutional claims that cannot be raised on habeas corpus are Fourth Amendment exclusionary rule claims that have had a full and fair opportunity to be litigated in state court.

6. Has There Been a Procedural Default, and If So, Is There Either Cause and Prejudice or an Adequate Showing of Actual Innocence?

Criminal defendants are required to raise their constitutional claims during their trials and direct appeals. The failure to do so is deemed a procedural default. The question is whether such procedural defaults bar a convicted defendant from then raising the issue on habeas corpus.

The law has changed dramatically over the past half century concerning when a defendant may present a matter on habeas corpus that was not litigated at the trial. Under the Warren Court's decisions, a defendant was allowed to raise matters not argued in the state courts unless it could be demonstrated that the defendant deliberately chose to bypass the state court procedures. In other words, there was a strong presumption that procedural defaults would not bar federal habeas corpus review.

In Fay v. Noia, 372 U.S. 391 (1963), the Supreme Court held that an individual convicted in state court may raise on habeas issues that were not presented at trial, unless it can be demonstrated that he or she deliberately chose to bypass the state procedures. In *Fay*, three codefendants were convicted. Two of the defendants appealed and were successful in having their convictions overturned because of the manner in which their confessions were obtained. Noia, the third defendant, then tried to obtain relief in the New York state courts. The New York courts, however, denied Noia's motion to have his conviction overturned because his failure to appeal constituted a procedural default precluding review.

The United States Supreme Court rejected the argument that failure to comply with state procedures bars federal court review on habeas corpus. The Court concluded that "a forfeiture of remedies does not legitimize the unconstitutional conduct by which . . . [a] conviction was procured." In *Fay*, the Court perceived its role and the purpose of habeas corpus as preventing the detention of individuals whose conviction resulted from unconstitutional conduct. The Court said that a habeas petitioner would be foreclosed from raising an issue on the ground that it was not presented at trial only if he or she "deliberately bypassed the orderly procedure of the state courts."

In sharp contrast, the Burger and Rehnquist Courts departed from and ultimately overruled *Fay*. The Court held that a defendant could present matters on habeas corpus that were not raised at the trial only if the defendant could demonstrate either actual innocence or good "cause" for the procedural default, and either "prejudice" from the federal court's refusal to hear the matter or a showing of actual innocence. Under this approach, there is a strong presumption that procedural defaults in state court will preclude habeas corpus litigation.

Wainwright v. Sykes was the key Supreme Court case signaling a departure from Fay v. Noia and a different approach to handling procedural defaults on habeas corpus. In reading Wainwright v. Sykes, it is important to consider how it rests on different assumptions than Fay v. Noia concerning why procedural defaults happen and the fairness of precluding constitutional claims from being raised.

WAINWRIGHT v. SYKES

433 U.S. 72 (1977)

Justice REHNQUIST delivered the opinion of the Court.

We granted certiorari to consider the availability of federal habeas corpus to review a state convict's claim that testimony was admitted at his trial in violation of his rights under Miranda v. Arizona (1966), a claim which the Florida courts have previously refused to consider on the merits because of noncompliance with a state contemporaneous-objection rule.

Respondent Sykes was convicted of third-degree murder after a jury trial in the Circuit Court of DeSoto County. He testified at trial that on the evening of January 8, 1972, he told his wife to summon the police because he had just shot Willie Gilbert. Other evidence indicated that when the police arrived at respondent's trailer home, they found Gilbert dead of a shotgun wound, lying a few feet from the front porch. Shortly after their arrival, respondent came from across the road and volunteered that he had shot Gilbert, and a few minutes later respondent's wife approached the police and told them the same thing. Sykes was immediately arrested and taken to the police station.

Once there, it is conceded that he was read his *Miranda* rights, and that he declined to seek the aid of counsel and indicated a desire to talk. He then made a statement, which was admitted into evidence at trial through the testimony of the two officers who heard it, to the effect that he had shot Gilbert from the front porch of his trailer home. There were several references during the trial to respondent's consumption of alcohol during the preceding day and to his apparent state of intoxication, facts which were acknowledged by the officers who arrived at the scene. At no time during the trial, however, was the admissibility of any of respondent's statements challenged by his counsel on the ground that respondent had not understood the *Miranda* warnings. Nor did the trial judge question their admissibility on his own motion or hold a factfinding hearing bearing on that issue.

Respondent appealed his conviction, but apparently did not challenge the admissibility of the inculpatory statements. He later filed in the trial court a motion to vacate the conviction and, in the State District Court of Appeals and Supreme Court, petitions for habeas corpus. These filings, apparently for the first time, challenged the statements made to police on grounds of involuntariness. In all of these efforts respondent was unsuccessful.

The simple legal question before the Court calls for a construction of the language of 28 U.S.C. §2254(a), which provides that the federal courts shall entertain an application for a writ of habeas corpus "in behalf of a person in custody pursuant to the judgment of a state court only on the ground that he is in custody in violation of the Constitution or laws or treaties of the United States." But, to put it mildly, we do not write on a clean slate in construing this statutory provision.

As to the role of adequate and independent state grounds, it is a well-established principle of federalism that a state decision resting on an adequate foundation of state substantive law is immune from review in the federal courts. The application of this principle in the context of a federal habeas proceeding has therefore excluded from consideration any questions of state substantive law, and thus effectively barred federal habeas review where questions of that sort are either the only ones raised by a petitioner or are in themselves dispositive of his case. The area of controversy which has developed has concerned the reviewability of federal claims which the state court has declined to pass on because not presented in the manner prescribed by its procedural rules.

We conclude that Florida procedure did, consistently with the United States Constitution, require that respondents' confession be challenged at trial or not at all, and thus his failure to timely object to its admission amounted to an independent and adequate state procedural ground which would have prevented direct review here. We thus come to the crux of this case. Shall the rule of Francis v. Henderson, supra, barring federal habeas review absent a showing of "cause" and "prejudice" attendant to a state procedural waiver, be applied to a waived objection to the admission of a confession at trial? We answer that question in the affirmative.

[S]ince Brown v. Allen (1953), it has been the rule that the federal habeas petitioner who claims he is detained pursuant to a final judgment of a state court in violation of the United States Constitution is entitled to have the federal habeas court make its own independent determination of his federal claim, without being bound by the determination on the merits of that claim reached in the state proceedings. This rule of Brown v. Allen is in no way changed by our holding today. Rather, we deal only with contentions of federal law which were not resolved on the merits in the state proceeding due to respondent's failure to raise them there as required by state procedure. We leave open for resolution in future decisions the precise definition of the "cause"-and-"prejudice" standard, and note here only that it is narrower than the standard set forth in dicta in Fay v. Noia, which would make federal habeas review generally available to state convicts absent a knowing and deliberate waiver of the federal constitutional contention. It is the sweeping language of Fay v. Noia, going far beyond the facts of the case eliciting it, which we today reject.

The reasons for our rejection of it are several. The contemporaneous-objection rule itself is by no means peculiar to Florida, and deserves greater respect than *Fay* gives it, both for the fact that it is employed by a coordinate jurisdiction within the federal system and for the many interests which it serves in its own right. A contemporaneous objection enables the record to be made with respect to the constitutional claim when the recollections of witnesses are freshest, not years later in a federal habeas proceeding. It enables the judge who observed the demeanor of those witnesses to make the factual determinations necessary for properly deciding the federal constitutional question.

A contemporaneous-objection rule may lead to the exclusion of the evidence objected to, thereby making a major contribution to finality in criminal litigation. Without the evidence claimed to be vulnerable on federal constitutional grounds, the jury may acquit the defendant, and that will be the end of the case; or it may nonetheless convict the defendant, and he will have one less federal constitutional claim to assert in his federal habeas petition. Subtler considerations as well militate in favor of honoring a state contemporaneous-objection rule. An objection on the spot may force the prosecution to take a hard look at its whole card, and even if the prosecutor thinks that the state trial judge will admit the evidence he must contemplate the possibility of reversal by the state appellate courts or the ultimate issuance of a federal writ of habeas corpus based on the impropriety of the state court's rejection of the federal constitutional claim.

We think that the rule of Fay v. Noia, broadly stated, may encourage "sandbagging" on the part of defense lawyers, who may take their chances on a verdict of not guilty in a state trial court with the intent to raise their constitutional claims in a federal habeas court if their initial gamble does not pay off. The refusal of federal habeas courts to honor contemporaneous-objection rules may also make state courts themselves less stringent in their enforcement. Under the rule of Fay v. Noia, state appellate courts know that a federal constitutional issue raised for the first time in the proceeding before them may well be decided in any event by a federal habeas tribunal. Thus, their choice is between addressing the issue notwithstanding the petitioner's failure to timely object, or else face the prospect that the federal habeas court will decide the question without the benefit of their views.

The failure of the federal habeas courts generally to require compliance with a contemporaneous-objection rule tends to detract from the perception of the trial of a criminal case in state court as a decisive and portentous event. A defendant has been accused of a serious crime, and this is the time and place set for him to be tried by a jury of his peers and found either guilty or not guilty by that jury. To the greatest extent possible all issues which bear on this charge should be determined in this proceeding: the accused is in the court-room, the jury is in the box, the judge is on the bench, and the witnesses, having been subpoenaed and duly sworn, await their turn to testify. Society's resources have been concentrated at that time and place in order to decide, within the limits of human fallibility, the question of guilt or innocence of one of its citizens. Any procedural rule which encourages the result that those proceedings be as free of error as possible is thoroughly desirable, and the contemporaneous-objection rule surely falls within this classification.

We believe the adoption of the [cause and prejudice] rule in this situation will have the salutary effect of making the state trial on the merits the "main event," so to speak, rather than a "tryout on the road" for what will later be the determinative federal habeas hearing. There is nothing in the Constitution or in the language of §2254 which requires that the state trial on the issue of guilt or innocence be devoted largely to the testimony of fact witnesses directed to the elements of the state crime, while only later will there occur in a federal habeas hearing a full airing of the federal constitutional claims which were not raised in the state proceedings. If a criminal defendant thinks that an action of the state trial court is about to deprive him of a federal constitutional right there is every reason for his following state procedure in making known his objection.

The "cause"-and-"prejudice" exception will afford an adequate guarantee, we think, that the rule will not prevent a federal habeas court from adjudicating for the first time the federal constitutional claim of a defendant who in the absence of such an adjudication will be the victim of a miscarriage of justice. Whatever precise content may be given those terms by later cases, we feel confident in holding without further elaboration that they do not exist here. Respondent has advanced no explanation whatever for his failure to object at trial, and, as the proceeding unfolded, the trial judge is certainly not to be faulted for failing to question the admission of the confession himself. The other evidence of guilt presented at trial, moreover, was substantial to a degree that would negate any possibility of actual prejudice resulting to the respondent from the admission of his inculpatory statement.

Justice BRENNAN, with whom Justice MARSHALL joins, dissenting.

Over the course of the last decade, the deliberate-bypass standard announced in Fay v. Noia (1963), has played a central role in efforts by the federal judiciary to accommodate the constitutional rights of the individual with the States' interests in the integrity of their judicial procedural regimes. The Court today decides that this standard should no longer apply with respect to procedural defaults occurring during the trial of a criminal defendant. In its place, the Court adopts the two-part "cause"-and-"prejudice" test. [T]oday's decision makes no effort to provide concrete guidance as to the content of those terms. More particularly, left unanswered is the thorny question that must be recognized to be central to a realistic rationalization of this area of law: How should the federal habeas court treat a procedural default in a state court that is attributable purely and simply to the error or negligence of a defendant's trial counsel? Because this key issue remains unresolved, I shall attempt in this opinion a re-examination of the policies that should inform and in *Fay* did inform the selection of the standard governing the availability of federal habeas corpus jurisdiction in the face of an intervening procedural default in the state court.

I

I begin with the threshold question: What is the meaning and import of a procedural default? If it could be assumed that a procedural default more often than not is the product of a defendant's conscious refusal to abide by the duly constituted, legitimate processes of the state courts, then I might agree that a regime of collateral review weighted in favor of a State's procedural rules would be warranted. *Fay*, however, recognized that such rarely is the case; and therein lies *Fay*'s basic unwillingness to embrace a view of habeas jurisdiction that results in "an airtight system of (procedural) forfeitures."

This, of course, is not to deny that there are times when the failure to heed a state procedural requirement stems from an intentional decision to avoid the presentation of constitutional claims to the state forum. *Fay* was not insensitive to this possibility. Indeed, the very purpose of its bypass test is to detect and enforce such intentional procedural forfeitures of outstanding constitutionally based claims. *Fay* does so through application of the long-standing rule used to test whether action or inaction on the part of a criminal defendant should be construed as a decision to surrender the assertion of rights secured by the Constitution: To be an effective waiver, there must be "an intentional relinquishment or abandonment of a known right or privilege." Johnson v. Zerbst (1938). Incorporating this standard, *Fay* recognized that if one "understandingly and knowingly forewent the privilege of seeking to vindicate his federal claims in the state courts, whether for strategic, tactical or any other reasons that can fairly be described as the deliberate by-passing of state procedures, then it is open to the federal court on habeas to deny him all relief. . . ." For this reason, the Court's assertion that it "think[s]" that the *Fay* rule encourages intentional "sandbagging" on the part of the defense lawyers is without basis; certainly the Court points to no cases or commentary arising during the past 15 years of actual use of the *Fay* test to support this criticism. Rather, a consistent reading of case law demonstrates that the bypass formula has provided a workable vehicle for protecting the integrity of state rules in those instances when such protection would be both meaningful and just.

But having created the bypass exception to the availability of collateral review, *Fay* recognized that intentional, tactical forfeitures are not the norm upon which to build a rational system of federal habeas jurisdiction. In the ordinary case, litigants simply have no incentive to slight the state tribunal, since constitutional adjudication on the state and federal levels are not mutually exclusive. Brown v. Allen (1953). Under the regime of collateral review recognized since the days of Brown v. Allen, and enforced by the *Fay* bypass test, no rational lawyer would risk the "sandbagging" feared by the Court. If a constitutional challenge is not properly raised on the state level, the explanation generally will be found elsewhere than in an intentional tactical decision.

In brief then, any realistic system of federal habeas corpus jurisdiction must be premised on the reality that the ordinary procedural default is born of the inadvertence, negligence, inexperience, or incompetence of trial counsel. *Fay*'s answer thus is plain: the bypass test simply refuses to credit what is essentially a lawyer's mistake as a forfeiture of constitutional rights. I persist in the belief that the interests of Sykes and the State of Florida are best rationalized by adherence to this test, and by declining to react to inadvertent defaults through the creation of an "airtight system of forfeitures."

II

What are the interests that Sykes can assert in preserving the availability of federal collateral relief in the face of his inadvertent state procedural default? Two are paramount.

As is true with any federal habeas applicant, Sykes seeks access to the federal court for the determination of the validity of his federal constitutional claim. Since at least Brown v. Allen, it has been recognized that the "fair effect [of] the habeas corpus jurisdiction as enacted by Congress" entitles a state prisoner to such federal review. While some of my Brethen may feel uncomfortable with this congressional choice of policy, the Legislative Branch nonetheless remains entirely free to determine that the constitutional rights of an individual subject to state custody are best preserved by interposing the federal courts between the states and the people, as guardians of the people's federal rights.

With respect to federal habeas corpus jurisdiction, Congress explicitly chose to effectuate the federal court's primary responsibility for preserving federal rights and privileges by authorizing the litigation of constitutional claims and defenses in a district court after the State vindicates its own interest through trial of the substantive criminal offense in the state courts. This, of course, was not the only course that Congress might have followed: As an alternative, it might well have decided entirely to circumvent all state procedure through the expansion of existing federal removal statutes such as 28 U.S.C. §§1442(a)(1) and 1443, thereby authorizing the pretrial transfer of all state criminal cases to the federal courts whenever federal defenses or claims are in issue. But liberal posttrial federal review is the redress that Congress ultimately chose to allow and the consequences of a state procedural default should be evaluated in conformance with this policy choice. Certainly, we can all agree that once a state court has assumed jurisdiction of a criminal case, the integrity of its own process is a matter of legitimate concern. The *Fay* bypass test, by seeking to discover intentional abuses of the rules of the state forum, is, I believe, compatible with this state institutional interest. But whether *Fay* was correct in penalizing a litigant solely for his intentional forfeitures properly must be read in light of Congress' desired norm of widened posttrial access to the federal courts. If the standard adopted today is later construed to require that the simple mistakes of attorneys are to be treated as binding forfeitures, it would serve to subordinate the fundamental rights contained in our constitutional charter to inadvertent defaults of rules promulgated by state agencies, and would essentially leave it to the States, through the enactment of procedure and the certification of the competence of local attorneys, to determine whether a habeas applicant will be permitted the access to the federal forum that is guaranteed him by Congress.

Thus, I remain concerned that undue deference to local procedure can only serve to undermine the ready access to a federal court to which a state defendant otherwise is entitled. But federal review is not the full measure of Sykes' interest, for there is another of even greater immediacy: assuring that his constitutional claims can be addressed to some court. For the obvious consequence of barring Sykes from the federal courthouse is to insulate Florida's alleged constitutional violation from any and all judicial review because of a lawyer's mistake. From the standpoint of the habeas petitioner, it is a harsh rule indeed that denies him "any review at all where the state has granted none," particularly when he would have enjoyed both state and federal consideration had his attorney not erred.

In sum, I believe that *Fay*'s commitment to enforcing intentional but not inadvertent procedural defaults offers a realistic measure of protection for the habeas corpus petitioner seeking federal review of federal claims that were not litigated before the State. The threatened creation of a more "airtight system of forfeitures" would effectively deprive habeas petitioners of the opportunity for litigating their constitutional claims before any forum and would disparage the paramount importance of constitutional rights in our system of government. Such a restriction of habeas corpus jurisdiction should be countenanced, I submit, only if it fairly can be concluded that *Fay*'s focus on knowing and voluntary forfeitures unduly interferes with the legitimate interests of state courts or institutions. The majority offers no suggestion that actual experience has shown that *Fay*'s bypass test can be criticized on this score.

III

A regime of federal habeas corpus jurisdiction that permits the reopening of state procedural defaults does not invalidate any state procedural rule as such; Florida's courts remain entirely free to enforce their own rules as they choose, and to deny any and all state rights and remedies to a defendant who fails to comply with applicable state procedure. The relevant inquiry is whether more is required specifically, whether the fulfillment of important interests of the State necessitates that federal courts be called upon to impose additional sanctions for inadvertent noncompliance with state procedural requirements such as the contemporaneous-objection rule involved here.

Florida, of course, can point to a variety of legitimate interests in seeking allegiance to its reasonable procedural requirements, the contemporaneous-objection rule included. The question remains, however, whether any of these policies or interests are efficiently and fairly served by enforcing both intentional and inadvertent defaults pursuant to the identical stringent standard. I remain convinced that when one pierces the surface justifications for a harsher rule posited by the Court, no standard stricter than *Fay*'s deliberate-bypass test is realistically defensible.

Punishing a lawyer's unintentional errors by closing the federal courthouse door to his client is both a senseless and misdirected method of deterring the slighting of state rules. It is senseless because unplanned and unintentional action of any kind generally is not subject to deterrence; and, to the extent that it is hoped that a threatened sanction addressed to the defense will induce greater care and caution on the part of trial lawyers, thereby forestalling negligent conduct or error, the potential loss of all valuable state remedies would be sufficient to this end. And it is a misdirected sanction because even if the penalization of incompetence or carelessness will encourage more thorough legal training and trial preparation, the habeas applicant, as opposed to his lawyer, hardly is the proper recipient of such a penalty. Especially with fundamental constitutional rights at stake, no fictional relationship of principal-agent or the like can justify holding the criminal defendant accountable for the naked errors of his attorney. This is especially true when so many indigent defendants are without any realistic choice in selecting who ultimately represents them at trial. Indeed, if responsibility for error must be apportioned between the parties, it is the State, through its attorney's admissions and certification policies, that is more fairly held to blame for the fact that practicing lawyers too often are ill-prepared or ill-equipped to act carefully and knowledgeably when faced with decisions governed by state procedural requirements.

Hence, while I can well agree that the proper functioning of our system of criminal justice, both federal and state, necessarily places heavy reliance on the professionalism and judgment of trial attorneys, I cannot accept a system that ascribes the absolute forfeiture of an individual's constitutional claims to situations where his lawyer manifestly exercises no professional judgment at all where carelessness, mistake, or ignorance is the explanation for a procedural default. Of course, it is regrettable that certain errors that might have been cured earlier had trial counsel acted expeditiously must be corrected collaterally and belatedly. I can understand the Court's wistfully wishing for the day when the trial was the sole, binding and final "event" of the adversarial process although I hesitate to agree that in the eyes of the criminal defendant it has ever ceased being the "main" one. But it should be plain that in the real world, the interest in finality is repeatedly compromised in numerous ways that arise with far greater frequency than do procedural defaults.

In short, I believe that the demands of our criminal justice system warrant visiting the mistakes of a trial attorney on the head of a habeas corpus applicant only when we are convinced that the lawyer actually exercised his expertise and judgment in his client's service, and with his client's knowing and intelligent participation where possible. This, of course, is the precise system of habeas review established by Fay v. Noia.

––––––––––

Although *Wainwright* and its progeny implicitly overruled *Fay*, it was not until Coleman v. Thompson, 501 U.S. 722 (1991), that *Fay* was explicitly overturned and the Court held that all procedural defaults are to be evaluated under the cause and prejudice test. Justice O'Connor, writing for the majority, declared:

> We now make it explicit: in all cases in which a state prisoner has defaulted his federal claims in state court pursuant to an independent and adequate state procedural rule, federal habeas review of the claim is barred unless the prisoner can demonstrate cause for the default and actual prejudice as a result of the alleged violation of federal law, or demonstrate that the failure to consider the claim will result in a fundamental miscarriage of justice.

In *Coleman*, a defendant in a capital case was denied appeal to the state court of appeals of his state habeas petition because he filed the notice of appeals three days late. The issue was whether the procedural error precluded federal habeas review. The Supreme Court explained that Wainwright v. Sykes effectively had overruled Fay v. Noia and that the petitioner's procedural default would preclude federal habeas review unless he could show cause and prejudice or a likelihood of actual innocence. In May 1992, Coleman was executed in Virginia despite some evidence that he was actually innocent.[43] No federal court ever heard Coleman's claim.

While the *Wainwright* decision clearly adopted the "cause" and "prejudice" test for habeas corpus review, the Court explicitly avoided defining these two terms. Subsequent cases have given content to this test. Several decisions have focused on what is sufficient "cause" to excuse a state court procedural default and permit a habeas corpus petitioner to raise matters not presented in the state courts.

Engle v. Isaac, 456 U.S. 107 (1982), indicated how difficult it is to show "cause." In *Engle*, a defendant used habeas corpus to challenge the constitutionality of the jury instructions used in his trial. In a case decided subsequent to his conviction, the Ohio Supreme Court held that the type of jury instructions given violated Ohio law and that its ruling applied retroactively to all cases in which they had been used. Nonetheless, the Supreme Court held that the issue could not be raised on habeas corpus because the defense counsel did not object at trial, even though at that time there was no reason to think that the instructions were unconstitutional. Justice O'Connor, writing for the majority, concluded, "[T]he futility of presenting an objection to the state courts cannot alone constitute cause for failure to object at trial. . . . Even a state court that has previously rejected a constitutional argument may decide, upon reflection, that the contention is valid."

The Court in *Engle* made it clear that it took a very different view of habeas corpus than had the Warren Court. Justice O'Connor expressed great reservations about the availability of habeas corpus because it imposes "significant costs" on society, including "undermin[ing] the usual principles of finality" and "cost[ing] society the right to punish admitted offenders." According to the Court, these cost considerations outweigh the value of providing relief to an individual who was convicted and incarcerated as a result of admittedly unconstitutional jury instructions.

Two years after *Engle*, in Reed v. Ross, 468 U.S. 1 (1984), the Supreme Court recognized that under limited circumstances, "where a constitutional claim is so novel that its legal basis is not reasonably available to counsel," a defendant may present matters on habeas that were not raised at trial. *Reed* was a 5-4 decision, with four of the justices who were in the majority in *Engle*—Justices Burger, Blackmun, O'Connor, and Rehnquist—dissenting.

---

43. *See* Jill Smolowe, *Must This Man Die?*, Time, May 18, 1992, at 40.

Like *Engle*, *Reed* involved a challenge to jury instructions about the burden of
proof for a claim of self-defense. The majority distinguished *Reed* from *Engle*
based on the time the trial occurred. The trial took place in *Engle* after the
Supreme Court's 1970 decision in In re Winship, 397 U.S. 358 (1969), which
required the state to prove every element of a crime beyond a reasonable
doubt. Thus, the *Engle* Court concluded that in light of *Winship* and
subsequent lower court cases interpreting it, the defendant's attorney
should have thought to object to the jury instructions. But in *Ross*, the
trial occurred in 1969, before *Winship*, and the Court decided that it
would be inappropriate to require the defense attorney to anticipate a
major Supreme Court decision.

In allowing the defendant to challenge the jury instruction on habeas
corpus, the Supreme Court in *Reed* identified circumstances in which habeas
petitioners can raise issues based on cases decided after their trial but
applied retroactively. The Court's criteria indicated the breadth of the
Engle holding and the narrowness of the *Reed* exception. Justice Brennan,
writing for a plurality, said that a defendant could present claims that
became apparent subsequent to the trial when there was a Supreme Court
decision that explicitly overrules precedent, or when the decision overturns
"a longstanding and widespread practice to which the Court has not spoken," or when the decision disapproves "a practice this Court arguably has
sanctioned in prior cases." In short, even in distinguishing *Engle*, the *Reed*
Court affirmed its conclusion that mere novelty of a claim is not sufficient
cause for a defense counsel's failure to present it at trial. As Professor Resnik
notes, "[a]lthough the *Ross* plurality found a crevice in the seeming impregnable 'cause' requirement of *Isaac*, the aperture is narrow. . . . Under *Ross*,
the hurdle of 'cause' only can be surmounted in rare instances."

In a subsequent decision concerning the meaning of "cause," Lee v.
Kemna, 534 U.S. 362 (2002), the Supreme Court found that there was a
sufficient basis for allowing a federal habeas petition to be heard despite
a state procedural default. At a murder trial in Missouri state court, a
defendant asked for an overnight continuance when key witnesses were
not present in the courtroom. The trial judge denied the request for a continuance, explaining that he had a daughter in the hospital and another trial
scheduled to begin the next day. After the defendant was convicted, his
appeal for a violation of due process was denied on the grounds that he
did not follow the Missouri law requiring that requests for continuances
be in writing and supported by affidavits. The federal district court denied
habeas corpus based on the failure to comply with state procedures, and the
United States Court of Appeals for the Eighth Circuit affirmed.

The Supreme Court reversed. Justice Ginsburg, writing for the Court, said
that "[t]here are . . . exceptional cases in which exorbitant application of a
generally sound rule renders the state ground inadequate." Ginsburg
explained that a written motion for a continuance would not have made
any difference; it would not have overcome the reasons why the judge denied
the continuance. Also, the Court said that nothing in Missouri law required

compliance with the procedural rules in a circumstance where there is an unexpected disappearance of a key witness. Finally, the Court emphasized that Lee had substantially complied with the state rules through his motion for a continuance and his explanation of the reasons for the request. Lee v. Kemna is important because it clearly holds that in some circumstances the failure to comply with state procedures will not preclude a subsequent habeas corpus petition.

In its most recent decision concerning procedural default, the Court found that abandonment by a defense lawyer, as opposed to negligence, is sufficient to excuse a procedural default.

MAPLES v. THOMAS

132 S. Ct. 912 (2012)

Justice GINSBURG delivered the opinion of the Court.

Cory R. Maples is an Alabama capital prisoner sentenced to death in 1997 for the murder of two individuals. At trial, he was represented by two appointed lawyers, minimally paid and with scant experience in capital cases. Maples sought postconviction relief in state court, alleging ineffective assistance of counsel and several other trial infirmities. His petition, filed in August 2001, was written by two New York attorneys serving *pro bono*, both associated with the same New York-based large law firm. An Alabama attorney, designated as local counsel, moved the admission of the out-of-state counsel *pro hac vice.* As understood by New York counsel, local counsel would facilitate their appearance, but would undertake no substantive involvement in the case.

In the summer of 2002, while Maples' postconviction petition remained pending in the Alabama trial court, his New York attorneys left the law firm; their new employment disabled them from continuing to represent Maples. They did not inform Maples of their departure and consequent inability to serve as his counsel. Nor did they seek the Alabama trial court's leave to withdraw. Neither they nor anyone else moved for the substitution of counsel able to handle Maples' case.

In May 2003, the Alabama trial court denied Maples' petition. Notices of the court's order were posted to the New York attorneys at the address of the law firm with which they had been associated. Those postings were returned, unopened, to the trial court clerk, who attempted no further mailing. With no attorney of record in fact acting on Maples' behalf, the time to appeal ran out.

Thereafter, Maples petitioned for a writ of habeas corpus in federal court. The District Court and, in turn, the Eleventh Circuit, rejected his petition, pointing to the procedural default in state court, *i.e.,* Maples' failure timely to appeal the Alabama trial court's order denying him postconviction relief. Maples, it is uncontested, was blameless for the default.

The sole question this Court has taken up for review is whether, on the extraordinary facts of Maples' case, there is "cause" to excuse the default. Maples maintains that there is, for the lawyers he believed to be vigilantly representing him had abandoned the case without leave of court, without informing Maples they could no longer represent him, and without securing any recorded substitution of counsel. We agree. Abandoned by counsel, Maples was left unrepresented at a critical time for his state postconviction petition, and he lacked a clue of any need to protect himself *pro se.* In these circumstances, no just system would lay the default at Maples' death-cell door. Satisfied that the requisite cause has been shown, we reverse the Eleventh Circuit's judgment.

I

Alabama sets low eligibility requirements for lawyers appointed to represent indigent capital defendants at trial. Appointed counsel need only be a member of the Alabama bar and have "five years' prior experience in the active practice of criminal law." Experience with capital cases is not required. Nor does the State provide, or require appointed counsel to gain, any capital-case-specific professional education or training.

Appointed counsel in death penalty cases are also undercompensated. Until 1999, the State paid appointed capital defense attorneys just "$40.00 per hour for time expended in court and $20.00 per hour for time reasonably expended out of court in the preparation of [the defendant's] case." Although death penalty litigation is plainly time intensive, the State capped at $1,000 fees recoverable by capital defense attorneys for out-of-court work. Even today, court-appointed attorneys receive only $70 per hour.

Nearly alone among the States, Alabama does not guarantee representation to indigent capital defendants in postconviction proceedings. The State has elected, instead, "to rely on the efforts of typically well-funded [out-of-state] volunteers." Thus, as of 2006, 86% of the attorneys representing Alabama's death row inmates in state collateral review proceedings "either worked for the Equal Justice Initiative (headed by NYU Law professor Bryan Stevenson), out-of-state public interest groups like the Innocence Project, or an out-of-state mega-firm." On occasion, some prisoners sentenced to death receive no postconviction representation at all.

This system was in place when, in 1997, Alabama charged Maples with two counts of capital murder; the victims, Stacy Alan Terry and Barry Dewayne Robinson II, were Maples' friends who, on the night of the murders, had been out on the town with him. Maples pleaded not guilty, and his case proceeded to trial, where he was represented by two court-appointed Alabama attorneys. Only one of them had earlier served in a capital case. Neither counsel had previously tried the penalty phase of a capital case. Compensation for each lawyer was capped at $1,000 for time spent out-of-court preparing Maples' case, and at $40 per hour for in-court services.

Finding Maples guilty on both counts, the jury recommended that he be sentenced to death. The vote was 10 to 2, the minimum number Alabama requires for a death recommendation. Accepting the jury's recommendation, the trial court sentenced Maples to death. On direct appeal, the Alabama Court of Criminal Appeals and the Alabama Supreme Court affirmed the convictions and sentence.

Two out-of-state volunteers represented Maples in postconviction proceedings: Jaasi Munanka and Clara Ingen-Housz, both associates at the New York offices of the Sullivan & Cromwell law firm. At the time, Alabama required out-of-state attorneys to associate local counsel when seeking admission to practice *pro hac vice* before an Alabama court, regardless of the nature of the proceeding. The Alabama Rule further prescribed that the local attorney's name "appear on all notices, orders, pleadings, and other documents filed in the cause," and that local counsel "accept joint and several responsibility with the foreign attorney to the client, to opposing parties and counsel, and to the court or administrative agency in all matters [relating to the case]."

Munanka and Ingen-Housz associated Huntsville, Alabama attorney John Butler as local counsel. Notwithstanding his obligations under Alabama law, Butler informed Munanka and Ingen-Housz, "at the outset," that he would serve as local counsel only for the purpose of allowing the two New York attorneys to appear *pro hac vice* on behalf of Maples. Given his lack of "resources, available time [and] experience," Butler told the Sullivan & Cromwell lawyers, he could not "deal with substantive issues in the case." The Sullivan & Cromwell attorneys accepted Butler's conditions. This arrangement between out-of-state and local attorneys, it appears, was hardly atypical.

With the aid of his *pro bono* counsel, Maples filed a petition for postconviction relief under Alabama Rule of Criminal Procedure 32. Among other claims, Maples asserted that his court-appointed attorneys provided constitutionally ineffective assistance during both guilt and penalty phases of his capital trial. He alleged, in this regard, that his inexperienced and underfunded attorneys failed to develop and raise an obvious intoxication defense, did not object to several egregious instances of prosecutorial misconduct, and woefully underprepared for the penalty phase of his trial.

[I]n the summer of 2002, both Munanka and Ingen-Housz left Sullivan & Cromwell. Munanka gained a clerkship with a federal judge; Ingen-Housz accepted a position with the European Commission in Belgium. Neither attorney told Maples of their departure from Sullivan & Cromwell or of their resulting inability to continue to represent him. In disregard of Alabama law, neither attorney sought the trial court's leave to withdraw. Compounding Munanka's and Ingen-Housz's inaction, no other Sullivan & Cromwell lawyer entered an appearance on Maples' behalf, moved to substitute counsel, or otherwise notified the court of any change in Maples' representation.

Another nine months passed. During this time period, no Sullivan & Cromwell attorneys assigned to Maples' case sought admission to the Alabama bar, entered appearances on Maples' behalf, or otherwise advised the Alabama court that Munanka and Ingen-Housz were no longer Maples' attorneys. Thus, Munanka and Ingen-Housz (along with Butler) remained Maples' listed, and only, "attorneys of record."

There things stood when, in May 2003, the trial court, without holding a hearing, entered an order denying Maples' Rule 32 petition. The clerk of the Alabama trial court mailed copies of the order to Maples' three attorneys of record. He sent Munanka's and Ingen-Housz's copies to Sullivan & Cromwell's New York address, which the pair had provided upon entering their appearances.

When those copies arrived at Sullivan & Cromwell, Munanka and Ingen-Housz had long since departed. The notices, however, were not forwarded to another Sullivan & Cromwell attorney. Instead, a mailroom employee sent the unopened envelopes back to the court. "Returned to Sender— Attempted, Unknown" was stamped on the envelope addressed to Munanka. A similar stamp appeared on the envelope addressed to Ingen-Housz, along with the handwritten notation "Return to Sender—Left Firm."

Upon receiving back the unopened envelopes he had mailed to Munanka and Ingen-Housz, the Alabama court clerk took no further action. In particular, the clerk did not contact Munanka or Ingen-Housz at the personal telephone numbers or home addresses they had provided in their *pro hac vice* applications. Nor did the clerk alert Sullivan & Cromwell or Butler. Butler received his copy of the order, but did not act on it. He assumed that Munanka and Ingen-Housz, who had been "CC'd" on the order, would take care of filing an appeal.

Meanwhile, the clock ticked on Maples' appeal. Under Alabama's Rules of Appellate Procedure, Maples had 42 days to file a notice of appeal from the trial court's May 22, 2003 order denying Maples' petition for postconviction relief. No appeal notice was filed, and the time allowed for filing expired on July 7, 2003.

A little over a month later, on August 13, 2003, Alabama Assistant Attorney General Jon Hayden, the attorney representing the State in Maples' collateral review proceedings, sent a letter directly to Maples. Hayden's letter informed Maples of the missed deadline for initiating an appeal within the State's system, and notified him that four weeks remained during which he could file a federal habeas petition. Hayden mailed the letter to Maples only, using his prison address. No copy was sent to Maples' attorneys of record, or to anyone else acting on Maples' behalf.

Upon receiving the State's letter, Maples immediately contacted his mother. She telephoned Sullivan & Cromwell to inquire about her son's case. *Ibid.* Prompted by her call, Sullivan & Cromwell attorneys Marc De Leeuw, Felice Duffy, and Kathy Brewer submitted a motion, through Butler, asking the trial court to reissue its order denying Maples' Rule 32 petition, thereby restarting the 42-day appeal period.

The trial court denied the motion. Maples next petitioned the Alabama Court of Criminal Appeals for a writ of mandamus, granting him leave to file an out-of-time appeal. Rejecting Maples' plea, the Court of Criminal Appeals determined that, although the clerk had "assumed a duty to notify the parties of the resolution of Maples's Rule 32 petition," the clerk had satisfied that obligation by sending notices to the attorneys of record at the addresses those attorneys provided.

Having exhausted his state postconviction remedies, Maples sought federal habeas corpus relief. Addressing the ineffective-assistance-of-trial-counsel claims Maples stated in his federal petition, the State urged that Maples had forever forfeited those claims. The District Court determined that Maples had defaulted his ineffective-assistance claims, and that he had not shown "cause" sufficient to overcome the default. A divided panel of the Eleventh Circuit affirmed.

II

A

As a rule, a state prisoner's habeas claims may not be entertained by a federal court "when (1) 'a state court [has] declined to address [those] claims because the prisoner had failed to meet a state procedural requirement,' and (2) 'the state judgment rests on independent and adequate state procedural grounds.'" The bar to federal review may be lifted, however, if "the prisoner can demonstrate cause for the [procedural] default [in state court] and actual prejudice as a result of the alleged violation of federal law."

Given the single issue on which we granted review, we will assume, for purposes of this decision, that the Alabama Court of Criminal Appeals' refusal to consider Maples' ineffective-assistance claims rested on an independent and adequate state procedural ground: namely, Maples' failure to satisfy Alabama's Rule requiring a notice of appeal to be filed within 42 days from the trial court's final order. Accordingly, we confine our consideration to the question whether Maples has shown cause to excuse the missed notice of appeal deadline.

Cause for a procedural default exists where "something *external* to the petitioner, something that cannot fairly be attributed to him[,] . . . 'impeded [his] efforts to comply with the State's procedural rule.'" Negligence on the part of a prisoner's postconviction attorney does not qualify as "cause." That is so because the attorney is the prisoner's agent, and under "well-settled principles of agency law," the principal bears the risk of negligent conduct on the part of his agent. Thus, when a petitioner's postconviction attorney misses a filing deadline, the petitioner is bound by the oversight and cannot rely on it to establish cause. We do not disturb that general rule.

A markedly different situation is presented, however, when an attorney abandons his client without notice, and thereby occasions the default. Having severed the principal-agent relationship, an attorney no longer acts, or fails to act, as the client's representative. His acts or omissions therefore "cannot fairly be attributed to [the client]."

We agree that, under agency principles, a client cannot be charged with the acts or omissions of an attorney who has abandoned him. Nor can a client be faulted for failing to act on his own behalf when he lacks reason to believe his attorneys of record, in fact, are not representing him. We therefore inquire whether Maples has shown that his attorneys of record abandoned him, thereby supplying the "extraordinary circumstances beyond his control," necessary to lift the state procedural bar to his federal petition.

B

From the time he filed his initial Rule 32 petition until well after time ran out for appealing the trial court's denial of that petition, Maples had only three attorneys of record: Munanka, Ingen-Housz, and Butler. Unknown to Maples, not one of these lawyers was in fact serving as his attorney during the 42 days permitted for an appeal from the trial court's order.

The State contends that Sullivan & Cromwell represented Maples throughout his state postconviction proceedings. Accordingly, the State urges, Maples cannot establish abandonment by counsel continuing through the six weeks allowed for noticing an appeal from the trial court's denial of his Rule 32 petition. We disagree. It is undisputed that Munanka and Ingen-Housz severed their agency relationship with Maples long before the default occurred. Both Munanka and Ingen-Housz left Sullivan & Cromwell's employ in the summer of 2002, at least nine months before the Alabama trial court entered its order denying Rule 32 relief. Their new employment—Munanka as a law clerk for a federal judge, Ingen-Housz as an employee of the European Commission in Belgium—disabled them from continuing to represent Maples. Hornbook agency law establishes that the attorneys' departure from Sullivan & Cromwell and their commencement of employment that prevented them from representing Maples ended their agency relationship with him.

Furthermore, the two attorneys did not observe Alabama's Rule requiring them to seek the trial court's permission to withdraw. By failing to seek permission to withdraw, Munanka and Ingen-Housz allowed the court's records to convey that they represented Maples. As listed attorneys of record, they, not Maples, would be the addressees of court orders Alabama law requires the clerk to furnish.

Maples' only other attorney of record, local counsel Butler, also left him abandoned. Indeed, Butler did not even begin to represent Maples. Butler informed Munanka and Ingen-Housz that he would serve as local counsel only for the purpose of enabling the two out-of-state attorneys to appear *pro hac vice*. Lacking the necessary "resources, available time [and] experience," Butler told the two Sullivan & Cromwell lawyers, he would not "deal with substantive issues in the case." That the minimal participation he undertook was inconsistent with Alabama law, underscores the absurdity of holding Maples barred because Butler signed on as local counsel.

In sum, the record admits of only one reading: At no time before the missed deadline was Butler serving as Maples' agent "in any meaningful sense of that word."

Not only was Maples left without any functioning attorney of record, the very listing of Munanka, Ingen-Housz, and Butler as his representatives meant that he had no right personally to receive notice. He in fact received none or any other warning that he had better fend for himself. Had counsel of record or the State's attorney informed Maples of his plight before the time to appeal ran out, he could have filed a notice of appeal himself or enlisted the aid of new volunteer attorneys. Given no reason to suspect that he lacked counsel able and willing to represent him, Maples surely was blocked from complying with the State's procedural rule.

C

"The cause and prejudice requirement," we have said, "shows due regard for States' finality and comity interests while ensuring that 'fundamental fairness [remains] the central concern of the writ of habeas corpus.'" In the unusual circumstances of this case, principles of agency law and fundamental fairness point to the same conclusion: There was indeed cause to excuse Maples' procedural default. Through no fault of his own, Maples lacked the assistance of any authorized attorney during the 42 days Alabama allows for noticing an appeal from a trial court's denial of postconviction relief. As just observed, he had no reason to suspect that, in reality, he had been reduced to *pro se* status. Maples was disarmed by extraordinary circumstances quite beyond his control. He has shown ample cause, we hold, to excuse the procedural default into which he was trapped when counsel of record abandoned him without a word of warning.

Justice SCALIA, with whom Justice THOMAS joins, dissenting.

Our doctrine of procedural default reflects, and furthers, the principle that errors in state criminal trials should be remedied in state court. As we have long recognized, federal habeas review for state prisoners imposes significant costs on the States, undermining not only their practical interest in the finality of their criminal judgments, but also the primacy of their courts in adjudicating the constitutional rights of defendants prosecuted under state law. We have further recognized that "[t]hese costs are particularly high ... when a state prisoner, through a procedural default, prevents adjudication of his constitutional claims in state court." For that reason, and because permitting federal-court review of defaulted claims would "undercu[t] the State's ability to enforce its procedural rules," we have held that when a state court has relied on an adequate and independent state procedural ground in denying a prisoner's claims, the prisoner ordinarily may not obtain federal habeas relief.

To be sure, the prohibition on federal-court review of defaulted claims is not absolute. A habeas petitioner's default in state court will not bar federal habeas review if "the petitioner demonstrates cause and actual prejudice," — "cause" constituting "something *external* to the petitioner, something that cannot fairly be attributed to him," that impeded compliance with the State's procedural rule. As a general matter, an attorney's mistakes (or omissions) do not meet the standard "because the attorney is the petitioner's agent when acting, or failing to act, in furtherance of the litigation, and the petitioner must 'bear the risk of attorney error.'"

In light of the principles just set out, the Court is correct to conclude that a habeas petitioner's procedural default may be excused when it is attributable to abandonment by his attorney. I likewise agree with the Court's conclusion that Maples' two out-of-state attorneys of record, Jaasi Munanka and Clara Ingen-Housz, had abandoned Maples by the time the Alabama trial court entered its order denying his petition for postconviction relief.

It is an unjustified leap, however, to conclude that Maples was left unrepresented during the relevant window between the Alabama trial court's dismissal of his postconviction petition and expiration of the 42-day period for filing a notice of appeal. Start with Maples' own allegations: In his amended federal habeas petition, Maples alleged that, at the time he sought postconviction relief in Alabama trial court, he "was represented by Sullivan & Cromwell of New York, New York." Although the petition went on to identify Munanka and Ingen-Housz as "the two Sullivan lawyers handling the matter," its statement that Maples was "represented" by the firm itself strongly suggests that Maples viewed himself as having retained the services of the firm as a whole, a perfectly natural understanding. "When a client retains a lawyer who practices with a firm, the presumption is that both the lawyer and the firm have been retained."

In any case, even if Maples had no attorney-client relationship with the Sullivan & Cromwell firm, Munanka and Ingen-Housz were surely not the only Sullivan & Cromwell lawyers who represented Maples on an individual basis. In sum, there is every indication that when the trial court entered its order dismissing Maples' postconviction petition in May 2003, Maples continued to be represented by a team of attorneys in Sullivan & Cromwell's New York office.

But even leaving aside the question of Maples' "unadmitted" attorneys at Sullivan & Cromwell, Maples had a fully admitted attorney, who had entered an appearance, in the person of local counsel, John Butler. There is no support for the Court's conclusion that Butler "did not even begin to represent Maples." True, the affidavit Butler filed with the Alabama trial court in the proceeding seeking extension of the deadline stated that he had "no substantive involvement" with the case, and that he had "agreed to serve as local counsel only." But a disclaimer of "substantive involvement" in a case, whether or not it violates a lawyer's ethical obligations, see is not equivalent to a denial of any agency role at all. A local attorney's "nonsubstantive" involvement would surely include, *at a minimum*, keeping track of local court orders and advising "substantive" counsel of impending deadlines. Nor did Butler's explanation for his failure to act when he received a copy of the trial court's order sound in abandonment. Butler did not say, for instance, that he ignored the order because he did not consider Maples to be his client. Instead, based on "past practice" and the content of the order, Butler "assumed" that Maples' lawyers at Sullivan & Cromwell would receive a copy.

One suspects that today's decision is motivated in large part by an understandable sense of frustration with the State's refusal to waive Maples' procedural default in the interest of fairness. Indeed, that frustration may well explain the Court's lengthy indictment of Alabama's general procedures for providing representation to capital defendants, a portion of the Court's opinion that is so disconnected from the rest of its analysis as to be otherwise inexplicable.

But if the interest of fairness justifies our excusing Maples' procedural default here, it does so whenever a defendant's procedural default is caused by his attorney. That is simply not the law — and cannot be, if the states are to have an orderly system of criminal litigation conducted by counsel. Our precedents allow a State to stand on its rights and enforce a habeas petitioner's procedural default even when counsel is to blame. Because a faithful application of those precedents leads to the conclusion that Maples has not demonstrated cause to excuse his procedural default; and because the reasoning by which the Court justifies the opposite conclusion invites future evisceration of the principle that defendants are responsible for the mistakes of their attorneys; I respectfully dissent.

———————

Beginning in two decisions decided on the same day — Murray v. Carrier, 477 U.S. 478 (1986), and Smith v. Murray, 477 U.S. 27 (1986) — the Supreme Court has held that as an alternative to demonstrating cause, a habeas petitioner may raise matters not argued in the state courts by demonstrating that he or she is probably innocent of the charges.

The issue in Murray v. Carrier was whether a habeas petitioner could show cause for a procedural default by demonstrating that the defense counsel inadvertently failed to raise an issue. The inadvertence, however, did not amount to ineffective assistance of counsel. In *Murray*, the defense attorney inadvertently omitted an important issue from the notice of appeal. Under the pertinent state law, a failure to include an issue in the notice of appeal was deemed a waiver. Hence, the state courts refused to hear or rule on the omitted issue. The Supreme Court concluded that there was not sufficient cause to permit the defendant to raise the issue in a federal court habeas proceeding.

The *Murray* Court did indicate, however, one alternative to demonstrating cause. The Court said that a state prisoner who could show that he or she is probably actually innocent should be able to secure relief regardless of the reason for the state court procedural default. Justice O'Connor explained that "in an extraordinary case, where a constitutional violation has probably resulted in the conviction of one who is actually innocent, a federal habeas court may grant the writ even in the absence of a showing of cause for the procedural default."

In two cases, below, Herrara v. Collins and House v. Bell, the Court considered when actual innocence can excuse a procedural default. In reading these cases, it is important to note that the Court was considering two different uses of "actual innocence": as a "gateway" to raise a procedurally defaulted claim and as a "freestanding" claim that would justify overturning a conviction on habeas corpus. In reading these cases, consider how the justices approach the questions of what is the standard for showing actual innocence as a gateway to raising a procedurally defaulted claim. Also, is executing an innocent person unconstitutional so as to allow "freestanding" claims of innocence? And if so, what is the standard for freestanding claims of innocence?

HERRERA v. COLLINS
506 U.S. 390 (1993)

Chief Justice REHNQUIST delivered the opinion of the Court.

Petitioner Leonel Torres Herrera was convicted of capital murder and sentenced to death in January 1982. He unsuccessfully challenged the conviction on direct appeal and state collateral proceedings in the Texas state courts, and in a federal habeas petition. In February 1992 — 10 years after his conviction — he urged in a second federal habeas petition that he was "actually innocent" of the murder for which he was sentenced to death, and that the Eighth Amendment's prohibition against cruel and unusual punishment and the Fourteenth Amendment's guarantee of due process of law therefore forbid his execution. He supported this claim with affidavits tending to show that his now-dead brother, rather than he, had been the perpetrator of the crime. Petitioner urges us to hold that this showing of innocence entitles him to relief in this federal habeas proceeding. We hold that it does not.

Shortly before 11 P.M. on an evening in late September 1981, the body of Texas Department of Public Safety Officer David Rucker was found by a passer-by on a stretch of highway about six miles east of Los Fresnos, Texas, a few miles north of Brownsville in the Rio Grande Valley. Rucker's body was lying beside his patrol car. He had been shot in the head.

At about the same time, Los Fresnos Police Officer Enrique Carrisalez observed a speeding vehicle traveling west towards Los Fresnos, away from the place where Rucker's body had been found, along the same road. Carrisalez, who was accompanied in his patrol car by Enrique Hernandez, turned on his flashing red lights and pursued the speeding vehicle. After the car had stopped briefly at a red light, it signaled that it would pull over and did so. The patrol car pulled up behind it. Carrisalez took a flashlight and walked toward the car of the speeder. The driver opened his door and exchanged a few words with Carrisalez before firing at least one shot at Carrisalez' chest. The officer died nine days later.

Petitioner Herrera was arrested a few days after the shootings and charged with the capital murder of both Carrisalez and Rucker. He was tried and found guilty of the capital murder of Carrisalez in January 1982, and sentenced to death. In July 1982, petitioner pleaded guilty to the murder of Rucker.

At petitioner's trial for the murder of Carrisalez, Hernandez, who had witnessed Carrisalez' slaying from the officer's patrol car, identified petitioner as the person who had wielded the gun. A declaration by Officer Carrisalez to the same effect, made while he was in the hospital, was also admitted. Through a license plate check, it was shown that the speeding car involved in Carrisalez' murder was registered to petitioner's "live-in" girlfriend. Petitioner was known to drive this car, and he had a set of keys to the car in his pants pocket when he was arrested. Hernandez identified the car as the vehicle from which the murderer had emerged to fire the fatal shot. He also testified that there had been only one person in the car that night.

The evidence showed that Herrera's Social Security card had been found alongside Rucker's patrol car on the night he was killed. Splatters of blood on the car identified as the vehicle involved in the shootings, and on petitioner's blue jeans and wallet were identified as type A blood — the same type which Rucker had. (Herrera has type O blood.) Similar evidence with respect to strands of hair found in the car indicated that the hair was Rucker's and not Herrera's. A handwritten letter was also found on the person of petitioner when he was arrested, which strongly implied that he had killed Rucker.

Petitioner appealed his conviction and sentence, arguing, among other things, that Hernandez' and Carrisalez' identifications were unreliable and improperly admitted. The Texas Court of Criminal Appeals affirmed, and we denied certiorari. Petitioner's application for state habeas relief was denied. Petitioner then filed a federal habeas petition, again challenging the identifications offered against him at trial. This petition was denied, and we again denied certiorari.

Petitioner next returned to state court and filed a second habeas petition, raising, among other things, a claim of "actual innocence" based on newly discovered evidence. In support of this claim petitioner presented the affidavits of Hector Villarreal, an attorney who had represented petitioner's brother, Raul Herrera, Sr., and of Juan Franco Palacious, one of Raul, Senior's former cellmates. Both individuals claimed that Raul, Senior, who died in 1984, had told them that he — and not petitioner — had killed Officers Rucker and Carrisalez. The State District Court denied this application, finding that "no evidence at trial remotely suggest[ed] that anyone other than [petitioner] committed the offense."

In February 1992, petitioner lodged the instant habeas petition — his second — in federal court, alleging, among other things, that he is innocent of the murders of Rucker and Carrisalez, and that his execution would thus violate the Eighth and Fourteenth Amendments. In addition to proffering the above affidavits, petitioner presented the affidavits of Raul Herrera,

Jr., Raul Senior's son, and Jose Ybarra, Jr., a schoolmate of the Herrera brothers. Raul, Junior, averred that he had witnessed his father shoot Officers Rucker and Carrisalez and petitioner was not present. Raul, Junior, was nine years old at the time of the killings. Ybarra alleged that Raul, Senior, told him one summer night in 1983 that he had shot the two police officers. Petitioner alleged that law enforcement officials were aware of this evidence, and had withheld it in violation of Brady v. Maryland (1963).

Petitioner asserts that the Eighth and Fourteenth Amendments to the United States Constitution prohibit the execution of a person who is innocent of the crime for which he was convicted. This proposition has an elemental appeal, as would the similar proposition that the Constitution prohibits the imprisonment of one who is innocent of the crime for which he was convicted. After all, the central purpose of any system of criminal justice is to convict the guilty and free the innocent. But the evidence upon which petitioner's claim of innocence rests was not produced at his trial, but rather eight years later. In any system of criminal justice, "innocence" or "guilt" must be determined in some sort of a judicial proceeding. Petitioner's showing of innocence, and indeed his constitutional claim for relief based upon that showing, must be evaluated in the light of the previous proceedings in this case, which have stretched over a span of 10 years.

A person when first charged with a crime is entitled to a presumption of innocence, and may insist that his guilt be established beyond a reasonable doubt. In re Winship (1970). Other constitutional provisions also have the effect of ensuring against the risk of convicting an innocent person. All of these constitutional safeguards, of course, make it more difficult for the State to rebut and finally overturn the presumption of innocence which attaches to every criminal defendant. But we have also observed that "[d]ue process does not require that every conceivable step be taken, at whatever cost, to eliminate the possibility of convicting an innocent person." To conclude otherwise would all but paralyze our system for enforcement of the criminal law.

Once a defendant has been afforded a fair trial and convicted of the offense for which he was charged, the presumption of innocence disappears. Here, it is not disputed that the State met its burden of proving at trial that petitioner was guilty of the capital murder of Officer Carrisalez beyond a reasonable doubt. Thus, in the eyes of the law, petitioner does not come before the Court as one who is "innocent," but, on the contrary, as one who has been convicted by due process of law of two brutal murders.

Based on affidavits here filed, petitioner claims that evidence never presented to the trial court proves him innocent notwithstanding the verdict reached at his trial. Such a claim is not cognizable in the state courts of Texas. For to obtain a new trial based on newly discovered evidence, a defendant must file a motion within 30 days after imposition or suspension of sentence. The Texas courts have construed this 30-day time limit as jurisdictional.

Claims of actual innocence based on newly discovered evidence have never been held to state a ground for federal habeas relief absent an independent constitutional violation occurring in the underlying state criminal proceeding. This rule is grounded in the principle that federal habeas courts sit to ensure that individuals are not imprisoned in violation of the Constitution — not to correct errors of fact.

The dissent fails to articulate the relief that would be available if petitioner were to meet its "probable innocence" standard. Would it be commutation of petitioner's death sentence, new trial, or unconditional release from imprisonment? The typical relief granted in federal habeas corpus is a conditional order of release unless the State elects to retry the successful habeas petitioner, or in a capital case a similar conditional order vacating the death sentence. Were petitioner to satisfy the dissent's "probable innocence" standard, therefore, the District Court would presumably be required to grant a conditional order of relief, which would in effect require the State to retry petitioner 10 years after his first trial, not because of any constitutional violation which had occurred at the first trial, but simply because of a belief that in light of petitioner's new-found evidence a jury might find him not guilty at a second trial.

Yet there is no guarantee that the guilt or innocence determination would be any more exact. To the contrary, the passage of time only diminishes the reliability of criminal adjudications. Under the dissent's approach, the District Court would be placed in the even more difficult position of having to weigh the probative value of "hot" and "cold" evidence on petitioner's guilt or innocence.

This is not to say that our habeas jurisprudence casts a blind eye toward innocence. In a series of cases, we have held that a petitioner otherwise subject to defenses of abusive or successive use of the writ may have his federal constitutional claim considered on the merits if he makes a proper showing of actual innocence. This rule, or fundamental miscarriage of justice exception, is grounded in the "equitable discretion" of habeas courts to see that federal constitutional errors do not result in the incarceration of innocent persons. But this body of our habeas jurisprudence makes clear that a claim of "actual innocence" is not itself a constitutional claim, but instead a gateway through which a habeas petitioner must pass to have his otherwise barred constitutional claim considered on the merits.

Petitioner in this case is simply not entitled to habeas relief based on the reasoning of this line of cases. For he does not seek excusal of a procedural error so that he may bring an independent constitutional claim challenging his conviction or sentence, but rather argues that he is entitled to habeas relief because newly discovered evidence shows that his conviction is factually incorrect. The fundamental miscarriage of justice exception is available "only where the prisoner supplements his constitutional claim with a colorable showing of factual innocence." We have never held that it extends to freestanding claims of actual innocence. Therefore, the exception is inapplicable here.

Petitioner asserts that this case is different because he has been sentenced to death. But we have "refused to hold that the fact that a death sentence has been imposed requires a different standard of review on federal habeas corpus."

Alternatively, petitioner invokes the Fourteenth Amendment's guarantee of due process of law in support of his claim that his showing of actual innocence entitles him to a new trial, or at least to a vacation of his death sentence. "[B]ecause the States have considerable expertise in matters of criminal procedure and the criminal process is grounded in centuries of common-law tradition," we have "exercis[ed] substantial deference to legislative judgments in this area." Thus, we have found criminal process lacking only where it "'offends some principle of justice so rooted in the traditions and conscience of our people as to be ranked as fundamental.'" We cannot say that Texas' refusal to entertain petitioner's newly discovered evidence eight years after his conviction transgresses a principle of fundamental fairness "rooted in the traditions and conscience of our people."

This is not to say, however, that petitioner is left without a forum to raise his actual innocence claim. For under Texas law, petitioner may file a request for executive clemency. Clemency is deeply rooted in our Anglo-American tradition of law, and is the historic remedy for preventing miscarriages of justice where judicial process has been exhausted.

Executive clemency has provided the "fail safe" in our criminal justice system. It is an unalterable fact that our judicial system, like the human beings who administer it, is fallible. But history is replete with examples of wrongfully convicted persons who have been pardoned in the wake of after-discovered evidence establishing their innocence. In his classic work, Professor Edwin Borchard compiled 65 cases in which it was later determined that individuals had been wrongfully convicted of crimes. Clemency provided the relief mechanism in 47 of these cases; the remaining cases ended in judgments of acquittals after new trials. E. Borchard, Convicting the Innocent (1932). Recent authority confirms that over the past century clemency has been exercised frequently in capital cases in which demonstrations of "actual innocence" have been made. See M. Radelet, H. Bedau, & C. Putnam, In Spite of Innocence 282-356 (1992).

As the foregoing discussion illustrates, in state criminal proceedings the trial is the paramount event for determining the guilt or innocence of the defendant. Federal habeas review of state convictions has traditionally been limited to claims of constitutional violations occurring in the course of the underlying state criminal proceedings. Our federal habeas cases have treated claims of "actual innocence," not as an independent constitutional claim, but as a basis upon which a habeas petitioner may have an independent constitutional claim considered on the merits, even though his habeas petition would otherwise be regarded as successive or abusive. History shows that the traditional remedy for claims of innocence based on new evidence, discovered too late in the day to file a new trial motion, has been executive clemency.

We may assume, for the sake of argument in deciding this case, that in a capital case a truly persuasive demonstration of "actual innocence" made after trial would render the execution of a defendant unconstitutional, and warrant federal habeas relief if there were no state avenue open to process such a claim. But because of the very disruptive effect that entertaining claims of actual innocence would have on the need for finality in capital cases, and the enormous burden that having to retry cases based on often stale evidence would place on the States, the threshold showing for such an assumed right would necessarily be extraordinarily high. The showing made by petitioner in this case falls far short of any such threshold.

The affidavits filed in this habeas proceeding were given over eight years after petitioner's trial. No satisfactory explanation has been given as to why the affiants waited until the 11th hour — and, indeed, until after the alleged perpetrator of the murders himself was dead — to make their statements. Equally troubling, no explanation has been offered as to why petitioner, by hypothesis an innocent man, pleaded guilty to the murder of Rucker. Moreover, the affidavits themselves contain inconsistencies, and therefore fail to provide a convincing account of what took place on the night Officers Rucker and Carrisalez were killed.

This is not to say that petitioner's affidavits are without probative value. Had this sort of testimony been offered at trial, it could have been weighed by the jury, along with the evidence offered by the State and petitioner, in deliberating upon its verdict. Since the statements in the affidavits contradict the evidence received at trial, the jury would have had to decide important issues of credibility. But coming 10 years after petitioner's trial, this showing of innocence falls far short of that which would have to be made in order to trigger the sort of constitutional claim which we have assumed, arguendo, to exist.

Justice O'CONNOR, with whom Justice KENNEDY joins, concurring.

I cannot disagree with the fundamental legal principle that executing the innocent is inconsistent with the Constitution. Regardless of the verbal formula employed — "contrary to contemporary standards of decency," "shocking to the conscience," or offensive to a "'principle of justice so rooted in the traditions and conscience of our people as to be ranked as fundamental,'" — the execution of a legally and factually innocent person would be a constitutionally intolerable event. Dispositive to this case, however, is an equally fundamental fact: Petitioner is not innocent, in any sense of the word.

As the Court explains, petitioner is not innocent in the eyes of the law because, in our system of justice, "the trial is the paramount event for determining the guilt or innocence of the defendant." In petitioner's case, that paramount event occurred 10 years ago. He was tried before a jury of his peers, with the full panoply of protections that our Constitution affords criminal defendants. At the conclusion of that trial, the jury found petitioner guilty beyond a reasonable doubt. Petitioner therefore does not appear before us as an innocent man on the verge of execution. He is instead a legally guilty one who, refusing to accept the jury's verdict, demands a hearing in which to have his culpability determined once again.

Consequently, the issue before us is not whether a State can execute the innocent. It is, as the Court notes, whether a fairly convicted and therefore legally guilty person is constitutionally entitled to yet another judicial proceeding in which to adjudicate his guilt anew, 10 years after conviction, notwithstanding his failure to demonstrate that constitutional error infected his trial. In most circumstances, that question would answer itself in the negative. Our society has a high degree of confidence in its criminal trials, in no small part because the Constitution offers unparalleled protections against convicting the innocent. The question similarly would be answered in the negative today, except for the disturbing nature of the claim before us. Petitioner contends not only that the Constitution's protections "sometimes fail," but that their failure in his case will result in his execution — even though he is factually innocent and has evidence to prove it.

Exercising restraint, the Court and Justice White assume for the sake of argument that, if a prisoner were to make an exceptionally strong showing of actual innocence, the execution could not go forward. Justice Blackmun, in contrast, would expressly so hold; he would also announce the precise burden of proof. Resolving the issue is neither necessary nor advisable in this case. The question is a sensitive and, to say the least, troubling one. It implicates not just the life of a single individual, but also the State's powerful and legitimate interest in punishing the guilty, and the nature of state-federal relations. Indeed, as the Court persuasively demonstrates, throughout our history the federal courts have assumed that they should not and could not intervene to prevent an execution so long as the prisoner had been convicted after a constitutionally adequate trial. The prisoner's sole remedy was a pardon or clemency.

Nonetheless, the proper disposition of this case is neither difficult nor troubling. No matter what the Court might say about claims of actual innocence today, petitioner could not obtain relief. The record overwhelmingly demonstrates that petitioner deliberately shot and killed Officers Rucker and Carrisalez the night of September 29, 1981; petitioner's new evidence is bereft of credibility. Indeed, despite its stinging criticism of the Court's decision, not even the dissent expresses a belief that petitioner might possibly be actually innocent. Nor could it: The record makes it abundantly clear that petitioner is not somehow the future victim of "simple murder," but instead himself the established perpetrator of two brutal and tragic ones.

Ultimately, two things about this case are clear. First is what the Court does not hold. Nowhere does the Court state that the Constitution permits the execution of an actually innocent person. Instead, the Court assumes for the sake of argument that a truly persuasive demonstration of actual innocence would render any such execution unconstitutional and that federal habeas relief would be warranted if no state avenue were open to process the claim. Second is what petitioner has not demonstrated. Petitioner has failed to make a persuasive showing of actual innocence. Not one judge — no state court judge, not the District Court Judge, none of the three judges of the Court of Appeals, and none of the Justices of this Court — has expressed doubt about petitioner's guilt. Accordingly, the Court has no reason to pass on, and appropriately reserves, the question whether federal courts may entertain convincing claims of actual innocence. That difficult question remains open. If the Constitution's guarantees of fair procedure and the safeguards of clemency and pardon fulfill their historical mission, it may never require resolution at all.

Justice SCALIA, with whom Justice THOMAS joins, concurring.

We granted certiorari on the question whether it violates due process or constitutes cruel and unusual punishment for a State to execute a person who, having been convicted of murder after a full and fair trial, later alleges that newly discovered evidence shows him to be "actually innocent." I would have preferred to decide that question, particularly since, as the Court's discussion shows, it is perfectly clear what the answer is: There is no basis in text, tradition, or even in contemporary practice (if that were enough) for finding in the Constitution a right to demand judicial consideration of newly discovered evidence of innocence brought forward after conviction. In saying that such a right exists, the dissenters apply nothing but their personal opinions to invalidate the rules of more than two-thirds of the States, and a Federal Rule of Criminal Procedure for which this Court itself is responsible. If the system that has been in place for 200 years (and remains widely approved) "shock[s]" the dissenters' consciences, perhaps they should doubt the calibration of their consciences, or, better still, the usefulness of "conscience shocking" as a legal test.

I nonetheless join the entirety of the Court's opinion, including the final portion, because there is no legal error in deciding a case by assuming, arguendo, that an asserted constitutional right exists, and because I can understand, or at least am accustomed to, the reluctance of the present Court to admit publicly that Our Perfect Constitution lets stand any injustice, much less the execution of an innocent man who has received, though to no avail, all the process that our society has traditionally deemed adequate. With any luck, we shall avoid ever having to face this embarrassing question again, since it is improbable that evidence of innocence as convincing as today's opinion requires would fail to produce an executive pardon.

Justice WHITE, concurring in the judgment.

In voting to affirm, I assume that a persuasive showing of "actual innocence" made after trial, even though made after the expiration of the time provided by law for the presentation of newly discovered evidence, would render unconstitutional the execution of petitioner in this case. To be entitled to relief, however, petitioner would at the very least be required to show that based on proffered newly discovered evidence and the entire record before the jury that convicted him, "no rational trier of fact could [find] proof of guilt beyond a reasonable doubt." For the reasons stated in the Court's opinion, petitioner's showing falls far short of satisfying even that standard, and I therefore concur in the judgment.

Justice BLACKMUN, with whom Justice STEVENS and Justice SOUTER join, dissenting.

Nothing could be more contrary to contemporary standards of decency, or more shocking to the conscience, than to execute a person who is actually innocent.

I therefore must disagree with the long and general discussion that precedes the Court's disposition of this case. That discussion, of course, is dictum because the Court assumes, "for the sake of argument in deciding this case, that in a capital case a truly persuasive demonstration of 'actual innocence' made after trial would render the execution of a defendant unconstitutional." Without articulating the standard it is applying, however, the Court then decides that this petitioner has not made a sufficiently persuasive case. Because I believe that in the first instance the District Court should decide whether petitioner is entitled to a hearing and whether he is entitled to relief on the merits of his claim, I would reverse the order of the Court of Appeals and remand this case for further proceedings in the District Court.

The Court's enumeration of the constitutional rights of criminal defendants surely is entirely beside the point. These protections sometimes fail.[44] We really are being asked to decide whether the Constitution forbids the execution of a person who has been validly convicted and sentenced but who, nonetheless, can prove his innocence with newly discovered evidence. Despite the State of Texas' astonishing protestation to the contrary, I do not see how the answer can be anything but "yes."

The Eighth Amendment prohibits "cruel and unusual punishments." This proscription is not static but rather reflects evolving standards of decency. I think it is crystal clear that the execution of an innocent person is "at odds with contemporary standards of fairness and decency." Indeed, it is at odds with any standard of decency that I can imagine.

This Court has ruled that punishment is excessive and unconstitutional if it is "nothing more than the purposeless and needless imposition of pain and suffering," or if it is "grossly out of proportion to the severity of the crime." It has held that death is an excessive punishment for rape, and for mere participation in a robbery during which a killing takes place. If it is violative of the Eighth Amendment to execute someone who is guilty of those crimes, then it plainly is violative of the Eighth Amendment to execute a person who is actually innocent. Executing an innocent person epitomizes "the purposeless and needless imposition of pain and suffering."

---

44. One impressive study has concluded that 23 innocent people have been executed in the United States in this century, including one as recently as 1984. Bedau & Radelet, Miscarriages of Justice in Potentially Capital Cases, 40 Stan. L. Rev. 21, 36, 173-179 (1987); Radelet, Bedau, & Putnam, In Spite of Innocence 282-356 (1992). The majority cites this study to show that clemency has been exercised frequently in capital cases when showings of actual innocence have been made. But the study also shows that requests for clemency by persons the authors believe were innocent have been refused. See, e.g., Bedau & Radelet, 40 Stan. L. Rev., at 91 (discussing James Adams who was executed in Florida on May 10, 1984); Radelet, Bedau, & Putnam, In Spite of Innocence, at 5-10 (same). [Footnote by the Court.]

The protection of the Eighth Amendment does not end once a defendant has been validly convicted and sentenced. Respondent and the United States as amicus curiae argue that the Eighth Amendment does not apply to petitioner because he is challenging his guilt, not his punishment. Whether petitioner is viewed as challenging simply his death sentence or also his continued detention, he still is challenging the State's right to punish him. Respondent and the United States would impose a clear line between guilt and punishment, reasoning that every claim that concerns guilt necessarily does not involve punishment. Such a division is far too facile. What respondent and the United States fail to recognize is that the legitimacy of punishment is inextricably intertwined with guilt.

The Court also suggests that allowing petitioner to raise his claim of innocence would not serve society's interest in the reliable imposition of the death penalty because it might require a new trial that would be less accurate than the first. This suggestion misses the point entirely. The question is not whether a second trial would be more reliable than the first but whether, in light of new evidence, the result of the first trial is sufficiently reliable for the State to carry out a death sentence. Furthermore, it is far from clear that a State will seek to retry the rare prisoner who prevails on a claim of actual innocence. I believe a prisoner must show not just that there was probably a reasonable doubt about his guilt but that he is probably actually innocent. I find it difficult to believe that any State would choose to retry a person who meets this standard.

I believe it contrary to any standard of decency to execute someone who is actually innocent. Because the Eighth Amendment applies to questions of guilt or innocence, and to persons upon whom a valid sentence of death has been imposed, I also believe that petitioner may raise an Eighth Amendment challenge to his punishment on the ground that he is actually innocent.

Execution of the innocent is equally offensive to the Due Process Clause of the Fourteenth Amendment.

The majority's discussion of petitioner's constitutional claims is even more perverse when viewed in the light of this Court's recent habeas jurisprudence. Beginning with a trio of decisions in 1986, this Court shifted the focus of federal habeas review of successive, abusive, or defaulted claims away from the preservation of constitutional rights to a fact-based inquiry into the habeas petitioner's guilt or innocence. The Court sought to strike a balance between the State's interest in the finality of its criminal judgments and the prisoner's interest in access to a forum to test the basic justice of his sentence. In striking this balance, the Court adopted the view of Judge Friendly that there should be an exception to the concept of finality when a prisoner can make a colorable claim of actual innocence. Friendly, *Is Innocence Irrelevant? Collateral Attack on Criminal Judgments*, 38 U.Chi.L.Rev. 142, 160 (1970).

Having adopted an "actual-innocence" requirement for review of abusive, successive, or defaulted claims, however, the majority would now take the position that "a claim of 'actual innocence' is not itself a constitutional claim, but instead a gateway through which a habeas petitioner must pass to have his otherwise barred constitutional claim considered on the merits." In other words, having held that a prisoner who is incarcerated in violation of the Constitution must show he is actually innocent to obtain relief, the majority would now hold that a prisoner who is actually innocent must show a constitutional violation to obtain relief. The only principle that would appear to reconcile these two positions is the principle that habeas relief should be denied whenever possible.

The Eighth and Fourteenth Amendments, of course, are binding on the States, and one would normally expect the States to adopt procedures to consider claims of actual innocence based on newly discovered evidence. The majority's disposition of this case, however, leaves the States uncertain of their constitutional obligations.

Whatever procedures a State might adopt to hear actual-innocence claims, one thing is certain: The possibility of executive clemency is not sufficient to satisfy the requirements of the Eighth and Fourteenth Amendments. The majority correctly points out: "'A pardon is an act of grace.'" The vindication of rights guaranteed by the Constitution has never been made to turn on the unreviewable discretion of an executive official or administrative tribunal.

Like other constitutional claims, Eighth and Fourteenth Amendment claims of actual innocence advanced on behalf of a state prisoner can and should be heard in state court. If a State provides a judicial procedure for raising such claims, the prisoner may be required to exhaust that procedure before taking his claim of actual innocence to federal court. See 28 U.S.C. §§2254(b) and (c). Furthermore, state-court determinations of factual issues relating to the claim would be entitled to a presumption of correctness in any subsequent federal habeas proceeding. See §2254(d).

Texas provides no judicial procedure for hearing petitioner's claim of actual innocence and his habeas petition was properly filed in district court under §2254. The district court is entitled to dismiss the petition summarily only if "it plainly appears from the face of the petition and any exhibits annexed to it that the petitioner is not entitled to relief." §2254 Rule 4. If, as is the case here, the petition raises factual questions and the State has failed to provide a full and fair hearing, the district court is required to hold an evidentiary hearing.

The question that remains is what showing should be required to obtain relief on the merits of an Eighth or Fourteenth Amendment claim of actual innocence. I agree with the majority that "in state criminal proceedings the trial is the paramount event for determining the guilt or innocence of the defendant." I also think that "a truly persuasive demonstration of 'actual innocence' made after trial would render the execution of a defendant unconstitutional." The question is what "a truly persuasive demonstration" entails, a question the majority's disposition of this case leaves open.

In articulating the "actual-innocence" exception in our habeas jurisprudence, this Court has adopted a standard requiring the petitioner to show a "'fair probability that, in light of all the evidence . . . , the trier of the facts would have entertained a reasonable doubt of his guilt.'" In other words, the habeas petitioner must show that there probably would be a reasonable doubt.

I think the standard for relief on the merits of an actual-innocence claim must be higher than the threshold standard for merely reaching that claim or any other claim that has been procedurally defaulted or is successive or abusive. I would hold that, to obtain relief on a claim of actual innocence, the petitioner must show that he probably is innocent. This standard is supported by several considerations. First, new evidence of innocence may be discovered long after the defendant's conviction. Given the passage of time, it may be difficult for the State to retry a defendant who obtains relief from his conviction or sentence on an actual-innocence claim. The actual-innocence proceeding thus may constitute the final word on whether the defendant may be punished. In light of this fact, an otherwise constitutionally valid conviction or sentence should not be set aside lightly. Second, conviction after a constitutionally adequate trial strips the defendant of the presumption of innocence.

In considering whether a prisoner is entitled to relief on an actual-innocence claim, a court should take all the evidence into account, giving due regard to its reliability. Because placing the burden on the prisoner to prove innocence creates a presumption that the conviction is valid, it is not necessary or appropriate to make further presumptions about the reliability of newly discovered evidence generally. Rather, the court charged with deciding such a claim should make a case-by-case determination about the reliability of the newly discovered evidence under the circumstances. The court then should weigh the evidence in favor of the prisoner against the evidence of his guilt. Obviously, the stronger the evidence of the prisoner's guilt, the more persuasive the newly discovered evidence of innocence must be.

It should be clear that the standard I would adopt would not convert the federal courts into "'forums in which to relitigate state trials.'" I believe that if a prisoner can show that he is probably actually innocent, in light of all the evidence, then he has made "a truly persuasive demonstration," and his execution would violate the Constitution. I would so hold.

———————————

Thus, there are two ways in which "actual innocence" might be raised: as a "gateway" to allow procedurally defaulted claims to be raised or as a "freestanding" basis for overturning a conviction. Herrera v. Collins is unclear as to whether the latter is allowed. There is only one case in which the Supreme Court ever has found a sufficient showing of actual innocence: House v. Bell. In it, the Court clarified and applied the standard for "actual innocence" as a "gateway" for raising procedurally defaulted claims and also discussed the standard for "freestanding" claims of innocence.

HOUSE v. BELL
----
547 U.S. 518 (2006)

Justice KENNEDY delivered the opinion of the Court.

Some 20 years ago in rural Tennessee, Carolyn Muncey was murdered. A jury convicted petitioner Paul Gregory House of the crime and sentenced him to death, but new revelations cast doubt on the jury's verdict. House, protesting his innocence, seeks access to federal court to pursue habeas corpus relief based on constitutional claims that are procedurally barred under state law. Out of respect for the finality of state-court judgments federal habeas courts, as a general rule, are closed to claims that state courts would consider defaulted. In certain exceptional cases involving a compelling claim of actual innocence, however, the state procedural default rule is not a bar to a federal habeas corpus petition. *See* Schlup v. Delo (1995). After careful review of the full record, we conclude that House has made the stringent showing required by this exception; and we hold that his federal habeas action may proceed.

I

We begin with the facts surrounding Mrs. Muncey's disappearance, the discovery of her body, and House's arrest. Around 3 P.M. on Sunday, July 14, 1985, two local residents found her body concealed amid brush and tree branches on an embankment roughly 100 yards up the road from her driveway. Mrs. Muncey had been seen last on the evening before, when, around 8 P.M., she and her two children—Lora Muncey, age 10, and Matthew Muncey, age 8—visited their neighbor, Pam Luttrell. According to Luttrell, Mrs. Muncey mentioned her husband, William Hubert Muncey, Jr., known in the community as "Little Hube" and to his family as "Bubbie." As Luttrell recounted Mrs. Muncey's comment, Mr. Muncey "had gone to dig a grave, and he hadn't come back, but that was all right, because [Mrs. Muncey] was going to make him take her fishing the next day." Mrs. Muncey returned home, and some time later, before 11:00 P.M. at the latest, Luttrell "heard a car rev its motor as it went down the road," something Mr. Muncey customarily did when he drove by on his way home. Luttrell then went to bed.

Around 1 A.M., Lora and Matthew returned to Luttrell's home, this time with their father, Mr. Muncey, who said his wife was missing. Muncey asked Luttrell to watch the children while he searched for his wife. After he left, Luttrell talked with Lora. While Lora was talking, Luttrell recalled, "Matt kept butting in, you know, on us talking, and he said—sister they said daddy had a wreck, they said daddy had a wreck."

Lora testified that after leaving Luttrell's house with her mother, she and her brother "went to bed." Later, she heard someone, or perhaps two different people, ask for her mother.

Lora did not describe hearing any struggle. Some time later, Lora and her brother left the house to look for their mother, but no one answered when they knocked at the Luttrells' home, and another neighbor, Mike Clinton, said he had not seen her. After the children returned home, according to Lora, her father came home and "fixed him a bologna sandwich and he took a bit of it and he says — sissy, where is mommy at, and I said — she ain't been here for a little while." Lora recalled that Mr. Muncey went outside and, not seeing his wife, returned to take Lora and Matthew to the Luttrells' so that he could look further.

The next afternoon Billy Ray Hensley, the victim's first cousin, heard of Mrs. Muncey's disappearance and went to look for Mr. Muncey. As he approached the Munceys' street, Hensley allegedly "saw Mr. House come out from under a bank, wiping his hands on a black rag." Just when and where Hensley saw House, and how well he could have observed him, were disputed at House's trial. Hensley admitted on cross-examination that he could not have seen House "walking up or climbing up" the embankment; rather, he saw House, in "[j]ust a glance," "appear out of nowhere," "next to the embankment." On the Munceys' street, opposite the area where Hensley said he saw House, a white Plymouth was parked near a sawmill. Another witness, Billy Hankins, whom the defense called, claimed that around the same time he saw a "boy" walking down the street away from the parked Plymouth and toward the Munceys' home. This witness, however, put the "boy" on the side of the street with the parked car and the Munceys' driveway, not the side with the embankment.

Hensley, after turning onto the Munceys' street, continued down the road and turned into their driveway. "I pulled up in the driveway where I could see up toward Little Hube's house," Hensley testified, "and I seen Little Hube's car wasn't there, and I backed out in the road, and come back [the other way]." As he traveled up the road, Hensley saw House traveling in the opposite direction in the white Plymouth. House "flagged [Hensley] down" through his windshield, and the two cars met about 300 feet up the road from the Munceys' driveway. According to Hensley, House said he had heard Mrs. Muncey was missing and was looking for her husband. Though House had only recently moved to the area, he was acquainted with the Munceys, had attended a dance with them, and had visited their home. He later told law enforcement officials he considered both of the Munceys his friends. According to Hensley, House said he had heard that Mrs. Muncey's husband, who was an alcoholic, was elsewhere "getting drunk."

As Hensley drove off, he "got to thinking to [him]self — he's hunting Little Hube, and Little Hube drunk — what would he be doing off that bank. . . ." His suspicion aroused, Hensley later returned to the Munceys' street with a friend named Jack Adkins. The two checked different spots on the embankment, and though Hensley saw nothing where he looked, Adkins found Mrs. Muncey. Her body lay across from the sawmill near the corner where House's car had been parked, dumped in the woods a short way down the bank leading toward a creek.

Around midnight, Dr. Alex Carabia, a practicing pathologist and county medical examiner, performed an autopsy. Dr. Carabia put the time of death between 9 and 11 P.M. Mrs. Muncey had a black eye, both her hands were bloodstained up to the wrists, and she had bruises on her legs and neck. Dr. Carabia described the bruises as consistent with a "traumatic origin," i.e., a fight or a fall on hard objects. Based on the neck bruises and other injuries, he concluded Mrs. Muncey had been choked, but he ruled this out as the cause of death. The cause of death, in Dr. Carabia's view, was a severe blow to the left forehead that inflicted both a laceration penetrating to the bone and, inside the skull, a severe right-side hemorrhage, likely caused by Mrs. Muncey's brain slamming into the skull opposite the impact. Dr. Carabia described this head injury as consistent either with receiving a blow from a fist or other instrument or with striking some object.

The county sheriff, informed about Hensley's earlier encounter with House, questioned House shortly after the body was found. That evening, House answered further questions during a voluntary interview at the local jail. Special Agent Ray Presnell of the Tennessee Bureau of Investigation (TBI) prepared a statement of House's answers, which House signed. Asked to describe his whereabouts on the previous evening, House claimed — falsely, as it turned out — that he spent the entire evening with his girlfriend, Donna Turner, at her trailer. Asked whether he was wearing the same pants he had worn the night before, House replied — again, falsely — that he was. House was on probation at the time, having recently been released on parole following a sentence of five years to life for aggravated sexual assault in Utah. House had scratches on his arms and hands, and a knuckle on his right ring finger was bruised. He attributed the scratches to Turner's cats and the finger injury to recent construction work tearing down a shed. The next day House gave a similar statement to a different TBI agent, Charles Scott.

In fact House had not been at Turner's home. After initially supporting House's alibi, Turner informed authorities that House left her trailer around 10:30 or 10:45 P.M. to go for a walk. According to Turner's trial testimony, House returned later — she was not sure when — hot and panting, missing his shirt and his shoes. House, Turner testified, told her that while he was walking on the road near her home, a vehicle pulled up beside him, and somebody inside "called him some names and then they told him he didn't belong here anymore." House said he tried to ignore the taunts and keep walking, but the vehicle pulled in behind him, and "one of them got out and grabbed him by the shoulder . . . and [House] swung around with his right hand" and "hit something." According to Turner, House said "he took off down the bank and started running and he said that he — he said it seemed forever where he was running. And he said they fired two shots at him while he took off down the bank. . . ." House claimed the assailants "grabbed ahold of his shirt," which Turner remembered as "a blue tank top, trimmed in yellow," and "they tore it to where it wouldn't stay on him and he said — I just throwed it off when I was running." Turner, noticing House's bruised knuckle, asked how he hurt it, and House told her "that's where he hit." Turner testified that she "thought maybe my ex-husband had something to do with it."

Although the white Plymouth House drove the next day belonged to Turner, Turner insisted House had not used the car that night. No forensic evidence connected the car to the crime; law enforcement officials inspected a white towel covering the driver seat and concluded it was clean. Turner's trailer was located just under two miles by road, through hilly terrain, from the Muncey residence.

Law enforcement officers also questioned the victim's husband. Though Mrs. Muncey's comments to Luttrell gave no indication she knew this, Mr. Muncey had spent the evening at a weekly dance at a recreation center roughly a mile and a half from his home. In his statement to law enforcement — a statement House's trial counsel claims he never saw — Mr. Muncey admitted leaving the dance early, but said it was only for a brief trip to the package store to buy beer. He also stated that he and his wife had had sexual relations Saturday morning.

Late in the evening on Monday, July 15 — two days after the murder — law enforcement officers visited Turner's trailer. With Turner's consent, Agent Scott seized the pants House was wearing the night Mrs. Muncey disappeared. The heavily soiled pants were sitting in a laundry hamper; years later, Agent Scott recalled noticing "reddish brown stains" he "suspected" were blood. Around 4 P.M. the next day, two local law enforcement officers set out for the Federal Bureau of Investigation in Washington, D.C., with House's pants, blood samples from the autopsy, and other evidence packed together in a box. They arrived at 2:00 A.M. the next morning. On July 17, after initial FBI testing revealed human blood on the pants, House was arrested.

II

The State of Tennessee charged House with capital murder. At House's trial, the State presented testimony by Luttrell, Hensley, Adkins, Lora Muncey, Dr. Carabia, the sheriff, and other law enforcement officials. Through TBI Agents Presnell and Scott, the jury learned of House's false statements. Central to the State's case, however, was what the FBI testing showed — that semen consistent (or so it seemed) with House's was present on Mrs. Muncey's nightgown and panties, and that small bloodstains consistent with Mrs. Muncey's blood but not House's appeared on the jeans belonging to House.

Regarding the semen, FBI Special Agent Paul Bigbee, a serologist, testified that the source was a "secretor," meaning someone who "secrete[s] the ABO blood group substances in other body fluids, such as semen and saliva" — a characteristic shared by 80 percent of the population, including House.

Agent Bigbee further testified that the source of semen on the gown was blood-type A, House's own blood type. As to the semen on the panties, Agent Bigbee found only the H blood-group substance, which A and B blood-type secretors secrete along with substances A and B, and which O-type secretors secrete exclusively. Agent Bigbee explained, however — using science an amicus here sharply disputed — that House's A antigens could have "degraded" into H. Agent Bigbee thus concluded that both semen deposits could have come from House, though he acknowledged that the H antigen could have come from Mrs. Muncey herself if she was a secretor — something he "was not able to determine," — and that, while Mr. Muncey was himself blood-type A (as was his wife), Agent Bigbee was again "not able to determine his secretor status." Agent Bigbee acknowledged on cross-examination that "a saliva sample" would have sufficed to determine whether Mr. Muncey was a secretor; the State did not provide such a sample, though it did provide samples of Mr. Muncey's blood.

As for the blood, Agent Bigbee explained that "spots of blood" appeared "on the left outside leg, the right bottom cuff, on the left thigh and in the right inside pocket and on the lower pocket on the outside." Agent Bigbee determined that the blood's source was type A (the type shared by House, the victim, and Mr. Muncey). He also successfully tested for the enzyme phosphoglucomutase and the blood serum haptoglobin, both of which "are found in all humans" and carry "slight chemical differences" that vary genetically and "can be grouped to differentiate between two individuals if those types are different." Based on these chemical traces and on the A blood type, Agent Bigbee determined that only some 6.75 percent of the population carry similar blood, that the blood was "consistent" with Mrs. Muncey's (as determined by testing autopsy samples), and that it was "impossible" that the blood came from House.

A different FBI expert, Special Agent Chester Blythe, testified about fiber analysis performed on Mrs. Muncey's clothes and on House's pants. Although Agent Blythe found blue jean fibers on Mrs. Muncey's nightgown, brassier, housecoat, and panties, and in fingernail scrapings taken from her body (scrapings that also contained trace, unidentifiable amounts of blood), he acknowledged that, as the prosecutor put it in questioning the witness, "blue jean material is common material," so "this doesn't mean that the fibers that were all over the victim's clothing were necessarily from [House's] pair of blue jeans." On House's pants, though cotton garments both transfer and retain fibers readily, Agent Blythe found neither hair nor fiber consistent with the victim's hair or clothing.

As Turner informed the jury, House's shoes were found several months after the crime in a field near her home. Turner delivered them to authorities. Though the jury did not learn of this fact (and House's counsel claims he did not either), the State tested the shoes for blood and found none. House's shirt was not found.

The State's closing argument suggested that on the night of her murder, Mrs. Muncey "was deceived. . . . She had been told [her husband] had had an accident." The prosecutor emphasized the FBI's blood analysis, noting that "after running many, many, many tests," Agent Bigbee: "was able to tell you that the blood on the defendant's blue jeans was not his own blood, could not be his own blood. He told you that the blood on the blue jeans was consistent with every characteristic in every respect of the deceased's, Carolyn Muncey's, and that ninety-three (93%) percent of the white population would not have that blood type. . . . He can't tell you one hundred (100%) percent for certain that it was her blood. But folks, he can sure give you a pretty good — a pretty good indication."

In addition the government suggested the black rag Hensley said he saw in House's hands was in fact the missing blue tank top, retrieved by House from the crime scene. And the prosecution reiterated the importance of the blood. "[D]efense counsel," he said, "does not start out discussing the fact that his client had blood on his jeans on the night that Carolyn Muncey was killed. . . . He doesn't start with the fact that nothing that the defense has introduced in this case explains what blood is doing on his jeans, all over his jeans, that is scientifically, completely different from his blood." The jury found House guilty of murder in the first degree.

The trial advanced to the sentencing phase. As aggravating factors to support a capital sentence, the State sought to prove: (1) that House had previously been convicted of a felony involving the use or threat of violence; (2) that the homicide was especially heinous, atrocious, or cruel in that it involved torture or depravity of mind; and (3) that the murder was committed while House was committing, attempting to commit, or fleeing from the commission of, rape or kidnaping. After presenting evidence of House's parole status and aggravated sexual assault conviction, the State rested.

[III]

As a general rule, claims forfeited under state law may support federal habeas relief only if the prisoner demonstrates cause for the default and prejudice from the asserted error. The rule is based on the comity and respect that must be accorded to state-court judgments. The bar is not, however, unqualified. In an effort to "balance the societal interests in finality, comity, and conservation of scarce judicial resources with the individual interest in justice that arises in the extraordinary case," the Court has recognized a miscarriage-of-justice exception.

"'[I]n appropriate cases,'" the Court has said, "the principles of comity and finality that inform the concepts of cause and prejudice 'must yield to the imperative of correcting a fundamentally unjust incarceration.'"

In *Schlup*, the Court adopted a specific rule to implement this general principle. It held that prisoners asserting innocence as a gateway to defaulted claims must establish that, in light of new evidence, "it is more likely than not that no reasonable juror would have found petitioner guilty beyond a reasonable doubt." This formulation, *Schlup* explains, "ensures that petitioner's case is truly 'extraordinary,' while still providing petitioner a meaningful avenue by which to avoid a manifest injustice." In the usual case the presumed guilt of a prisoner convicted in state court counsels against federal review of defaulted claims. Yet a petition supported by a convincing *Schlup* gateway showing "raise[s] sufficient doubt about [the petitioner's] guilt to undermine confidence in the result of the trial without the assurance that that trial was untainted by constitutional error"; hence, "a review of the merits of the constitutional claims" is justified.

For purposes of this case several features of the *Schlup* standard bear emphasis. First, although "[t]o be credible" a gateway claim requires "new reliable evidence — whether it be exculpatory scientific evidence, trust-worthy eyewitness accounts, or critical physical evidence — that was not pre-sented at trial," the habeas court's analysis is not limited to such evidence. There is no dispute in this case that House has presented some new reliable evidence; the State has conceded as much. In addition, because the District Court held an evidentiary hearing in this case, and because the State does not challenge the court's decision to do so, we have no occasion to elaborate on *Schlup*'s observation that when considering an actual-innocence claim in the context of a request for an evidentiary hearing, the District Court need not "test the new evidence by a standard appropriate for deciding a motion for summary judgment," but rather may "consider how the timing of the submission and the likely credibility of the affiants bear on the probable reliability of that evidence." Our review in this case addresses the merits of the *Schlup* inquiry, based on a fully developed record, and with respect to that inquiry *Schlup* makes plain that the habeas court must consider "'all the evidence,'" old and new, incriminating and exculpatory, without regard to whether it would necessarily be admitted under "rules of admissibility that would govern at trial." Based on this total record, the court must make "a probabilistic determination about what reasonable, properly instructed ju-rors would do." The court's function is not to make an independent factual determination about what likely occurred, but rather to assess the likely impact of the evidence on reasonable jurors.

Second, it bears repeating that the *Schlup* standard is demanding and permits review only in the "'extraordinary'" case. At the same time, though, the *Schlup* standard does not require absolute certainty about the peti-tioner's guilt or innocence. A petitioner's burden at the gateway stage is to demonstrate that more likely than not, in light of the new evidence, no reasonable juror would find him guilty beyond a reasonable doubt — or, to remove the double negative, that more likely than not any reasonable juror would have reasonable doubt.

The State also argues that the District Court's findings in this case tie our hands, precluding a ruling in House's favor absent a showing of clear error as to the District Court's specific determinations. This view overstates the effect of the District Court's ruling. Deference is given to a trial court's assessment of evidence presented to it in the first instance. Yet the *Schlup* inquiry, we repeat, requires a holistic judgment about "'all the evidence,'" and its likely effect on reasonable jurors applying the reasonable-doubt standard. As a general rule, the inquiry does not turn on discrete findings regarding disputed points of fact, and "[i]t is not the district court's independent judgment as to whether reasonable doubt exists that the standard addresses." Here, although the District Court attentively managed complex proceedings, carefully reviewed the extensive record, and drew certain conclusions about the evidence, the court did not clearly apply *Schlup*'s predictive standard regarding whether reasonable jurors would have reasonable doubt. As we shall explain, moreover, we are uncertain about the basis for some of the District Court's conclusions — a consideration that weakens our reliance on its determinations.

With this background in mind we turn to the evidence developed in House's federal habeas proceedings.

DNA EVIDENCE

First, in direct contradiction of evidence presented at trial, DNA testing has established that the semen on Mrs. Muncey's nightgown and panties came from her husband, Mr. Muncey, not from House. The State, though conceding this point, insists this new evidence is immaterial. At the guilt phase at least, neither sexual contact nor motive were elements of the offense, so in the State's view the evidence, or lack of evidence, of sexual assault or sexual advance is of no consequence. We disagree. In fact we consider the new disclosure of central importance.

From beginning to end the case is about who committed the crime. When identity is in question, motive is key. The point, indeed, was not lost on the prosecution, for it introduced the evidence and relied on it in the final guilt-phase closing argument. Referring to "evidence at the scene," the prosecutor suggested that House committed, or attempted to commit, some "indignity" on Mrs. Muncey that neither she "nor any mother on that road would want to do with Mr. House." Particularly in a case like this where the proof was, as the State Supreme Court observed, circumstantial, we think a jury would have given this evidence great weight. Quite apart from providing proof of motive, it was the only forensic evidence at the scene that would link House to the murder.

Law and society, as they ought to do, demand accountability when a sexual offense has been committed, so not only did this evidence link House to the crime; it likely was a factor in persuading the jury not to let him go free. At sentencing, moreover, the jury came to the unanimous conclusion, beyond a reasonable doubt, that the murder was committed in the course of a rape or kidnaping. The alleged sexual motivation relates to both those determinations. This is particularly so given that, at the sentencing phase, the jury was advised that House had a previous conviction for sexual assault.

A jury informed that fluids on Mrs. Muncey's garments could have come from House might have found that House trekked the nearly two miles to the victim's home and lured her away in order to commit a sexual offense. By contrast a jury acting without the assumption that the semen could have come from House would have found it necessary to establish some different motive, or, if the same motive, an intent far more speculative. When the only direct evidence of sexual assault drops out of the case, so, too, does a central theme in the State's narrative linking House to the crime. In that light, furthermore, House's odd evening walk and his false statements to authorities, while still potentially incriminating, might appear less suspicious.

BLOODSTAINS

The other relevant forensic evidence is the blood on House's pants, which appears in small, even minute, stains in scattered places. As the prosecutor told the jury, they were stains that, due to their small size, "you or I might not detect[,] [m]ight not see, but which the FBI lab was able to find on [House's] jeans." The stains appear inside the right pocket, outside that pocket, near the inside button, on the left thigh and outside leg, on the seat of the pants, and on the right bottom cuff, including inside the pants. Due to testing by the FBI, cuttings now appear on the pants in several places where stains evidently were found. (The cuttings were destroyed in the testing process, and defense experts were unable to replicate the tests.) At trial, the government argued "nothing that the defense has introduced in this case explains what blood is doing on his jeans, all over [House's] jeans, that is scientifically, completely different from his blood." House, though not disputing at this point that the blood is Mrs. Muncey's, now presents an alternative explanation that, if credited, would undermine the probative value of the blood evidence.

Other evidence confirms that blood did in fact spill from the vials. It appears the vials passed from Dr. Carabia, who performed the autopsy, into the hands of two local law enforcement officers, who transported it to the FBI, where Agent Bigbee performed the enzyme tests. The blood was contained in four vials, evidently with neither preservative nor a proper seal. The vials, in turn, were stored in a styrofoam box, but nothing indicates the box was kept cool. Rather, in what an evidence protocol expert at the habeas hearing described as a violation of proper procedure, the styrofoam box was packed in the same cardboard box as other evidence including House's pants (apparently in a paper bag) and other clothing (in separate bags). The cardboard box was then carried in the officers' car while they made the 10-hour journey from Tennessee to the FBI lab. Dr. Blake stated that blood vials in hot conditions (such as a car trunk in the summer) could blow open; and in fact, by the time the blood reached the FBI it had hemolyzed, or spoiled, due to heat exposure. By the time the blood passed from the FBI to a defense expert, roughly a vial and a half were empty, though Agent Bigbee testified he used at most a quarter of one vial. Blood, moreover, had seeped onto one corner of the styrofoam box and onto packing gauze inside the box below the vials.

In addition, although the pants apparently were packaged initially in a paper bag and FBI records suggest they arrived at the FBI in one, the record does not contain the paper bag but does contain a plastic bag with a label listing the pants and Agent Scott's name—and the plastic bag has blood on it. The blood appears in a forked streak roughly five inches long and two inches wide running down the bag's outside front. Though testing by House's expert confirmed the stain was blood, the expert could not determine the blood's source. Speculations about when and how the blood got there add to the confusion regarding the origins of the stains on House's pants.

Faced with these indications of, at best, poor evidence control, the State attempted to establish at the habeas hearing that all blood spillage occurred after Agent Bigbee examined the pants. Were that the case, of course, then blood would have been detected on the pants before any spill — which would tend to undermine Dr. Blake's analysis and support using the bloodstains to infer House's guilt.

In sum, considering "'all the evidence,'" on this issue, we think the evidentiary disarray surrounding the blood, taken together with Dr. Blake's testimony and the limited rebuttal of it in the present record, would prevent reasonable jurors from placing significant reliance on the blood evidence. We now know, though the trial jury did not, that an Assistant Chief Medical Examiner believes the blood on House's jeans must have come from autopsy samples; that a vial and a quarter of autopsy blood is unaccounted for; that the blood was transported to the FBI together with the pants in conditions that could have caused vials to spill; that the blood did indeed spill at least once during its journey from Tennessee authorities through FBI hands to a defense expert; that the pants were stored in a plastic bag bearing both a large blood stain and a label with TBI Agent Scott's name; and that the styrofoam box containing the blood samples may well have been opened before it arrived at the FBI lab. Thus, whereas the bloodstains, emphasized by the prosecution, seemed strong evidence of House's guilt at trial, the record now raises substantial questions about the blood's origin.

A DIFFERENT SUSPECT

Were House's challenge to the State's case limited to the questions he has raised about the blood and semen, the other evidence favoring the prosecution might well suffice to bar relief. There is, however, more; for in the post-trial proceedings House presented troubling evidence that Mr. Muncey, the victim's husband, himself could have been the murderer.

At trial, as has been noted, the jury heard that roughly two weeks before the murder Mrs. Muncey's brother received a frightened phone call from his sister indicating that she and Mr. Muncey had been fighting, that she was scared, and that she wanted to leave him. The jury also learned that the brother once saw Mr. Muncey "smac[k]" the victim. House now has produced evidence from multiple sources suggesting that Mr. Muncey regularly abused his wife.

Of most importance is the testimony of Kathy Parker and her sister Penny Letner. They testified at the habeas hearing that, around the time of House's trial, Mr. Muncey had confessed to the crime. Parker recalled that she and "some family members and some friends [were] sitting around drinking" at

Parker's trailer when Mr. Muncey "just walked in and sit down." Muncey, who had evidently been drinking heavily, began "rambling off . . . [t]alking about what happened to his wife and how it happened and he didn't mean to do it." According to Parker, Mr. Muncey "said they had been into [an] argument and he slapped her and she fell and hit her head and it killed her and he didn't mean for it to happen." Parker said she "freaked out and run him off."

Other testimony suggests Mr. Muncey had the opportunity to commit the crime. According to Dennis Wallace, a local law enforcement official who provided security at the dance on the night of the murder, Mr. Muncey left the dance "around 10:00, 10:30, 9:30 to 10:30." Although Mr. Muncey told law enforcement officials just after the murder that he left the dance only briefly and returned, Wallace could not recall seeing him back there again. Later that evening, Wallace responded to Mr. Muncey's report that his wife was missing. Muncey denied he and his wife had been "a fussing or a fighting"; he claimed his wife had been "kidnapped."

In the habeas proceedings, then, two different witnesses (Parker and Letner) described a confession by Mr. Muncey; two more (Atkins and Lawson) described suspicious behavior (a fight and an attempt to construct a false alibi) around the time of the crime; and still other witnesses described a history of abuse.

The evidence pointing to Mr. Muncey is by no means conclusive. If considered in isolation, a reasonable jury might well disregard it. In combination, however, with the challenges to the blood evidence and the lack of motive with respect to House, the evidence pointing to Mr. Muncey likely would reinforce other doubts as to House's guilt.

OTHER EVIDENCE

Certain other details were presented at the habeas hearing. First, Dr. Blake, in addition to testifying about the blood evidence and the victim's head injury, examined photographs of House's bruises and scratches and concluded, based on 35 years' experience monitoring the development and healing of bruises, that they were too old to have resulted from the crime. In addition Dr. Blake claimed that the injury on House's right knuckle was indicative of "[g]etting mashed"; it was not consistent with striking someone.

The victim's daughter, Lora Muncey (now Lora Tharp), also testified at the habeas hearing. She repeated her recollection of hearing a man with a deep voice like her grandfather's and a statement that her father had had a wreck down by the creek. She also denied seeing any signs of struggle or hearing a fight between her parents, though she also said she could not recall her parents ever fighting physically. The District Court found her credible, and this testimony certainly cuts in favor of the State.

Finally, House himself testified at the habeas proceedings. He essentially repeated the story he allegedly told Turner about getting attacked on the road. The District Court found, however, based on House's demeanor, that he "was not a credible witness."

CONCLUSION

This is not a case of conclusive exoneration. Some aspects of the State's evidence — Lora Muncey's memory of a deep voice, House's bizarre evening walk, his lie to law enforcement, his appearance near the body, and the blood on his pants — still support an inference of guilt. Yet the central forensic proof connecting House to the crime — the blood and the semen — has been called into question, and House has put forward substantial evidence pointing to a different suspect. Accordingly, and although the issue is close, we conclude that this is the rare case where — had the jury heard all the conflicting testimony — it is more likely than not that no reasonable juror viewing the record as a whole would lack reasonable doubt.

V

In addition to his gateway claim under *Schlup*, House argues that he has shown freestanding innocence and that as a result his imprisonment and planned execution are unconstitutional. In *Herrera*, decided three years before *Schlup*, the Court assumed without deciding that "in a capital case a truly persuasive demonstration of 'actual innocence' made after trial would render the execution of a defendant unconstitutional, and warrant federal habeas relief if there were no state avenue open to process such a claim." House urges the Court to answer the question left open in *Herrera* and hold not only that freestanding innocence claims are possible but also that he has established one.

We decline to resolve this issue. We conclude here, much as in *Herrera*, that whatever burden a hypothetical freestanding innocence claim would require, this petitioner has not satisfied it. To be sure, House has cast considerable doubt on his guilt — doubt sufficient to satisfy *Schlup*'s gateway standard for obtaining federal review despite a state procedural default. In *Herrera*, however, the Court described the threshold for any hypothetical freestanding innocence claim as "extraordinarily high." The sequence of the Court's decisions in *Herrera* and *Schlup* — first leaving unresolved the status of freestanding claims and then establishing the gateway standard — implies at the least that *Herrera* requires more convincing proof of innocence than *Schlup*. It follows, given the closeness of the *Schlup* question here, that House's showing falls short of the threshold implied in *Herrera*.

House has satisfied the gateway standard set forth in *Schlup* and may proceed on remand with procedurally defaulted constitutional claims.

Chief Justice ROBERTS, with whom Justice SCALIA and Justice THOMAS join, concurring in the judgment in part and dissenting in part.

To overcome the procedural hurdle that Paul House created by failing to properly present his constitutional claims to a Tennessee court, he must demonstrate that the constitutional violations he alleges "ha[ve] probably resulted in the conviction of one who is actually innocent," such that a federal court's refusal to hear the defaulted claims would be a "miscarriage of justice." Schlup v. Delo (1995). To make the requisite showing of actual innocence, House must produce "new reliable evidence" and "must show that it is more likely than not that no reasonable juror would have convicted him in the light of the new evidence." The question is not whether House was prejudiced at his trial because the jurors were not aware of the new evidence, but whether all the evidence, considered together, proves that House was actually innocent, so that no reasonable juror would vote to convict him. Considering all the evidence, and giving due regard to the District Court's findings on whether House's new evidence was reliable, I do not find it probable that no reasonable juror would vote to convict him, and accordingly I dissent.

Because I do not think that House has satisfied the actual innocence standard set forth in *Schlup*, I do not believe that he has met the higher threshold for a freestanding innocence claim, assuming such a claim exists. *See* Herrera v. Collins (1993). I therefore concur in the judgment with respect to the Court's disposition of that separate claim.

I

Critical to the Court's conclusion here that House has sufficiently demonstrated his innocence are three pieces of new evidence presented to the District Court: DNA evidence showing that the semen on Carolyn Muncey's clothing was from her husband, Hubert Muncey, not from House; testimony from new witnesses implicating Mr. Muncey in the murder; and evidence indicating that Mrs. Muncey's blood spilled from test tubes containing autopsy samples in an evidence container. To determine whether it should open its door to House's defaulted constitutional claims, the District Court considered this evidence in a comprehensive evidentiary hearing. As House presented his new evidence, and as the State rebutted it, the District Court observed the witnesses' demeanor, examined physical evidence, and made findings about whether House's new evidence was in fact reliable. This fact-finding role is familiar to a district court. "The trial judge's major role is the determination of fact, and with experience in fulfilling that role comes expertise."

The State did not contest House's new DNA evidence excluding him as the source of the semen on Mrs. Muncey's clothing, but it strongly contested the new testimony implicating Mr. Muncey, and it insisted that the blood spillage occurred after the FBI tested House's jeans and determined that they were stained with Mrs. Muncey's blood.

At the evidentiary hearing, sisters Kathy Parker and Penny Letner testified that 14 years earlier, either during or around the time of House's trial, they heard Mr. Muncey drunkenly confess to having accidentally killed his wife when he struck her in their home during an argument, causing her to fall and hit her head. *Schlup* provided guidance on how a district court should assess this type of new evidence: The court "may consider how the timing of the submission and the likely credibility of the affiants bear on the probable reliability of that evidence," and it "must assess the probative force of the newly presented evidence in connection with the evidence of guilt adduced at trial." Consistent with this guidance, the District Court concluded that the sisters' testimony was not credible. The court noted that it was "not impressed with the allegations of individuals who wait over ten years to come forward." It also considered how the new testimony fit within the larger web of evidence, observing that Mr. Muncey's alleged confession contradicted the testimony of the Munceys' "very credible" daughter, Lora Tharp, who consistently testified that she did not hear a fight in the house that night, but instead heard a man with a deep voice who lured her mother from the house by saying that Mr. Muncey had been in a wreck near the creek.

The District Court engaged in a similar reliability inquiry with regard to House's new evidence of blood spillage. At the evidentiary hearing, House conceded that FBI testing showed that his jeans were stained with Mrs. Muncey's blood, but he set out to prove that the blood spilled from test tubes containing autopsy samples, and that it did so before the jeans were tested by the FBI. The District Court summarized the testimony of the various witnesses who handled the evidence and their recollections about bloodstains and spillage; it acknowledged that House's expert, Dr. Cleland Blake, disagreed with FBI Agent Paul Bigbee about how to interpret the results of Agent Bigbee's genetic marker analysis summary; and it summarized the testimony of the State's blood spatter expert, Paulette Sutton. After reviewing all the evidence, the District Court stated: "Based upon the evidence introduced during the evidentiary hearing . . . the court concludes that the spillage occurred after the FBI crime laboratory received and tested the evidence."

Normally, an appellate court reviews a district court's factual findings only for clear error. The majority essentially disregards the District Court's role in assessing the reliability of House's new evidence. The majority's assessment of House's new evidence is precisely the summary judgment-type inquiry *Schlup* said was inappropriate. By casting aside the District Court's factual determinations made after a comprehensive evidentiary hearing, the majority has done little more than reiterate the factual disputes presented below. Witnesses do not testify in our courtroom, and it is not our role to make credibility findings and construct theories of the possible ways in which Mrs. Muncey's blood could have been spattered and wiped on House's jeans. The District Court did not painstakingly conduct an evidentiary hearing to compile a record for us to sort through transcript by transcript and photograph by photograph, assessing for ourselves the reliability of what we see. *Schlup* made abundantly clear that reliability determinations were essential, but were for the district court to make. We are to defer to the better situated District Court on reliability, unless we determine that its findings are clearly erroneous. We are not concerned with "the district court's independent judgment as to whether reasonable doubt exists," but the District Court here made basic factual findings about the reliability of

House's new evidence; it did not offer its personal opinion about whether it doubted House's guilt. *Schlup* makes clear that those findings are controlling unless clearly erroneous.

I have found no clear error in the District Court's reliability findings. Not having observed Ms. Parker and Ms. Letner testify, I would defer to the District Court's determination that they are not credible, and the evidence in the record undermining the tale of an accidental killing during a fight in the Muncey home convinces me that this credibility finding is not clearly erroneous. Dr. Alex Carabia, who performed the autopsy, testified to injuries far more severe than a bump on the head: Mrs. Muncey had bruises on the front and back of her neck, on both thighs, on her lower right leg and left knee, and her hands were bloodstained up to the wrists; her injuries were consistent with a struggle and traumatic strangulation. And, of course, Lora Tharp has consistently recalled a deep-voiced visitor arriving late at night to tell Mrs. Muncey that her husband was in a wreck near the creek.

I also find abundant evidence in the record to support the District Court's finding that blood spilled within the evidence container after the FBI received and tested House's jeans. Agent Bigbee testified that there was no leakage in the items submitted to him for testing. The majority's entire analysis on this point assumes the agent flatly lied, though there was no attack on his credibility below.

It is also worth noting that the blood evidently spilled inside the evidence container when the jeans were protected inside a plastic zip lock bag, as shown by the presence of a bloodstain on the outside of that bag. House's expert tested the exterior and interior of that plastic bag for bloodstains using an "extremely sensitive" test, and only the exterior of the bag tested positive for blood. The evidence in the record indicates that the jeans were placed in the plastic bag after they arrived at the FBI: FBI records show that the jeans arrived there in a paper bag, and the plastic bag has FBI markings on it.

II

With due regard to the District Court's reliability findings, this case invites a straightforward application of the legal standard adopted in *Schlup*. A petitioner does not pass through the *Schlup* gateway if it is "more likely than not that there is any juror who, acting reasonably, would have found the petitioner guilty beyond a reasonable doubt."

The majority states that if House had presented just one of his three key pieces of evidence — or even two of the three — he would not pass through the *Schlup* gateway. According to the majority, House has picked the trifecta of evidence that places conviction outside the realm of choices any juror, acting reasonably, would make. Because the case against House remains substantially unaltered from the case presented to the jury, I disagree.

Given the District Court's reliability findings about the first two pieces of evidence, the evidence before us now is not substantially different from that considered by House's jury. I therefore find it more likely than not that in light of this new evidence, at least one juror, acting reasonably, would vote to convict House. The evidence as a whole certainly does not establish that House is actually innocent of the crime of murdering Carolyn Muncey, and accordingly I dissent.

7. May the Federal Court Hold an Evidentiary Hearing?

Assuming that all of the above hurdles have been overcome, the issue then can arise as to whether a federal court may hold an evidentiary hearing or is limited to deciding the matter based on the record from the state court. This is addressed in 28 U.S.C. §2254(e), which states:

> (1) In a proceeding instituted by an application for a writ of habeas corpus by a person in custody pursuant to the judgment of a State court, a determination of a factual issue made by a State court shall be presumed to be correct. The applicant shall have the burden of rebutting the presumption of correctness by clear and convincing evidence.
> (2) If the applicant has failed to develop the factual basis of a claim in State court proceedings, the court shall not hold an evidentiary hearing on the claim unless the applicant shows that —
> (A) the claim relies on —
> (i) a new rule of constitutional law, made retroactive to cases on collateral review by the Supreme Court, that was previously unavailable; or
> (ii) a factual predicate that could not have been previously discovered through the exercise of due diligence; and
> (B) the facts underlying the claim would be sufficient to establish by clear and convincing evidence that but for constitutional error, no reasonable fact-finder would have found the applicant guilty of the underlying offense.

In Cullen v. Pinholster, the Court gave this a restrictive interpretation, which leaves open the issue of when, if ever, there can be an evidentiary hearing in federal court on habeas corpus.

CULLEN v. PINHOLSTER

131 S. Ct. 1388 (2011)

Justice THOMAS delivered the opinion of the Court.

Scott Lynn Pinholster and two accomplices broke into a house in the middle of the night and brutally beat and stabbed to death two men who happened to interrupt the burglary. A jury convicted Pinholster of first-degree murder, and he was sentenced to death.

After the California Supreme Court twice unanimously denied Pinholster habeas relief, a Federal District Court held an evidentiary hearing and granted Pinholster habeas relief under 28 U.S.C. §2254. The District Court concluded that Pinholster's trial counsel had been constitutionally ineffective at the penalty phase of trial. Sitting en banc, the Court of Appeals for the Ninth Circuit affirmed. Considering the new evidence adduced in the District Court hearing, the Court of Appeals held that the California Supreme Court's decision "was contrary to, or involved an unreasonable application of, clearly established Federal law."

I

On the evening of January 8, 1982, Pinholster solicited Art Corona and Paul David Brown to help him rob Michael Kumar, a local drug dealer. On the way, they stopped at Lisa Tapar's house, where Pinholster put his buck knife through her front door and scratched a swastika into her car after she refused to talk to him. The three men, who were all armed with buck knives, found no one at Kumar's house, broke in, and began ransacking the home. They came across only a small amount of marijuana before Kumar's friends, Thomas Johnson and Robert Beckett, arrived and shouted that they were calling the police.

Pinholster and his accomplices tried to escape through the rear door, but Johnson blocked their path. Pinholster backed Johnson onto the patio, demanding drugs and money and repeatedly striking him in the chest. Johnson dropped his wallet on the ground and stopped resisting. Beckett then came around the corner, and Pinholster attacked him, too, stabbing him repeatedly in the chest. Pinholster forced Beckett to the ground, took both men's wallets, and began kicking Beckett in the head. Meanwhile, Brown stabbed Johnson in the chest, "'bury[ing] his knife to the hilt.'" Johnson and Beckett died of their wounds.

Pinholster was arrested shortly thereafter and threatened to kill Corona if he did not keep quiet about the burglary and murders. Corona later became the State's primary witness. The prosecution brought numerous charges against Pinholster, including two counts of first-degree murder.

The California trial court appointed Harry Brainard and Wilbur Dettmar to defend Pinholster on charges of first-degree murder, robbery, and burglary. Before their appointment, Pinholster had rejected other attorneys and insisted on representing himself. During that time, the State had mailed Pinholster a letter in jail informing him that the prosecution planned to offer aggravating evidence during the penalty phase of trial to support a sentence of death. The jury convicted Pinholster on both counts of first-degree murder.

Before the penalty phase, Brainard and Dettmar moved to exclude any aggravating evidence on the ground that the prosecution had failed to provide notice of the evidence to be introduced, as required. At a hearing on April 24, Dettmar argued that, in reliance on the lack of notice, he was "not presently prepared to offer anything by way of mitigation." The trial court asked whether a continuance might be helpful, but Dettmar declined, explaining that he could not think of a mitigation witness other than Pinholster's mother and that additional time would not "make a great deal of difference." Three days later, after hearing testimony, the court found that

Pinholster had received notice while representing himself and denied the motion to exclude.

The penalty phase was held before the same jury that had convicted Pinholster. The prosecution produced eight witnesses, who testified about Pinholster's history of threatening and violent behavior, including resisting arrest and assaulting police officers, involvement with juvenile gangs, and a substantial prison disciplinary record. Defense counsel called only Pinholster's mother, Burnice Brashear. She gave an account of Pinholster's troubled childhood and adolescent years, discussed Pinholster's siblings, and described Pinholster as "a perfect gentleman at home." Defense counsel did not call a psychiatrist, though they had consulted Dr. John Stalberg at least six weeks earlier. Dr. Stalberg noted Pinholster's "psychopathic personality traits," diagnosed him with antisocial personality disorder, and concluded that he "was not under the influence of extreme mental or emotional disturbance" at the time of the murders.

After 2½ days of deliberation, the jury unanimously voted for death on each of the two murder counts. On mandatory appeal, the California Supreme Court affirmed the judgment.

In August 1993, Pinholster filed his first state habeas petition. Represented by new counsel, Pinholster alleged ineffective assistance of counsel at the penalty phase of his trial. He alleged that Brainard and Dettmar had failed to adequately investigate and present mitigating evidence, including evidence of mental disorders. Pinholster supported this claim with school, medical, and legal records, as well as declarations from family members, Brainard, and Dr. George Woods, a psychiatrist who diagnosed Pinholster with bipolar mood disorder and seizure disorders. Dr. Woods criticized Dr. Stalberg's report as incompetent, unreliable, and inaccurate. The California Supreme Court unanimously and summarily denied Pinholster's penalty-phase ineffective-assistance claim "on the substantive ground that it is without merit."

Pinholster filed a federal habeas petition in April 1997. He reiterated his previous allegations about penalty-phase ineffective assistance and also added new allegations that his trial counsel had failed to furnish Dr. Stalberg with adequate background materials. In support of the new allegations, Dr. Stalberg provided a declaration stating that in 1984, Pinholster's trial counsel had provided him with only some police reports and a 1978 probation report. Dr. Stalberg explained that, had he known about the material that had since been gathered by Pinholster's habeas counsel, he would have conducted "further inquiry" before concluding that Pinholster suffered only from a personality disorder. He noted that Pinholster's school records showed evidence of "some degree of brain damage." Dr. Stalberg did not, however, retract his earlier diagnosis. The parties stipulated that this declaration had never been submitted to the California Supreme Court, and the federal petition was held in abeyance to allow Pinholster to go back to state court.

In August 1997, Pinholster filed his second state habeas petition, this time including Dr. Stalberg's declaration and requesting judicial notice of the documents previously submitted in support of his first state habeas petition.

His allegations of penalty-phase ineffective assistance of counsel mirrored those in his federal habeas petition. The California Supreme Court again unanimously and summarily denied the petition "on the substantive ground that it is without merit."

Having presented Dr. Stalberg's declaration to the state court, Pinholster returned to the District Court. In November 1997, he filed an amended petition for a writ of habeas corpus. The District Court concluded that the Antiterrorism and Effective Death Penalty Act of 1996 (AEDPA), did not apply and granted an evidentiary hearing.

The District Court granted habeas relief. Applying pre-AEDPA standards, the court granted the habeas petition "for inadequacy of counsel by failure to investigate and present mitigation evidence at the penalty hearing." After *Woodford v. Garceau* (2003), clarified that AEDPA applies to cases like Pinholster's, the court amended its order but did not alter its conclusion.

II

We first consider the scope of the record for a §2254(d)(1) inquiry. The State argues that review is limited to the record that was before the state court that adjudicated the claim on the merits. Pinholster contends that evidence presented to the federal habeas court may also be considered. We agree with the State.

As amended by AEDPA, 28 U.S.C. §2254 sets several limits on the power of a federal court to grant an application for a writ of habeas corpus on behalf of a state prisoner. If an application includes a claim that has been "adjudicated on the merits in State court proceedings," §2254(d), an additional restriction applies. Under §2254(d), that application "shall not be granted with respect to [such a] claim . . . unless the adjudication of the claim": "(1) resulted in a decision that was contrary to, or involved an unreasonable application of, clearly established Federal law, as determined by the Supreme Court of the United States; or (2) resulted in a decision that was based on an unreasonable determination of the facts in light of the evidence presented in the State court proceeding." This is a "difficult to meet," and "highly deferential standard for evaluating state-court rulings, which demands that state-court decisions be given the benefit of the doubt." The petitioner carries the burden of proof.

We now hold that review under §2254(d)(1) is limited to the record that was before the state court that adjudicated the claim on the merits. Section 2254(d)(1) refers, in the past tense, to a state-court adjudication that "resulted in" a decision that was contrary to, or "involved" an unreasonable application of, established law. This backward-looking language requires an examination of the state-court decision at the time it was made. It follows that the record under review is limited to the record in existence at that same time *i.e.*, the record before the state court.

This understanding of the text is compelled by "the broader context of the statute as a whole," which demonstrates Congress' intent to channel prisoners' claims first to the state courts. "The federal habeas scheme leaves primary responsibility with the state courts. . . ."

Limiting §2254(d)(1) review to the state-court record is consistent with our precedents interpreting that statutory provision. Our cases emphasize that review under §2254(d)(1) focuses on what a state court knew and did. State-court decisions are measured against this Court's precedents as of "the time the state court renders its decision." To determine whether a particular decision is "contrary to" then-established law, a federal court must consider whether the decision "applies a rule that contradicts [such] law" and how the decision "confronts [the] set of facts" that were before the state court. If the state-court decision "identifies the correct governing legal principle" in existence at the time, a federal court must assess whether the decision "unreasonably applies that principle to the facts of the prisoner's case." It would be strange to ask federal courts to analyze whether a state court's adjudication resulted in a decision that unreasonably applied federal law to facts not before the state court.

Pinholster's contention that our holding renders §2254(e)(2) superfluous is incorrect. Section 2254(e)(2) imposes a limitation on the discretion of federal habeas courts to take new evidence in an evidentiary hearing. Like §2254(d)(1), it carries out "AEDPA's goal of promoting comity, finality, and federalism by giving state courts the first opportunity to review [a] claim, and to correct any constitutional violation in the first instance."[45]

Section 2254(e)(2) continues to have force where §2254(d)(1) does not bar federal habeas relief. For example, not all federal habeas claims by state prisoners fall within the scope of §2254(d), which applies only to claims "adjudicated on the merits in State court proceedings." At a minimum, therefore, §2254(e)(2) still restricts the discretion of federal habeas courts to consider new evidence when deciding claims that were not adjudicated on the merits in state court.

Although state prisoners may sometimes submit new evidence in federal court, AEDPA's statutory scheme is designed to strongly discourage them from doing so. Provisions like §§2254(d)(1) and (e)(2) ensure that "[f]ederal courts sitting in habeas are not an alternative forum for trying facts and issues which a prisoner made insufficient effort to pursue in state proceedings."

Accordingly, we conclude that the Court of Appeals erred in considering the District Court evidence in its review under §2254(d)(1). [The Court then considered and rejected Pinholster's claim of ineffective assistance of counsel.]

---

45. Justice Sotomayor's argument that §2254(d)(1) must be read in a way that "accommodates" §2254(e)(2) rests on a fundamental misunderstanding of §2254(e)(2). The focus of that section is not on "preserving the opportunity" for hearings, but rather on *limiting* the discretion of federal district courts in holding hearings. We see no need in this case to address the proper application of §2254(e)(2). [Footnote by the Court.]

Justice ALITO, concurring in part and concurring in the judgment.

Although I concur in the Court's judgment, I agree with the conclusion reached in Part I of the dissent, namely, that, when an evidentiary hearing is properly held in federal court, review under 28 U.S.C. §2254(d)(1) must take into account the evidence admitted at that hearing. As the dissent points out, refusing to consider the evidence received in the hearing in federal court gives §2254(e)(2) an implausibly narrow scope and will lead either to results that Congress surely did not intend or to the distortion of other provisions of the Antiterrorism and Effective Death Penalty Act of 1996 (AEDPA), 110 Stat. 1214, and the law on "cause and prejudice."

Under AEDPA evidentiary hearings in federal court should be rare. The petitioner generally must have made a diligent effort to produce in state court the new evidence on which he seeks to rely. If that requirement is not satisfied, the petitioner may establish the factual predicate for a claim in a federal-court hearing only if, among other things, "the facts underlying the claim would be sufficient to establish by clear and convincing evidence that but for constitutional error, no reasonable factfinder would have found the applicant guilty of the underlying offense." §2254(e)(2)(B).

Even when the petitioner does satisfy the diligence standard, a hearing should not be held in federal court unless the new evidence that the petitioner seeks to introduce was not and could not have been offered in the state-court proceeding.

In this case, I would hold that the federal-court hearing should not have been held because respondent did not diligently present his new evidence to the California courts.

Justice SOTOMAYOR, dissenting.

Some habeas petitioners are unable to develop the factual basis of their claims in state court through no fault of their own. Congress recognized as much when it enacted the Antiterrorism and Effective Death Penalty Act of 1996 (AEDPA) and permitted therein the introduction of new evidence in federal habeas proceedings in certain limited circumstances. See 28 U.S.C. §2254(e)(2). Under the Court's novel interpretation of §2254(d)(1), however, federal courts must turn a blind eye to new evidence in deciding whether a petitioner has satisfied §2254(d)(1)'s threshold obstacle to federal habeas relief—even when it is clear that the petitioner would be entitled to relief in light of that evidence. In reading the statute to "compe[l]" this harsh result, the Court ignores a key textual difference between §§2254(d)(1) and 2254(d)(2) and discards the previous understanding in our precedents that new evidence can, in fact, inform the §2254(d)(1) inquiry. I therefore dissent from the Court's first holding.

The Court first holds that, in determining whether a state-court decision is an unreasonable application of Supreme Court precedent under §2254(d)(1), "review . . . is limited to the record that was before the state court that adjudicated the claim on the merits." New evidence adduced at a federal evidentiary hearing is now irrelevant to determining whether a petitioner has satisfied §2254(d)(1). This holding is unnecessary to pro-mote

AEDPA's purposes, and it is inconsistent with the provision's text, the structure of the statute, and our precedents.

To understand the significance of the majority's holding, it is important to view the issue in context. AEDPA's entire structure — which gives state courts the opportunity to decide factual and legal questions in the first instance — ensures that evidentiary hearings in federal habeas proceedings are very rare. See N. King, F. Cheesman, & B. Ostrom, Final Technical Report: Habeas Litigation in U.S. District Courts 35-36 (2007) (evidentiary hearings under AEDPA occur in 0.4 percent of noncapital cases and 9.5 percent of capital cases). Even absent the new restriction created by today's holding, AEDPA erects multiple hurdles to a state prisoner's ability to introduce new evidence in a federal habeas proceeding.

First, "[u]nder the exhaustion requirement, a habeas petitioner challenging a state conviction must first attempt to present his claim in state court." With certain narrow exceptions, federal courts cannot consider a claim at all, let alone accept new evidence relevant to the claim, if it has not been exhausted in state court. The exhaustion requirement thus reserves to state courts the first opportunity to resolve factual disputes relevant to a state prisoner's claim.

Second, the exhaustion requirement is "complement[ed]" by the standards set forth in §2254(d). Under this provision, a federal court may not grant habeas relief on any "claim that was adjudicated on the merits in State court proceedings" unless the adjudication "(1) resulted in a decision that was contrary to, or involved an unreasonable application of, clearly established Federal law, as determined by the Supreme Court of the United States; or (2) resulted in a decision that was based on an unreasonable determination of the facts in light of the evidence presented in the State court proceeding. These standards "control whether to grant habeas relief." Accordingly, we have said, if the factual allegations a petitioner seeks to prove at an evidentiary hearing would not satisfy these standards, there is no reason for a hearing. In such a case, the district court may exercise its "discretion to deny an evidentiary hearing." This approach makes eminent sense: If district courts held evidentiary hearings without first asking whether the evidence the petitioner seeks to present would satisfy AEDPA's demanding standards, they would needlessly prolong federal habeas proceedings.

Third, even when a petitioner seeks to introduce new evidence that would entitle him to relief, AEDPA prohibits him from doing so, except in a narrow range of cases, unless he "made a reasonable attempt, in light of the information available at the time, to investigate and pursue claims in state court." Thus, §2254(e)(2) provides: "If the applicant has failed to develop the factual basis of a claim in State court proceedings, the court shall not hold an evidentiary hearing on the claim unless the applicant shows that — (A) the claim relies on — (i) a new rule of constitutional law, made retroactive to cases on collateral review by the Supreme Court, that was previously unavailable; or (ii) a factual predicate that could not have been previously discovered through the exercise of due diligence; and (B) the facts underlying the claim would be sufficient to establish by clear and convincing evidence that but for constitutional error, no reasonable factfinder would have found the applicant guilty of the underlying offense."

The majority's interpretation of §2254(d)(1) finds no support in the provision's text or the statute's structure as a whole. Section 2254(d)(1) requires district courts to ask whether a state-court adjudication on the merits "resulted in a decision that was contrary to, or involved an unreasonable application of, clearly established Federal law, as determined by the Supreme Court of the United States." Because this provision uses "backward-looking language" — *i.e.*, past-tense verbs — the majority believes that it limits review to the state-court record. But both §§2254(d)(1) and 2254(d)(2) use "backward-looking language," and §2254(d)(2) — unlike §2254(d)(1) — expressly directs district courts to base their review on "the evidence presented in the State court proceeding." If use of the past tense were sufficient to indicate Congress' intent to restrict analysis to the state-court record, the phrase "in light of the evidence presented in the State court proceeding" in §2254(d)(2) would be superfluous. The majority's construction of §2254(d)(1) fails to give meaning to Congress' decision to include language referring to the evidence presented to the state court in §2254(d)(2).

Unlike my colleagues in the majority, I refuse to assume that Congress simply engaged in sloppy drafting. The inclusion of this phrase in §2254(d)(2) — coupled with its omission from §2254(d)(2)'s partner provision, §2254(d)(1) — provides strong reason to think that Congress did not intend for the §2254(d)(1) analysis to be limited categorically to "the evidence presented in the State court proceeding."

The "'broader context of the statute as a whole,'" reinforces this conclusion. In particular, Congress' decision to include in AEDPA a provision, §2254(e)(2), that permits federal evidentiary hearings in certain circumstances provides further evidence that Congress did not intend to limit the §2254(d)(1) inquiry to the state-court record in every case.

We have long recognized that some diligent habeas petitioners are unable to develop all of the facts supporting their claims in state court. As discussed above, in enacting AEDPA, Congress generally barred evidentiary hearings for petitioners who did not "exercise diligence in pursuing their claims" in state court.

The majority charts a novel course that, so far as I am aware, no court of appeals has adopted: §2254(d)(1) continues to apply when a petitioner has additional evidence that he was unable to present to the state court, but the district court cannot consider that evidence in deciding whether the petitioner has satisfied §2254(d)(1). The problem with this approach is its potential to bar federal habeas relief for diligent habeas petitioners who cannot present new evidence to a state court.

Consider, for example, a petitioner who diligently attempted in state court to develop the factual basis of a claim that prosecutors withheld exculpatory witness statements in violation of *Brady v. Maryland* (1963). The state court denied relief on the ground that the withheld evidence then known did not rise to the level of materiality required under *Brady*. Before the time for filing a federal habeas petition has expired, however, a state court orders the State to disclose additional documents the petitioner had timely requested under the State's public records Act. The disclosed documents reveal that the State withheld other exculpatory witness statements, but state law would not permit the petitioner to present the new evidence in a successive petition.

Under our precedent, if the petitioner had not presented his *Brady* claim to the state court at all, his claim would be deemed defaulted and the petitioner could attempt to show cause and prejudice to overcome the default. If, however, the new evidence merely bolsters a *Brady* claim that was adjudicated on the merits in state court, it is unclear how the petitioner can obtain federal habeas relief after today's holding. What may have been a reasonable decision on the state-court record may no longer be reasonable in light of the new evidence. Because the state court adjudicated the petitioner's *Brady* claim on the merits, §2254(d)(1) would still apply. Yet, under the majority's interpretation of §2254(d)(1), a federal court is now prohibited from considering the new evidence in determining the reasonableness of the state-court decision.

The majority's interpretation of §2254(d)(1) thus suggests the anomalous result that petitioners with new claims based on newly obtained evidence can obtain federal habeas relief if they can show cause and prejudice for their default but petitioners with newly obtained evidence supporting a claim adjudicated on the merits in state court cannot obtain federal habeas relief if they cannot first satisfy §2254(d)(1) without the new evidence. That the majority's interpretation leads to this anomaly is good reason to conclude that its interpretation is wrong.

The majority responds to this anomaly by suggesting that my hypothetical petitioner "may well [have] a new claim." This suggestion is puzzling. New evidence does not usually give rise to a new claim; it merely provides additional proof of a claim already adjudicated on the merits.

The majority's reading of §2254(d)(1) appears ultimately to rest on its understanding that state courts must have the first opportunity to adjudicate habeas petitioners' claims. I fully agree that habeas petitioners must attempt to present evidence to state courts in the first instance. Where I disagree with the majority is in my understanding that §2254(e)(2) already accomplishes this result. By reading §2254(d)(1) to do the work of §2254(e)(2), the majority gives §2254(e)(2) an unnaturally cramped reading. As a result, the majority either has foreclosed habeas relief for diligent petitioners who, through no fault of their own, were unable to present exculpatory evidence to the state court that adjudicated their claims or has created a new set of procedural complexities for the lower courts to navigate to ensure the availability of the Great Writ for diligent petitioners.

I fear the consequences of the Court's novel interpretation of §2254(d)(1) for diligent state habeas petitioners with compelling evidence supporting their claims who were unable, through no fault of their own, to present that evidence to the state court that adjudicated their claims.

8.   May the Federal Court Grant the Habeas Corpus Petition?

Assuming the habeas petitioner makes it through the previous seven hurdles, the issue then becomes whether the federal court may grant the habeas petition. The Antiterrorism and Effective Death Penalty Act imposed a significant new restriction on the ability of a federal court to grant relief to state prisoners. Section 2254(d) provides that a

> writ of habeas corpus on behalf of a person in custody pursuant to a judgment of a State court shall not be granted with respect to any claim that was adjudicated on the merits in a State court proceeding unless the adjudication of the claim:
> (1) resulted in a decision that was contrary to, or involved an unreasonable application of clearly established Federal law, as determined by the Supreme Court of the United States; or
> (2) resulted in a decision that was based on an unreasonable determination of the facts in light of the evidence presented in the State court proceeding.

As for the former, the key question concerns when a state court decision is "contrary to, or an unreasonable application of clearly established federal law." Williams v. Taylor is the key Supreme Court case defining this phrase.

WILLIAMS v. TAYLOR
529 U.S. 362 (2000)

Justice STEVENS announced the judgment of the Court and delivered the opinion of the Court with respect to Parts I, III, and IV, and an opinion with respect to Parts II and V. Justice SOUTER, Justice GINSBURG, and Justice BREYER join this opinion in its entirety. Justice O'CONNOR and Justice KENNEDY join Parts I, III, and IV of this opinion.

The questions presented are whether Terry Williams' constitutional right to the effective assistance of counsel as defined in Strickland v. Washington (1984), was violated, and whether the judgment of the Virginia Supreme Court refusing to set aside his death sentence "was contrary to, or involved an unreasonable application of, clearly established Federal law, as determined by the Supreme Court of the United States," within the meaning of 28 U.S.C. §2254(d)(1). We answer both questions affirmatively.

I

On November 3, 1985, Harris Stone was found dead in his residence on Henry Street in Danville, Virginia. Finding no indication of a struggle, local officials determined that the cause of death was blood alcohol poisoning, and the case was considered closed. Six months after Stone's death, Terry Williams, who was then incarcerated in the "I" unit of the city jail for an unrelated offense, wrote a letter to the police stating that he had killed "that man down on Henry Street" and also stating that he "'did it'" to that "lady down on West Green Street" and was "'very sorry.'" The letter was unsigned, but it closed with a reference to "I cell." The police readily identified Williams as its author, and, on April 25, 1986, they obtained several statements from him. In one Williams admitted that, after Stone refused to lend him "'a couple of dollars,'" he had killed Stone with a mattock and taken the money from his wallet. In September 1986, Williams was convicted of robbery and capital murder.

The jury found a probability of future dangerousness and unanimously fixed Williams' punishment at death. The trial judge concluded that such punishment was "proper" and "just" and imposed the death sentence. The Virginia Supreme Court affirmed the conviction and sentence.

In 1988 Williams filed for state collateral relief in the Danville Circuit Court. The petition was subsequently amended, and the Circuit Court (the same judge who had presided over Williams' trial and sentencing) held an evidentiary hearing on Williams' claim that trial counsel had been ineffective. Based on the evidence adduced after two days of hearings, Judge Ingram found that Williams' conviction was valid, but that his trial attorneys had been ineffective during sentencing. Among the evidence reviewed that had not been presented at trial were documents prepared in connection with Williams' commitment when he was 11 years old that dramatically described mistreatment, abuse, and neglect during his early childhood, as well as testimony that he was "borderline mentally retarded," had suffered repeated head injuries, and might have mental impairments organic in origin. The habeas hearing also revealed that the same experts who had testified on the State's behalf at trial believed that Williams, if kept in a "structured environment," would not pose a future danger to society.

Counsel's failure to discover and present this and other significant mitigating evidence was "below the range expected of reasonable, professional competent assistance of counsel." Counsel's performance thus "did not measure up to the standard required under the holding of Strickland v. Washington (1984), and [if it had,] there is a reasonable probability that the result of the sentencing phase would have been different." Judge Ingram therefore recommended that Williams be granted a rehearing on the sentencing phase of his trial.

The Virginia Supreme Court did not accept that recommendation. Although it assumed, without deciding, that trial counsel had been ineffective, it disagreed with the trial judge's conclusion that Williams had suffered sufficient prejudice to warrant relief.

Having exhausted his state remedies, Williams sought a federal writ of habeas corpus pursuant to 28 U.S.C. §2254. After reviewing the state habeas hearing transcript and the state courts' findings of fact and conclusions of law, the federal trial judge agreed with the Virginia trial judge: The death sentence was constitutionally infirm.

The Federal Court of Appeals reversed. It construed §2254(d)(1) as prohibiting the grant of habeas corpus relief unless the state court "'decided the question by interpreting or applying the relevant precedent in a manner that reasonable jurists would all agree is unreasonable.'" Applying that standard, it could not say that the Virginia Supreme Court's decision on the prejudice issue was an unreasonable application of the tests developed in [earlier cases]. It explained that the evidence that Williams presented a future danger to society was "simply overwhelming," and it characterized the state court's understanding of the facts in this case as "reasonable."

II

The warden here contends that federal habeas corpus relief is prohibited by the amendment to 28 U.S.C. §2254, enacted as a part of the Antiterrorism and Effective Death Penalty Act of 1996 (AEDPA). The relevant portion of that amendment provides:

> (d) An application for a writ of habeas corpus on behalf of a person in custody pursuant to the judgment of a State court shall not be granted with respect to any claim that was adjudicated on the merits in State court proceedings unless the adjudication of the claim—
> (1) resulted in a decision that was contrary to, or involved an unreasonable application of, clearly established Federal law, as determined by the Supreme Court of the United States. . . .

In this case, the Court of Appeals read the amendment as prohibiting federal courts from issuing the writ unless:

> (a) the state court decision is in "square conflict" with Supreme Court precedent that is controlling as to law and fact or (b) if no such controlling decision exists, "the state court's resolution of a question of pure law rests upon an objectively unreasonable derivation of legal principles from the relevant [S]upreme [C]ourt precedents, or if its decision rests upon an objectively unreasonable application of established principles to new facts."

Accordingly, it held that a federal court may issue habeas relief only if "'the state courts have decided the question by interpreting or applying the relevant precedent in a manner that reasonable jurists would all agree is unreasonable.'" We are convinced that that interpretation of the amendment is incorrect. It would impose a test for determining when a legal rule is clearly established that simply cannot be squared with the real practice of decisional law. It would apply a standard for determining the "reasonableness" of state-court decisions that is not contained in the statute itself, and that Congress surely did not intend. And it would wrongly require the federal courts, including this Court, to defer to state judges' interpretations of federal law.

As the Fourth Circuit would have it, a state-court judgment is "unreasonable" in the face of federal law only if all reasonable jurists would agree that the state court was unreasonable. Thus, in this case, for example, even if the

Virginia Supreme Court misread our opinion in [an earlier case], we could not grant relief unless we believed that none of the judges who agreed with the state court's interpretation of that case was a "reasonable jurist." But the statute says nothing about "reasonable judges," presumably because all, or virtually all, such judges occasionally commit error; they make decisions that in retrospect may be characterized as "unreasonable." Indeed, it is most unlikely that Congress would deliberately impose such a requirement of unanimity on federal judges. As Congress is acutely aware, reasonable lawyers and lawgivers regularly disagree with one another. Congress surely did not intend that the views of one such judge who might think that relief is not warranted in a particular case should always have greater weight than the contrary, considered judgment of several other reasonable judges.

The inquiry mandated by the amendment relates to the way in which a federal habeas court exercises its duty to decide constitutional questions; the amendment does not alter the underlying grant of jurisdiction in §2254(a). When federal judges exercise their federal-question jurisdiction under the "judicial Power" of Article III of the Constitution, it is "emphatically the province and duty" of those judges to "say what the law is." Marbury v. Madison (1803). At the core of this power is the federal courts' independent responsibility—independent from its coequal branches in the Federal Government, and independent from the separate authority of the several States—to interpret federal law. A construction of AEDPA that would require the federal courts to cede this authority to the courts of the States would be inconsistent with the practice that federal judges have traditionally followed in discharging their duties under Article III of the Constitution. If Congress had intended to require such an important change in the exercise of our jurisdiction, we believe it would have spoken with much greater clarity than is found in the text of AEDPA.

This basic premise informs our interpretation of both parts of §2254(d)(1): first, the requirement that the determinations of state courts be tested only against "clearly established Federal law, as determined by the Supreme Court of the United States," and second, the prohibition on the issuance of the writ unless the state court's decision is "contrary to, or involved an unreasonable application of," that clearly established law. We address each part in turn.

THE "CLEARLY ESTABLISHED LAW" REQUIREMENT

In Teague v. Lane (1989), we held that the petitioner was not entitled to federal habeas relief because he was relying on a rule of federal law that had not been announced until after his state conviction became final. The anti-retroactivity rule recognized in *Teague*, which prohibits reliance on "new rules," is the functional equivalent of a statutory provision commanding exclusive reliance on "clearly established law." Because there is no reason to believe that Congress intended to require federal courts to ask both whether a rule sought on habeas is "new" under *Teague*—which remains the law—and also whether it is "clearly established" under AEDPA, it seems safe to assume that Congress had congruent concepts in mind. It is perfectly clear that AEDPA codifies *Teague* to the extent that *Teague* requires federal habeas courts to deny relief that is contingent upon a rule of law not clearly established at the time the state conviction became final. *Teague*'s core principles are therefore relevant to our construction of this requirement. *Teague* established some guidance for making this determination, explaining that a federal habeas court operates within the bounds of comity and finality if it applies a rule "dictated by precedent existing at the time the defendant's conviction became final." A rule that "breaks new ground or imposes a new obligation on the States or the Federal Government," falls outside this universe of federal law.

To this, AEDPA has added, immediately following the "clearly established law" requirement, a clause limiting the area of relevant law to that "determined by the Supreme Court of the United States." If this Court has not broken sufficient legal ground to establish an asked-for constitutional principle, the lower federal courts cannot themselves establish such a principle with clarity sufficient to satisfy the AEDPA bar. In this respect, we agree with the Seventh Circuit that this clause "extends the principle of *Teague* by limiting the source of doctrine on which a federal court may rely in addressing the application for a writ."

A rule that fails to satisfy the foregoing criteria is barred by *Teague* from application on collateral review, and, similarly, is not available as a basis for relief in a habeas case to which AEDPA applies.

In the context of this case, we also note that, as our precedent interpreting *Teague* has demonstrated, rules of law may be sufficiently clear for habeas purposes even when they are expressed in terms of a generalized standard rather than as a bright-line rule. Moreover, the determination whether or not a rule is clearly established at the time a state court renders its final judgment of conviction is a question as to which the "federal courts must make an independent evaluation."

THE "CONTRARY TO, OR AN UNREASONABLE APPLICATION OF," REQUIREMENT

The message that Congress intended to convey by using the phrases "contrary to" and "unreasonable application of" is not entirely clear. The prevailing view in the Circuits is that the former phrase requires de novo review of "pure" questions of law and the latter requires some sort of "reasonability" review of so-called mixed questions of law and fact.

We are not persuaded that the phrases define two mutually exclusive categories of questions. Most constitutional questions that arise in habeas corpus proceedings — and therefore most "decisions" to be made — require the federal judge to apply a rule of law to a set of facts, some of which may be disputed and some undisputed. For example, an erroneous conclusion that particular circumstances established the voluntariness of a confession, or that there exists a conflict of interest when one attorney represents multiple defendants, may well be described either as "contrary to" or as an "unreasonable application of" the governing rule of law. In constitutional adjudication, as in the common law, rules of law often develop incrementally as earlier decisions are applied to new factual situations. But rules that depend upon such elaboration are hardly less lawlike than those that establish a bright-line test.

Indeed, our pre-AEDPA efforts to distinguish questions of fact, questions of law, and "mixed questions," and to create an appropriate standard of habeas review for each, generated some not insubstantial differences of opinion as to which issues of law fell into which category of question, and as to which standard of review applied to each. The statutory text likewise does not obviously prescribe a specific, recognizable standard of review for dealing with either phrase. Significantly, it does not use any term, such as "de novo" or "plain error," that would easily identify a familiar standard of review. Rather, the text is fairly read simply as a command that a federal court not issue the habeas writ unless the state court was wrong as a matter of law or unreasonable in its application of law in a given case.

On the other hand, it is significant that the word "deference" does not appear in the text of the statute itself. Neither the legislative history nor the statutory text suggests any difference in the so-called "deference" depending on which of the two phrases is implicated. Whatever "deference" Congress had in mind with respect to both phrases, it surely is not a requirement that federal courts actually defer to a state-court application of the federal law that is, in the independent judgment of the federal court, in error.

In sum, the statute directs federal courts to attend to every state-court judgment with utmost care, but it does not require them to defer to the opinion of every reasonable state-court judge on the content of federal law. If, after carefully weighing all the reasons for accepting a state court's judgment, a federal court is convinced that a prisoner's custody — or, as in this case, his sentence of death — violates the Constitution, that independent judgment should prevail. Otherwise the federal "law as determined by the Supreme Court of the United States" might be applied by the federal courts one way in Virginia and another way in California. In light of the well-recognized interest in ensuring that federal courts interpret federal law in a uniform way, we are convinced that Congress did not intend the statute to produce such a result.

III

In this case, Williams contends that he was denied his constitutionally guaranteed right to the effective assistance of counsel when his trial lawyers failed to investigate and to present substantial mitigating evidence to the sentencing jury. The threshold question under AEDPA is whether Williams seeks to apply a rule of law that was clearly established at the time his state-court conviction became final. That question is easily answered because the merits of his claim are squarely governed by our holding in Strickland v. Washington (1984). [The Court then explained why there was ineffective assistance of counsel in this case.]

V

In our judgment, the state trial judge was correct both in his recognition of the established legal standard for determining counsel's effectiveness, and in his conclusion that the entire postconviction record, viewed as a whole and cumulative of mitigation evidence presented originally, raised "a reasonable probability that the result of the sentencing proceeding would have been different" if competent counsel had presented and explained the significance of all the available evidence. It follows that the Virginia Supreme Court rendered a "decision that was contrary to, or involved an unreasonable application of, clearly established Federal law." Williams' constitutional right to the effective assistance of counsel as defined in Strickland v. Washington was violated.

Justice O'CONNOR delivered the opinion of the Court with respect to Part II, concurred in part, and concurred in the judgment. Justice KENNEDY joins this opinion in its entirety. THE CHIEF JUSTICE and Justice THOMAS join this opinion with respect to Part II. Justice SCALIA joins this opinion with respect to Part II.

The Court holds today that the Virginia Supreme Court's adjudication of Terry Williams' application for state habeas corpus relief resulted in just such a decision. I agree with that determination and join Parts I, III, and IV of the Court's opinion. Because I disagree, however, with the interpretation of §2254(d)(1) set forth in Part II of Justice Stevens' opinion, I write separately to explain my views.

I

Before 1996, this Court held that a federal court entertaining a state prisoner's application for habeas relief must exercise its independent judgment when deciding both questions of constitutional law and mixed constitutional questions (i.e., application of constitutional law to fact). In other words, a federal habeas court owed no deference to a state court's resolution of such questions of law or mixed questions.

If today's case were governed by the federal habeas statute prior to Congress' enactment of AEDPA in 1996, I would agree with Justice Stevens that Williams' petition for habeas relief must be granted if we, in our independent judgment, were to conclude that his Sixth Amendment right to effective assistance of counsel was violated.

II

Williams' case is not governed by the pre-1996 version of the habeas statute. Because he filed his petition in December 1997, Williams' case is governed by the statute as amended by AEDPA. Justice Stevens' opinion in Part II essentially contends that §2254(d)(1) does not alter the previously settled rule of independent review. Indeed, the opinion concludes its statutory inquiry with the somewhat empty finding that §2254(d)(1) does no more than express a "'mood' that the Federal Judiciary must respect." For Justice Stevens, the congressionally enacted "mood" has two important qualities. First, "federal courts [must] attend to every state-court judgment with utmost care" by "carefully weighing all the reasons for accepting a state court's judgment." Second, if a federal court undertakes that careful review and yet remains convinced that a prisoner's custody violates the Constitution, "that independent judgment should prevail."

Justice Stevens' interpretation of §2254(d)(1) gives the 1996 amendment no effect whatsoever. The command that federal courts should now use the "utmost care" by "carefully weighing" the reasons supporting a state court's judgment echoes our pre-AEDPA statement that federal habeas courts "should, of course, give great weight to the considered conclusions of a coequal state judiciary."

That Justice Stevens would find the new §2254(d)(1) to have no effect on the prior law of habeas corpus is remarkable given his apparent acknowledgment that Congress wished to bring change to the field. That acknowledgment is correct and significant to this case. It cannot be disputed that Congress viewed §2254(d)(1) as an important means by which its goals for habeas reform would be achieved.

Justice Stevens arrives at his erroneous interpretation by means of one critical misstep. He fails to give independent meaning to both the "contrary to" and "unreasonable application" clauses of the statute. By reading §2254(d)(1) as one general restriction on the power of the federal habeas court, Justice Stevens manages to avoid confronting the specific meaning of the statute's "unreasonable application" clause and its ramifications for the independent-review rule. It is, however, a cardinal principle of statutory construction that we must "'give effect, if possible, to every clause and word of a statute.'"

Section 2254(d)(1) defines two categories of cases in which a state prisoner may obtain federal habeas relief with respect to a claim adjudicated on the merits in state court. Under the statute, a federal court may grant a writ of habeas corpus if the relevant state-court decision was either (1) "contrary to . . . clearly established Federal law, as determined by the Supreme Court of the United States," or (2) "involved an unreasonable application of . . . clearly established Federal law, as determined by the Supreme Court of the United States."

The Court of Appeals for the Fourth Circuit properly accorded both the "contrary to" and "unreasonable application" clauses independent meaning. The Fourth Circuit held that a state-court decision can be "contrary to" this Court's clearly established precedent in two ways. First, a state-court decision is contrary to this Court's precedent if the state court arrives at a conclusion opposite to that reached by this Court on a question of law.

Second, a state-court decision is also contrary to this Court's precedent if the state court confronts facts that are materially indistinguishable from a relevant Supreme Court precedent and arrives at a result opposite to ours.

The word "contrary" is commonly understood to mean "diametrically different," "opposite in character or nature," or "mutually opposed." Webster's Third New International Dictionary 495 (1976). The text of §2254(d)(1) therefore suggests that the state court's decision must be substantially different from the relevant precedent of this Court. The Fourth Circuit's interpretation of the "contrary to" clause accurately reflects this textual meaning. A state-court decision will certainly be contrary to our clearly established precedent if the state court applies a rule that contradicts the governing law set forth in our cases. On the other hand, a run-of-the-mill state-court decision applying the correct legal rule from our cases to the facts of a prisoner's case would not fit comfortably within §2254(d)(1)'s "contrary to" clause.

The Fourth Circuit's interpretation of the "unreasonable application" clause of §2254(d)(1) is generally correct. That court held that a state-court decision can involve an "unreasonable application" of this Court's clearly established precedent in two ways. First, a state-court decision involves an unreasonable application of this Court's precedent if the state court identifies the correct governing legal rule from this Court's cases but unreasonably applies it to the facts of the particular state prisoner's case. Second, a state-court decision also involves an unreasonable application of this Court's precedent if the state court either unreasonably extends a legal principle from our precedent to a new context where it should not apply or unreasonably refuses to extend that principle to a new context where it should apply.

A state-court decision that correctly identifies the governing legal rule but applies it unreasonably to the facts of a particular prisoner's case certainly would qualify as a decision "involv[ing] an unreasonable application of . . . clearly established Federal law."

The Fourth Circuit also held that state-court decisions that unreasonably extend a legal principle from our precedent to a new context where it should not apply (or unreasonably refuse to extend a legal principle to a new context where it should apply) should be analyzed under §2254(d)(1)'s "unreasonable application" clause. Although that holding may perhaps be correct, the classification does have some problems of precision. Just as it is sometimes difficult to distinguish a mixed question of law and fact from a question of fact, it will often be difficult to identify separately those state-court decisions that involve an unreasonable application of a legal principle (or an unreasonable failure to apply a legal principle) to a new context. Indeed, on the one hand, in some cases it will be hard to distinguish a decision involving an unreasonable extension of a legal principle from a decision involving an unreasonable application of law to facts. On the other hand, in many of the same cases it will also be difficult to distinguish a decision involving an unreasonable extension of a legal principle from a decision that "arrives at a conclusion opposite to that reached by this Court on a question of law." Today's case does not require us to decide how such "extension of legal principle" cases should be treated under §2254(d)(1). For now it is sufficient to hold that when a state-court decision unreasonably applies the law of this Court to the facts of a prisoner's case, a federal court applying §2254(d)(1) may conclude that the state-court decision falls within that provision's "unreasonable application" clause.

There remains the task of defining what exactly qualifies as an "unreasonable application" of law under §2254(d)(1). The Fourth Circuit held that a state-court decision involves an "unreasonable application of . . . clearly established Federal law" only if the state court has applied federal law "in a manner that reasonable jurists would all agree is unreasonable." The placement of this additional overlay on the "unreasonable application" clause was erroneous.

Defining an "unreasonable application" by reference to a "reasonable jurist," however, is of little assistance to the courts that must apply §2254(d)(1) and, in fact, may be misleading. Stated simply, a federal habeas court making the "unreasonable application" inquiry should ask whether the state court's application of clearly established federal law was objectively unreasonable. The federal habeas court should not transform the inquiry into a subjective one by resting its determination instead on the simple fact that at least one of the Nation's jurists has applied the relevant federal law in the same manner the state court did in the habeas petitioner's case. The "all reasonable jurists" standard would tend to mislead federal habeas courts by focusing their attention on a subjective inquiry rather than on an objective one.

The term "unreasonable" is no doubt difficult to define. That said, it is a common term in the legal world and, accordingly, federal judges are familiar with its meaning. For purposes of today's opinion, the most important point is that an unreasonable application of federal law is different from an incorrect application of federal law.

Throughout this discussion the meaning of the phrase "clearly established Federal law, as determined by the Supreme Court of the United States" has been put to the side. That statutory phrase refers to the holdings, as opposed to the dicta, of this Court's decisions as of the time of the relevant state-court decision. In this respect, the "clearly established Federal law" phrase bears only a slight connection to our *Teague* jurisprudence. With one caveat, whatever would qualify as an old rule under our *Teague* jurisprudence will constitute "clearly established Federal law, as determined by the Supreme Court of the United States" under §2254(d)(1). The one caveat, as the statutory language makes clear, is that §2254(d)(1) restricts the source of clearly established law to this Court's jurisprudence.

In sum, §2254(d)(1) places a new constraint on the power of a federal habeas court to grant a state prisoner's application for a writ of habeas corpus with respect to claims adjudicated on the merits in state court. Under §2254(d)(1), the writ may issue only if one of the following two conditions is satisfied — the state-court adjudication resulted in a decision that (1) "was contrary to . . . clearly established Federal law, as determined by the Supreme Court of the United States," or (2) "involved an unreasonable application of . . . clearly established Federal law, as determined by the Supreme Court of the United States." Under the "contrary to" clause, a federal habeas court may grant the writ if the state court arrives at a conclusion opposite to that reached by this Court on a question of law or if the state court decides a case differently than this Court has on a set of materially indistinguishable facts. Under the "unreasonable application" clause, a federal habeas court may grant the writ if the state court identifies the correct governing legal principle from this Court's decisions but unreasonably applies that principle to the facts of the prisoner's case.

III

Although I disagree with Justice Stevens concerning the standard we must apply under §2254(d)(1) in evaluating Terry Williams' claims on habeas, I agree with the Court that the Virginia Supreme Court's adjudication of Williams' claim of ineffective assistance of counsel resulted in a decision that was both contrary to and involved an unreasonable application of this Court's clearly established precedent.

Chief Justice REHNQUIST, with whom Justice SCALIA and Justice THOMAS join, concurring in part and dissenting in part.

I agree with the Court's interpretation of 28 U.S.C. §2254(d)(1) (opinion of O'Connor, J.), but disagree with its decision to grant habeas relief in this case. There is "clearly established Federal law, as determined by [this Court]" that governs petitioner's claim of ineffective assistance of counsel: Strickland v. Washington (1984). Thus, we must determine whether the Virginia Supreme Court's adjudication was "contrary to" or an "unreasonable application of" *Strickland*. [Chief Justice Rehnquist then argued that there was not ineffective assistance of counsel in this case.]

Subsequently, though, in Harrington v. Richter, 131 S. Ct. 770 (2011), the Court said that "[a]s a condition for obtaining habeas corpus from a federal court, a state prisoner must show that the state court's ruling on the claim being presented in federal court was so lacking in justification that there was an error well understood and comprehended in existing law beyond any possibility for fairminded disagreement." This statement appears to adopt the standard that the Court had rejected in *Williams*, but the Court does so without acknowledging the change in the law. In a case after *Harrington*, the Court reiterated and applied this standard to overrule a lower court's granting a habeas petition. Bobby v. Dixon, 132 S. Ct. 26 (2011).

C. STATUTES AND RULES GOVERNING HABEAS CORPUS

Federal statutes prescribe the availability of habeas corpus relief and define the procedures to be followed in federal habeas corpus proceedings. In addition, in 1977, the Rules Governing Section 2254 Cases in the United States District Courts went into effect. The statutes and rules describe many important aspects of federal habeas corpus litigation.

First, a writ of habeas corpus may be granted by "the Supreme Court, any justice thereof, the district courts and any circuit judge within their respective jurisdictions." 28 U.S.C. §2241(a). If a petition for a writ of habeas corpus is filed with the Supreme Court, a Supreme Court justice, or a federal court of appeals judge, the petition may be transferred to the district court having jurisdiction to entertain it.

Second, habeas corpus petitions must be in writing, signed, and verified by the person for whom relief is requested or by someone acting on his or her behalf. 28 U.S.C. §2242. The petition must describe the facts concerning the "applicant's commitment or detention," including the basis for requesting the writ. Because the writ, if granted, directs the person holding the petitioner to release him or her from custody, the petition should name the custodian — such as the warden — as the respondent.

Third, the person must be in "custody" in order to bring a habeas corpus petition. Over the last half century, the Court has broadly defined "custody." The Court has held that individuals may use habeas corpus petitions to challenge any restriction of liberty, such as parole; habeas petitions may be heard even if an individual will not necessarily be released because of consecutive or concurrent sentences; and habeas petitions should not be dismissed as moot even after a person is released from prison.

Jones v. Cunningham, 371 U.S. 286 (1963), which held that a person may present a habeas corpus petition while on parole, is a crucial case liberalizing the definition of "in custody." In *Jones,* an individual filed a habeas corpus petition while in prison but was paroled while the matter was pending in federal court. The United States Court of Appeals for the Fourth Circuit dismissed the petition because the individual was no longer in custody but, in fact, free on parole. The Supreme Court reversed. In an opinion by Justice Black, the Court observed that "[h]istory, usage, and precedent can leave no doubt that, besides physical imprisonment, there are other restraints on a man's liberty." The Court catalogued the many restrictions on liberty suffered by a person on parole — ranging from limits on travel to required visits from and meetings with a parole officer. In fact, under the state's law, a person granted parole was "'under the custody and control of the . . . Parole Board.'" The Court said that because parole imposes restraints "not shared by the public generally," a person on parole should be regarded as in custody.

Similarly, the Court held in Hensley v. Municipal Court, 411 U.S. 34 (1973), that individuals could seek habeas corpus even when they were released on bail or on their own recognizance. The court of appeals, in accord with prior Supreme Court rulings, concluded that a person could not seek habeas corpus until incarceration began. The Supreme Court reversed and emphasized that because all appeals in the state court system had been exhausted, incarceration was imminent. The Court said that there was no reason to require a person to spend "[ten] minutes in jail" in order to file a habeas corpus petition. The Court explained that the petitioner's movement was restricted because he was required to appear at the demand of any competent court and the failure to appear was itself a crime.

Although the requirement for actual incarceration has been eliminated, habeas corpus petitions still must be brought to challenge restrictions on liberty. Habeas corpus may not be used to challenge the imposition of fines or payment of restitution as part of a sentence.

Fourth, courts have authority to grant habeas corpus to individuals held in custody "within their respective jurisdictions." 28 U.S.C. §2241(a). In Padilla v. Rumsfeld, 542 U.S. 426 (2004), the Court reaffirmed that a habeas petition must be brought in the judicial district where a person is detained. Jose Padilla was apprehended in Chicago's O'Hare Airport and detained as an enemy combatant on suspicion that he was planning to build and detonate a "dirty bomb." He was initially taken to New York, where he was held as a material witness. A habeas petition was filed on his behalf from there. He was transferred to a military prison in South Carolina, but the habeas petition continued to be litigated in the Southern District of New York and then the Second Circuit, which ruled in his favor.

The Supreme Court, in a 5-4 decision, reversed and held that the habeas petition needed to be brought in the federal district court in South Carolina, where the immediate custodian over his person was located.

Federal prisoners must file petitions pursuant to §2255 with the court that imposed the sentence. Previously, federal prisoners also could file petitions with courts located in the areas where they were confined. This proved inconvenient both for the courts and the prisoners. Courts in areas where federal prisons are located were deluged with petitions, whereas courts in areas without prisons received no petitions. Also, petitioners often were confined far from the court where the trial occurred and hence were removed from the witnesses and documents they might need for their habeas petition. Consequently, federal prisoners, pursuant to 28 U.S.C. §2255, must return to the court that sentenced them and thus have less of a choice as to where to file their habeas petitions.

Fifth, the federal statutes authorize the federal court in ruling on a habeas corpus petition to "dispose of the matter as law and justice require." 28 U.S.C. §2243. Generally, the federal court in granting a habeas corpus petition either orders the release of an individual from custody or, more commonly, orders the individual released unless a new trial is held within a reasonable amount of time.

Finally, in general, the final order of a judge in a habeas proceeding is subject to review on appeal by the court of appeals in the circuit where the federal district court is located. However, a major limitation on the right to appeal is that a state prisoner whose petition for habeas corpus is denied may appeal only if the federal district court judge or a court of appeals judge issues a certificate of appealability.[46] Before the Antiterrorism and Effective Death Penalty Act this was termed a certificate of probable cause. A court can issue a certificate of appealability only if "the applicant has made a substantial showing of the denial of a constitutional right." In other words, absent a certification of appealability, a state prisoner may not appeal the denial of habeas corpus. Although the text of the act seems to say that district court judges cannot issue such certificates, most courts have ruled to the contrary and concluded that either a district court or a court of appeals can authorize review.

In Miller-El v. Cockrell, 537 U.S. 322 (2003), the Supreme Court held that a certificate of appealability should be granted if "reasonable jurists could debate" whether the petition should have been granted. This "does not require a showing that the appeal will succeed." Nor is there to be full consideration of the merits. But the certificate should be granted if it presents a debatable issue for the court of appeals to consider.

D. HABEAS CORPUS AND THE WAR ON TERRORISM

In recent years, there has been a major debate over whether federal courts should be able to exercise habeas corpus over those who are detained as part of the war on terrorism, especially those held in Guantánamo Bay, Cuba. After the United States government began to detain individuals there in January 2002, habeas corpus petitions were filed on their behalf. In Rasul v. Bush, the Supreme Court held that federal courts have jurisdiction to hear habeas petitions by those detained in Guantánamo.

---

46. Section 2253(c) provides:

(1) Unless a circuit justice or judge issues a certificate of appealability, an appeal may not be taken to the court of appeals from — (A) the final order in a habeas corpus proceeding in which the detention complained of arises out of process issued by a state court; or (B) the final order is a proceeding under section 2255. (2) A certificate of appealability may issue under paragraph (1) only if the applicant has made a substantial showing of the denial of a constitutional right. (3) The certificate of appealability under paragraph (1) shall indicate which specific issue or issues satisfy the showing required by paragraph (2).

RASUL v. BUSH
542 U.S. 466 (2004)

Justice STEVENS delivered the opinion of the Court.

These two cases present the narrow but important question whether United States courts lack jurisdiction to consider challenges to the legality of the detention of foreign nationals captured abroad in connection with hostilities and incarcerated at the Guantanamo Bay Naval Base, Cuba.

I

On September 11, 2001, agents of the al Qaeda terrorist network hijacked four commercial airliners and used them as missiles to attack American targets. While one of the four attacks was foiled by the heroism of the plane's passengers, the other three killed approximately 3,000 innocent civilians, destroyed hundreds of millions of dollars of property, and severely damaged the U.S. economy. In response to the attacks, Congress passed a joint resolution authorizing the President to use "all necessary and appropriate force against those nations, organizations, or persons he determines planned, authorized, committed, or aided the terrorist attacks . . . or harbored such organizations or persons." Acting pursuant to that authorization, the President sent U.S. Armed Forces into Afghanistan to wage a military campaign against al Qaeda and the Taliban regime that had supported it.

Petitioners in these cases are 2 Australian citizens and 12 Kuwaiti citizens who were captured abroad during hostilities between the United States and the Taliban. Since early 2002, the U.S. military has held them — along with, according to the Government's estimate, approximately 640 other non-Americans captured abroad — at the naval base at Guantanamo Bay. The United States occupies the base, which comprises 45 square miles of land and water along the southeast coast of Cuba, pursuant to a 1903 Lease Agreement executed with the newly independent Republic of Cuba in the aftermath of the Spanish-American War. Under the agreement, "the United States recognizes the continuance of the ultimate sovereignty of the Republic of Cuba over the [leased areas]," while "the Republic of Cuba consents that during the period of the occupation by the United States . . . the United States shall exercise complete jurisdiction and control over and within said areas." In 1934, the parties entered into a treaty providing that, absent an agreement to modify or abrogate the lease, the lease would remain in effect "[s]o long as the United States of America shall not abandon the . . . naval station of Guantanamo."

In 2002, petitioners, through relatives acting as their next friends, filed various actions in the U.S. District Court for the District of Columbia challenging the legality of their detention at the base. All alleged that none of the petitioners has ever been a combatant against the United States or has ever engaged in any terrorist acts. They also alleged that none has been charged with any wrongdoing, permitted to consult with counsel, or provided access to the courts or any other tribunal.

Construing all [these] actions as petitions for writs of habeas corpus, the District Court dismissed them for want of jurisdiction. The court held, in reliance on our opinion in Johnson v. Eisentrager (1950), that "aliens detained outside the sovereign territory of the United States [may not] invok[e] a petition for a writ of habeas corpus." The Court of Appeals affirmed.

II

Congress has granted federal district courts, "within their respective jurisdictions," the authority to hear applications for habeas corpus by any person who claims to be held "in custody in violation of the Constitution or laws or treaties of the United States." Consistent with the historic purpose of the writ, this Court has recognized the federal courts' power to review applications for habeas relief in a wide variety of cases involving executive detention, in wartime as well as in times of peace. The Court has, for example, entertained the habeas petitions of an American citizen who plotted an attack on military installations during the Civil War, Ex parte Milligan (1866), and of admitted enemy aliens convicted of war crimes during a declared war and held in the United States, Ex parte Quirin (1942), and its insular possessions, In re Yamashita (1946).

The question now before us is whether the habeas statute confers a right to judicial review of the legality of executive detention of aliens in a territory over which the United States exercises plenary and exclusive jurisdiction, but not "ultimate sovereignty."

III

Respondents' primary submission is that the answer to the jurisdictional question is controlled by our decision in *Eisentrager*. In that case, we held that a Federal District Court lacked authority to issue a writ of habeas corpus to 21 German citizens who had been captured by U.S. forces in China, tried and convicted of war crimes by an American military commission headquartered in Nanking, and incarcerated in the Landsberg Prison in occupied Germany. The Court of Appeals in *Eisentrager* had found jurisdiction, reasoning that "any person who is deprived of his liberty by officials of the United States, acting under purported authority of that Government, and who can show that his confinement is in violation of a prohibition of the Constitution, has a right to the writ." In reversing that determination, this Court summarized the six critical facts in the case: "We are here confronted with a decision whose basic premise is that these prisoners are entitled, as a constitutional right, to sue in some court of the United States for a writ of habeas corpus. To support that assumption we must hold that a prisoner of our military authorities is constitutionally entitled to the writ, even though he (a) is an enemy alien; (b) has never been or resided in the United States; (c) was captured outside of our territory and there held in military custody as a prisoner of war; (d) was tried and convicted by a Military Commission sitting outside the United States; (e) for offenses against laws of war committed outside the United States; (f) and is at all times imprisoned outside the United States." On this set of facts, the Court concluded, "no right to the writ of habeas corpus appears."

Petitioners in these cases differ from the *Eisentrager* detainees in important respects: They are not nationals of countries at war with the United States, and they deny that they have engaged in or plotted acts of aggression against the United States; they have never been afforded access to any tribunal, much less charged with and convicted of wrongdoing; and for more than two years they have been imprisoned in territory over which the United States exercises exclusive jurisdiction and control.

Not only are petitioners differently situated from the *Eisentrager* detainees, but the Court in *Eisentrager* made quite clear that all six of the facts critical to its disposition were relevant only to the question of the prisoners' constitutional entitlement to habeas corpus. The Court had far less to say on the question of the petitioners' statutory entitlement to habeas review. Its only statement on the subject was a passing reference to the absence of statutory authorization: "Nothing in the text of the Constitution extends such a right, nor does anything in our statutes."

IV

[R]espondents contend that we can discern a limit on §2241 through application of the "longstanding principle of American law" that congressional legislation is presumed not to have extraterritorial application unless such intent is clearly manifested. Whatever traction the presumption against extraterritoriality might have in other contexts, it certainly has no application to the operation of the habeas statute with respect to persons detained within "the territorial jurisdiction" of the United States. By the express terms of its agreements with Cuba, the United States exercises "complete jurisdiction and control" over the Guantanamo Bay Naval Base, and may continue to exercise such control permanently if it so chooses. Respondents themselves concede that the habeas statute would create federal-court jurisdiction over the claims of an American citizen held at the base. Considering that the statute draws no distinction between Americans and aliens held in federal custody, there is little reason to think that Congress intended the geographical coverage of the statute to vary depending on the detainee's citizenship. Aliens held at the base, no less than American citizens, are entitled to invoke the federal courts' authority under §2241.

Application of the habeas statute to persons detained at the base is consistent with the historical reach of the writ of habeas corpus. At common law, courts exercised habeas jurisdiction over the claims of aliens detained within sovereign territory of the realm, as well as the claims of persons detained in the so-called "exempt jurisdictions," where ordinary writs did not run, and all other dominions under the sovereign's control.

In the end, the answer to the question presented is clear. Petitioners contend that they are being held in federal custody in violation of the laws of the United States. No party questions the District Court's jurisdiction over petitioners' custodians. Section 2241, by its terms, requires nothing more. We therefore hold that §2241 confers on the District Court jurisdiction to hear petitioners' habeas corpus challenges to the legality of their detention at the Guantanamo Bay Naval Base.

Justice KENNEDY, concurring in the judgment.

The Court is correct, in my view, to conclude that federal courts have jurisdiction to consider challenges to the legality of the detention of foreign nationals held at the Guantanamo Bay Naval Base in Cuba. While I reach the same conclusion, my analysis follows a different course.

The decision in *Eisentrager* indicates that there is a realm of political authority over military affairs where the judicial power may not enter. The existence of this realm acknowledges the power of the President as Commander in Chief, and the joint role of the President and the Congress, in the conduct of military affairs. A faithful application of *Eisentrager*, then, requires an initial inquiry into the general circumstances of the detention to determine whether the Court has the authority to entertain the petition and to grant relief after considering all of the facts presented. A necessary corollary of *Eisentrager* is that there are circumstances in which the courts maintain the power and the responsibility to protect persons from unlawful detention even where military affairs are implicated.

The facts here are distinguishable from those in *Eisentrager* in two critical ways, leading to the conclusion that a federal court may entertain the petitions. First, Guantanamo Bay is in every practical respect a United States territory, and it is one far removed from any hostilities. The opinion of the Court well explains the history of its possession by the United States. In a formal sense, the United States leases the Bay; the 1903 lease agreement states that Cuba retains "ultimate sovereignty" over it. At the same time, this lease is no ordinary lease. Its term is indefinite and at the discretion of the United States. What matters is the unchallenged and indefinite control that the United States has long exercised over Guantanamo Bay. From a practical perspective, the indefinite lease of Guantanamo Bay has produced a place that belongs to the United States, extending the "implied protection" of the United States to it.

The second critical set of facts is that the detainees at Guantanamo Bay are being held indefinitely, and without benefit of any legal proceeding to determine their status. In *Eisentrager*, the prisoners were tried and convicted by a military commission of violating the laws of war and were sentenced to prison terms. Having already been subject to procedures establishing their status, they could not justify "a limited opening of our courts" to show that they were "of friendly personal disposition" and not enemy aliens. Indefinite detention without trial or other proceeding presents altogether different considerations. It allows friends and foes alike to remain in detention. It suggests a weaker case of military necessity and much greater alignment with the traditional function of habeas corpus. Perhaps, where detainees are taken from a zone of hostilities, detention without proceedings or trial would be justified by military necessity for a matter of weeks; but as the period of detention stretches from months to years, the case for continued detention to meet military exigencies becomes weaker.

In light of the status of Guantanamo Bay and the indefinite pretrial detention of the detainees, I would hold that federal-court jurisdiction is permitted in these cases. This approach would avoid creating automatic statutory authority to adjudicate the claims of persons located outside the United States, and remains true to the reasoning of *Eisentrager*. For these reasons, I concur in the judgment of the Court.

Justice SCALIA, with whom THE CHIEF JUSTICE and Justice THOMAS join, dissenting.

The Court today holds that the habeas statute, 28 U.S.C. §2241, extends to aliens detained by the United States military overseas, outside the sovereign borders of the United States and beyond the territorial jurisdictions of all its courts. This is not only a novel holding; it contradicts a half-century-old precedent on which the military undoubtedly relied, Johnson v. Eisentrager (1950). This is an irresponsible overturning of settled law in a matter of extreme importance to our forces currently in the field. I would leave it to Congress to change §2241, and dissent from the Court's unprecedented holding.

Eisentrager's directly-on-point statutory holding makes it exceedingly difficult for the Court to reach the result it desires today.

In abandoning the venerable statutory line drawn in *Eisentrager,* the Court boldly extends the scope of the habeas statute to the four corners of the earth. The consequence of this holding, as applied to aliens outside the country, is breathtaking. It permits an alien captured in a foreign theater of active combat to bring a §2241 petition against the Secretary of Defense. Over the course of the last century, the United States has held millions of alien prisoners abroad. A great many of these prisoners would no doubt have complained about the circumstances of their capture and the terms of their confinement. The military is currently detaining over 600 prisoners at Guantanamo Bay alone; each detainee undoubtedly has complaints — real or contrived — about those terms and circumstances. The Court's unheralded expansion of federal-court jurisdiction is not even mitigated by a comforting assurance that the legion of ensuing claims will be easily resolved on the merits.

Today's carefree Court disregards, without a word of acknowledgment, the dire warning of a more circumspect Court in *Eisentrager:* "To grant the writ to these prisoners might mean that our army must transport them across the seas for hearing. This would require allocation for shipping space, guarding personnel, billeting and rations. It might also require transportation for whatever witnesses the prisoners desired to call as well as transportation for those necessary to defend legality of the sentence. The writ, since it is held to be a matter of right, would be equally available to enemies during active hostilities as in the present twilight between war and peace. Such trials would hamper the war effort and bring aid and comfort to the enemy. They would diminish the prestige of our commanders, not only with enemies but with wavering neutrals. It would be difficult to devise more effective fettering of a field commander than to allow the very enemies he is ordered to reduce to submission to call him to account in his own civil courts and divert his efforts and attention from the military offensive abroad to the legal defensive at home. Nor is it unlikely that the result of such enemy litigiousness would be a conflict between judicial and military opinion highly comforting to enemies of the United States."

Departure from our rule of stare decisis in statutory cases is always extraordinary; it ought to be unthinkable when the departure has a potentially harmful effect upon the Nation's conduct of a war. The Commander in Chief and his subordinates had every reason to expect that the internment of combatants at Guantanamo Bay would not have the consequence of bringing the cumbersome machinery of our domestic courts into military affairs. Congress is in session. If it wished to change federal judges' habeas jurisdiction from what this Court had previously held that to be, it could have done so. And it could have done so by intelligent revision of the statute, instead of by today's clumsy, countertextual reinterpretation that confers upon wartime prisoners greater habeas rights than domestic detainees. For this Court to create such a monstrous scheme in time of war, and in frustration of our military commanders' reliance upon clearly stated prior law, is judicial adventurism of the worst sort. I dissent.

In 2005, in response to Rasul v. Bush, Congress enacted the Detainee Treatment Act, which provided that those held in Guantánamo shall not have access to federal courts via a writ of habeas corpus; they must go through military commissions and then seek review in the District of Columbia Circuit.[47] In Hamdan v. Rumsfeld, 548 U.S. 557 (2006), the Supreme Court ruled that this provision applies only prospectively, not retroactively, to those petitions that already were pending in federal court at the time that the law was enacted.

In the fall of 2006, Congress responded by enacting the Military Commissions Act of 2006, which makes clear that the restrictions on habeas corpus in the Detainee Treatment Act apply retroactively.[48] The act provides, "No court, justice, or judge shall have jurisdiction to hear or consider an

47. 119 Stat. 2739, codified at 10 U.S.C. §801.
48. Pub. L. No. 109-366, 120 Stat. 2600 (2006).

application for a writ of habeas corpus filed by or on behalf of an alien detained by the United States who has been determined by the United States to have been properly detained as an enemy combatant or is awaiting such determination."[49] The act is explicit about its retroactive application and says that it "shall apply to all cases, without exception, pending on or after the date of the enactment of this Act which relate to any aspect of the detention, transfer, treatment, trial, or conditions of detention of an alien detained by the United States since September 11, 2001."[50]

In Boumediene v. Bush, the Supreme Court declared this unconstitutional as an impermissible suspension of the writ of habeas corpus.

BOUMEDIENE v. BUSH
553 U.S. 723 (2008)

Justice KENNEDY delivered the opinion of the Court.

Petitioners are aliens designated as enemy combatants and detained at the United States Naval Station at Guantanamo Bay, Cuba. There are others detained there, also aliens, who are not parties to this suit.

Petitioners present a question not resolved by our earlier cases relating to the detention of aliens at Guantanamo: whether they have the constitutional privilege of habeas corpus, a privilege not to be withdrawn except in conformance with the Suspension Clause, Art. I, §9, cl. 2. We hold these petitioners do have the habeas corpus privilege. Congress has enacted a statute, the Detainee Treatment Act of 2005 (DTA), that provides certain procedures for review of the detainees' status. We hold that those procedures are not an adequate and effective substitute for habeas corpus. Therefore §7 of the Military Commissions Act of 2006 (MCA), operates as an unconstitutional suspension of the writ. We do not address whether the President has authority to detain these petitioners nor do we hold that the writ must issue. These and other questions regarding the legality of the detention are to be resolved in the first instance by the District Court.

I

Under the Authorization for Use of Military Force (AUMF), the President is authorized "to use all necessary and appropriate force against those nations, organizations, or persons he determines planned, authorized, committed, or aided the terrorist attacks that occurred on September 11, 2001, or harbored such organizations or persons, in order to prevent any future acts of international terrorism against the United States by such nations, organizations or persons."

49. 28 U.S.C. §2241(e).
50. Id.

In Hamdi v. Rumsfeld (2004), five Members of the Court recognized that detention of individuals who fought against the United States in Afghanistan "for the duration of the particular conflict in which they were captured, is so fundamental and accepted an incident to war as to be an exercise of the 'necessary and appropriate force' Congress has authorized the President to use." After Hamdi, the Deputy Secretary of Defense established Combatant Status Review Tribunals (CSRTs) to determine whether individuals detained at Guantanamo were "enemy combatants," as the Department defines that term. A later memorandum established procedures to implement the CSRTs. The Government maintains these procedures were designed to comply with the due process requirements identified by the plurality in Hamdi.

Interpreting the AUMF, the Department of Defense ordered the detention of these petitioners, and they were transferred to Guantanamo. Some of these individuals were apprehended on the battlefield in Afghanistan, others in places as far away from there as Bosnia and Gambia. All are foreign nationals, but none is a citizen of a nation now at war with the United States. Each denies he is a member of the al Qaeda terrorist network that carried out the September 11 attacks or of the Taliban regime that provided sanctuary for al Qaeda. Each petitioner appeared before a separate CSRT; was determined to be an enemy combatant; and has sought a writ of habeas corpus in the United States District Court for the District of Columbia.

The first actions commenced in February 2002. We granted certiorari and reversed, holding that 28 U.S.C. §2241 extended statutory habeas corpus jurisdiction to Guantanamo. See Rasul v. Bush (2004). After Rasul, petitioners' cases were consolidated and entertained in two separate proceedings. In the first set of cases, Judge Richard J. Leon granted the Government's motion to dismiss, holding that the detainees had no rights that could be vindicated in a habeas corpus action. In the second set of cases Judge Joyce Hens Green reached the opposite conclusion, holding the detainees had rights under the Due Process Clause of the Fifth Amendment.

While appeals were pending from the District Court decisions, Congress passed the DTA. Subsection (e) of §1005 of the DTA amended 28 U.S.C. §2241 to provide that "no court, justice, or judge shall have jurisdiction to hear or consider . . . an application for a writ of habeas corpus filed by or on behalf of an alien detained by the Department of Defense at Guantanamo Bay, Cuba." Section 1005 further provides that the Court of Appeals for the District of Columbia Circuit shall have "exclusive" jurisdiction to review decisions of the CSRTs. Ibid.

In Hamdan v. Rumsfeld (2006), the Court held this provision did not apply to cases (like petitioners') pending when the DTA was enacted. Congress responded by passing the MCA.

II

As a threshold matter, we must decide whether MCA §7 denies the federal courts jurisdiction to hear habeas corpus actions pending at the time of its enactment. We hold the statute does deny that jurisdiction, so that, if the statute is valid, petitioners' cases must be dismissed.

As amended by the terms of the MCA, 28 U.S.C.A. §2241(e) now provides:

> (1) No court, justice, or judge shall have jurisdiction to hear or consider an application for a writ of habeas corpus filed by or on behalf of an alien detained by the United States who has been determined by the United States to have been properly detained as an enemy combatant or is awaiting such determination.
>
> (2) Except as provided in [§§1005(e)(2) and (e)(3) of the DTA] no court, justice, or judge shall have jurisdiction to hear or consider any other action against the United States or its agents relating to any aspect of the detention, transfer, treatment, trial, or conditions of confinement of an alien who is or was detained by the United States and has been determined by the United States to have been properly detained as an enemy combatant or is awaiting such determination.

Section 7(b) of the MCA provides the effective date for the amendment of §2241(e). It states: "The amendment made by [MCA §7(a)] shall take effect on the date of the enactment of this Act, and shall apply to all cases, without exception, pending on or after the date of the enactment of this Act which relate to any aspect of the detention, transfer, treatment, trial, or conditions of detention of an alien detained by the United States since September 11, 2001."

If this ongoing dialogue between and among the branches of Government is to be respected, we cannot ignore that the MCA was a direct response to Hamdan's holding that the DTA's jurisdiction-stripping provision had no application to pending cases. The Court of Appeals was correct to take note of the legislative history when construing the statute, and we agree with its conclusion that the MCA deprives the federal courts of jurisdiction to entertain the habeas corpus actions now before us.

III

In deciding the constitutional questions now presented we must determine whether petitioners are barred from seeking the writ or invoking the protections of the Suspension Clause either because of their status, i.e., petitioners' designation by the Executive Branch as enemy combatants, or their physical location, i.e., their presence at Guantanamo Bay. The Government contends that noncitizens designated as enemy combatants and detained in territory located outside our Nation's borders have no constitutional rights and no privilege of habeas corpus. Petitioners contend they do have cognizable constitutional rights and that Congress, in seeking to eliminate recourse to habeas corpus as a means to assert those rights, acted in violation of the Suspension Clause.

A

The Framers viewed freedom from unlawful restraint as a fundamental precept of liberty, and they understood the writ of habeas corpus as a vital instrument to secure that freedom. Experience taught, however, that the common-law writ all too often had been insufficient to guard against the abuse of monarchial power. That history counseled the necessity for specific language in the Constitution to secure the writ and ensure its place in our legal system.

That the Framers considered the writ a vital instrument for the protection of individual liberty is evident from the care taken to specify the limited grounds for its suspension: "The Privilege of the Writ of Habeas Corpus shall not be suspended, unless when in Cases of Rebellion or Invasion the public Safety may require it." Art. I, §9, cl. 2. The word "privilege" was used, perhaps, to avoid mentioning some rights to the exclusion of others. (Indeed, the only mention of the term "right" in the Constitution, as ratified, is in its clause giving Congress the power to protect the rights of authors and inventors. See Art. I, §8, cl. 8.) Surviving accounts of the ratification debates provide additional evidence that the Framers deemed the writ to be an essential mechanism in the separation-of-powers scheme.

In our own system the Suspension Clause is designed to protect against these cyclical abuses. The Clause protects the rights of the detained by a means consistent with the essential design of the Constitution. It ensures that, except during periods of formal suspension, the Judiciary will have a time-tested device, the writ, to maintain the "delicate balance of governance" that is itself the surest safeguard of liberty. The Clause protects the rights of the detained by affirming the duty and authority of the Judiciary to call the jailer to account.

B

The broad historical narrative of the writ and its function is central to our analysis, but we seek guidance as well from founding-era authorities addressing the specific question before us: whether foreign nationals, apprehended and detained in distant countries during a time of serious threats to our Nation's security, may assert the privilege of the writ and seek its protection. The Court has been careful not to foreclose the possibility that the protections of the Suspension Clause have expanded along with post-1789 developments that define the present scope of the writ. But the analysis may begin with precedents as of 1789, for the Court has said that "at the absolute minimum" the Clause protects the writ as it existed when the Constitution was drafted and ratified.

To support their arguments, the parties in these cases have examined historical sources to construct a view of the common-law writ as it existed in 1789 — as have amici whose expertise in legal history the Court has relied upon in the past. Diligent search by all parties reveals no certain conclusions. In none of the cases cited do we find that a common-law court would or would not have granted, or refused to hear for lack of jurisdiction, a petition for a writ of habeas corpus brought by a prisoner deemed an enemy combatant, under a standard like the one the Department of

Defense has used in these cases, and when held in a territory, like Guantanamo, over which the Government has total military and civil control.

Both arguments are premised, however, upon the assumption that the
historical record is complete and that the common law, if properly understood, yields a definite answer to the questions before us. There are reasons
to doubt both assumptions. Recent scholarship points to the inherent short-
comings in the historical record. And given the unique status of Guantanamo Bay and the particular dangers of terrorism in the modern age, the
common-law courts simply may not have confronted cases with close parallels to this one. We decline, therefore, to infer too much, one way or the
other, from the lack of historical evidence on point. Cf. Brown v. Board of
Education (1954) (noting evidence concerning the circumstances surrounding the adoption of the Fourteenth Amendment, discussed in the parties'
briefs and uncovered through the Court's own investigation, "convince us
that, although these sources cast some light, it is not enough to resolve the
problem with which we are faced. At best, they are inconclusive").

IV

Drawing from its position that at common law the writ ran only to territories
over which the Crown was sovereign, the Government says the Suspension
Clause affords petitioners no rights because the United States does not claim
sovereignty over the place of detention.

Guantanamo Bay is not formally part of the United States. And under the
terms of the lease between the United States and Cuba, Cuba retains
"ultimate sovereignty" over the territory while the United States exercises
"complete jurisdiction and control." Under the terms of the 1934 Treaty,
however, Cuba effectively has no rights as a sovereign until the parties agree
to modification of the 1903 Lease Agreement or the United States abandons
the base.

The United States contends, nevertheless, that Guantanamo is not within its
sovereign control. This was the Government's position well before the events
of September 11, 2001. And in other contexts the Court has held that questions of sovereignty are for the political branches to decide. Even if this were a
treaty interpretation case that did not involve a political question, the President's construction of the lease agreement would be entitled to great respect.

We therefore do not question the Government's position that Cuba, not
the United States, maintains sovereignty, in the legal and technical sense of
the term, over Guantanamo Bay. But this does not end the analysis. Our cases
do not hold it is improper for us to inquire into the objective degree of
control the Nation asserts over foreign territory. Accordingly, for purposes
of our analysis, we accept the Government's position that Cuba, and not the
United States, retains de jure sovereignty over Guantanamo Bay. As we did in
Rasul, however, we take notice of the obvious and uncontested fact that the
United States, by virtue of its complete jurisdiction and control over the base,
maintains de facto sovereignty over this territory.

Were we to hold that the present cases turn on the political question doctrine, we would be required first to accept the Government's premise that de jure sovereignty is the touchstone of habeas corpus jurisdiction. This premise, however, is unfounded. For the reasons indicated above, the history of common-law habeas corpus provides scant support for this proposition; and, for the reasons indicated below, that position would be inconsistent with our precedents and contrary to fundamental separation-of-powers principles.

A

The Court has discussed the issue of the Constitution's extraterritorial application on many occasions. These decisions undermine the Government's argument that, at least as applied to noncitizens, the Constitution necessarily stops where de jure sovereignty ends.

Practical considerations weighed heavily as well in Johnson v. Eisentrager (1950), where the Court addressed whether habeas corpus jurisdiction extended to enemy aliens who had been convicted of violating the laws of war. The prisoners were detained at Landsberg Prison in Germany during the Allied Powers' postwar occupation. The Court stressed the difficulties of ordering the Government to produce the prisoners in a habeas corpus proceeding. It "would require allocation of shipping space, guarding personnel, billeting and rations" and would damage the prestige of military commanders at a sensitive time.

True, the Court in Eisentrager denied access to the writ, and it noted the prisoners "at no relevant time were within any territory over which the United States is sovereign, and [that] the scenes of their offense, their capture, their trial and their punishment were all beyond the territorial jurisdiction of any court of the United States." The Government seizes upon this language as proof positive that the Eisentrager Court adopted a formalistic, sovereignty-based test for determining the reach of the Suspension Clause. We reject this reading for three reasons.

First, we do not accept the idea that the above-quoted passage from Eisentrager is the only authoritative language in the opinion and that all the rest is dicta. The Court's further determinations, based on practical considerations, were integral to Part II of its opinion and came before the decision announced its holding.

Second, because the United States lacked both de jure sovereignty and plenary control over Landsberg Prison, it is far from clear that the Eisentrager Court used the term sovereignty only in the narrow technical sense and not to connote the degree of control the military asserted over the facility. The Justices who decided Eisentrager would have understood sovereignty as a multifaceted concept. That the Court devoted a significant portion of Part II to a discussion of practical barriers to the running of the writ suggests that the Court was not concerned exclusively with the formal legal status of Landsberg Prison but also with the objective degree of control the United States asserted over it. Even if we assume the Eisentrager Court considered the United States' lack of formal legal sovereignty over Landsberg Prison as the decisive factor in that case, its holding is not inconsistent with a functional approach to questions of extraterritoriality. The formal legal status of a given territory affects, at least to some extent, the political branches' control over that territory. De jure sovereignty is a factor that bears upon which constitutional guarantees apply there.

Third, if the Government's reading of Eisentrager were correct, the opinion would have marked not only a change in, but a complete repudiation of, the Insular Cases' functional approach to questions of extraterritoriality. We cannot accept the Government's view. Nothing in Eisentrager says that de jure sovereignty is or has ever been the only relevant consideration in determining the geographic reach of the Constitution or of habeas corpus.

B

The Government's formal sovereignty-based test raises troubling separation-of-powers concerns as well. The political history of Guantanamo illustrates the deficiencies of this approach. The United States has maintained complete and uninterrupted control of the bay for over 100 years. Yet the Government's view is that the Constitution had no effect there, at least as to noncitizens, because the United States disclaimed sovereignty in the formal sense of the term. The necessary implication of the argument is that by surrendering formal sovereignty over any unincorporated territory to a third party, while at the same time entering into a lease that grants total control over the territory back to the United States, it would be possible for the political branches to govern without legal constraint.

Our basic charter cannot be contracted away like this. Even when the United States acts outside its borders, its powers are not "absolute and unlimited" but are subject "to such restrictions as are expressed in the Constitution." Abstaining from questions involving formal sovereignty and territorial governance is one thing. To hold the political branches have the power to switch the Constitution on or off at will is quite another. The former position reflects this Court's recognition that certain matters requiring political judgments are best left to the political branches. The latter would permit a striking anomaly in our tripartite system of government, leading to a regime in which Congress and the President, not this Court, say "what the law is." Marbury v. Madison (1803).

These concerns have particular bearing upon the Suspension Clause question in the cases now before us, for the writ of habeas corpus is itself an indispensable mechanism for monitoring the separation of powers. The test for determining the scope of this provision must not be subject to manipulation by those whose power it is designed to restrain.

C

In addition to the practical concerns discussed above, the Eisentrager Court found relevant that each petitioner:

(a) is an enemy alien; (b) has never been or resided in the United States; (c) was captured outside of our territory and there held in military custody as a prisoner of war; (d) was tried and convicted by a Military Commission sitting outside the United States; (e) for offenses against laws of war committed outside the United States; (f) and is at all times imprisoned outside the United States.

Based on this language from Eisentrager, and the reasoning in our other extraterritoriality opinions, we conclude that at least three factors are relevant in determining the reach of the Suspension Clause: (1) the citizenship and status of the detainee and the adequacy of the process through which that status determination was made; (2) the nature of the sites where apprehension and then detention took place; and (3) the practical obstacles inherent in resolving the prisoner's entitlement to the writ.

Applying this framework, we note at the onset that the status of these detainees is a matter of dispute. The petitioners, like those in Eisentrager, are not American citizens. But the petitioners in Eisentrager did not contest, it seems, the Court's assertion that they were "enemy alien[s]." In the instant cases, by contrast, the detainees deny they are enemy combatants. They have been afforded some process in CSRT proceedings to determine their status; but, unlike in Eisentrager, there has been no trial by military commission for violations of the laws of war. The difference is not trivial. The records from the Eisentrager trials suggest that, well before the petitioners brought their case to this Court, there had been a rigorous adversarial process to test the legality of their detention. The Eisentrager petitioners were charged by a bill of particulars that made detailed factual allegations against them. To rebut the accusations, they were entitled to representation by counsel, allowed to introduce evidence on their own behalf, and permitted to cross-examine the prosecution's witnesses.

In comparison the procedural protections afforded to the detainees in the CSRT hearings are far more limited, and, we conclude, fall well short of the procedures and adversarial mechanisms that would eliminate the need for habeas corpus review. Although the detainee is assigned a "Personal Representative" to assist him during CSRT proceedings, the Secretary of the Navy's memorandum makes clear that person is not the detainee's lawyer or even his "advocate." The Government's evidence is accorded a presumption of validity. The detainee is allowed to present "reasonably available" evidence, but his ability to rebut the Government's evidence against him is limited by the circumstances of his confinement and his lack of counsel at this stage. And although the detainee can seek review of his status determination in the Court of Appeals, that review process cannot cure all defects in the earlier proceedings.

As to the second factor relevant to this analysis, the detainees here are similarly situated to the Eisentrager petitioners in that the sites of their apprehension and detention are technically outside the sovereign territory of the United States. As noted earlier, this is a factor that weighs against finding they have rights under the Suspension Clause. But there are critical differences between Landsberg Prison, circa 1950, and the United States Naval Station at Guantanamo Bay in 2008. Unlike its present control over the naval station, the United States' control over the prison in Germany was neither absolute nor indefinite. Like all parts of occupied Germany, the prison was under the jurisdiction of the combined Allied Forces. Guantanamo Bay, on the other hand, is no transient possession. In every practical sense Guantanamo is not abroad; it is within the constant jurisdiction of the United States.

As to the third factor, we recognize, as the Court did in Eisentrager, that there are costs to holding the Suspension Clause applicable in a case of military detention abroad. Habeas corpus proceedings may require expenditure of funds by the Government and may divert the attention of military personnel from other pressing tasks. While we are sensitive to these concerns, we do not find them dispositive. Compliance with any judicial process requires some incremental expenditure of resources. Yet civilian courts and the Armed Forces have functioned along side each other at various points in our history. The Government presents no credible arguments that the military mission at Guantanamo would be compromised if habeas corpus courts had jurisdiction to hear the detainees' claims. And in light of the plenary control the United States asserts over the base, none are apparent to us.

The situation in Eisentrager was far different, given the historical context and nature of the military's mission in post-War Germany. When hostilities in the European Theater came to an end, the United States became responsible for an occupation zone encompassing over 57,000 square miles with a population of 18 million. In addition to supervising massive reconstruction and aid efforts the American forces stationed in Germany faced potential security threats from a defeated enemy. In retrospect the post-War occupation may seem uneventful. But at the time Eisentrager was decided, the Court was right to be concerned about judicial interference with the military's efforts to contain "enemy elements, guerilla fighters, and 'werewolves.'"

Similar threats are not apparent here; nor does the Government argue that they are. The United States Naval Station at Guantanamo Bay consists of 45 square miles of land and water. The base has been used, at various points, to house migrants and refugees temporarily. At present, however, other than the detainees themselves, the only long-term residents are American military personnel, their families, and a small number of workers. The detainees have been deemed enemies of the United States. At present, dangerous as they may be if released, they are contained in a secure prison facility located on an isolated and heavily fortified military base.

There is no indication, furthermore, that adjudicating a habeas corpus petition would cause friction with the host government. No Cuban court has jurisdiction over American military personnel at Guantanamo or the enemy combatants detained there. While obligated to abide by the terms of the lease, the United States is, for all practical purposes, answerable to no other sovereign for its acts on the base. Were that not the case, or if the detention facility were located in an active theater of war, arguments that issuing the writ would be "impracticable or anomalous" would have more weight. Under the facts presented here, however, there are few practical barriers to the running of the writ. To the extent barriers arise, habeas corpus procedures likely can be modified to address them.

We hold that Art. I, §9, cl. 2, of the Constitution has full effect at Guantanamo Bay. If the privilege of habeas corpus is to be denied to the detainees now before us, Congress must act in accordance with the requirements of the Suspension Clause.

V

In light of this holding the question becomes whether the statute stripping jurisdiction to issue the writ avoids the Suspension Clause mandate because Congress has provided adequate substitute procedures for habeas corpus.

The gravity of the separation-of-powers issues raised by these cases and the fact that these detainees have been denied meaningful access to a judicial forum for a period of years render these cases exceptional.

Our case law does not contain extensive discussion of standards defining suspension of the writ or of circumstances under which suspension has occurred. This simply confirms the care Congress has taken throughout our Nation's history to preserve the writ and its function. Indeed, most of the major legislative enactments pertaining to habeas corpus have acted not to contract the writ's protection but to expand it or to hasten resolution of prisoners' claims.

We do not endeavor to offer a comprehensive summary of the requisites for an adequate substitute for habeas corpus. We do consider it uncontroversial, however, that the privilege of habeas corpus entitles the prisoner to a meaningful opportunity to demonstrate that he is being held pursuant to "the erroneous application or interpretation" of relevant law. And the habeas court must have the power to order the conditional release of an individual unlawfully detained — though release need not be the exclusive remedy and is not the appropriate one in every case in which the writ is granted.

Where a person is detained by executive order, rather than, say, after being tried and convicted in a court, the need for collateral review is most pressing. A criminal conviction in the usual course occurs after a judicial hearing before a tribunal disinterested in the outcome and committed to procedures designed to ensure its own independence. These dynamics are not inherent in executive detention orders or executive review procedures. In this context the need for habeas corpus is more urgent. The intended duration of the detention and the reasons for it bear upon the precise scope of the inquiry. Habeas corpus proceedings need not resemble a criminal trial, even when the detention is by executive order. But the writ must be effective. The habeas court must have sufficient authority to conduct a meaningful review of both the cause for detention and the Executive's power to detain.

To determine the necessary scope of habeas corpus review, therefore, we must assess the CSRT process, the mechanism through which petitioners' designation as enemy combatants became final. Whether one characterizes the CSRT process as direct review of the Executive's battlefield determination that the detainee is an enemy combatant — as the parties have and as we do — or as the first step in the collateral review of a battlefield determination makes no difference in a proper analysis of whether the procedures Congress put in place are an adequate substitute for habeas corpus. What matters is the sum total of procedural protections afforded to the detainee at all stages, direct and collateral.

Petitioners identify what they see as myriad deficiencies in the CSRTs. The most relevant for our purposes are the constraints upon the detainee's ability to rebut the factual basis for the Government's assertion that he is an enemy combatant. As already noted, at the CSRT stage the detainee has limited means to find or present evidence to challenge the Government's case against him. He does not have the assistance of counsel and may not be aware of the most critical allegations that the Government relied upon to order his detention. The detainee can confront witnesses that testify during the CSRT proceedings. But given that there are in effect no limits on the admission of hearsay evidence — the only requirement is that the tribunal deem the evidence "relevant and helpful," the detainee's opportunity to question witnesses is likely to be more theoretical than real.

Even if we were to assume that the CSRTs satisfy due process standards, it would not end our inquiry. Habeas corpus is a collateral process that exists, in Justice Holmes' words, to "cu[t] through all forms and g[o] to the very tissue of the structure. It comes in from the outside, not in subordination to the proceedings, and although every form may have been preserved opens the inquiry whether they have been more than an empty shell." Even when the procedures authorizing detention are structurally sound, the Suspension Clause remains applicable and the writ relevant.

Although we make no judgment as to whether the CSRTs, as currently constituted, satisfy due process standards, we agree with petitioners that, even when all the parties involved in this process act with diligence and in good faith, there is considerable risk of error in the tribunal's findings of fact. And given that the consequence of error may be detention of persons for the duration of hostilities that may last a generation or more, this is a risk too significant to ignore.

For the writ of habeas corpus, or its substitute, to function as an effective and proper remedy in this context, the court that conducts the habeas proceeding must have the means to correct errors that occurred during the CSRT proceedings. This includes some authority to assess the sufficiency of the Government's evidence against the detainee. It also must have the authority to admit and consider relevant exculpatory evidence that was not introduced during the earlier proceeding. Federal habeas petitioners long have had the means to supplement the record on review, even in the post-conviction habeas setting. Here that opportunity is constitutionally required.

The extent of the showing required of the Government in these cases is a matter to be determined. We need not explore it further at this stage. We do hold that when the judicial power to issue habeas corpus properly is invoked the judicial officer must have adequate authority to make a determination in light of the relevant law and facts and to formulate and issue appropriate orders for relief, including, if necessary, an order directing the prisoner's release.

C

We now consider whether the DTA allows the Court of Appeals to conduct a proceeding meeting these standards. The DTA does not explicitly empower the Court of Appeals to order the applicant in a DTA review proceeding released should the court find that the standards and procedures used at his CSRT hearing were insufficient to justify detention. This is troubling. Yet, for present purposes, we can assume congressional silence permits a constitutionally required remedy.

The absence of a release remedy and specific language allowing AUMF challenges are not the only constitutional infirmities from which the statute potentially suffers, however. The more difficult question is whether the DTA permits the Court of Appeals to make requisite findings of fact. Assuming the DTA can be construed to allow the Court of Appeals to review or correct the CSRT's factual determinations, as opposed to merely certifying that the tribunal applied the correct standard of proof, we see no way to construe the statute to allow what is also constitutionally required in this context: an opportunity for the detainee to present relevant exculpatory evidence that was not made part of the record in the earlier proceedings.

On its face the statute allows the Court of Appeals to consider no evidence outside the CSRT record. Under the DTA the Court of Appeals has the power to review CSRT determinations by assessing the legality of standards and procedures. This implies the power to inquire into what happened at the CSRT hearing and, perhaps, to remedy certain deficiencies in that proceeding. But should the Court of Appeals determine that the CSRT followed appropriate and lawful standards and procedures, it will have reached the limits of its jurisdiction. There is no language in the DTA that can be construed to allow the Court of Appeals to admit and consider newly discovered evidence that could not have been made part of the CSRT record because it was unavailable to either the Government or the detainee when the CSRT made its findings. This evidence, however, may be critical to the detainee's argument that he is not an enemy combatant and there is no cause to detain him.

By foreclosing consideration of evidence not presented or reasonably available to the detainee at the CSRT proceedings, the DTA disadvantages the detainee by limiting the scope of collateral review to a record that may not be accurate or complete.

Although we do not hold that an adequate substitute must duplicate §2241 in all respects, it suffices that the Government has not established that the detainees' access to the statutory review provisions at issue is an adequate substitute for the writ of habeas corpus. MCA §7 thus effects an unconstitutional suspension of the writ. In view of our holding we need not discuss the reach of the writ with respect to claims of unlawful conditions of treatment or confinement.

VI

The real risks, the real threats, of terrorist attacks are constant and not likely soon to abate. The ways to disrupt our life and laws are so many and unforeseen that the Court should not attempt even some general catalogue of crises that might occur. Certain principles are apparent, however. Practical considerations and exigent circumstances inform the definition and reach of the law's writs, including habeas corpus. The cases and our tradition reflect this precept.

In cases involving foreign citizens detained abroad by the Executive, it likely would be both an impractical and unprecedented extension of judicial power to assume that habeas corpus would be available at the moment the prisoner is taken into custody. If and when habeas corpus jurisdiction applies, as it does in these cases, then proper deference can be accorded to reasonable procedures for screening and initial detention under lawful and proper conditions of confinement and treatment for a reasonable period of time. Domestic exigencies, furthermore, might also impose such onerous burdens on the Government that here, too, the Judicial Branch would be required to devise sensible rules for staying habeas corpus proceedings until the Government can comply with its requirements in a responsible way. Here, as is true with detainees apprehended abroad, a relevant consideration in determining the courts' role is whether there are suitable alternative processes in place to protect against the arbitrary exercise of governmental power.

The cases before us, however, do not involve detainees who have been held for a short period of time while awaiting their CSRT determinations. Were that the case, or were it probable that the Court of Appeals could complete a prompt review of their applications, the case for requiring temporary abstention or exhaustion of alternative remedies would be much stronger. These qualifications no longer pertain here. In some of these cases six years have elapsed without the judicial oversight that habeas corpus or an adequate substitute demands. And there has been no showing that the Executive faces such onerous burdens that it cannot respond to habeas corpus actions. To require these detainees to complete DTA review before proceeding with their habeas corpus actions would be to require additional months, if not years, of delay. The detainees in these cases are entitled to a prompt habeas corpus hearing.

Our decision today holds only that the petitioners before us are entitled to seek the writ; that the DTA review procedures are an inadequate substitute for habeas corpus; and that the petitioners in these cases need not exhaust the review procedures in the Court of Appeals before proceeding with their habeas actions in the District Court. The only law we identify as unconstitutional is MCA §7. Accordingly, both the DTA and the CSRT process remain intact. Our holding with regard to exhaustion should not be read to imply that a habeas court should intervene the moment an enemy combatant steps foot in a territory where the writ runs. The Executive is entitled to a reasonable period of time to determine a detainee's status before a court entertains that detainee's habeas corpus petition.

In considering both the procedural and substantive standards used to impose detention to prevent acts of terrorism, proper deference must be accorded to the political branches. There are further considerations, however. Security subsists, too, in fidelity to freedom's first principles. Chief among these are freedom from arbitrary and unlawful restraint and the personal liberty that is secured by adherence to the separation of powers. It is from these principles that the judicial authority to consider petitions for habeas corpus relief derives.

Our opinion does not undermine the Executive's powers as Commander in Chief. On the contrary, the exercise of those powers is vindicated, not eroded, when confirmed by the Judicial Branch. Within the Constitution's separation-of-powers structure, few exercises of judicial power are as legitimate or as necessary as the responsibility to hear challenges to the authority of the Executive to imprison a person. Some of these petitioners have been in custody for six years with no definitive judicial determination as to the legality of their detention. Their access to the writ is a necessity to determine the lawfulness of their status, even if, in the end, they do not obtain the relief they seek.

Because our Nation's past military conflicts have been of limited duration, it has been possible to leave the outer boundaries of war powers undefined. If, as some fear, terrorism continues to pose dangerous threats to us for years to come, the Court might not have this luxury. This result is not inevitable, however. The political branches, consistent with their independent obligations to interpret and uphold the Constitution, can engage in a genuine debate about how best to preserve constitutional values while protecting the Nation from terrorism.

It bears repeating that our opinion does not address the content of the law that governs petitioners' detention. That is a matter yet to be determined. We hold that petitioners may invoke the fundamental procedural protections of habeas corpus. The laws and Constitution are designed to survive, and remain in force, in extraordinary times. Liberty and security can be reconciled; and in our system they are reconciled within the framework of the law. The Framers decided that habeas corpus, a right of first importance, must be a part of that framework, a part of that law.

Justice SOUTER, with whom Justice GINSBURG and Justice BREYER join, concurring.

I join the Court's opinion in its entirety and add this afterword only to emphasize two things one might overlook after reading the dissents.

Four years ago, this Court in Rasul v. Bush (2004) held that statutory habeas jurisdiction extended to claims of foreign nationals imprisoned by the United States at Guantanamo Bay, "to determine the legality of the Executive's potentially indefinite detention" of them. Subsequent legislation eliminated the statutory habeas jurisdiction over these claims, so that now there must be constitutionally based jurisdiction or none at all. But no one who reads the Court's opinion in Rasul could seriously doubt that the jurisdictional question must be answered the same way in purely constitutional cases, given the Court's reliance on the historical background of habeas generally in answering the statutory question.

A second fact insufficiently appreciated by the dissents is the length of the disputed imprisonments, some of the prisoners represented here today having been locked up for six years. Hence the hollow ring when the dissenters suggest that the Court is somehow precipitating the judiciary into reviewing claims that the military (subject to appeal to the Court of Appeals for the District of Columbia Circuit) could handle within some reasonable period of time. These suggestions of judicial haste are all the more out of place given the Court's realistic acknowledgment that in periods of exigency the tempo of any habeas review must reflect the immediate peril facing the country. After six years of sustained executive detentions in Guantanamo, subject to habeas jurisdiction but without any actual habeas scrutiny, today's decision is no judicial victory, but an act of perseverance in trying to make habeas review, and the obligation of the courts to provide it, mean something of value both to prisoners and to the Nation.

Chief Justice ROBERTS, with whom Justice SCALIA, Justice THOMAS, and Justice ALITO join, dissenting.

Today the Court strikes down as inadequate the most generous set of procedural protections ever afforded aliens detained by this country as enemy combatants. The political branches crafted these procedures amidst an ongoing military conflict, after much careful investigation and thorough debate. The Court rejects them today out of hand, without bothering to say what due process rights the detainees possess, without explaining how the statute fails to vindicate those rights, and before a single petitioner has even attempted to avail himself of the law's operation. And to what effect? The majority merely replaces a review system designed by the people's representatives with a set of shapeless procedures to be defined by federal courts at some future date. One cannot help but think, after surveying the modest practical results of the majority's ambitious opinion, that this decision is not really about the detainees at all, but about control of federal policy regarding enemy combatants.

The majority is adamant that the Guantanamo detainees are entitled to the protections of habeas corpus—its opinion begins by deciding that question. I regard the issue as a difficult one, primarily because of the unique and unusual jurisdictional status of Guantanamo Bay. I nonetheless agree with Justice Scalia's analysis of our precedents and the pertinent history of the writ, and accordingly join his dissent. The important point for me, however, is that the Court should have resolved these cases on other grounds. Habeas is most fundamentally a procedural right, a mechanism for contesting the legality of executive detention. The critical threshold question in these cases, prior to any inquiry about the writ's scope, is whether the system the political branches designed protects whatever rights the detainees may possess. If so, there is no need for any additional process, whether called "habeas" or something else.

Congress entrusted that threshold question in the first instance to the Court of Appeals for the District of Columbia Circuit, as the Constitution surely allows Congress to do. But before the D.C. Circuit has addressed the issue, the Court cashiers the statute, and without answering this critical threshold question itself. The Court does eventually get around to asking whether review under the DTA is, as the Court frames it, an "adequate substitute" for habeas, but even then its opinion fails to determine what rights the detainees possess and whether the DTA system satisfies them. The majority instead compares the undefined DTA process to an equally undefined habeas right-one that is to be given shape only in the future by district courts on a case-by-case basis. This whole approach is misguided.

It is also fruitless. How the detainees' claims will be decided now that the DTA is gone is anybody's guess. But the habeas process the Court mandates will most likely end up looking a lot like the DTA system it replaces, as the district court judges shaping it will have to reconcile review of the prisoners' detention with the undoubted need to protect the American people from the terrorist threat — precisely the challenge Congress undertook in drafting the DTA. All that today's opinion has done is shift responsibility for those sensitive foreign policy and national security decisions from the elected branches to the Federal Judiciary.

I believe the system the political branches constructed adequately protects any constitutional rights aliens captured abroad and detained as enemy combatants may enjoy. I therefore would dismiss these cases on that ground. With all respect for the contrary views of the majority, I must dissent.

The majority's overreaching is particularly egregious given the weakness of its objections to the DTA. Simply put, the Court's opinion fails on its own terms. The majority strikes down the statute because it is not an "adequate substitute" for habeas review, but fails to show what rights the detainees have that cannot be vindicated by the DTA system.

Because the central purpose of habeas corpus is to test the legality of executive detention, the writ requires most fundamentally an Article III court able to hear the prisoner's claims and, when necessary, order release. Beyond that, the process a given prisoner is entitled to receive depends on the circumstances and the rights of the prisoner. After much hemming and hawing, the majority appears to concede that the DTA provides an Article III court competent to order release. The only issue in dispute is the process the Guantanamo prisoners are entitled to use to test the legality of their detention. Hamdi concluded that American citizens detained as enemy combatants are entitled to only limited process, and that much of that process could be supplied by a military tribunal, with review to follow in an Article III court. That is precisely the system we have here. It is adequate to vindicate whatever due process rights petitioners may have.

The Court reaches the opposite conclusion partly because it misreads the statute. The majority appears not to understand how the review system it invalidates actually works—specifically, how CSRT review and review by the D.C. Circuit fit together. After briefly acknowledging in its recitation of the facts that the Government designed the CSRTs "to comply with the due process requirements identified by the plurality in Hamdi," the Court proceeds to dismiss the tribunal proceedings as no more than a suspect method used by the Executive for determining the status of the detainees in the first instance.

The majority is equally wrong to characterize the CSRTs as part of that initial determination process. They are instead a means for detainees to challenge the Government's determination. The Executive designed the CSRTs to mirror Army Regulation 190-8, the very procedural model the plurality in Hamdi said provided the type of process an enemy combatant could expect from a habeas court. The CSRTs operate much as habeas courts would if hearing the detainee's collateral challenge for the first time: They gather evidence, call witnesses, take testimony, and render a decision on the legality of the Government's detention. If the CSRT finds a particular detainee has been improperly held, it can order release.

The majority insists that even if "the CSRTs satisf[ied] due process standards," full habeas review would still be necessary, because habeas is a collateral remedy available even to prisoners "detained pursuant to the most rigorous proceedings imaginable." This comment makes sense only if the CSRTs are incorrectly viewed as a method used by the Executive for determining the prisoners' status, and not as themselves part of the collateral review to test the validity of that determination. The majority can deprecate the importance of the CSRTs only by treating them as something they are not.

In short, the Hamdi plurality concluded that this type of review would be enough to satisfy due process, even for citizens. Congress followed the Court's lead, only to find itself the victim of a constitutional bait and switch.

Given the statutory scheme the political branches adopted, and given Hamdi, it simply will not do for the majority to dismiss the CSRT procedures as "far more limited" than those used in military trials, and therefore beneath the level of process "that would eliminate the need for habeas corpus review." The question is not how much process the CSRTs provide in comparison to other modes of adjudication. The question is whether the CSRT procedures—coupled with the judicial review specified by the DTA—provide the "basic process" Hamdi said the Constitution affords American citizens detained as enemy combatants.

To what basic process are these detainees due as habeas petitioners? We have said that "at the absolute minimum," the Suspension Clause protects the writ "'as it existed in 1789.'" The majority admits that a number of historical authorities suggest that at the time of the Constitution's ratification, "common-law courts abstained altogether from matters involving prisoners of war." If this is accurate, the process provided prisoners under the DTA is plainly more than sufficient—it allows alleged combatants to challenge both the factual and legal bases of their detentions.

Assuming the constitutional baseline is more robust, the DTA still provides adequate process, and by the majority's own standards. The DTA system—CSRT review of the Executive's determination followed by D.C. Circuit review for sufficiency of the evidence and the constitutionality of the CSRT process—meets these criteria.

All told, the DTA provides the prisoners held at Guantanamo Bay adequate opportunity to contest the bases of their detentions, which is all habeas corpus need allow. The DTA provides more opportunity and more process, in fact, than that afforded prisoners of war or any other alleged enemy combatants in history.

Despite these guarantees, the Court finds the DTA system an inadequate habeas substitute, for one central reason: Detainees are unable to introduce at the appeal stage exculpatory evidence discovered after the conclusion of their CSRT proceedings. The Court hints darkly that the DTA may suffer from other infirmities, but it does not bother to name them, making a response a bit difficult. As it stands, I can only assume the Court regards the supposed defect it did identify as the gravest of the lot.

If this is the most the Court can muster, the ice beneath its feet is thin indeed. As noted, the CSRT procedures provide ample opportunity for detainees to introduce exculpatory evidence—whether documentary in nature or from live witnesses—before the military tribunals. And if their ability to introduce such evidence is denied contrary to the Constitution or laws of the United States, the D.C. Circuit has the authority to say so on review.

For all its eloquence about the detainees' right to the writ, the Court makes no effort to elaborate how exactly the remedy it prescribes will differ from the procedural protections detainees enjoy under the DTA. The Court objects to the detainees' limited access to witnesses and classified material, but proposes no alternatives of its own. Indeed, it simply ignores the many difficult questions its holding presents. What, for example, will become of the CSRT process? The majority says federal courts should generally refrain from entertaining detainee challenges until after the petitioner's CSRT proceeding has finished. But to what deference, if any, is that CSRT determination entitled?

There are other problems. Take witness availability. What makes the majority think witnesses will become magically available when the review procedure is labeled "habeas"? Will the location of most of these witnesses change—will they suddenly become easily susceptible to service of process? Or will subpoenas issued by American habeas courts run to Basra? And if they did, how would they be enforced? Speaking of witnesses, will detainees be able to call active-duty military officers as witnesses? If not, why not?

The majority has no answers for these difficulties. What it does say leaves open the distinct possibility that its "habeas" remedy will, when all is said and done, end up looking a great deal like the DTA review it rejects.

The majority rests its decision on abstract and hypothetical concerns. Step back and consider what, in the real world, Congress and the Executive have actually granted aliens captured by our Armed Forces overseas and found to be enemy combatants:

- The right to hear the bases of the charges against them, including a summary of any classified evidence.
- The ability to challenge the bases of their detention before military tribunals modeled after Geneva Convention procedures. Some 38 detainees have been released as a result of this process.
- The right, before the CSRT, to testify, introduce evidence, call witnesses, question those the Government calls, and secure release, if and when appropriate.
- The right to the aid of a personal representative in arranging and presenting their cases before a CSRT.
- Before the D.C. Circuit, the right to employ counsel, challenge the factual record, contest the lower tribunal's legal determinations, ensure compliance with the Constitution and laws, and secure release, if any errors below establish their entitlement to such relief.

In sum, the DTA satisfies the majority's own criteria for assessing adequacy. This statutory scheme provides the combatants held at Guantanamo greater procedural protections than have ever been afforded alleged enemy detainees—whether citizens or aliens—in our national history.

So who has won? Not the detainees. The Court's analysis leaves them with only the prospect of further litigation to determine the content of their new habeas right, followed by further litigation to resolve their particular cases, followed by further litigation before the D.C. Circuit—where they could have started had they invoked the DTA procedure. Not Congress, whose attempt to "determine—through democratic means—how best" to balance the security of the American people with the detainees' liberty interests, has been unceremoniously brushed aside. Not the Great Writ, whose majesty is hardly enhanced by its extension to a jurisdictionally quirky outpost, with no tangible benefit to anyone. Not the rule of law, unless by that is meant the rule of lawyers, who will now arguably have a greater role than military and intelligence officials in shaping policy for alien enemy combatants. And certainly not the American people, who today lose a bit more control over the conduct of this Nation's foreign policy to unelected, politically unaccountable judges.

Justice SCALIA, with whom THE CHIEF JUSTICE, Justice THOMAS, and Justice ALITO join, dissenting.

Today, for the first time in our Nation's history, the Court confers a constitutional right to habeas corpus on alien enemies detained abroad by our military forces in the course of an ongoing war. The Chief Justice's dissent, which I join, shows that the procedures prescribed by Congress in the Detainee Treatment Act provide the essential protections that habeas corpus guarantees; there has thus been no suspension of the writ, and no basis exists for judicial intervention beyond what the Act allows. My problem with today's opinion is more fundamental still: The writ of habeas corpus does not, and never has, run in favor of aliens abroad; the Suspension Clause thus has no application, and the Court's intervention in this military matter is entirely ultra vires.

I shall devote most of what will be a lengthy opinion to the legal errors contained in the opinion of the Court. Contrary to my usual practice, however, I think it appropriate to begin with a description of the disastrous consequences of what the Court has done today.

America is at war with radical Islamists. The enemy began by killing Americans and American allies abroad: 241 at the Marine barracks in Lebanon, 19 at the Khobar Towers in Dhahran, 224 at our embassies in Dar es Salaam and Nairobi, and 17 on the USS Cole in Yemen. On September 11, 2001, the enemy brought the battle to American soil, killing 2,749 at the Twin Towers in New York City, 184 at the Pentagon in Washington, D. C., and 40 in Pennsylvania. It has threatened further attacks against our homeland; one need only walk about buttressed and barricaded Washington, or board a plane anywhere in the country, to know that the threat is a serious one. Our Armed Forces are now in the field against the enemy, in Afghanistan and Iraq. Last week, 13 of our countrymen in arms were killed.

The game of bait-and-switch that today's opinion plays upon the Nation's Commander in Chief will make the war harder on us. It will almost certainly cause more Americans to be killed. That consequence would be tolerable if necessary to preserve a time-honored legal principle vital to our constitutional Republic. But it is this Court's blatant abandonment of such a principle that produces the decision today. The President relied on our settled precedent in Johnson v. Eisentrager (1950), when he established the prison at Guantanamo Bay for enemy aliens. Citing that case, the President's Office of Legal Counsel advised him "that the great weight of legal authority indicates that a federal district court could not properly exercise habeas jurisdiction over an alien detained at [Guantanamo Bay]." Memorandum from Patrick F. Philbin and John C. Yoo, Deputy Assistant Attorneys General, Office of Legal Counsel, to William J. Haynes II, General Counsel, Dept. of Defense (Dec. 28, 2001). Had the law been otherwise, the military surely would not have transported prisoners there, but would have kept them in Afghanistan, transferred them to another of our foreign military bases, or turned them over to allies for detention. Those other facilities might well have been worse for the detainees themselves.

In the long term, then, the Court's decision today accomplishes little, except perhaps to reduce the well-being of enemy combatants that the

Court ostensibly seeks to protect. In the short term, however, the decision is devastating. At least 30 of those prisoners hitherto released from Guantanamo Bay have returned to the battlefield. See S.Rep. No. 110-90, pt. 7, p. 13 (2007) (Minority Views of Sens. Kyl, Sessions, Graham, Cornyn, and Coburn) (hereinafter Minority Report). Some have been captured or killed. See also Mintz, Released Detainees Rejoining the Fight, Washington Post, Oct. 22, 2004, pp. A1, A12. But others have succeeded in carrying on their atrocities against innocent civilians. In one case, a detainee released from Guantanamo Bay masterminded the kidnapping of two Chinese dam workers, one of whom was later shot to death when used as a human shield against Pakistani commandoes. Another former detainee promptly resumed his post as a senior Taliban commander and murdered a United Nations engineer and three Afghan soldiers. Mintz, supra. Still another murdered an Afghan judge. It was reported only last month that a released detainee carried out a suicide bombing against Iraqi soldiers in Mosul, Iraq. See White, Ex-Guantanamo Detainee Joined Iraq Suicide Attack, Washington Post, May 8, 2008, p. A18.

These, mind you, were detainees whom the military had concluded were not enemy combatants. Their return to the kill illustrates the incredible difficulty of assessing who is and who is not an enemy combatant in a foreign theater of operations where the environment does not lend itself to rigorous evidence collection. Astoundingly, the Court today raises the bar, requiring military officials to appear before civilian courts and defend their decisions under procedural and evidentiary rules that go beyond what Congress has specified. As The Chief Justice's dissent makes clear, we have no idea what those procedural and evidentiary rules are, but they will be determined by civil courts and (in the Court's contemplation at least) will be more detainee-friendly than those now applied, since otherwise there would no reason to hold the congressionally prescribed procedures unconstitutional. If they impose a higher standard of proof (from foreign battlefields) than the current procedures require, the number of the enemy returned to combat will obviously increase.

But even when the military has evidence that it can bring forward, it is often foolhardy to release that evidence to the attorneys representing our enemies. And one escalation of procedures that the Court is clear about is affording the detainees increased access to witnesses (perhaps troops serving in Afghanistan?) and to classified information. During the 1995 prosecution of Omar Abdel Rahman, federal prosecutors gave the names of 200 unindicted co-conspirators to the "Blind Sheik's" defense lawyers; that information was in the hands of Osama Bin Laden within two weeks. In another case, trial testimony revealed to the enemy that the United States had been monitoring their cellular network, whereupon they promptly stopped using it, enabling more of them to evade capture and continue their atrocities.

And today it is not just the military that the Court elbows aside. A mere two Terms ago in Hamdan v. Rumsfeld (2006), when the Court held (quite amazingly) that the Detainee Treatment Act of 2005 had not stripped habeas jurisdiction over Guantanamo petitioners' claims, four Members of today's five-Justice majority joined an opinion saying the following: "Nothing prevents the President from returning to Congress to seek the authority [for trial by military commission] he believes necessary."

Turns out they were just kidding. For in response, Congress, at the President's request, quickly enacted the Military Commissions Act, emphatically reasserting that it did not want these prisoners filing habeas petitions. It is therefore clear that Congress and the Executive — both political branches — have determined that limiting the role of civilian courts in adjudicating whether prisoners captured abroad are properly detained is important to success in the war that some 190,000 of our men and women are now fighting. As the Solicitor General argued, "the Military Commissions Act and the Detainee Treatment Act . . . represent an effort by the political branches to strike an appropriate balance between the need to preserve liberty and the need to accommodate the weighty and sensitive governmental interests in ensuring that those who have in fact fought with the enemy during a war do not return to battle against the United States."

But it does not matter. The Court today decrees that no good reason to accept the judgment of the other two branches is "apparent." "The Government," it declares, "presents no credible arguments that the military mission at Guantanamo would be compromised if habeas corpus courts had jurisdiction to hear the detainees' claims." What competence does the Court have to second-guess the judgment of Congress and the President on such a point? None whatever. But the Court blunders in nonetheless. Henceforth, as today's opinion makes unnervingly clear, how to handle enemy prisoners in this war will ultimately lie with the branch that knows least about the national security concerns that the subject entails.

Today the Court warps our Constitution in a way that goes beyond the narrow issue of the reach of the Suspension Clause, invoking judicially brainstormed separation-of-powers principles to establish a manipulable "functional" test for the extraterritorial reach of habeas corpus (and, no doubt, for the extraterritorial reach of other constitutional protections as well). It blatantly misdescribes important precedents, most conspicuously Justice Jackson's opinion for the Court in Johnson v. Eisentrager. It breaks a chain of precedent as old as the common law that prohibits judicial inquiry into detentions of aliens abroad absent statutory authorization. And, most tragically, it sets our military commanders the impossible task of proving to a civilian court, under whatever standards this Court devises in the future, that evidence supports the confinement of each and every enemy prisoner.

The Nation will live to regret what the Court has done today. I dissent.

However, since *Boumediene*, the United States Court of Appeals for the District of Columbia Circuit has denied relief in every case. Following the Supreme Court's decision, federal district court judges in the District of

Columbia granted relief to a number of Guantánamo detainees. But in each instance so far, the D.C. Circuit reversed, and then the Supreme Court denied review.

For example, in Kiyemba v. Obama, a federal district court ordered the release of five Chinese Muslim (Uighur) detainees who had been cleared for release from Guantánamo. But the D.C. Circuit reversed, 561 F.3d 509 (D.C. Cir. 2009), and held that a federal judge lacks the power to order the transfer of Guantánamo detainees to the United States. Subsequently, in the same case, the D.C. Circuit, 605 F.3d 1046 (D.C. Cir. 2010), denied federal judges the power to regulate transfers of Guantánamo detainees to elsewhere in the world. The Supreme Court denied review. 131 S. Ct. 1631 (2011).

In Latif v. Obama, 666 F.3d 746 (D.C. Cir. 2011), the D.C. Circuit ruled that federal district judges must "presume" that government intelligence reports used to justify detention are reliable and accurate. Adnan Farhan Abdul Latif, a Yemeni man, was picked up near the border between Afghanistan and Pakistan in December 2001. The government has relied on an intelligence report prepared at the time to justify holding him ever since. The district court ordered his release saying that the report was not sufficiently reliable to warrant keeping him imprisoned. But the D.C. Circuit, while acknowledging problems with the report, said that it was entitled to "a presumption of regularity." In dissent, D.C. Circuit Judge David Tatel said that this would mean that the government would win virtually every case and that "it is hard to see what is left of the Supreme Court's command in Boumediene." The Supreme Court denied certiorari. 132 S. Ct. 2741 (2012).

TABLE OF CASES

Italics indicate principal cases.

INDEX